TOWARD
A
FEMINIST TRADITION

GARLAND REFERENCE LIBRARY
OF THE HUMANITIES
(VOL. 201)

TOWARD
A
FEMINIST TRADITION
An Annotated Bibliography
of
Novels in English
by Women
1891–1920

Diva Daims
Janet Grimes

with the editorial assistance of
Doris Robinson

GARLAND PUBLISHING, INC. • NEW YORK & LONDON
1982

The preparation of this volume was made possible (in part) by a grant from the Program for Research Tools and Reference Works of the National Endowment for the Humanities, an independent federal agency, Russell Sage College, and the State University of New York at Albany.

Library of Congress Cataloging in Publication Data

Daims, Diva.
    Toward a feminist tradition.

    (Garland reference library of the humanities ; v. 201)
    Includes index.
    1. English fiction—Women authors—Bibliography.
2. American fiction—Women authors—Bibliography.
I. Grimes, Janet. II. Robinson, Doris. III. Title.
IV. Series.
Z2013.5.W6D34 [PR830.W62]   016.823′912   82-15496
ISBN 0-8240-9523-5

Printed on acid-free, 250-year-life paper
Manufactured in the United States of America

Contents ～

Introduction ⌒

Toward a Feminist Tradition is an annotated list of English language novels by women published during the period 1891–1920. It contains 3,407 titles by 1,723 authors. Fifty-one anonymous novels have been included as well as novels by 136 authors (identified by asterisks) whose names do not clearly indicate they are women and about whom we have found no other information. These novels have been selected from *Novels in English by Women** for the purpose of providing a broad basis for subsequent research by women's studies scholars leading to analysis and definition of a feminist tradition in women's novels of the period. Novels identified as juvenile have been excluded, but we have occasionally included short stories when they appear to be novelistic in their focus on a central character or theme. English translations of novels by women have been included if the first translation was published during the period.

The principal idea governing our selection of the novels was the unconventional treatment of women characters which focuses attention either on the efforts of women to control their lives or on social attitudes and conditions functioning as counterforces to that achievement. One could reasonably argue that not all variation of this sort is feminist, and we would agree. However, in the absence of a general agreement on what is or is not feminist, we have adopted this inclusive concept in our search for novels in the feminist tradition.

Our information about the novels is based on reviews for the period. We have not attempted to evaluate the feminism of the author, although some reviewers have done so, and we have included some of their comments on the subject as well as some of their opinions on feminism and women writers. The overall quality of their opinions has led us to be somewhat skeptical of their social and literary judgment. However, we have occasionally included brief comments like "sentimental" and "for girls" as indications of literary quality or point of view. Where reviewers' opinions differ, we have tried to reflect these differences in our annotations.

The kinds of novels we looked for in making our selections were those, first of all, that varied from the portrayal of the conventional heroine both in her qualifications and the limits of her activity. Briefly described, the conventional heroine we have in mind is in her late teens, beautiful, pure, and so childlike in her delicacy and dependence that she requires the constant protection of men. She usually passes from dependence on her father to dependence on her husband. (In one category of novels the male guardian functions first as father and then as husband.) She achieves an education and develops skills ("accomplishments") not in order to lead an independent life, but in preparation for her primary job which is to wait in attractive passiveness in order to allure and be captured by a handsome and unattached male who will make her an object of love and protection.

The conventional heroine is severely limited in her activity and relations to other people. Her relations to the men in the novel other than the hero are usually confined to the roles of mother, sister, daughter, nurse, and assistant, and her relation to other women characters is frequently one of competition for the hero. Her principal functions once she has won the hero's affection are to reform, inspire, serve, and marry him and to sacrifice all to his home and children. Because of her beauty, purity, and training, she would under ordinary circumstances have no difficulty fulfilling this destiny, and her story is generally one of external complications, such as the schemings of another character, which impede her progress. One variation on this theme is the heroine who finds herself in a loveless relationship because she has been forced by circumstances into a marriage or has been deceived by her lover into believing he is a suitable mate. The conventional response is acceptance, which may in time be rewarded by a revelation of his basic goodness or his reform, either of which will permit love to flourish, or by his death, which will permit her to marry the right man.

Conventionally, women characters who go beyond these limits are unsympathetically portrayed. If they seek fuller education and careers or if they choose to live alone, they are criticized; if they have sex outside of marriage, they are punished; if they have children outside of marriage, they and their children are condemned; if they leave a marriage, they are shunned by society; and if they avoid marriage, they are made objects of pity or ridicule. These women characters are the dark mirror images of the conventional women—the neurotic women, the fallen women, and the old maids.

Where the reviews we read described novels with women

characters in conventional roles but suggested that the characters were subjects of analysis or psychological study, we included these novels. They are most frequently studies of problems, such as oppressive relations with men, difficult relations between mothers and daughters, contrasts between two women, and physical, mental and emotional problems of disability and of aging. We included all novels that depict unhappy marriages and novels in diary or autobiographical form on the assumption that such novels are apt to describe experiences from the woman's point of view.

The unconventional heroine, as represented by our selections, is apt to be any age, but characteristically is beyond 20. She is often described as plain and may even have a physical deformity. She is not restricted to women's traditional roles in her efforts to define her life, and she is often consciously aware of the limits of these roles. Her actions to define her life are perceived as legitimate stages of development. In some novels, her actions may achieve fantastic proportions, as contrasted with the novels of realism wherein the heroine's single action may be one of resistance. Her course of action may include study, work, travel, wearing male attire, separation from parents, commitment to a cause, and defying convention and law. She determines her relations to men; she may even be the sexually aggressive one. She looks at marriage realistically, often choosing to remain single, childless or to be a single parent. If she marries, she often proposes or makes her own terms; she may have a love relationship outside of marriage or initiate a separation or divorce or a course which combines family and career. She is capable of great acts of heroism, seeks adventure, and may, in fact, have occult or superhuman powers which are not necessarily benevolent. She may be highly moral, immoral, or amoral; she may be a social reformer, cynic, or she may be obsessed with personal justice. Her efforts may meet with complete defeat or wild success. Since we have included all novels whose heroines work outside the home, a year or two on her own may be all that distinguishes her from the conventional heroine.

The world of this unconventional heroine, again as defined by the novels listed here, extends to relations between women and to broad social concerns related to women. Some novels show friendships between women, love of women for each other, women living in communities, women working with women, women in different cultures, and women in prisons, convents, schools, and asylums. Some novels consider such subjects related to women as prostitution, betrayal of women, male tyranny, legal reforms, suffrage and working conditions; others criticize systems that oppress women, such as war and political ideologies. Many of the novels we have included tend to be "hybrids" of the conventional and unconventional: a heroine may act heroically but be punished, resigned, or remorseful in the final pages. Many of the novels include love stories, the inclusion of which may represent a compromise with convention or a recognition of social reality.

The annotations describing the novels are summaries of the reviews we read for each novel. We have frequently loosely paraphrased or quoted in order to preserve the original wording and not lose the quality of the expression. Where the quotation is lengthy and substantively critical, we have provided a citation. Except for an occasional surrender to the urge to reject the language of the period, we have retained such expressions as indiscretion, lover, betrayal, liaison, adventuress, desertion, hoyden, and spinster. Many of these expressions currently have new meanings, are in poor taste, or are no longer used. A few entries are listed without annotations. These are entries for which no reviews were found, but the titles themselves suggested that the novels met our criteria. This may seem like slim evidence for including these novels, but in keeping with our intention to be inclusive, we preferred to list them rather than to omit them.

To locate the best sources for information about feminist characters and subjects, we first turned to the feminist journals of the period, but found few book reviews. We then identified the major review sources (see list which follows). To determine the content of the novels, we made a systematic search of these sources.

The entries are arranged alphabetically by the last name of the author. Authors' names have been entered in the fullest form available. Where the information was available and when the name used by the author on the title page differs from the fullest form of the name under which her works are entered, the pen name follows the title, and a see reference is provided. The decision to treat the authors' names in this manner was arrived at only with much consideration and reflects an attempt to provide as much information as possible about the author without sacrificing access. We would have preferred to enter the novels under the author's pen name with see references to other pen names used by the author, but the largest portion of the novels are British publications, and the British Museum's *General Catalogue of Printed Books* does not consistently provide that information. We are aware that many of the authors would have preferred to be known by the names given them at birth, rather than losing their identity in names acquired by marriage; others would object to losing their marital names. Neither the Library of Congress nor the British Museum has been consistent in the form of author entries, apparently having applied different rules at different times. We considered arranging the entries alphabetically by title and thereby avoiding the problems inherent in the form of women's names, but our final decision was to aim for the fullest information and consistency possible.

In alphabetizing the names, we have adhered to the following rules. Hyphenated names are alphabetized by the second part of the name; surnames preceded by a preposition or article are alphabetized by the preposition or article. No honorific titles are included except where such titles are parts of pen names or where the title helps represent the fullest form of the name provided by the catalogs, such as Mrs. E. Young. In these cases "Mrs." is considered part of the name and alphabetized accordingly. Where an initial is given in place of a first name but where the second name is clearly that of a woman (S. Emily Clark), such a name is assumed to be a woman's. Initial only names (A.F.D.) are considered pseudonyms, but where the author's name is represented by words like the epithets "A Spinster" or "Exponent," such works are considered anonymous and are entered under the author heading "Anonymous Authors—Not Identified." In order to alphabetize correctly, it was necessary to standardize the spelling of all names beginning with Mc and M' to Mac and St. to Saint. Abbreviations are alphabetized as spelled.

Copyright dates are given only where the imprint dates are not available. If the novel was published in England and the United States, both publishers are included. Catalog locations follow the date of publication.

The source of this bibliography is *Novels in English by Women, 1891-1920; a Preliminary Checklist*, a near complete list of English language novels by women for the period. It contains 5,267 authors and the titles of 15,174 novels, 75% of which are annotated. To prepare *Novels in English by Women* we searched for all male pseudonyms used by women authors during the period. Then we searched through all issues of *Publishers' Weekly* and *Bookseller* (the two journals of record for book publishing during the period) and selected all novels which might have been written by women. This file was then carefully checked against the British Museum's *General Catalogue of Printed Books,* the *National Union Catalog, pre-1956 Imprints,* and Robert Glenn Wright's *Bibliography of English Language Fiction in the Library of Congress through 1950* to verify the bibliographic accuracy of the entry and to establish the names of the authors. Place of birth or residence and birth and death dates were added as found in the above works as well as in Lyle Wright's *American Fiction, 1876–1900.* Those novels by authors whose names were not definitely female were further checked in a number of biographical sources.

NOTE

*Grimes, Janet, and Diva Daims. *Novels in English by Women, 1891–1920: A Preliminary Checklist.* New York: Garland, 1981.

Acknowledgments ~

In a seminar on publishing held in 1974 by David L. Mitchell, Assistant Professor, Library and Information Science, State University of New York at Albany, a search for feminist novels published in 1913 proved to be the pilot project for an annotated bibliography of feminist novels from 1891–1920. During that spring and summer Mitchell provided us with guidance concerning sources and methods and the sympathy and enthusiasm necessary to launch the project. During that same year Ann Prentice, then Assistant Professor, Library and Information Science, SUNYA, advised us on the design of our research. The importance of their help in establishing a basically sound research design proved to be particularly important as the scope of our research widened to include the earlier period of time, 1781–1890, as well as the work published as *Novels in English by Women*. We also remember their companionship in sharing our early excitement.

We did our research at the New York State Library, developing our method by identifying male pseudonyms used by women writers, determining those periodicals whose reviews would give us the best information on the writers, and compiling the file of all novels written by women during the thirty year period. We have spent several years working in the New York State Library, and we are most grateful to the staff for their efforts in providing us with the working space and materials needed. The Cataloging Department provided an area for use and access to their copies of the *National Union Catalog* and the British Museum's *General Catalogue of Printed Books* during those months the library was closed. Eric Daims greatly facilitated the compilation of entries by his careful and accurate recording of thousands of titles.

In 1976 we realized that funding would help us complete the work sooner. It was then we applied to the National Endowment for the Humanities under the generous sponsorship of Russell Sage College. Christopher Reaske, Provost, Russell Sage College, gave us full encouragement by his wholehearted support of our grant proposal, a support which he has continued to give the project. When the National Endowment for the Humanities funded one year of full-time research, 1977–78, Gerald Tyson gave us very special assistance through all stages of the work during and after the grant period. In addition we had the generous help and counsel of Melissa E. Fountain, Director of Sponsored Programs, Russell Sage College.

We are indebted to John C. Gerber, Chair, English Department, SUNYA, and John W. Shumaker, Dean, College of Humanities and Fine Arts, SUNYA. At the SUNYA Computing Center we have had excellent help and advisement from Steven Greenstein, Program Analyst, and Stephen J. Rogowski, Manager, Documentation Services and Typesetting.

During the past five years, our work has been based at the Albany Campus Library of Russell Sage. We are indebted to the library staff, in particular to Deborah Priest for processing numerous inter-library loan requests. We have also had the full cooperation of the Inter-library Loan Office of SUNYA, especially that of Jacqueline Mitnick.

Finally, we are especially grateful to Florence Boos and William Grimes for their contributions.

Diva Daims
Janet Grimes
Doris Robinson

List of Sources
and Abbreviations ~

MAJOR REVIEW SOURCES

Academy and Literature. London, October 9, 1869–Sept. 1916. (Title varies.)

Athenaeum: a Journal of Literature, Science, the Fine Arts, Music and the Drama. London, Jan. 2, 1828–Feb.11, 1921. (Subtitle varies.)

Baker, Ernest Albert. *A Descriptive Guide to the Best Fiction, British and American, Including Translations from Foreign Languages.* London: S. Sonnenschein, 1903.

————. *A Guide to the Best Fiction, English and American, Including Translations from Foreign Languages,* rev. ed. London: G. Routledge, 1913.

————. *A Guide to the Best Fiction, English and American, Including Translations from Foreign Languages,* rev. ed. London: G. Routledge, 1932.

Bookman. London, Oct. 1891–Dec. 1934.

Bookman; a Review of Books and Life. New York, Feb. 1895–Mar. 1933.

Critic; an Illustrated Monthly Review of Literature, Art, and Life. New York, Jan. 15, 1881–Sept. 1906.

Literary World. Boston, June 1870–1904.

New York Times Book Review. New York, Oct. 10, 1896–.

Publishers' Weekly. New York, 1872–.

Saturday Review. London, 1855–July 16, 1938.

Spectator. London, July 5, 1828–.

Times Literary Supplement. London, 1902–.

OTHER SOURCES

Arena. Boston, etc., Dec. 1889–Aug. 1909.

Book Monthly. London, Oct. 1903–June 1920.

Book News Monthly. Philadelphia, Sept. 1882–Aug. 1918.

Book Review Digest. New York: Wilson, 1905–.

Dial. Chicago, New York, May 1880–July 1929.

Franklin, Margaret Ladd. *The Case for Woman Suffrage; a Bibliography.* New York: National College Equal Suffrage League, 1913.

Godey's Magazine. Philadelphia, July 1830–Aug. 1898.

Harper's Magazine. New York, June 1850–.

Independent. New York, Boston, Dec. 7, 1848–Oct. 13, 1928.

Johnson, Reginald Brimley. *The Women Novelists.* London: W. Collins, 1918.

Literature. London, Oct. 23, 1897–Jan. 11, 1902.

Literature. [American ed.] New York, Oct. 23, 1897–Nov. 24, 1899.

Nation. New York, 1865–.

Overton, Grant. *The Women Who Make Our Novels,* rev. ed. New York: Dodd, Mead, 1928.

Review of Reviews. London, 1890–Feb. 1936.

Wellington, Amy. *Women Have Told; Studies in the Feminist Tradition.* Boston: Little, Brown, 1930.

Woman's Journal. (National American Woman Suffrage Association). Boston, Chicago, 1870–May 26, 1917.

BIBLIOGRAPHIC SOURCES

Bookseller. London, 1858–.

British Museum. Department of Printed Books. *General Catalogue of Printed Books.* Photolithographic edition to 1955. London: Trustees, 1959–66.

English Catalogue of Books. London, 1864–.

National Union Catalog, pre-1956 Imprints. London: Mansell, 1968–.

Publishers' Weekly. New York, 1872–.

The United States Catalog, 1899, 1912, and 1928. New York: H. W. Wilson.

Wright, Lyle Henry. *American Fiction, 1876–1900; a Contribution toward a Bibliography.* San Marino, California: Huntington Library, 1966.

Wright, Robert Glenn. *Author Bibliography of English Language Fiction in the Library of Congress through 1950.* Boston: G. K. Hall, 1973.

BIOGRAPHICAL SOURCES

Adams, Oscar Fay. *A Dictionary of American Authors,* 5th ed. Detroit: Gale Research Company, 1969.

American Women; The Standard Biographical Dictionary of Notable Women. Teaneck, N. J.: Zephyrus Press, 1974.

Browning, David Clayton. *Everyman's Dictionary of Literary Biography, English and American*. London: Dent; New York: Dutton, [1958].

Burke, William Jeremiah and Will D. Howe. *American Authors and Books, 1640 to the Present Day*. New York: Crown Publishers, [1962].

The Dictionary of National Biography. Edited by Sir Leslie Stephen and Sir Sidney Lee. London: Oxford University Press, 1921–22.

Halkett, Samuel and John Laing. *Dictionary of Anonymous and Pseudonymous English Literature*, new and enlarged edition. Edinburgh and London: Oliver and Boyd, 1926–1934.

Havlice, Patricia P. *Index to Literary Biography*. Metuchen, N. J.: Scarecrow Press, 1975.

Kunitz, Stanley J. and Howard Haycraft. *Twentieth Century Authors; a Biographical Dictionary of Modern Literature*. New York: Wilson, 1942.

Sharp, Harold S. *Handbook of Pseudonyms and Personal Nicknames*. Metuchen, N. J.: Scarecrow, 1972. Supplement, 1975.

Wallace, William Stewart. *A Dictionary of North American Authors Deceased before 1950*. Toronto: Ryerson Press, [1951].

Who Was Who in America; a Companion Biographical Reference Work to Who's Who in America, historical vol., rev. ed., and vol. 1–6. Chicago: Marquis, 1967–1976.

Who Was Who in Literature, 1906–1934. Detroit: Gale Research Company, 1979.

Who's Who among Living Authors of Older Nations, vol. 1. Los Angeles: Golden Syndicate Publishing Company, 1931–32.

Who's Who among North American Authors, vol. 3. Los Angeles: Golden Syndicate Publishing Company, 1927–28.

ABBREVIATIONS

BMC	British Museum. *General Catalogue of Printed Books*
BS	*Bookseller*
EC	*English Catalogue of Books*
LC	Robert Glenn Wright. *Author Bibliography...*
NUC	*National Union Catalog*
PW	*Publishers' Weekly*
USC	*United States Catalog*
W	Lyle Henry Wright. *American Fiction...*

THE BIBLIOGRAPHY ∼

ABBOTT, HELEN RAYMOND. See BEALS, HELEN RAYMOND (ABBOTT).

ABBOTT, JANE LUDLOW (DRAKE). B. 1881. United States.

1 HAPPY HOUSE. Philadelphia and London: J.B. Lippincott, 1920 BMC NUC.
Two college friends change places, the one with the "jolly careless disposition" visiting the relatives, leaving the other free to go to Siberia as a teacher.

ABBOTT, LUCY HESTER (THURSTON). B. 1883. United States.

2 NAOMI OF THE ISLAND. Boston: L. C. Page, 1912 NUC.
Young woman earns her way through school and college.

ADALET [pseud.].*

3 HADJIRA: A TURKISH LOVE STORY. BY ADALET. London: E. Arnold, 1896 NUC BMC.
Minute study of the harem. Publisher says identity of author cannot be revealed; it would endanger her personal safety. Allusions to cruelty of the women to their slaves.

ADAMS, ELLINOR DAVENPORT.

4 MISS SECRETARY ETHEL: A STORY FOR GIRLS OF TODAY. London: Hurst and Blackett, 1898 BMC.
She's educated in science, history and politics; she is a reporter, a brilliant orator, and an ideal private secretary.

ADAMS, JANE.

5 THE TEST. London: J. Long, 1910 BMC.
A male publisher's reader steals the plot of a woman's

novel. She later falls for him, marries him. Book is a chronicle of their unhappy marriage. Final reconciliation.

ADAMS, MARY. See WARD, ELIZABETH STUART (PHELPS).

ADDISON, JULIA DE WOLF (GIBBS). B. 1866. United States.

6   MRS. JOHN VERNON; A STUDY OF A SOCIAL SITUATION. Boston: R. G. Badger, 1909 NUC.
Social life of artistic and musical people in Boston. Main character is a rich widow who married after birth of daughter. The scandal forced her out of society and onto the stage.

ADELAIDE, SISTER MAGDALENE. See SHEPHERD, MARGARET LISLE.

AGATHA, SISTER.

7   CONFESSIONS OF A NUN. Philadelphia: Jordon, [n.d.] USC, 1891 PW.
Sister Agatha is in a convent because of her family's misfortunes and the loss of the man she loved. Her experiences in the French convent as well as the stories of other inmates. Attacks convent life.

AGNEW, ALEXANDRA GEORGETTE.

8   THE BREAD UPON THE WATERS. BY GEORGETTE AGNEW. London: W. Heinemann, 1911 BMC.
Iris Hawthorne becomes a successful artist because of her hard work and excellent talent. When she falls in love, she leaves the man to help her father who had been good to her when she was studying art. Another woman character is Kitty O'Kelly, an artist's model.

9   THE NIGHT THAT BRINGS OUT STARS. BY GEORGETTE AGNEW. London: W. Heinemann, 1908 BMC.
Unhappy wife, "unconventional, impulsive, and full of

imagination," leaves her husband and goes to London to make her living. She eventually becomes a successful novelist, has a love affair with her publisher.

AGNEW, GEORGETTE. See AGNEW, ALEXANDRA GEORGETTE.

AGRESTI, OLIVIA ROSSETTI AND HELENE ROSSETTI ANGELI.

10 A GIRL AMONG THE ANARCHISTS. BY ISABEL MEREDITH. London: Duckworth, 1903 BMC.
The young woman joins the anarchists in London and edits an anarchist journal. She, the anarchists, their ideals and their doings are all treated sympathetically.

AINSLIE, NOEL. See LISTER, EDITH.

ALAN, MIRIAM.

11 WEDNESDAY'S CHILD. London: S. Low, 1891 BMC.
Autobiography of Hester Steele, a depressing story of her gruesome experiences. The author's purpose is to denounce and expose "the practice of publicly and shamefully whipping girls," a practice she believed was common in Irish Roman Catholic convent schools.

ALBANESI, E. MARIA. See ALBANESI, EFFIE ADELAIDE MARIA.

ALBANESI, EFFIE ADELAIDE MARIA. 1866-1936. United Kingdom.

12 DIANA FALLS IN LOVE. London: Ward, Lock, 1919 BMC.
Several interesting women: Diana who prefers independence to living off relatives. She can enjoy life even in shabby clothes. She gives up her job as nursery governess to become a secretary. Her employer is a level-headed manager of an important business, and a woman

who on the other hand is infatuated with her young husband who married her for her money. Marlie Carrew, a "bachelor girl" living on her own in London, is very fond of her close friend Diana.

13 ENVIOUS ELIZA. London: E. Nash, 1909 BMC.
Lady Eliza writes serial shockers. She is a bit envious of women who have children. She is also envious of all the great writers because she is only a writer of popular fiction.

14 THE KINGDOM OF A HEART. BY EFFIE ADELAIDE ROWLANDS. London: G. Routledge, [1899] BMC.
Heroine is married three times before she is 21. All three husbands are wrong for her; all three are killed. One is shot to avenge his betrayal and desertion of a young woman. She married him on the condition that he leave her absolutely alone for a year.

15 ONE OF THE CROWD. A NOVEL. London: Chapman and Hall, 1913 BMC.
Celia is an actor's daughter, left by her father in her aunt's care, then saved from drudgery by her stepmother, a woman addicted to drugs. She is educated in a French school. Later she becomes a musical comedy actress and finally a success in serious drama. Story describes her Bohemian friends, her love, and career.

16 PATRICIA AND LIFE. BY E. MARIA ALBANESI. London and Melbourne: Ward, Lock, 1920 BMC NUC.
Patricia is an "accurate model of emancipated energetic girlhood today." She took destiny in her own hands and found a more suitable husband than the scoundrel she was doomed to wed.

17 THE WOMAN'S FAULT. BY EFFIE ADELAIDE ROWLANDS. London: Hurst & Blackett, 1915 BMC.
Unhappily married, leaves, becomes successful opera singer, returns to husband.

18 A YOUNG MAN FROM THE COUNTRY. London: Hurst & Blackett, 1906 BMC.
Unhappy marriage. Unattractive wife most interesting character in book.

ALBERT, MARY.

19 BROOKE FINCHLEY'S DAUGHTER. London: Chatto and Windus, 1891 BMC.

Mrs. Finchley simply makes a fresh start when her husband returns after a long absence. Thinking him dead, she had wiped him out of her mind, married and been widowed. On his return, a changed man, she accepts him, they enjoy a second honeymoon, and no fuss is made about her other marriage.

ALDEN, CYNTHIA MAY (WESTOVER). 1862-1931.

20 BUSHY; A ROMANCE FOUNDED ON FACT. BY CYNTHIA M. WESTOVER. New York: Morse, 1896 NUC.

Becky, daughter of a geologist, accompanies him on his trips. The story is an account of her adventures from four to sixteen: her escapes from drowning and scalping, her killing of buffalo, rattlesnakes, and Indians. She has all the adventures of a pioneer, trapper, and cowboy.

ALDEN, ISABELLA (MACDONALD). 1841-1930. United States.

21 MARA. BY PANSY. (MRS. G. R. ALDEN). Boston: Lothrop, [1903] NUC.

The love fortunes of four schoolmates. One's fiance marries another woman; one's husband dies on her wedding day; the third learns her fiance is cheating and throws him over; and the fourth marries a man who turns out to be a Mormon with six other wives. The three single women (two are now teachers and one is a nurse) come to her rescue, save her and one other wife. And a train just happens to run over her Mormon husband!

22 PAULINE. BY PANSY. (MRS. G. R. ALDEN). Boston: Lothrop, [c1900] NUC. London: C. H. Kelly, 1901 BMC.

"The flight of a high-spirited young wife from her husband." Ends in peace and reunion.

23 TWENTY MINUTES LATE. BY PANSY. Boston: D. Lothrop, 1893 NUC. London: C. H. Kelly, 1893 BMC.

Caroline Bryant's life takes a different direction when she gets on the wrong train. She ends up in Philadelphia where she learns stenography and typing.

ALDEN, MRS. G. R. See ALDEN, ISABELLA (MACDONALD).

ALDIS, MARY (REYNOLDS). 1872-1949. United States.

24   DRIFT. New York: Duffield, 1918 NUC.
"Minutely analyzed," Eileen Picardy is a "complex character, a woman weak and restless, possessed of many gifts, yet absolutely futile." She drifts through life and marriage.

ALERAMO, SIBILLA. See FACCIO, RINA (COTTINO).

ALEXANDER, MIRIAM. United Kingdom.

25   THE PORT OF DREAMS. New York: G. P. Putnam's Sons, 1912 NUC. London: A. Melrose, 1912 NUC BMC.
Story of the Irish support of the Jacobite cause and John Clavering's cowardice on three critical occasions. The young Irish heroine Kathleen Desmond is full of enthusiasm for the cause. It becomes the most important consideration of her life, at the expense, as one reviewer put it, of "what nature demands of women." She is "deficient in some of the finest attributes of her sex. Her unbalanced mind might, in the present day, have rendered her responsible for window smashing and pillar-box outrages."

26   THE RIPPLE. New York & London: G. P. Putnam's Sons, 1913 NUC. London: A. Melrose, 1913 BMC.
Dierdre's daring adventures and pursuit of hated kinsman across Europe. Set in late 17th century Ireland and northern Germany, when the Jacobites were in turmoil and the Irish hated. Dierdre, raised to hate her Irish country-people, is a spit-fire, equal to the perils she faces. Includes her love story.

ALEXANDER, MRS. See HECTOR, ANNIE (FRENCH).

ALIEN. See BAKER, LOUISA ALICE, also HUMPHREYS, ELIZA MARGARET J. (GOLLAN) AND LOUISA ALICE BAKER.

ALLATINI, R. See SCOTT, ROSE LAURE (ALLATINI).

ALLEN, EMMA SARAH (GAGE). B. 1859. United States.

27 THE HOUSE OF GLADNESS. Philadelphia: G. W. Jacobs, [1915] NUC. London: R. T. S., [1921] BMC.
"Superficially a love story. In reality a plea for the education of girls along useful lines." Because Virginia Tyrell did receive the most adequate kind of education, she is able to support herself when the time comes.

ALLEN, FRANCES NEWTON (SYMMES). B. 1865. United States.

28 HER WINGS. Boston: Houghton Mifflin, 1914 NUC.
Georgia Frame and her friend are feminists. They share an apartment and work for the movement. Georgia has a friend from college who is an impoverished widow with a family. A serious work which upholds feminism and marriage.

ALLEN, LINDA MARGUERITE SANGREE. United States.

29 FLORINE; OR, THE INNER LIFE OF ONE OF THE "FOUR HUNDRED." BY THE AUTHOR OF "MIGNONNETTE," "THE DEVIL AND I," ETC. [ANONYMOUS]. New York: G. W. Dillingham, 1891 NUC.
A journal covering Florine's life from age nine to age thirty. It is meant for her daughter to read some day.

ALLONBY, EDITH.

30 THE FULFILLMENT. London: Greening, 1905 BMC.
Heroine is a teacher and a novelist. Reviewer thinks novel

is a product of a disordered mind. "Miss Allonby died in order that her book might be issued exactly as she wrote it," and considering the "circumstances pity to publish the book at all."

ALMAZ, E. F.*

31 COPPER UNDER THE GOLD. London: Chatto and Windus, 1907 BMC.

Mary is the secret mistress of a married publisher whose wife had agreed to a separation and is travelling abroad. Mary has a child, and later believing the child is dead, she leaves the publisher whom she no longer loves. Years go by, and she meets a doctor who learns about her past. They marry. But when she chances to meet and to be reunited with her daughter, she again feels love for the publisher. The moral seems to be, says one reviewer, "carry on as you like; all comes out right in the end."

ALSOP, GULIELMA FELL. B. 1881.

32 MY CHINESE DAYS. Boston: Little, Brown, 1918 BMC NUC. London: Hutchinson, [1920] BMC.

An American woman doctor in China, her adventures in fire and flood.

AMBER, MILES. See SICKERT, ELLEN MELICENT (COBDEN).

AMES, ELEANOR MARIA (EASTERBROOK). 1831-1908. United States.

33 LIBRA: AN ASTROLOGICAL ROMANCE. BY ELEANOR KIRK. Brooklyn: Eleanor Kirk, [1896] NUC.

The personalities of Elizabeth and the hero reveal astrological influence. Elizabeth, a Libra, longs for freedom; he, a Capricorn, desires control. The story concludes with her refusal to promise to obey the man she is going to marry.

ANDERSON, ADA (WOODRUFF). B. 1860. United States.

34 THE HEART OF THE RED FIRS; A STORY OF THE
PACIFIC NORTHWEST. Boston: Little, Brown, 1908
NUC.
Alice, of Puget Sound, becomes a teacher, fights a forest
fire, rescues her husband, and finds his lost claim.

ANDERSON, MRS. FINLEY. United States.

35 A WOMAN WITH A RECORD: A NOVEL. New York:
G. W. Dillingham, 1896 NUC.
First person account of the life of an adventuress. Lenoir
lives in New York, is witty, cynical, enjoys gambling,
dinners, theater etc. One of her lovers is stabbed by a
jealous friend.

ANDERSON, STELLA (BENSON). 1892-1933. United
Kingdom.

36 I POSE. BY STELLA BENSON. London: Macmillan, 1915
NUC BMC. New York: Macmillan, 1916 NUC.
The heroine is a militant suffragist who travels for awhile
with a man but leaves him for her work. The author
confesses that she loves her heroine very much. Still she
shows the heroine attracted to a very unworthy young
man. The author constantly interrupts with comments and
asides and even with descriptions of her own experiences.

37 LIVING ALONE. BY STELLA BENSON. London:
Macmillan, 1919 BMC NUC.
A fantasy about Angela, a witch. She operates a small
general store that combines the functions of convent,
monastery, nursing home and college for people who wish
to live alone. It is a magic boarding house on an island on
the Thames. Angela gets around on a broomstick, hexes
committee meetings, the lives of policemen and grocers,
and gets respectable women doing all sorts of
unconventional things. "Satire of a civilization that
engages illogically in war...mingled with uproarious
farce...."

38 THIS IS THE END. BY STELLA BENSON. London: Macmillan, 1917 BMC NUC.

Jay and her brother are wards of Mrs. Gustus, a robust feminist novelist who is quite domestic in real life and who turns her whole life into material for novels. Jay and her brother leave their guardian to work with people in the slums. Jay has high ideals. She questions everything, takes nothing for granted. She is a rebel against conventions, proves her independence in becoming a bus conductor in London during the war and seriously considers living with a man. Jay holds on to her ideals, her belief in her freedom until the war shatters all her ideals. Her brother dies, and she gives up by marrying for respectability.

ANDREWS, ANNULET. See OHL, MAUDE ANNULET (ANDREWS).

ANGELI, HELENE ROSSETTI, jt. au. See AGRESTI, OLIVIA ROSSETTI AND HELENE ROSSETTI ANGELI.

ANGELL, BRYAN MARY (DOYLE). B. 1877.

39 THE SECRET OF THE MOOR COTTAGE. BY H. RIPLEY CROMARSH. Boston: Small, Maynard, 1906 NUC. London: Ward, Lock, 1907 BMC.

Mystery involving a beautiful young woman who killed her husband—a wicked Russian count.

ANGELLOTTI, MARION POLK. B. 1887. United States.

40 THE BURGUNDIAN; A TALE OF OLD FRANCE. New York: Century, 1912 BMC NUC.

Historical romance. Rosemonde of Provence, disguised as a man, becomes the best swordsman in Provence. She goes to Paris, schemes with the craftiest of princes, fights with the mightiest of warriors.

ANICHKOVA, ANNA MITROFANOVNA (AVINOVA). Russia.

41 THE SHADOW OF THE HOUSE. BY IVAN STRANNIK. New York: McClure, Phillips, 1906 BMC NUC. (Tr. by Emma A. Clinton.)

Because of the typical ignorance in which European women are raised, an ardent, unconventional young woman marries a blackguard. When she asks for a divorce, he insists on his legal right to the child. She resigns herself to a life of misery.

ANNA CATHARINA. See REBEK, LILLIE.

ANNE [pseud.].*

42 THE BACHELOR GIRL'S COLONIAL BEAU. BY ANNE. New York: Neale, 1904 NUC.

"Musings on the compensations of 'single blessedness.'"

ANNE, EDITH CHARLTON.

43 A WOMAN OF MOODS: A SOCIAL CINEMATOGRAPHE. London: Burns and Oates, 1897 BMC.

Valeria Villiers, a good and beautiful woman, learns years after she is married that her father died mad. Her children, according to her wish, take vows of celibacy. She founds a new order based on the theory that "as there are more women than can marry, only the healthiest in mind and body should undertake the responsibility of continuing the race." Her end is extremely tragic. She shuts herself up, studies the subject of heredity, then one night, kisses her husband goodbye, cuts her mother's throat, delivers a still-born, and throws herself in the river.

ANNESLEY, MAUDE. United Kingdom.

44 ALL AWRY. London: Mills and Boon, 1911 BMC.

Clo Mayne hates being a girl, hates being courted. She goes to sea disguised as a man, becomes the assistant purser of a ship that is shipwrecked. A romance follows.

45 THE SPHINX IN THE LABYRINTH. New York: Duffield, 1913 NUC. London: Mills and Boon, 1913 BMC.

Menage-a-trois shared by two women friends. One is an invalid, married to the man. The man loves both women, but when the wife dies, her friend refuses to marry him out of loyalty to the wife.

46 WIND ALONG THE WASTE. New York: J. Lane, 1910 NUC. London: Methuen, 1910 BMC.

Although Gonda, an American artist in Paris, ultimately pays dearly for her escapades, she leads an exciting life. Dissastisfied with her painting, she meets a group of Apaches and tries to flirt with one of them; he knocks her down. She then adopts a disguise and becomes honored in Apache circles as "Verre Bleu." She leads a double life as his companion, escapes from prison, and when his life is taken by the guillotine, she takes up with his son.

47 THE WINE OF LIFE. London and New York: J. Lane, 1908 NUC BMC.

Concerns divorce and a woman's revolt against the charges made against her of which she is innocent. But her new freedom begins with a voyage and includes romantic adventures.

ANONYMOUS AUTHORS—NOT IDENTIFIED.

48 ALTOGETHER JANE. BY HERSELF. New York: M. Kennerley, 1914 NUC.

Written in the form of an autobiography, Jane describes her life, beginning with childhood and ending with Jane "middle-aged and somewhat battered and bruised." Speaking with neither "gush nor morbidity," Jane tells of her literary work, and the possibility of happiness in friendship with a man.

49 THE AUTOBIOGRAPHY OF A HAPPY WOMAN. New York: Moffat, Yard, 1914 NUC. London: G. Allen & Unwin, 1915 BMC NUC.

The thoughts and feelings of a woman in autobiographical form. Segments of her life—her university education, her work as teacher, newspaper writer—mixed with observations about women very much in keeping with feminist ideas. She stresses the joy of work, supports divorce and remains single.

50 CHRYSTAL: THE NEWEST OF WOMEN. BY AN EXPONENT. London: Digby, Long, [1896] BMC.
Chrystal "claims the right to choose fathers for her children." Reviewers don't find this a new idea.

51 THE CONFESSION OF A REBELLIOUS WIFE. Boston: Small, Maynard, [1910] NUC.
The autobiography of a marriage. There is a seeming happiness, yet the wife is raising her son to be completely different from his father; she cannot bear to see any resemblance between them.

52 THE CONFESSIONS OF A DANCING GIRL. BY HERSELF. London: Heath, Cranton & Ouseley, 1913 EC.
Account of the training for the profession of an acrobat and dancer, the conditions and the ups and downs of a career. Set in Spain, Portugal, and South America as well as England.

53 THE CONFESSIONS OF A WOMAN. London: Griffith, Farran, 1893 BMC.
Married woman describes her various relations with other men and her passionate nature. One man, she says, gave her peace until he "buried his teeth in her neck." She describes herself as sensuous, subject to "great tides of emotion." "Purity is only ignorance," she declares and confesses she "has touched pitch."

54 CONFESSIONS OF MARGUERITE; THE STORY OF A GIRL'S HEART. New York: Rand, McNally, [1903] NUC.

Tries many ways to earn a living—artist, stage, publishing, etc., fails, goes home and marries "right man."

55 ELBOW LANE. BY THE AUTHOR OF "ALTOGETHER JANE". New York: M. Kennerley, 1915 BMC NUC.
Love story of a famous woman sculptor.

56   THE EMPTY HOUSE. New York: Macmillan, 1917 NUC.
     Joan grows up seeing mother a prisoner to too frequent
     pregnancies; fears marriage and marries only with
     understanding that there will be no children. All goes
     well, husband has his job, but she becomes restless. She
     begins to prod him to be more successful, pushes him so
     that he dies from the strain. According to one reviewer,
     the theme is that women who have no children become
     terribly destructive people.

57   A FAIR FIELD AND NO FAVOR. TO THE WOMEN OF
     ENGLAND, THIS VOLUME IS OFFERED. BY ONE OF
     THEMSELVES. London: H.J. Drane, [1912] BMC.
     Written to "illustrate the claim for a 'fair field' etc. for
     women." One reviewer says that "the style is such that it
     will be accepted with gratitude by few."

58   THE FLAW IN THE MARBLE. London: Hutchinson,
     [1896] BMC. New York and London: F. A. Stokes,
     [c1896] NUC.
     Madeleine LeFagon, a famous actress, provokes a passion
     in a sculptor for whom she has posed. She then finds the
     strength of his feeling for her a threat to her career and
     leaves him. He smashes the statue he has made of her
     because of the "flaw in the marble."

59   FOR A GOD DISHONOURED. BY AUTHOR OF
     *******. London: J. Long, 1899 BMC.
     A utopian socialist settlement: the members called the Just
     advocate domestic independence, women's rights and
     vegetarianism. Clothilde, the heroine, resembles her
     husband whose identity she assumes in the House of Lords
     and elsewhere. She inherits a peerage in her own right in
     the end.

60   FROM BEHIND THE PALE. London: Methuen, 1915
     BMC.
     Woman leaves her husband and child and takes a lover.
     Years later she tells her story to her seventeen-year-old
     daughter whom she never knew.

61 HARCOURT. BY THE AUTHOR OF "DAUGHTERS OF THE CITY". London: Simpkin, Marshall, 1899 BMC.

Tony conspires with her mother to go through life as a man in order to beat the Salic principle of law that makes a male heir inherit over a female. Triumphant in winning the inheritance, she keeps the disguise, fools all her friends, and goes on to take up feminist causes, posing as the male champion of suffrage. She mixes easily with men as their companion and equal, has a fighting bout with a big burly ruffian whom she defeats, and enters Parliament where her great speeches are generously applauded. The book is "a prolonged wail of pity for the poor, miserable, downtrodden, despised English wives and mothers and incidentally an impeachment of the anti-feminist tyrant—stupid, unintelligent man."

62 THE HARD WAY. BY A PEER. London: J. Long, 1908 BMC.

Heroine is married to a homocidal maniac. She leaves him and works in a tea shop. She marries again, bigamously; the author makes the marriage work out alright.

63 THE HIGHROAD; BEING THE AUTOBIOGRAPHY OF AN AMBITIOUS MOTHER. Chicago: H. S. Stone, 1904 NUC.

Story of a widow who had to support her family and how she did it. Details of her evolution from a West Virginia farm house to mother of English peeress are curious in their frankness.

64 HIS FAULT OR HERS? A NOVEL. BY THE AUTHOR OF "A HIGH LITTLE WORLD". London: R. Bentley, 1897 BMC.

Girl seduced, dies in childbirth: Achsa Mary, "child in years," is "caught into the whirring wheels of passion only to be flung out a crushed and withered flower." Her father's wild grief. The "beautiful charity" of her father and others.

65 HIS NAME.

Esther refuses to marry Wayland, a clergyman, because of

her liberty, art, and theosophy. Offers to find a wife for him but at book's end they marry. Watered-down Sarah Grand.

66 THE HOME-BREAKERS (AN ANTI-MILITANT SUFFRAGIST NOVEL). BY A LOOKER-ON. London: Hurst & Blackett, 1913 BMC.

Joan Campion and others abandon their lives for the Cause. Meantime, Joan's husband falls in love with someone else. The militants figure as the noblest and most self-sacrificing of women.

67 HUNGERHEART. THE STORY OF A SOUL. London: Methuen, 1915 BMC.

The full life of heroine John Wingfield—her unfortunate childhood, her studies at Oxford, and her work as secretary, saleswoman in a bookshop, writer of musical criticism, and actress. When she sickens of her drab life, she tries a relation with a married man for the experience of passion. When she half-heartedly becomes a suffragette, she is radicalized in the riot at Westminster. She comes to hate men but to have a large capacity for women friends. One reviewer says she realizes in the end that she is a cruel, selfish absurd creature.

68 HUSBAND AND BROTHER: A FEW CHAPTERS IN A WOMAN'S LIFE OF TO-DAY, AND FROM KEY-NOTE TO DOMINANT. Bristol: Arrowsmith, 1894 BS.

A young woman must earn her own way in the title story. In From Key Note to Dominant a woman does unconventional things but draws the line when it comes to doing wrong, "and that means only one thing in the feminine novel." "When it comes to that kind of freedom, women characters act as though Heavenly Twins never existed. Perhaps Miss Conway, B.A. really means to show what twaddle most of the talk about the rights and wrongs of the New Woman really is."

69 I; IN WHICH A WOMAN TELLS THE TRUTH ABOUT HERSELF. New York: D. Appleton, 1904 NUC BMC.

The story of her mental, moral and physical development, relates her marital infidelity, etc.

70 IN A SILENT WORLD; THE LOVE STORY OF A DEAF MUTE. BY THE AUTHOR OF "VIEWS OF ENGLISH SOCIETY". London: Hutchinson, 1896 BMC. New York: Dodd, Mead, 1896 NUC.

The inner history of a young woman who is deaf and dumb, in diary form.

71 IN STATU PUPILLARI. London: Sonnenschein, 1907 BMC.

Close study of a women's college at Cambridge from a woman's point of view. The women are modern, restless, self-reliant, serious, and ambitious. Eva's career shows her development from a fresher to high academic success in classical tripos. The love story is slight.

72 IN THE YEAR OF WAITING. BY A PEER, AUTHOR OF "THE HARD WAY". London: J. Long, [1916] BMC.

German spy novel. German governess involved; she's an incognito countess.

73 JULIE'S DIARY; A PERSONAL RECORD. Boston: J. W. Luce, 1908 NUC.

An adventuress similar to Bashkirtseff "teems with passionate thoughts about love." "Passes through the fires of hell unscorched," sweeter than ever.

74 LESLIE: A NOVEL. BY THE AUTHOR OF "A MODERN MILKMAID" ETC. London: Digby, Long, [1891] BMC.

A study of Leslie at a particular time in her life. She has just lost her mother and is grief-stricken. She is 22, "an atheist, a thinker of considerable power." She initiates a passionate relationship with her doctor and allows his wife to attempt to cross a rotten bridge and be swept away by the river. "For the short remnant of her life she is either bathed in the sheet lightning of passion or has murder running in her veins." At the end, she is stabbed.

75 LETTERS OF AN ACTRESS. London: E. Arnold, 1902 BMC. New York: F. A. Stokes, [1902] NUC.

Written to several men, one of whom she marries in the end. Describes the trials of her stage career and her life as an actress.

76 THE LETTERS OF THOMASINA ATKINS, PRIVATE (W.A.A.C.)—ON ACTIVE SERVICE. G. H. Doran, [c1918] NUC. London: T. F. Fisher, [1918] BMC.

Thomasina is a member of the Women's Auxiliary Army Corps (the "WAACS"); formerly she had been an actress leading a comfortable luxurious life. Description of the unromantic, hard, useful work the women do, of "regulations purposely made more severe than those of any boarding school, that there may be no possible shadow of justification for such vile rumors as those circulated by Hun propaganda, rumors which enrage her who knows so well that they are lies."

77 LETTERS TO MYSELF. BY A WOMAN OF FORTY. London: T. W. Laurie, [1912] BMC.

Views on the sex question.

78 THE MAHATMA: A TALE OF MODERN THEOSOPHY. London: Downey, 1895 BMC.

"The Countess and Mrs. Fleeting Montgomery (her accomplice) are...fair examples of the female trickster, who in these days takes to 'spooks' as formerly she took to husband hunting." Concerns theosophy.

79 THE MAIDS' COMEDY; A CHIVALRIC ROMANCE IN THIRTEEN CHAPTERS. London: S. Swift, 1911 BMC.

In this chivalric romance Dorothea DeVilliers is the knight, and a headstrong young woman named Dota Filjee is her Sancho Panza.

80 MERCILESS LOVE. BY THE AUTHOR OF "FOR A GOD DISHONOURED". London: J. Long, 1900 BMC.

She is an active anti-vivisectionist, writing articles and attending meetings, when a friend leaves her money for the cause, on the provision that she doesn't marry. She marries but either suicides or fakes her death (reviewers conflict) to keep the fortune from falling into the hands of vivisectionists.

81 A MOTHER IN EXILE. London: Everett, [c1914] BMC NUC. Boston: Little, Brown, 1914 NUC.

Her husband deserts her and takes the children. In letters to her daughter whom she is not allowed to see she tells the story of her marriage. One reviewer describes her as "a deranged mind suffering from the hallucination that everyone is against her."

82 THE MOTHER-LIGHT, A NOVEL. New York: D. Appleton, 1905 BMC NUC. London: Hutchinson, 1905 BMC.
Widow who loses her job joins the Mother of Light religious movement when her child dies. She starts out as a secretary in the movement, but as Mother Light the leader ages, the widow begins to take her place. When she falls in love, her passion for the religion makes her give up the man.

83 MY WIFE'S HIDDEN LIFE. London: Hodder and Stoughton, [c1913] BMC NUC. Chicago: Randy, McNally, [c1913] NUC.
The unhappy marriage of Hester and Gilbert, told by the husband out of painful regret that he never understood his wife. Her diary comes to his attention after she is dead. In it he discovers she was not a commonplace woman with narrow interests but a complex, unusual person.

84 THE MYSTERY OF A CORNISH MOOR. BY A NEW AUTHOR. Bristol: J. W. Arrowsmith, [1891] BMC.
Passionate Nita poisons her wicked grandfather, and while she is waiting for him to die, she talks to him with "great plainness of speech."

85 NORMANSTOWE. London: R. Bentley, 1895 BMC NUC.

Ella Lyell, on her own after father dies, takes a job as ballad singer in a music hall and matron of a boarding house. She's a strong, self-reliant woman.

86 ON HEATHER HILLS. Paisley: A. Gardner, 1891 NUC BMC.
The hero, not the heroine, is self-sacrificing. Mary Mellis from Australia marries a Scot, Malcolm Strong. He has a strong urge to protect her after her parents die. They have an idyllic honeymoon, but their marriage is unhappy. When Mary takes a fancy to Malcolm's cousin and elopes with him, Malcolm gets out of her life by pretending he

drowned. When this cousin, now Mary's husband, proves to be a dangerous drunk, Malcolm disguises himself as a servant to protect her. And when Mary's new husband dies and she goes back to Australia, Malcolm does nothing to stop her.

87 THE OPAL, A NOVEL. Boston: Houghton, Mifflin, 1905 NUC.

A woman who is nothing in herself takes her feelings from others, has every virtue but no individuality, marries and is unhappy.

88 THE OTHER KIND OF GIRL. New York: B. W. Huebsch, 1914 NUC.

Written in autobiographical form, the story of a factory worker who became a prostitute, not for economic motives but because "there comes an ache in your nerves to dance and dance when you do long factory work that can only be rested by aching your nerves some other way."

89 PAID IN FULL. BY THE AUTHOR OF "LOVE WILL FIND OUT THE WAY". London: The Family Story Teller, [1892] BMC.

Heroine is treated by father "with fiendish cruelty." She escapes him, has further adventures, happy ending.

90 PILLARS OF SMOKE. New York: Sturgis & Walton, 1915 NUC.

The love story of a new woman.

91 THE SORROWS OF BESSIE SHERIFF. London: Constable, 1912 BMC.

Nervous, sensitive, idealistic heroine. When her family is ruined, she works as a teacher and a journalist. Her romance is fruitless. "Depressing."

92 STAR OF THE MORNING; A CHRONICLE OF KARYL THE GREAT, AND THE REVOLT OF 1920-22. BY THE AUTHOR OF THE TRUTH ABOUT MAN. London: T. Burleigh, 1906 BMC.

Karyl was the great queen through whom "England made her women co-equal in power with her men."

93   A SUFFRAGETTE'S LOVE LETTERS. London: Chatto & Windus, 1907 BMC.

One reviewer says the author of the letters is in favor of the vote. Another says she gives up "the poor, dear, dull, mischief-making, silly dead old cause."

94   THEO. BY A PEER, AUTHOR OF "THE HARD WAY". London: J. Long, 1911 BMC NUC.

Story of her neglected childhood, her efforts to support herself, her "sordid" life in musical comedy and her unhappy marriage with an alcoholic husband.

95   TIME'S FOOL; AN ENGLISH IDYLL. Edinburgh: D. Douglas, 1901 BMC.

Romance of a woman who is a postmaster.

96   THE TRUTH ABOUT MAN. BY A SPINSTER. ILLUSTRATED BY FACTS FROM HER OWN PRIVATE HISTORY. London: Hutchinson, 1905 BMC.

A diatribe against men; shows innocent women how to deal with men; suggests women should stick to platonic relations.

97   UNVEILING A PARALLEL: A ROMANCE. BY TWO WOMEN OF THE WEST. Boston: Arena, 1893 W. (W: The Names "Jones (Alice Ilgenfritz)" and "Merchant (Ella)" are written on title page of the [Huntington Library] copy as though they were the authors.)

"A satire on modern civilization and a plea for justice to women, presented under the semblance of a picture of social life on the planet Mars." A person from earth visits two Martian cities: Thursia and Caskia where "the same code of morals applies to both sexes. In Thursia the women vote, legislate, engage in every kind of business, offer themselves in marriage and indulge in all the vices and amusements commonly reserved for men."

98   A WOMAN'S CRUSADE. BY A DAME OF THE PRIMROSE LEAGUE. London: Kegan Paul, 1893 BMC.

Lady Ethelhyrst is bored with the trivial activities that make up her life. She becomes a leader in county society and starts a crusade to help other women bring serious concerns into their lives. She starts a salon—a series of meetings where women discuss serious subjects. Her plan is a brilliant success.

ANSTRUTHER, E. H. See SQUIRE, EILEEN HARRIET ANSTRUTHER (WILKINSON).

ANTHONY, GERALDINE. D. 1912. United States.

99 A VICTIM OF CIRCUMSTANCES. New York & London: Harper, 1901 BMC NUC.
Madame Trevor is an "indomitable old lady" who "governs her family with an iron hand."

ANTROBUS, SUZANNE. See ROBINSON, SUZANNE (ANTROBUS).

APLINGTON, KATE ADELE (SMITH). B. 1859. United States.

100 PILGRIMS OF THE PLAINS. A ROMANCE OF THE SANTA FE TRAIL. Chicago: F. G. Browne, 1913 BMC NUC.
In her diary, Delia Randall describes her journey with a trading caravan traveling across the prairie in Kit Carson's day. She travels with her brother who is not strong. She tells of their adventures which include her love story.

ARDEN, JOAN.

101 A CHILDHOOD. Cambridge: Bowes and Bowes, 1913 BMC NUC.
Account of a young woman's childhood experiences and feelings at a London boarding school.

ARMFIELD, ANNE CONSTANCE (SMEDLEY). 1881-1941. United Kingdom.

102 AN APRIL PRINCESS. BY CONSTANCE SMEDLEY. New York: Dodd, Mead, 1903 NUC. London: Cassell, 1903 BMC.

Bright, witty young English woman outrages everyone with her boldness. Completely impatient with domesticity, she is more than unconventional. In her daring adventures with several men, her "pals," she lives her philosophy: escape convention, fall in love as often as possible—for new sensations. "In real life she would shake to its centre the most tolerant society. Only bolts and bars could protect her reputation."

103 COMMONERS' RIGHTS; A NOVEL. BY CONSTANCE SMEDLEY (MRS. MAXWELL ARMFIELD). London: Chatto & Windus, 1912 BMC NUC.

The story is concerned with family life in its relation to the individual and to the community. People's rights is the theme; women's suffrage is touched on. "Aesthetic radicalism" is the author's creed."

104 CONFLICT. BY CONSTANCE SMEDLEY. London: A. Constable, 1907 BMC. New York: Moffat, Yard, 1907 NUC.

Attacks the false ideals of womanhood, insisting that women need love and work. Mary von Heyton is such a good stenographer that her boss leaves her the business. She loves her work, ignores the emphasis on beauty that takes up so much of her women friends' time. The conflict concerns feminist ideas in a modern society as shown in the contrast ·between Mary, her individuality, energy, responsibility and another woman who lives only for and through men.

105 THE DAUGHTER; A LOVE STORY. BY CONSTANCE SMEDLEY. New York: Moffat, Yard, 1908 NUC. London: A. Constable, 1908 BMC.

Delia Willett is a suffragist and a socialist and is actively involved in both causes. She marries a man for 10,000 pounds to be donated to the Suffragist Society and converts him. The portrayal of various kinds of feminists contrasts conflicting ideals within the movement.

106 THE EMOTIONS OF MARTHA. London: Religious Tract Society, 1911 BMC.

Martha is restless at home. She yearns for an independent life in London in order to study art. She gets to London and to her studies, but the training proves too much for her. She must give up her hope of a career in art.

107 THE JUNE PRINCESS. London: Chatto & Windus, 1909 BMC.

She is a frank, independent, up-to-date young woman determined to have a career as the only worthwhile way to live her life. She takes a position which promises her greater independence and a flat of her own. She also organizes an international society to bring together women of all countries. Much good dialogue on the subject of women.

108 ON THE FIGHTING LINE. BY CONSTANCE SMEDLEY. London & New York: G. P. Putnam's Sons, 1915 BMC NUC.

Not a war story, but the battle of women to earn a living. Minnie Blunt's journal is a commentary on working women in London. Her own work as expert stenographer pays 25 shillings a week, three of which she banks every Saturday. At first Minnie is proud to work for Alliance Trust, proud of her nation at war, proud of big business, of success and of womanly women. Then she meets a suffragette who radicalizes all her thinking—especially about women.

109 REDWING: A NOVEL. BY CONSTANCE SMEDLEY. London: G. Allen & Unwin, 1916 BMC NUC.

Typifies the modern revolt of women. The story of Mimsy who left home at 17. Includes discussion of a women's club.

110 SERVICE. A DOMESTIC NOVEL. London: Chatto & Windus, 1910 BMC.

A daring, almost malicious book which challenges, by implication, the whole idea of the family. The story is of Phebe, a maid in a middle-class family. When her mother died, she was offered a poultry farm, turned it down and became a servant.

111 UNA AND THE LIONS. A NOVEL. London: Chatto & Windus, 1914 BMC.

In diary form, the story of a young schoolteacher who wins a month's trip to Italy in a limerick contest. Her adventures, mostly among other women.

ARMFIELD, MRS. MAXWELL. See ARMFIELD, ANNE CONSTANCE (SMEDLEY).

ARMSTRONG, ANNE AUDUBON (WETZELL). 1872-1958. United States.

112 THE SEAS OF GOD; A NOVEL. New York: Hearst's International Library, [c1915] NUC. London: Mills & Boon, 1916 BMC.

Character study of Lydia: after her father dies, she refuses the support of friends because she wants to arrange a wider and freer life for herself. First, she travels for a publishing firm and is in charge of hiring book salesmen. Then she meets and lives with a young married man. When she and her child are deserted, she becomes a prostitute. There is nothing of the white slavery theory here. Lydia knows what she's doing; for her prostitution is purely a business matter. The story is told simply, plainly, and powerfully; men make a bad showing in her story.

ARMSTRONG, ANNIE E.

113 MONA ST. CLAIRE. London & New York: F. Warne, 1897 BMC.

She inherits money from her grandfather and can at last do the philanthropic work she wants to do: she establishes a home for convalescents.

ARMSTRONG, ELISA. See BENGOUGH, ELISA (ARMSTRONG).

ARMSTRONG, ESTELLE AUBREY. United States.

114 THE INDIAN SPECIAL. New York: H. Lechner, [c1912] NUC.

Young woman works on Indian reservation.

ARNOLD, ADELAIDE VICTORIA (ENGLAND). United Kingdom.

115 FIRE I' THE FLINT. London: A. Rivers, 1911 BMC.

Esther Smith develops from a village dancer to an artiste in London and Paris.

116 REQUITAL. BY MRS. J. O. ARNOLD. London: Methuen, [1913] NUC BMC.

Subplot concerns two women authors—Jane Buchanan and Mrs. Wylde. Focus on Beatrice, the sacrifices demanded by her ambition and her loveless unhappy marriage to rich old Sir Henry Dacre.

ARNOLD, BIRCH. See BARTLETT, ALICE ELINOR (BOWEN).

ARNOLD, ETHEL M.

117 PLATONICS. A STUDY. London: Osgood, McIlvaine, 1894 NUC BMC.

The story of a friendship between two cultured women. Ronald loves Susan, a widow, whose "theories of life" forbid marriage. Her best friend Kit meets Ronald, loves him, and marries him. Susan and Kit part over this, but just as Susan is not completely able to give up her love for Ronald, so Kit cannot give up her friendship for Susan.

ARNOLD, LILIAN S. United Kingdom.

118 ALSO JOAN. London: John Long, 1911 BMC.

Careers of two sisters, one a teacher. A man comes near wrecking one's life.

ARNOLD, MAUD. B. 1873. United Kingdom.

119   BLOOD ROYAL. London: Greening, 1908 BMC.

Described as sentimental and morbid, the story is of a typewriter and her past, which includes a dead baby. Her lover's horror, when this is revealed to him, causes her flight and insanity.

ARNOLD, MRS. J. O. See ARNOLD, ADELAIDE VICTORIA (ENGLAND).

ASHTON, WINIFRED. United Kingdom. 1888-1965.

120   FIRST THE BLADE; A COMEDY OF GROWTH. BY CLEMENCE DANE. London: W. Heinemann, 1918 BMC. New York: Macmillan, 1918 NUC.

Laura and Justin are childhood playmates; the development of character is followed in the pair. When they come of age, Laura finds Justin lacking in certain qualities, and the book ends on a note of discord. "The sense of a half-pathetic, half-ironic comedy of human relationships is admirably sustained all through the book." The author may have exaggerated Justin's "male shortcomings."

121   LEGEND. BY CLEMENCE DANE. London: W. Heinemann, 1919 BMC NUC. New York: Macmillan, 1920 NUC.

Madala Grey's literary group gets the news one evening that she is dead at 28. Though Madala is the chief character, she never appears; her character is developed through the conversations of the group about her on the occasion of her death. She was a novelist who wrote about prostitutes and sex. She died in childbirth one year after leaving the group to marry a commonplace doctor. The discussion about her centers upon the question of why she gave up her art for a mere man. Only two in the group understand her, and they are silent. She appears in a vision to both of them at the end. The rest do not know her, yet she will be remembered only through the eyes of one of them—Anita Serle who is to write Madala Grey's biography.

122 REGIMENT OF WOMEN. BY CLEMENCE DANE. London: W. Heinemann, [1917] BMC NUC. New York: Macmillan, 1917 NUC.

Study of the "abnormal" psychological manifestation of the crush. Set in a girls' school. Clare Hartill, a teacher, is a tyrant over her colleagues and students, but she can win the love and devotion of her students at will—to feed her vanity and love of power. Thirteen-year- old Louise Denny kills herself because Clare seems to pet her one minute, bully her the next. Alwynne must choose between Clare and the man she loves. Psychoanalysis is used to cure one young woman of like obsession. Yet the author never allows us to forget the beauty of Clare and the attractiveness of her.

ASHWORTH, MARION.*

123 A SENTIMENTAL PILGRIM. London: Chapman & Hall, 1915 BMC.

Ida goes to Paris to study opera, and she is a grand success. She is accompanied by her mother Emily, who is too fully occupied with other men to watch Ida, and by her quiet sister whose premature death brings their father to Paris. The author seems to approve of the characters' behavior.

ASKWITH, ELLEN GRAHAM.

124 THE DISINHERITED OF THE EARTH. BY MRS. HENRY GRAHAM. London: A. Rivers, 1908 BMC.

Lady Verrier has a system of raising children which proves disastrous: her daughter is sentenced for murdering her child. Earnest and gloomy.

ATHERTON, GERTRUDE FRANKLIN (HORN). 1857-1948. United States.

125 AMERICAN WIVES AND ENGLISH HUSBANDS; A NOVEL. New York: Dodd, Mead, 1898 NUC. London: Service & Paton, 1898 BMC NUC.

"...by creating a living woman, who is human and not a

mere bag of views, she makes intelligible the point which Sarah Grand and others wish to make, and goes far towards proving it. She brings her heroine from America, where the women are, as a rule, far better educated than in England, and where they have far more independence of thought and initiative; she makes her deeply in love with her English husband, who, in his stolid, somewhat limited way, is a fine honest gentleman, and, in spite of their real love and respect for one another, she shows how the woman's individuality is being gradually crushed out by the husband's obtuseness in not seeing that, while loving him, she may have interests of her own in addition to her interest in his ambitions." The Athenaeum, 12 (1898), 597.

126 ANCESTORS: A NOVEL. New York & London: Harper, 1907 NUC. London: J. Murray, 1907 BMC.

Isobel Otis closes the door on the question of sex. She refuses marriage with its economic dependence on men to whom she declares: "I want nothing that your sex has to offer." Instead she proudly runs her ranch alone, travels by herself in Europe, and turns to politics, resolved to be a leader of women. The story is an analysis of her character contrasted to those of bored dependent wives of a community that insists women marry.

127 A DAUGHTER OF THE VINE. London & New York: J. Lane, 1899 NUC. London: Service & Paton, 1899 BMC.

The "gradual degradation of a beautiful and gifted woman." Nina Randolph's mother was a barmaid, who took to drink and who fed the infant Nina alcohol when her husband deserted them. Nina falls in love and has a child outside of marriage by a man who is indifferent to her. She marries a disreputable doctor and, after he dies, returns to her mother whom she has come to hate. Nina gradually yields to her passion for drink and dies. California in the 60s.

128 THE DOOMSWOMAN. New York: Tait, Sons, [c1893] NUC. London: Hutchinson, [1895] BMC.

Title refers to Chonita's supposed power to curse or heal humanity and is based also on the superstition that a woman who is a twin is doomed. Chonita is a beautiful, proud woman living in California in old Spanish days. Her keen mind hungers for knowledge and struggles against all the superstitions of her family. She falls in love with a man who is the enemy of her family, but precisely because he has great power over her, she knows she will never marry him.

129   JULIA FRANCE AND HER TIMES; A NOVEL. New York: Macmillan, 1912 NUC. London: J. Murray, 1912 BMC.

The intellectual and political evolution of a modern woman during the early 1900's, the obstacles met by the suffrage leader in the movement of those years, and the social and legal oppression of English women of that time.

130   MRS. BALFAME; A NOVEL. New York: F. A. Stokes, [1916] NUC. London: J. Murray, 1916 BMC.

Mrs. Belfame is accused of poisoning her husband. Although she didn't do it, she had thought about it. The women in her club support her even though they believe her guilty and constitute a body of "sob-sisters" around her in court.

131   PATIENCE SPARHAWK AND HER TIMES: A NOVEL. London and New York: J. Lane, 1897 BMC NUC.

"A defiant portrait of a defiant woman" with a "strong belief in the sanitary influence of brains." Her life from her early days on a western ranch—her experience among W.C.T.U. women, her friendship with Rosita, a variety actress, her career as a newspaper woman in New York and her attacks on yellow journalism, her poisoning of her husband, her trial—to the moment she is rescued from the electric chair.

132   PERCH OF THE DEVIL. New York: F.A. Stokes, [1914] NUC. London: J. Murray, 1914 BMC.

Ida's unlimited adaptability is contrasted with her husband's self-centeredness. She is an elemental, untutored young woman from Butte, Montana. He soon wearies of her and half scornfully offers to pay for lessons to make her a suitable wife for a man in the position he will someday fill as he advances. She takes him at his word and takes lessons from an older woman who is destined to be her rival. Her character develops under this tutelage, as does the rivalry between the two women.

133 A QUESTION OF TIME. New York: U. S. Book, [c1891] NUC. London: Gay and Bird, [1892] BMC.

In the first story, Boradil Trevor, a beautiful widow of 46, meets and marries a young man of 22. She is a talented painter as well as a good musician. The author approves of such marriages. In the second story, four men propose to the same woman, a widow, on the same morning.

134 SENATOR NORTH. New York and London: J. Lane, 1900 BMC NUC.

Betty, 29 year old heroine, is daughter of socially elite Washington family. She is extremely interested in politics, studies the Congressional Record, and wishes to establish a political salon, much to her mother's dismay. She has an unconventional relationship with the 60 year old married Senator North and eventually marries him. Atherton's views on the insolubility of the problem of marriages of mixed blood are explicit in the tragedy of Betty's half sister Harriet, an octaroon.

135 THE TRAVELLING THIRDS. London and New York: Harper, 1905 NUC BMC.

Catalina Shore shocks her conventional fellow travellers on their tour of Spain. She is completely contemptuous of ordinary conventions. The author criticizes different types of women, especially U.S. women. The mood is humorous rather than serious.

136 THE WHITE MORNING: A NOVEL OF THE POWER OF GERMAN WOMEN IN WARTIME. New York: F. A. Stokes, [c1918] NUC.

Gisela, a young American woman, goes to Germany as a writer. War breaks out and she becomes a nurse. Disillusionment with Germany follows, and she becomes the leader of German women in a revolt against the war which leads to the abdication of the emperor. They establish universal peace through the holocaust of their rebellion.

ATHERTON, MAIMIE.

137 GREY SAND. London: Everett, [1915] BMC.

A young woman is seduced by a man who tries to cover up what he has done by setting up a mock marriage. His political career is at stake, but he comes to a bad end.

ATKINSON, ELEANOR (STACKHOUSE). 1863-1942. United States.

138 HEARTS UNDAUNTED; A ROMANCE OF FOUR FRONTIERS. New York and London: Harper, [1917] NUC.

Eleanor Lytle is kidnapped and raised by Indians, taught woodcraft and Indian lore. After she returns to the colony, she marries. All the hardships she endures as a frontier wife, the escapes and dangers, the ordeal of the war of 1812, the courage demanded of her are fully described.

AUDOUX, MARGUERITE. 1863-1937. France.

139 MARIE CLAIRE. New York: Doran, 1911 NUC. London: Chapman & Hall, 1911 NUC BMC. (Tr. by J. N. Raphael.)

Autobiography of an orphan. After 10 years in an orphanage, she is moved to a farm where she works as a shepherdess and a domestic worker. The humiliation she undergoes drives her back to the orphanage, then to Paris where she becomes a seamstress.

140 MARIE CLAIRE'S WORKSHOP. New York: T. Seltzer, 1920 NUC. London: Chapman & Hall, 1920 NUC BMC. (Tr. by F. S. Flint.)

Sequel to Marie Claire. Realistic picture of small Parisian workshop and the lives of the women workers, the grim, ugly, remorseless toil.

AUSTIN, MARY (HUNTER). 1868-1934. United States.

141 THE LOVELY LADY. Garden City, New York: Doubleday, Page, 1913 NUC.

Built around a parable about types of women. Peter, the knight, seeks the lovely lady, who comes in many forms: a prostitute whom he treats as a person and who responds in kind; a typewriter who believes women should propose; a social-climber who finally refuses to play the marry-rich game, tells him he's unsuitable and returns his gifts; and finally Savina, who is not the ideal lady but a fine, intelligent young woman, Peter's equal. The novel ends in marriage, but one with a realistic attitude on both sides and no moondust.

142   NO. 26 JAYNE STREET. Boston: Houghton Mifflin, 1920 NUC.

Heroine leaves home for small apartment in New York.

143   A WOMAN OF GENIUS. Garden City, N.Y.: Doubleday, Page, 1912 NUC.

Written in autobiographical form, the struggle of a talented actress to satisfy conventional demands made of her and the demands of her art. Her deepest conflict lies in the obligations of her marriage and that part of her which refuses to be submerged.

AYRES, DAISY (FITZHUGH).

144   THE CONQUEST. New York: Neale, 1907 NUC.

This novel is a fearless tale of a very modern and daring woman. Determined to discover why her husband is attracted to another woman, she goes to Washington where her husband serves as senator, takes an assumed name, makes herself popular in official circles, and catches an Italian count. The author dissects her motives and her love for her husband in this psychological study of "love logic."

AYRES, RUBY MILDRED. 1883-1955. United Kingdom.

145   THE ROAD THAT BENDS. London and New York: Cassell, [1916] NUC BMC.

A woman who ran away from a brutal husband lives with a man and has a child—Millicent. Millicent, as illegitimate, is not accepted in society. She in turn marries a cruel and sullen man and later meets a man she loves.

BABCOCK, BERNIE (SMADE). B. 1868. United States.

146　JUSTICE TO THE WOMAN. Chicago: A.C. McClurg, 1901 NUC.

The women's clubs in the community discover the betrayer to be none other than the candidate for the U.S. Senate. They resolve to defeat his campaign. Learning this, he proposes to the woman who flatly rejects him to face poverty alone with her child. And later she's saved from suicide by the doctor she marries.

BABCOCK, WINNIFRED (EATON). B. 1879. United States.

147　ME: A BOOK OF REMEMBRANCE [ANONYMOUS]. New York: Century, 1915 NUC. London: T. F. Unwin, 1915 BMC.

Covers a year in the life of a young woman who leaves home to make her own way. Nora Ascough is one of 16 children; her mother was a tight-rope dancer. Nora goes to New York with $10 confident of her talent as a writer, makes her way in the business world, does newspaper work. She feels that writing is her work in life. She is engaged to three men at the same time, but loves a fourth.

148　TAMA. BY ONOTO WATANNA. New York and London: Harper, 1910 BMC NUC.

A mysterious fox woman, a blind girl shunned and detested as a witch, condemned to an awful isolation. Contemporary Japan. Sentimental.

BABCOCK, WINNIFRED (EATON) AND SARA BOSSE. B. 1879. United States.

149　MARION; THE STORY OF AN ARTIST'S MODEL. BY HERSELF AND THE AUTHOR OF "ME" [ANONYMOUS]. New York: W. J. Watt, [c1916] NUC.

She is engaged to a law student but earns her own living

as a model, actress or "any unconventional and hazardous thing that comes to hand." She is ready at one point to live with a man outside of marriage. She has many thrilling adventures and hair-breadth escapes "from want and infamy."

BACK, BLANCHE EATON. United Kingdom.

150   THE SIN AND THE WOMAN: A STUDY FROM LIFE. BY DEREK VANE. London and Sydney: Remington, 1893 BMC.

Eleanor Monroe is the woman who commits the sin "conveying" to get money to publish her novel. She becomes a famous novelist.

151   THE SOUL OF A MAN. BY DEREK VANE. London: Holden and Hardingham, [1913] BMC.

Neglected wife leaves her husband, divorces and remarries. Then she learns she prefers husband number one. Author arranges a convenient death for number two.

BACON, DOLORES. See BACON, MARY SCHELL (HOKE).

BACON, JOSEPHINE DODGE (DASKAM). 1876-1961. United States.

152   THE DOMESTIC ADVENTURERS. New York: Charles Scribner's Sons, 1907 NUC.

The wild adventures of three older single women in New York City; one is forty. One housekeeps for the other two—a teacher and an editor. The novel does not end in marriage.

153   OPEN MARKET. New York and London: D. Appleton, 1915 BMC NUC.

Evelyn Jaffrey gives up her youth to care for her aunt for years. She is left nothing when her aunt dies. She uses her small savings to buy clothes, gets invited to the Adirondacks, and meets a very unsophisticated backwoodsman, a cripple who has never seen a woman, and she proposes to him. She takes him around the world, educates him. In the end he is cured and all is well. In marrying, Evelyn was fully aware she was entering upon a new kind of slavery, different from her slavery to her aunt.

154 TO-DAY'S DAUGHTER. New York and London: D. Appleton, 1914 BMC NUC.

Lucia is nationally known for her work in prison reform. At 30 her father objects to her taking her work seriously and working regular hours just like a man compelled to earn a living. She ought to be content house-keeping for him or another man. She loves her father and ends up marrying a broad-minded surgeon she does not love enough to marry, but is still completely absorbed in her work. Her attitude changes with motherhood.

BACON, MARY SCHELL (HOKE). 1870-1934. United States.

155 IN HIGH PLACES. BY DOLORES BACON. London & New York: Doubleday, Page, 1907 BMC NUC.

Jean Meredith is an up-to-date young woman and a competent stenographer. She earns $10,000 in her position with an overworked businessman whose jealous wife almost ruins him. Because of the wife's jealousy, Jean is forced to leave her job. Nevertheless, through her good advice, she saves the business.

BAGNOLD, ENID. See JONES, ENID (BAGNOLD).

BAILEY, IRENE TEMPLE. 1880-1953. United States.

156 CONTRARY MARY. BY TEMPLE BAILEY. Philadelphia: Penn, 1914 NUC. London: Duckworth, [1916] BMC.

She is contrary because she prefers her job in a government office and her economic independence to marriage for the sake of support or a home which would mean economic dependence. She has modern ideas about love in keeping with her passion for work and freedom. Eventually she marries and helps her husband "face the world."

BAILEY, MAY HELEN MARION (EDGINTON). B. 1883.
United Kingdom.

157 THE MAN WHO BROKE THE RULE. London: Cassell,
[1919] BMC.

Rich elderly widow falls desperately in love with a man in
his 20's, proposes to him, and marries him. Her love and
jealousy of him and her death.

158 MARRIED LIFE; OR, THE TRUE ROMANCE. BY MAY
EDGINTON. London and New York: Cassell, [1917] BMC
NUC.

Realistic account of a man and woman whose first year of
marriage is happy. The next six are miserable because his
earnings must support five, she is worn out from
housekeeping and childbearing, and he becomes selfish and
morose, finally welcoming the chance to go off to the U.
S. on business. She refuses to take him back when he
returns because she liked her freedom so. Turnabout
ending with money solving their problems and differences.

159 THE SIN OF EVE. BY MAY EDGINTON. London, New
York: Hodder and Stoughton, [1913] BMC NUC. (Also
published as A Modern Eve. By May Edginton. New
York: F. A. Stokes, [1913] NUC.)

Ellen Flamartin is determined never to marry until the
wrongs against women are righted and the vote is won. A
militant suffragist, ardent organizer for the W.S.P.U.

BAILEY, TEMPLE. See BAILEY, IRENE TEMPLE.

BAINES, MINNIE WILLIS. See MILLER, MINNIE (WILLIS)
BAINES.

BAKER, JOSEPHINE (TURCK). D. 1942. United States.

160 THE BURDEN OF THE STRONG. Evanston, Ill.: Correct
English Pub. Co., [c1915] NUC.

Julia considers divorce but remains with her husband for
her child's sake.

BAKER, LOUISA ALICE. B. 1858. United States.

161 ANOTHER WOMAN'S TERRITORY. BY ALIEN. New York: T. Y. Crowell 1901 NUC. Westminster: A. Constable, 1901 BMC.
Friendship between two women who can be very honest with each other. One is a wife estranged from her husband; the other is the "other" woman.

162 A DAUGHTER OF THE KING. BY "ALIEN". London: Hutchinson, 1894 BMC. Chicago: F. T. Neely, 1894 NUC.

Florence, a violinist, marries the wrong man to please her adopted mother. The story is a fair presentation of what marriage without love means to a strong character. She keeps her daughter away from her husband by "accusing herself of immorality."

163 HIS NEIGHBOURS' LANDMARK. BY "ALIEN". London: Digby, Long, 1907 BMC.
New Zealand. Woman becomes a famous opera singer.

164 NOT IN FELLOWSHIP: A NOVEL. BY "ALIEN," AUTHOR OF "THE UNTOLD HALF". London: Digby, Long, 1902 BMC.
Heroine's marriage is a sacrifice for her uncle's sake. When her uncle dies, she divorces, eventually remarries.

BALBACH, JULIA ANNA NENNINGER. B. 1852. United States.

165 CUPID INTELLIGENT. New York: [Press of J. J. Little and Ives], 1910 NUC.
Equal education for women is one of the themes in a novel about intelligent people with a social conscience.

BALDWIN, M. E.*

166 THE HEIRESS OF BEECHFIELD: A NOVEL. London: Digby, Long, [1891] BMC.
She almost marries a bigamist, unknowingly, but does marry a moral young man instead. She writes literary criticism and reflects on the solar system.

BALDWIN, MARY RUTH. United States.

167 ALONG THE ANATAW. THE RECORD OF A CAMPAIGN. New York: Hunt and Eaton, 1891 BMC NUC.
Jessie Ward and her deacon husband campaign vigorously against the drinking of alcohol in the town of Masson.

BALFOUR, M. C. See BALFOUR, MARIE CLOTHILDE.

BALFOUR, MARIE CLOTHILDE. United States.

168 MARIS STELLA. Boston: Roberts, 1896 NUC. London: J. Lane, 1896 BMC.
'Poldine, because of her narrow conventionality, is unable to accept her husband Laumec's illegitimate child. Laumec, a French sailor, admires her virtuous superiority, but when the child's mother dies, conflict results. He leaves in anger; neither will yield. After losing him, she devotes her life to the child whom she has "rendered imbecile" with an angry blow. The last part of the book is a study of her developing insanity.

169 WHITE SAND. THE STORY OF A DREAMER AND HIS DREAM. BY M. C. BALFOUR. London: T.F. Unwin, 1896 BMC. New York: Merriam, [c1896] NUC.
Sylvia is married to an elderly man who had loved and lost her mother. She is "as unstable and shiftless as white sand." She runs away to Paris and then returns to her understanding husband who feels she needs his protection. Claire marries a man who is incapable of fidelity, in order to protect him. One reviewer calls the book "fin de siecle," finds the author "determined" to be flippant and emancipated. Another reviewer praises her "largeness and wholesomeness."

BALL, HYLDA (RHODES).

170 THE SECRET BOND. London: J. Long, [1917] BMC.
Lenore Mortimer struggles against poverty, is betrayed by

a man, comes under a hypnotist's power and goes on stage. Her past haunts her and fills her with guilt until she finds a man who has also "sinned." Then she is happy. Includes a description of a communist village.

171 THE UNHALLOWED VOW. London: J. Long, [1918] BMC.

Occult. Woman utilizes powers of darkness in carrying out her vow of vengeance against a man with whom she lived, would not marry her and is now a widower.

BALL, OONA HOWARD (BUTLIN). B. 1867.

172 A QUIET HOLIDAY. London: Cassell, 1912 BMC NUC.

She is commissioned to write a country book and retires to village in search of rural matter.

BAMFORD, MARY ELLEN. B. 1857. United States.

173 MISS MILLIE'S TRYING. New York: Hunt and Eaton, 1893 NUC.

Millie, through writing articles for the press, provides herself and her sister with the meager necessities of life. An unexpected bargain with a real estate agent ends her struggles.

BANKS, ELIZABETH L. 1870-1938. United States.

174 CAMPAIGNS OF CURIOSITY. JOURNALISTIC ADVENTURES OF AN AMERICAN GIRL IN LONDON. London: Cassell, 1894 BMC. Chicago: F. T. Neely, 1894 BMC NUC.

A young American journalist astonishes the British press with her unique campaign to get the news. She impersonates a servant in order to learn what the servant-master relation is like; she also takes the disguise of an heiress to learn about the aristocracy and of a laundry girl to learn about the work. Offers "various examples of women's emancipation."

175 THE MYSTERY OF FRANCES FARRINGTON. London: Hutchinson, 1909 BMC. New York: 1909 NUC.

As Margaret Allison, she writes light comedy; as Frances

Farrington, serious stories. She can't succeed as a serious writer because of her reputation as a popular writer. Comic murder trial; serious attack on American judicial system.

BANNING, MARGARET (CULKIN). B. 1891. United States.

176 THIS MARRYING. London: Hodder and Stoughton, [1920] BMC. New York: G. H. Doran, [c1920] NUC.

Horatia is a dedicated journalist; she prefers a career to taking care of children. The theme is the claims of men on women and vice versa. Described as sentimental.

BARBARA. See WRIGHT, MABEL (OSGOOD).

BARCLAY, FLORENCE LOUISA (CHARLESWORTH). 1862-1921. United Kingdom.

177 THE BROKEN HALO. London and New York: G. P. Putnam's Sons, 1913 BMC NUC.

Woman of 60, twice widowed, marries a man of 28 who later turns his attentions to a younger widow. Sentimental.

178 THE FOLLOWING OF THE STAR; A ROMANCE. London and New York: G. P. Putnam's Sons, 1911 BMC NUC.

Diana Rivers is very up-to-date. She does not believe in marriage; in fact, she will have nothing to do with men except as good friends. But she must marry in order to keep her fortune. Therefore, she proposes to a young minister who needs money for missionary work. They go through with the marriage service after which they part. She devotes her life to social causes. Eventually they fall in love.

BARCYNSKA, COUNTESS HELENE. See EVANS, MARGUERITE FLORENCE HELENE (JERVIS).

BARKER, ELLEN (BLACKMAR) MAXWELL. 1853?-1938. United States.

179 THREE OLD MAIDS IN HAWAII. BY ELLEN BLACKMAR MAXWELL. New York: Curts and Jennings, 1896 NUC. New York: Eaton & Mains, 1896 BMC.

Three women travel to Hawaii. Describes native customs, superstitions, scenes of native life.

180 THE WAY OF FIRE. BY ELLEN BLACKMAR MAXWELL. New York: Dodd, Mead, 1897 NUC.

Eurasian woman married to an English doctor realizes she is her husband's "intellectual inferior." "Domestic cares, child-bearing, natural limitations—many causes conspire to prevent her overtaking her freer and stronger mate in the race of life." She goes away to England in order to be properly schooled, and with the help of a young Englishwoman, Helen Sunderland, she rises to her husband's level.

BARKER, HELEN MANCHESTER (GATES) GRANVILLE.
D. 1950. United States.

181 EASTERN RED. BY HELEN HUNTINGTON. New York and London: Putnam, 1918 BMC NUC.

A study of the modern woman who has not outgrown dependence and is not yet ready for freedom. Rose is not able to hurt her husband by leaving him so kills herself; Elsie is not able to face the publicity of a divorce. A good deal is heard of the suffrage movement.

182 THE SOVEREIGN GOOD. BY HELEN HUNTINGTON. New York and London: G. P. Putnam, 1908 BMC NUC.

A story which deals with the social gaieties of the New York smart set. Friendship between rich American woman and poor European man twelve years younger. He marries a younger woman. Study of the older woman.

BARKER, S. DARLING.*

183 MARS. London: Hutchinson, 1898 BMC.

The heroine is described as a "noisy young Amazon" with the language of a "brainless stable boy," an "exaggerated specimen" of the modern cigarette-smoking heroine. She seeks revenge on the man who ruined her father.

BARMBY, BEATRICE HELEN. D. 1904. United States.

184   BETTY MARCHAND. New York: G. H. Doran, [c1918] BMC NUC.

The story of Betty's life from 6 to 35. Left alone at 17, she enters the business world as a stenographer and after a difficult struggle becomes a successful business woman.

185   SUNRISE FROM THE HILLTOP. New York: G. H. Doran, [c1919] BMC NUC.

Marriage for this young Englishwoman means a complete uprooting. She must give up her beloved English home to live in a New York apartment. The story describes all the painful adjustments she is forced to make.

BARNETT, ADA.

186   FOR THE LIFE OF OTHERS: A NOVEL. BY G. CARDELLA. London: Sonnenschein, 1897 BMC.

Heroine devotes her life to preaching that persons cursed with hereditary insanity as she is should avoid marriage for the sake of others. She establishes a hospital and a settlement.

187   THE PERFECT WAY OF HONOUR. BY G. CARDELLA. London: S. Sonnenschein, 1894 BMC.

Mary Carruthers discovers her husband has an illegitimate son older than their own. She forces him to acknowledge his son publicly, treating him "in the grand style of the modern young woman destined to regenerate the world."

BARNETT, ANNIE.

188   DRIFTING THISTLEDOWN. BY MRS. P. A. BARNETT AND ANOTHER. London, New York: Longmans, Green, 1910 BMC NUC.

The heroine, an "incorrigible flirt," believes that the single professional woman has the advantage of financial independence, and that when all the professions are open to women, marriage will have to be made more attractive to compete.

BARNETT, EDITH A. United Kingdom.

189   A CHAMPION IN THE SEVENTIES: BEING THE TRUE RECORD OF SOME PASSAGES IN A CONFLICT OF SOCIAL FAITHS. Chicago: H.S. Stone, 1898 NUC. London: W. Heinemann, 1898 BMC.

Tabitha was a champion of women's independence in the 1870's. She broke away from her family to escape the idleness imposed on her at home and went to London where she edited the Woman's Patriot, worked for the social betterment of women, and almost starved. The author says, "Her life and her death proved as to women's strength of body nothing except that this woman never had a fair chance. They proved a good deal to some of us as to one woman's strength of mind, and she will be the first to say that her life and her work were not wasted, if they gained for women less strong than herself the right to try in an easier way." One reviewer comments that since the conditions of the 70's are part of history, this might make women contented with what they have now.

190   DR. AND MRS. GOLD: AN EPISODE IN THE LIFE OF A CAUSE. London: Sonnenschein, 1891 BMC.

Inner life of an anarchist community and the conflict in a woman's mind between devotion to the cause and love. Clara David becomes the mistress of Dr. Gold who has deserted his wife. But she is an earnest anarchist while he has none of her passion for the cause. She gives her full devotion as a revolutionary to the cause of social anarchism. "Poor Clara's doom might easily have been more terrible than it was," says one reviewer.

191   THE FETICH OF THE FAMILY. A RECORD OF HUMAN SACRIFICE. London: W. Heinemann, 1902 BMC NUC.

This painful 30-year history of a family focuses upon the mother and her two daughters. The first born is retarded; the second, normal. The mother sacrifices the second to her resolve that no difference will be made between the two. The second daughter devotes her life to her sister out of duty but leads a sad, shut-away life.

192   SUNNINGHAM AND THE CURATE. London: Chapman and Hall, 1899 BMC.

In the Cranford mode, a semi-suburban neighborhood in the 60's.

193   A WILDERNESS WINNER. London: Methuen, 1907 BMC.

Realistic picture of what the life of a woman in the American West was really like and Phoebe's crushing disillusionment with the gloom of it all.

BARNETT, MRS. P. A. See BARNETT, ANNIE.

BARR, AMELIA EDITH (HUDDLESTON). 1831-1919. United States.

194   THE BLACK SHILLING: A TALE OF BOSTON TOWNS. New York: Dodd, Mead, 1903 NUC. London: T.F. Unwin, 1904 BMC.

The witchcraft trials. Cotton Mather drawn as a savage.

195   CECILIA'S LOVERS. New York: Dodd, Mead, 1905 NUC. London: T.F. Unwin, [1905] BMC.

Cecelia, makes an intelligent choice of one of the lovers at the end of the novel. She is a young woman on her own. Her first ambition is to be a great cook and make lots of money. But she becomes a secretary to an artist.

196   CHRISTINE, A FIFE FISHER GIRL. New York and London: D. Appleton, 1917 BMC NUC.

Christine Ruleson is a fisherman's daughter whose Scottish parents are ambitious for their son Neil because they believe he is the brightest. But it is Christine who tutored Neil. She is a strong generous person who chooses a fisherman husband over a lord of a nearby manor. Her marriage is happy. She discovers she can write, has stories and poems published, and becomes a well-known novelist.

197   THE FLOWER OF GALA WATER: A NOVEL. New York: R. Bonner's Sons, 1895 NUC. London: S. Low, 1895 BMC.

Though her guardian promises her in marriage to his nephew, Katherine Janfarie chooses her own partner.

198 THE HEART OF JESSY LAURIE. New York: Dodd, Mead, 1907 NUC. London: C. Brown, 1907 BMC.

Young woman, tricked into thinking she's married, has a child. As it turns out, the marriage is valid, the seducer-husband drowns, and she's free to marry her faithful lover.

199 JOAN; A ROMANCE OF AN ENGLISH MINING VILLAGE. New York and London: D. Appleton, 1917 BMC NUC.

Study of Joan, a middle-class English woman living in a Yorkshire coal-mining town. When trouble develops in the mines, Joan organizes the women to fight for the welfare of their children. Study of miners and their home life, much of it in dialect.

200 AN ORKNEY MAID. New York and London: D. Appleton, 1918 BMC NUC.

One of the two heroines goes to the front as a nurse to take care of her lover. Crimean War. Founding of the Red Cross.

201 A SINGER FROM THE SEA. New York: Dodd, Mead, [c1893] NUC. New York and London: B. F. Stevens, [1893] BMC.

Dena Penelles, daughter of simple Cornish fishing couple, has a beautiful voice. She is lured away from home by a man who promises her a singing career. She earns her living singing and supports her husband and child. When both die, she wanders for a while, then returns home. In the end she marries an old faithful lover.

202 A SONG OF A SINGLE NOTE; A LOVE STORY. New York: Dodd, Mead, 1902 NUC. London: B.F. Stevens and Brown, 1902 BMC.

Maria's tyrannical father forces her to marry against her will, but at the altar, she says no.

203 WAS IT RIGHT TO FORGIVE? A DOMESTIC ROMANCE. Chicago and New York: H. S. Stone, 1899 NUC BMC. London: T. F. Unwin, 1900 BMC.

"Theorizes very fully on the separate standard of morality

required of men and women. Two married women, one strong, the other a weak woman who drinks, are contrasted. The first forgives her frivolous unfaithful husband, and the second is forgiven by her husband though she ruins his reputation.

BARRINGTON, EMILIE ISABEL (WILSON). 1842-1933. United Kingdom.

204 LENA'S PICTURE. A STORY OF LOVE. Edinburgh: D. Douglas, 1892 NUC. London: Osgood, McIlvaine, 1893 BMC.

Both Lena's mother and sister are insane. The novel is a character study of Lena, her recognition that she cannot marry, her repugnance at the idea that she could be happy in a love affair while her sister is suffering alone. She arrives at a state of peace and serenity and strength, derived from a non-defined spiritual source, a mysterious light.

BARSTOW, EMMA MAGDALENA ROSALIA MARIA JOSEFA BARBARA ORCZY. 1865-1947. United Kingdom.

205 THE EMPEROR'S CANDLESTICKS. BY THE BARONESS EMMUSKA ORCZY. London: C.A. Pearson, 1899 BMC. New York: C.H. Doscher, [c1908] NUC.

A Russian woman of high rank is a spy.

206 LADY MOLLY OF SCOTLAND YARD. BY THE BARONESS ORCZY. London, New York: Cassell, 1910 BMC NUC.

Lady Molly solves a series of mysteries. In the last she clears her husband of a murder charge and retires from detective work.

BARTLETT, ALICE ELINOR (BOWEN). 1848-1920. United States.

207 A NEW ARISTOCRACY. BY BIRCH ARNOLD. New York: Bartlett, 1891 NUC.

Two daughters and a son of a minister must make their

own living when their father dies. They begin kitchen farming. One daughter becomes a cook for a wealthy family, and the other organizes a society of universal brotherhood and gives lectures "in the midst of a socialist movement among workers of a great city." She is the "new aristocracy" wherein "moral worth and purpose count first with brain and healthy digestion a good second. Idealistic.

BARTLETT, LUCY RE.

208 TRANSITION. A PSYCHOLOGICAL ROMANCE. BY LUCY RE. London: Longmans, Green, 1914 NUC BMC.

Novel is a defense of militant feminism. Described as a "morbid and neurotic girl," Maimie prefers earning her own living to marrying. Author presents people with mystical powers, contrasting "their special views, special feelings, special tensity and rapidity of psychological development," with the "stolid restiveness of the ordinary type."

BARTLETT, VANDA WATHEN.

209 HEART'S DESIRE. London: J. Lane, 1899 BMC.

Vail Glannock is unhappy in her marriage to Norman and very much attracted to Mr. Beauvigne. The story consists of her meetings and discussions with this man that hide their true passion. In the end, Gail chooses to remain with her husband. "An instance of what a woman writer is capable of when she conscientiously analyzes the feelings of a woman." The author "boldly faced the truth that a woman whose heart is not satisfied by her husband's affections can love another, acknowledging it to herself, but not finally succumbing to its power."

BARTLEY, NALBRO ISADORAH. B. 1888. United States.

210 PARADISE AUCTION. Boston: Small, Maynard, [1917] BMC NUC.

For the sake of her son, Darley Heath gives up her stage career once she gets her divorce. She watches him grow to make a poor marriage and to degenerate. She asks herself whether her son was worth all her sacrificing. An admirable, sympathetic character.

211 A WOMAN'S WOMAN. Boston: Small, Maynard, [c1919] NUC BMC. London: Hodder and Stoughton, [1920] BMC.
At 37, Denise feels "shabby" and "dowdy," and her family considers her the same. Step by step the changes of her life: she joins several women's clubs, goes to women's conventions, and finally becomes the best known woman in the U.S. Her family, on the other hand, suffers. At the end, she realizes she has neglected her family.

BARTON, MARION T. (DAVIS).

212 AN EXPERIMENT IN PERFECTION. London and New York: Doubleday, Page, 1907 BMC NUC.
The experiment is a marriage between a young woman and man who were sweethearts from childhood and who took up careers. She studied nursing; he prepared for the ministry. The marriage lasts only six months because the husband dies of overwork. The wife has a very close woman friend with whom she shares all her thinking.

BASCOM, LEE. United States.

213 A GOD OF GOTHAM: A ROMANCE FROM THE LIFE OF A WELL-KNOWN ACTRESS. New York: G. W. Dillingham, 1891 NUC.
Donita Lorraine is a celebrated actress in New York. Her love story involves a man in high society.

BASKERVILLE, BEATRICE C. United Kingdom.

214 WHEN SUMMER COMES AGAIN. London: Simpkin, Marshall, 1915 BMC.
Young Irish woman is penniless and alone after her father's suicide. She takes a position as companion with a Jewish family in Vienna. Here she becomes involved in espionage. She marries but suffers because her German husband is unworthy. She is mistreated by a German secret service agent, but escapes to Russia. In the end she

marries again—her first husband died—but with the full sympathy of the author who regrets her loss of independence.

BATEMAN, MAY GERALDINE FRANCES.

215 FARQUAHARSON OF GLUNE. London: Chapman & Hall, 1908 BMC.

About politics and women in politics.

216 THE GLOWWORM. London: W. Heinemann, 1901 BMC NUC.

We follow the development of Aseneth's character from childhood to her death. Passionate and eager in nature, she's already a rebel at five, leaves home at seventeen, becomes an agnostic, makes an unsuccessful marriage, writes novels, and achieves fame as an author.

BATES, MARGRET HOLMES (ERNSPERGER). 1844-1927. United States.

217 THE PRICE OF THE RING. BY MARGRET HOLMES. Chicago: F. J. Schulte, [1892] NUC.

Plea for social purity and one code of morals for both husband and wife. Involves infidelity on both sides.

BATSON, HENRIETTA M. United Kingdom.

218 THE EARTH CHILDREN. London: Hutchinson, [1897] BMC.

Set in Wessex. Lil Goodeve and Dick Jennings love each other from childhood. A commercial traveller named Clement Drury seduces Lil and sets up a mock marriage. Lil eventually leaves him, wanders through Wessex looking for work, returns to faithful Dick and murders the wicked Drury.

219 SUCH A LORD IS LOVE: A WOMAN'S HEART TRAGEDY. London: A.D. Innes, 1893 BMC.

Lord Love leads the four Miss Temples to different lives. One marries and has ten babies. But the focus is on the other three: the widow who had married for love and suffered and who then proposes to a vicar with very strict ideas about obedience in wives. Adria who marries a squire though he had an affair with a married woman and renews the relationship. She leaves him but is persuaded to return and to keep forgiving him for unfaithfulness. And Elizabeth who writes. She jilts her fiance almost at the altar and later weds an Oxford don. They live in "stuffy Oxford quarters...where she has to write to make ends meet."

BAXENDALE, FLORENCE.

220 THE DISENCHANTMENT OF NURSE DOROTHY: A STORY OF HOSPITAL LIFE. London: Skeffington, 1900 BMC.

An expose of faults in the hospital system. One reviewer thinks Dorothy suffers most from a house surgeon's love.

BAYLISS, HELEN.

221 A WOMAN IN THE CITY: A NOVEL. London: J. Long, 1903 BMC.

A woman of strong passions and impulses, without any standard of moral action, has one desire—to be luxuriously free. She's shown in various moods and under different influences.

BAYLY, ADA ELLEN. 1857-1903. United Kingdom.

222 DOREEN: THE STORY OF A SINGER. BY EDNA LYALL. London: Longmans, 1894 BMC. New York: Longmans, Green, 1894 NUC.

An Irish patriot by heredity and conviction, she is also a great popular singer and helps the cause by her singing. She is imprisoned and loses her voice because of an illness brought on by her imprisonment. The book closes with her marriage to an Englishman who was in the same prison.

223 WAYFARING MEN; A NOVEL. BY EDNA LYALL. New York: Longmans, 1897 NUC. London: Longmans, 1897 BMC.

Concerns actresses and actors. The author confers her

benediction on the acting profession, at the same time "urges the iniquity of English divorce laws." Christine Greville makes a marriage for money rather than love and cannot get a divorce when her husband proves unfaithful.

BAYNTON, BARBARA. Australia.

224 HUMAN TOLL. London: Duckworth, 1907 NUC BMC.
Grim, realistic study of Ursula's childhood—infancy to dawning womanhood. Set in Australia.

BAZAN, EMILIA PARDO. 1852-1921. Spain.

225 A CHRISTIAN WOMAN. New York: Cassell, [c1891] BMC NUC. (Tr. by Mary Springer.)
Carmen refuses to stay in her father's house because to do so would condone the fact that he keeps a mistress. Therefore she marries an old man she does not love and remains faithful to him though she is greatly tempted by her love for Salustio, her husband's nephew. The question the novel asks is "How much more virtuous was she than the girl who does not exact the wedding ring as a prelude to her diamonds and her brougham?"

226 MIDSUMMER MADNESS. Boston, Mass.: C. M. Clark, 1907 NUC. (Tr. from the Spanish by Amparo Loring.)
Intense and unconventional love story set in Spain. The author is "an ardent upholder of equal rights...educational, social and political. Her theories are exploited by the hero throughout the novel."

227 MORRINA (HOMESICKNESS). New York: Cassell, [c1891] BMC NUC. (Tr. by Mary J. Serrano.)
Morrina, as a servant in the household of Dona Autora, is lonesome, friendless, and homesick. After she is seduced by Dona Autora's son, she suffers terrible melancholy and kills herself.

228 THE SWAN OF VILAMORTA. New York: Cassell, [c1891] NUC. (Tr. by Mary J. Serrano.)
Two women love the "swan"—a young selfish Galacian poet. Leocadia is a middle aged teacher whose love for the

poet makes her ignore her crippled child and finally brings her to ruin and suicide. Hers was an intellectual love, love for his art. Madrilena, on the other hand, has a quick passionate affair with the poet and proceeds to forget him. Her old husband dies when he learns of the affair.

229 A WEDDING TRIP. New York: Cassell, [c1891] NUC. (Tr. by Mary J. Serrano.)

Lucia, sold by father for social position to old worn-out rake and married by rake for her money, is accidentally separated from him shortly after the wedding. Thinking he deserted her, she falls in love with a young man. Old husband torments her with his jealousy. A second character Pilar is a fine portrait of a "modern hysterical girl."

BEACON, EVELYN.*

230 ONCE OF THE ANGELS. London: Methuen, 1913 BMC. Concerns white slave traffic. "Crudely written."

BEALS, HELEN RAYMOND (ABBOTT). B. 1888. United States.

231 THE MERRY HEART. BY HELEN RAYMOND ABBOTT. New York: Century, 1918 NUC BMC.

Anne Carew, the oldest of three sisters living on New England farm, is self-sacrificing, living her life for the sake of the family, until the day she asserts herself and leaves.

BEAUFORT, E. V.*

232 SATAN FINDS SOME MISCHIEF STILL: A CHARACTER STUDY. London: T. Fisher Unwin, 1899 BMC.

"Study of modern, emancipated" Herrice. One reviewer describes her story as "harmless"; another says she "brings ruin on other people's lives as she advances with sure steps in her brilliant and selfish career."

BECKETT, CECIL (GRIFFITH).

233 CORINTHIA MARAZION. BY CECIL GRIFFITH (MRS. S. BECKETT). London: Chatto and Windus, 1892 BMC. Philadelphia: J. B. Lippincott, [1892] NUC.

Corinthia, an educated and intelligent woman, is forced into marrying a clergyman she doesn't love because she was compromised by having to spend a night on an island with him. She is an agnostic and the literary associate of her adopted father, a scientist. The clergyman, after an eight-month struggle between loving his wife and loving his soul, dies. Three years later she makes a good marriage.

BECKETT, MRS. S. See BECKETT, CECIL (GRIFFITH).

BECKLEY, ZOE. D. 1961. United States.

234 A CHANCE TO LIVE. New York: MacMillan, 1918 NUC.

At 14, Annie Hargan becomes the head of her poor family with the death of her father. She provides for her family first by earning $2 a week as a cash girl. She then moves up to a factory job at $10. When the factory burns down, she is safe but jobless. She gets a job as a switchboard operator, then office work at $6, and finally as a stenographer she earns $12 a week: the whole struggle of this young woman from the slums trying to earn a subsistence wage. Even love and marriage bring no relief from her hardships.

BEDFORD, H. LOUISA.

235 HIS WILL AND HER WAY. London: S. Paul, 1911 BMC. Jennie King inherits a mill from her father while her worthless brother inherits only an annuity. Describes her dealings with her manager and with the young women who work in her factory.

BEDFORD, JESSIE. United Kingdom.

236 CORNISH DIAMONDS. BY ELIZABETH GODFREY. London: Bentley, 1895 NUC BMC.

Love versus career. Jenifer Lyon studies the violin. Her

young man loses interest in her for a slight reason, becomes engaged to a widow, but returns to Jenifer when the widow jilts him. Jenifer refuses him, saying she loves her violin more. For a long time she holds out for music but marries in the end.

237 THE CRADLE OF A POET. BY ELIZABETH GODFREY. New York and London: John Lane, 1910 BMC NUC.

Therese, impulsive, marries an architect who goes downhill; she takes up Greek dancing to support them. She finally marries someone else—an old lover.

238 A STOLEN IDEA: A NOVEL. BY ELIZABETH GODFREY. London: Jarrold, 1899 BMC.

Delicia Watson, aspiring author, steals a plot and writes a successful novel. Author of the idea finds his work a success but himself unknown. Then Delicia falls in love with him, and they reach a good conclusion.

239 'TWIXT WOOD AND SEA. London: Chapman and Hall, 1892 BMC.

Contemplative, melancholy autobiographic account of Eleanor Baxdale's life—her childhood, girlhood, her two marriages.

BEECHER, CAROLYN. United States.

240 MAID AND WIFE. New York: Britton, [c1919] BMC NUC.

A young woman raised in luxury is forced to earn her own living when her father dies and the family is left penniless. First she holds a job as a saleswoman in a large department store—until she is fired ostensibly for stealing but actually for not playing up to the floorwalker. Then she marries, but finds the life so dull that she returns to New York to take up her business career again. By the end, she returns home.

241 ONE WOMAN'S STORY; A NOVEL. New York: Britton, [c1919] BMC NUC.

Margaret Drayton knows nothing about housework when she marries because her family is quite well-to-do. Her great interest is music. Her lawyer husband expects her to cook and to put up with his wining and dining of women clients, but she refuses to do either. She devotes her time to music much to his frustration. The arguments go on until the very end when a tragedy ends their estrangement.

BELDEN, JESSIE PERRY (VAN ZILE). 1857-1910. United States.

242 FATE AT THE DOOR. Philadelphia: J. B. Lippincott, 1895 NUC.

Mrs. Courtlandt, suspecting her husband is losing interest in her, tries to establish a platonic relationship with a man. Her conversations and meetings with him make up most of the novel which ends with her conviction that platonic relations between men and women are impossible.

BELL, EVA MARY (HAMILTON). B. 1878. United Kingdom.

243 IN THE WORLD OF BEWILDERMENT. A NOVEL. BY JOHN TRAVERS. London: Duckworth, 1912 BMC.

Story of a marital triangle which touches on women's suffrage.

244 SECOND NATURE: A STUDY IN CONTRASTS. BY JOHN TRAVERS. London: Duckworth, 1914 BMC.

The hero, to inherit his fortune, must marry a woman who has been sentenced to a term in prison. He does so, but since society is shocked by his wife's manners, he takes her to a lonely station on the Indian frontier.

BELL, FLORENCE EVELEEN ELEANORE (OLLIFFE). 1851-1930. United Kingdom.

245 THE GOOD SHIP BROMPTON CASTLE, A NOVEL. BY LADY BELL. London: Mills & Boon, [1915] NUC BMC.

Author simply reverses the sex roles of the traditional love story. The young woman is the naval officer. She pursues Ralph at his club till she gets to talk to him and leads him to the altar aboard ship. To show how bold Hildred really is, the author creates Antonia who also loves Ralph but is completely passive, reticent and lady-like.

246 THE STORY OF URSULA. BY MRS. HUGH BELL. London: Hutchinson, 1895 BMC NUC.
At 22, Ursula Vane loses her position as governess when she is discovered being kissed by her employer's son. She is persuaded to marry her aged second employer, but soon tires of him and leaves with plans to join her friend Leila Witherell. Leila doesn't show up, but Ursula meets and spends the night at the Dover Hotel with her old flame Dick Mariner. Ursula has a child, but lets her husband believe he's the father. Twelve years later she tells him the truth; he forgives her and that is that: "so nauseous an ending."

BELL, GERTRUDE.

247 TRUE TO THE PRINCE: A TALE OF THE SIXTEENTH CENTURY 1567-1575. London: Digby, Long, 1892 BMC.
Catherine Van Baardhoven dressed as a page carries messages to the Prince of Orange through crowded streets of Antwerp. From this she goes on to further adventures. Historical romance.

BELL, LADY. See BELL, FLORENCE EVELEEN ELEANORE (OLLIFFE).

BELL, LILIAN LIDA. See BOGUE, LILIAN LIDA (BELL).

BELL, MRS. HUGH. See BELL, FLORENCE EVELEEN ELEANORE (OLLIFFE).

BELL, PEARL DOLES. United States.

248 GLORIA GRAY, LOVE PIRATE. Chicago: Roberts, [c1914] NUC.
Gloria attends business college and enters business at seventeen. Her love affairs.

249   HIS HARVEST. New York and London: J. Lane, 1915 NUC.

Conflict of love versus career of singer.

BENGOUGH, ELISA (ARMSTRONG). United States.

250   THE TEACUP CLUB. BY ELIZA ARMSTRONG. Chicago: Way and Williams, 1897 NUC.

Young woman organizes a women's club for the advancement of women. The members discuss women in politics, men's real attitudes toward women's progress, the new woman, etc. Gentle satire.

251   THE VERY YOUNG MAN AND THE ANGEL CHILD. BY ELISA ARMSTRONG. New York: Dodge, [c1900] NUC.

Two young women in a flat are objects of curiosity to the janitor and their neighbors, who annoy them. Two of the most annoying are mentioned in the title.

BENGOUGH, M. A. See BENGOUGH, MARION AGNES.

BENGOUGH, MARION AGNES.

252   IN A PROMISED LAND; A NOVEL. BY M. A. BENGOUGH. London: Bentley, 1893 BMC. New York: Harper, 1893 NUC.

Sarah Bowman and Mattie Williams, raised in the sheltered life of the Primitive Gospellers, are sent to South Africa to marry uncultured laborers. Sarah only slowly comes to love her philistine husband; Mattie is unfaithful to her husband whose strong passion for her makes him look the other way.

253   SO NEAR AKIN, A NOVEL. London: R. Bentley, 1891 NUC BMC.

Completely sympathetic portrayal of a lively young woman who runs away from home to live with the black sheep of the family. Anne Paton leaves her respectable religious family at a young age to join her Uncle Will and the strolling players. She has many experiences "closed to respectable young women." When she is brought back home, she runs off again to escape marriage to Sir Henry

Stephens. She finally marries a cousin who is concerned about her reputation.

BENNETT, ALICE HORLOCK. B. 1866. United States.

254 THE OTHER MRS. SCARLETTE. London: K. Paul, [1917] BMC.

She is the newly appointed secretary of the Ladies Helpers Assoc. Sly and sarcastic portrayal of the advanced ladies who form the association's committee.

BENNETT, MAISIE. See NIXSON, EDITH MAY MAYER.

BENNETT, MARY E. B. 1841? United States.

255 JEFFERSON WILDRIDER. BY ELIZABETH GLOVER. New York: Baker and Taylor, [c1898] NUC.

History of a New England family headed by Jefferson Wildrider who breaks one woman's heart by marrying another and whose wife is driven mad by the effort to support his children.

BENNETT, MRS. ROLF.

256 FELICITY. BY KATHERINE HARRINGTON. London: G. Alden & Unwin, 1919 BMC.

Brutal puritan father keeps young woman from being a school teacher after she had worked for a scholarship. She goes into service. End is conventional.

BENNING, HOWE. See HENRY, MARY H.

BENSON, STELLA. See ANDERSON, STELLA (BENSON).

BERESFORD, LESLIE.* B. 1899. United Kingdom.

257 THE FURNACE. BY PAN. London: Odhams, [1920] BMC NUC.

The marriage of an actress to a millionaire. She is at first content with her wealth and freedom but becomes increasingly dissatisfied.

258 LOVE, THE MAGNET. BY PAN, AUTHOR OF WHITE HEAT. London: Mills & Boon, [1916] BMC.
Dancer marries politician who exposes her cabaret act to the newspaper in puritanical campaign.

259 WONDERFUL LOVE: BEING THE ROMANTIC ADVENTURES OF GLORY WEST, ACTRESS. BY PAN, AUTHOR OF WHITE HEAT. London: Mills and Boon, 1916 BMC.

BERGENGREN, ANNA (FARQUHAR). B. 1865. United States.

260 A SINGER'S HEART. BY ANNA FARQUHAR. Boston: Roberts, 1897 NUC.
Eleanora Dean is bent upon a career as an opera singer. Love interferes when she meets a married German musician. But she leaves him and New England to study with a master in England. Her second love relation ends tragically—the man dies. For Eleanora everything, even love, comes second to her art.

BERINGER, AIMEE (DANIELL). B. 1856.

261 THE NEW VIRTUE. London: W. Heinemann, 1896 BMC.
Margaret faints during a thunderstorm and is raped by Teddy who is immediately killed by a bolt of lightning. Soon after she is wooed and married by Henry. One month later he discovers she is pregnant. In despair, he consults a doctor, who succeeds in reestablishing his faith in his wife as a symbol of purity. "The women still clamor for mercy and justice both, and demand more than the old sale and barter. How tired readers are of this new, or rather old, cry in fiction!"

BETHUNE, ANNE FLORENCE LOUISE MAY PATTON.

262 BACHELOR TO THE RESCUE. London: Remington, 1894 BMC.
Lena is an old-fashioned villain. She smokes cigarettes, drinks brandy, murders inconvenient husbands, stabs a half-hearted lover. She goes mad, and while attempting to murder her rival, she is killed by Bachelor, a dog.

BETTS, LILLIAN WILLIAMS.

263 THE STORY OF AN EAST-SIDE FAMILY. New York: Dodd, Mead, 1903 NUC.

Mary, daughter of an alcoholic woman, becomes a leader and acknowledged power in her community—"a person to be reckoned with in times of elections." She has three grown children. The novel studies closely her relation to each as one by one they fail her.

BEWSHER, MRS. M. E.

264 MISCHIEF-MAKERS; OR THE STORY OF ZIPPORAH. London: [1891] BMC. Sydney: Griffith, Farran, Okeden and Welsh, [1891] NUC.

Zipporah is sent to Rome as a delegate of the Greeks. She undergoes many dangers, including two abductions by Mark Antony.

BIANCHI, MARTHA GILBERT (DICKINSON). 1866-1943. United States.

265 THE KISS OF APOLLO. New York: Duffield, 1915 NUC.

Brilliant, unusual Judith—her marriage that is no marriage, her work in philanthropy, her "comrade" Julian. As a girl she liked to playact stories from mythology—except the Kiss of Apollo. The kiss became her dread; she becomes "intensely, fiercely virginal." After her boyfriend steals a kiss, she cries, "I am going to give my whole life to helping girls not to love men...women are happy and good until some man kisses them...." To work out her plan she marries, in name only, to be freer to move about. Apparently, she gives up her ideas in the end.

BIANCO, MARGERY (WILLIAMS). 1880-1944. United States.

266 THE LATE RETURNING. BY MARGERY WILLIAMS. New York, London: Macmillan, 1902 NUC. London: W. Heinemann, 1902 BMC.

Vanda becomes mistress of a president, deserts him for the

people during an uprising, disguises herself as a man and is shot as a rebel.

267 SPENDTHRIFT SUMMER. London: Heinemann, 1903 BMC.

Marital difficulties. The woman resents the affection between her husband and his brother. "A quiet tragedy" results in this subtle study of these three people.

BIGELOW, EDITH EVELYN (JAFFRAY). 1861-1932. United States.

268 THE MIDDLE COURSE. BY MRS. POULTNEY BIGELOW. New York: Smart Set, 1903 NUC.

An American woman, dissatisfied after eight years of marriage to her brutal English husband, becomes involved with an artist with whom she tries to establish a new kind of relationship—a bond somewhere between friendship and love. The artist won't take this "middle course," but as they decide to part, the husband discovers the relationship and gets a divorce.

269 WHILE CHARLEY WAS AWAY. BY MRS. POULTNEY BIGELOW. New York: D. Appleton, 1901 NUC. London: W. Heinemann, 1901 BMC.

Describes a woman's hunger for love, the constant demands of her vanity, and her feverish craving for excitement.

BIGELOW, MRS. POULTNEY. See BIGELOW, EDITH EVELYN (JAFFRAY).

BIGOT, MARIE (HEALY). B. 1843.

270 AN ARTIST. BY MADAME JEANNE MAIRET. New York: Cassell, [c1891] NUC. (Tr. by Anna D. Page.)

Diane is an artist studying with a French artist, Bernard Ozanne, who teaches her that for a woman love and art don't mix. For a time she won't marry him but keeps to her career. And when she does marry, he is selfishly jealous of her career but finally adjusts to the fact that she will not give it up.

BIRD, MARY (PAGE). B. 1866. United States.

271 . WEDDED TO A GENIUS. BY NEIL CHRISTISON. London: R. Bentley, 1894 BMC.

Judith married a doctor (the genius of the title) after Phelan, the man she loved, did not return as he had promised. Most of the reviewers are in agreement that the doctor subjected her to harrowing mental torture, while coldly observing her scientifically and making it appear reasonable, sometimes even to her. He turns his child into an idiot and separates him from his mother. "His superior way of treating her and speaking to her is naturally a little galling, but she makes it more galling than it need have been by keeping her mind constantly fixed upon it. She does not give him instinctive love, or submission, or accomodation, but is always asking herself, 'Why this chasm between me and this strange man? How is it that he does not think more with me and of me?' Domestic bliss does not flow in that channel. The husband is undoubtedly a trying person, but the author has not made him bad enough to earn our full sympathy for the wife. It is true that Dr. Courtney pins her down to a rather harrowing and perilous situation in order to test and study her, as he might study a moth on a cork. Yet the reader may see reason to conclude that she pinned herself down, and insisted on part of her torture." The Athenaeum, 104 (1894), 218.

BIRDSALL, ANNA HUNTINGTON.

272 A CONFLICT OF SEX: A NOVEL. London and New York: F. T. Neely, [1898] NUC.

Katherine, poor, marries millionaire. At the end she is Lady Superior of a convent in Ireland.

BIRKHEAD, ALICE. United Kingdom.

273 DESTINY'S DAUGHTER. London, New York: J. Lane, 1915 NUC.

A private secretary becomes a successful actress.

274   THE MASTER-KNOT. London, New York: J. Lane, 1908 BMC.

The story of two brilliantly educated and talented women. One is driven by slander into marriage with a country doctor. The other, a distinguised actress, loses her sight, and broken-hearted, marries a suitor she had previously scorned.

275   SHIFTING SANDS. London: J. Lane, 1914 BMC.

The heroine is a bluestocking and an altruist. She fails first as a secretary (she couldn't stand the horrible monotony of working in an office), becomes an actress, fails to fulfill her aspirations.

BISHOP, CONSTANCE E. United Kingdom.

276   A VISION SPLENDID. London: Heath, Cranton, [1917] BMC.

The novel concerns two Eurasian women. Jinny is the self-sacrificing woman; Clyte becomes a doctor. Each of the heroines is provided with a love story.

BISHOP, MRS. GEORGE.

277   TWO MEN AND A WOMAN. A NOVEL. London: Ward & Downey, 1893 BMC.

Muriel Lascelles is unhappy with her brutish, unfaithful, profligate husband. Author gives a long discourse on the text "Men were deceivers ever." "Mrs. Bishop should know," says one reviewer, "that as the law stands, simple adultery, unaccompanied by physical cruelty or lengthened desertion, does not enable a wife to get a divorce."

BLACK, CLEMENTINA. United States.

278   THE PRINCESS DESIREE. London: Longmans, 1896 BMC.

Beautiful German princess of strong principle refuses arranged marriage, asserts herself and triumphs.

BLACK, MARGARET HORTON (POTTER). 1881-1911.
United States.

279 THE CASTLE OF TWILIGHT. BY MARGARET HORTON POTTER. Chicago: A. C. McClurg, 1903 NUC. London: C.F. Cazenove, 1903 BMC.

Women living alone in feudal castle with no meaningful activities, their despair, revolt, and sympathy and support for one another.

280 THE FIRE OF SPRING. BY MARGARET POTTER. New York: D. Appleton, 1905 BMC NUC.

Young Virginia marries an elderly millionaire on her mother's urging. She loves all the wedding preparations, but is disgusted by her old husband. Bored and restless, she takes a young lover. Her mother is tortured with regret for having arranged the marriage. The author treats both women sympathetically.

281 THE GOLDEN LADDER; A NOVEL. BY MARGARET POTTER. New York & London: Harper, 1908 BMC NUC.

Sympathetic portrait of businessman's wife and of Kitty, an actress who becomes a desperate unwed mother. Title refers to American middle class values.

282 ISTER OF BABYLON, A PHANTASY. BY MARGARET HORTON POTTER. New York & London: Harper, 1902 BMC NUC.

A goddess who expresses many modern sentiments.

BLACK, MARGARET MOYES.

283 DISINHERITED. Edinburgh & London: Oliphant, 1891 BMC.

Old Lady Hernhurst is nearly ninety. For over fifty years of widowhood she has hated her husband's family and her grandchildren, even though she is in every other way a kind and charitable woman.

BLACKMAN, FRANCES.

284 LOVE IN A LIFE. London: Drane's, [1913] BMC.

Young woman from a poor family becomes a nurse. She

marries a man she has known all her life.

BLAKE, MABEL P. United Kingdom.

285 HOYA. BY FARREN LE BRETON. London: Holden and
Hardingham, [1914] BMC.

Heroine leaves her husband who has mistreated her, takes
up music as a profession. She meets a governess who has
also suffered because of her husband. Ends with a second
marriage.

BLAKE, MARGARET. See SCHEM, LIDA CLARA.

BLANCHARD, AMY ELLA. 1856-1926. United States.

286 GIRLS TOGETHER. Philadelphia: J.B. Lippincott, 1896
BMC NUC.

Two young women, one an art student, the other a music
student, live Bohemian lives together in New York.

287 TAKING A STAND. Philadelphia: G.W. Jacobs, 1896
BMC NUC.

Robina and her brother take over the management of the
family fortunes and save them.

288 TALBOT'S ANGLES. Boston: D. Estes, [c1911] NUC.

Old estate in legal trouble; heroine must leave to earn her
own living.

289 TWO MARYLAND GIRLS. Philadelphia: G. W. Jacobs,
[1903] NUC.

Story of a strong sisterly love.

BLAND, EDITH (NESBIT). 1858-1924. United Kingdom.

290 THE INCREDIBLE HONEYMOON. BY E. NESBIT. New
York & London: Harper, [1916] NUC. London:
Hutchinson, [1921] BMC.

A young woman from a conventional family longs for
freedom, hates housework, will not marry the middle-aged
man her father chose for her, leaves home with a young

man with whom she has a mock marriage—one which will leave each of them free to travel her/his own way when she/he wishes—travels through England with him, and gradually comes to love him.

291   THE RED HOUSE: A NOVEL. BY E. NESBIT. New York & London: Harper, 1902 NUC. London: Methuen, 1902 BMC.

Young married couple share domestic jobs. "One gathers that his (the husband's) heart lay in the dishpan, and that he was happiest when washing up the tea things," comments one reviewer.

292   SALOME   AND   THE   HEAD: A   MODERN MELODRAMA. London: A. Rivers, 1909 BMC. (Also published as The House With No Address. By E. Nesbit. New York: Doubleday, Page, 1909 NUC.)

A macabre story which begins with Sylvia's childhood. She becomes a professional dancer in London and hides away from her husband in a secret apartment. She dances Salome's dance, and one night actually has a real head in her hands—her husband's. Sylvia had killed him; another man confesses to the murder, but he is freed of the charge.

293   THE SECRET OF KYRIELS. BY E. NESBIT. London: R. Tuck, [1896] NUC. London: Hurst and Blackett, 1899 BMC.

Secret is an insane wife, Jane Eyre school.

BLENEAU, ADELE. United States.

294   THE NURSE'S STORY, IN WHICH REALITY MEETS ROMANCE. Indianapolis: Bobbs-Merrill, [1915] BMC NUC.

A Red Cross nurse narrates this anti-war story. She describes her work in a field hospital where she saves the life of an English officer whom she eventually marries. But the action concerns her capture by Germans, her continued career as a nurse for German soldiers, and her adventures as a German spy, work she is forced to do by the Germans.

BLINN, EDITH. United States.

295   THE ASHES OF MY HEART. New York: Mark-well Pub.
Co., 1916 BMC NUC.

Rhoda soon after her marriage is overcome with the
passion for drugs and gambling. When she seems past
help, a surgeon restores her through science and mind
control. He turns out to be her husband—(they didn't
recognize each other through the cure!). Rhoda is
described as having a dual personality.

296   THE EDGE OF THE WORLD. New York: Britton, [c1919]
NUC. London: H. Jenkins, 1921 BMC.

Elderly woman runs a restaurant for woodchoppers and
trappers; she cares for everyone and preaches all the time.

BLISSETT, NELLIE K. United Kingdom.

297   THE   BINDWEED;   A   ROMANTIC   NOVEL
CONCERNING THE LATE QUEEN OF SERVIA. London,
New   York: M.   Vynne,   1904   NUC.   Westminster:
Constable, 1904 BMC.

Woman marries man she does not love, runs away with
another, husband kills himself, king is attracted to her and
lover persuades her to become a queen. Tragedy at end.

298   BRASS: A NOVEL. London: Hutchinson, 1899 BMC.

Young woman marries, runs off with an Austrian
archduke, goes on the Variety stage, and is rescued by a
painter.

299   THE CONCERT-DIRECTOR. London: Macmillan, 1898
NUC BMC.

Tarasca, a widowed opera singer, is the victim of a plot
to persuade her to return to her career.

300   THE WISDOM OF THE SIMPLE. London: A.D. Innes,
1896 BMC.

Quiet, plain, colorless, puritanical woman married to
egotistical man with "advanced views" writes book of the
season anonymously. She tells no one but a French poet
of her authorship.

BLODGETT, MABEL LOUISE (FULLER). 1869-1959. United States.

301   AT THE QUEEN'S MERCY. Boston, New York, and London: Lamson, Wolffe, 1897 NUC.

Supernatural horrors. Queen Lah has her reluctant lover devoured alive by the Mad Man of the moon.

BLOEDE, GERTRUDE. 1845-1905. United States.

302   THE STORY OF TWO LIVES. BY STUART STERNE. New York: Cassell, [c1891] NUC.

The journal of a woman of thirty. Describes her home life and her study of sculpture with a man she comes to love later when they meet on a steamer and she is an artist in her own right.

BLOUNT, MELESINA MARY. United Kingdom.

303   LADY FANNY. BY MRS. GEORGE NORMAN. London: Methuen, 1911 BMC.

After seven years of happy married life, Lady Fanny is dissatisfied and restless. Her doctor orders her to go abroad and find other male companionship—by way of a tonic. She leaves her husband, travels in Switzerland by herself, meets the man she should have married, but returns to her husband who now loves her more than ever where he had taken her for granted and was negligent. But Lady Fanny is only slightly consoled by his renewed devotion.

304   THE SILVER DRESS. BY MRS. GEORGE NORMAN. London: Methuen, [1912] BMC NUC. New York: Duffield, 1913 NUC.

Eve Martindale is a study of a different kind of heroine, not the young heroine of 18, but a woman of 35 who has led a very quiet life of teas and luncheons with her old aunt and women like herself. Then she leaves that secluded life, gets out in the world and meets a man younger than herself. Eve learns she's very much a woman alive at 35.

BLUNDELL, AGNES. United Kingdom.

305 PENSION KRAUS. London: Herbert & Daniel, [1912] BMC NUC.

Humorous story of an English widow in a German pension which includes the romance of elderly Lili Broun—"prettily told."

BLUNDELL, MARY E. (SWEETMAN). 1857-1930. United Kingdom.

306 THE DUENNA OF A GENIUS. BY M. E. FRANCIS. London: Harper, 1898 BMC. Boston: Little, Brown, 1898 NUC.

The love stories of two sisters, Hungarian musicians in London. Margot, the duenna, is very proper. Valerie serenades her lover with her violin.

307 FLANDER'S WIDOW; A NOVEL. BY M. E. FRANCIS (MRS. FRANCIS BLUNDELL). New York, London: Longmans, Green, 1901 BMC NUC.

Heroine 18 homeless, "familyless" marries a man of 58. He dies; she gets a farm. She has many marriage offers, accepts none. She proposes to an old man who really plots to bring his nephew and her together. Happily ever after ending.

308 MAIME O' TH' CORNER: A NOVEL. BY M. E. FRANCIS. New York: Burr, 1897 NUC. London and New York: Harper, 1898 BMC.

The grinding poverty of a woman of Thornleigh: Maime is taken from the workhouse, raised by Mrs. Prescott, jilted by Mrs. Prescott's son, marries a poor farm worker, is near starvation with her husband but there is no agency to help—except the workhouse.

309 MISS ERIN: A NOVEL. BY M. E. FRANCIS. New York: Benziger, 1898 NUC. London: Methuen, 1898 BMC.

Spirited Irish orphan who writes patriotic poetry burns to become the Irish Joan of Arc, finally wins this distinction, "on rather slender grounds" one reviewer comments, before settling down.

310   SIMPLE ANNALS. BY M. E. FRANCIS (MRS. FRANCIS BLUNDELL). London, New York and Bombay: Longmans, Green, 1906 NUC.

Light stories portraying working women in Dorset. Includes Mrs. Angel, midwife.

311   THE STORY OF MARY DUNNE. BY M. E. FRANCIS (MRS. FRANCIS BLUNDELL). London: J. Murray, 1913 BMC NUC. New York: Longmans, Green, 1913 NUC.

Young Irish woman, whose fiance goes to U.S. to earn money to marry her, takes a job as servant, is kidnapped by white slavers in Liverpool, and tries to kill herself. Her fiance kills the man responsible for her downfall, but scorns her until she "lays her soul bare" on the witness stand trying to defend him.

312   WHITHER? A NOVEL. BY M. E. FRANCIS. London: Griffith, Farran, 1892 BMC.

Virginia Wentworth, tried and barely let off for her uncle's murder, becomes a governess. Under an assumed name she tries to escape her past in rural Lancashire at the time of the Reformation.

BLUNDELL, MRS. FRANCIS. See BLUNDELL, MARY E. (SWEETMAN).

BLUNDERLAND.*

313   THE ADVENTURES OF A RUNAWAY GIRL ON A DESERT ISLAND. Simpkin Marshall, 1905 BS.

Tom Sawyer-like experiences of a young woman in male attire. She has all the ingenuity and resourcefulness to cope with life on a desert island, and her experiences there are ones that few boys have ever had. The novel has an anti-home-life theme.

BOCHKAREVA, MARIIA LEONTIEVNA (FROLKOVA). B. 1889.

314   YASHKA, MY LIFE AS PEASANT, OFFICER AND EXILE. BY MARIA BOTCHKAREVA, COMMANDER OF

THE RUSSIAN WOMEN'S BATTALION OF DEATH, AS SET DOWN BY ISAAC DON LEVINE. New York: F. A. Stokes, [c1919] NUC BMC. London: Constable, [1919] NUC BMC.

An incredible saga of a Russian woman. Seduced at 15, she pretends to be ill to keep her father from punishing her. She marries, runs away from her husband, later tries to kill him with an ax. Is freed from one marriage, makes another. Is violated by a man and attempts suicide. Her new husband hangs her, but repents and cuts her down in time. She takes part in the war, walks 130 miles living on bread and water, joins a regiment and takes part in hand-to-hand combat with Germans. Organizes a Women's Battalion of Death whose sole objective is to kill Germans. Joins with Kerensky but won't follow orders, suspected of Bolshevism, escapes to U.S. Nonfiction?

BODDINGTON, HELEN.

315 A VOICE FROM THE VOID. London: Hurst and Blackett, 1904 BMC.

The love story of a young woman novelist.

BOEGLI, LINA.

316 FORWARD; LETTERS WRITTEN ON A TRIP AROUND THE WORLD. Philadelphia and London: J. B. Lippincott, 1904 BMC.

Young woman without money spends ten years traveling around the world.

BOEHME, MARGARETE. B. 1869.

317 THE DEPARTMENT STORE; A NOVEL OF TO-DAY. New York and London: D. Appleton, 1912 NUC BMC. (Tr. by Ethel C. Mayne.)

Portrayal of juggernaut role of store over crushed and broken lives. Bird's-eye view of manners and customs. Life history of a dozen families. Karen, an orphan, works her way up from shop girl, to head of art department, marries proprietor's son.

BOGGS, SARA ELISABETH (SIEGRIST). B. 1843. United States.

318 SANDPEEP. Boston: Little, Brown, 1906 BMC NUC.
"Fisher girl" of Maine becomes a governess and gets involved in a mystery. For girls.

BOGGS, WINIFRED. B. 1882. United States.

319 THE SALE OF LADY DAVENTRY [ANONYMOUS]. London: H. Jenkins, 1913 BMC NUC. New York: Brentano's, 1914 NUC.
Young woman married to an old nobleman in his 70's has a child outside of marriage. Ends in her suicide.

320 SALLY ON THE ROCKS. London: H. Jenkins, 1915 BMC. New York: Brentano's, 1915 NUC.
She spends six years in Paris trying to establish herself as an artist, but fails. Returns to hometown to get a husband—her competition with a young widow for a rich banker.

321 VAGABOND CITY. New York and London: G. P. Putnam's Sons, 1911 NUC BMC.
After three days of marriage, male novelist and his conventional wife "feel the galling of their chains." Then Elf enters their lives. She's an artist genius. Triangle and tragedy.

322 YESTERDAY: BEING THE CONFESSIONS OF BARBARA. London: H. Jenkins, 1919 BMC NUC.
Barbara is raised by a tyrannical grandfather, but after his death, she moves to London and takes up a literary career. The novel describes her various adventures with publishers.

BOGUE, LILIAN LIDA (BELL). 1867-1929. United States.

323 THE INTERFERENCE OF PATRICIA. BY LILIAN BELL. Boston: L. C. Page, 1903 BMC NUC.
Rides like Buffalo Bill and talks like a cowboy. Shocks Denver society with her daring ways. Also love story full of surprises.

324 A LITTLE SISTER TO THE WILDERNESS. BY LILIAN LIDA BELL. Chicago: Stone and Kimball, 1895 NUC. London: S. Low, 1895 BMC.

Realistic account of life in small hamlet in malarial bottom lands of west Tennessee with focus on Mag's relatives and friends and atypical Mag herself. She is superior, misunderstood, a young woman with a mind out of place in the dull environment of "poor whites" and lack of culture from which she is rescued by a lady revivalist preacher who reads to her. Mag comes to know a life of love and service. Use of dialect.

BOND, AIMEE. United Kingdom.

325 MONA-LISA-NOBODY. London: H. Jenkins, 1920 BMC NUC.

Struggles of a young woman who is left alone after her grandfather's death. She moves to New Orleans and tries to earn her living as a journalist. In the end she marries a journalist.

326 A PAIR OF VAGABONDS. London: H. Jenkins, 1919 BMC NUC.

Two English women operate a canteen in France near the front line.

BONE, FLORENCE. United Kingdom.

327 A BURDEN OF ROSES. London: R.T.S., 1913 BMC.

A foundling goes to London to seek her fortune, fails bravely, finds love and happiness.

BONE, GERTRUDE HELENA (DODD). B. 1876. United Kingdom.

328 WOMEN OF THE COUNTRY. London: Duckworth, [1913] BMC NUC.

Character studies of hard working and poor English women. The chief character is Anne Hilton who feels responsible for others. She adopts the child of a young woman who was seduced and abandoned and who died in childbirth in the workhouse. The novel shows all the misery of the workhouse, the women's wards full of old and young women with babies. But it also shows the quality of human nature that endures that misery.

BONNER, GERALDINE. 1870-1930. United States.

329 THE BLACK EAGLE MYSTERY. New York, London: D. Appleton, 1916 NUC BMC.

Molly Babbitts, retired from her position as telephone operator after her marriage, is recalled by the Whitney offices to help detectives solve a murder mystery.

330 THE BOOK OF EVELYN. Indianapolis: Bobbs-Merrill, [c1913] NUC BMC.

After a short and unhappy marriage, Evelyn Drake, widow of 33, returns to New York to live in an apartment house among arty people. She becomes close friends with Lizzie Harris whose morals are different from her own. Evelyn is very proper; Lizzie lives with a man who is helping her with her career. Evelyn's friend Roger falls in love with Lizzie or rather an ideal he believes is Lizzie, but though Evelyn cares for him, she does nothing to dissuade him. Lizzie suffers greatly when the man she lives with leaves her, but never regrets sleeping with him. Her suffering, in fact, improves her art, and she becomes a great success throughout Europe. In the end, Evelyn marries Roger, but the heroine is Lizzie: what began as Evelyn's diary becomes the story of Lizzie and her career.

331 THE GIRL AT CENTRAL. New York and London: D. Appleton, 1915 NUC BMC.

A telephone operator gathers clues that lead to the solution of a mystery and incidentally to a romance. She's an independent, energetic young woman, shrewd in her judgment. First person narrator.

332 HARD-PAN: A STORY OF BONANZA FORTUNES. New York: Century, 1900 NUC BMC.

Letitia, high spirited and strong-minded, discovers her father, who has lost his fortune, has borrowed money from her rich lover. She insists that they repay the money, sell their house, and move to another city. She makes her own choice of lovers.

333   MISS MAITLAND, PRIVATE SECRETARY. New York, London: D. Appleton, 1919 BMC NUC.
Molly Babbitts is the young woman detective who clears up the double mystery of a kidnapping and the theft of Miss Maitland's employer's jewels. Molly is a woman of perseverence and quick wit.

334   TOMORROW'S TANGLE. Indianapolis: Bobbs-Merrill, [1903] NUC BMC. London: Cassell, 1904 BMC.
A Mormon, on his way West, exchanges his wife and baby for a fresh team of horses. The child becomes a music teacher with only a small income, but refuses her inheritance because of her father's cruelty to her mother. The story includes a self-reliant woman journalist.

BOOTH, MAUD BALLINGTON (CHARLESWORTH). 1865-1948.

335   THE RELENTLESS CURRENT. BY M. E. CHARLESWORTH. New York: G. P. Putnam's Sons, 1912 BMC NUC.
Young woman marries man in prison who has been convicted of murder. Reviewers variously describe her activities: one says she devotes her life to helping falsely accused men, another says she finds another husband, while a third says she observes her surgeon uncle until she is able to enlighten world famous doctors on details of their cases.

BOSHER, KATE LEE (LANGLEY). 1865-1932. United States.

336   PEOPLE LIKE THAT: A NOVEL. New York and London: Harper, [1916] BMC NUC.
Danbridge moves to the slums to work for those who have been socially wronged, especially women and children. She comes to the conclusion that until women recognize less fortunate women as their sisters, there is no hope for improvement.

BOTCHKAREVA, MARIA. See BOCHKAREVA, MARIIA LEONTIEVNA (FROLKOVA).

BOTTOME, PHYLLIS. 1884-1963. United Kingdom.

337 "BROKEN MUSIC". London: Hutchinson, 1914 NUC BMC. Boston: Houghton Mifflin, 1914 NUC.

Judith St. Calvert owns an apartment in Hammersmith. She lives by herself and works as a secretary in London. Another character is Sonia, a great dancer. She represents a very convincing portrait of a genius.

338 THE CAPTIVE. London: Chapman & Hall, 1915 BMC NUC.

A fine study of young Rosamund Beaumont, a painter, who is never really able to free herself from the conventional ways impressed upon her by her upbringing and by tradition though she moves around in the Bohemian world of Rome. She shares an apartment with Maisie who in contrast is a struggling but happy art student. Rosamund marries, but her marriage is a fiasco. At the end of the novel, neither of their lives is right or happy.

339 THE IMPERFECT GIFT. London: J. Murray, 1907 BMC NUC. New York: Dutton, 1907 PW.

Close analysis of two sisters: the younger is described as dark, strange and plain. She marries a man who drinks heavily. In contrast, Marjory Delamaine is fair with perfect features. She goes on the stage and achieves great success. The title refers to the actor-manager that Marjory marries. He is the imperfect gift because he has had previous affairs with women.

340 LIFE, THE INTERPRETER. New York: Longmans, Green, 1902 BMC NUC.

Heroine is an independent woman who has forsaken "society" for the slums and club work.

341 THE SECOND FIDDLE. New York: Century, 1917 NUC.

Marian refuses to marry Julian when he goes off to war and again when he returns crippled. But the focus of the novel is on Stella Waring, Marian's friend and Julian's secretary. She is the second fiddle because she falls in love with Julian after Marian refuses him. They marry and are happy. She is a woman who does her own thinking. She's modern because she never absorbed the old ideas concerning women. And she's the main support of her family.

342   A SERVANT OF REALITY. London: Hodder & Stoughton, 1919 BMC. New York: Century, 1919 NUC.

"No record of war's physical or material devastation could be more appalling than this account of spiritual warping, or the casting away of a life like Kitty's." Kitty was raised by a father who taught her her most important purpose was to be attractive to men. Kitty falls in love, but goes to pieces when her lover is reported missing in action. She becomes a prostitute and dies of cancer. Captain Anthony Arden returns shattered by the war. He realizes people at home have no idea what war means. The novel tells of the tortures he suffered in action and as a prisoner of war.

BOUCICAULT, RUTH (HOLT). United States.

343   THE ROSE OF JERICHO. New York and London: G. P. Putnam's, 1920 NUC BMC.

She is an actress, finally famous. Story of her life from time of her marriage until she is 40. Poverty and relations which end in bigamy or separation are among the themes.

BOULGER, THEODORA (HAVERS). D. 1889. United Kingdom.

344   WRECKED AT THE OUTSET. BY THEO. GIFT. London: Jarrold, 1894 BMC.

Three stories, all sad. In two of the stories women's lives are "wrecked through the deliberate vice or callow selfishness of the monster man."

BOULNOIS, HELEN MARY.

345 SOME SOLDIERS AND LITTLE MAMMA. London: J. Lane, 1919 NUC BMC. New York: J. Lane, 1919 NUC BMC.

Letters of a young woman who entertained soldiers in France in World War I.

BOULTON, HELEN M.

346 BATS AT TWILIGHT. London: W. Heinemann, 1904 BMC.

Portrayal of the life and world of a young woman who is deaf—her childhood, her half-perceptions of the world, its misinterpretations and animosities, and finally her unhappy marriage to a ne'er do well twice her age.

347 JOSEPHINE CREWE: A NOVEL. London: Longmans, 1895 BMC NUC.

Tells her own rags-to-riches story. Born illegitimate in wretched London slums where her alcoholic mother dies. Later in life she tries to save the man she loves from alcohol, but fails. Ends as wife of gentleman. "Only God's mercy saved her from making a total wreck of her life, and we leave her bitterly regretting that she was saved."

BOURCHIER, HELEN.

348 THE WHITE LADY OF THE ZENANA. London: H. J. Drane, [1904] BMC.

Anglo-Indian marriage. The lady is very unhappy; a slave girl loses her life in helping her escape, a deed which is made successful through the efforts of an English champion.

BOURGOIN, SAIDEE.

349 SARAH MARTHA IN PARIS: A NOVEL. New York: Merriam, [c1895] NUC.

Sarah Martha studies voice in Paris where she is allowed much freedom because of the fact that her chaperone drinks. Many "questionable episodes" result.

BOURKE, MRS. HUBERT.

350 A POLITICAL WIFE. London: Eden, Remington, 1891 BMC.

Margaret Broughton holds strong conservative political views and acts on them. She does extensive canvassing for the political candidate of her choice. Though she loves a man whose political convictions are radical, she does not budge an inch. He is the one who changes his views completely to suit her. Story ends inconclusively.

BOWEN, MARJORIE. See LONG, GABRIELLE MARGARET VERE (CAMPBELL) COSTANZO.

BOWER, B. M. See SINCLAIR, BERTHA (MUZZY).

BOWLES, EVELYN MAY (CLOWES) WIEHE. 1877-1942. United Kingdom.

351 THE COST OF IT. BY ELEANOR MORDAUNT. New York: Sturgis & Walton, 1912 NUC. London: W. Heinemann, 1912 BMC NUC.

Study of a marriage in which the wife lives in terror awaiting the birth of their child, uncertain whether the father's Creole blood will be evident. "A novel which no white American can read without wishing to throw it into the fire. Such a book is hopelessly immoral—the more so because it is well-written."

352 THE FAMILY. BY ELINOR MORDAUNT. New York: John Lane, 1915 NUC. London: Methuen, [1915] BMC NUC.

Tragic study of a conventional family of eleven children, focusing on one daughter and one son—the only two of the eleven who show any sympathy for each other. The mother lives only for the family which is nevertheless a failure. Author is concerned with how sexual questions should be presented to children.

353 LU OF THE RANGES. BY ELENOR MORDAUNT. London: W. Heinemann, 1913 NUC BMC. New York: Sturgis & Walton, 1913 NUC.

As a child, Lu is left to care for her two brothers, one a

baby. The three are saved from starvation in Australian bush country by a vagabond English writer, Julien Orde, who then seduces and deserts Lu. But Lu refuses to be defeated. She leaves farm work and moves to town to start life anew. She has a brilliant career as a dancer; at the end she returns to the bush. The story expresses bitter resentment against "sensual man."

354   THE PARK WALL. BY ELINOR MORDAUNT. London: Cassell, 1916 BMC.
Alice Ingpen marries a "total cad." She decides to leave him. She tells him that she is pregnant by another man so that she can raise her child independently and without knowing his father. He divorces her immediately. When she returns home, her family closes their doors, and she works in a factory. She succeeds in raising the child by herself.

355   THE ROSE OF YOUTH. BY ELINOR MORDAUNT. New York: John Lane, 1915 NUC. London: Cassell, [1915] NUC BMC.
Celia Fielding, heiress, and young man of lower class meet, love, and bring great reforms to a business establishment.

356   A SHIP OF SOLACE. BY ELEANOR MORDAUNT. New York: Sturgis & Walton, 1911 NUC. London: W. Heinemann, 1911 BMC NUC.
The comforts and discomforts of a sailing voyage to Australia taken by two young women. Lively, humorous, with two love stories woven in.

BOWLES, JANET BYFIELD (PAYNE).

357   GOSSAMER TO STEEL. New York: Dunstan, [c1917] NUC.
Tragic story of psychical disturbances and reactions of a young woman.

BOWLES, M.*

358   CHARLOTTE LEYLAND. G. Richards, 1900 BS.
She is an orphan, a bachelor girl making a living by

secretarial work in London. She marries, disagrees with her husband. Although they are reconciled, nine tenths of the book is "insurrectionary formula." An advance on the author's previous work.

BOWLES, MAMIE.

359 THE AMAZING LADY. London: W. Heinemann, 1899 BMC.

"The social historian, when he comes to the early 90's and would deal with a certain feminine type which belonged to them, will find the records of the thoughts, words and actions of Magda Stacpoole of priceless service. For it is a little epic of Beardsleyism. The whole 'Yellow' movement is focussed in this amazing lady—its emotions, its preferences, its dislikes, and its vocabulary." The Academy, 56 (1899), 327. The author presents a minute and accurate psychological study of the decadent woman and the way she complicates the lives of two men. "Her delicacy of body and decadence of mind are dwelt upon with obvious enjoyment on every page and intended to enhance her attractions."

360 GILLETTE'S MARRIAGE. London: W. Heinemann, 1901 BMC. (Also published as The Supreme Sacrifice; or Gillette's Marriage. New York: G. W. Dillingham, 1901 NUC.)

An excellent character study of an unhappy wife—Gillette whose husband married her for her money. Their unsuccessful marriage leads first to a separation, then to divorce.

361 SEVEN LADIES AND AN OFFER OF MARRIAGE; A COMEDY OF THE CRINOLINE PERIOD. London: Duckworth, 1902 NUC BMC.

Seven women play joke on minister by sending him an anonymous proposal of marriage. The message states that the writer can be identified by her manner of dress. Then all seven women wear the same costume.

BOWYER, EDITH M. (NICHOLL). United States.

362 THE HUMAN TOUCH, A TALE OF THE GREAT
SOUTHWEST. BY EDITH NICHOLL. London: K. Paul,
1905 BMC. Boston: Lothrop, [1905] NUC.

Sylvia sports a six-shooter, rides the trail coolly as bullets
whiz by, rescues and marries a wealthy cattle king whose
wife is reported dead. But the wife (mismatched to the
man from the start) returns from her travels, and Sylvia,
scorned by the community, moves away. Soon the wife
wearies of her husband, gets a quick divorce, and Sylvia
and the man are reunited. The author makes these events
seem perfectly natural and satisfactory.

BOYCE, NEITH. See HAPGOOD, NEITH BOYCE.

BOYD, MARY STUART. B. 1860.

363 THE FIRST STONE. London: Hodder and Stoughton,
1909 BMC.

Woman leaves her unfaithful minister husband. Most of
the novel concerns her life alone in a farmhouse. She falls
in love with another man but returns to her husband,
even though he is physically repulsive to her. She does so
in order to keep her minister husband from further
wrongdoing.

BOYLAN, GRACE (DUFFIE). 1862-1935. United States.

364 THE SUPPLANTER. Boston: Lothrop, Lee & Shepard,
[1913] BMC NUC.

Janet Allen, nurse, adopts and raises child of an insane
woman. Later Janet rescues this same woman when she
sets a house on fire. The shock restores the woman's
reason, and Janet returns the boy to her. Eventually the
boy chooses to return to Janet. Included in list ot "New
Feminist Books for sale at the headquarters of the
Women's Political Union."

BOYLE, C. NINA. See BOYLE, CONSTANCE ANTONINA.

BOYLE, CONSTANCE ANTONINA. B. 1865. United Kingdom.

365 OUT OF THE FRYING PAN. BY C. NINA BOYLE. London: G. Allen and Unwin, 1920 BMC. New York: T. Seltzer, 1923 NUC.

Maisie Pleydele, well-educated, is brought to live with her mother for the first time. She gradually becomes aware that she is living in a gambling house and worse. She subsequently leaves and looks up her father, only to find he is a criminal. Her adventures do not end when she becomes a private secretary to a politician.

BOYLE, VIRGINIA (FRAZER). 1863-1938. United States.

366 SERENA; A NOVEL. New York: A. S. Barnes, 1905 NUC BMC.

Educated, courageous Serena—more manly than her twin brother—disguises herself as her brother when he turns coward and deserts. She leads his men of the Confederate army to victory.

BRABY, MAUD (CHURTON). United Kingdom.

367 DOWNWARD: "A SLICE OF LIFE". London: T.W. Laurie, [1910] NUC BMC. New York: W. Rickey, 1912 NUC.

The heroine takes one wrong step and has a child out of wedlock. A chain of misery follows. The author tries to make a "brighter horizon with a happy ending."

368 THE HONEY OF ROMANCE: BEING THE TRAGIC LOVE-STORY OF A PUBLISHER'S WIFE. [London]: T. W. Laurie, [1915] BMC NUC.

Marriage, unhappiness, another man, divorce.

BRADDON, M. E. See MAXWELL, MARY ELIZABETH (BRADDON).

BRADLEY, MARY WILHELMINA (HASTINGS). United States.

369   THE PALACE OF DARKENED WINDOWS. New York, London: D. Appleton, 1914 NUC BMC.

An American woman in Egypt, accustomed to the freedom of her own country, does not realize that her actions may be misinterpreted in another society. She meets a Turkish officer who falls in love with her; their cultural differences lead to misunderstanding and an abduction. She is rescued by an engineer whom she subsequently marries.

370   THE SPLENDID CHANCE. New York, London: D. Appleton, 1915 NUC BMC.

Katherine King refuses to marry. She goes to Paris to study music. Two men pursue her there. When the war comes, one of the men is blinded in battle. Strong anti-war novel showing the effects of war on individual people.

371   THE WINE OF ASTONISHMENT. New York and London: D. Appleton, 1919 NUC BMC.

Evelyn Day's socially ambitious mother makes her break her engagement to a young man she met in college and loves in order to marry a wealthy man. But it's a marriage in name only, for Evelyn finds him a sad contrast to the lover she gave up and marriage intolerable. When her husband dies, she cannot marry her former love because she cannot face poverty and he refuses to live on the money she inherited from her husband. Unknown to each other, Evelyn and the young man go off to find an independent life in the U. S. service in France.

BRADSHAW, ANNIE. United Kingdom.

372   ASHES TELL NO TALES. A DRAMATIC STORY. London: Greening, 1899 BMC.

Old fashioned villain, good with poisons, wrecks all her friends' domestic peace, locks up her husband in insane asylum, is betrayed by her maid and pretty much forgiven by her gentlemen friends and the author.

373 FALSE GODS. London: Henry, 1897 BMC.

Flavia Thornton loves money and clothes—above all else. Though she is married and has a child, she walks out without a word when she learns she can inherit money if she is single. After her husband dies, she marries a fine man who loves her for herself, knowing all about her. "We feel that poetic justic has hardly been served," says one reviewer.

374 THE GATES OF TEMPTATION. A NATURAL NOVEL. London and Amsterdam: L. Greening, 1898 BMC.

Orphan heroine supports family by singing on the stage. She becomes engaged to an English merchant, then falls in love with a French artist. Conflict between love and duty leads to suicide.

BRAINERD, ELEANOR (HOYT). 1868-1942. United States.

375 CONCERNING BELINDA. London, New York: Doubleday, Page, 1905 BMC NUC.

Teacher in girls' finishing school and the typical boarding school types.

376 HOW COULD YOU, JEAN? Garden City, New York: Doubleday, Page, 1917 NUC. London: T. Nelson, [1920] BMC.

Raised in luxury, now penniless, takes job as cook. Includes romance.

377 THE PERSONAL CONDUCT OF BELINDA. New York: Doubleday, Page, 1910 NUC. London: Hodder & Stoughton, 1910 BMC.

Described as silly by one reviewer, the story relates Belinda's adventures in conducting a small group of young women students on a tour through Europe. Belinda, a teacher of literature, is "safely married" at the end.

BRAMSTON, MARY. B. 1841. United Kingdom.

378 TOO FAIR A DAWN. London: Hurst and Blackett, 1896 BMC.

Crystal Rowhurst so impresses her lover with her purity

that he mends his ways. But she in the meantime takes up the ways he gave up. Story of her deterioration, gambling, and theft of a diamond necklace.

BRANDON, BEATRIX.

379   LADY MAUD. London: Digby, Long, [1895] BMC.
Sensational. Wicked Lady Maud gets rid of her drunken "half idiotic" husband by having him burned. She then marries the unscrupulous Dr. Morgan. Their child is an idiot who resembles the late husband.

BRASS, THEOPHILUS [pseud.].*

380   A CHAPTER FROM THE STORY OF PAULINE PARSONS. BY THEOPHILUS BRASS. Ashland, Mass.: W. P. Morrison, 1916 NUC.
Records conversations between rich young woman and her advisors who want to keep her from sharing profits with her employees.

BREDA, G. H.*

381   FROM ONE MAN'S HAND TO ANOTHER. London: T. F. Unwin, 1907 BMC.
A woman of 40 studying art falls in love with young Irish artist of 18. She tries to discourage him but finally they live together. Her refusal to marry him is based upon their ages. She leaves him, and he paints a picture of her.

BREWER, ANNETTE (FITCH).

382   THE STORY OF A MOTHER-LOVE. Akron, O.: New Werner, [c1913] NUC.
Narrative of a divorced woman's fight for the custody of her son. Non-fiction?

BRIDGES, MRS. COLONEL. United Kingdom.

383   DEAREST. BY MRS. FORRESTER. London: Hurst & Blackett, 1893 BMC. New York: Tait, [c1893] NUC.
She is Rachel Le Breton, governess employed by Eva

Huntingtower, who soon takes over the English country family. She wants social rank and money, and she gets what she wants through marriage to her pupil's wealthy brother, the squire. She only pretends to love him to win him, but ends up really loving him. She lies and schemes to get her way, and only once comes near confessing, an impulse she checks instantly.

384 TOO LATE REPENTED. BY MRS. FORRESTER. London: Hurst and Blackett, 1895 BMC.

Ethel and her husband once loved each other but are now hopelessly alienated. He believes she takes too much upon herself; she thinks he married her for her money. They agree to part, but once parted they seek each other. However, her husband dies at sea, and she meets a man she will be happier with.

BRIGGS, OLIVE MARY. B. 1873. United States.

385 THE BLACK CROSS. New York: Moffat, Yard, 1909 NUC.

The Countess Kaya as a member of the nihilist society called The Black Cross is called upon to assassinate the Grand Duke. She meets him at a ball and shoots him. She escapes with a violinist named Velasco whom she marries as a temporary safeguard. She disguises herself as a boy gypsy in order to make good the escape. Once she's safe, she leaves Velasco despite his protests. They are reunited one night when she's singing the part of Brunhilde gloriously and he happens to be leading the orchestra, and she learns she is indeed not a murderess but that the Grand Duke is in the audience.

386 THE FIR AND THE PALM. New York: C. Scribner's Sons, 1910 NUC.

Heroine is a lion-tamer, part of a travelling show. She marries a great physician, scorns his appeals to leave the show and get an education. She eventually leaves him.

BRIGHT, MARY CHAVELITA (DUNNE) MELVILLE CLAIRMONTE GOLDING. 1860-1945. Australia.

387 DISCORDS. BY GEORGE EGERTON. London: J. Lane, 1894 BMC. Boston: Roberts, 1894 NUC.

Studies of three women, two of them alcoholics, and their relationships with men. One starts a "foundling establishment."

388 KEYNOTES. BY GEORGE EGERTON. London: E. Mathews and J. Lane, 1893 BMC. Boston: Roberts, 1893 NUC.

Studies, not stories, of sexuality—"introspective studies of women's impulses which are acknowledged without false shame." She says nothing new about women's sexuality, but the work does have a "tingling sense of indecency" which is powerful. "To many of us that little volume came with a fine air of discovery; we felt we had at last a woman writer rising out of the multitude of women writers; an almost masculine strength of conception...."

389 SYMPHONIES. BY GEORGE EGERTON. London: J. Lane, 1897 BMC. London and New York: 1897 NUC.

Studies of "feminine temperament and of erotics." The purpose of "At the Heart of the Apple" is to depict "women, and there are many, to whom the child is first, the man always second." "Nobody loves well enough to marry or to be faithful; the lovers love and ride away. The loveresses commit suicide or console themselves with maternity—or other lovers."

390 THE WHEEL OF GOD. BY GEORGE EGERTON. London: G. Richards, 1898 BMC. New York: Putnam's Sons, 1898 NUC.

A psychological study of Mary, the book is divided into three parts: (1) a poetic young woman, she struggles as a shop girl (2) her ideals are shattered by two marriages (3) middle-aged and disillusioned, she has a "fund of love and tenderness for other women into whose struggles and dreary lives she has gained great insight." She concludes that "The men we women today need, or who need us, are not of our time—it lies in the mothers to rear them for the women who follow us."

BROAKER, JULIA FREDERIKA (LUTH). United States.

391 THE YOUNGER MRS. COURTNEY. A NOVEL. BY
MRS. FRANK BROAKER. New York: Alwood, 1903
BMC NUC.

"A novel of broken marriage vows, with a number of
sensational climaxes." Degenerate husband and virtuous
wife. Divorce.

BROAKER, MRS. FRANK. See BROAKER, JULIA
FREDERIKA (LUTH).

BRODHEAD, EVA WILDER (MACGLASSON). 1870-1915.
United States.

392 AN EARTHLY PARAGON: A NOVEL. BY EVA WILDER
MCGLASSON. New York: Harper, 1892 NUC.

Sylvia thinks of herself as a "thin and insufficient person";
she is not beautiful but is interesting. She moves to
Chamouni, Kentucky, lives in a hotel. She is disappointed
in the people she meets, says she is "tired of having to
form the literary taste of every man she meets." She says
of marriage, "people are happy...in proportion as they are
too stupid to find each other out or clever enough to keep
up prenuptial illusions." "She seems, without any intention
of so doing, to leave a blight wherever she moves."

BROOKE, E. F. See BROOKE, EMMA FRANCES.

BROOKE, EMMA FRANCES. D. 1926. United Kingdom.

393 TRANSITION, A NOVEL. BY THE AUTHOR OF A
SUPERFLUOUS WOMAN [ANONYMOUS]. Philadelphia:
J. B. Lippincott, 1895 NUC. London: W. Heinemann, 1895
BMC.

Honora Kemball, fresh from a brilliant career at
Cambridge, returns home ready to improve her father's
rectory and continue her studies but finds her father has
given up his titles to the church. She then takes a position
in charge of a girls' school in London. Story traces her
growth toward socialism, her suitors, one of whom is a

socialist, and her career at the school. Author believes in "constructive socialism."

394 THE ENGRAFTED ROSE; A NOVEL. London: Hutchinson, 1899 BMC. Chicago: H. S. Stone, 1900 NUC.

Development of Rosamunda's strong character. She grows up with uncultured mill-owners in rural England 1847-1867. At 17, her original artistic abilities come through, and she becomes completely devoted to playing the violin. At 20 she learns that her real mother, deserted by Rosamunda's father, died in the house of a midwife and that the midwife changed the babies. Mrs. Thorsbye, who raises her, is a fresh, unique character.

395 LIFE THE ACCUSER, A NOVEL IN TWO PARTS. BY E. F. BROOKE. London: Heinemann, 1896 NUC. New York: E. Arnold, 1896 NUC.

Author states that sensual passivity in women is a fallacy; when treated as a fact, it is tragic in its effect. The wife tells her husband that her passion for him, not her purity, has kept her faithful to him. He is horrified. Touches rather closely on facts of sex which it is more usual to wrap up in silences and conventions.

396 THE POET'S CHILD. London: Methuen, 1903 BMC.

Married woman has child outside of marriage.

397 A SUPERFLUOUS WOMAN. A NOVEL [ANONYMOUS]. London: W. Heinemann, 1894 BMC NUC. New York: Cassell, [c1894] NUC.

One reviewer defines the superfluous woman as being one who has found neither her mate nor her work, an odd woman, as Gissing put it. Jessamine, after a severe illness, longs for a simple life and serviceable work. She goes to a Scotch village and falls passionately in love with a farmer. They meet at night; he mistakes her confession of "unconditional surrender" as expressing terror rather than passion and responds by saying he has no intention of violating her honor. In turn, she mistakes this as a rejection of her love and, humiliated, flees back to London. Emotionally distraught, she agrees to marry Lord Heriot, a vicious and effete aristocrat, from whom she suffers acute mental torture, finally dying in labor with her third idiot child.

BROOKE, MAGDALEN. See CAPES, HARRIET MAY (MOTHER MARY REGINALD).

BROOKFIELD, FRANCES MARY (GROGAN). United Kingdom.

398 THE DIARY OF A YEAR; PASSAGES IN THE LIFE OF A WOMAN OF THE WORLD. EDITED BY MRS. CHARLES BROOKFIELD. Boston: L. C. Page, 1903 NUC. London: E. Nash 1909 BMC.

Woman, travelling alone, describes the sorrows and disagreements of her marriage, her husband's infidelity, and her own entanglement with another man. And she discusses divorce.

BROOKFIELD, MRS. CHARLES. See BROOKFIELD, FRANCES MARY (GROGAN).

BROOKS, HILDEGARD. B. 1875. United States.

399 THE DAUGHTERS OF DESPERATION. New York: McClure, Phillips, 1904 NUC. Edinburgh and London: W. Blackwood, 1904 BMC.

Comedy about three sisters who are "amateur" anarchists.

400 WITHOUT A WARRANT. New York: C. Scribner's Sons, 1901 NUC.

Kate is "another recruit to the evergrowing ranks of heroines in boys' clothes." Brave, high-spirited, full of wit and resource, a spitfire, she—not the hero—captures and subdues the villain singlehanded.

BROUGHTON, RHODA. 1840-1920. United Kingdom.

401 A BEGINNER; A NOVEL. New York: D. Appleton, 1894 NUC. London: R. Bentley, 1894 BMC.

Emma Jocelyn brashly writes a novel treating the interaction of the passions. It has an upsetting effect on her family. She enters into an innocent flirtation with the first literary man she has ever met, Edgar Hatcheson. The reviewers kill her novel; the publishers finally recall it.

She decides to become a wife instead of a novelist and seldom entertains literary people. Lesbia, a frisky matron, is a foil to Emma's staidness.

402   CONCERNING A VOW. London: S. Paul, 1914 BMC NUC. Leipzig: B. Tauchnitz, 1914 NUC.

Sally vowed to her dying sister that she would never have anything to do with Edward, who had jilted them both. She doesn't really break the vow, says one reviewer, she lives with him without marriage. Another reviewer says she does break the vow, makes her husband's life miserable, and eventually suicides.

403   DEAR FAUSTINA; A NOVEL. New York: D. Appleton, 1897 NUC. London: R. Bentley, 1897 BMC.

Faustina Bateson is an "up-to-date energetic woman of quick intelligence who joined the extreme left wing of the emancipation movement and by virtue of her vulgar tongue and facile pen, her tireless energy and indomitable self-assertion, has won for herself a prominent position in the ranks of professional philanthropists." Those young society women like Althea Vane who follow her to the slums to do social work become disillusioned with Faustina's methods, her insincerity and desire for personal glory. At the same time they meet women in like work who are the best models. Althea herself becomes such a social worker.

404   A FOOL IN HER FOLLY. London: Odhams Press, [1920] BMC NUC.

Heroine sets out to write novel that shall reveal for the first time what it is to love, without knowing anything about love herself. Her premature attempt at authorship is followed by an attempt to live by her theories, with disastrous results. Autobiographic study in disillusionment.

405   THE GAME AND THE CANDLE. London: Macmillan, 1899 NUC. New York: D. Appleton, 1899 NUC.

At 17, Jane Etheredge marries a famous wealthy scientist 30 years her senior, but she loves John Miles. After eight years of marriage, her husband at his death threatens to leave her penniless unless she promises never to marry Miles. She refuses; he leaves his wealth to his sister. A year later, Miles comes back into Jane's life, but she discovers he is a flirt, unworthy of her. The novel ends there.

406   MRS. BLIGH; A NOVEL. London: R. Bentley, 1892 NUC. New York: D. Appleton, 1892 NUC.

Mrs. Bligh is a 29 year old widow, angular, plain, self-conscious, clever, shrewish, with a geat capacity for enjoying life. Pamela Capel-Smith worships her; part of the story describes the rise and fall of their youthful infatuation. Together they visit an old school friend of Mrs. Bligh who has married a celebrity. His family are slaves to him, to the wonderment of Mrs. Bligh and Pamela.

407   A WAIF'S PROGRESS. London: Macmillan, 1905 NUC BMC. New York: Macmillan, 1905 NUC.

When her mother dies of drink at 34, this 17-year old orphan is already well-educated in the demi-monde of Paris where she was raised among outcasts. Wise, amoral, impulsive, she is a woman who knows everything and says and does daring things. She becomes an actress, makes a place for herself in proper society, and creates havoc in a straight-laced English family.

BROWER, LORRAINE CATLIN. United States.

408   THE VALE OF ILLUSION. Chicago: Reilly and Britton, [1915] NUC.

Eleanor rejects one man because he had had sexual relations with women. She marries Paul believing he's pure until a woman from his past shows up with his child. Eleanor leaves Paul. She travels, falls in love with another man. Fate brings them back together when he's fighting a drug habit, and they live together for months as friends.

BROWN, ALICE. 1857-1948. United States.

409   BROMLEY NEIGHBORHOOD. New York: Macmillan, 1917 BMC NUC.

Two interesting character studies. Ellen Brock marries a man for whom she feels no sexual attraction. She comes to the realization that she loves a man that was her friend from childhood and that he loves her. In the end, she leaves her husband not to join this man but to give her energies to war relief work. Mary Neale is another strong woman, a mother of grown sons. She is fundamentally a loving, giving person, but life with her cold narrow husband has cramped her and made her an introvert. When she was younger, she had more of the rebel in her. And in middle age she still rebels but takes no action.

410 THE COURT OF LOVE. Boston: Houghton, Mifflin, 1906 NUC.

Julia Leigh has spent most of her twenties as a companion to her great-uncle. When he dies, she buys a house and calls it "The Court of Love." A wide variety of people come to stay. The local people consider it a madhouse. Julia discovers her friend Kate is a neglected wife and persuades her to stay with her. Although this is essentially a romantic comedy, Julia is an untypical heroine, being both spirited and independent. Kate illustrates the pitfalls of a marriage in which the wife lives for the sake of her husband.

411 THE DAY OF HIS YOUTH. Boston and New York: Houghton, Mifflin, 1897 NUC.

Reversal of roles: The young hero, a simple child of nature, is raised in isolation seeing no outsiders for years. The heroine comes with a camping party to his village. She is the hard, disillusioned woman of the world who does not believe his vow of eternal love. The rest of the novel is in the form of letters between the two. The hero's end is tragic.

412 JOHN WINTERBOURNE'S FAMILY. Boston: Houghton Mifflin, 1910 BMC NUC.

The story of a family in which the "level-headed" adopted daughter "takes command" and "does things instead of talking."

413 JUDGMENT, A NOVEL. New York and London: Harper, 1903 NUC BMC.

Sensitive Helen Markham is anything but the wicked stepmother type. She almost sacrifices her life for her step-daughter; she averts a disaster involving her step-son's engagement; and she makes her husband see what an unbending tyrant he is.

414 THE MANNERINGS. Boston: Houghton, Mifflin, 1903 NUC. London: E. Nash, 1903 BMC.

A strong, capable woman is married to a selfish dullard. She revolts agains her marriage and plans to leave her husband. She writes a story meant for him alone explaining the reasons for her actions. He publishes the story anonymously.

415 MARGART WARRENER. Boston: Houghton, Mifflin, 1901 NUC.

Margaret Warrener begins to see all her husband's weaknesses, and he becomes interested in another woman. As she gets stronger in her art, he loses his talent. Their marriage ends in his death. Laura, the journalist, is another member of the group of Bohemian artists and writers. She's a heartless Titan, an egoist "with the brain of a man."

416 MY LOVE AND I. BY MARTIN REDFIELD. New York: Macmillan, 1912 NUC. London: Constable, 1912 BMC.

Narrated by Martin, who discovers his wife's bankbook contains an amount of money not possible on his income. After years of cold toleration of her presence, he looks at her pale, prematurely aged face and realizes that even though she had thrown away his love, he should have given her compassion.

417 ROSE MACLEOD. Boston and London: Houghton, Mifflin, 1908 NUC BMC. London: A. Constable, 1908.

Although Rose, an independent young woman in conflict with her mesmeric father, is the heroine, the secondary heroine, Electra's grandmother, a "frisky old lady" whose novels are no longer popular and whose memoirs are a fake, is the most complex and interesting character.

418 THE STORY OF THYRZA. London: A. Constable, 1909 BMC. Boston and London: Houghton Mifflin, 1909 BMC NUC.

Sympathetic portrayal of a young woman who has a child

outside of marriage—the father marries her sister. When she meets a man she loves, she decides to remain single rather than to identify the father of her child and ruin her sister's life. She supports her son by sewing and eventually sends him to college.

419 THE WIND BETWEEN THE WORLDS. New York: Macmillan, 1920 NUC BMC. London: E. Nash, 1921 BMC.

In this novel which is concerned with the possibility of communication with the spirits of the dead, Mme. Brooke, a woman of 80, "physically active and with a mind like a sharp-edged sword," is the "real heroine of the book." She believes psychic research is dangerous to the individual involved.

BROWN, ANNA ROBESON. See BURR, ANNA ROBESON (BROWN).

BROWN, ANNIE G. United States.

420 FIRESIDE BATTLES: A STORY. Chicago: Laird and Lee, [1900] NUC.

Struggles of "thoughtless but lovable" mother and daughter in overcoming poverty, ill-will, and discouragement after the death of the father.

BROWN, CAROLINE. See KROUT, CAROLINE VIRGINIA.

BROWN, DEMETRA (VAKA). 1877-1946. United States.

421 THE GRASP OF THE SULTAN. Boston: Houghton Mifflin, 1916 NUC. London: Cassell, 1917 BMC.

Young Greek woman in Turkish harem defies the Sultan when he tries to take her child from her. She eventually escapes with help of young English tutor.

422 HAREMLIK; SOME PAGES FROM THE LIFE OF TURKISH WOMEN. BY DEMETRA VAKA (MRS. KENNETH-BROWN). Boston: Houghton Mifflin, 1909 NUC. (Also published as Some Pages From the Life of

Turkish Women. By Demetra Vaka (Mrs. Kenneth-Brown). London: Constable, 1909, NUC.)

Ten typical episodes "based upon fact" of women living in the seclusion of Turkish harems.

423   IN THE SHADOW OF ISLAM. BY DEMETRA VAKA (MRS. KENNETH-BROWN). London: Constable, 1911 BMC. Boston: Houghton Mifflin, 1911 NUC.

American Radcliffe graduate Millicent Grey visits Turkey with the idea of helping to liberate Turkish women. In spite of herself she is attracted to a Turk, but finds that he is well aware of the wrongs done to women of his race though he is unable to help them. Millicent also becomes good friends with a young Greek woman.

BROWN, HELEN DAWES. 1857-1941. United States.

424   HER SIXTEENTH YEAR. Boston: Houghton, Mifflin, 1901 NUC.

Autobiography of a bright young woman from the age of seven till she arrives at Harvard.

425   THE PETRIE ESTATE. Boston and New York: Houghton, Mifflin, 1893 NUC.

Miss Coverdale inherits the estate, houses in New York as well as money that she uses to improve the lives of poor people in the slums. She institutes several reforms on her newly acquired estate. She works as head assistant mistress of the Mill Hill Seminary. She represents the highest ideal of the modern woman—"the best of man and woman is contained in her. It is our unbiased opinion that no living woman has yet reached Miss Coverdale's height, but we have little doubt that if all women keep on shouting, some one athletic woman will get there someday, then immediately and gladly die." Minor characters include Miss Bisbee an "unconventional Shakespeare philosopher" and Miss Devine the "society elocutionist."

BROWN, KATHARINE HOLLAND. 1876-1931. United States.

426 THE HALLOWELL PARTNERSHIP. New York: C. Scribner's Sons, 1912 NUC.

Marian, a Wellesley student whose illness has forced her to leave school, is persuaded to go to Illinois with her brother on a business trip. She is spoiled and fond of luxury, but when they are faced with hardships, she comes through and becomes her brother's business partner. No love interest.

427 UNCERTAIN IRENE. New York: Duffield, 1911 NUC.

Irene Kemper Bradbury, a brilliant professor, goes on a tour of the Mediterranean with her companion, Philura, who narrates the story. Philura's parents (who are rivals in business) have sent Philura abroad to forget a man who proposed to her. Irene goes to forget a relation with an admirer that involved knocking him down, having him arrested, and shooting him. She turns to study of archeology.

BROWN, LILIAN KATE ROWLAND. 1863-1959. United Kingdom.

428 THE STORY OF CHRIS. BY ROWLAND GREY. AUTHOR OF "IN SUNNY SWITZERLAND," "BY VIRTUE OF HIS OFFICE," "LINDENBLUMEN," "JACOB'S LETTER". London: Methuen, 1892 NUC BMC.

"The girl journalist, whose single romance is robbed by fate of its ordinary fulfillment, is one of the freshest and most charming of recent heroines; and among many other things for which she is to be thanked Rowland Grey deserves the gratitude of all sensible readers for doing what in her lies to dispose of the sentimental fiction that if a woman cannot marry the man she loves, her life must either end or be spoiled." (James Ashcroft Noble) The Academy, 41 (1892), 226-7.

BROWN, MRS. KENNETH. See BROWN, DEMETRA (VAKA).

BROWN, S. A.* United States.

429 THE DISSOLUTION: A PROJECTED DRAMA. BY RITTER DANDELYON. New York: G. W. Dillingham, 1894 NUC.

"Condemns all marriages without love as unnatural and unholy. Offers as a solution the establishment by law of Platonic unions which shall become intimate only with the consent of the woman. Story, which takes place in mythological times, illustrates this theory in the heroine's actions."

BROWNELL, ANNA GERTRUDE (HALL). B. 1863. United States.

430 AURORA THE MAGNIFICENT. BY GERTRUDE HALL. New York: Century, 1917 BMC NUC.

Aurora is a woman of crude upbringing, impossible manners, loud, a philistine, but magnificent in heart. She has an unhappy marriage. She and Estelle Madison burst upon Florentine society. They want everything—house, servants, horses. Aurora is outgoing by nature, jovial, generous and very rich.

431 MISS INGALIS. BY GERTRUDE HALL. New York: Century, 1918 BMC NUC. London: Skeffington, [1919] BMC.

Grace, an artist, meets Clarence on a cruise, falls in love. They visit his family, the Overcomes, who are well-mannered on the surface but ruthless underneath. She clashes with them, "steel meeting steel." She decides to leave, is held prisoner for awhile, but eventually escapes Clarence and his family.

432 THE TRUTH ABOUT CAMILLA. BY GERTRUDE HALL. New York: Century, 1913 NUC. London: W. Heinemann, 1913 BMC.

History of Camilla from age 8 to 50, daughter of a poor unmarried woman and a noble—who is made to provide for her education but otherwise disowns her. She is self-sufficient, ambitious with no respect for truth, a woman of fiery emotions who wants to make something of her life. First she teaches for a pitifully small wage; then she becomes in turn a paid companion to a novelist and a proprietor of a lace shop. Past 40, love comes for the first time to this Italian adventuress. Set in Italy.

BRUERE, MARTHA S. (BENSLEY). B. 1879. United States.

433 MILDRED CARVER, U.S.A. New York: Macmillan, 1919 NUC.

Story of the future, when young people will be required to give a year's service to their country. Those from the city will work in the country and vice versa. Mildred Carter, a very rich New Yorker, along with a young woman from the East Side and one from Greenwich Village, is ordered to service. She goes to work in a flour mill in Minnesota where she runs a tractor. When the year is up, she returns to New York society but finds life dull. She takes a job in a factory and then in a steel mill.

BRUNKHURST, HARRIET. United States.

434 THE WINDOW IN THE FENCE. New York: G. H. Doran, [1916] NUC. London: Hodder & Stoughton, 1916 BMC.

Thirty-five year old female artist has been married to a writer for fifteen years. Their lives are bland, there is no hope for fame and their love has faded. Then they discover "the window in the fence." "Sentiment and pathos are pleasantly balanced."

BRYANT, MARGUERITE. See MUNN, MARGUERITE (BRYANT).

BRYANT, ROSE CULLEN. United States.

435 RUTH ANNE. Philadelphia and London: J. B. Lippincott, 1913 NUC.

"The modern young woman...staunch, brave-hearted...with as much courage and fortitude as a militant engaged in a hunger strike (yet) the timidity and trembling shyness of an early Victorian maid...comes into her heritage of modernness through the awakening of her conscience." She is committed to a life of service first as a nurse and then as a settlement worker. Dr. Hollander is drawn to her because he shares her ideals.

BRYCE, MRS. CHARLES.

436   THE LONG SPOON. London, New York: J. Lane, 1917 NUC BMC.

Thirza Averill is married to a brutish husband who terrorizes her. After many narrow escapes from death at his hands, she comes upon a witch who can get rid of undesirable husbands. Through the mysteries of necromancy, the husband first disappears and then dies. Lady Averill ultimately finds happiness.

BRYHER, W. See ELLERMAN, ANNIE WINIFRED.

BUCHAN, ANNA. D. 1948. United Kingdom.

437   OLIVIA IN INDIA. THE ADVENTURES OF A CHOTA MISS SAHIB. BY O. DOUGLAS. London, New York: Hodder and Stoughton, [1913] BMC NUC.

Olivia's letters to her fiance from India where she has gone to visit her brother, but more to test her attachment to her fiance. Her letters show she is well read, is candid, appreciates other women, and has a passion for mountain climbing. They show her life on the liner, in everyday social activity in Calcutta and camping in the jungle.

438   PENNY PLAIN. BY O. DOUGLAS. New York: G. H. Doran, [c1920] NUC. London: Hodder and Stoughton, [1920] BMC.

Cranford-like village in Scotland. All nice people. Mrs. Hope makes age seem lovely and desirable.

BUCHANAN, EMILY HANDASYDE. B. 1872. United Kingdom.

439   FOR THE WEEK END. BY HANDASYDE. London: J. Lane, 1907 BMC NUC.

Three weekends during which Blanche and Mortimer meet. Blanche is married to easy-going husband. Tragedy comes.

BUCKROSE, J. E. See JAMESON, ANNIE EDITH (FOSTER).

BUDGETT, FRANCES ELIZABETH JANES. 1873-1928.
United States.

440 THE LIFE-BUILDERS. A NOVEL. BY ELIZABETH
DEJEANS. New York and London: Harper, 1915 BMC
NUC.

Sympathetic psychological study of a woman who believes
the ideal relationship between a man and wife is
comradeship—mutual understanding and respect and equal
sharing of the duties of marriage. But when she marries,
she finds her husband ridicules her ideal. Eventually, she
finds a man who shares her idea. Story concerns the
working out of this problem.

441 THE TIGER'S COAT. BY ELIZABETH DEJEANS.
Indianapolis: Bobbs-Merrill, [c1917] NUC. London: T.
Butterworth, 1923 BMC.

Marie is a mysterious worldly refugee from Belgium, a
dancer who becomes a successful movie star.

442 THE WINNING CHANCE. BY ELIZABETH DEJEANS.
Philadelphia and London: J. B. Lippincott, 1909 NUC.
London: J. Milne, 1909 BMC.

Character study of Janet Carew who becomes a
stenographer and supports her blind mother and lame
brother. For money, she becomes her boss' mistress, but
when he finally offers marriage, she rejects him because
she has fallen in love with a man from her past.

BUNKER, JANE. United States.

443 DIAMOND CUT DIAMOND. Indianapolis: Bobbs-
Merrill, [c1913] BMC NUC.

The central character of this wild adventure story of plots
and intrigues and an international gang of jewel thieves is
a middle-aged woman, the unwilling chaperone of a young
girl bound for Paris and New York. All through the
excitement, mystery, and nervewracking days, she finds
quiet hours to devote to her new book on travel "Belgium
Byways" even while she conceals a million dollars in
jewels.

BURMESTER, FRANCES G.

444   DAVINA. London: Smith, Elder, 1909 BMC.
Unusual heroine. She's half child, half woman, odd in her manner, deaf. She's married to a man who doesn't love her but who feels responsible for her deafness.

445   A NOVEMBER CRY. London: Smith, Elder, 1904 BMC.
Two women together run a farm in Essex. One is also an aspiring novelist. She falls in love with a publisher's reader who has rejected her manuscript but doesn't admit it.

BURN, IRENE.

446   GENEROUS GODS. Leek: W. H. Eaton, 1908 BMC. London: Simpkin, Marshall, 1908 BMC.
Cassandra Fallowfield has a B.A. in Greek and a marriage of "comradeship." Her husband deserts her to find love; she, too, seeks a lover.

447   THE UNKNOWN STEERSMAN. London: T. F. Unwin, 1912 BMC. New York: Brentano's, 1912 NUC.
A novel with a purpose concerning the education of women, the social conditions of women in India, and the relationship of white men to them.

BURNESIDE, MARGARET.

448   THE DELUSION OF DIANA. London: E. Arnold, 1898 BMC.
Talented composer and her friend both love a weak musician. In the style of Charlotte Yonge.

BURNETT, FRANCES HODGSON. See TOWNESEND, FRANCES ELIZA (HODGSON) BURNETT.

BURNHAM, CLARA LOUISE (ROOT). 1854-1927. United States.

449   DR. LATIMER: A STORY OF CASCO BAY. Boston and New York: Houghton, Mifflin, 1893 NUC.
"An encouraging book for women breadwinners." Three

women without money and families begin a kindergarten in a little flat on the outskirts of Boston.

450   A GREAT LOVE. Boston and New York: Houghton, Mifflin, 1898 NUC.

Love affairs of two heroines, one from Colorado studying music in Boston (slangy and amusing) and one a beautiful socialite with a unique voice who wants to make music her profession.

451   THE WISE WOMAN: A NOVEL. Boston and New York: Houghton, Mifflin, 1895 NUC.

She is an older woman who believes "there is no true foundation for the generally received conventionalities of society." She finds class distinction in the U.S. to be absurd and helps bring about changes in the lives of a workman and a milliner named Marguerite. She puts her efforts toward influencing young women.

BURR, ANNA ROBESON (BROWN). 1872-1941. United States.

452   A COSMOPOLITAN COMEDY. BY ANNA ROBESON BROWN. New York: D. Appleton, 1899 NUC.

Comedy about a valuable pearl and a Russian artiste who disguises herself as a young man.

453   THE JESSOP BEQUEST. Boston: Houghton Mifflin, 1907 NUC.

Diane is a sculptor of great talent. Analysis of mental processes. Makes an appeal to the intellect rather than emotions.

454   THE WINE-PRESS. BY ANNA ROBESON BROWN. New York: D. Appleton, 1905 NUC BMC.

In this "study in feminine psychology," Vanna Gaoletti is a serious student in a women's college. Her half sister—younger, impulsive, "wayward"—comes to study, and Vanna assumes full responsibility and almost sacrifices her life for her even though she knows her sister is the daughter of her father's mistress. Vanna is a man-hater because the men at the adjoining college won't give women university privileges and because of her father. The story follows the lives of these half-sisters as they share an apartment and become teacher and musician.

BURR, JANE. See WINSLOW, ROSE GUGGENHEIM.

BURT, KATHARINE (NEWLIN). B. 1882. United States.

455 THE BRANDING IRON. Boston: Houghton Mifflin, 1919 NUC. London: Constable, 1919 BMC.

Joan Landis is a woman of the mountains, raised by her father to be ignorant of the world and isolated from it because he feared she would turn bad like her mother—whom he killed. The story opens in Wyoming. Joan is 18, married, intelligent, gifted with a magnificent voice. She meets a minister who lends her books to read. After her husband's fit of jealous rage, she leaves him believing he's dead. She moves to New York where she becomes a great and famous actress.

456 THE RED LADY. London: Constable, 1920 BMC. Boston: Houghton Mifflin, 1920 NUC.

In this Gothic mystery set in a lonely country house in North Carolina, the young housekeeper Janice courageously solves the mystery surrounding the Red Lady—the famous detective hired for the purpose suspects Janice. The Red Lady turns out to be Janice's mother—a brilliant international criminal whose crimes have always been attributed to the less ingenious men with whom she has worked. The Red Lady admires Janice's courage and intelligence in a penultimate scene in which she is preparing, with some regret, to kill her. In the final chapter Janice forgives the detective his suspicions and marries him.

BUTT, BEATRICE MAY. United Kingdom.

457 THE GREAT RECONCILER. BY THE AUTHOR OF "MISS MOLLY" [ANONYMOUS]. London: Methuen, 1903 BMC.

Character studies of two women both married to alcholics.

BYNG, EVELYN (MORETON) BYNG. 1870-1949.

458 ANNE OF THE MARSHLAND. BY THE LADY BYNG OF VIMY. London: Holden and Hardingham, [1914] BMC. Toronto: McClelland and Steward, [c1921] NUC.
She's married to a village squire and she's bored with married life in the country. She leaves her husband for an exciting young journalist who also happens to be married.

459 BARRIERS. BY THE HONORABLE MRS. JULIAN BYNG. London: Holden and Hardingham, [1912] BMC NUC. Toronto: McClelland and Stewart, [c1921] NUC.
"Calm and masterful Clover" becomes pregnant. The father is a soldier and is killed. One reviewer says that it is impossible that such a woman should go down "before a man mediocre in everything but his passions. Women may, for all we know, be subject to such crises of physical emotion, but we should doubt that such crises come so disastrously to women so well equipped for life." The story ends with her marriage to a crippled soldier.

BYNG, MRS. JULIAN. See BYNG, EVELYN (MORETON) BYNG.

BYRD, EVIE SARTOR. United States.

460 A MODERN EVIL. New York: Broadway, 1907 NUC.
Tangled fates of several young people all unhappily married. Some choose to stick it out; others choose divorce. The author supports the divorce solution.

BYRON, GERTRUDE.

461 "POOR ANGELA". London: A. Melrose, [1920] BMC.
Angela is brilliant and the "darling of intellectuals." She has an accident and becomes an invalid. This enhances her central position in her circle of friends, and she prolongs the appearance of invalidism after she has ceased to be an invalid in reality. The secret finally has to be revealed, but the story ends with her engagement to the man who had first admired her "early promise." Charlotte Bronte style.

CABOT, ELISABETH LYMAN. United States.

462   IN PLAIN AIR. New York: H. Holt, 1897 NUC.

In every way Marion is different from her relatives and neighbors in Brookfield. She has seen the world outside that small town and finds her values are different from the narrow standards of the provincial townspeople. Her actions lead immediately to scandal. She has the pluck to befriend three young men that the town turns its back upon, one of whom she sends to Europe to be educated.

CAFFYN, KATHLEEN MANNINGTON (HUNT). D. 1926. United Kingdom.

463   ANNE MAULEVERER. BY IOTA. London: Methuen, 1899 BMC. Philadelphia: J. B. Lippincott, 1899 NUC.

She is an emancipated and eccentric Irish woman working and studying in Italy. By the end of chapter one, the man she loves marries another woman, is miserable as a consequence, and dies. Anne adopts his son who becomes her constant companion. From then on she is a friend to every man she meets, but the story leaves her celibate by choice. Her achievements run from "sculpture to diagnosis of curb wholly undiscovered by stud-groom or vet." She is commissioned by the King of Italy to purchase horses for him in Ireland. And "she can stem a revolution as easily as you can call a cab."

464   CHILDREN OF CIRCUMSTANCE: A NOVEL. BY "IOTA". London: Hutchinson, 1894 BMC. New York: D. Appleton, 1894 NUC.

Margaret Dering works in East London, rescuing fallen women. She gives the women supper parties, does not preach. "No man could endure to see his girl-sister or girl-cousin in such a place...." Margaret loves a married man; his wife and Margaret meet to discuss it, become friends. "Studies of emotion in the fantastic and distorted shapes which it assumes in neurotically diseased females."

465   A COMEDY IN SPASMS. BY IOTA. New York: F. A. Stokes, [1895] NUC. London: Hutchinson, [1895] BMC.

Introspective study of Elizabeth Marrable—moody,

thoughtful, high-strung, clever and quick-witted. She admires physical beauty and strength. She moves from Australia to England after her father dies and marries a physically weak but very intellectual man—to help solve the family's financial problems. Then she meets her ideal—a Hercules-Adonis type of man beautiful and strong—and is about to break free of her marriage when he stops her. She remains in her unhappy loveless marriage.

466 DORINDA AND HER DAUGHTER. London: Hurst and Blackett, 1910 BMC.
Passion in middle life of Lady Dorinda for youthful lover.

467 HAPPENINGS OF JILL. BY IOTA. London: Hutchinson, 1901 BMC.
Jill is brilliant, noble, unconquerable in spirit, strong, powerful in intellect, and unconventional. She's misunderstood, suffers in her marriage and out of it.

468 HE FOR GOD ONLY. London: Hurst and Blackett, 1903 BMC.
Wife of minister finally acknowledges to herself and others that her minister-husband has neglected his duty to her when he calls upon her to sacrifice her health and turn out her child for the good of the parish.

469 MAGIC OF MAY. BY IOTA. London: Nash, 1908 BMC.
A woman, described by one reviewer as "so far from living her own life (as to be) not alive at all except in and for this husband" is "studied to the depths."

470 MARY MIRRILIES. London: Hurst and Blackett, 1916 BMC.
The heroine, an intellectual, is married to a soldier in India and has "vague aspirations" for something more than children. They separate but are eventually reconciled.

471 PATRICIA: A MOTHER. BY "IOTA". London: Hutchinson, 1905 BMC. New York: D. Appleton, 1905 NUC.
Patricia's husband—a miserable man whose cast-off

mistress and child Patricia supports—dies, and by his will makes his mother legal guardian of both Pat and their son. Pat's mother-in-law is a saintly sacrificing mother; Pat is red-haired, rebellious and magnificent (she also hunts, fishes, and swims). The courage that makes her easy victor in the struggle between the two is part of this full, graphic characterization.

472 POOR MAX. BY IOTA. Philadelphia: Lippincott, 1898 NUC. London: Hutchinson, 1898 BMC.

Judith, "frank and impulsive and a passionate fighter for the truth" is married to Max, a self-indulgent artist who responds to life as aesthetic sensation, shrinks from pain, and whose indiscriminate generosity leads to desperate financial straits. Judith becomes his nurse and protector, faces their need for money. "She adopts a pitying, half-tolerant attitude to her husband...like Sarah Grand and others, Iota seems to imagine that no woman has any real dignity who does not adopt this attitude of crushed, and yet tolerant, martyr to the inferior sex."

473 "WHOSO BREAKETH AN HEDGE". BY MRS. MANNINGTON CAFFYN ("IOTA"). London: Hurst and Blackett, 1909 NUC BMC.

Audrey is variously described by reviewers as petulant, audacious, pagan, appallingly voluble, exasperating, vulgar, and much admired by the author. Audrey struggles between duty to husband and love for another man.

474 A YELLOW ASTER: A NOVEL. BY IOTA. New York: D. Appleton, 1894 NUC. London: Hutchinson, 1894 BMC.

On the subject of maternal love. Gwen is the "newest, most fashionable heroine." She is the child of agnostic parents who have devoted their lives to writing philosophical treatises. Gwen is educated, very intelligent, described by one reviewer disparagingly as having a hot brain and a cold heart. She marries, is unhappy, and leaves her husband, loving neither him nor her child. Then, on her deathbed, her mother confides her remorse in having missed the supreme pleasure of life, that of being a mother to Gwen and loving her more. This occasion is an awakening for Gwen, and her life takes on a dimension it had lacked.

CAFFYN, MRS. MANNINGTON. See CAFFYN, KATHLEEN MANNINGTON (HUNT).

CAIRD, MONA (ALISON). United Kingdom.

475 THE DAUGHTERS OF DANAUS. London: Bliss, Sands, 1894 BMC NUC.

Hadria, a musician, is insulted by all that is expected of women. She likes her husband, but dislikes marriage. She says of her two sons, "they are the tribute exacted of my womanhood. It is through them I am to be subdued and humbled." She doesn't think it matters who raises the children; it would be better if she were not there to mother them. She leaves her family to study in Paris; she wants to start a revolution. She returns eventually because of her mother's illness, but she still feels the same.

476 THE PATHWAY OF THE GODS: A NOVEL. London: Skeffington, 1898 BMC.

A study of Anna, a strong woman who has a capacity for passion larger than her lover's. An exacting, attractive, strenuous, exhausting, intelligent, quite intolerable neurotic young woman. Reviewers are confused about the meaning of the book; one calls it serious literature.

477 A ROMANCE OF THE MOORS. Bristol: [1891] BMC. New York: H. Holt, 1891 NUC.

Young woman from a Yorkshire farm is engaged to young farmer who has been reading and is influenced by Shelley. A woman artist comes from London to sketch the moors, and the young man falls in love with her. When he reveals his engagment, the widow artist feels sympathy for her rival. Both women give him up to his newly found interest in Shelley. All the action in the novel takes place in a week.

478 THE STONES OF SACRIFICE. London: Simpkin, Marshall, 1915 BMC.

Small group of modern young women and men discuss

their advanced ideas about society, family life, and feminism.

CALLAHAN, DORIS EGERTON (JONES). Australia.

479   THE COCOANUT PLANTER. BY D. EGERTON JONES. London and New York: Cassell, [1916] NUC BMC.

Cynthia Shale is barely surviving, teaching in a girls' school in Sydney, when she inherits 1,000 pounds. Believing the man she secretly married three years before to be dead, she sets out for Papua where she has leased 1,000 acres of land which she intends to cultivate for cocoanuts. The close of the book finds her independently developing her land, but she has also fallen in love with a man who turns out to be the cousin of her husband who is not dead. They are best friends and go off to war together, leaving her to her cocoanuts.

480   PETER PIPER. London: Cassell, 1913 BMC. Philadelphia: G. W. Jacobs, [191-?] NUC.

Peter Piper was raised in the Australian bush by a father who treats and dresses her as a boy and tells her nothing of her mother. She is seduced by a young lawyer who rides off. Her father then sends her into society where she makes a hit, becomes engaged to a man who rejects her on hearing of her past, and again meets the lawyer. In diary form.

481   THE YEAR BETWEEN. London: Cassell, 1918 BMC. Philadelphia: G. W. Jacobs, [c1919] NUC.

January Ellice, 17, is the widow of a drunken miner of West Australia. Reviewer says the most normal person is a woman lawyer.

CALVERT, F. XAVIER.* United Kingdom.

482   A MODERN ROSALIND. A STORY. Chicago: Rand, McNally, 1891 NUC.

Louise Parrish acts after the manner of Rosalind when she dresses as a man; she becomes a student at Harvard.

CAMBRIDGE, ADA. See CROSS, ADA (CAMBRIDGE).

CAMERON, EMILY (SHARP). D. 1921. United Kingdom.

483 A BACHELOR'S BRIDAL. BY MRS. H. LOVETT CAMERON. London: F. V. White, 1894 BMC. Philadelphia: J. B. Lippincott, 1897 NUC.

Young woman escapes guardian, arrives at solicitor's chambers in London late at night. He feels bound in honor to marry her and does so, but immediately after ceremony he sends her to a solitary mansion in the country, "a proceeding utterly inexplicable to the doting bride." A sad marriage and tragic ending follow.

484 DEVIL'S APPLES. London: F. V. White, 1898 BMC.

Reggie, a spoiled only child, under the influence of his parents abandons Jane Maxwell, who is pregnant. Blanche Tompkins proposes to him, progresses from extreme healthiness of body and mind to homicidal mania under the influence of his cruelty and treachery.

485 LITTLE LADY LEE. London: F. V. White, 1896 BMC.

A young woman is married to a vicious and cruel man three times older than herself. When she does not give him an heir, he moves his mistress on to the estate. He dies eventually and she remarries.

486 A SISTER'S SIN. A NOVEL. BY MRS. LOVETT CAMERON. London: F. V. White, 1893 BMC. Philadelphia: J. B. Lippincott, 1893 NUC.

Lilian Garnier is a poor half invalid motherless young woman who spends most of her time on a couch and whose only knowledge of the world comes through novels. She falls in love with Eric Denison who seduces her but refuses to marry her when she gets pregnant because she is of lower class. Lilian commits suicide, and her sister Daphne, who raises Lil's child, gives up her own fiance, swearing to seek Eric and avenge her sister's death.

CAMERON, MARGARET. See KILVERT, MARGARET (CAMERON).

CAMERON, MRS. H. LOVETT. See CAMERON, EMILY (SHARP).

CAMPBELL, DAISY RHODES. 1845-1927. United States.

487   THE FIDDLING GIRL: THE STORY OF VIRGINIA HAMMOND. Boston: Page, 1914 NUC.

Virginia is a country girl about to meet her step-mother for the first time. The story is of their relationship, of how the new mother encourages Virginia to go to a city school and through education begin her transition from "fiddling girl" to violinist.

488   THE PROVING OF VIRGINIA. Boston: Page, 1915 NUC.

Three years of her college life and her setting out to earn money in order to study music in Paris.

489   THE VIOLIN LADY. Boston: Page, 1916 NUC.

Heroine studies music in Paris; the story is of her success as a violinist and her romance.

CAMPBELL, H. M. F.*

490   THE STAR OF DESTINY. London: Odhams, [1920] BMC.

Stella, a young Englishwoman in India, becomes involved in a political intrigue which includes a female German spy. The author shows Stella as a bit of a prig, but is sympathetic to her enthusiasm and intellectual attitude.

CAMPBELL, HARRIETTE (RUSSELL). B. 1883. United States.

491   IS IT ENOUGH? A ROMANCE OF MUSICAL LIFE. New York and London: Harper, 1913 BMC NUC.

Young woman has a great passion for music and hopes to be a great singer. But her mother pushes her to marry a musical genius. Immediately she's unhappy because she sees he has old-fashioned ideas about wives. As husband and wife, they are strangers; as fellow musicians, they are comrades. There are long discussions of the degradation of wives having to ask husbands for money. Against his wishes, she goes away for a weekend much in the spirit of Nora, and when he shuts her out, friends urge a divorce. In their separation, he experiences many hardships including being tried for a bombing. When he is released and they are reunited, he writes a great opera in which she sings. They are famous at the end, and it is then enough to be his wife.

CAMPBELL, HELEN (STUART). 1839-1918. United States.

492   BALLANTYNE; A NOVEL. Boston: Little, Brown, 1901 NUC BMC.

Between two Americans, one a young educated woman disillusioned with American society and the other a man who loves America, rages a conflict for mastery as each fights for a principle in discussing modern social, political and economic theories. The woman passes for a man, deceiving intimate associates and housemates for years in this "inner history" of communal life.

CAMPBELL, JOSEPHINE ELISABETH.

493   OF THIS DEATH. London: Ward and Downey, 1891 BMC.

A young woman's "distorted soul and body shown in painful precision and uncompromising detail." History of Phyllis Eden.

494   THE PROBLEM OF PREJUDICE. BY MRS. VERE CAMPBELL. London: T. F. Unwin, 1896 BMC NUC.

Margaret Marey is irrevocably unhappy with husband. Opportunity for release comes in a dignified and moral form. Work and liberty are available to her. She chooses to remain with her husband. "It is the very depth of brutality in her husband, his bestiality, which has left him helpless and alone, which appeals to her."

CAMPBELL, MRS. VERE. See CAMPBELL, JOSEPHINE ELISABETH.

CAMPBELL, R. W.* United States.

495   DOROTHY V.A.D. AND THE DOCTOR. London: W. & R. Chambers, 1918 BMC NUC.

Life of a volunteer nurse in a military hospital recorded in letters. Includes a love story.

496   WINNIE MCLEOD. London: Hutchinson, [1920] NUC BMC.

A sympathetic portrayal of Winnie's life, first as a typist with a few inconsequential love affairs, then as mistress of a rich man. She later loves a man who is killed in the war. She goes on to become the manager of a munitions factory and eventually marries its owner.

CANFIELD, DOROTHY. See FISHER, DOROTHEA FRANCES (CANFIELD).

CAPES, HARRIET MAY (MOTHER MARY REGINALD). B. 1849.

497   THE STORY OF ELEANOR LAMBERT. BY MAGDALEN BROOKE. London: T. F. Unwin, 1891 NUC BMC. New York: Cassell, [1891] NUC.

"The moral must be that in a woman's world men are of no importance." Felicia Gray is engaged to a man who inspite of himself loves her bosom friend Eleanor. Felicia begs Eleanor to give him up and she does. They marry, and the women meet ten years later when the dying man wants to see Eleanor.

CARD, SUSAN.

498   AGNES'S DILEMMA. London: Drane's, 1913 BMC.

Dangers that beset young unprotected women in London.

CARDELLA, G. See BARNETT, ADA.

CAREY, ALICE V.

499   PARADISE WOLD. New York: G.W. Dillingham, 1896 NUC.

Virginia, hated by her half-sister who has attempted to drown her, flees from her home in Kentucky. She goes first to Washington, then to Los Angeles, where she has found employment. On route she is attacked by robbers, is carried off by their captain, and has many adventures.

CARLETON-MILECETE. See JONES, SUSAN CARLETON AND HELEN MILECETE.

CARNIE, ETHEL. United Kingdom.

500 MISS NOBODY. London: Methuen, [1913] NUC BMC.

Part I presents the drab life of working class people, focusing upon Caroline Evelyn Brown in her grimy surroundings. She sells oysters, reads penny novelettes, and aspires to a better life. She moves to Manchester to work in a factory, and we are given vivid descriptions of her work. Then she marries a man she hardly knows, leaves him, but they are eventually reconciled. In part II she is left a large fortune, and the novel leaves her with almost grown children.

CAROLIN, EMILY OLIVIA.

501 THE VERGE OF TWILIGHT. London: Hurst & Blackett, 1911 BMC.

Story of an aunt and her niece in slum setting. The aunt is a sombre passionate woman with "a sour secret longing for love." She rages at her own plainness and hates her niece for her beauty. Ends miserably.

CARR, ALICE VANSITTART (STRETTEL). B. 1850. United Kingdom.

502 THE ARM OF THE LORD. London: Duckworth, 1899 BMC.

Like her mother, Nancy is bold and defiant. When her fanatical Methodist grandfather forces her to church meetings and arranges a marriage with a churchman for her, Nancy mocks his religion and defies all. There is a rakish squire and Nancy is "wayward," but her grandfather is relentlessly tyrannical and unforgiving, though he loves her in his strange way and wants to save her from damnation. He casts her out and even at the end refuses to admit her dead body into his house.

CARR, MILDRED EMILY. B. 1877. United Kingdom.

503   GEORGE GORING'S DAUGHTERS. London: Smith, Elder, 1903 BMC.

Ann Goring tells the story of the early influences on her two daughters: their lonely moorland life and the romantic ideas from books. Their only contact with the "real" world is their father's visits until their 20's when they go forth to be educated among ordinary women. They come to love the same man whom Lucy rejects because of his previous relations with women. They discover their father's cruelty to their mother.

CARRUTH, FRANCES WESTON. See PRINDLE, FRANCES WESTON (CARRUTH).

CARRY, MABEL D.

504   BETTY MOORE'S JOURNAL. Chicago: Rand, McNally, 1912 NUC.

Betty is unhappy in her marriage. In her journal she considers the questions of what the middle-class married woman's job is, salaries for housework, and women's management in government. She is married to a man who drinks and while drunk injures their child. She redeems him, and he is persuaded that votes for women and women in government would be a great social improvement.

CARSON, NORMA (BRIGHT). B. 1883. United States.

505   TRUEHEART MARGERY. New York: G. H. Doran, [c1917] NUC.

Father resents daughter because mother died at her birth. When she refuses to marry the man he chooses, he disinherits her. Her marriage doesn't go well; when her husband leaves, she supports self and child, dies. Father reconciled with her daughter.

CARSWELL, CATHERINE ROXBURGH (MACFARLANE).
1879-1946. United Kingdom.

506 OPEN THE DOOR! New York: Harcourt, Brace & Howe, 1920 NUC. London: A. Melrose, [1920] NUC BMC.
Joanna's sexual history from age 7 to 27. Described as eminently a feminist novel. Joanna moves from the severe piety of a Glasgow family to more unconventional freedom. Her emotional odyssey is described by a quote from the novel itself, as the lavishing of "unreciprocated passion on individuals of both sexes."

CARTER, MARION HAMILTON.* United States.

507 SOULS RESURGENT. New York: C. Scribner's Sons, 1916 NUC.
After ten years away from home at college and at work, Dora returns when her father dies. He has made her the executor of his estate and guardian of two younger children. Dora, whose mother was Irish and whose father was Norwegian and Scotch, finds that her sister and brother have none of the cultural ideals of their parents. The author sees the social "melting pot" as a failure, in which the dominant American value is the American dollar.

508 THE WOMAN WITH EMPTY HANDS: THE EVOLUTION OF A SUFFRAGETTE [ANONYMOUS]. New York: Dodd, Mead, 1913 NUC.
Her conversion to the women's movement as a result of personal circumstances, stress and need: what the author calls "the horror of that desolation, the conviction of utter uselessness." Story opens with her selling "The Woman Voter" on Broadway. Flashback to her married life in Virginia, the death of her husband and child, her despondency, and the successive stages of her psychological development from her first obsession with the idea of widowhood to the comprehension of women as a community; the stages include meeting a suffragette,

learning about the sisterhood, becoming a militant suffragette, rescuing a victim of white slavery, and realizing once and for all that men can not be trusted to legislate for women and that women must remake the laws.

CARTER, WINIFRED. United Kingdom.

509 ASHES OF EDEN. London: Simpkin, Marshall, 1915 BMC.

Perils facing independent young woman; Katherine ends up on poultry farm that minister sets up to save young women.

CASE, FRANCES POWELL. United States.

510 THE HOUSE ON THE HUDSON. BY FRANCES POWELL. New York: C. Scribner, 1903 NUC. London: Harper, 1903 BMC.

Naive heroine, a bit of a pagan, orphaned, becomes housekeeper and companion and is drawn into a mesh of horrors.

511 AN OLD MAID'S VENGEANCE. BY FRANCES POWELL. New York: C. Scribner, 1911 NUC.

Vengeance against a man who made love to her because of her money and then jilted her.

CASSAVETTI, CECILE.

512 ANTHEA: A TRUE STORY OF THE GREEK WAR OF INDEPENDENCE. London: Cassell, [1892] BMC.

Realistic narrative of the flight of a widow and her children from the rapacious Ali Pasha who has killed her husband. "Painfully graphic."

CASTLE, AGNES (SWEETMAN). D. 1922. United Kingdom.

513 MY LITTLE LADY ANNE. BY MRS. EGERTON CASTLE. London: J. Lane, 1896 BMC. Philadelphia: H. Altemus, 1896 NUC.

Anne, a half wit, is manipulated by her mother into a

financially advantageous marriage with a dissipated cousin. Anne's nurse narrates how the marriage totally destroys Anne's reason and eventually kills her.

CASTLE, MRS. EGERTON. See CASTLE, AGNES (SWEETMAN).

CATHARINA, ANNA. See REBEK, LILLIE.

CATHER, WILLA SIBERT. 1873-1947. United States.

514 MY ANTONIA. Boston: Houghton Mifflin, 1906 NUC. London: W. Heinemann, 1919 NUC BMC.

Immigrant family from Bohemia settle in Nebraska: the Shimerdas, focus on Antonia. Male narrator. The women are strong and independent. They move from farms to the town. Frances Harley has a good business mind. She keeps her family going when her husband is away. Lena Lingard refuses to relate to men except as friends and becomes a successful dressmaker. Tiny Soderball refuses love and marriage, travels to Alaska and makes a fortune. Antonia returns to the land. She represents the strong solid pioneer spirit.

515 O PIONEERS! Boston: Houghton Mifflin, 1913 NUC. London: W. Heinemann, 1913 NUC BMC.

Scandinavian and Bohemian pioneers in Nebraska. Alexandra Bergson "a new woman who succeeds in the western plains where her father had failed." At 18 she is in charge of the family. The farm prospers in her care, and she becomes the richest and most influential citizen of her county. Her friend Marie is different, tragic, but strong too. "Possibly some might call it a feminist novel, for the two heroines are stronger, cleverer and better balanced than their husbands and brothers—but we are sure that Miss Cather had nothing so inartistic in mind." The New York Times Review of Books, 5 January 1913, p. 466.

516 THE SONG OF THE LARK. Boston: Houghton Mifflin, 1915 NUC BMC. London: J. Murray, 1916 NUC.

Thea Kronberg struggles to succeed as an artist. At 11, studies piano. At 17 moves to Chicago to study seriously.

Her teacher discovers her beautiful voice. She meets a young man who wishes to help her in her career; she borrows money to study in Germany, is successful in opera abroad and in New York. At the very end she marries the young man but keeps her career.

CAUMONT, MARY.

517 A DISH OF MATRIMONY. London: E. Stock, 1894 BMC.

Clerks in a London suburb, a woman adulterer. "Not a pleasing picture of manners or values," comments reviewer.

CAUSTON, SELINA MARY.

518 TWIXT TWO ETERNITIES. London: Routledge, 1893 BMC.

Lady Katherine is a brilliant aristocratic woman who is devoted to good works. She turns her living room over to lectures and visits the slums. Centers on a love story.

CAVALIER, Z. LANGRANA.*

519 THE SOUL OF THE ORIENT. London: Murray and Evenden, [1913] BMC.

Helen, a wealthy young astrologist, converts her fiance to her new philosophy, a new religious creed that will reform the whole world. Together with her sister, another convert, Helen performs many charitable deeds.

CAVENDISH, PAULINE BRADFORD (MACKIE) HOPKINS. B. 1873. United States.

520 A GEORGIAN ACTRESS. BY PAULINE BRADFORD MACKIE (MRS. HERBERT MUELLER HOPKINS). Boston: L. C. Page, 1900 NUC.

The life and adventures of a talented actress during the reign of George III.

521   YE   LYTTLE   SALEM   MAIDE: A   STORY   OF
       WITCHCRAFT.   BY   PAULINE   BRADFORD   MACKIE.
       Boston and London: Lamson, Wolffe, 1898 NUC.
       A study of Salem witchcraft.

CHAMBERLAIN, LUCIA.

522   SON OF THE WIND. Indianapolis: Bobbs-Merrill, [c1910]
       NUC.
       Story of a rancher and a woman who feel opposite ways
       about a wild horse; he would tame it; she would keep it
       free. They quarrel, part when he gets his way. The horse
       breaks its back trying to throw the man.

CHAMBERS, ROSA. B. 1886. United States.

523   THE   HIPPODROME;   A   NOVEL.   BY   RACHEL
       HAYWARD. London: W. Heinemann, 1913 BMC NUC.
       New York: G.H. Doran, [c1913] NUC.
       When her Irish-Austrian family loses a fortune, Fatalite
       comes to Barcelona to ride in the Hippodrome. She soon
       meets and joins a band of terrorists devoted to the cause
       of liberty. She becomes a close comrade to one of the
       anarchists and loves another. Study of her contradictory
       nature, her meeting with the terrorists and their plans.

524   LETTERS   FROM   LA-BAS.   BY   RACHEL   HAYWARD.
       Boston: J. W. Luce, 1914 NUC. London: W. Heinemann,
       [1914] BMC.
       Letters from "a large-hearted woman to a cold-hearted
       man," expressing opinions on love, marriage, and
       feminism. Her last letter announces her departure for Paris
       with a lover.

CHAMBLIN, JEAN.

525   LADY BOBS, HER BROTHER, AND I. A ROMANCE OF
       THE AZORES. New York and London: G. P. Putnam's
       Sons, 1905 BMC NUC.
       Actress's letters about the Azores.

CHAMPION, JESSIE. United Kingdom.

526 THE FOOLISHNESS OF LILIAN. London: J. Lane, 1918 NUC BMC. New York: J. Lane, 1918 NUC BMC.

Lilian (from the slums but actually of "superior" birth) goes from factory work to the stage, to literature, to nursing in the war, and then to a happy marriage.

CHAMPNEYS, ADELAIDE MARY. United Kingdom.

527 BRIDE ELECT. London: E. Arnold, 1913 BMC.

Psychological study of Audrey, a rebellious young woman who is devoted to her mother's memory. She is put in the care of her aunt who soon packs her off to a second rate girls' school. Here she keeps a diary and is infuriated when her teacher attempts to take it from her. At 17 her guardian who is three times her age offers marriage. She accepts but only out of gratitude. Just before the wedding, she learns of his infatuation with an actress and breaks the engagement. She ends up in a convent.

528 THE RECOILING FORCE. London: E. Arnold, 1914 BMC.

Madeline rejects an arranged marriage when her fiance drives off after running over a child. She instead marries Ralph Helger, but their marriage is unhappy and she rebels. A secondary character, "Dulcie—good-hearted, common, sensible, womanly—is our refuge; but even Dulcie is a practising feminist, and rest from feminism is the one temporary mercy we owe to perfidious Prussia."

CHANCELLOR, LOUISE ISABEL (BEECHER). 1871-1908. United States.

529 THE PLAYERS O' LONDON. A TALE OF AN ELIZABETHIAN [SIC] SMART SET. New York: B. W. Dodge, [1909] NUC BMC.

Phyllis, twin of boy player in Lord Leicester's Company, takes the part of Juliet.

CHANCELLOR, OLIVE.

530 THE LADY GARDENER. A ROMANCE OF SIX MONTHS. London: Drane's, [1914] BMC.

CHANNING, BLANCHE MARY. 1863-1902.

531 WINIFRED WEST. A STORY. Boston: W. A. Wilde, 1901 NUC.

Heroine studies violin.

CHANNON, ETHEL MARY. B. 1875. United Kingdom.

532 THE AUTHORESS. London: Hutchinson, 1909 BMC.

Vivia Mortlake wrongly gains authorship of a book—"pathetic story."

533 MISS KING'S PROFESSION. London: Mills and Boon, 1913 BMC.

Satire. Young woman writes "second rate" novels and by so doing sacrifices her family. One reviewer says she's "justly punished in the end by marrying a priggish clergyman."

534 THE STRENGTH OF WEAKNESS. London: Mills & Boon, 1915 BMC.

A girl is raised very much like a boy by a father who wants a son. When she is older, she loves a man who is attracted elsewhere because he finds she is not feminine enough. But she soon wins him back because he finds he is miserable married to the true woman type.

CHANTER, GRATIANA. See KNOCKER, GRATIANA LONGWORTH.

CHAPIN, ANNA ALICE. 1880-1920. United States.

535 JANE. New York and London: G. P. Putnam's Sons, 1920 BMC NUC.

Young Irish woman turned out by her father joins acting troupe and becomes successful actress.

536   THE UNDER TRAIL. Boston: Little, Brown, 1912 NUC. London: I. Pitman, 1912 BMC.

Melodrama. Narration of love of an educated nurse for a primitive man. Hair-raising adventures in the mountains.

CHARLESWORTH, M. E. See BOOTH, MAUD BALLINGTON (CHARLESWORTH).

CHARTRES, A. VIVANTI. See CHARTRES, ANITA (VIVANTI).

CHARTRES, ANITA (VIVANTI). 1868-1942. United Kingdom.

537   THE DEVOURERS. BY A. VIVANTI CHARTRES. New York: G. P. Putnam's Sons, 1910 NUC. London: W. Heinemann, 1910 BMC NUC.

A talented and intellectual woman's career is interrupted by the birth of a daughter who, like her mother, is a genius. The mother sacrifices her aspirations for the child whom she raises to womanhood. The daughter is on her way to fulfilling her talent as a poet when she is faced with the birth of a child, another genius. The book closes: "In the shadowy cradle the baby opened its eyes and said, 'I am hungry.'"

538   VAE VICTIS. London: E. Arnold, 1917 BMC. (Also published as The Outrage. New York: A. A. Knopf, 1918 NUC.)

A child, a young girl and a young married woman are attacked by German soldiers in Belgium. The child becomes deaf and dumb because of the terror of the experience. The girl and the woman are raped and become pregnant. One has an abortion by an English surgeon. The other keeps her child.

CHARTRES, ANNIE. See CHARTRES, ANITA.

CHASE, JESSIE (ANDERSON). 1865-1949. United States.

539 THREE FRESHMEN: RUTH, FRAN AND NATHALIE.
Chicago: A. C. McClurg, 1898 NUC.
One from Chicago, one from Boston, one from the South
at Smith; merry, studious, and happy.

CHATTERTON, G. G. United Kingdom.

540 THE HUMAN STARLING. A STUDY OF A WOMAN'S
NATURE. London: J. Long, [1918] BMC.
Barbara, a "caged starling," struggles unsuccessfully for
independence in different jobs and love affairs,
culminating in an unhappy marriage.

CHEEVER, HARRIET ANNA. Fl. 1890-1911. United States.

541 GIPSY JANE. Boston: D. Estes, [1903] NUC.
She is a talented dancer and musician who goes on the
stage.

542 JOSIE BEAN: FLAT STREET. Boston: D. Estes, [c1905]
NUC.
Josie Bean is an uneducated but ambitious and talented
young woman who starts her career as a milliner's
assistant and rises from poverty to become a prominent
artist. At 18 she faces a happy and prosperous future.

CHILDS, CARRIE GOLDSMITH. United States.

543 AND THE SWORD FELL. Floral Park, N.Y.: Mayflower,
1895 NUC.
Woman tells the story of her marriage through her
journal: the few years of happiness followed by suspicion
and estrangement.

544 LOST LINEAGE. Floral Park, N.Y.: Mayflower, 1897
NUC.
Young woman, married secretly, is about to have a child.
Her father calls the doctor to the remote farmhouse with
the intention of having the child killed because he is angry
about his daughter's marriage.

CHILDS, ELEANOR STUART (PATTERSON). 1876-1920. United States.

545   AVERAGES: A STORY OF NEW YORK. BY ELEANOR STUART. New York: D. Appleton, 1899 NUC BMC.

Two women, both unhappily married: Jane Dupuis works to help working women. She edits the Day Star, organ of the Early Bird Circle of World's Workers. Cornelia writes a novel under a pen name that is published in England. Jane reads the book, writes to the author, and the two women correspond. But when Jane learns that the author is her nearest neighbor and friend, their friendship ends.

546   STONEPASTURES. BY ELEANOR STUART. New York: D. Appleton, 1895 NUC BMC.

Heroine is a barber. On her wedding day, her new husband is critically injured in an explosion because his rival fails to warn him of the impending danger. Story traces the couple's lives from there on. Set in Soot City, Pennsylvania.

CHOLMONDELEY, ALICE. See RUSSELL, MARY ANNETTE (BEAUCHAMP) ARNIM RUSSELL.

CHOLMONDELEY, MARY. 1859-1925. United Kingdom.

547   NOTWITHSTANDING. London: J. Murray, 1913 NUC BMC. (Also published as After All. New York: D. Appleton, 1913 NUC.)

Annette is raised by three aunts, one of whom is a popular novelist. At 21, she goes to live with her father, but leaves because he tries to sell her first to a musician, then to another man. We first meet her meditating suicide. She is saved by a man and goes away with him, and she is "saved" from him because he immediately falls ill. The plot turns on a will, and the novel ends with Annette's marriage to the cousin of the man who saved her from throwing herself into the Seine.

548 PRISONERS; FAST BOUND IN MISERY AND IRON. New York: Dodd, Mead, 1906 NUC. London: Hutchinson, 1906 BMC NUC.

Sympathetic study of the character development of a miserably weak woman who allows a man to remain in jail for a murder he didn't commit.

549 RED POTTAGE. London: E. Arnold, 1899 BMC. New York and London: Harper, 1899 NUC.

Contrast between two women: Rachel West an heiress who loves Hugh Scarlett but learns in time he is a scoundrel and Hester Gresley an intellectually emancipated modern woman who is a novelist.

CHOPIN, KATE (O'FLAHERTY). 1851-1904. United States.

550 THE AWAKENING. Chicago and New York: H. S. Stone, 1899 NUC.

Edna, 28 and mother of two sons, spends a summer at Grand Isle in the company of "mother women" like Adele and two men who "stir her emotional nature for a short time." Here she realizes her life as wife and mother does not satisfy her. The end is tragic.

CHRISTIAN, SYDNEY. See LORD, MARIA L.

CHRISTISON, NEIL. See BIRD, MARY PAGE.

CHURCHILL, LIDA ABBIE. B. 1859. United States.

551 A GRAIN OF MADNESS: A ROMANCE. New York, London: The Abbey Press, [1902] NUC.

The illegitimate child of a priest becomes the pupil of an artist on the condition that she not marry for ten years and then only an artist greater than herself. He then falls in love with her, but she is a better painter than he is.

CLARE, FRANCES. United Kingdom.

552 WILD JUSTICE. London: A. Melrose, 1912 BMC. New York: Duffield, 1913 PW.

Marriage martyrdom. The characters remain married only because it is their ideal of the way in which obligations already assumed must be met. "Tame" chronicle of the relations between two men and two women.

CLARK, GEORGINA BINNIE. Canada.

553 A SUMMER ON THE CANADIAN PRAIRIE. New York: Longman's, Green, 1910 NUC. London: E. Arnold, 1910 BMC.

Two women and their brother develop a free grant of land in the Northwest.

CLARK, IMOGEN. D. 1936. United States.

554 GOD'S PUPPETS; A STORY OF OLD NEW YORK. Toronto: W. J. Gage, 1901 BMC. New York: C. Scribner's Sons, 1901 NUC.

Peggy, a madcap, is a jockey.

CLARK, MURIEL.

555 SISTER JEFFERIES. London: J. Nisbet, 1914 BMC.

A woman journalist gives up career and love on joining the Salvation Army.

CLEEVE, LUCAS. See KINGSCOTE, ADELINE GEORGINA ISABELLA (WOLFF).

CLEGHORN, SARAH NORCLIFFE. 1876-1959. United States.

556 THE SPINSTER; A NOVEL WHEREIN A NINETEENTH CENTURY GIRL FINDS HER PLACE IN THE TWENTIETH. New York: H. Holt, 1916 NUC.

The evolution of a sentimental schoolgirl to a contented, fulfilled spinster. Ellen Graham grows up in Vermont and goes to Radcliffe. She has a passion for literature. She develops a sense of social justice and becomes a socialist. She has a love affair which comes to nothing and in the end devotes her pen to the cause of justice.

CLEGHORN, SARAH NORCLIFFE AND DOROTHEA FRANCES (CANFIELD) FISHER.

557 FELLOW CAPTAINS. BY SARAH N. CLEGHORN AND DOROTHY CANFIELD FISHER. New York: H. Holt, 1916 NUC.

Five middle-aged women of different types meet twice a week for conversations. The novel begins with one woman telling how she took control of her own life—became captain of her soul—and contains appropriate poems for "reading in different emergencies."

CLEMENT, ELLIS (MEREDITH). B. 1865. United States.

558 HEART OF MY HEART. BY ELLIS MEREDITH. New York: McClure, Phillips, 1904 NUC. London: Methuen, 1905 BMC.

Diary of experiences, plans, etc. of woman expecting first child. Treatment is frank and free.

559 THE MASTER-KNOT OF HUMAN FATE. BY ELLIS MEREDITH. Boston: Little, Brown, 1901 BMC NUC.

The woman, a successful opera star, divorced, is an "idealized, feminized Robinson Crusoe." She and a man live as comrades on an island alone for a year. Then they fall in love. They question whether to start the human race over again. The decision, left to the new Eve, remains unsettled at the end.

560 UNDER THE HARROW. BY ELLIS MEREDITH. Boston: Little, Brown, 1907 NUC.

The chances of success of women earning their living by their brains in New York City. The experiences and disappointments of three women writers and illustrators, the returned MS's and illustrations, the financial problems, etc.

CLIFFORD, ELIZABETH LYDIA ROSABELLE (BONHAM) DE LA PASTURE. 1866-1945. United Kingdom.

561 PETER'S MOTHER. BY MRS. HENRY DE LA PASTURE. New York: E.P. Dutton, 1905 NUC. London: Smith, Elder, 1905 BMC NUC.

In this study of tragic motherhood, the woman finally says enough! She marries, much too young, a squire who makes life unbearably miserable and dull. When he dies, the son who inherits his father's "dense masculine selfishness" goes on making her suffer. Finally, at middle-age, after twenty years of all that, she has the courage to leave.

562 THE TYRANT. BY MRS. HENRY DE LA PASTURE. London: Methuen, [1909] BMC NUC. New York: E.P. Dutton, 1910 NUC.

Welch woman blamed by tyrant husband for her inner revolt (though she's self-sacrificing), by her children for her lack of courage, and by the world for her subservience.

CLIFFORD, LUCY (LANE). 1854-1929. United Kingdom.

563 AUNT ANNE. BY MRS. W. K. CLIFFORD. London: R. Bentley, 1892 BMC. New York: Harper, 1892 NUC.

Aunt Ann is a sympathetic portrait of a 60 year old woman who needs love and companionship. She accepts a marriage proposal from a young fortune seeker. "An old woman is not generally considered an attractive object. Neither in life nor in fiction is opinion very favorable to her." Aunt Anne is a "curious, delicate real being," "perfectly independent," and "never for a moment ridiculous even when she makes us laugh."

564 A FLASH OF SUMMER: THE STORY OF A SIMPLE WOMAN'S LIFE. BY MRS. W. K. CLIFFORD. New York: D. Appleton, 1894 NUC. London: Methuen, 1895 BMC.

Character study of Katherine. Raised in a lonely household, she leads a solitary life with dreary walks to school, haunted by an unknown terror. She is forced to marry a brutal man by her equally brutal uncle. After a year of physical and mental abuse, she leaves her husband and travels with friends, concealing the fact that she is married. Then she meets and loves Jim Alford who convinces her to return to her husband. She agrees—more out of love for him than duty to her husband. But at this very time Jim dies. Katherine throws herself before a speeding train.

565 THE HOUSE IN MARYLEBONE; A CHRONICLE. London: Duckworth, 1917 BMC NUC.

All the tenants of this lodging house are working women. Studies of different women, different kinds of work, descriptions of parties and of private struggles in gaining independence. Most of the women end up married.

566 LOVE-LETTERS OF A WORLDLY WOMAN. BY MRS. W. K. CLIFFORD. London: E. Arnold, [1891] BMC. New York: Harper, 1892 NUC.

Three sets of letters by three very modern women—Marie Bashkirtseff types. The author of the first set, "A Modern Correspondence," is a "visionary, impulsive, ill-regulated femme incomprise of the latter end of the century." She does not marry the old-fashioned, healthy-minded Englishman. The second woman is thrown over by the man she loves, marries an aging baronet, and finds happiness—not in love, but in companionship. She looks foward not to children, but to the power her salon will eventually have. The writer of the third set "On the Wane" is like the first author but less aggressive. Gwen is first in love with a man who jilts her and then wants her. She refuses him because her views of life have changed. About the first woman one critic says, "The contrast between the visionary idealizing love of an unconventional young girl, and the practical point of view of the average beefy Englishman—who is looking for a wife—has never been better brought out."

567 MISS FINGAL. BY MRS. W. K. CLIFFORD. Edinburgh and London: W. Blackwood, 1919 NUC BMC. New York: C. Scribner's Sons, 1919 NUC.

At 21, Alice leads a life of solitude in her small flat, speaking to no one but her cleaning woman, reading novels and watching people from her balcony. Then her whole life changes. She inherits an estate and becomes obsessed with the story surrounding a small cottage she particularly likes. She learns of the unhappy marriage of the former tenants, traces their whereabouts and becomes friends with Linda Alliston, the wife who is dying of a mysterious disease and who is divorced from her unfaithful husband. Alice so identifies with Linda that when Linda dies Alice falls unconscious and awakens completely changed. She has taken over Linda's personality completely. Her one object is to gain custody of the children. The husband dies in war; Alice adopts the children.

568   A WOMAN ALONE. THREE STORIES. BY MRS. W. K. CLIFFORD. New York, London: Macmillan, 1898 NUC. London: Methuen, 1901 BMC.
Three stories, theme of isolation in marriage.

CLIFFORD, MRS. W. K. See CLIFFORD, LUCY (LANE).

CLOSE, EVELYNE. B. 1874. United Kingdom.

569   CHERRY ISLE. Philadelphia: C. W. Jacobs, [c1920] NUC. London: G. Richards, 1920 BMC NUC.
The career of a singer and her religious regeneration.

CLOWES, ALICE ADA.

570   MONA: A NOVEL. London: S. Sonnenschein, 1899 BMC NUC.
Beautiful young Irish woman marries and makes England her new home. But she learns her husband gambles, and though she is pregnant, she leaves him to make her own living. In the end she forgives her husband for her child's sake.

CLYDE, CONSTANCE. New Zealand.

571   A PAGAN'S LOVE. London: T. Unwin, 1905 BMC.
Dorothea, a social worker, has a very close friendship

with another woman, a journalist. The slums, the boarding houses, the lives of social workers—all the social conditions—including maternity—of modern Australia are well described.

CLYDE, IRENE.

572 BEATRICE THE SIXTEENTH. London: G. Bell, 1909 BMC.

Feminist science fiction. The narrator called Mere finds herself in an Eastern country where people know nothing about our world, where the sexes are treated exactly alike, where most of the people are called "she," and where there is a weekly supply of babies from a nearby barbarian country that keeps up the population.

COBDEN, ELLEN MELICENT. See SICKERT, ELLEN MELICENT (COBDEN).

COCAYNE, EDITH K. United States.

573 SUE MCFARLAND, SCHOOLMARM. Baltimore, Md.: Saulsbury, [1918] NUC.

A young woman leaves home to teach out West.

COHN, CLARA (VIEBIG). 1860-1952. Germany.

574 ABSOLUTION. BY CLARA VIEBIG. London, New York: J. Lane, 1908 NUC BMC. (Tr. by H. Raahauge.)

Poland—young woman given to a coarse elderly man whom she loathes and tries to kill. Finally he kills himself. She is the only calm one at his grave. She loves another man. Author seems to sympathize with her.

575 OUR DAILY BREAD. BY CLARA VIEBIG. New York: J. Lane, 1909 BMC. London: J. Lane, 1909 BMC NUC. (Tr. by Margaret L. Clarke.)

Two young women go to Berlin and enter domestic service. Realistic view of the painful aspects of their lives.

COLE, SOPHIE. 1862-1947. United Kingdom.

576 ARROWS FROM THE DARK. London: Mills and Boon, [1909] NUC BMC.

Sympathetic portrayal of Eugenia, a widow who publishes love letters her husband received from a woman whose name she does not reveal. Her only purpose is to make money. The letters cause a sensation as well as complications.

577 THE GATE OF OPPORTUNITY. London: Mills and Boon, [1918] BMC.

Heroine is an educated young woman who works for a living.

578 THE LOITERING HIGHWAY. London: Mills and Boon, 1916 BMC.

Valeria, an illegitimate young woman, becomes an actor.

579 PENELOPE'S DOORS. London: Mills and Boon, 1913 BMC.

After losing her money, Penelope saves herself from disaster by opening up a shop. Eventually the business fails, and she falls in love.

580 A PLAIN WOMAN'S PORTRAIT. London: Mills and Boon, [1912] BMC NUC.

Beginning as an office worker, the heroine at 37 is an established and successful novelist. She subsequently finds happiness in marriage.

581 SKIRTS OF STRAW. London: Mills and Boon, 1915 BMC NUC.

Rhoda is a "maid-of-all-work" raised in a work house. She loses her small son who was the center of her life. She has artistic talent which is recognized by a young male artist. At the end of the book, Rhoda is still unmarried.

COLERIDGE, CHRISTABEL ROSE. 1843-1921. United Kingdom.

582 AMETHYST: THE STORY OF A BEAUTY. London: A. D. Innes, 1891 BMC. New York: D. Appleton, 1892 NUC.

Beauty is all but fatal for Amethyst Haredale. She is the daughter of a man who squandered his fortune. As a result, Amethyst was sent to live with her aunt. She was well-educated. She passed the exams at Cambridge with distinction and wanted to teach, but her aunt sent her back to her family and the social whirl of marriage-making organized by her mother. "In a couple of years she has been battered into something very like a professional beauty." Study of her character, her struggle between principle and instinct, her descent into the competitive social world of the marriage market and the struggle out of it.

583 FIFTY POUNDS: A SEQUEL TO "THE GREEN GIRLS OF GREY THORPE". London: National Society's Depository, [1891] BMC. New York: T. Whittaker, [1891] BMC.

Linda Inglewood is very restless in her grandfather's house and with the common duties of her everyday life. She writes novels about highborn heroes and heroines and their uncommon adventures, and she wants a successful career in literature.

584 THE TENDER MERCIES OF THE GOOD. London: Isbister, 1895 BMC NUC.

The Fairford family and Hilda who at 38 had never thought of independent action until she at last realizes that her position as "one of the girls" is intolerable. "An eloquent indictment of the dangers of domestic repression."

COLERIDGE, M. E. See COLERIDGE, MARY ELIZABETH.

COLERIDGE, MARY ELIZABETH. 1861-1907. United Kingdom.

585 THE KING WITH TWO FACES. BY M. E. COLERIDGE. London: E. Arnold, 1897 BMC. New York: J. Lane, 1898 NUC.

Madame de Stael's salon and conversations figure strongly in this historic romance.

COLLIN, GRACE LATHROP.

586 PUTNAM PLACE. New York and London: Harper, 1903 BMC NUC.

Portraits of older women in a New York town.

COLLINS, E. BURKE. See SHARKEY, EMMA AUGUSTA (BROWN).

COLLINS, E. LEUTY.*

587 HADASSEH; OR, "FROM CAPTIVITY TO THE PERSIAN THRONE". New York: Cassell, [1891] NUC. London: T. F. Unwin, 1891 BMC.

Story of Esther from captivity to the Persian throne. "How the queen saved the Hebrew people in Persia from the bloodthirsty rage of Haman, the King's minister."

COLLINS, MABEL. See COOK, MABEL (COLLINS).

COLMORE, G. See WEAVER, BAILLE GERTRUDE RENTON (COLMORE).

COLVILL, HELEN HESTER.

588 LADY JULIA'S EMERALD. New York: J. Lane, 1908 BMC. London: J. Lane, 1908 BMC NUC.

Described as an intricate narrative of the career of a heroine of independent character and artistic gifts—not to be taken for the ordinary missing jewels story.

COMBE, MRS. KENNETH. See COMBE, THEODORA (WILLIAMSON).

COMBE, THEODORA (WILLIAMSON). United Kingdom.

589 THE UPWARD FLIGHT. BY MRS. KENNETH COMBE. London: Skeffington, [c1919] BMC.

Philippa Ferrington is separated from her husband, in love with another man, but refuses to consider divorce because her religion upholds the sanctity of marriage. Author suggests that she is the product of propaganda and that until women take part in making laws, there will be no progress.

COMFORT, BESSIE (MARCHANT). 1862-1941. United Kingdom.

590 THE ADVENTURES OF PHYLLIS; A STORY OF THE ARGENTINE. London: Cassell, [1910] BMC. New York: Funk & Wagnall, 1914 PW.

Phyllis answers an advertisement for a nursery governess and finds herself amongst strange people in a remote place. In a series of adventures she solves a number of mysteries.

591 FROM THE SCOURGE OF THE TONGUE. London: A. Melrose, [1901] BMC.

Two orphaned sisters reorder their lives: they successfully run a farm.

COMPTON, C. G.* United Kingdom.

592 HER OWN DEVICES. London: W. Heinemann, 1896 BMC. New York: E. Arnold, 1896 NUC.

Actress looking for a husband aims for a weak flabby man. He escapes.

593 THE HOUSE OF BONDAGE. London: W. Heinemann, 1911 BMC NUC.

Laura Henderson is single, has two children, each with a different father, yet becomes a peeress when she marries a duke—all with the approval of her author.

COMSTOCK, HARRIET THERESA (SMITH). B. 1860. United States.

594 MAM'SELLE JO. Garden City, N. Y.: Doubleday, Page, 1918 NUC. London: Hodder and Stoughton, 1924 BMC.

Jo Morey, at 40, is finally able to pay off her father's debts and has turned the run-down property into a modestly prosperous farm. She adopts a child, Donelle, from the local orphanage. There is a mystery about her birth, and the town believes that Donelle is Jo's illegitimate daughter. When Donelle is old enough to hear and understand this gossip, she believes it also, and her loyalty to Jo causes her to turn down an opportunity to become trained as a musician. The end of the story is happy for both women. They are very different but both strong and independent and each sympathetic and supportive to the other throughout.

595 THE MAN THOU GAVEST. Garden City, N. Y.: Doubleday, Page, 1917 NUC. London: Hodder and Stoughton, [1924] BMC.

Nellie Rose, young country woman living in the hills, is loved and left by a man from the city. She has a child, but no problem, for her old love understands everything. They marry. Lydia is the sophisticated woman the city man returns to. She is economically independent, intends to be on an equal basis in marriage and arranges an unusual marriage. The two will live apart. When she wants a child, she adopts the hill-woman's child, by mutual agreement.

596 THE PLACE BEYOND THE WINDS. Garden City, N.Y.: Doubleday, Page, 1914 NUC. London: C. Brown, 1914 BMC.

Priscilla Glenn is raised in a Canadian community by a father who is a bigot and a tyrant. In spite of him she gets an education and becomes a nurse. Then she is faced with a decision which means the renunciation of her profession. She reveals to a friend the medical condition of a male patient whom the friend is about to marry.

597 A SON OF THE HILLS. Garden City, N. Y.: Doubleday, Page, 1913 NUC.

Story focuses upon the hero, Martin Morley, but Marcia Lowe, a minor character, is a doctor from Massachusetts who comes to the hill country in Virginia to help the "poor whites." "Her appeal to Martin Morley is an illuminating epitome of much of the feminist movement."

598　UNBROKEN LINES. New York: Doubleday, 1919 NUC.
Author explores the problem of whether a woman should remain married to a man she is unsuited for. Gwen was raised by her father to be unsophisticated. She marries the wrong man, one who would completely change her. At the same time, she has a male friend, a "comrade" who would keep her exactly as she is.

COMSTOCK, SARAH. D. 1960. United States.

599　THE SODDY. Garden City, N.Y.: Doubleday, Page, 1912 NUC.
Jerry first struggles to care for the younger children when her parents die, then to stick to the farm in spite of failures, fire, drought, and winds. The man from the East whom she marries gives up and goes home but eventually returns.

600　THE VALLEY OF VISION. Garden City, N.Y.: Doubleday, Page, 1919 NUC BMC.
Marcia Warren "should have been a boy." She's energetic, tempestuous; she digs earthworms and cares nothing for clothes. Only one boy understands her, but he goes off to school. Isolated and unhappy, she reads voraciously and at 21 becomes a nurse in order to do welfare work. She meets the boy now grown and married. The two rebel against the narrow puritans of Banbury by planning to reform the town and factory.

CONKLIN, JENNIE MARIA (DRINKWATER). 1841-1900. United States.

601　LOOKING SEAWARD. BY JENNIE M. DRINKWATER. Boston: A. I. Bradley, [c1893] NUC.
Helen Kline decides to remain single because "a single middleaged woman has glorious opportunities. I honor the wife and mother, but there is much she cannot do for her girls." Consequently she devotes her life to working for girls and young women of all types.

602 THREE-AND-TWENTY. BY JENNIE M. DRINKWATER. Boston: A. I. Bradley, 1895 NUC.

The girlhood of Leah Ritchie in New England, her life as a journalist in New York, and the proposal of marriage she receives at 23.

CONNEY, MRS.

603 JUDY, A JILT: A NOVEL. London: Jarrold, 1897 BMC.

She is the "impossible, tempestuous daughter of a ballet dancer, more at home in the hunting field than in the drawing room." But she knows her face is her fortune and believes marriage is her only reason for living. She becomes engaged to an old colonel, but loves another whom she tries to trick into marriage. The novel ends with her drowning.

604 PEGGY'S PERVERSITY. London: Hurst and Blackett, 1891 BMC.

Peggy Treherne, angular and gawky, is transformed in six months from tomboy to "lady of her brother's house." But she vacillates between this "proper" way of life and the active life with candid friendships with men.

CONSTANCE, E.

605 ALONG THE ROAD. A NOVEL. London: Hutchinson, 1899 BMC NUC.

Ella is a straight-from-the-shoulder young woman, completely unsentimental and candid. She is popular with the children at the wretched sea-side school where she teaches, but she is frank about preferring the company of adults. Her bold statements about children shock her friends. At the end she approaches her marriage to an ordinary but good-natured man coldly and clearly. She has doubts but is ready to make the best of it.

CONVERSE, FLORENCE. B. 1871. United States.

606 THE BURDEN OF CHRISTOPHER. Boston: Houghton, Mifflin, 1900 NUC.

Christopher, a manufacturer who believes in sharing

profits equally with his workers rather than benevolently donating to charities, fails in modern competition. The value of women's labor especially is discussed.

607 THE CHILDREN OF LIGHT. Boston: Houghton-Mifflin, 1912 NUC. London: J.M. Dent, 1912 BMC.

Clara, raised in a cooperative settlement, and filled with idealism and enthusiasm, joins two young male idealists. They start a paper, become active in political work, and get involved in a strike which results in death for one of the men and imprisonment for the other. Narrated by Clara, in autobiographical form.

608 DIANA VICTRIX: A NOVEL. Boston and New York: Houghton, Mifflin, 1897 NUC.

Two "bachelor girls" from New England visit the impoverished Creole Dumaris family in New Orleans for a winter. "Their aversion to marriage is as unnatural as their absorbing love for each other. Of course, the young Southerners fall in love with them, but being what they are, the damsels prefer each other, although Sylvia quite loses her head as well as her heart." One is a teacher and lecturer of social science in Boston, who has come to involve her old schoolmate in a more active life. The eldest son of the Dumaris family falls in love with her. "The action of this self-sufficient woman is thereafter interesting; she is last seen living contentedly in a Boston tenement."

CONYERS, DOROTHEA (SMYTH). 1873-1949. United Kingdom.

609 B. E. N. London: Methuen, 1919 BMC.

Fox hunting Irish stories linked together by B. E. N., a young woman making her own way as a whip. She is poor, self-reliant. She has tried several war jobs without success. She becomes the second whip to the West Cara Hounds but becomes ill from the hard work.

610 TWO IMPOSTERS AND TINKER. London: Hutchinson, 1910 NUC BMC. New York: E. P. Dutton, 1911 NUC.

Irish hunting and a young woman who "dresses as a young man and conquers the country."

COOK, GRACE LOUISE.

611   WELLESLEY STORIES. Boston: R.G. Badger, 1901 NUC.
Seven stories describing friendships between college
women who are intellectually involved in their studies.

COOK, MABEL (COLLINS). 1851-1927. United Kingdom.

612   JULIET'S LOVERS. BY MABEL COLLINS. London: Ward
and Downey, 1893 BMC.
Sensational story of theatrical life as well as a protest
against bringing up girls ignorant of sex. Juliet's father
keeps a mistress, and his illegitimate daughter becomes
Juliet's friend. Juliet becomes a successful actress, marries
an actor, and on her wedding day confronts another
woman claiming his name. Contains many sensational
episodes such as shootings. One minor character is a
wicked woman director who wears a live snake as a
bracelet.

613   THE STAR SAPPHIRE. BY MABEL COLLINS. London:
Downey, 1896 BMC. Boston: Roberts, 1896 NUC.
"Drunkenness in an educated woman is as horrible as it
fortunately is rare. Even a great master could not make
the subject anything but offensive; but when, as here, it is
treated as a mere theme for the most commonplace of
society novels, it becomes positively bothersome." The
Athenaeum, 108 (1896), 753. Another review indicates that
the best part of the book is Laurence Monkwell's
experience as a hospital nurse.

COOKE, GRACE (MACGOWAN). B. 1863. United States.

614   THE POWER AND THE GLORY. New York: Doubleday,
Page, 1910 NUC.
Johnnie, a mill-worker, is desperately ambitious for the
sake of the younger children in her family who also work
in the mill. She loves machinery and has invented an
improvement of the loom. After a half-hour driving
lesson, she successfully drives an automobile through a
dare-devil chase down a mountain side. She has a love
story.

COOKE, GRACE (MACGOWAN) AND ALICE MACGOWAN.

615 AUNT HULDAH; PROPRIETOR OF THE WAGON-TIRE HOUSE AND GENIAL PHILOSOPHER OF THE CATTLE COUNTRY. London: Hodder and Stoughton, 1904 BMC. Indianapolis: Bobbs-Merrill, [1904] NUC.

Aunt Huldah is a widow with orphans who runs a coffeehouse in the West and is kind to all.

616 THE STRAIGHT ROAD [ANONYMOUS]. New York: G. H. Doran, [c1917] NUC.

Taking her child, Callie leaves her husband to start a new life and to earn a living. "The narrative is a true story of a pretty woman's fight against predatory men. Includes recognizable incidents such as the white-slave traffic and the riot in the hop fields of California."

617 WILD APPLES, A CALIFORNIA STORY. BY THE AUTHOR OF "THE STRAIGHT ROAD" [ANONYMOUS]. New York: G. H. Doran, [1918] NUC.

Julian, 19, has an affair with a 17 year old factory worker, Lynnie. She refuses to marry him; his family buys her family off, not wishing to see him tied for life to her. He runs away; all is eventually resolved.

COOKE, MARJORIE BENTON. 1876-1920. United States.

618 BAMBI. Garden City, N. Y.: Doubleday, Page, 1914 NUC. London: Jarrold's, 1915 NUC.

Bambi is married to an impractical and unsuccessful playwright. She braves theatrical managers and wins success for him. In her spare moments she writes a successful novel pseudonymously and persuades a manager to let her husband dramatize it. During her husband's correspondence with the unknown novelist, he falls in love with her, not realizing until the conclusion of the book that she is his wife.

619 CINDERELLA JANE. Garden City, N. Y.: Doubleday, Page, 1917 BMC NUC. [London]: Jarrolds, [1917] BMC.

Career of a remarkable woman writer. From the first Jane

is sure of her ability; she is recognized in her hometown as a writer. When she moves to New York, she writes for five years without attempting to publish, while she works as a cook for a group of Greenwich village artists. She marries one because she believes marriage and maternity will give her experiences she needs as a writer—as she tells her husband. She is determined to be a modern wife: she holds her own in her arguments with her husband, makes her career solely her own business, has her own work room where she writes, leaving him to mind the baby. She is a genius, finally recognized by her husband and the public. She takes two publishing houses by storm with her remarkable novel and even acts the part of Salome on stage. Her woman friend is a successful sculptor.

620   THE CLUTCH OF CIRCUMSTANCE. New York: G. H. Doran, [c1918] NUC. London: Skeffington, [1919] BMC.
Lady Roberta Trask, raised in the United States, is of the opinion that this country "grabs and orates." When World War I breaks out, she becomes a German agent. She and an Irish officer are accused and court-martialed, and she makes a confession. One reviewer describes the conclusion: "Forthwith the people who had unmasked her wept and humbly apologized for interfering with her. She forgave them nobly...and expired in an odor of sanctity. The author seems to admire her immensely. The book is dull, and more than a little pro-German in tendency."

621   DR. DAVID. Chicago: A. C. McClurg, 1911 NUC.
Nannette Brandon is married to a man who is all wrapped up in his business. She is bored and restless. Then she gets pregnant. Childbirth leaves her blind, she falls in love with her eye doctor, hates and blames her child for her blindness. Her husband, aware of all of her feelings, waits. Then all turns out well. The doctor marries another woman, and Nanette, her husband and child are reconciled.

622   THE DUAL ALLIANCE. Garden City, New York: Doubleday, Page, 1915 NUC.
Barbara Garratry supports herself and sick father at age

15, goes on to become a reporter, a short story writer, and an interior decorator. She marries a successful lawyer on the basis that they live separate lives. She makes a sensational political speech in New York which helps land her husband in the governor's chair. At 24, she's a famous actress and noted playwright.

623   THE GIRL WHO LIVED IN THE WOODS. Chicago: A.C. McClurg, 1910 NUC. [London]: Jarrolds, 1917 BMC.

The first experiences in society of Celia Carne, artist, carpenter, gardener, a young woman independent and full of socialist ideals, living and managing well by herself alone in a cabin in the woods.

624   THE THRESHOLD. A STORY. Garden City, New York: Doubleday, Page, 1918 NUC. [London]: Jarrolds, [1918] BMC.

Joan from the working class fought for her education and now, a social housekeeper to a mill owner, fights for the mill workers. The results of her efforts include a strike and the building of a model village and factory. Described by one reviewer as the "saccharine type of fiction."

COOKE, MATILDA VANCE. United States.

625   THE ZIG-ZAG PATHS OF LIFE: A NOVEL. Chicago: C. H. Kerr, 1895 NUC.

Woman leaves her Methodist minister husband when she learns he "ruined" a young woman. The minister is later murdered by the brother of his third victim.

COOKSON, SYBIL IRENE ELEANOR (TAYLOR). B. 1890. United Kingdom.

626   THE AUCTION MART. BY SYDNEY TREMAYNE. London: J. Lane, 1915 BMC. New York: J. Lane, 1915 NUC.

Jacqueline's father is convinced all women are vampires. He is her unwed father, teaches her to "be very expensive" and to find satisfaction in shallow desires, all he feels women are capable of. Jacqueline resents her father's ideas, leaves home, becomes a private secretary, then a famous dancer. She does return home when he's sick and dying.

COOLIDGE, ASENATH CARVER. B.1830. United States.

627 HUMAN BEINGS VS. THINGS. Watertown, N. Y.: Hungerford-Holbrook, 1910 NUC.

Heroine comes to the realization that women spend too much of their time with things and too little with people (like the poor who need help) and that there is too much commercialism; she also attacks men who make instruments of war.

628 THE MODERN BLESSING FIRE. New York, London: Abbey Press, [1902] NUC.

A novel with strong-minded women; both men and women characters are in favor of suffrage and equality for women.

629 PROPHET OF PEACE. Watertown, N. Y.: Hungerford-Holbrook, 1907 NUC.

A woman who is a member of the Society of Friends and who emigrates to the U.S. is dedicated to the cause of peace, to equal rights and to dress reform.

COOPER, ELIZABETH. 1877-1945. United States.

630 LIVING UP TO BILLY. New York: F. A. Stokes, [c1915] NUC.

Girlish letters to sister imprisoned for theft tell of career in East Side dance halls and Broadway shows. She raises her sister's baby.

631 MY LADY OF THE CHINESE COURTYARD. New York: F.A. Stokes, [1914] NUC.

The author has saturated herself with the point of view of the high-caste Chinese woman. The first part of the book is about a young wife—her subjection to her mother-in-law, her many duties in the patriarchal family. The second half is about her middle age. "Brings home how near akin are the wives and mothers of East and West."

CORBETT, ELIZABETH BURGOYNE. B. 1846.

632 DEB O'MALLY'S. London: Hurst and Blackett, 1895 BMC.
Deborah Pendlebury is the daughter of unmarried parents. She leaves Lancashire to work in a factory but is dissatisfied with the work. She is determined to educate herself so that she can properly denounce her father. In London, she becomes a successful novelist and social success in smart society. She gets a proposal from her own father who does not know who she is.

633 THE MARRIAGE MARKET: A SERIES OF CONFESSIONALS COMPILED FROM THE DIARY OF A SOCIETY GO-BETWEEN. London: R. A. Everett, 1905 BMC.

634 WHEN THE SEA GIVES UP ITS DEAD: A THRILLING DETECTIVE STORY. London: Tower, 1894 BMC NUC.
Annie Cory and her father are detectives.

CORBETT, ELIZABETH FRANCES. B. 1887. United States.

635 CECILY AND THE WIDE WORLD; A NOVEL OF AMERICAN LIFE TODAY. New York: H. Holt, 1916 NUC. London: Hurst and Blackett, 1918 BMC.
Avery and Cecily develop different interests. She goes to a distant city and becomes a successful business woman, supporting herself and the two children. He follows a "splendid new woman" into an apprenticeship in "health education." Divorce follows and new liaisons for both. They eventually remarry, both better off for their experiences.

636 PURITAN AND PAGAN. New York: H. Holt, 1920 NUC.
A story of two independent women in New York, one an actress, the other a painter.

637 THE VANISHED HELGA. New York: G. H. Doran, [c1918] NUC BMC.
Zoe Lenox is an Olympian, a superwoman so much in control of herself and her life that men believe her to be

passionless. The story, narrated by John Whittaker, describes a voyage he takes by Zoe's invitation on her yacht Helga and its consequences. She "marries" him while they are lost at sea, revealing a depth of physical passion which exceeds his, and then she separates from him when the ship is rescued, preferring to live without him. He is devastated by losing her; he describes his attempts to love other women, his mental and physical collapse, his half recovery, and years of waiting until Zoe chooses to share her life with him.

CORELLI, MARIE. See MACKAY, MARY.

CORKEY, ETHEL.

638 THE WAY OF THE HUNDRED STARS. London: R.T.S., 1918 BMC.

Love of a young woman (who becomes a famous artist) is threatened by a danger from heredity, but ends happily.

CORKRAN, HENRIETTE. D. 1911. United Kingdom.

639 ROUND OUR SQUARE. London: Hurst & Blackett, 1906 BMC.

Female artist tells story of Bohemian life.

CORY, MATILDA WINIFRED MURIEL (GRAHAM). C. 1875-1950. United Kingdom.

640 THE ENEMY OF WOMAN. BY WINIFRED GRAHAM. London: Mills and Boon, [1910] BMC NUC. New York: M. Kennerley, 1914 NUC.

Meg, twin sister of Lionel Marsh the famous opponent of suffrage, takes his place in disguise in Parliament and pleads eloquently for the movement. She is a militant willing to die for the cause. They separate, and Lionel for a time turns to Mrs. Bruce, a widow. When by accident he discovers her reputation, he persuades Meg to return. Thus scorned, Mrs. Bruce joins the militant suffragists declaring that "a man must die." She hurls a bomb at

Lionel and is taken to an insane asylum. In the end Meg merges her own career in her brother's, and agrees with him that she has been her own worst enemy. Described as anti-suffrage.

641 JUDAS OF SALT LAKE. London: E. Nash, 1916 BMC.
Mormon preacher lures two young women to Utah.

642 THE LOVE STORY OF A MORMON. BY WINIFRED GRAHAM. London: Mills and Boon, [1911] BMC NUC.
Mormon agent tries to abduct a young Englishwoman. Written frankly to warn young women against Mormons.

643 MERESIA. London: Hurst and Blackett, 1898 BMC.
Meresia murdered her husband, a Spanish judge who supervised the torture of anarchist prisoners. The reader is invited to sympathize with her.

CORY, VIVIAN. United Kingdom.

644 ANNA LOMBARD. BY VICTORIA CROSS. London: J. Long, [1901] BMC NUC. New York: Kensington Press, [190-?] NUC.
Anna Lombard expects to continue her affair with one man after her marriage to another, and she gets her fiance to agree. Anna shocked the critics who called her "horrible," hysterically sexual" and described her "ill-regulated sensuality" as "disgusting." But her author wants us to admire her.

645 THE ETERNAL FIRES. BY VICTORIA CROSS. New York: Kennerley, [c1910] NUC. London: T. W. Laurie, [c1910] NUC BMC.
Irene, a school teacher, travels through the heavens and becomes Apollo's bride. She must return to Earth and live as a mortal. Pregnant, she is forced to leave her position and to attempt to survive in London by selling her poetry and working as an artist's model. She refuses to marry or to love men but is friends with several, one an artist with whom she lives. When her child is born, she agrees to spend six months with a rich man, posing as his mistress

in return for an income for her son that will provide for his future.

646 A GIRL OF THE KLONDIKE. BY VICTORIA CROSS. London: W. Scott, [1899] BMC.

Katrine, daughter of a Polish saloon keeper, drinks and gambles. She marries a young man educated as a missionary who tries his best to reform her, but the monotony of her marriage is unbearable. She returns to the saloon, and the reforming has to begin all over again. Ends in a shoot-out at the saloon.

647 THE GREATER LAW. BY VICTORIA CROSS. London: J. Long, [1914] NUC BMC.

Narrated by a male artist in love with his cousin, an independent woman composer. The story is a study of their relationship, the working out of a love relationship which will provide each of them the freedom and independence which they both require. He learns he can be happy loving a woman without totally possessing her. Trash, according to one reviewer, and typical of Cross, this novel glorifies the illicitly passionate woman. The author relates her sympathy for conventional people who, "suffering and agonized, like poor helpless slaves driven chained to the market-place, go to the altar."

648 THE LIFE SENTENCE. BY VICTORIA CROSS. London: J. Long, 1912 BMC. New York: Macaulay, [1914] NUC.

Against divorce laws, as "surveyed from the plane of unbridled passion."

649 LIFE'S SHOP WINDOW. BY VICTORIA CROSS. London: T. W. Laurie, 1907 BMC. New York: M. Kennerley, [1907] NUC.

Detailed account of the passions and emotions in the life of a young woman. When she finds her husband dull, she leaves him, takes a lover, and almost leaves the lover when he in turn tires her.

650 THE NIGHT OF TEMPTATION. BY VICTORIA CROSS. London: T.W. Laurie, [1912] BMC. New York: Macaulay, 1914 NUC.

Described as "foolish and unwholesome," a story of

passionate women and men.

651 PAULA: A SKETCH FROM LIFE. BY VICTORIA CROSS. London: W. Scott, [1897] BMC. New York: G. Munro, [1898] NUC.

Paula is described as a "brat who takes herself and her exaggerated emotions too seriously." She is "an exponent of the new selfishness and new self-consciousness." She smokes, beats a record at walking, and, while her brother makes tea and keeps the place tidy, she reads novels and writes plays. She agrees to marry a man in order to get one of her plays produced, but soon runs off with a lover. She has her blood transfused into the veins of this anemic lover and dies.

652 SELF AND THE OTHER. BY VICTORIA CROSS. New York: [Press of W. G. Hewitt], 1911 NUC. London: T. W. Laurie, [1911] BMC.

Male college student sacrifices career for young Indian woman—a nurse.

653 TO-MORROW? BY VICTORIA CROSS. London: W. Scott, 1904 BMC NUC.

The narrator is a novelist who is engaged to his cousin, an artist. His father disapproves of their marriage and refuses to give it his financial support unless his son gets a job or succeeds in publishing one of his novels (which he doesn't think possible). He does eventually publish a novel in France (his writing is too daring for English taste), but when he returns triumphant to his cousin, he finds that she has burned herself out in her work. Within the year she is dead. She was too passionate to wait for him indefinitely and too single-minded to turn to someone else.

654 A WOMAN WHO DID NOT. BY VICTORIA CROSS. London: J. Lane, 1895 BMC. Boston: Roberts, 1895 NUC.

Married woman falls in love with a man she meets aboard ship, but she refuses to sleep with him. Their relationship ends with "her laughing indifference" to their separation. Reviewers call him "coarse and tawdry" and "a cad" and describe the subject as one that "offends propriety," "concerns the back slums of social life" and "positively reeks of whiskeys and sodas and of physical passion."

COSTANTINI, ANNA MILLER. B. 1880. Europe.

655 RAGNA, A NOVEL. New York: Sturgis & Walton, 1910 NUC. London: Greening, 1910 BMC.

Young Swedish woman's passions are awakened by a count and she becomes pregnant. The social distance between them is such that marriage is out of the question. She marries an Italian, remains with him in spite of his physical brutality to the children and herself.

COTES, MRS. EVERARD. See COTES, SARA JEANNETTE (DUNCAN).

COTES, SARA JEANNETTE (DUNCAN). 1862?-1922. Canada.

656 AN AMERICAN GIRL IN LONDON. BY SARA JEANNETTE DUNCAN. London: Chatto and Windus, 1891 BMC. New York: D. Appleton, 1891 NUC.

Mamie Wick of Chicago goes to London alone. (Her father is busy with politics, and her mother is an invalid.) On the steamer she escapes one motherly woman's efforts to curb her freedom. In England she finds her relatives cold, makes friends with the thoroughly unconventional Miss Peter Corke, is shocked to learn one Englishman interprets her relation to him as an engagment, compares English conventionality to U.S. freedom, and criticizes women for being slaves to convention.

657 THE BURNT OFFERING. BY MRS. EVERARD COTES (SARA JEANNETTE DUNCAN). London: Methuen, 1909 BMC. New York: John Lane, 1910 NUC.

Joan Mills represents modern womanhood with its advanced ideas in all directions. She is a socialist with earnest sympathy toward the people of India. She and her father go to India where she devotes herself to the cause of the Indian people. She falls in love with a native who dies during a bombing. The novel ends abruptly with his death and her return to England.

658 THE CONSORT. BY MRS. EVERARD COTES (SARA JEANNETTE DUNCAN). London: S. Paul, [189-?] NUC BMC.

Mary Pargeter, the head of a great banking house, is married to a weak but lovable man. Her marriage is unhappy—a psychological study.

659 A DAUGHTER OF TO-DAY: A NOVEL. BY MRS. EVERARD COTES (SARAH JEANNETTE DUNCAN). London: Chatto & Windus, 1894 BMC. New York: D. Appleton, 1894 NUC.

Elfrida Bell is an artist, a writer, and a wife who kills herself and writes her own epitaph: "Pas femme—artiste." Although only a few reviewers see her as a sympathetic portrait, there is general agreement that she could not reconcile her literary and artistic idealism and ambitions with experience. One reviewer concludes: the moral is that opposition to "customs and institutions by the restraints of which civilization painfully protects itself from the beast" can cause disaster.

660 HILDA: A STORY OF CALCUTTA. BY SARAH JEANETTE DUNCAN (MRS. EVERARD COTES). New York: F. A. Stokes, [c1898] NUC. (Also published as The Path of a Star. London: Methuen, 1899 BMC.)

Light satire focusing on two women: Laura Filbert is a captain in the Salvation Army. She loves a business man until she finds a man she likes more. Hilda is the more modern, unconventional woman—a brilliant actress and leading lady in Calcutta. For a time she is so taken by a priest that she gives up the stage for the nursing sisterhood to be near him, but the author "has to kill the priest to save Hilda for her art." Hilda wants money and fame; she expects big things from herself and is honestly devoted to her art. Anglo-Indian life.

661 THE SIMPLE ADVENTURES OF A MEMSAHIB. BY SARA JEANNETTE DUNCAN. London: Chatto and Windus, 1893 BMC. New York: D. Appleton, 1893 NUC.

Young Englishwoman marries and makes her home in

India. Her simple adventures, the unusual customs and native ideas concerning housekeeping. (A Memsahib is a married woman.)

662 VERNON'S AUNT: BEING THE ORIENTAL EXPERIENCES OF MISS LAVINIA MOFFAT. BY MRS. EVERARD COTES (SARA JEANNETTE DUNCAN). New York: D. Appleton, 1895 NUC.

Lavinia Moffat "spinster" after years of quiet existence in a small rural English parish, goes off uninvited to visit her brother in the Orient. All her fascinating experiences and "some grotesque situations" follow her arrival, when she is met by an elephant she must mount.

663 A VOYAGE OF CONSOLATION (BEING IN THE NATURE OF A SEQUEL TO THE EXPERIENCES OF "AN AMERICAN GIRL IN LONDON"). BY SARA JEANNETTE DUNCAN (MRS. EVERARD COTES). London: Methuen, 1898 BMC. New York: D. Appleton, 1898 NUC.

Mamie, on her return to the United States quarrels with her betrothed Yale professor over her Anglomania and his accent. She sweeps her parents off to Europe and with others they travel, a feminine Tramp Abroad. Satire, wit. Reconciliation at end.

COTTERELL, CONSTANCE. United Kingdom.

664 THE HONEST TRESPASS. London: E. Nash, 1911 BMC.

Young wife whose husband is in a mental institution takes a former suitor as her lover. Author makes Lesbia an attractive, sympathetic character.

665 AN IMPOSSIBLE PERSON. London: T. F. Unwin [Autonym Library], 1896 BMC NUC.

"Brilliant sketch of an 'intense' and gushing school-girl, married to an elderly gourmand whom she idealizes and adores, neglecting his dinners in her worship of the great soul she insists on ascribing to him."

666 THE PERPETUAL CHOICE. London: Methuen, 1915 BMC.

Ambitious young woman, a budding novelist, sets up

housekeeping with a woman composer. She faces problems of love and poverty, but there is a radiant future before her.

667 TEMPE: A NOVEL. London: R. Bentley, 1893 BMC. New York: Harper, 1894 NUC.

Tempe is a novelist, a genius rebellious against conventions. She expounds her views on love, marriage, the duty of opposing public opinion, the absurdity of religious belief. She analyzes herself and others—like her uncle whose embraces she describes as a bit too passionate. "Vivid and sympathetic understanding of the partially veiled and hidden springs of action with maiden fancy free and fancy bound." "Elaborate study of the type recently labelled as the 'revolting daughter.'"

COTTRELL, MARIE. See HARLAN, MRS. M. R.

COUVREUR, JESSIE CATHERINE (HUYBERS). 1848-1897. Australia.

668 A FIERY ORDEAL. BY TASMA. London: R. Bentley, 1897 BMC. New York: Appleton, 1898 NUC.

Ruth Fenton is an orphan of a French political refugee. She teaches school in Australia, but "escapes that drudgery" by an early marriage. Unfortunately her husband drinks and gambles, and by the time Ruth is 21, her child is dead and her husband is bankrupt. On a mission to see the man who holds their mortgage, Ruth meets that man's son, and the two fall in love. She leaves her husband who tries to set his rival's house on fire, but is himself killed instead.

669 A KNIGHT OF THE WHITE FEATHER. BY TASMA. London: W. Heinemann, 1891 BMC. Leipzig: Heinemann and Balestier, 1893 NUC.

The heroine, trained in Positivism by a French professor, settles in Melbourne, Australia. She has three male admirers, marries the one she comes closest to loving. He is a coward; the marriage is unhappy. After his death she feels remorse that she cannot grieve for him as though she had fully loved him, but she knows this is unreasonable as she has damaged her own life as well.

670 NOT COUNTING THE COST. BY TASMA. AUTHOR OF "UNCLE PIPER OF PIPER'S HILL" "IN HER EARLIEST YOUTH" "A KNIGHT OF THE WHITE FEATHER" ETC. London: R. Bentley, 1895 BMC NUC. New York: Appleton, 1895 NUC.

Eila Croft has all but forgotten the man she married when she was little more than a child and who has been in an insane asylum for years. She is an independent free-thinking young woman who seriously considers her rich cousin's offer—to live with him if he will help her family. She is not repulsed by the offer nor by her cousin who is deformed. Includes a beauty show in Paris.

671 THE PENANCE OF PORTIA JAMES. BY TASMA. London: W. Heinemann, 1891 BMC NUC. New York: J. W. Lovell, 1891 NUC.

Almost from childhood, Portia James is betrothed to a man she never loves. She can not shake herself free of him; she cannot admit that she loves someone else. On her wedding day, she learns that her husband betrayed a poor young woman. She leaves her husband and departs secretly on a wedding trip all her own. She supports herself as a model. In the end she returns to her husband, but reviewers do not agree why. One says she does penance for leaving him by sacrificing her own happiness to care for his child. Another says she does penance because she discovers the gossip about her husband was lies. A third claims she chooses "submission to social customs and laws." A fourth says her penance is to return to her husband after the betrayed woman dies, but it is not clear what her sin is.

COVERTSIDE, NAUNTON. See DAVIES, NAUNTON.

COX, ANNE. United Kingdom.

672 THE MYSTIC NUMBER SEVEN. BY ANNABEL GRAY. London: Simpkin, Marshall, [1900] BMC.

"Gorgeous melodrama. The heroine had been born over a

muffin shop in Bow, but comes into our ken possessed of hats, gowns, jewels, horses, carriages, and corsets at extravagant prices...a cellar of costly vintages, a refined maid who knew her business...her gold stoppered scent bottles were inlaid with diamonds...her sables were valued at 5,000 pounds...she looked lovely on the stage...twisting her costly diamond rings or arranging roses with diamonds in them to represent dewdrops in her hair...Glen shuddered as she thought of ordinary life."

COX, CHARLOTTE CRISMAN. United States.

673 IONE: A SEQUEL TO "VASHTI". Boston: Eastern, 1900 NUC.

Argument for the setting aside of the word obedient in marriage service.

COX, EMILY. United States.

674 COURTSHIP AND CHEMICALS. London: Ward, Lock, [1898] BMC.

Lois, reserved and studious, and Francesca, merry and bold, are students at Newnham. Their love stories.

COXON, MRS. SIDNEY. See COXON, MURIEL (HINE).

COXON, MURIEL (HINE). United Kingdom.

675 APRIL PANHASARD. BY MURIEL HINE (MRS. SIDNEY COXON). London: J. Lane, 1913 BMC. New York: J. Lane, 1913 NUC.

Shows injustice to women of English divorce laws. Lady Essendine divorces her unfaithful dissipated husband, escapes the scandal by moving to a quiet village and assuming the name April Panhasard. She meets an American she is attracted to, but her husband shows up before the six months necessary to make the divorce absolute. She is finally freed through a strange accident and marries the American.

676 AUTUMN. BY MURIEL HINE (MRS. SIDNEY COXON). New York: J. Lane, 1917 NUC. London: J. Lane, 1917 BMC NUC.

Dierdre Carodoc is nearly 40 and very attractive. She is married to a man who runs around and neglects her and has such a bad temper that she finally leaves him to live in her own country cottage. She meets Rollo and falls in love with him, but the romance is shortlived for he drowns. Another unhappy marriage is depicted; the characters uphold the sanctity of love above all else.

677 THE BEST IN LIFE. BY MURIEL HINE (MRS. SIDNEY COXON). London: J. Lane, 1918 BMC NUC. New York: J. Lane, 1918 NUC.

A dressmaker's model who inherits some money travels, a fairly innocent adventuress who comes to a traditional happy ending.

678 THE BREATHLESS MOMENT. BY MURIEL HINE. London: J. Lane, 1920 BMC NUC. New York: J. Lane, 1920 NUC.

Sabine, housekeeper to a pacifist, seduces the nephew of her employer just before he leaves for the war. The "breathless moment" lasts a month—until she realizes she is pregnant. A few years pass before complications of nephew's wife and amnesia are straightened out and they are united in marriage. One reviewer says the author's point of view is "tolerant and broad-minded, without being lax."

679 EARTH. BY MURIEL HINE (MRS. SIDNEY COXON). New York: J. Lane, 1912 BMC NUC. London: J. Lane, 1912 NUC.

Diana carves out a career for herself, wants to keep sex out of her life, learns that her body has needs too.

680 THE HIDDEN VALLEY. BY MURIEL HINE. London: J. Lane, 1919 NUC BMC. New York: J. Lane, 1919 NUC BMC.

The fortunes of Sheila Travers. At 19, she leads a sheltered life, rich, ignorant of the world. She is athletic—swims, rows and rides. She longs to live life as men do. Very modern in her views, she looks for a certain kind of man. She breaks off her first marriage; her second husband dies in the war; finally number three is the right one. She works for suffrage.

681 THE INDIVIDUAL. BY MURIEL HINE (MRS. SIDNEY COXON). London: J. Lane, 1916 BMC NUC. New York: J. Lane, 1916 BMC NUC.

Elizma Tavernet is a fine violinist and a poet married to a surgeon who is a firm believer in eugenics. She wants a child, but he refuses because there is insanity in her family. Elizma rebels, for she sees no point in marriage without children. She learns she is pregnant, and while he is away, she has her child. All works out in the end with the threat to the child removed.

CRAIG, DORIN.*

682 MIST IN THE VALLEY. London: Long, 1916 BMC.
Nurse Merion solves murder mystery.

CRAIGIE, PEARL MARY TERESA (RICHARDS). 1867-1906. United Kingdom.

683 THE DREAM AND THE BUSINESS. BY JOHN OLIVER HOBBES. London: T.F. Unwin, 1906 BMC NUC. New York: D. Appleton, 1906 NUC.

The portrayal of three women and their mismatched lovers; one is an author, another an actress. One reviewer feels they are too fully realized intellectually. The final message is religious and anti-divorce, according to a second reviewer.

684 THE GODS, SOME MORTALS AND LORD WICKENHAM. BY JOHN OLIVER HOBBES. New York: D. Appleton, 1895 NUC. London: Henry, 1895 BMC NUC.

Of the "school of scold" tradition—angry unwomanly women speaking back. Centers on Anne Delaware, a weak sensualist of crude vulgarity. The "excessive filthiness of her mind is not rendered credible enough to make its loathsomeness tolerable." Anne marries a young doctor Simon Warre after three meetings. But the marriage is not consummated because her husband learns on their wedding day that she had an affair. She leaves him; he goes off to the tropics and works himself to death.

685 LOVE AND THE SOUL HUNTERS. BY JOHN OLIVER HOBBES. New York: Funk & Wagnalls, 1902 NUC. London: T.F. Unwin, 1902 BMC NUC.

Wife deserts husband and becomes successful actress, rears idealistic daughters. The story includes a morganatic marriage.

686 ROBERT ORANGE. BEING A CONTINUATION OF THE HISTORY OF ROBERT ORANGE, M.P., AND A SEQUEL TO "THE SCHOOL FOR SAINTS". BY JOHN OLIVER HOBBES. London: T. F. Unwin, 1900 BMC NUC. New York: F. A. Stokes, [c1900] NUC.

Tragic consequences of Robert's marriage to Mrs. Parflete. Immediately after marriage, news comes that Mr. Parflete is alive. Robert becomes a priest, she an actress. Then Parflete dies. She does not tell Robert as she refuses to blunt his resolve. She stays in her profession.

687 THE SCHOOL FOR SAINTS. BY JOHN OLIVER HOBBES. New York: Century, 1896 BMC. London: T. F. Unwin, 1897 BMC NUC.

Although the focus is on Robert and political life of the 1860's, the women characters have public roles, and such issues as divorce and marriage are "fearlessly discussed."

688 THE SERIOUS WOOING: A HEART'S HISTORY. BY JOHN OLIVER HOBBES. London: Methuen, 1901 BMC NUC. New York: F.A. Stokes, [1901] NUC.

Married young and then separated from insane husband, the heroine falls in love with a socialist and agrees to live openly with him. When her socialist lover goes off on a mission and relatives intercept their letters, she marries, thinking he has forgotten her. But when he returns, she leaves this husband without hesitation.

689 SOME EMOTIONS AND A MORAL. BY JOHN OLIVER HOBBES. London: T. F. Unwin, 1891 BMC NUC. New York: Cassell, [c1891] NUC.

Several finely drawn characters. Cynthia Heathcote marries for success and fame but succeeds only in being unhappy with wealth and mediocrity. Her husband is unfaithful and the author condemns unsuitable marriages.

690 A STUDY IN TEMPTATIONS. BY JOHN OLIVER HOBBES. London: T. F. Unwin, 1893 BMC NUC. New York: Cassell, [c1893] NUC.

Sophia Jeyn is raised by her father's artist friend. Her mother died at Sophia's birth and her father committed suicide. Sophia is an impulsive young woman who becomes an actress. At 30 she marries the artist who raised her, but their marriage is kept secret for the sake of her career.

CRAIK, GEORGIANA M. See MAY, GEORGIANA MARION (CRAIK).

CRANSTON, RUTH. United States.

691 ASHES OF INCENSE, A NOVEL. BY THE AUTHOR OF "MASTERING FLAME" [ANONYMOUS]. London: Mills and Boon, 1912 BMC. New York: M. Kennerley, 1912 NUC.

A woman's wifely existence is made tolerable by her spirit of mischief which feeds on itself until she has "ended her mad career by compassing her own murder." She awakens to the fact that her life has been one long outrage.

692 THE BEST PEOPLE. BY ANNE WARWICK. New York: J. Lane, [c1918] NUC.

Nancy, a young widow, searches for a meaningful, independent life. She has a friendship with an older woman who is worldly and sensible. She considers a marriage of convenience but decides freedom would not be possible in this marriage. She tries and fails in an acting career. She turns to works of service and an old friend who is a labor reformer. They marry; she believes this marriage will provide the greatest opportunity for freedom.

693   THE CHALK LINE. BY ANNE WARWICK. New York: J. Lane, 1915 NUC.

Hilary Comer, concert singer, leaves staid husband for Pembroke, the passion of her life. Goes to his bungalow, but their lips hardly meet before John Brent, an earlier lover who used to preach mutual freedom of sexes comes and tries to get Hilary to go home. Her husband arrives, cholera breaks out in the servants' quarters, and the four are quarantined together in a few rooms.

694   THE UNKNOWN WOMAN. BY ANNE WARWICK. New York: J. Lane, 1912 BMC NUC.

Sandra is an artist, a "beautiful, passionless egoist." She is still "unfailingly alluring at thirty-nine." One reviewer says the author "has been playing ducks and drakes with ethics and morality."

695   VICTORY LAW. BY ANNE WARWICK. New York: J. Lane, 1914 BMC NUC. Toronto: Bell and Cockburn, 1914 BMC.

Victory marries, is forced by her husband to give up her career as an actress. She endures for a year or two and returns to acting. This novel "need not detain us long. It is simply one more variant upon a theme which has become a sort of obsession with all the women writers of today who happen to be interested in the feministic movement. It once again raises the familiar battlecry of woman's inalienable rights to self expression; if a husband interferes with a career, let her cut out the husband...."

CRAVEN, HELEN EMILY.

696   KATHARINE CROMER. London: A.D. Innes, 1897 BMC.

Narrated by a woman friend of Katharine, the story

focuses on Katharine's marriage to an opera singer. She marries him against her father's wishes not because she's in love with him but because she is in sympathy with him. The story does not end happily ever after, but with the conclusion that the marriage is an experiment.

CRAVEN, PRISCILLA. See SHORE, FLORENCE TEIGNMOUTH.

CRAWFORD, AMY JOSEPHINE (BAKER). B. 1895. United Kingdom.

697 I TOO HAVE KNOWN. London: J. Long, 1911 BMC.
Two teachers up-country in South Africa.

698 THE IMPENITENT PRAYER. London: J. Long, 1913 BMC.
Unusual love relation and career. Elizabeth Baring was educated in a convent school. At 25 she is still unsophisticated. When she falls in love with a much older and much more worldly man, she puts off marriage until the question of another woman Eva Sheldon is resolved. Elizabeth's career is in scientific work.

699 THE SNAKE GARDEN; A TALE OF SOUTH AFRICA. London: J. Long, 1915 BMC.
Theo Hambridge is an independent young woman who runs her own estate and who has had a very unconventional love experience.

CREED, SIBYL. United Kingdom.

700 THE FIGHT: A NOVEL. Edinburgh and London: W. Blackwood, 1904 BMC.
Tale of a young woman's rise after fighting against squalid circumstances and sordid men to a position of ease and happiness. A novel of serious workmanship.

CRICHTON, FRANCES ELIZABETH (SINCLAIR). 1877-1918. United States.

701 THE SOUNDLESS TIDE. London: E. Arnold, 1911 BMC NUC.

Gillian Ward makes a loveless marriage and is later "awakened" by a man young enough to be her son. When her husband dies, she confesses her love. A humiliating rejection follows. Touching study of the anguished soul of a bright, witty woman of "wayward mind."

CRICHTON, MADELINE.

702 LIKE A SISTER. London: Digby, Long, [1893] BMC.

Unfortunate love stories of two sisters. Begins with Kathleen Tredennick jumping into the harbor at Hong Kong to save her sister and finding when she surfaces that her sister and the ship are gone. Amy is the reckless one, passionate for pleasure and excitement. She makes a bad marriage and suffers till her husband dies. Kathleen is the more reserved idealist. She suffers in her romance due to a misunderstanding.

CRIM, MARTHA JANE. United States.

703 ADVENTURES OF A FAIR REBEL. BY MATT CRIM. New York: C. L. Webster, 1891 NUC. London: Chatto & Windus, 1892 NUC BMC.

Rachel is a staunch rebel for the Confederate cause in the Civil War, travels through the South with an amateur theatrical group for the cause, and has many unusual experiences. She is from Georgia. She falls in love with a Union soldier.

704 ELIZABETH, CHRISTIAN SCIENTIST. BY MATT CRIM. New York: C. L. Webster, 1893 NUC.

She is a school teacher with strong feelings for the pains of other people. She cures a bad case of sprained ankle, lameness, drunkenness and various other physical disorders. Includes a love story.

CRIM, MATT. See CRIM, MARTHA JANE.

CRISPE, WINIFRED.

705 SNARES: A NOVEL. London: Hutchinson, 1904 BMC.
Diary of a 30 year old woman unattractive and "with strong sexual feelings and a somewhat morbid longing to attract a man."

CROAL, FRANCES A.

706 THE FLY IN THE OINTMENT. BY FRANCES HAMMOND. London: Chapman and Hall, 1912 BMC.
Theodora, a hunchback, in her longing for love finds only suffering. She finally finds a spiritual strength which saves her from bitterness.

707 LET THEM SAY! BY FRANCES HAMMOND. London: Chapman and Hall, 1913 BMC.
Unconventional heroine who has her doubts about marriage adopts a child who happens to resemble her. The community assumes she is an unwed mother, and they turn against her. In the end she marries.

708 THE MAGIC FIRE. BY FRANCES HAMMOND. London: Chapman and Hall, 1913 BMC.
The heroine Norma Dundas is an unmarried mother who did not know at first that the man is married—to an insane woman. After much suffering, a happy solution.

CROKER, B. M. See CROKER, BITHIA MARY (SHEPPARD).

CROKER, BITHIA MARY (SHEPPARD). D. 1920. United Kingdom.

709 ANGEL: A SKETCH IN INDIAN INK. BY B. M. CROKER. New York: Dodd, Mead, 1901 NUC. London: Methuen, 1901 BMC.
Angel runs off to India to escape a hated marriage. She is

clever, shrewd and impulsive, a woman with masterful self-control.

710　THE CAT'S PAW. BY B. M. CROKER. Philadelphia: J. B. Lippincott, 1902 NUC. London: Chatto and Windus, 1902 BMC.

Heroine is lured to India on false pretences and refuses to marry the imposter. She supports herself in various positions, including nurse and companion, and finally marries man of her choice.

711　THE CHAPERONE. London: Cassell, [1920] BMC.

Reminiscences of a divorcee.

712　FAME. London: Mills & Boon, 1910 BMC. London: 1910 NUC.

Novelist in an attempt to gain attention of the literary women's world is reduced to meannesses to recover her position. She claims as her own a great novel written by her cousin.

713　INTERFERENCE: A NOVEL. London: F. V. White, 1891 BMC. Philadelphia: J. B. Lippincott, 1906 NUC.

Betty is a splendid, fearless horserider who is sacrificed by her aunt who cares only for her own daughter. Betty and her cousin Belle love the same man, but Betty alone has reason to believe the man, now in India, returns her love. Her aunt, who is anxious for Belle to marry at any cost, intercepts the letter of proposal meant for Betty and sends Belle to India to marry the man who has been told the lie that Betty is already engaged. Belle leaves Ireland ignorant of her mother's plot and on her arrival is married, the man feeling compelled to accept her. The novel follows Belle's voyage, reception, and discovery of the truth, her emotional outbursts, signs of approaching madness, and death.

714　KATHERINE THE ARROGANT. London: 1902 NUC. London: Methuen, 1909 BMC.

A story of "the woman who has to conquer the world for

herself." Born of a good family but orphaned with a small income, Katherine lives in a dreary London boarding house. Unwilling to settle for the monotony of this existence, she talks her way into the position of companion to a woman who travels. Adventures and complications follow.

715 MARRIED OR SINGLE? BY B. M. CROKER. London: Chatto and Windus, 1895 BMC NUC. [New York]: [P. F. Collier], c1895 NUC.

Madeline West teaches in a fashionable boarding school. When she marries a poor young barrister, she cares for him during his illness and nurses her sickly child. Then her father who was missing returns with millions but threatens to give her nothing if she marries a poor man. Madeline takes off her wedding ring, deserts her husband and child who dies, and resumes her maiden name. She uses her father's money to send her husband to the country to convalesce. In the end she tells her father the truth and is reunited with her husband, with her father's blessing. "One suspects the author of thinking it a pardonable and even amiable weakness in a pretty young woman to prefer diamonds and flattery to the company of a kind husband and a delicate child."

716 THE SERPENT'S TOOTH. BY B. M. CROKER. London: Hutchinson, 1912 NUC BMC. Leipzig: B. Tauchnitz, 1912 NUC.

Unhappy marriage, lover, divorce. When daughter grows up leaves mother for rich father.

717 A THIRD PERSON: A NOVEL. BY B. M. CROKER. London: F. V. White, 1893 BMC NUC. Philadelphia: J. B. Lippincott, 1899 NUC.

Mrs. Baggett at 60 is younger than her daughter. She rides, flirts, smokes, and admits to owning a chestnut toupee.

CROMARSH, H. RIPLEY. See ANGELL, BRYAN MARY (DOYLE).

CROMMELIN, MARIA HENRIETTA DE LA CHEROIS. D. 1934. United Kingdom.

718 CRIMSON LILIES. London: J. Long, 1903 BMC.

We first find heroine as a boy acrobat in a travelling fair; leave her a great lady and heiress.

719 DUST BEFORE THE WIND: A NOVEL. London: Bliss, Sands and Foster, 1894 BMC NUC.

Story of a "thoroughly depraved woman" who, married to a man twice her age, does not endure nobly. He in turn elopes with her daughter whom she idolizes.

720 FOR THE SAKE OF THE FAMILY. BY MAY CROMMELIN. New York: J. W. Lovell, [c1891] BMC NUC. London and Sydney: Eden, Remington, 1892 BMC.

Heroine takes on a crime for family's sake. She goes to South Africa as a companion, is shipwrecked, decides she must marry a "worthless fellow" for his money; he is murdered, and she is implicated.

721 THE HOUSE OF HOWE. London: J. Long, 1907 BMC.

Mainly an account of a tour in Palestine of a spinster and her guardian.

722 "I LITTLE KNEW!" London: J. Milne, [1908] BMC.

Story of an elderly woman who travels around the world. Sentimental.

723 KINSAH: A DAUGHTER OF TANGIER. London: J. Long, 1899 BMC.

Heroine is native of Tangiers, her story from childhood to entrance of harem.

CROMMELIN, MAY. See CROMMELIN, MARIA HENRIETTA DE LA CHEROIS.

CROSBIE, MARY. United Kingdom.

724 DISCIPLES. London: Methuen, 1907 BMC.

Contrasts two women: Maev has a child-like mind and

writes poetry; Denise is unconventional, detached, egoistic, cold. She is determined to seek "the nakedness of things" and rejects a doctor's love for her "heroic faiths."

725 KINSMEN'S CLAY. London: Methuen, [1910] BMC.

Menage a trois, in the tradition of George Eliot. Focus is on the two women, one of whom is crippled.

CROSS, ADA (CAMBRIDGE). 1844-1926. Australia.

726 THE DEVASTATORS. BY ADA CAMBRIDGE. London: Methuen, 1901 BMC NUC. New York: D. Appleton, 1901 NUC.

Husbands and wives who devastate marriage.

727 A HAPPY MARRIAGE. BY ADA CAMBRIDGE. London: Hurst & Blackett, 1906 BMC. London and Bombay: G. Bell, [n.d.] NUC.

The author's point of view is that there probably is no such thing. Study of a marriage.

728 A HUMBLE ENTERPRISE. BY ADA CAMBRIDGE. London: Ward, Lock and Bowden, 1896 BMC NUC.

Young heroine supports herself, her sister, and her mother by running a tea shop until wealthy suitor comes along. Author views marriage as an "unfortunate necessity."

729 THE MAKING OF RACHEL ROWE. BY ADA CAMBRIDGE. London and New York: Cassell, 1914 BMC NUC.

The Australian heroine while visiting relatives in Yorkshire makes a disastrous union with a man wanted for bigamy. She has a son. Her character is developed by the experience. An Australian doctor who loves her takes her home to happiness.

730 MATERFAMILIAS. BY ADA CAMBRIDGE. London and New York: Ward, Lock, [1898] BMC. New York: D. Appleton, 1898 NUC.

The autobiography of an Australian middle-aged matron; impressionable, indiscreet, jealous but affectionate mother and wife is one reviewer's description. Another is surprised a woman author would choose a type so frequently satirized by male writers, a puppet rather than a person, and states that her "rare examples of virtue cannot blind the reader to the hatefulness of such a woman."

731 NOT ALL IN VAIN. BY ADA CAMBRIDGE. London: Heinemann, 1892 BMC. New York: D. Appleton, 1892 NUC.

Katherine follows a man who has killed another in protecting her from violence to Melbourne where he is serving a twenty year prison term. While she is waiting for him, she opens a hospital and makes it a success. When he is released, however, he falls for a younger woman. Katherine marries a surgeon with whom she works.

732 THE THREE MISS KINGS: AN AUSTRALIAN STORY. BY ADA CAMBRIDGE. London: Heinemann, 1891 BMC. New York: D. Appleton, 1891 NUC.

Three sisters left to support themselves go to Melbourne to earn a living. They were raised in the isolated backwoods of Australia where "their graceful and athletic forms had never worn stays." All were taught by their mother to play the piano beautifully. One is a musical genius. All are well read, but unsophisticated. From Melbourne, they go to Europe. Elizabeth marries a middle-age preacher; Patty a newsman. Eleanor also marries. They later inherit a great deal of money. Sisterly love and much writing about women's lives.

CROSS, MARGARET BESSIE.

733 LOVE AND OLIVIA. London: Hurst and Blackett, 1899 BMC. (Bookseller subtitle: Being the Sentimental Troubles of a Clever Woman.)

Olivia Wynworth, a very modern and talented blue stocking, wins honors at Cambridge where she does her research in Persephone. She almost marries a young man shortly after graduation, but they are separated for seven years. When they meet again, the man is a bit uncomfortable with the brilliant and famous Olivia. He turns to a sweet old-fashioned feminine woman out of fear of Olivia's superiority. Olivia has won distinction and literary fame as a lecturer in the classics. She marries a rival lecturer in classical archeology.

734 NEWLY FASHIONED. London: Hurst and Blackett, 1895 BMC.

Beatrice Hayes steals a purse from her employer, a woman she served as companion. She is accused of stealing, tried, and released. In court she meets Jim Fyffe who is convinced of her innocence and believes she is his "ideal." They marry, and she does become that ideal. She eventually tells him the truth, and the novel ends with the two struggling for their lives in the ocean—one with a broken leg, the other with a wounded head.

735 A QUESTION OF MEANS. London and Edinburgh: Thomas Nelson & Sons, [1917] BMC.

Rose Oliphant struggles with many babies in this story of a marriage. The couple face new financial problems with the arrival of each child. There is much conflict between the parents; each is treated with sympathy.

736 THE SAFFRON ROBE. London: Hurst and Blackett, 1893 BMC.

Focuses on Diana Moore, her thoughts and feelings. She is a wise, quick witted young woman whose friendship with Dick is a fencing match. They have been friends since childhood, and Diane wants their relationship to be a "comradeship"—not a romantic sentimental love. "We are told a great deal more than we want to know about Diane's thoughts and feelings."

737 STOLEN HONEY. London: Hurst and Blackett, 1892 BMC.

Susie marries Major Blake and discovers her marriage to be bigamous when his alcoholic wife dies. Susie is pregnant. She goes through a legal marriage ceremony, but from this point on she refuses to be a wife in anything but name. She takes a lover. Reviewers are not sympathetic to her; one feels that Major Blake is "essentially good."

738 UP TO PERRIN'S. London: Chatto & Windus, 1912 BMC NUC.

The story of a woman writer in an English fishing village. Tragic end.

CROSS, VICTORIA. See CORY, VIVIAN.

CROUCH, FRANCES.

739 FEMININE FINANCE. New York: B.W. Dodge, 1907 NUC.

Amusing story of how two women help a third out of difficulty. First one visits the farmer who owes the woman money in order to collect. The next day the second one calls on him, and when he refuses, she pelts him with stones. They are then successful; the farmer pays the promisory note.

CRUGER, JULIE GRINNELL (STORROW). D. 1920. United States.

740 EAT NOT THY HEART. BY JULIEN GORDON. Chicago and London: H. S. Stone, 1897 BMC NUC.

Elizabeth Bush, farmer's wife, reads the Sunday papers and follows the life of a socialite Mrs. Marston, tries to copy that woman's life. Then her husband gets a position on the Marston estate, and her envy slowly "rises into an insanity of destructive rage"; she sets fire to the Marston house. One reviewer says she loses her mind at the end because she learns how ridiculous she is.

741 MRS. CLYDE: THE STORY OF A SOCIAL CAREER. BY JULIEN GORDON. New York: D. Appleton, 1901 BMC NUC. London: Methuen, 1902 BMC.

Love plays a minor part in this study of a whole woman

from youth to old age. It follows her from her humble beginning through her long and successful social career. Throughout her life, "her selfhood panted for expansion." The novel includes a study of the mother-daughter relation.

742 POPPAEA. BY JULIEN GORDON. Philadelphia and London: J. B. Lippincott, 1895 BMC NUC.

She is a very modern woman who longs for every pleasure the world offers. She marries an old man for his money, gets all the material luxuries she wants, is about to leave him because she falls in love with another man; then the crash comes. Her husband dies, but Poppaea does not marry the other man. Here her real story begins. She becomes half-insane, doing all sorts of strange unreasonable, reckless and mad things.

CRUIKSHANK, JULIA.

743 WHIRLPOOL HEIGHTS. THE DREAM-HOUSE ON THE NIAGARA RIVER. London: G. Allen and Unwin, [1915] BMC NUC.

Woman writes a diary of her every day life as wife in house on Niagara River.

CRUTTWELL, MAUDE.

744 FIRE AND FROST. New York: J. Lane, 1913 NUC. London: J. Lane, 1913 BMC NUC.

Out of pity and self sacrifice, an Englishwoman marries an Egyptian prince and gives up her career in writing to do so. The result is mutual unhappiness, ending in divorce. She is then free to pursue her writing career.

CUDLIP, ANNIE HALL (THOMAS). 1838-1918. United Kingdom.

745 COMRADES TRUE. BY ANNIE THOMAS (MRS. PENDER CUDLIP). London: Chatto and Windus, 1900 BMC. New York: F. M. Buckles, 1900 NUC.

One of the heroines is a singer.

746 A LOVER OF THE DAY. A NOVEL. London: Digby, Long, [1895] BMC.

Sholto Graham, "a profligate and selfish vulgarian," worms his way into a young woman's affections, jilts her, marries an older woman for money, kills her by his neglect and deserts his child.

747 A PRETENDER. London: Digby, Long, 1905 BMC.

An adventuress presented in a sympathetic light. "If this sort of girl is going to be the future heroine of many novels, what is to become of one's ideal of true girlhood?" asks one reviewer.

CUDLIP, MRS. PENDER. See CUDLIP, ANNIE HALL (THOMAS).

CULTER, MARY NANTZ (MACCRAE). B. 1858. United States.

748 THE GIRL WHO KEPT UP. Boston: Lee and Shepard, 1903 NUC.

Two young people are close friends and keen intellectual rivals through high school where she wins the contest much of the time. When they graduate, she must help at home; he goes to college. But she's determined to keep up with her friend in securing an education, and she succeeds.

CUMMINS, G. D. See CUMMINS, GERALDINE DOROTHY.

CUMMINS, GERALDINE DOROTHY. 1890-1960. United Kingdom.

749 THE LAND THEY LOVED. BY G. D. CUMMINS. London: Macmillan, 1919 BMC NUC. New York: Macmillan, 1919 NUC.

Kate Carmody is a self reliant individual—tough and sharp-tongued. She leaves Ireland for the U.S. where she works as a domestic servant for five years—refusing always to be treated as a drudge. She returns to Ireland to work on her brother's farm and almost marries, but discovers in time that the young man does not suit her. She then returns to domestic work, this time in Dublin, but in the end again feels the strong attraction to the land.

CUNINGHAME, CAROLINE MADELINA FAIRLIE.

750 A SIN OF THE SOUL. London: H. Cox, 1895 BMC.

Woman married to a "gay dog" who gambles away their money and mistreats her. Her mother throws the husband, Stephen Beauclerk, overboard and causes his death, a fate he "richly deserves."

CURRY, E. S.*

751 CAN SHE FORGIVE? New York: E. & J.B. Young, 1893 PW. London: Society for Promoting Christian Knowledge, [1894] BMC.

Points out morals against hasty marriage, intemperance and gambling. Wife discovers husband drinks and gambles, leaves him. After long separation, he repents; they are reunited.

CURTIS, ALICE (TURNER). United States.

752 A CHALLENGE TO ADVENTURE. BY MRS. IRVING CURTIS. Boston: M. Jones, 1919 NUC.

Young woman helps a man seeking a patent on airplane equipment; she also helps uncover a German spy plot.

CURTIS, MARGUERITE.

753 MARCIA: A TRANSCRIPT FROM LIFE. Edinburgh and London: W. Blackwood, 1909 BMC.

Sympathetic and insightful psychological study of a dual personality—one good; one evil. Marcia begins to feel cursed rather than ill because she cannot control actions that she finds repulsive.

CURTIS, MRS. IRVING. See CURTIS, ALICE (TURNER).

CURTISS, ALICE EDDY. United States.

754 NEIGHBORS IN BARTON SQUARE. Boston: Congregational Sunday School & Pub. Soc., [c1892] NUC.

Story of lovable, hard-working, self-sacrificing dressmaker.

755 THE SILVER CROSS, A STORY OF THE KING'S DAUGHTERS; AND, MISS MARIGOLD'S TITHES. Boston: Congregational Sunday School & Pub. Soc., [c1891] NUC.

In the first story, Mary, poor almost invalid, works wonders on Conner St., a rough neighborhood. In the second, a "sunny old maid" does kindly acts.

CUTTING, MARY STEWART (DOUBLEDAY). 1851-1924. United States.

756 THE UNFORSEEN. Garden City, New York: Doubleday, Page, 1910 NUC. London: Hodder & Stoughton, 1910 BMC.

Evelyn Gaynor becomes editor of New York magazine. She has a disheartening struggle, almost decides to go home when two men come into her life. She is rescued from poverty by marriage.

DALE, DARLEY. See STEELE, FRANCESCA MARIA.

DALE, LUCY AND GERTRUDE MINNIE FAULDING.

757 MERELY PLAYERS. BY LUCY DALE AND G. M. FAULDING. London: T. F. Unwin, [1917] BMC NUC.

Psychological study of Judith and Madeleine. Madeleine, impulsive and light-hearted, is a playwright too wrapped up in her productions to give much time to her husband. He finds happiness with calm and repressed Judith.

758 TIME'S WALLET. BY LUCY DALE AND G. M. FAULDING. London: Sidgwick and Jackson, 1913 BMC NUC.

Nan Bosanquet and Helen Daventry, single, independent,

well educated, free to travel, read and work, write to each other. Their letters are "a pleasant presentment of modern educated femininity...independent and sane."

DALE, MARY. See DAWSON, MARJORIE.

DALLAS, MARY (KYLE). 1830-1897. United States.
759 BILLTRY. New York: Merriam, [c1895] NUC BMC.
Parody on "Trilby," reversing the characters of that novel. The three artists are young professional women of Gotham; their model is male, not female. Farcical, racey, humorous.

DALLYN, VIOLA (MEYNELL). 1886-1956. United Kingdom.
760 COLUMBINE. BY VIOLA MEYNELL. London: M. Secker, [1915] BMC NUC. London: G.P. Putnam's Sons, 1915 NUC.
Two women very different from each other are loved in turn by the same man. Lily Peak is a beautiful vulgar chorus girl, artificial, empty-headed. Jennifer Watts is an efficient conscientious hard-working secretary who has a very complex relation with Dixon. She dies at the end.

D'ALPENS, MARQUESA. See WILLIAMSON, ALICE MURIEL (LIVINGSTON).

DALTON, MORAY.* United Kingdom.
761 OLIVE IN ITALY. London: T.F. Unwin, 1909 BMC.
Painful struggle of young woman trying to earn her own living. She teaches in Siena, is a governess in Florence and an artist's model in Rome. Happy ending.

DALZIEL, L. BEITH. See DILL, BESSIE.

DANBY, FRANK. See FRANKAU, JULIA (DAVIS).

DANDELYON, RITTER. See BROWN, S. A.

DANE, CLEMENCE. See ASHTON, WINIFRED.

D'ANETHAN, ELEANORA MARY (HAGGARD). B. 1860.
United Kingdom.

762 IT HAPPENED IN JAPAN. London: Brown, Langham,
1906 BMC.
Heroine divorces unbearable husband,, is victim of
slander, leaves England and goes to Tokyo hoping for
peace. Three years pass and an old lover appears;
complications follow which end in her death.

763 TWO WOMEN. London: T.F. Unwin, 1909 BMC.
The diaries of a mother and her daughter: Lady Beaumont
reveals that her husband is not the father of her daughter.
She eventually leaves her offensive husband. Her daughter
Ruby marries not for love, but for money.

DANILEVSKAIA, NADEZHDA ALEKSANDROVNA
(LIUTKEVICH) LAPPO. B. 1876. Europe.

764 MICHAIL; OR, THE HEART OF A RUSSIAN. A NOVEL
IN FOUR PARTS. BY A RUSSIAN LADY
[ANONYMOUS]. London: W. Heinemann, [1917] NUC.
World of the highest society—"where the mistakes of legal
marriage are ignored and its members live in monogamy,
polygamy, promiscuity or polyandry."

DANVIN, CATHERINE RADZIWILL KOLB.

765 THE DISILLUSIONS OF A CROWN PRINCESS; BEING
THE STORY OF THE COURTSHIP AND MARRIED LIFE
OF CECILE, EX-CROWN PRINCESS OF GERMANY.
New York and London: J. Lane, 1920 BMC.
Account of an unhappy marriage told by an intimate
friend.

DARDAY, OLGA.

766   CRAB APPLES; HUNGARIAN SOCIETY SKETCHES. London: M. Goschen, 1914 BMC.

Described as a "suffrage pamphlet" of Hungarian origin, a collection of sketches and stories of discontented wives.

DARING, HOPE. See JOHNSON, ANNA.

DART, EDITH C. M. United Kingdom.

767   LIKENESS. London: Mills & Boon, 1911 BMC.

A close resemblance between two women enables a poor typewriter to impersonate the other at a fashionable ball.

768   SAREEL. London: P. Allan, 1920 BMC. New York: Boni and Liviright, [c1922] NUC.

The story of a young woman in a workhouse who becomes a farm servant. The development of her character, careful workmanship, like that of Dorothy Richardson.

DASHWOOD, EDMEE ELIZABETH MONICA (DE LA PASTURE). 1890-1943. United Kingdom.

769   CONSEQUENCES. BY E. M. DELAFIELD. London and New York: Hodder & Stoughton, [1919] BMC NUC.

Alex Clare is the blacksheep of her aristocratic family. Extremely self-conscious, clumsy and gauche, she feels she's a failure in her parents' eyes because the only proposal she gets is from a man she finds too stupid to tolerate. Giving up hope of marriage, she enters a convent but suffers such loneliness that after ten years she begs to be released. She returns to the world but has no skill to earn her money. Facing poverty, she embezzles and consequently loses the few friends she had left. With nowhere to turn and no place for her in this world's economy, she drowns herself.

770 THE PELICANS. BY E. M. DELAFIELD. London: W. Heinemann, [1919] BMC NUC. New York: A.A. Knopf, 1919 NUC.

"When Bertha misunderstands her unfortunate protegees, she is like an elephant trampling down their souls with joyful trumpetings." Bertha is the guardian of three young women, all of whom eventually defy their overbearing mother and determine their own lives. One dies in a convent; the author describes it as an "inhuman world."

771 TENSION. BY E. M. DELAFIELD. London: Hutchinson, [1920] BMC. New York: Macmillan, 1920 NUC.

Pauline, the superintendent of a commercial college, breaks her engagement to a soldier who retires from the war disabled. She is willing to live with a man whose wife has been institutionalized for alcoholism, but he is concerned about their social status. Described as a "humorous novel concerning the defenses put up by two fine and sensitive spirits against a society of vulgarians."

772 THE WAR-WORKERS. BY E. M. DELAFIELD. New York: A.A. Knopf, 1918 NUC. London: Heinemann, [1918] NUC BMC.

A satire on women war workers who find the war an opportunity to inflate their egos. Miss Vivian often needlessly overworks herself and others because she is actuated not by a passionate patriotism but by a love of exercising authority, being admired, feeling indispensable. Of her staff, only Miss Jones sees through her. Two men play minor parts, otherwise all women. There is "kindness and tolerance beneath the satire."

773 ZELLA SEES HERSELF. BY E. M. DELAFIELD. New York: A.A. Knopf, 1917 NUC. London: W. Heinemann, [1917] NUC BMC.

Character study of Zella from 7-19, drawn with sympathetic understanding. Through her childhood she tries to be charming by agreeing with everyone. She always poses and depends exclusively on the opinions of others—until she develops an unreal self. At 19, she is about to marry a man just like herself when she gets a true perspective of her personality. She refuses to marry the man. The novel ends there.

DASKEIN, TARELLA (QUIN). Australia.

774   KERNO. A STONE. London: W. Heinemann, 1914 BMC.
Kerno is a remote but prosperous sheep farm in Australia, owned by Wynne Holland, an elegant lawyer who lives off its income but resides in Melbourne. Judith Acton, fleeing from a brutal husband, seeks rest there, and draws Wynne back to Kerno. They have a child, but the attraction of the city proves too strong for Wynne. He escapes Kerno only to die.

DAVIDGE, FRANCES.

775   THE GAME AND THE CANDLE. New York: D. Appleton, 1905 BMC NUC.
Wife wants a divorce.

776   THE MISFIT CROWN. New York: D. Appleton, 1904 BMC NUC.
Unhappy marriage.

DAVIDSON, LILLIAS CAMPBELL. United Kingdom.

777   THE LOST MILLIONAIRE. London: Cassell, 1908 BMC.
An inheritance plot in which a woman doctor is involved.

778   SECOND LIEUTENANT CELIA. London: Bliss, Sands, 1898 BMC.
Puts on her brother's uniform and takes his place in camp when he outstays his leave. Descriptions of her beauty and frocks. For schoolgirls.

DAVIES, HELEN. See TAINTER, HELEN (DAVIES).

DAVIES, NAUNTON.*

779 THE SECRET OF A HOLLOW TREE: A NOVEL. BY NAUNTON COVERTSIDE. London: Digby, Long, [1898] BMC.

A murder in which Matskalla, the "wisest woman of the Romani," is the "leading agent" in its solution.

DAVIESS, MARIA (THOMPSON). 1872-1924. United States.

780 BLUE-GRASS AND BROADWAY. New York: Century, 1919 BMC NUC.

Young woman from a small town in Kentucky moves to New York City and becomes involved in theater work.

781 THE DAREDEVIL. Chicago: Reilly and Britton, [c1916] NUC BMC.

Modern young heroine disguises herself as the Marquis de Grez, comes to the U.S. to get her rich uncle's help for herself and lame brother, becomes her uncle's secretary (still dressed as a man) and has an adventurous career in that position and in her male attire.

782 THE GOLDEN BIRD. New York: Century, 1918 NUC.

Ann leaves Mathew and his wealth to return home and restore her family's fortunes by raising chickens. Counselled by Adam, she is successful.

783 THE MATRIX. New York: Century, 1920 BMC NUC.

The author states that Nancy Hanks as a weaver and dyer was "probably the first woman in Kentucky to enter trade and secure her own financial independence." This is also a story of her courtship and marriage.

784 THE TINDER-BOX. New York: Century, 1913 BMC NUC.

Evelina has been to college and has studied art in Paris. She returns to her hometown in Harpeth Valley, Tennessee, bringing all her advanced ideas and commitment to women's rights with her with the aim of putting them into practice. She begins by proposing to the man she loves and encouraging other women to do the same. Jane Mathers is a New England millionaire, a new woman and a firebrand in the community. The town grows to like the feminists, and the Equality League helps shape the future of the town. Light and humorous.

DAVIS, ELIZABETH S.

785 ROPES OF SAND. New York: Guarantee Pub. Co., [1906] NUC.

A young woman from Kentucky meets a visiting preacher, becomes pregnant. Years later they meet.

DAVIS, ETHEL. United States.

786 WHEN LOVE IS DONE: A NOVEL. Boston: Estes & Lauriat, 1895 NUC.

"The title stands for a problem that looms up large in some women's lives." Set near Boston, a modern and very personal story of Mary Eldredge's quiet tragedy—which is "women's tragedy."

DAVIS, JESSIE AINSWORTH.

787 WHEN HALF-GODS GO. Edinburgh and London: W. Blackwood, 1907 BMC.

After her mother and brother die and her father remarries, Mary lives with Beaton who promises but puts off marriage. She runs off in terror that someone will discover her "sin." In the end she marries a man who considers her fear ridiculous. Character study.

DAVIS, REBECCA (HARDING). 1831-1910. United States.

788 FRANCES WALDEAUX: A NOVEL. New York: Harper, 1897 NUC. London: Osgood, McIlvaine, 1897 BMC.

"It was long ago decided by the most infallible of masculine critics that there never has been, was not, and never could be a woman possessed of a sense of humor like unto a man's sense of humor. So that this little woman, who makes a living for herself and her son by writing a daily column of Rabelaisian fun, cannot, of course, find any correspondence in reality," says one reviewer. When her son marries a vulgar unscrupulous woman, Frances in a fit of madness considers murdering the woman to save her son. Powerful and sympathetic study of her later life.

DAWSON, MARJORIE. United States.

789 MISS EAGLE, THE SUFFRAGETTE. BY MARY DALE. New York: Aberdeen, 1909 NUC.

The issue of women's suffrage discussed by birds: Miss Eagle is the leading suffragette; the Magpie, the Raven, Mrs. Barnyard, the Owl, and the rest join in.

DEAKIN, DOROTHEA. United Kingdom.

790 THE POET AND THE PIERROT. London: Chatto and Windus, 1905 BMC.

Older sister supports younger one by writing serial stories. Pierette, the younger, shocks the villagers with her unconventional behavior. She also shocks her admirers by admitting that her love for each of them cannot last.

791 THE SMILE OF MELINDA. New York and London: Harper, 1903 BMC.

On her lonely African homestead, Melinda is a completely different woman from the sweet 18 year old she was when she first married. She "trifles with the maternal instinct" and almost deserts her child. All the while, her husband is blind to the change. To him she remains the sweet loveable wife.

792 THE YOUNG COLUMBINE. London: Methuen, 1908 BMC.

A young actress, disgusted with her profession, seeks her fortune elsewhere. But because of her past as an actress, she cannot succeed. "Sad, augmented by the stamp of truth."

DEAN, MRS. ANDREW. See SIDGWICK, CECILY (ULLMANN).

DEAN, TERESA H. United States.

793   REVERIES OF A WIDOW. New York: Town Topics, 1899 NUC. London: G. Routledge, [1899] BMC.
Heroine's first husband dies; she divorces the second.

DEANE, MARY BATHURST.

794   EVE'S APPLE. London: R. Bentley, 1894 BMC.
Vivienne, during the French Revolution, writes a political satire, is arrested, tried, and sentenced to deportation. She is part of the old society, an aristocrat, but is a pioneer in the new society.

DEARMER, JESSIE MABEL (WHITE). 1872-1915. United Kingdom.

795   THE ALIEN SISTERS. London: Smith, Elder, 1908 BMC.
"The real purpose of the book is to attack the conditions which allow women to starve upon wages of 5 shillings or 7 shillings and sixpence a week at honest work and so force them to 'pick up' what they can in the streets." The story is of two sisters, one legitimate, the other not.

DEBARRIOS, ADELAIDE.

796   THE SHEPHERDESS OF TODAY. New York: Aberdeen, 1910 PW.
The heroine, a Christian Scientist, sets up an office across from a medical doctor. She is so successful she is able to establish a church in the community.

DE BREMONT, ANNA (DUNPHY).

797 DAUGHTERS OF PLEASURE: BEING THE HISTORY OF NEARA, A MUSICIAN, ATHENE, AN ACTRESS, AND HERA, A SINGER. London: Greening, 1900 BMC.

The three heroines, unrelated, have all "unclassed themselves"; they tell their histories. Because they are all endowed with genius, they are reinstated in society, each becomes famous for her art. They all get husbands.

798 LADY LILIAN'S LUCK. A ROMANCE OF OSTEND. London: Greening, 1907 BMC.

She gambles in order to make enough money to marry as she likes.

799 THE LIONESS OF MAYFAIR. London: Everett, 1909 BMC.

Woman is a sculptor who marries.

DE BURY, F. BLAZE.

800 PHANTOM FIGURES. London: F. V. White, 1907 BMC.

Love outside of marriage and divorce.

801 THE STORM OF LONDON: A SOCIAL RHAPSODY. London: J. Long, 1904 BMC NUC. Boston: Turner, 1905 NUC.

A dream in which London after a storm is devoid of all material goods. Everyone is naked, and as people become accustomed to their state, class distinctions vanish and marriage becomes obsolete. A "typical modern woman" is one of the chief speakers.

DE CARRET, ALICE. United States.

802 FLAMES AND ASHES. New York: G. W. Dillingham, 1898 NUC.

New England governess marries a Cuban and goes with

him to Cuba. She suffers all kinds of indignities and loves another, but they decide they must try to forget each other. By the time she is a widow he has succeeded.

DE COULEVAIN, HELENE FAVRE. 1871-1913. France.

803   AMERICAN NOBILITY. BY PIERRE DE COULEVAIN. New York: Scribner, 1897 NUC. London and Cambridge, Mass.: Sampson Low, Marston, 1898 BMC.
A French aristocrat marries an American woman and subsequently takes a mistress. This is intolerable for his wife who is contrasted with French women. There are several chapters on the superior status of women in the United States.

804   THE HEART OF LIFE. BY PIERRE DE COULEVAIN. New York: E. P. Dutton, [1912] NUC. (Tr. by Alys Hallard, pseud.)
The slight story of Maia who hastily divorced her husband and eventually returned to him. Most of the book, however, is the author's self-analysis and a rather copious journal of her day to day existence.

805   ON THE BRANCH. BY PIERRE DE COULEVAIN. New York: Knickerbocker Press, 1903 NUC. London: E. Nash, 1909 NUC. (Tr. by Alys Hallard, pseud.)
Written in the first person, the detailed account of the life of a widow whose literary career has begun at 50, and who has given up her home to live "on the branch," in hotel rooms, travelling alone.

DE COULEVAIN, PIERRE. See DE COULEVAIN, HELENE FAVRE.

DE GROOT, J. MORGAN.* B. 1868. United Kingdom.

806   A LOTUS FLOWER. Edinburgh and London: W. Blackwood, 1898 BMC.
Sympathetic study of a neurotic woman.

DEHAN, RICHARD. See GRAVES, CLOTILDE INEZ MARY.

DE JAN, WINIFRED LEWELLIN JAMES. 1876-1941. Australia.

807 BACHELOR BETTY. BY WINIFRED JAMES. London: A. Constable, 1907 BMC. New York: Dutton, 1907 NUC.

She comes to England from Australia to seek fame as a novelist, furnishes a flat, struggles for independence, but in the end marries.

808 LETTERS OF A SPINSTER. BY WINIFRED JAMES. London: Chapman & Hall, 1911 BMC. London: G. Bell, 1911 NUC.

DE JANVILLE, SYBILLE GABRIELLE MARIE ANTOINETTE (DE RIQUETTI DE MIREBEAU) MARTEL. 1849-1932. France.

809 CHIFFON'S MARRIAGE. BY GYP. Chicago: E. A. Weeks, [c1895] NUC. London: Hutchinson, Zeit-geist Library, 1895 BMC. (Am. ed. tr. by Nora Teller; Eng. ed. tr. by Mrs. Patchett Martin.)

Chiffon is a "slangy, impulsive tomboy," half child, half woman, innocent, self willed and outspoken. She is hardly more than a child when her mother plots to marry her to an old duke. But Chiffon knows what marriage is, refuses the old man though everyone presses for the match, and chooses her own love.

810 GINETTE'S HAPPINESS. BY "GYP". London: T. F. Unwin, 1896 BMC. New York: R. F. Fenno, [c1896] NUC. (Tr. by Ralph Derechef.)

For fifteen years she has managed her husband's stud farm and his political campaigns in this marriage of convenience, but when their political views are no longer harmonious, she refuses to be involved.

811 AN INFATUATION. BY GYP. New York: R.F. Fenno, [1895] NUC. (Tr. by Elise Paul.)

The heroine is unhappily married and bored with her

various admirers. She has a "strong desire to do some loving on her own account"—especially since she learns her husband is unfaithful. She "forms her own code of ethics" and pursues the man of her choice, apparently unsuccessfully. Ends in suicide.

DEJEANS, ELIZABETH. See BUDGETT, FRANCES ELIZABETH JANES.

DE JOUVENAL, SIDONIE GABRIELLE (COLETTE) GAUTHER-VILLARS. 1873-1954. France.

812 THE VAGRANT. BY COLETTE WILLY. London: E. Nash, 1912 BMC. (Tr. from the French by Charlotte Remfrey Kidd.)

Story of an actress in autobiographical form. The "morbid introspection and self revelation will produce a depressing effect on the average English reader."

DE KOVEN, ANNA (FARWELL). 1860-1953. United States.

813 A SAWDUST DOLL. BY MRS. REGINALD DE KOVEN. Chicago: Stone and Kimball, 1895 NUC. London: G. Routledge, 1895 BMC.

Helen Rivington was 20 when she married a man of 50, and she is lonely, unhappy and bored with her life. She falls in love with a young artist but lies to him concerning her feelings. They part.

DE KOVEN, MRS. REGINALD. See DE KOVEN, ANNA (FARWELL).

DELAFIELD, E. M. See DASHWOOD, EDMEE ELIZABETH MONICA (DE LA PASTURE).

DELAIRE, JEAN.*

814 A DREAM OF FAME. London: Long, 1899 BMC.

Story of Giuseppa whose artistic "genius flickered out amid the petty cares of married life." She dies because she is not "allowed to live for painting." She leaveş one wonderful painting of the Resurrection; part of the story concerns the ironical fate of this painting.

815   TWO GIRLS AND A DREAM. London: Ward, Lock, 1901 BMC.

Two women, an artist and a writer, struggle in their careers. The artist "reviles" the world that won't accept her work; the writer has much trouble publishing hers. In the end, one marries; the other goes on with her career to fame.

DELAND, MARGARET WADE (CAMPBELL). 1857-1945. United States.

816   THE AWAKENING OF HELENA RICHIE. New York and London: Harper, 1906 BMC NUC.

Helena Richie has left her husband, an alcoholic responsible for the death of their child, and has for a number of years been the mistress of a man who passes as her brother. Helena is portrayed with great sympathy, but the development of the story demonstrates the author's beliefs that extra-marital love is harmful to all who are involved, even tangentially.

817   AN ENCORE. New York and London: Harper, 1907 BMC NUC.

Lettie Norris meets her old lover after 25 years. Both are widowed with grown children, and their Indian summer romance is complicated by the respective children.

818   THE IRON WOMAN. New York and London: Harper, 1911 BMC NUC.

The story of a strong woman whose joy in life is the efficient management of her iron mill. She loves her son, but he is envious of his friend whose mother is more womanly and sensitive.

819   AN OLD CHESTER SECRET. New York and London: Harper, [c1920] NUC BMC.

Lydia, a "timid, gallant, little old maid," refuses to marry a man she doesn't respect, refuses to try to conceal her poverty, and is indifferent to her shabbiness. Her adoption of a child results in gossip.

820 PARTNERS. New York and London: Harper, 1913 BMC NUC.

Widow and her older single daughter are joint postmasters in Vermont. For twenty years they find pride in their work, lead peaceful, interesting lives, and share a stong bond of love. With the election of Cleveland comes a new postmaster, but the painful prospect of changing the lives of these women is averted by setting up a partnership of three.

821 PHILIP AND HIS WIFE. Boston and New York: Houghton, Mifflin, 1894 NUC BMC. London: Longmans and Green, 1894 BMC.

Cecilla is married to Philip; reviewers concur that he is a prig who insists that she live up to his ideals. They are both unhappy; she joins the Women's Pushahead Club, seeking the support of other women, but finds that they judge women harshly. She and Philip separate, but conclude that the only way out of a bad marriage is through it; their lives cannot be put back to where they were before. Cecilla's sister Alicia in her self-sacrifice to her invalid mother is accused by Mrs. Deland of "immoral unselfishness...characteristic of many women...abnegation of their comforts, their rights, their necessities even."

822 THE RISING TIDE. London: J. Murray, 1916 BMC. New York and London: Harper, [1916] NUC.

The conflict of ideas of young feminists and older women as portrayed in the relationship of Freddy, a militant suffragist, and her mother. Her brother is an imbecile because of her father's venereal disease. She advocates birth control. She is a monster in her mother's eyes. She proposes to a man who turns her down.

823 THE STORY OF A CHILD. Boston and New York: Houghton, Mifflin, 1892 NUC BMC. London: Longmans, Green, 1892 BMC.

A study of the workings of a lively mind, showing the effects of heredity and environment on Ellen, the heroine, but also showing her unique imagination. She can withdraw at will into herself, has pagan instincts like those of Marie Bashkirtseff. She runs away from a strict grandmother, eventually returns. One reviewer suggests the story is autobiographical.

DELANO, EDITH (BARNARD). D. 1946. United States.

824 TO-MORROW MORNING; CHRONICLE OF THE NEW EVE AND THE SAME OLD ADAM. Boston: Houghton Mifflin, 1917 NUC.

Martha Ramsey is 30ish, competent, bright; she serves on several committees, is active in the suffrage movement—in short, she is thoroughly modern. At the same time she finds her husband is still "like old Adam, making a fool of himself over a pretty face." In other matters, Martha believes "Women are learning to keep step with men...ready for them as we never were before."

825 WHEN CAREY CAME TO TOWN. New York: Dodd, Mead, 1916 NUC.

Carey, raised by two aunts on an isolated plantation in Virginia, believes that "a gentleman is ready and willing to help a lady—a woman, all women. You need never be afraid of anything, not of anything at all, when there's a gentleman near to protect you." In this romantic comedy which involves a mill town and a srike, she is befriended by a woman who devotes her considerable energies to women's rights.

DE LA PASTURE, MRS. HENRY. See CLIFFORD, ELIZABETH LYDIA ROSABELLE (BONHAM) DE LA PASTURE.

DE LASZOWSKA, JANE EMILY (GERARD) AND DOROTHEA (GERARD) LONGARD DE LONGGARDE.

826 A SENSITIVE PLANT. BY E. AND D. GERARD. London: K. Paul, 1891 BMC. New York: D. Appleton, 1891 NUC.

Life of a woman who from childhood is painfully shy. As

a girl Janet Sinclair is alone much of the time, sitting in the garden watching the flowers grow. Her mother dies; she grows up, still very frightened and timid. She struggles to support herself in Venice. The rest of the story concerns the misunderstanding between her and her fiance.

DE LA VAL, JEANNETTE.

827 THE HUMAN OCTOPUS. London: Murray and Evenden, [1915] BMC.
Concerns white slave traffic.

828 SCARLET BY FATE. London: Murray and Evenden, 1913 BMC.
Two divorce suits.

DELEDDA, GRAZIA. See MADESANI, GRAZIA COSIMA (DELEDDA).

DELL, ETHEL MAY. 1881-1939. United Kingdom.

829 THE HUNDREDTH CHANCE. New York and London: G.P. Putnam's Sons, 1917 NUC. London: Hutchinson, 1917 BMC.
Aristocratic Maud Brian marries a race horse trainer because of insufferable conditions for herself and her brother, but she loves Lord Saltash. The marriage is miserable because the two are unsuited. But the end is happy.

DE LONGGARDE, DOROTHEA (GERARD) LONGARD. 1855-1915. United Kingdom.

830 THE ETERNAL WOMAN. BY DOROTHEA GERARD (MADAME LONGARD DE LONGGARDE). New York: Brentano's, 1903 NUC. London: Hutchinson, 1903 BMC.
Poverty drives Clara to set a trap to win a husband. She is penniless and completely on her own, living by her wits. She is in turn a circus performer, a governess, work she gives up because men will not leave her alone, and a nurse. She sets out to get a certain man whom she ends

up loving.

831 A FORGOTTEN SIN. BY DOROTHEA GERARD (MADAME LONGARD DE LONGGARDE). Edinburgh & London: W. Blackwood, 1898 BMC. New York: D. Appleton, 1898 NUC.

Morell, a lady's man, married for money when he became 30 and his hair started to thin. After spending his wife's fortune and on the brink of financial ruin, he sees his salvation in the marriage of his daughter, Esme, to a wealthy man. The man, however, is distracted by La Belveda, a dancer. Morell appeals to her and discovers that the proud woman is his illegitimate daughter. Vengeance is in her hands, although she eventually relents and allows Esme to marry. The shock, however, is too much for Morell, and he kills himself. La Belveda wins the reader's sympathy and admiration.

832 A GLORIOUS LIE. London: J. Long, 1912 BMC. Leipzig: B. Tauchnitz, 1912 NUC.

The heroine, who unknowingly has married a soldier who has a wife, says she is his mistress to save his life. The novel then goes on to describe her career as a singer.

833 THE INEVITABLE MARRIAGE. BY DOROTHEA GERARD (MADAME LONGARD DE LONGGARDE). London: J. Long, [1911] BMC NUC. Leipzig: B. Tauchnitz, 1911 NUC.

Winnie Mowbray tries to support herself in India, but poverty and illness force her to marry. Eventually she learns to love her husband.

834 MISS PROVIDENCE: A NOVEL. BY DOROTHEA GERARD. London: Jarrold, 1897 BMC. New York: D. Appleton, 1897 NUC.

Florence Crossly breaks her engagement when she learns her fiance once loved a governess. She sends him off to marry that young woman, but he learns the governess has a husband. Florence and he are reunited.

835 ONE YEAR. BY DOROTHEA GERARD. Edinburgh and London: W. Blackwood, 1899 BMC. New York: Dodd, Mead, 1900 NUC.

English governess tells the story of her year with a wealthy Polish family in East Galacia and of the wayward unconventional Jadwiga, raised in a hothouse atmosphere, her rival lovers, and her unhappy marriage: "the mental and nervous fibres of the Polish girl who commits suicide at 20."

836 PASSION AND FAITH. BY DOROTHEA GERARD (MADAME LONGARD DE LONGGARDE). London: S. Paul, [1915] NUC BMC.

Marian Scott is a married woman who meets the man who awakens her to true love. She lives with him until she is attracted to Roman Catholicism. Conflict of passion and religion.

837 A QUEEN OF CURDS AND CREAM. BY DOROTHEA GERARD. London: Eden, Remington, 1892 BMC. New York: D. Appleton, 1892 NUC.

Ulrica, the daughter of an Austrian count and a peasant mother, is left at her father's death with a title and a huge debt. She is strong, honest, and courageous (an "untrained savage" who remains unsoftened). She runs a dairy farm to pay off her father's debt, defends herself with her fists. When she inherits money and meets London society, she can handle that too.

838 A SPOTLESS REPUTATION. BY DOROTHEA GERARD (MADAME LONGARD DE LONGGARDE). Edinburgh: W. Blackwood, 1897 BMC. New York: D. Appleton, 1897 NUC.

Geraldine Nolebrook, raised in complete isolation and married at 17 to the first man she ever knew, hits London and Vienna society like a thunderbolt because of her great beauty. She is also a cold, emotionless woman, empty of passion. She soon learns the power of her beauty and lures six men to their ruin. She dies of an overdose of arsenic taken from a quack doctor to regain her complexion after her face is burned in an accident.

839 THE WRONG MAN. BY DOROTHEA GERARD. Edinburgh and London: W. Blackwood, 1895 BMC. New York: D. Appleton, 1896 NUC.

Traces development of Antonina, one of the three principal characters, from girl to woman. She has an active mind, warm heart, and energetic will, and she works to bring socialistic reforms to the village. But the story is depressingly sombre.

DE LONGGARDE, DOROTHEA (GERARD) LONGARD, jt. au. See DE LASZOWSKA, JANE EMILY (GERARD) AND DOROTHEA (GERARD) LONGARD DE LONGGARDE.

DE LONGGARDE, MADAME LONGARD. See DE LONGGARDE, DOROTHEA (GERARD) LONGARD.

DELTA.*

840 A FASCINATING SINNER. F. Tennyson Neely, 1897 USC.

While her husband is away, a conventional wife is persuaded to taste of "forbidden pastimes." She learns in the whirl of a London season that men "lead other people's womankind into mischief and keep their own out of it. "There are many differences of opinion between this woman and her husband when he returns. Should be "excluded from all libraries."

DEMAREST, VIRGINIA.

841 THE FRUIT OF DESIRE; A NOVEL. New York and London: Harper, 1910 NUC BMC.

The heroine is a woman with strong convictions against marriage. She meets, travels and lives with a man, an ex-convict, who was innocent of the crime he paid for. Heroine works out her own lifestyle.

DEMENS, INNA. United States.

842 HE WHO BREAKS. New York: Dodd, Mead, 1918 NUC.
Elsa, a musician, lives in the country with Theodore, an artist. But his art absorbs him, and she realizes the limits of his love. After a trial period she refuses marriage and finds happiness living alone with her child.

DE MEYER, MAHRAH (CARACCIOLO). B. 1875. United States.

843 NADINE NARSKA. New York: Wilmarth, 1916 NUC.
Nadine's girlhood is "darkened by her mother's irregular mode of life." She is gifted, marries unhappily, and leaves her husband who then divorces her. Her other relations with men are also unhappy.

DENISON, MARY (ANDREWS). 1826-1911. United States.

844 CAPTAIN MOLLY: A LOVE STORY. Boston: Lee and Shepard, 1897 NUC.
A rich spoiled young woman gives up her life of ease to join the Salvation Army, but gives up that work to marry in the end.

DE PRATZ, CLAIRE. D. 1934. United Kingdom.

845 THE EDUCATION OF JACQUELINE. New York: Duffield, 1910 NUC. London: Mills & Boon, [1910] BMC NUC.
A young widow raises her daughter to be an independent thinker, well-educated. She doesn't want her to be like her own generation of women who lived only to serve others. She has an experience which "no mother would wish a young girl to go through." Traditions concerning women in France are contrasted with those in the United States.

846 ELIZABETH DAVENAY. London: Mills & Boon, [1909] NUC BMC. New York: M. Kennerley, 19—? [] NUC.
She is a feminist of advanced ideas living in Paris. She has no thoughts of love, marriage or children. Instead she

devotes herself to her career as Professor of English at the Lycee George Sand until feminist politics call her to edit La Revolte, a feminist newspaper started and run solely by women. Then she falls in love, and her feelings clash with her ideals. But she gives up the man because she fears she will lose her individuality if she marries. She goes to England to work for her sisters. Much discussion of feminism.

847 EVE NORRIS. London: W. Heinemann, 1907 BMC.

She has a beautiful voice, but her family has neither appreciation nor understanding of her gift. She revolts against the dullness of suburban life and escapes to Paris where she drifts into a relationship with a man out of a desire to live. But most of the novel concerns her life as a voice student. A positive and sympathetic portrayal.

DERVILLE, LESLIE.*

848 THE OTHER SIDE OF THE STORY. A NOVEL. New York: G. W. Dillingham, [1904] NUC. London: T. F. Unwin, 1904 BMC.

A young woman working in Washington as a government clerk is finally driven to suicide by the problems of sexual discrimination and the attitudes of her male supervisor.

DE SAVALLO, DONA TERESA. See WILLIAMSON, ALICE MURIEL (LIVINGSTON).

DE SELINCOURT, ANNE DOUGLAS (SEDGWICK). 1873-1935. United Kingdom.

849 AMABEL CHANNICE. BY ANNE DOUGLAS SEDGWICK. New York: Century, 1908 NUC. London: E. Arnold, 1908 BMC.

Lady Channice has married young and cannot love her husband. She leaves him for a young artist. The result of this infatuation is a child, whom she raises by herself. The problems she encounters are the subject of the book.

850   THE CONFOUNDING OF CAMELIA. BY ANNE DOUGLAS SEDGWICK. London: Heinemann, 1899 BMC. New York: C. Scribner's Sons, 1899 NUC.

Character novel focusing upon the relation between Camelia and her cousin Mary. Camelia has everything—brains, beauty, cabinet ministers at her feet. She's egotistical and arrogant, particularly cruel to Mary, her "inferior" in all ways. She preys on her cousin, competes with her for a man. Then Camelia realizes what she has done and tries to atone for her cruelty. Mary forgives her at her (Mary's) death.

851   THE DULL MISS ARCHINARD. BY ANNE DOUGLAS SEDGWICK. London: Heinemann, 1898 BMC. New York: C. Scribner, 1898 NUC.

Hilda is a painter, and after spending the mornings working in her studio, she teaches art for the rest of the day, using this income to buy clothes for her sister, luxuries for her invalid mother, and to supplement her father's income. She is considered dull because she is too tired to go out in society. Peter Odd, a widower, also believes her dull and almost makes the mistake of marrying her sister.

852   THE ENCOUNTER. BY ANNE DOUGLAS SEDGWICK (MRS. BASIL DE SELINCOURT). London: E. Arnold, 1914 BMC. New York: Century, 1914 NUC.

Persis, an intellectual neophyte, a "chill and shallow moon" around whom revolve a Nietzschean philosopher and his two German disciples. She is really not in love with any of them and remains her cool, quiet self. A "contemporary product of transitory feministic ideas."

853   A FOUNTAIN SEALED. BY ANNE DOUGLAS SEDGWICK (MRS. BASIL DE SELINCOURT). New York: Houghton Mifflin, [c1907] BMC NUC. New York: Century, 1907 BMC. (Also published as Valerie Upton. By Anne Douglas Sedgwick. London: Constable, 1908 BMC NUC.)

An analysis of the painful relationship between Valerie

and her daughter, Imogen, a selfish egoist. Valerie leaves her husband and Imogen to lead their "superior" lives. She returns when her husband dies. Imogen attempts to raise her mother morally while luring on her mother's old suitor.

854 PATHS OF JUDGMENT. New York: Century, 1904 NUC. London: A. Constable, 1904 BMC.
An in-depth analysis of the relationships between a young woman, her father, two men, and another woman. The subjection (and exploitation) of feminine strength to masculine weakness.

855 THE RESCUE. BY ANNE DOUGLAS SEDGWICK. New York: Century Co., 1902 NUC. London: J. Murray, 1902 BMC.
Study of the relationships between a 47 year old widow, her beautiful daughter, and a young man who has fallen in love with a youthful picture of the mother.

856 TANTE. BY ANNE DOUGLAS SEDGWICK (MRS. BASIL DE SELINCOURT). New York: Century, 1911 NUC. London: E. Arnold, 1911 BMC NUC.
Character study of Mercedes Okraska, a 46 year old concert pianist of world-wide fame, an egoist. Crisis comes when her ward Karen becomes engaged to a lawyer. In style of Henry James.

DE SELINCOURT, IRENE RUTHERFORD (MACLEOD). B. 1891.

857 GRADUATION: A NOVEL. BY IRENE RUTHERFORD MCLEOD. London: Chatto & Windus, 1918 BMC NUC.
Frieda is involved in art, social work, and suffrage. A "too intimate accounting" of her progress and methods in love.

DE SELINCOURT, MRS. BASIL. See DE SELINCOURT, ANNE DOUGLAS (SEDGWICK).

DEVAURIARD, G.*

858 MATED IN SOUL. London: Hurst & Blackett, 1912 BMC.
Written with the purpose of marriage reform, the story is
"a sympathetic study of a sensitive and highly-strung
woman." Alice meets her soul-mate after her marriage. She
leaves her husband for him. The question of the paternity
of her child "concerns the physiologist rather than the
novelist," remarks one reviewer.

859 THE SIBYL OF BOND STREET. London: Everett, 1907
BMC.
Adventuress transforms lives of three elderly female
cousins.

DEVI, SRIMATI SVARNA KUMARI. See GHOSAL,
SRIMATI SVARNA KUMARI DEVI.

DE VILLENEUVE, LOUIS. See GIBBONS, LOUISE ELISE.

DEWING, E. B. See KAUP, ELIZABETH BARTOL (DEWING).

DI CADHILAC, MARGARET ISABELLA (COLLIER)
GALLETTI.

860 THE SCHOOL OF ART. BY ISABEL SNOW. London: T.
F. Unwin, 1891 BMC NUC.
Emmeline Harris, "plain," intensely practical, is an artistic
genius. In art school, a gross injustice is done to her when
it is suggested that the work she exhibited is not her own.
The signs of her genius first attract the man she marries, a
Royal academician who visits the school.

DICKENS, MARY ANGELA (EVANS). 1838-1896. United
Kingdom.

861   CROSS CURRENTS: A NOVEL. London: Chapman and
      Hall, 1891 BMC NUC. New York: D. Appleton, 1892
      NUC.
      Selma, who has "considerable dramatic talent," decides on
      an acting career rather than the marriage she has been
      contemplating. She devotes herself to her art, and it does
      not fail her. "She refuses every offer of marriage, and we
      leave her a sweetly grave woman who finds her pure
      satisfactions in high dedication to her art."

862   A MERE CYPHER: A NOVEL. London and New York:
      Macmillan, 1893 BMC NUC.
      Unique study of a tame, withdrawn woman who reveals
      her true strength in a time of crisis. Leila Custance is
      overwhelmed by the tyranny of her villain doctor husband
      to whom she is a helpless slave. When Norman Strange
      comes to live with them to be cured of alcoholism, it is
      she, not the doctor, who cures him. And later when
      Norman becomes rich and her husband tries to frame him
      to extort money, Leila murders her husband. She dies in
      prison.

DICKINSON, EVELYN ELIZABETH. Australia.

863   HEARTS IMPORTUNATE. London: Heinemann, 1899
      BMC. New York: Dodd, Mead, 1900 NUC.
      Avis has a hatred of sex; she wishes there were only
      slightly materialized angels—rather than men and women.
      There is something strange about Avis' past: "Heroine is
      distant, unlovable, detached from her surroundings, and
      morbidly conscious of a past which is in truth dead."
      There is a man in her life who knows of this past but
      who loves her steadfastly. Avis finally yields to him. "The
      author is sympathetically disposed toward the highly
      educated Amazon of today." The following is a quotation
      from the novel: "Hazell knew, as all men know, that
      woman has fair cause of complaint against man and
      against society. He knew that it was required of her to be
      an exquisite kind of paradox—good and pure, steadfast in
      her constancy, and yet abundant in a piquant sauce of

coquetry and wiles; and should the one part predominate, she is heavy, unattractive; and should the other, she is light, unworthy. To be fascinating, the reason of her being—she must maintain unstable equilibrium. Man, were he asked to do this, would refuse the endless effort." Set in Australia.

864 A VICAR'S WIFE. London: Methuen, 1892 BMC NUC.

The author shows a "fury of resentment against the hypocrisies of society" in this history of a madman. The vicar is a monster. His wife leaves him. He horsewhips his 17 year old daughter. He "soon after expires (with unpleasant detail) in his own gore."

DICKINSON, MARY (LOWE). 1839-1914. United States.

865 FROM HOLLOW TO HILLTOP? Philadelphia: American Baptist Society, 1896 NUC.

Mrs. Burke returns to the village where she once taught school.

DICKSON, F. THORALD* AND MARY PECHELL.

866 A RULER OF IND. London: Digby, Long, [1895] BMC.

Anglo-Indian life, restless wives. Heroine, to some degree a new woman, makes a bad marriage.

DIEHL, ALICE (MANGOLD). 1844-1912. United Kingdom.

867 THE CONFESSIONS OF PERPETUA. London: Stanley Paul, [1912] BMC.

An unhappy marriage, a divorce, and the prospect of a new marriage.

868 DR. PAULL'S THEORY: A ROMANCE. BY MRS. A. M. DIEHL. Bristol: J. W. Arrowsmith, [1893] BMC. New York: D. Appleton, 1893 NUC.

His theory involves the education of his daughter Lilia who is kept prisoner in their country home away from all contacts and as a result becomes an extremely sensitive, introspective and delicate person completely without a sense of herself. The most disastrous effect of this education comes when she marries. She attaches herself completely to her husband, living solely through him. She dies shortly after her marriage.

869   ELSIE'S ART LIFE: A NOVEL. BY MRS. A. M. DIEHL. London: R. Bentley, 1893 BMC NUC.

Elsie Gerhard is a pianist of great ability. She is "discovered" and brought to fame by Frank Clare, an unhappily married man. But we lose sympathy with Frank Clare "when he makes this born artist sacrifice her art in order that she fill a void in his life."

870   THE GARDEN OF EDEN. London: Digby, Long, 1907 BMC.

Althea has a beautiful voice and becomes a famous singer. The course of her career and her love for Clifford to a dramatic close.

871   MISS STRANGEWAYS. London: J Long,, [1909] BMC NUC.

Unhappy couple: husband was a criminal; wife comes close to poisoning him in the end.

872   A WOMAN'S WHIM: A NOVEL. London: Hutchinson, 1894 BMC.

Teresa, dedicated to becoming an opera singer, gives up home, rank, and fortune to do so. In spite of love affairs she persists in her career.

DIEHL, MRS. A. M. See DIEHL, ALICE (MANGOLD).

DILL, BESSIE.

873   THE STORY OF BELL. BY L. BEITH DALZIEL. London: Ward and Downey, 1896 BMC.

A mild touch of fin-de-siecle freedom. The heroine keeps up an unlawful attachment with her cousin's husband after he marries. Suicide.

DILLINGHAM, LUCY. United States.

874 THE MISSING CHORD: A NOVEL. New York: G. W. Dillingham, 1894 NUC.

Juliet is the daughter of a woman devoted to social pleasure. She decides to study music in Berlin for a year before making her debut. Love changes her artistic bent; she marries an American professor devoted to the improvement of his fellow men. After a short year of marriage her life is once more wholly changed.

DILLON, MARY C. (JOHNSON). D. 1923. United States.

875 THE AMERICAN. New York: Century, 1919 BMC NUC.

Helen Seymour is a social worker in the slums. She is head resident of the Sunshine House, well-liked in the community and successful in her work. She comes from a well off family and must choose between a lover of that world and one of the world of her new life. The war solves the problem—one dies saving the other. Sentimental.

876 COMRADES. New York: Century, 1918 NUC BMC.

A group of students in a German pension, all good friends. War breaks out. Male narrator, English, is in love with American, Beatrice. He enlists, she goes to the front to drive a motor ambulance. They marry, reuniting the group at their wedding, including the German who is now a POW in England.

877 IN OLD BELLAIRE. New York: Century, 1906 NUC BMC.

Love story of a woman school teacher.

DITSON, LINA BARTLETT. United States.

878 THE SOUL AND THE HAMMER: A TALE OF PARIS. New York: G. A. S. Wieners, 1900 NUC.

Narrated by a Dutch-American painter, who was rescued from suicide by heroine, a famous writer and singer who lives with her mother in Paris. Later he helps her care for a blind husband and little child.

DIVER, KATHERINE HELEN MAUD (MARSHALL). 1867-1945. United Kingdom.

879 AWAKENING; A STUDY IN POSSIBILITIES. BY MAUD DIVER. New York: J. Lane, 1911 NUC.

Sympathetic portrayal of a young Hindu woman who comes West to study medicine, marries an English artist, and has difficulties adjusting to English manners and role of wife. She almost commits suicide when she learns of her husband's fear of having a dark child.

880 CANDLES IN THE WIND. BY MAUD DIVER. New York: J. Lane, 1909 NUC. Edinburgh: W. Blackwood, 1909 BMC.

Author never tires of praising Lyndsay Vereker, poet and artist. She marries a Eurasian doctor not knowing he is part Indian. She is unhappy in India and in her marriage. When her husband dies, she remarries. Much space is given to her emotions and difficulties and to her women friends.

DIVER, MAUD. See DIVER, KATHERINE HELEN MAUD (MARSHALL).

DIX, BEULAH MARIE. B. 1876. United States.

881 THE BATTLE MONTHS OF GEORGE DAURELLA. New York: Duffield, 1916 NUC.

War from the pacifist point of view. Heroine is a nurse working in a military hospital.

882 LITTLE FAITHFUL. London: Mills and Boon, 1914 BMC.

Betty is a successful novelist and playwright but discovers that without love life is barren.

883 THE LITTLE GOD EBISU. New York: Duffield, 1914 NUC.

The old-fashioned love story of a young woman who

hated teaching.

884 MOTHER'S SON; A NOVEL. New York: Holt, 1913 NUC.

Betty Willard is a successful playwright who befriends Hugo—so good looking a young man that everyone spoils him. She takes him seriously finally. He is saved in the Titanic disaster.

DIX, GERTRUDE. United States.

885 THE GIRL FROM THE FARM. Boston: Roberts, 1895 NUC. London: J. Lane, 1895 BMC NUC.

"This is one of those wearisome books that deal with the modern daughter of emancipated views." Young woman, daughter of a dean who is blind, returns home after graduating with honors at Cambridge. She is bent on working in the reform movements of the day but torn between her duty to parents and need to do philanthropic work. The girl from the farm who is seduced helps the heroine decide to leave home for rescue work. Shows "the compatibility of higher education and true womanhood."

886 THE IMAGE BREAKERS. New York: F. A. Stokes, [c1900] NUC. London: W. Heinemann, 1900 BMC.

Rosalind, married to a wealthy manufacturer, and Leslie, an artist, become socialists. They leave their homes together and devote their lives to social reform, particularly to raising the position of women. Neither of them, ultimately, is able to make the personal sacrifices required by their ideals, and tragedy results. One reviewer says the author has lent a peculiar pathos and dignity to that generally unpopular kind of woman who outrages public opinion in the name of Duty.

DIXIE, FLORENCE CAROLINE (DOUGLAS). 1857-1905. United Kingdom.

887 IZRA; A CHILD OF SOLITUDE. London: J. Long, [1906] BMC.

A manifesto proclaiming love of animals, hatred of sport

and gambling, social tyrannies, religion, and championship of women.

DIXON, ELLA HEPWORTH. D. 1932. United Kingdom.

888 MY FLIRTATIONS. BY MARGARET WYNMAN. London: Chatto & Windus, 1892 BMC. Philadelphia: J. B. Lippincott, 1893 NUC.

Satirical humorous sketches of a dozen or so men of various types, all of whom admire the heroine.

889 THE STORY OF A MODERN WOMAN. London: W. Heinemann, 1894 BMC. New York: Cassell, [1894] NUC.

Mary Erle is "an earnest, patient woman who accepts her life and makes one of the great army of working women, unnoticed in their heroism and endurance," "a gentle and essentially feminine creature who only took to journalism and a solitary life in London lodgings owing to outward circumstances." She is jilted by her lover, refuses him when he comes back.

DOBBIN, GERTRUDE (PAGE). 1873-1922. United Kingdom.

890 THE EDGE O' BEYOND. BY GERTRUDE PAGE. London: Hurst and Blackett, 1908 BMC. London: G. Bell, 1908 NUC.

Described as sentimental this is the story of a wife who runs away with another man and lives happily.

891 THE PATHWAY. BY GERTRUDE PAGE. London: Ward, Lock, 1914 BMC NUC.

Sympathetic to the lot of the woman pioneer, this story portrays the important role of woman in the work of empire building of Rhodesia.

892 SOME THERE ARE—. BY GERTRUDE PAGE. London: Hurst and Blackett, 1916 NUC BMC.

Alastair, a mysogynist, is visited by two women, Doris and Doreen. Doris, who was sacrificed young to an unhappy marriage, has been travelling the world since her husband died. Doreen, waiting for a dream-lover, discovers a submarine base on the coast of Northern Scotland and almost loses her life in a heroic attempt to inform authorities in southern England.

893 TWO LOVERS AND A LIGHTHOUSE. London: Hurst and Blackett, 1910 BMC.

An irregular alliance between a cabinet minister whose wife is in a home for inebriates and a woman who has escaped from an unhappy marriage. The story is narrated by the woman; she tells of his rescuing her from the streets.

894 THE VELDT TRAIL. BY GERTRUDE PAGE. London: Cassell, 1919 BMC. London and New York: Cassell, [1921] NUC.

Young woman separates from husband when she learns he cheated during their engagement, insists he go abroad—he's mauled to death by leopard. She takes up with his partner but he's repulsed by her and leaves her.

895 WHERE THE STRANGE ROADS GO DOWN. BY GERTRUDE PAGE. London: Hurst and Blackett, 1913 BMC NUC.

Describes the difficulties of women who marry and move to a wholly new country. Joe, the heroine, is a young Englishwoman who comes to the wilds of Rhodesia as the wife of a Rhodesian settler. Her trials and disillusionment as well as those of another woman are described.

896 WINDING PATHS. BY GERTRUDE PAGE. London: Hurst and Blackett, 1911 NUC BMC. New York: D. Appleton, 1911 NUC.

Illustrates the status of working women in London in the early 1900s. Hal Pritchard is a strong young woman who makes a place for herself as a journalist. And Lorraine Vivian is one of London's leading actresses. The author obviously admires these women, especially Hal. Both women practice freely the habit of being pals with men. There is much discussion concerning suffrage and women's independence.

DODD, ANNA BOWMAN (BLAKE). 1855-1929. United States.

897 ON THE BROADS. London and New York: Macmillan, 1896 BMC NUC.

A cruise on the Broads and a love story. The skipper, a "practical old lady."

DODD, CATHERINE ISABEL. 1860-1932. United Kingdom.

898 A VAGRANT ENGLISHWOMAN. London: Smith, Elder, 1905 BMC NUC.

No love motif. A handful of German university people, an Englishwoman among them, hold discussions which focus upon the emancipation of German women. The Englishwoman is conscious that her sisters have much to put up with, and that men are "unsatisfactory creatures."

DODGE, JANET.

899 AN INN UPON THE ROAD. London: Sidgwick and Jackson, 1913 BMC.

Intimate analysis of Natalie Herbert, an extremely sensitive young woman who is so frightened of sex that she breaks off her marriage to the one man who awakened her sexually. Her "masculine" friend Helen who smokes a pipe believes that marriage is only an inn, a stop rather than the whole end of women's lives.

900 TONY UNREGENERATE. London: Duckworth, 1912 BMC.

Tony does not believe in marriage. She has a child; the father is a weakling and she tells him off, although she is not sorry she has known him.

DORSET, G.*

901 A SUCCESSFUL WIFE. A STORY. New York and London: Harper, 1910 NUC. (Also published as The Confessions of a Successful Wife. London: W. Heinemann, 1910 BMC.)

Esther a stenographer brings up three brothers and sisters.

Marries an eccentric genius who drinks. She leaves him, but there is a reconciliation.

DOSTOEVSKAIA, LIUBOV FEDOROVNA. B. 1869. Russia.

902 THE EMIGRANT. BY L. F. DOSTOIEFFSKAYA. London: Constable, 1915 BMC NUC. New York: Brentano's, 1916 NUC. (Tr. by Vera Margolies.)

Irene, an idealistic Russian young woman leaves Russia after the Russo-Japanese War, disillusioned in any future reforms for her country. She becomes a nun but leaves the faith to marry, but the marriage ends in her suicide. "Gloomy but powerful."

DOSTOIEFFSKAYA, L. F. See DOSTOEVSKAIA, LIUBOV FEDOROVNA.

DOUDNEY, SARAH. 1843-1926. United Kingdom.

903 PILGRIMS OF THE NIGHT: A NOVEL. London: W. H. Addison, 1897 BMC.

Dulcie Daughton writes short stories. "That her husband should appreciate his wife's accomplishments indicates how he has been converted by her love."

DOUGALL, LILY. 1858-1923. Canada.

904 THE EARTHLY PURGATORY. London: Hutchinson, 1904 BMC.

A psychological study of the sufferings and suspicions of two sisters. Complete lack of love interest, the sisters are involved in a murder mystery.

905 THE MORMON PROPHET. London: A. and C. Black, 1899 BMC NUC. New York: D. Appleton, 1899 NUC.

Susannah Halsey is a strong woman whose love of justice makes her support the Mormon cause. She marries a Mormon and sees her husband and child killed by anti-Mormons. Though she remains skeptical about the faith, she joins them. And though she is fascinated with the leader Joseph Smith, she refuses his offer to be part of his harem.

DOUGLAS, AMANDA MINNIE. 1837-1916. United States.

906 THE HEIR OF SHERBURNE. New York: Dodd, Mead, [c1899] NUC.

Much of the novel is devoted to Gertrude Maurice—her character, her career as a secretary to a wealthy woman, and her sisters' lives.

907 HELEN GRANT, TEACHER. Boston: Lothrop, Lee and Shepard, [1909] NUC.

She is an earnest, capable, competent and affectionate teacher.

908 HELEN GRANT'S DECISION. Boston: Lothrop, Lee and Shepard, [c1910] NUC.

She gets an offer to teach in a college after two years of high school teaching but decides to stay where she is.

909 HELEN GRANT'S HARVEST YEAR. Boston: Lothrop, Lee and Shepard, [1911] NUC.

She travels abroad, marries, hates to give up her work to do housework, but in the end she does.

910 HER PLACE IN THE WORLD. Boston: Lee and Shepard, [c1897] NUC.

"...a gentle and perfectly lady like assault on the chains of convention which have barred a woman's horizon across her domestic hearth." Can be read with "perfect safety."

911 IN WILD ROSE TIME. Boston: Lee and Shepard, 1895 NUC.

Pictures life among the poor. Dilsey Quinn cares for her helpless sister Bessie.

DOUGLAS, O. See BUCHAN, ANNA.

DOUGLAS, THEO. See EVERETT, MRS. H. D.

DOWDALL, MARY FRANCES HARRIET (BORTHWICK). 1876-1939. United Kingdom.

912 SUSIE, YESTERDAY, TO-DAY, AND FOREVER. London: Duckworth, 1919 BMC.

"Portrayed with loving hatred," Susie is described by one reviewer as brainless, faithless, alluring, vain, and by her author as follows: "Susie went out very little and had no occupation at home. Her mind was a riot of femininity. She had been educated by elderly ladies in whose ideas men figured as professional rivals, or interesting friends, or dangers to the community, or pupils' fathers....Finding nothing in her education to explain the mysteries they suggested she thought about them...all day. Their admiration became a thing to work for like points scored in a game, and she played her cards to that end." Her great mission is motherhood, the father is expected to perform his function, no more. Marries successfully though she continues her relationship with an artist who loves her.

DOWIE, MENIE MURIEL. See FITZGERALD, MENIE MURIEL (DOWIE) NORMAN.

DOWSON, ROSINA (FILIPPI). B. 1866.

913 THE HEART OF MONICA. London: Cassell, 1914 BMC.

Letters to a male friend revealing the tragedy of her life, her union to a hopeless drunkard. (Withdrawn from sale first time published.)

DREW, SARA.

914 THE GIRL BEHIND: A STORY BASED UPON THE LIFE OF A SHOP-GIRL. London: J. Ouseley, 1908 BMC.

915 THE HARLOT IN HEAVEN. London: J. Ouseley, [1910] BMC. Orphaned young woman given good educaton by relatives, turned adrift in London for a month. Falls in hands of a dissolute artist and a scoundrel who makes her a "decoy of men." She falls for one such man, but he must rescue her from the man who wishes to keep her for business purposes.

DRINKWATER, JENNIE M. See CONKLIN, JENNIE MARIA (DRINKWATER).

DROWER, ETHEL STEFANA (STEVENS). 1879-1972. United Kingdom.

916   AND WHAT HAPPENED; BEING AN ACCOUNT OF SOME ROMANTIC MEALS. BY E. S. STEVENS. London: Mills and Boon, [c1916] BMC NUC.

Letty, a student of the Cradock School of Journalism, and her life in a group of Bohemian literary men and women. Pleasant and amusing.

917   THE LURE. BY E. S. STEVENS. London: Mills and Boon, 1912 BMC NUC. New York: J. Lane, 1912 NUC.

Anna, a journalist, becomes entangled with Huntley Goss, a villain who first is the editor of a society journal, then in Sudan the owner of a fraudulent crocodile farm. She is pursued by him even after her marriage to another man—she meets him on a trip on the Nile where he is slowly poisoning his middle-aged wife and making plans for doing away with his half-witted son. Fine character studies of Anna and Huntley, whom one can't help liking, remarks one reviewer.

918   MAGDALENE: A STUDY IN METHODS. BY E. S. STEVENS. London: Cassell, [1919] BMC NUC.

Kathleen, daughter of a cleric, had been seduced when she was 14. Now that she is 40 and married, she becomes involved in reforming the rescue homes. Attacks old fashioned punitive methods of conducting rescue homes for fallen women, arguing that the women need help and freedom from the repressed joyless life of these institutions.

919   SARAH EDEN. BY E. S. STEVENS. London: Mills and Boon, [1914] NUC. New York: Dodd, Mead, 1914 NUC.

Sarah goes to Jerusalem and founds a religious community which holds wealth in common, is celibate, does good

works, and waits the second coming. A conflict over her
daughter's lover is resolved.

920   THE VEIL; A ROMANCE OF TUNISIA. BY ETHEL
STEFANA STEPHENS. London: Mills and Boon, 1909
BMC. New York: F.A. Stokes, [c1909] NUC.

As a child Mabrouka, an Arab girl, gets a glimpse at the
relative freedom women have in western life. Later, as
part of a harem, she yearns for freedom. She escapes with
the help of a French officer, but when she learns he has
no intention of setting her free, she robs and kills him.
There follow her exciting adventures as a dancer and as a
spy.

DU BOIS, CONSTANCE GODDARD. United States.

921   THE SHIELD OF THE FLEUR DE LIS: A NOVEL. New
York: Merriam, [c1895] NUC.

In 1431 Jeanne d'Arc was burned at the stake. Three years
later a stranger comes to the place of her birth and learns
all the details of her life.

DUCHESS, THE. See HUNGERFORD, MARGARET WOLFE (HAMILTON).

DUDENEY, ALICE (WHITTIER). 1866-1945. United Kingdom.

922   CANDLELIGHT. BY MRS. HENRY DUDENEY. London:
Hurst and Blackett, [1918] BMC NUC.

Edith, married to Wilfred, conceives a child with George,
who is engaged to Wilfrid's sister. Psychological study of
Edith.

923   FOLLY CORNER. BY MRS. H. DUDENEY. London: W.
Heinemann, 1899 BMC. New York: H. Holt, 1899 NUC.

Character study of Pamela Crisp, an up-to-date
independent young woman of London. Jethro offers her
security; Edred, passion. She finally chooses the first, but
never loses her passion for the second.

924 GOSSIPS GREEN. London: Cassell, 1906 BMC. (Also published as The Battle of the Weak, or Gossips Green. By Mrs. Henry Dudeney. New York: G. W. Dillingham, [1906] NUC.)

A loveless marriage and its results. The husband, a country physician, is brutish, and his wife takes a lover, a wild untamed youth.

925 HAGAR OF HOMERTON. London: C. A. Pearson, 1898 BMC NUC.

Hagar is a suspected thief, a shop girl. A widow from the East End adopts her for diversion. Hagar does not adapt to Cheltenham Terrace. She likes the pretty frocks and leisure time, but she continues her ties with family and friends, marrying one of the young men.

926 THE HEAD OF THE FAMILY. BY MRS. HENRY DUDENEY. London: Methuen, [1917] BMC NUC.

Beausire Fillery rebels against her lifelong dependence on her aunt, and she finds her grand passion in William, a married man. Instead of being passive about her love, she goes after him openly and directly—until she realizes he is not worth the effort. She marries a different man.

927 A LARGE ROOM. BY MRS. HENRY DUDENEY. London: W. Heinemann, 1910 BMC NUC. New York: Brentano, 1911 NUC.

Amaza Meeks is precocious as a child, apart from other children. She is educated and poetic. She lives with two men before she marries a third.

928 MAID'S MONEY. BY MRS. HENRY DUDENEY. London: W. Heinemann, 1911 BMC NUC. New York: Duffield, 1912 NUC.

Two forty-year old cousins, both single, inherit money on the condition they will remain single and live together. Sarah Peacock was a paid companion; she is the more lively of the two. Amy was a governess in the best houses. Both are pleased that the inheritance attracts suitors but realize that the men are after their money. Close psychological study of their daily life and feelings like that of Sarah's longing for her cousin's death so that she actually believes that she has killed Amy. All characters are over 40.

929 A MAN WITH A MAID. BY MRS. HENRY DUDENEY. London: Heinemann, 1898 BMC NUC.
Described by one reviewer as "profoundly sad," the story is of Tom's betrayal of Tabbie, a "simple" milliner's assistant, and her subsequent suicide.

930 MANHOOD END. BY MRS. HENRY DUDENEY. London: Hurst and Blackett, [1920] NUC BMC.
Story of Rainbird and Sophy. He calls himself a priest but is married. She can't help being bored. She goes off with someone and returns. When her baby dies, she runs anywhere. She comes back, but they both die while planning another honeymoon.

931 THE MATERNITY OF HARRIOTT WICKEN. BY MRS. HENRY DUDENEY. London: W. Heinemann, 1899 BMC NUC. New York and London: Macmillan, 1899 NUC.
Good psychological study of Harriott Wicken whose family carries a disease in their blood. Harriott marries Darnell, and later when he is away, her child, a victim of heredity is born a hopeless idiot. The story traces her hatred for the child, her efforts to conceal it from her husband, a succession of tragedies through which she comes to love the child, and her death.

932 RACHEL LORIAN. BY MRS. HENRY DUDENEY. New York: Duffield, 1909 NUC. London: W. Heinemann, 1909 NUC BMC.
Rachel marries at 18. On her honeymoon her husband is mangled and disfigured in an accident. She remains with him for 15 years out of pity though she rebels against the conditions and in spite of the fact that she is awakened to a white heat kind of love by Patrick Rivers. When her husband dies, she still wishes to wait before marrying Patrick. On the eve of their marriage, she discovers he has had a mistress since her husband's death one year earlier. She refuses to marry him, adopts the child of his mistress with whom we leave her happy at the end.

933 ROBIN BRILLIANT. BY MRS. HENRY DUDENEY. London: Hodder and Stoughton, [1902] BMC. New York: Dodd, Mead, 1903 NUC.

Loyal, fearless, "high bred," unflinching, Robin Brilliant is not a heroine but a hero, more man-like than Loten, the man in the story, who does nothing till she pulls him after her. Robin gives him up to the other woman who is opposite her in all ways. She lives out her life alone.

934 A RUNAWAY RING. BY MRS. HENRY DUDENEY. New York: Duffield, 1913 PW. London: W. Heinemann, 1913 NUC BMC.

Contrast of two women's totally different kinds of lives. Aunt Frusannah is in reality Fanny's unmarried mother—as Fanny learns after she marries. Frusannah's lover was an Austrian duke. Now she is poor and addicted to drink. To escape this poverty, Fanny marries the son of Mrs. Baigent whose life and household represent stability, order and virtue. Fanny is enough like her mother to rebel against this order, the pressure on her to have children, the vulgarity of domesticity that claims her body and soul. Frusannah dies drunk in a railroad station.

935 THE SECRET SON. BY MRS. HENRY DUDENEY. London: Methuen, [1915] NUC BMC.

Nancy Pinyoun, a laundry maid, is seduced, made pregnant by a squire who, though he loves her, loves respectability more. He marries Enid and arranges for another man to marry Nancy. Nancy is repulsed by this idea, but because she is destitute, she marries the man, who soon drowns himself because of his unrequited love for Nancy. Nancy raises her secret son to manhood. This son discovers that his own wife is untrue and at the same time learns the truth about his own mother and scorns her. Nancy is represented as the only strong character among weaklings.

936 SET TO PARTNERS: A NOVEL. BY MRS. HENRY DUDENEY. London: Heinemann, 1913 NUC BMC. New York: Duffield, 1914 NUC.

At age ten, Angelina Peachey is precocious in her relations

with boys. When she later falls in love, she refuses to marry the man. She lives with him for seven years during which time all goes well. Then she falls in love with her lover's friend and runs off with him. When her new lover becomes paralyzed and her old one blind, she lives with the two of them who are wholly dependent upon her. She supports them by operating a second-hand furniture store.

937 SPINDLE AND PLOUGH. BY MRS. HENRY DUDENEY. New York: Dodd, Mead, 1901 NUC. London: W. Heinemann, 1901 NUC BMC.

Shalisha is a landscape gardener. What's more she's any man's equal in intellect, in magnificent physical strength, in lusty health, and physical activity. Sworn to celibacy, she is an "old maid by temperament, with a constitutional shrinking from men and matrimony," but she does marry in the end.

938 THE THIRD FLOOR. BY MRS. HENRY DUDENEY. London: Methuen, 1901 NUC BMC.

Valencia takes her child with her when she divorces her husband and becomes a platform woman.

939 THIS WAY OUT. BY MRS. HENRY DUDENEY. London: Methuen, [1917] BMC NUC.

Jane Vaguener, vulgar, loud and very industrious, makes a very comfortable living writing popular fiction. She also writes a brilliant play but never knows how good it was. Her brother knew, but he makes her believe she is through as a writer. He considers himself a great literary artist but lives off his sister whose writing he despises. Bizarre tragedy of Jane's death.

940 WHAT A WOMAN WANTS. BY MRS. HENRY DUDENEY. London: W. Heinemann, [1914] NUC BMC.

Chrismas Hamlyn, child of a Sussex farm, uneducated, never forgot the sailor who took her to tea when she was a young girl. Her mother dies, and she is finally left alone with the males of the family, the other women having left. When her brother dies and leaves her with a small inheritance, she goes to London and is robbed by a false lover. She returns to the farm and lives alone until years later the sailor returns as a tourist with his child. After a life of victimization she marries him: "I wants you. There's nothing else for women!"

941   THE WISE WOODS. BY MRS. HENRY DUDENEY. London: Heinemann, 1905 NUC BMC.

When Vashti marries, the wreck of it is a foregone conclusion. She's a woman capable of anything, anytime. The novel studies her humdrum suburban life with a dull husband, her rebellion against Christian values, and her escapes to the woods where she engages in free fights with men of her own gypsy tribe. "Hideous things happen to this abnormal character in this sordid tragedy."

DUDENEY, MRS. HENRY. See also DUDENEY, ALICE (WHITTIER).

942   ROUND THE CORNER. Hurst and Blackett, 1918 BS.

Drab realism. Wife and husband's closest friend have an affair; she has a child. This separates the four friends for twenty years.

DUFF, LILY GRANT.

943   PERIWINKLE. London: J. Murray, 1906 BMC.

Periwinkle, a freely sexual young woman, is intimate with men with whom she is not in love, finds her husband's care of her and respectability a restraint of her freedom. She excels Pam in her vitality and strength.

944   VACATION. London: J. Murray, 1910 BMC.

The story of two sisters. One with a physical disability becomes a successful painter, the other, an Anglican nun. Conflict of work and love; "the natural calls to maternity and paternity are not ignored, but at the close of the narrative there is not even the promise of fulfillment."

DUGANNE, PHYLLIS. United States.

945   PROLOGUE. New York: Harcourt, Brace and Howe, 1920 NUC.

Young woman at start of career in New York at the

beginning of the war.

DUGGAN, JANIE PRICHARD. United States.

946 A MEXICAN RANCH: OR BEAUTY FOR ASHES: A
PRIZE STORY. Philadelphia: American Baptist Society,
1894 NUC.

The adventures of Mary Summers, a Baptist missionary
working as nurse, teacher, and proselytizer in Mexico.

DUNBOYNE, LADY.

947 ROMANCE OF A LAWN TENNIS TOURNAMENT.
Trischler, 1891 BS.

Two sisters: one holds many advanced ideas; the other
has extraordinary skill in lawn tennis. Story of a week of
tournament and the two proposals the tennis player gets.

DUNCAN, FRANCES. See MANNING, FRANCES DUNCAN.

DUNCAN, SARA JEANNETTE. See COTES, SARA
JEANNETTE (DUNCAN).

DUNTZE, HARRIET ELIZABETH ISABELLA.

948 INFELIX: A SOCIETY STORY. London: Ward and
Downey, 1892 BMC. London: 1899 NUC.

The life story of Jetta, an impoverished young woman
who marries a rich man without love. She has a daughter
who dies. She grows to love her husband's friend, thinks
several times of running off with him, but a lack of
money prevents her. She refuses to be unfaithful to her
husband while living with him. Eventually the friend's
love grows cold, and she poisons herself.

DURANT, M.

949 REPENTANCE. London: Mills and Boon, 1917 BMC.

A wife quarrels with her husband, leaves to join the man
she loves, but writes to her husband immediately. The
husband divorces her though apparently he knew she had

not slept with the man. The wife makes no defense.

DURYEA, NINA LARREY (SMITH). 1874-1951. United States.

950 A SENTIMENTAL DRAGON. New York: G.H. Doran, [c1916] NUC.

Mrs. Bradish, who has made a fortune from an invention, decides to enter European society and succeeds in marrying her daughter to a European artist.

DUTTON, LOUISE ELIZABETH. United States.

951 THE GODDESS GIRL. New York: Moffat, Yard, 1915 NUC.

Rose Saxon moves from a small town to New York when her father becomes too poor to support her. In New York she joins a Bohemian group, gives up her "wholesome" conventional ideas, and encourages a lover who says he cannot marry her, insisting she can take care of herself. Apparently she does not go "all the way," however.

EASTMAN, REBECCA LANE (HOOPER). B. 1877. United States.

952 THE BIG LITTLE PERSON; A ROMANCE. New York and London: Harper, [1917] NUC.

Heroine is a deaf woman. Arathea loses her hearing and her fiance—because of her deafness. She sends away for a hearing aid, begins a correspondence with the inventor and eventually marries him.

EASTWICK, MRS. EGERTON.

953 "BEYOND THESE VOICES." A NOVEL. London: Burns and Oates, 1901 BMC.

Woman of modern views who works havoc on her uncle's old-fashioned ways. She has great personal ambition and is ready to go after what she wants. In the end she finds the way to perpetuate her ideas by establishing an institution of some kind.

EATON, ELIZABETH.

954 WHEN THE SHADOWS FALL. London: Wells Gardner, 1912 BMC.

Pretty and harmless diary of invalided young woman.

ECCOTT, W. J.* United Kingdom.

955 THE BACKGROUND. Edinburgh and London: W. Blackwood, 1909 BMC.

A woman whose husband is thought to have died in a fire remarries. When he shows up, she keeps her new husband because her first husband divorces her, preferring another woman who happens to look much like her. The heroine is a successful novelist who keeps her anonymity even from her husband.

956 THE HEARTH OF HUTTON. Edinburgh: W. Blackwood, 1906 BMC.

Unhappy marriage, separation, reconciliation. Historical romance.

957 THE RED NEIGHBOR. Edinburgh: W. Blackwood, 1908 BMC.

She is a woman of the people who has made a fortune in cosmetics and confidences.

EDGINTON, MAY. See BAILEY, MAY HELEN MARION (EDGINTON).

EDWARDS, ANNIE. D. 1896. United Kingdom.

958 A PLASTER SAINT. London: Chatto and Windus, 1899 BMC NUC.

Heroine tells of her earlier love for a rake who loved and left and who almost ruined her life. He went on to a miserable marriage and then to take holy orders.

EDWARDS, M. BETHAM. See EDWARDS, MATILDA BARBARA BETHAM.

EDWARDS, MATILDA BARBARA BETHAM. 1836-1919.
United Kingdom.

959 THE CURB OF HONOUR. BY M. BETHAM-EDWARDS. London: A. and C. Black, 1893 BMC. New York: Anglo-American, [c1893] NUC.

Lamenta marries late in life a younger man who has decided against having children because his physical weakness is hereditary. But Lamenta loves him, and they are really very well matched in their wit and temperaments.

960 A NORTH-COUNTRY COMEDY. BY M. BETHAM-EDWARDS. London: Henry, [1891] BMC. Philadelphia: J. B. Lippincott, 1892 NUC.

"Two maiden ladies no longer young": one gets married; both have financial fortune. Humorous.

961 A ROMANCE OF DIJON. London: A. and C. Black, 1894 BMC. New York: Macmillan, 1894 NUC.

Old-fashioned historical romance, French Revolution and the taking of the Bastile. Pernelle Nesmond, young tradeswoman at outbreak of Revolution, wants to marry a young man solely because he'll be useful in the business. She's super intelligent, business-like, self-contained and beautiful.

962 A STORM-RENT SKY: SCENES OF LOVE AND REVOLUTION. London: Hurst and Blackett, 1898 BMC NUC.

A small village in the Champagne district during the French Revolution and a "maiden of heroic mould who prefers patriotism to love and the common destiny of womankind." A "grande dame" adopts various disguises and is central character.

EDWARDS, MRS. BENNETT.

963 THE UNWRITTEN LAW. London: Simpkin, 1892 BS.

"Declamation against marriage of the ordinary kind."

EDWARDS, R. W. K.*

964 THE MERMAID OF INISH-UIG. London: E. Arnold, 1898 BMC.

Donegal. An orphaned young woman, abandoned by her lover and shunned by her neighbors, brings up her child in a seals' cave. The child, amphibious, is one day cut off from her mother by falling rocks, and she lives with the seals until she is mistaken for one by an islander and falls victim to his gun. Minutely circumstantial narrative given in the diary of the lighthousekeeper, the dupe of Black Kate's betrayer; reveals a sense of humor.

EDWOOD, MAY.

965 THE AUTOBIOGRAPHY OF A SPIN: A STORY OF ANGLO-INDIAN LIFE. Calcutta & London: Thacker, Spink, 1893 BMC.

"Spin" means spinster to one reviewer, a worn-out flirt who is "on the shelf" to another. Juanita Desmond is 29. Her story is "the brutally frank analysis of the thoughts, motives and feelings—or the want of them—of a thoughtlessly heartless flirt. She pretends that her heart was soured and hardened by the conduct of a man who was simply amusing himself with her and that she has avenged herself on the sex by amusing herself with subsequent admirers." The Athenaeum, 102 (1893), 551. Anglo-Indian setting.

EGERTON, GEORGE. See BRIGHT, MARY CHAVELITA (DUNNE) MELVILLE CLAIRMONTE GOLDING.

ELIOT, ANNIE. See TRUMBULL, ANNIE ELIOT.

ELISABETH, QUEEN CONSORT OF CHARLES I, KING OF RUMANIA. See PAULINE ELIZABETH OTTILIA LOUISA, QUEEN CONSORT OF CHARLES I, KING OF RUMANIA.

ELLERMAN, ANNIE WINIFRED. B. 1894. United Kingdom.

966   DEVELOPMENT; A NOVEL. BY W. BRYHER. London: Constable, 1920 BMC NUC. New York: Macmillan, 1920 NUC.

Written in autobiographical form, the story of Nancy who possesses "the intellect, the hopes, the ambitions of a man, unsoftened by any female attribute." She insists on studying paleontology at twelve. She also wants to be an artist. At eighteen she publishes a book of poetry.

ELLIOT, ANNE.

967   EVELYN'S CAREER: A NOVEL. BY THE AUTHOR OF "MY WIFE'S NIECE," "DR. EDITH ROMNEY." "AN OLD MAN'S FAVOR," ETC. [ANONYMOUS]. London: R. Bentley, 1891 BMC.

Evelyn Cunningham is adopted by her grandmother and raised to be a great lady. But at twenty, Evelyn becomes completely absorbed in the cause of working women. She goes to London to use her fortune to help the poor, opens a country rest home for them, and involves many young women in this project and others. Evelyn is agnostic but has a deep faith in people. Though she has discouraging experiences at first, she learns from them, and her work then is more successful. Part of her reform work involves lectures to the rich about the conditions of the poor. One reviewer insists that ultimately Evelyn fails in her work, "whether the author thinks so or not."

968   A MARTIAL MAID. London: Hurst and Blackett, 1900 BMC.

Clare goes to England with the child of a mother who has been shipwrecked to reclaim its birthrights, is considered an adventuress, fights till she succeeds.

969   THE MEMOIRS OF MIMOSA. BY HERSELF. EDITED BY ANNE ELLIOT. New York: Moffat, Yard, [1912] NUC. London: S. Paul, [1912] BMC.

Brilliant, undisciplined woman resolves to "live every

moment of her life."

970   WHERE THE REEDS WAVE. A STORY. London: R. Bentley, 1897 BMC.

Mother dares not interfere with her child's ruin because of sin in her own past.

971   WINNING OF MAY. BY THE AUTHOR OF "DR. EDITH ROMNEY" [ANONYMOUS]. London: Hurst and Blackett, 1893 BMC.

May Leslie is a novelist supporting herself in dingy lodgings in Fulham Road. She meets Arthur Beresford, a deformed man who is a supreme egoist. Both May and her friend Ernestine fall in love with him. When he is accused of murder, May's evidence saves his life but ruins her reputation. She then learns he became engaged to her out of gratitude not love; therefore, she leaves. But eventually they marry.

972   A WOMAN AT THE HELM. BY THE AUTHOR OF "DR. EDITH ROMNEY" [ANONYMOUS]. London: Hurst and Blackett, 1892 BMC.

Clare's dying father leaves the management of Thurston & Co. to her rather than her brother. She is capable, clear-headed, and shrewd, guides the business out of financial troubles into prosperity. The hero, in one reviewer's opinion, lacks Clare's "finer manliness." Another reviewer is not sure of the author's intention but suspects that it is "not well that a woman should be at the helm"; she is apt to have her attention distracted by romance.

ELLIOTT, DELIA BUFORD.

973   ADELE HAMILTON. New York: Neale, 1907 NUC.

When her husband's death leaves her penniless, a Southern woman takes her five children to California hoping to make a new start and to earn a good living.

ELLIOTT, EMILIA. See JACOBS, CAROLINE EMILIA.

ELLIOTT, SARAH BARNWELL. 1848-1928. United States.

974 THE DURKET SPERRET: A NOVEL. New York: H. Holt, 1898 NUC. (Also contains An Idle Man.)

Hannah is employed by a professor and his family as a waitress. She is ruined, at least the reverend thinks she is, but is not sure just how it happened. She is dismissed from the family. Tennessee mountains.

975 THE MAKING OF JANE; A NOVEL. New York: Scribner's Sons, 1901 NUC.

Study in individualism. Jane sacrifices luxury for independence, becomes a teacher, a milliner, a manager of a large department store.

ELLIS, BETH. See ELLIS, ELIZABETH.

ELLIS, EDITH MARY OLDHAM (LEES). 1861-1916. United Kingdom.

976 ATTAINMENT. BY MRS. HAVELOCK ELLIS. London: A. Rivers, 1909 NUC BMC.

Rachel Merton wants more from life. She moves to a London flat, works for the poor, and helps form the Brotherhood of the Perfect Life, a commune experiment in living equally with people of different classes.

977 KIT'S WOMAN; A CORNISH IDYLL. BY MRS. HAVELOCK ELLIS. London: A. Rivers, 1907 BMC NUC. (Revised edition of Seaweed.)

Kit is crippled by an accident after two years of marriage. "Question of a man allowing his wife to take a lover for the sake of posterity — the wife prefers the husband." Described as "morbid realism."

ELLIS, ELIZABETH. United States.

978 BARBARA WINSLOW, REBEL. BY BETH ELLIS. Edinburgh and London: W. Blackwood, 1903 BMC. New York: Dodd, Mead, 1906 NUC.

Barbara Winslow takes part in the Monmouth Rebellion.

She is no tame dove; she can "hold her own, and a rapier too, with any man." She defies the king and is pursued by his armies across England.

979 BLIND MOUTHS. BY BETH ELLIS. Edinburgh: W. Blackwood, 1907 BMC.

A woman organizes a movement against social vice. Concerns the struggle of labor and capital.

ELLIS, MRS. HAVELOCK. See ELLIS, EDITH MARY OLDHAM (LEES).

ELMORE, MAUD (JOHNSON).

980 THE REVOLT OF SUNDARAMMA. New York: F. H. Revell, [c1911] NUC BMC.

Hindu woman is married at 8 years old and revolts against the marriage, but fate, law and religion force her to submit. Later in life she learns a different religion and a different way women can live, and there is hope that she and her daughter can start a new life.

EMERY, FLORENCE (FARR). D. 1917.

981 THE DANCING FAUN. BY FLORENCE FARR. London: E. Mathews and J. Lane, 1894 BMC. Boston: Roberts, 1894 NUC.

Lady Geraldine offers a married cardsharp half her income if he will live with her. He explains he can do better financially by sticking with his wife, a promising actress. Lady Geraldine shoots him and is happy she has done so. The verdict is suicide, so she is not made to suffer.

982 THE SOLEMNIZATION OF JACKLIN. SOME ADVENTURES ON THE SEARCH FOR REALITY. BY FLORENCE FARR. London: A. C. Fifield, 1912 NUC BMC.

Jacklin divorces her husband and marries another, eventually goes back to first husband. All the women characters are "rakes or prigs."

ERSKINE, ANGELA SELINA BLANCHE (FORBES) SAINT CLAIR. B. 1876.

983 THE BROKEN COMMANDMENT. BY LADY ANGELA FORBES. London: E. Nash, 1910 BMC NUC.

Circulating Libraries censored this. Defends adultery on the grounds of personality.

984 PENELOPE'S PROGRESS. London: E. Nash, 1911 BMC.

She has an unconventional education, wins success on stage, breaks off engagement when she tells her fiance she's illegitimate. Ends happily.

ERSKINE, BEATRICE CAROLINE (STRONG). United Kingdom.

985 THE MAGIC PLUMES. London: Methuen, 1907 BMC.

Carlotta is a great opera singer.

ERSKINE, EMMA (PAYNE). 1854-1924. United States.

986 A GIRL OF THE BLUE RIDGE. BY PAYNE ERSKINE. Boston: Little, Brown, 1915 NUC BMC.

Two northern women establish a school in the southern mountains and influence the heroine—a sensitive and noble young woman growing up in the most sordid surroundings.

987 WHEN THE GATES LIFT UP THEIR HEADS; A STORY OF THE SEVENTIES. BY PAYNE ERSKINE. Boston: Little, Brown, 1901 NUC BMC.

Advocates interracial marriage. The heroine declares: "The great Caucasian race must stoop to these (Indians, Chinese, and Negroes) before it can rise higher. They have reached the boundary line past which they cannot move toward God's likeness until they have learned to place God's estimate of value upon a human soul of whatever race or condition...the heroine with a theory showing that it is really her duty to marry some one not of her own race is Miss Erskine's own discovery....Prophecy is dangerous, but it would not be surprising if the story marked a turning point in the subject of American fiction."

ERSKINE, PAYNE. See ERSKINE, EMMA (PAYNE).

ERVIN, MABEL CLARE. United States.

988 AS TOLD BY THE TYPEWRITER GIRL. New York: E. R. Herrick, [c1898] NUC.

A series of stories about "the intrigues of the profession of the typewriter girl," "a girl bachelor of the present day."

ESCHENBACH, MARIE VON EBNER. 1830-1916. Austria.

989 THE TWO COUNTESSES. London: T. F. Unwin, 1893 NUC BMC. New York: Cassell, [1893] NUC. (Tr. by Mrs. Waugh.)

Two German women very different from each other relate their experiences; one in letters to a friend; the other, in a journal. "In both cases the heroines have revolted against marriages made for them by their parents regardless of their personal feelings."

ESCOMBE, EDITH.

990 STUCCO AND SPECULATION. London: Remington, 1894 BMC.

Two stories. In Stucco the heroine is a woman of the very newest type. She and her husband believe in friendships outside marriage and support each other in this. One of her male friends babysits for them. In Speculation a young woman and man enter into a five-year marriage contract, with the consent of their parents.

991 A TALE THAT IS TOLD. London: Eden, Remington, 1893 BMC.

Helen Denham is very introspective and self analytical. When she marries, she is completely miserable. Another woman Hettie is unhappily married and amuses herself with her husband's friends. The story has no "ending" because the author believes endings are false. "A delicate and purposely inconclusive story of the temptations to which some of the most attractive women are subject."

ESLER, E. RENTOUL. See ESLER, ERMINDA (RENTOUL).

ESLER, ERMINDA (RENTOUL). D. 1924. United Kingdom.

992   'MID GREEN PASTURES. BY E. RENTOUL ESLER. New York: J. Pott, 1895 NUC. London: S. Low, 1895 BMC.
Grimpat. Another Cranford.

993   THE TRACKLESS WAY; THE STORY OF A MAN'S QUEST FOR GOD. London: R. B. Johnson, 1903 BMC.
Wife leaves out of boredom and jealousy.

994   THE WARDLAWS. London: Smith, Elder, 1896 BMC.
Novel divided into two parts. One concerns John, the other his half-sister who, when he went to England, remained in Ireland to operate a grocery shop.

EVANS, HOWEL.* United Kingdom.

995   A GIRL ALONE. London: G. Richards, 1917 BMC. New York and London: G. P. Putnam's Sons, 1918 NUC.
Ellice Mayne comes to England from Australia to claim an inheritance. Her suit fails, and she is left to make her own living in the sweatshops. "Realism that does not shrink from vulgar, harrowing or repulsive subjects."

EVANS, MARGUERITE FLORENCE HELENE (JERVIS). 1894-1964. United Kingdom.

996   CHICANE. BY OLIVER SANDYS. London: J. Long, 1912 BMC.
Heroine becomes a partner of Lady Webride in the business of cheating at bridge, stealing jewelry, and general swindling.

997 THE HONEY POT; A STORY OF THE STAGE. BY THE COUNTESS BARCYNSKA. London: Hurst and Blackett, 1916 BMC. New York: E. P. Dutton, 1916 NUC.

Two girls struggling on comic opera stage help each other through temptation. One succumbs and both find happiness in the end.

998 LOVE MAGGY. BY COUNTESS HELENE BARCYNSKA. London: Hurst and Blackett, 1918 BMC.

Sequel to Honey Pot. Misunderstandings arising out of Maggy's past, fights with husband, returns to stage, stardom.

999 ROSE O' THE SEA, A ROMANCE. BY THE COUNTESS BARCYNSKA. Boston: Houghton Mifflin, 1920 NUC.

Rose, an orphan, goes to London, becomes a flower girl. She repels the dishonorable advances of Denis, thereby winning his father with whom she falls in love but agrees, for love of him, to marry his son, who soon strays. She inherits a fortune in a necklace, loses it, but "in a month or so" becomes a movie star.

EVERETT, MRS. H. D. United States.

1000 MALEVOLA. London: Heath, Cranton and Ouseley, [1914] BMC.

An older woman is a musician and a vampire. She draws beauty and vitality from her victims through massage.

1001 WHITE WEBS. A ROMANCE OF SUSSEX. London: M. Secker, 1912 BMC.

Historical novel, 1746, in which the "threads of loyalty which sustained the cause of the White Rose were being woven at White Webs and elsewhere, largely by women's hands."

1002 A WHITE WITCH. BY THEO DOUGLAS. London: Hurst and Blackett, 1908 BMC.

Historical romance, witchcraft.

1003 WINDY GAP. BY THEO DOUGLAS. Bristol: J. W. Arrowsmith, [1898] BMC.

The heroine, alone in the world, wanders into a meeting house of a quaint, primitive sect. She hears a call for a sister to work in the West. Convinced that the call was meant for her, she goes to work as a missionary.

EVERETT, RUTH. United States.

1004 THAT MAN FROM WALL STREET; A STORY OF THE STUDIOS. New York: G. T. Long, [1908] BMC NUC.

Three women artists with "low moral standards."

EWELL, A. M. See EWELL, ALICE MAUDE.

EWELL, ALICE MAUDE. 1860-1946. United States.

1005 A WHITE GUARD TO SATAN: BEING AN ACCOUNT OF MINE OWN ADVENTURES AND OBSERVATION IN THAT TIME OF THE TROUBLE IN VIRGINIA NOW CALLED BACON'S REBELLION, WHICH SAME DID TAKE PLACE IN 1676, BY MISTRESS ELIZABETH GODSTOWE. RECOVERED BY A. M. EWELL. Boston and New York: Houghton, Mifflin, 1900 NUC.

Narrated by heroine, an account of an incident during Bacon's Rebellion when women and children were put in the front line of the attacking force.

EYLES, MARGARET LEONORA (PITCAIRN). 1890-1960. United Kingdom.

1006 MARGARET PROTESTS. London: E. Macdonald, 1919 BMC.

Begins "in a state of white-hot indignation against men." It pictures the monotonous lives of many married women, the selfishness of husbands, women's economic problems: "the only way a woman can get money is by selling herself to a man—either getting married or the other thing." Margaret's marriage, her early poverty-stricken widowhood, her unwanted child—"all a continuous and passionate protest on the subject of maternity...dissectingly frank." Ends with Margaret living a peaceful rural life with a compatible man.

F., M. See FISHER, MARY.

FABREGUE, AIMEE.

1007 CRUCIFIX. London: Tower Publishing, [1896] BMC. (Tr. by D. H. Fisher.)
Diary form. Story of "sentimental and candid" young woman whose mother has leprosy and who expects to be a leper herself.

FACCIO, RINA (COTTINO). 1876-1960. Italy.

1008 A WOMAN AT BAY (UNA DONNA). BY SIBILLA ALERAMO. New York and London: G.P. Putnam's Sons, 1908 NUC BMC. (Tr. by Maria H. Lansdale.)
Feminist analysis is present at each stage of the speaker's life. As a girl she is close to her aristocratic father. She is a free thinker, studies hard, loves her freedom. Gradually she understands her quiet mother, first through the shock of learning her father has a mistress, then through her mother's suicide attempt. As a young woman of 15 she takes a job in her father's factory, is raped by a man of 25, but interprets the act as a bond between them. They become engaged, though she sees all his failings clearly, knows very well she is miserable and that her freedom is over. As a wife and mother she lives with her husband's family away from the intellectual life she knew. Her jealous husband keeps her locked up. (Her mother is now in an asylum.) Her only joy is her child. Her husband beats her. Desperate she takes poison but is saved by her repentant husband. In convalescence, she again takes up intellectual life, reads, writes, gets articles published, has her consciousness raised by articles on feminism and socialism, feels a new hope — determines to write the great feminist novel. With her taking a job as a writer of articles, she is more estranged from her husband. They separate, but she learns that the law protects the father's rights not the mother's. At the end, she is in Rome alone teaching. Her women friends are journalists, one is a

doctor. She is part of a woman's group with no regrets and with full self respect.

FACILIS.*

1009 TWO WOMEN WHO POSED. New York: J. S. Ogilvie, 1897 PW, 1903 USC.

One is a society woman attracted to Bohemia; the other a professional model. Their relations with an artist.

FAHNESTOCK, HARRIETTE ZEPHINE (HUMPHREY). B. 1874. United States.

1010 THE HOMESTEAD. BY ZEPHINE HUMPHREY. New York: E.P. Dutton, [c1919] NUC.

The struggle between a woman's temperament and her environment: Barbara Marshall is raised on a New England farm where the environment is monotonous. She has inherited a love of travel along with the need for roots in her homestead. Love story is incidental.

FAIRBRIDGE, DOROTHEA. 1862?-1931. South Africa.

1011 THE TORCH BEARER. London: Mills & Boon, 1915 BMC. Capetown: J. C. Juta, [1915] NUC.

Agatha Lumsden spinster goes to South Africa to begin her work with women. Teaches them to cook. It turns out they cook better than she. She is always putting her foot in her mouth.

FAIRFAX, G. V.*

1012 THE WORKING-DAY WORLD; OR THE STRONGER PORTION OF HUMANITY. London: Digby, [1893] BMC.

Madge Merton is "a spirited, intellectually audacious young woman...who is mad on women's rights." Includes a murder and the solving of it by the accused man's wife.

FALCONER, LANOE. See HAWKER, MORWENNA PAULINE.

FALL, ANNA CHRISTY. B. 1855. United States.

1013 THE TRAGEDY OF A WIDOW'S THIRD. Boston: I. P.
Fox, 1898 NUC.
"A story illustrating the injustice of Massachusetts law
regarding a widow's rights in her husband's estate. Written
by a member of the Boston bar."

FARJEON, ELEANOR. 1881-1965. United Kingdom.

1014 GYPSY AND GINGER. London: J.M. Dent, 1920 BMC.
New York: E.P. Dutton, [c1920] NUC.
Whimsical. When Gypsy and Ginger marry, Gypsy
proposes they live in a one room house with two doors.
In fair weather she would go out her door and he would
do the cooking, etc., in foul weather, the reverse. Book
tells how the plan worked out.

FARMER, LYDIA HOYT. See PAINTER, LYDIA (HOYT)
FARMER.

FARQUHAR, ANNA. See BERGENGREN, ANNA
(FARQUHAR).

FARR, FLORENCE. See EMERY, FLORENCE (FARR).

FARRAR, GERALDINE. 1882-1967. United States.

1015 GERALDINE FARRAR: THE STORY OF AN AMERICAN
SINGER. BY HERSELF. New York and Boston: Houghton
Mifflin, 1916 BMC NUC.
Prima donna's career—years of struggle crowned with
success. Autobiography?

FAULDING, G. M. See DALE, LUCY AND GERTRUDE
MINNIE FAULDING.

FAULDING, GERTRUDE MINNIE, jt. au. See DALE, LUCY
AND GERTRUDE MINNIE FAULDING.

FEE, MARY HELEN. B. 1864. United States.

1016   THE LOCUSTS' YEARS. Chicago: A. C. McClurg, 1912 NUC.

Unhappy marriage between an American pearl fisher in the Philippines and a weary New England nurse.

FEILD, ELSIE. See STREATFEILD, LILIAN CECIL.

FELKIN, ELLEN THORNEYCROFT (FOWLER). 1860-1929. United Kingdom.

1017   CONCERNING ISABEL CARNABY. BY ELLEN THORNEYCROFT FOWLER. London: Hodder and Stoughton, 1898 BMC. New York: D. Appleton, 1899 NUC.

Isabel is witty and brilliant. She writes an anonymous novel which achieves a scandalous success; she later regrets its authorship. Her romance is a large part of the story.

1018   A DOUBLE THREAD. BY ELLEN THORNEYCROFT FOWLER. London: Hutchinson, 1899 BMC. New York: D. Appleton, 1899 NUC.

Heroine leads a double life of two very different women. As Ethel she is a poor governess; as Elfrida, a wealthy adopted daughter of a nobleman. Ethel falls in love with a captain to whom she reveals her double identity. At first he breaks their engagement, but later the two are reconciled.

1019   HER LADYSHIP'S CONSCIENCE. BY ELLEN THORNEYCROFT FOWLER (THE HONBLE. MRS. ALFRED FELKIN). New York and London: Hodder and Stoughton, [c1913] BMC NUC.

Lady Esther Wyvern is 40, not beautiful. Raised a Calvinist, she feels all pleasure is sinful. She falls deeply in love with a man of 28 but refuses to marry him because of the age difference. In fact she plots to get him married to a younger woman; when he does, he is unhappy. His young wife dies. Then Esther marries him. Full of discussion of feminism, especially about the equality of the sexes concerning marriage and the belief that a woman should as freely marry a younger man as a man marries a younger woman.

1020　THE WISDOM OF FOLLY. BY ELLEN THORNEYCROFT FOWLER (MRS. FELKINS). Boston: School of Printing, 1907 NUC. London: Hodder & Stoughton, 1910 BMC.

Two sisters in remote village. One murders her husband to save her baby; the other dies tragically.

FELKIN, HON. MRS. ALFRED. See FELKIN, ELLEN THORNEYCROFT (FOWLER).

FELKINS, MRS. See FELKIN, ELLEN THORNEYCROFT (FOWLER).

FENOLLOSA, MARY (MACNEIL). D. 1954. United States.

1021　RED HORSE HILL. BY SIDNEY MCCALL. Boston: Little, Brown, 1909 NUC.

Direct appeal for mill children and mill women: Maria Alden leaves brutal husband, thinking her child dead, and moves to Milltown where she discovers her child whose arm was crushed in millwork. A minor character, "a modern of moderns," is a woman who teaches sociology at a university.

1022　THE STIRRUP LATCH. BY SIDNEY MCCALL. Boston: Little, Brown, 1915 BMC NUC.

Compares a Victorian type of woman to an ultra-modern one. Cecily Dering married very young is left widowed with two daughters. Julia, her dear friend, is also a widow, with a son. The two meet as the story opens after Julia's long stay in England during which Cecily has become a household drudge and a slave to her daughters who ignore and abuse her. Julia, in contrast, is youthful, intelligent, alert and alive, a companion to her son who adores her. Julia sets out to rescue her friend Cicely.

1023   THE STRANGE WOMAN. BY SIDNEY MCCALL. New York: Dodd, Mead, 1914 NUC.

Inez, a divorced French widow, meets an American from a small town and together they write a novel expressing her views on marriage. She has vowed never to marry and believes in the full emancipation of women. They fall in love and return to a small mid-western town. The story is about the town's reception of this new woman.

1024   TRUTH DEXTER. BY SIDNEY MCCALL. Boston: Little, Brown, 1901 BMC NUC. London: C.A. Pearson, [1902] BMC.

Contrast between two women—Truth Dexter the much less interesting. Orchid is brilliant, sharp, loves danger, wants power, can discuss politics with great statesmen and overwhelm them, married but open about her love for Van. Truth is an ignorant Southern woman whom the lawyer Van marries so that he can make the legal decisions about her inheritance that she is too young to make. Her move from Alabama to Boston means a transformation in Truth—culture, courses at Radcliffe—but she is never a match for Orchid. Truth leaves Van out of jealousy because he can not give up Orchid. But in the end Truth and Van are reconciled.

FERBER, EDNA. 1887-1968. United States.

1025   DAWN O'HARA, THE GIRL WHO LAUGHED. New York: F. A. Stokes, [1911] NUC. London: Methuen, 1925 BMC.

For ten years, Dawn O'Hara supports herself as a journalist on a New York paper and pays the hospital bills for her insane husband. Then she has a nervous breakdown and recuperates in the care of her sister, her brother-in-law and a German doctor who loves her. She returns to work, and her husband now cured comes to claim her. She likes her newspaper work and her life alone but is also attracted to the traditional women's roles.

1026 EMMA MCCHESNEY AND CO. New York: F. A. Stokes, [1915] NUC BMC.
She has now reached the top as a business woman—a leader in women's fashions. She is married, a good mother and housewife, and a success in her work—a super woman.

1027 FANNY HERSELF. New York: F.A. Stokes, [1917] BMC NUC. London: Methuen, 1923 BMC.
The first half concerns Fanny's mother. Mrs. Brandeis runs a general store in a Western town after her husband dies. In her competent hands, the store prospers. Her buying trips and the relations between mother and daughter are described. The second part focuses upon Fanny. She helped her mother in the store, but after her mother's death, she wants to satisfy a longing that has grown in her for years. She wants to live a different life from her mother's; she would deny her Jewishness. She takes an important position in a mail-order house in Chicago, but is still restless. Then she makes a brilliant career as a cartoonist and falls in love.

1028 PERSONALITY PLUS; SOME EXPERIENCES OF EMMA MCCHESNEY AND HER SON, JOCK. New York: F.A. Stokes, 1914 BMC NUC.
Mrs. McChesney's experiences as a modern businesswoman make her a better mother in helping and understanding her son. She encounters problems in her career when a younger person challenges her methods as being old-fashioned.

1029 ROAST BEEF MEDIUM; THE BUSINESS ADVENTURES OF EMMA MCCHESNEY. New York: F.A. Stokes, [1913] NUC BMC. London: Methuen, 1920 BMC.
She is thirty six, divorced, devoted to her seventeen year

old son, a woman who gets things done, who knows how to take care of herself, a travelling saleswoman for petticoats, so good at her job that she becomes secretary of the firm.

FERGUSON, V. MUNRO.*

1030 MUSIC HATH CHARMS: A NOVEL. BY V. MUNRO FERGUSON ("V."). New York: Harper, 1894 NUC.

Victoria, modern and candid, is a famous singer. She and Dawnay struggle for power in their relationship. The last chapter is morbid and sensational.

FERRUGGIA, GEMMA. 1868-1930.

1031 WOMAN'S FOLLY. London: Heinemann, 1895 BMC. (Tr. by E. Zimmern.)

Introduction by Gosse: "leaves George Egerton and Sarah Grand panting far behind." "Characters are sadly lacking in imaginative justice towards man."

FESSENDEN, LAURA CANFIELD SPENCER (DAYTON). D. 1924. United States.

1032 BONNIE MACKIRBY: AN INTERNATIONAL EPISODE. Chicago: Rand, McNally, [c1898] NUC.

She at mother's request has married an impecunious Englishman. Realizes how bad marriage is after birth of children, but endures husband's brutality for their sake. He is addicted to arsenic and overdoses on it. She is accused of his murder and sentenced to life imprisonment.

FETHERSTONHAUGH, V.*

1033 MRS. JIM BAKER AND FROSTS OF JUNE. London: Chapman and Hall, 1899 BMC.

Mrs. Jim was raised as much like a boy as possible for the purpose of making her completely unsuitable for women's natural duties and, therefore, unmarriageable. By this upbringing, she is not "therefore rendered more perverse than the young woman of fiction whose mission is to make her husband miserable, and then repent and reform. This particular young woman's adventures are very brightly written." Set in Canadian Northwest.

FIASTRI, VIRGINIA GUICCIARDI. B. 1864. Italy.

1034   FROM OPPOSITE SHORES. London: M. Goschen, 1914 BMC NUC. (Tr. by Helene Antonelli.)

Dorinda, a devoutly religious Italian widow, sends her lover away because his socialist beliefs are in conflict with the church. She struggles as a washerwoman to educate her daughter at the convent. When she loses her daughter to the church, she gradually realizes she has been tricked by the priests and nuns.

FIELD, CHRISTINE. See LAURENCE, FRANCES ELSIE (FRY).

FIELD, LOUISE MAUNSELL. United States.

1035   THE LITTLE GODS LAUGH; A NOVEL. Boston: Little, Brown, 1917 BMC NUC.

Nita Wynne's life is one long period of disillusionment. First she discovers the true character of the man she loves and idolizes. Then she learns what New York society is really like and what the business world is like at its core. When she falls in love again, it is with a married man, and Nita must wait for him to be divorced.

FIFIELD, SALOME (HOCKING).

1036   BELINDA THE BACKWARD: A ROMANCE OF MODERN IDEALISM. BY SALOME HOCKING. London: A.C. Fifield, 1905 BMC NUC.

Belinda leaves home to join a settlement in which the simple life is practiced.

FIFINE [pseud.].*

1037   MAMZELLE GRANDMERE: A FRIVOLITY. BY FIFINE. London: Lawrence and Bullen, 1899 BMC NUC.

She is an adult young woman of at least 50 who is a

serious rival of her beautiful granddaughter. Two weddings at the end.

FINDLATER, JANE HELEN. 1866-1946. United Kingdom.

1038   THE LADDER TO THE STARS. London: Methuen, 1906 BMC. New York: D. Appleton, 1906 NUC.

Plain young woman from working class family becomes a journalist, concludes with a happy marriage.

FINDLATER, MARY. 1865-1946. United Kingdom.

1039   BETTY MUSGRAVE. London: Methuen, 1899 BMC. New York: E. P. Dutton, 1913 NUC.

Delicate character study of Mrs. Musgrave who wastes the family's resources to maintain her drinking habit. Betty and her mother move to a Bloomsbury boarding house in London where Betty cares for her mother.

1040   A BLIND BIRD'S NEST. London: Methuen, 1907 NUC BMC.

Agnes Sorel learns that when she was a small child her father went to prison for shooting the man who dishonored her sister Clare. She almost marries, but shame of her father prevents her. She becomes a woman's companion, later nurses her ill father, and wins her way to prosperity and happiness in this novel of strong characterization.

1041   A NARROW WAY. London: Methuen, 1901 BMC NUC. New York: E. P. Dutton, [n.d.] NUC.

Study of a new feminine type, a woman who is "impatient of calf love" and who is sanely and completely in control of her feelings.

1042   OVER THE HILLS. London: Methuen, 1897 BMC. New York: Dodd, Mead, 1897 NUC.

Six well contrasted women of a Scottish village, among them: Jane Anne—an admirable portrait of a gentle "old maid"; Dinah Jemington, a strong self reliant woman who elopes in an emigrant ship; and Annie Fraser, a young woman absolutely without scruples who jilts her fiance for his rival and lets her fiance go to prison for forgery she committed.

1043 THE ROSE OF JOY. New York: McClure, Phillips, 1903 NUC. London: Methuen, 1903 BMC.

Susan is a "plain" woman who doesn't dress well. In her marriage of convenience, she's totally unhappy. She leaves her selfish husband, refuses another proposal of marriage, preferring the single life. Free, she devotes herself to painting and is happy.

1044 TENTS OF A NIGHT. London: Smith, Elder, 1914 BMC. New York: E. P. Dutton, [1914] NUC.

Anne, a "self-centered young woman" who has found falling in love disappointing, is discontent and critical of life. Her awakening is a result of falling out of love and a realization she has all she needs to be happy. Barbara, ten years younger than Anne, is a flapper and an independent new spirit.

FINDLAY, JESSIE PATRICK.

1045 MICHAEL LAMONT, SCHOOLMASTER. London: Hodder & Stoughton, 1893 BMC.

"Phyllis Winter, the minister's daughter, with her keenness of perception and her pathetic longing for a career withheld from her by the narrow surroundings of her home, and the more insuperable obstacle of her bodily weakness, is a more complex and more interesting study" than that of Michael Lamont.

1046 NORMAN REID, M.A. New York: Hunt and Eaton, [1891] NUC. Edinburgh: Oliphant, Anderson and Ferrier, [1898] BMC.

Heroine is an artist who rejects the hero because she loves her work. The story concerns the troubles she has in pursuing her career and he in his career as a clergyman. Eventually they marry.

FINNEMORE, EMILY PEARSON.

1047   FATE'S HANDICAPS. London: Digby, Long, 1904 BMC.

Heroine through early training in cricket has lost the merely feminine attributes of vanity and self love. Becomes a professional carrier.

1048   TALLY. London: Hurst and Blackett, 1904 BMC.

Man and woman trapped in loveless marriages. The man accidentally kills her husband; she lets him go to the gallows rather than see the other woman keep him. Tragedy.

FISHER, DOROTHEA FRANCES (CANFIELD). 1879-1958. United States.

1049   THE SQUIRREL-CAGE. BY DOROTHY CANFIELD. New York: H. Holt, 1912 BMC NUC.

Wife is imprisoned by social conventions and ambitions of husband. When she becomes a widow, she tries to raise her children in a different way.

1050   UNDERSTOOD BETSY. BY DOROTHY CANFIELD. New York: Holt, 1917 NUC. London: Constable, 1922 BMC.

She was pampered by her aunt—never allowed to think things through for herself. Once she moves to Putney farm, she is expected to work by herself and think for herself. Suggests certain ideas about child rearing.

FISHER, DOROTHEA FRANCES (CANFIELD), jt. au. See CLEGHORN, SARAH NORCLIFFE AND DOROTHEA FRANCES (CANFIELD) FISHER.

FISHER, MARY. B. 1858. United States.

1051   KIRSTIE. BY M. F. New York: T. Y. Crowell, [1912] NUC.

Nurse in love with M.D. whose wife she has been engaged to care for; nurse sickens and dies.

FITZGERALD, ENA.

1052   AND THE STARS FOUGHT; A ROMANCE. London: Greening, 1912 BMC.

Murderer leaves his wife and daughter to join the priesthood. Mother and daughter are devoted, the latter a successful sculptor. Then mother meets father, sees that he has not expiated his sin and she loses faith in the church. At the same time the daughter loses her talent, apparently because of the symbiotic relationship of mother and daughter.

FITZGERALD, MENIE MURIEL (DOWIE) NORMAN. 1866-1945. United Kingdom.

1053   THE CROOK OF THE BOUGH. BY MENIE MURIEL DOWIE. London: Methuen, 1898 BMC. New York: Scribner, 1898 NUC.

Satire on the unemancipated young woman. Islay Netherdale, a dowdily dressed typewriter, travels to the Near East where she meets Captain Hassan. He mistakes her plainness for intelligence and usefulness and, tired of women who are merely ornaments, falls in love with her. As a result of the meeting, however, Islay begins to view her body as the "airy shining temple of her hopes" and becomes engrossed in feminine finery. When Captain Hassan meets her again, she is in her ornamental phase, and he abandons his suit.

1054   GALLIA. BY MENIE MURIEL DOWIE. London: Methuen, 1895 BMC. Philadelphia: J. B. Lippincott, 1895 NUC.

Gallia is a thoroughly independent, unconventional modern young woman "weighted down" with knowledge of all kinds. She has lived much by herself, thought for herself, has formed strong ideals, and lives by them. She has studied at Oxford and is a prodigious reader. "Femininity," we are informed, "reached her late, was resented fiercely, and fought and subdued promptly." She falls in love with a decadent Oxford fellow who is befuddled by her straightforward admission of love. She eventually falls out of love with him, but marries him, as she candidly explains to him, in order to have a father for her children. For Gallia has determined that love and marriage are separate. With her friends Miss Essex and Miss Janison, she discusses bold and forbidden subjects. The author "has gone further in sheer audacity of treatment of the sexual relations and sexual feelings of men and women than any woman before."

1055   A GIRL IN THE KARPATHIANS. BY MENIE MURIEL DOWIE. New York: Cassell, [1891] NUC. London: G. Philip, 1891 BMC.

Young Scottish woman of about 24 narrates her own story. She rides, swims, shoots, speaks French and German, drinks beer and smokes, and dresses like a man in order to travel more comfortably through East Galacia, Russia, Poland, Hungary and Austria. She travels alone, studies the people, and makes keen observations on what she sees.

1056   LOVE AND HIS MASK. BY MENIE MURIEL DOWIE. London: W. Heinemann, 1901 NUC BMC.

Leslie is a widow of 27, a modern wealthy complex woman who wants everything. She writes straightforward letters to a man pouring out the whole of her mind. She keeps her friendship with this man though she eventually marries another.

FLANDRAU, GRACE C. (HODGSON). D. 1971. United States.

1057   COUSIN JULIA. New York and London: D. Appleton, 1917 BMC NUC.

She is the wife of an ambitious businessman and is totally convinced that social success is all that matters. She is so determined to arrange wealthy marriages for her two daughters and she so dominates her daughter Virginia, particularly, that in the end Virginia believes she is doing exactly what she wants but is actually following her mother's plan.

FLANEUSE [pseud.].*

1058 DOUBLY TIED. A FARCE. BY FLANEUSE. London: Greening, [1913] BMC NUC.

Author states that she is intentionally funny, that we are meant to laugh at the audacious ex-barmaid Molly and her successful bigamy to a millionaire while her husband serves as the millionaires's valet and becomes his heir.

FLEMING, ALICE MACDONALD (KIPLING). B. 1868. United Kingdom.

1059 A PINCH-BECK GODDESS. BY MRS. J. M. FLEMING. London: Heinemann, 1897 BMC. New York: D. Appleton, 1897 NUC.

Penniless Madeline Norton is sent to India to visit a match-making matron in the hopes that she will find a husband. But when she is ignored, she rebels and returns to England where she unexpectedly inherits a fortune. She returns to India, but this time as Lilian Miles, a dashing, elegant, wigged widow. Now that she has a fortune, the men flock around, and Lilian amuses herself by having revenge on several for her past suffering. In the end she falls in love with one. Comedy.

FLEMING, MRS. J. M. See FLEMING, ALICE MACDONALD (KIPLING).

FLEMMING, HARFORD. See MACCLELLAN, HARRIET (HARE).

FLETCHER, MARGARET.

1060 THE FUGITIVES. London and New York: Longmans, Green, 1912 BMC NUC.

Three women art students in Paris. One, on the brink of success, is pulled by her family back into domestic servitude.

FLINT, ANNIE AUSTIN. B. 1866. United States.

1061 THE BREAKING POINT. New York: Broadway, 1915 NUC.

Tragedy of Rose Kreppel married to a man who is not the man she married. Her husband has a split personality.

1062 A GIRL OF IDEAS. London: Ward, Lock, 1903 BMC. New York: C. Scribner's Sons, 1903 NUC.

A college graduate and writer makes a great success of a unique business. From her office on Broadway, she sells ideas to authors. The novel describes her work with different kinds of writers as well as her close friendship with a woman. Always true to herself, intellectual, and noble, she's full of surprises right up to her triumphant exit.

FLOWERDEW [pseud.].*

1063 THE SEVENTH POSTCARD. BY FLOWERDEW. London: Greening, 1914 BMC.

The heroine, a successful writer of detective stories, sets out to expose the League of Personal Safety, a society that punishes by death any motorist who, though acquitted in court, has caused death.

FLOYD, ANNA.

1064 THE ROUGH ROAD TO THE STARS. London: T. W. Laurie, [1920] BMC.

The story of a woman who is driven to the streets to support her illegitimate child.

FOAKES, GERTRUDE M. FOXE.

1065 THE POOL OF GOLD. London: G. Allen and Unwin, 1915 BMC.

Vera Forwood is restless living at home near Moscow with her widowed mother and her sister. She marries a teacher who offers to train her voice and make her famous. Restless again, she runs off to England with an English composer. In the end she returns to Russia, fame, and her husband. All is forgiven.

FOLDAIROLLES, CLAIRE [pseud.].*

1066 PRIVATE LETTERS OF A FRENCH WOMAN. BY MADEMOISELLE CLAIRE FOLDAIROLLES (THE FRENCH GOVERNESS). New York: G. W. Dillingham, 1895 NUC.

The letters concern such subjects as "will the kiss become obsolete," "the woman's man," "professional love makers," and "elimination of the old maid from American society."

FOLEY, KATHLEEN P. (EMMETT).

1067 A GIRL SOLDIER. London: F. V. White, 1903 BMC.

Bert fights in the Boer War and keeps her unconventional ways in London society.

1068 THE SILVER ZONE: A HINDU NOVEL. London: J. Murray, 1908 BMC.

A portrayal of Hindu married life. "One sees how the marriage laws and customs and superstitious traditions decide the destinies of the women, weigh on their characters and imagination, and determine their love of or indifference to their children."

FOLKARD, MARY H.

1069 A SINLESS SINNER: A NOVEL. BY MARY H. TENNYSON. London: J. Macqueen, 1897 BMC.

A young girl, of wretchedly poor parents, poisons her sister. Her dreary life in a reformatory where she is tortured.

FOOTE, MARY (HALLOCK). 1847-1938. United States.

1070 EDITH BONHAM. Boston: Houghton Mifflin, 1917 NUC.

Strong bond between two women. Edith tells the story of her friendship with Nanny Aylesford in art school, Nanny's marriage, and her travels with her artist father.

Edith goes to Nanny to help her with her children but finds her dead. Edith raises Nanny's children and eventually marries Nanny's widower.

1071 THE GROUND-SWELL. Boston: Houghton Mifflin, 1919 NUC.

Katherine plans to marry Spanish-American hero with parental approval, but she dies of grippe in France on war duty just as Tony has spent his fortune on a home for her.

FORBES, ANNABELLA (KEITH). D. 1922. United Kingdom.

1072 HELENA; A NOVEL. BY MRS. H. O. FORBES. Edinburgh and London: W. Blackwood, 1905 BMC NUC.

Heroine is a "half caste" Maori.

FORBES, ETHEL M.

1073 A DAUGHTER OF THE DEMOCRACY. London: Cassell, 1911 BMC.

Betty is first a governess, then a social worker in the slums along with Aileen. They and their friends live like the poor, but are very idealistic. "Deals with present unrest in the minds of the modern woman and the desire to break from the old conventional life."

FORBES, EVELINE LOUISA MITCHELL (FARWELL). 1866-1924. United Kingdom.

1074 BLIGHT. London: Osgood, McIlvaine, 1897 BMC.

Author writes with "wide sympathies" about a woman who wants desperately to love and be loved, but has no way to show or inspire love. First as a governess she makes people uncomfortable, and then as Lady Easton she makes her children miserable and drives her husband to his grave.

1075 A GENTLEMAN. London: J. Murray, 1900 BMC.

Dressmaker struggles so son shall live as gentleman. He is unaware of her occupation, thinks she writes. Focus is on his travels; he is oblivious to her sacrifice.

1076   ,NAMELESS; A NOVEL. London: J. Murray, 1909 BMC.
Cecil Grey is a genius and she is a famous authoress. Part
of the novel involves a tragic marriage.

1077   VANE ROYAL. London: J. Long, 1908 BMC.
A sweet gentle woman married to an impossibly selfish
husband runs away with another man; tragedy results and
she dies.

FORBES, HELEN EMILY (CRAVEN). B. 1874.

1078   HIS EMINENCE; A STORY OF THE LAST CENTURY.
London: E. Nash, 1904 BMC.
Historical, struggle for power between cardinal and
duchess widow.

FORBES, LADY ANGELA. See ERSKINE, ANGELA SELINA BLANCHE (FORBES) SAINT CLAIR.

FORBES, MRS. H. O. See FORBES, ANNABELLA (KEITH).

FORD, ISABELLA O.

1079   ON THE THRESHHOLD. London: Arnold, 1895 NUC.
The entrance to womanhood of Kitty and Lucretia, "their
apprehension of the unknown sorrows and degradation of
existence, especially of the obscure lives of wandering
Londoners."

FORD, MARY HANFORD (FINNEY). B. 1856. United States.

1080   OTTO'S INSPIRATION. Chicago: S. C. Griggs, 1895
NUC BMC.
A wife and her husband devote their lives to the helpless.

1081   WHICH WINS? A STORY OF SOCIAL CONDITIONS.
Boston: Lee & Shephard, 1891 BMC NUC.
Attacks monopolies and all capitalist power and calls for
labor reform. Dedicated to the Farmer's Alliance, a third

political party that will give wives a partnership in their husbands' property and control of their own.

FORD, MAY.

1082 THE REVOKE OF JEAN RAYMOND. London: S. Swift, 1911 BMC.

Jean Gretton, independent, agnostic, decides to leave her husband because he bores her to death with talk of religion, Wordsworth and vivisection. She takes her child and goes to live with her socialist friend Mary Margetson with whom she is happy. There's a reconciliation at her husband's deathbed, and a former admirer nearby. Author claims all our sympathy for Jean.

FORD, PENELOPE.

1083 A PAGE IN A MAN'S HISTORY. London: J. Long, 1913 BMC.

That page concerns a wayward, selfish, rich young woman who was first a tomboy then a "wayward society belle" with a genius for dancing. She is loved by the man, but he refuses to marry her for fear marriage will hurt his career. She commits suicide. Her various states of mind are depicted with great insight.

FORRESTER, MRS. See BRIDGES, MRS. COLONEL.

FORSYTH, JEAN. See MACILWRAITH, JEAN NEWTON.

FOSDICK, GERTRUDE CHRISTIAN. United States.

1084 OUT OF BOHEMIA: A STORY OF PARIS STUDENT LIFE. New York: G. H. Richmond, 1894 NUC.

Heroine studies art in Paris, has adventures, but comes out unscathed.

FOSTER, BERTHA CLEMENTIA.

1085   THE HOUSE ON THE MINE. London: H. J. Drane,
        [1903] BMC.
        Young woman is "a vixen." She survives financial
        problems to become an immensely successful novelist.

FOSTER, FRANCES G. KNOWLES.

1086   JEHANNE OF THE GOLDEN LIPS. New York: J. Lane,
        1910 NUC. London: Mills & Boon, 1910 BMC.
        Queen Jehanne is "beautiful, wise, and a genius in
        government" in this historical romance.

FOSTER, MILDRED.

1087   A ROSE AMIDST SCOTCH THISTLES. London: J.
        Ouseley, [1912] BMC.
        The experiences of a nurse.

FOTHERGILL, CAROLINE. United Kingdom.

1088   THE COMEDY OF CECILIA; OR, AN HONOURABLE
        MAN. London: A. and C. Black, 1895 BMC NUC.
        "The novel of the 'new woman' with a vengeance." Cecilia
        must marry a medieval dullard she detests because he is
        her brother's choice, and she must marry with her
        brother's permission to secure her independent fortune.
        First she runs off to London determined to be free and to
        have a career. Then she goes through with the marriage
        but informs the groom on her wedding day that having
        secured her fortune, she means to lead an independent life
        and have a good time at it.

FOTHERGILL, JESSIE. 1851-1891. United Kingdom.

1089   ORIOLES' DAUGHTER. New York: Tait, [c1892] NUC.
        London: W. Heinemann, 1893 BMC.
        The author attacks the custom of pressing young women
        to marry for money. Fulvia is forced to marry a vulgar
        and repulsive man by her mother. She endures him for
        five years but then leaves him to live with Signor Orioles.

She is his illegitimate daughter.

FOWLER, EDITH HENRIETTA. See HAMILTON, EDITH HENRIETTA (FOWLER).

FOWLER, ELLEN THORNEYCROFT. See FELKIN, ELLEN THORNEYCROFT (FOWLER).

FOX, ALICE THEODORA (RAIKES) WILSON. B. 1863. United Kingdom.

1090   A REGULAR MADAM. London: Macmillan, 1912 BMC NUC.

Lady Barbara is "a little too mannish." She shoots a highwayman with his own pistol, runs off to Canada to search for her brother, finds him and a lover. Many adventures among the Indians. Time: close of 18th century. For girls.

FOX, MARION INEZ DOUGLAS (WARD). B. 1885. United Kingdom.

1091   THE BOUNTIFUL HOUR. London and New York: J. Lane, 1912 BMC NUC.

A young woman of the 18th century who thinks for herself has run away from home several times and is independent of her father.

FRANCIS, C. E. [pseud.].*

1092   EVERY DAY'S NEWS. BY C. E. FRANCIS. New York: G. P. Putnam, 1895 NUC. London: T. F. Unwin, 1895 BMC NUC.

A new woman writes and publishes rude stories that embarrass her husband—a pure-minded novelist. Variant on Elizabeth Robins' "George Mandeville's Husband."

FRANCIS, J.*

1093   ARCHIE CAREW. London: Ward and Downey, 1892
        BMC.
        When young wife discovers husband has not properly
        married her because he has not wanted family and friends
        to know he has married a farmer's daughter, she leaves
        him.

FRANCIS, M. E. See BLUNDELL, MARY E. (SWEETMAN).

FRANKAU, JULIA (DAVIS). 1864-1916. United Kingdom.

1094   BACCARAT. A NOVEL. BY FRANK DANBY. London:
        W. Heinemann, 1904 BMC. Philadelphia & London: J.B.
        Lippincott, 1904 NUC.
        The sympathetic story of a wife with a passion for
        gambling who leaves her husband and children for a
        croupier. Husband forgives her. The author believes that
        sexual passion is the most powerful force in men and
        women, remarks one reviewer.

1095   CONCERT PITCH. BY FRANK DANBY. London:
        Hutchinson, 1913 BMC NUC. New York: Macmillan, 1913
        NUC.
        Wealthy Manuella Wagner is only eighteen when she
        elopes with a musical genius. She marries primarily to
        avoid her stepmother's efforts to make a socially brilliant
        marriage for her. She does not love her husband, and on
        the first day of marriage, she learns she will be a
        subordinate to this man and his career. He later deserts
        her for an opera soprano and is shot by the singer's
        husband.

1096   THE HEART OF A CHILD. BEING PASSAGES FROM
        THE EARLY LIFE OF SALLY SNAPE, LADY
        KIDDERMINSTER. BY FRANK DANBY. London:
        Hutchinson, 1908 NUC BMC. New York: Macmillan,
        [c1908] NUC.
        Sally goes on the stage and becomes a successful dancer.
        One reviewer says that the author's thesis is that a woman
        can have a career on stage without losing her honor.

Another reviewer feels that "Sally owed her safety to the combination of her sexlessness and stupidity, one of which is so often closely related to the other."

1097   AN INCOMPLETE ETONIAN. BY FRANK DANBY. London: W. Heinemann, 1909 NUC BMC.

Vanessa Randall is a famous novelist just as her father was and just as she would have her son be. She is proud of her fame and wants the same for Sebastian. She despises her businessman husband and his work and is very jealous that her son and husband share so much. When her son leaves his studies to join his father's business, Vanessa is heartbroken and leaves. Study of her bitter disappointment in her son's choice of career and his marriage.

1098   JOSEPH IN JEOPARDY. BY FRANK DANBY. New York: Macmillan, 1912 NUC. London: Methuen, 1912 BMC.

The study of an unhappy marriage with a happy ending. Joseph is tempted by another woman; Mabel his wife develops into an interesting woman. (Danby defends fidelity in marriage and is anti-suffrage in this novel, note reviewers.)

1099   LET THE ROOF FALL IN. BY FRANK DANBY. New York: D. Appleton, 1910 NUC. London: Hutchinson, 1910 BMC.

Rosaleen O'Daly is seduced by a young Lord who is killed. To his cousin falls the "burden of shouldering Ranmore's sin against the girl."

1100   PIGS IN CLOVER. BY FRANK DANBY. London: W. Heinemann, 1903 BMC. Philadelphia: J. B. Lippincott, 1903 NUC.

The author paints a huge canvas, but central is the psychological study, "the subtle half-tones" of Joan's character. Joan is a novelist with a "clear virile brain." Estranged from her husband, she's lonely when she meets Louis. Their passionate affair is described with "merciless frankness." But then she learns he really wants the farm she will inherit when her husband dies. Refusing him outright, she gives up the farm and leaves—for fear her passion may make her give in. When she meets him months later, she's in control and resists him.

1101 TWILIGHT. BY FRANK DANBY. New York: Dodd, Mead, 1916 NUC. London: Hutchinson, 1916 BMC.

Woman novelist retires to house in London, ill with neuritis. Study first of her illness, then of her morphia dreams in which she learns the story of the previous occupant, a woman novelist. The doctor who is attending her continues to give her morphia because he loved the dead woman, is insane and wants to hear more about her through this woman's dreams. She becomes aware of his intent as he begins to confuse her with the dead woman.

FRASER, AGNES. 1859-1944. United Kingdom.

1102 RELICS. BY FRANCES MACNAB. London: W. Heinemann, 1893 BMC. New York: D. Appleton, 1893 NUC.

Reminiscenses of an elderly woman who marries late in life.

FRASER, AUGUSTA ZELIA (WEBB). D. 1925.

1103 LUCILLA: AN EXPERIMENT. BY ALICE SPINNER. London: K. Paul, Trench, Trubner, 1895 BMC NUC.

Lucilla St. John leaves England for San Jose to teach music to black girls in Grove Hill College where Miss Gale is the principal. Lucilla, not happy or successful at her work, gives it up to marry a fairly wealthy "half-breed." Though she is not an intelligent person nor an attractive character, she is made fully sympathetic for the social penalties that fall on a woman reckless enough to make such a marriage. She experiences all the evils of the prejudices of whites—beginning with the clergy who pretend illness when she wants to marry—the contempt and ostracism. The reverse situation is shown in cultured, refined Liris Morales, a Creole woman, "captured" by an English captain but saved by another Creole woman.

FRASER, MARY (CRAWFORD). 1851-1922. United Kingdom.

1104 A LITTLE GREY SHEEP; A NOVEL. Philadelphia: J. B. Lippincott, 1901 NUC. London: Hutchinson, 1901 BMC.

Nina is a well built, athletic woman totally without a conscience. This "almost violently modern story" concerns "the loves and emotions of a partly fashionable, partly artistic group rusticating on the banks of the river of pleasure," where virtue is made narrow and conventional.

1105 A MAID OF JAPAN. BY MRS. HUGH FRASER. New York: H. Holt, 1905 NUC.

Idyllic Madame Butterfly situation.

1106 PALLADIA. BY MRS. HUGH FRASER. London: 1896 BMC. New York and London: Macmillan, 1896 NUC BMC.

The daughter of an unwed gypsy, she is forced to marry a duke. They are wretched.

1107 THE SPLENDID PORSENNA. BY MRS. HUGH FRASER. London: Hutchinson, 1899 BMC. Philadelphia: J. B. Lippincott, 1900 NUC.

Modern Roman society. Porsenna is a wicked count who marries an English woman and bullies her. He tries "daggers, poison, pistols, and finally drops her into the vault." In the end he is killed in a duel; she marries an old friend.

FRASER, MRS. HUGH. See FRASER, MARY (CRAWFORD).

FREEMAN, MARY ELEANOR (WILKINS). 1852-1930. United States.

1108 THE BUTTERFLY HOUSE. New York: Dodd, Mead, 1912 NUC.

Bored woman in suburban commuting district of New York tries to do something worthwhile. She is secretly writing successful novels. Cranford-like.

1109 BY THE LIGHT OF THE SOUL; A NOVEL. New York and London: Harper, 1906 BMC NUC.

Maria sets out to find her impetuous half-sister who she fears is lost. She is forced to be away overnight with two friends, one a young man. Although they are both under 20, they are persuaded to marry to protect her reputation. She later becomes a teacher.

1110 THE JAMESONS. BY MARY E. WILKINS. New York and London: Doubleday, McClure, 1899 BMC NUC.

Mrs. Jameson, nervous, dyspeptic, "an emancipated New Yorker, the maitresse femme of a meek and unsuccessful merchant." The two descend on a small New England village, introduce Ibsen to the community, and transform it with their modern ideas of hygiene, dress, literature, etc. Humorous.

1111 JANE FIELD: A NOVEL. BY MARY E. WILKINS. London: Osgood & McIlvaine, 1892 BMC. New York: Harper, 1893 NUC.

Concerns older women—rough, strong, uneducated. Jane is a middle-aged widow with a school-teacher daughter Lois. The two are half-starved on what they earn, and Lois is sick from walking great distances in the sun to teach. When Jane gets a chance to impersonate her sister to gain an inheritance, she takes it, but the results are Lois' scorn when she learns of the deceit and Jane's overpowering sense of guilt. At the end Jane regains her sense, and Lois, her health.

1112 MADELON: A NOVEL. BY MARY E. WILKINS. New York: Harper, 1896 NUC. London: Osgood, 1896 BMC.

Passionate Madelon loves fickle Burr, is loved by him and Lot. In a burst of anger at a dance she stabs Burr but gets Lot by mistake. Burr is accused of the crime, no one believing Madelon's self-accusations. Lot recovers and saves Burr by stating that he stabbed himself, in exchange for Madelon's consenting to marry him. He releases her on the eve of their marriage; she goes back to Burr, but the crime still pursues them and Lot finally kills himself.

1113 PEMBROKE; A NOVEL. BY MARY E. WILKINS. London: Osgood, McIlvaine, 1894 BMC. New York: Harper, [c1894] NUC.

Characters with an incapacity for willing themselves to do what they want to do. Charlotte and Barney are kept apart by a quarrel between Barney and her father. Deborah, a sternly religious woman, kills her child after a doctor's warning not to rod him. Her daughter "falls" and for years after her marriage, lives in memory of her shame.

1114 THE PORTION OF LABOR. BY MARY E. WILKINS. New York and London: Harper, 1901 BMC NUC.

The novel studies Ellen's life—her growth from childhood. She's an independent and intelligent woman. Her interest in factory workers takes her very far from "the circle of home." She's a strike-leader. Ellen represents "the ideal of womanhood finding its highest recompense in work."

1115 THE SHOULDERS OF ATLAS; A NOVEL. New York and London: Harper, 1908 BMC NUC.

The study of the conscience of a plain New England woman who with her husband comes into the possession of a fortune which she doesn't believe is rightfully hers. Another woman attempts to poison two women of whom she is jealous.

FRENCH, ALICE. 1850-1934. United States.

1116 THE MAN OF THE HOUR. BY OCTAVE THANET. Indianapolis: Bobbs-Merrill, [c1905] NUC BMC.

A Russian princess with anarchistic views marries an American to get out of Russia. The two are completely incompatible; their child makes things worse. They compete for the child's affection, and the boy grows up torn between his parents and their political views. The woman leaves her husband; the son apparently chooses his father's politics.

FRENCH, ANNE RICHMOND (WARNER). 1869-1913. United States.

1117 IN A MYSTERIOUS WAY. BY ANNE WARNER. Boston: Little, Brown, 1909 NUC.

A woman who is postmaster, storekeeper, and dressmaker has a voice in the affairs of the town.

1118 THE REJUVENATION OF AUNT MARY. BY ANNE WARNER. Boston: Little, Brown, 1905 NUC. London: Gay & Bird, 1907 BMC.

Deaf, eccentric "maiden lady," guardian of several children. Wild fun.

1119 SUSAN CLEGG AND A MAN IN THE HOUSE. BY ANNE WARNER. Boston: Little, Brown, 1907 NUC.

Susan is outspoken about men and the restrictions marriage puts on women. She attends a woman's political convention and makes caustic comments about the Democrats and Republicans.

1120 WHEN WOMAN PROPOSES. BY ANNE WARNER. Boston: Little, Brown, 1911 NUC.

Woman shown as energetic and resourceful, ready to cope with any and all situations: Nathalie Arundel, a young widow, spies a stranger at a reception, takes off her wedding ring and announces: "I don't want it any more because I am going to marry that man down there." She takes extraordinary measures to get this soldier who won't marry her because she's very rich. She spends millions, stops an army in its tracks when it is ordered out to stop a strike, gets laws passed to revolutionize conditions of labor and to raise soldiers' pay.

FROTHINGHAM, EUGENIA BROOKS. B. 1874. United States.

1121 THE TURN OF THE ROAD. Boston: Houghton Mifflin, 1901 NUC.

An opera singer, ambitious and self-reliant, "walks unscathed through a thousand dangers." She's devoted to her art. Year after year she rejects her suitor who chases her in Paris where she studies until he goes blind and she realizes that she now cares for him.

1122 THE WAY OF THE WIND. Boston: Houghton Mifflin, 1917 NUC. London: Constable, 1917 BMC.

Janet Eversly is single, attractive, past 30. She spends the summer with her friend Fanny Chilworth whose profligate half brother is a trial to Fanny and objectionable to Janet. But she falls in love with him, though she is eight years older and meets his ex-mistress. Before they marry, Janet insists he lead a life of abstinence and return to her cleansed and acceptable.

FRY, E. N. LEIGH. See LEFROY, ELLA NAPIER.

FRY, SHEILA KAYE (SMITH). 1887-1956. United Kingdom.

1123 ISLE OF THORNS. BY SHEILA KAYE SMITH. London: Constable, 1913 BMC NUC. New York: E.P. Dutton, [1924] NUC.

Picaresque novel of Sally Adiarne's life on the open road. She is an unsuccessful novelist and a self-proclaimed "gentleman tramp," very modern—with no idea of conventional morality, a gypsy who has had some ugly experiences such as stabbing her lover and who takes up with show people. Sympathetic portrayal.

1124 LITTLE ENGLAND. BY SHEILA KAYE SMITH. London: Nisbet, [1918] BMC NUC.

Non-conformity in Sussex people under the influence of the war. One of the daughters becomes a tram-conductor; the other is a teacher.

1125 SPELL LAND. THE STORY OF A SUSSEX FARM. BY SHEILA KAYE SMITH. London: G. Bell, 1910 BMC NUC. New York: E. P. Dutton, [1926] NUC.

Unhappy love affair, reminiscent of Jude the Obscure. Title refers to a farm, Claude is the central figure. As a boy he meets Emily (of a different class). She marries and eventually leaves her unfaithful husband. When she and Claude decide to live together, they are cut off by family and friends. The novel is a study of their struggle to live in isolation on a farm and the gradual breaking down of their relationship and subsequent tragedy.

1126 SUSSEX GORSE: THE STORY OF A FIGHT. BY SHEILA KAYE SMITH. New York: A.A. Knopf, 1916 NUC. London: Nisbet, [1916] BMC NUC.

A farmer marries for the sole purpose of having children. He "slowly murdered" his wife. His children rebel against his tyranny, his son becoming a criminal, his daughter a prostitute.

FULLER, ANNA. 1853-1916. United States.

1127 A LITERARY COURTSHIP UNDER THE AUSPICES OF PIKE'S PEAK. New York, London: G. P. Putnam's Sons, 1893 NUC BMC.

Several members of a men's club discuss why women authors use pseudonyms. All but one agree it is because of the double standard in literary criticism. The one tries to prove them wrong by issuing his novel under the name Lilian Leslie Lamb. Another Lilian Leslie Lamb begins a correspondence with him, and amusing incidents follow.

FULLER, CAROLINE MACOMBER. B. 1873. United States.

1128 BRUNHILDE'S PAYING GUEST. A STORY OF THE SOUTH TODAY. New York: Century, 1907 BMC NUC.

Three young women take in New Yorker as boarder; landlady and he quarrel continually. He falls for "this modern Brunhilde" who is over 30 and eight years his senior.

FULTON, MARY. United Kingdom.

1129 BLIGHT. London: Duckworth, 1919 BMC.

Illustrates the blight of sexual passion where there is no love. Eileen Redfern was engaged to the man; her sister

Elsie married him; and Grace Manners had an affair with the same man. No happy end. Also traces career of a typewriting heroine.

1130 THE PLOUGH. London: Duckworth, [1919] NUC BMC.
Patricia refuses to marry the aristocrat her parents choose for her, and is successful in avoiding the marriage with the help of her cousin Sally, a dope addict who loves the man and who commits suicide. Pat marries a different man who is later killed in the war. She finds happiness with her child and with other women who return to the land.

FURMAN, LUCY S. 1870-1958. United States.

1131 MOTHERING ON PERILOUS. New York: Macmillan, 1913 NUC BMC.
Young woman works in Kentucky settlement school, "acquires a family" of twelve boys.

FYFE, ETHEL DUFF.

1132 WRITTEN ON OUR FOREHEADS. London: Chapman and Hall, 1913 BMC.
Story in three parts: child-wife of nine and the Bengali homes of her father and husband; girl-widow in English home of Indian station; her life in a convent and her second marriage.

FYTCHE, M. AMELIA. Canada.

1133 KERCHIEFS TO HUNT SOULS. New York: F.T. Neely, 1897 NUC.
A young Canadian woman, Doris Pembroke, goes to Europe to study after teaching school for five years. There she meets a young widower who offers her marriage on the basis of his friendship and respect. But Doris refuses him because she wants love. In Paris, she is loved by an artist who nearly breaks her heart.

GALE, ZONA. 1874-1938. United States.

1134   A DAUGHTER OF THE MORNING. Indianapolis: Bobbs-
       Merrill, [c1917] NUC BMC.
       Cosma Wakeley, an illiterate country girl, tells her own
       story, beginning with incoherent stammerings. She sees the
       tyranny around her and is determined to better her life,
       inspired by a man who understands the revolt of modern
       women against "the drudgery which love sometimes makes
       so sweet." She breaks with her country sweetheart and
       leaves the farm taking with her a woman, wife of a
       drunken brute, and the woman's child. She becomes
       educated and takes a job as secretary with the man who
       helped inspire her to improve her life. Eventually she
       marries this man, but refuses to be absorbed in
       housework. She convinces him that she is not a mother-
       woman, that instead she wants to devote her life to
       making the whole world right for all children.

1135   FRIENDSHIP VILLAGE. New York: Macmillan, 1908
       BMC NUC.
       An American Cranford.

1136   HEART'S KINDRED. New York: Macmillan, 1915 NUC
       BMC.
       Anti-war novel dedicated to those people who obey the
       commandment "Thou shall not kill." Author believes war
       is organized murder. Women from warring and neutral
       countries meet in Washington to demand that war be
       abolished. Parts of speeches from a real women's peace
       conference are included.

1137   MISS LULU BETT. New York and London: D. Appleton,
       1920 BMC NUC.
       Sympathetic portrait of a spinster who is the "beast of
       burden" in her sister and brother-in-law's household. Her
       sister's highest ambition is to make herself the mental and
       moral jellyfish that is her husband's ideal of a wife. She is
       treated by them as a nonentity. When the husband's well-
       travelled brother visits and treats her as a person, she sees

him as her only opportunity. She marries him, only to discover on their honeymoon that he already has a wife.

1138 MOTHERS TO MEN. New York: Macmillan, 1911 BMC NUC.

A young woman adopts an orphan, an action which causes the breaking of her engagement. Later she marries a professor who is devoted to social work.

1139 NEIGHBORHOOD STORIES. New York: Macmillan, 1914 BMC NUC.

An elderly woman, a prophet, creates a utopian communal village where there are no more social problems. One memorable scene describes her strong feelings when she views women marching and her inspiration to join the parade.

1140 WHEN I WAS A LITTLE GIRL. New York: Macmillan, 1913 BMC NUC.

A series of detached scenes taken from a young girl's life describing her feelings and her fantasies.

GARDENER, HELEN HAMILTON (CHENOWETH). 1853-1925. United States.

1141 PRAY YOU, SIR, WHOSE DAUGHTER? Boston, Mass.: Arena, 1892 NUC.

Author advocates political and intellectual freedom for women, introduces her novel by stating that marriage and maternity are incidental to woman's existence. The heroine, a college graduate, fights against holding a position of dependence in her father's household, a position to which her mother has become resigned.

GARDINER, RUTH (KIMBALL). 1872-1924. United States.

1142 THE HEART OF A GIRL. New York: A.S. Barnes, 1905 NUC BMC.

Home is scarcely a value to Margaret. She's aloof from her family, utterly secretive toward her mother and sister.

She's not a "nice girl." Boys have a place in her life unthought of by her mother. She defies teachers and God, for goodness has no appeal to her. Yet in this study of her friendships, disillusionments and self-realization, she is never censured by the author, but made noble and admirable.

1143 THE WORLD AND THE WOMAN. New York: A. S. Barnes, 1907 NUC.

Woman, deserted by her husband, teaches for 20 years. When her husband returns, she sends him about his business and goes to Washington to make her way with her daughter.

GARDNER, MRS. S. M. H. See GARDNER, SARAH M. H.

GARDNER, SARAH M. H.

1144 THE FORTUNES OF MARGARET WELD. BY MRS. S. M. H. GARDNER. Boston: Arena, 1894 NUC.

Artist at 28 loses the fortune left her by her father and attempts to earn her living, never hesitating to express her doubts of religion and to demand the same moral law for men and women.

GARVEY, INA.

1145 ROSAMOND'S STORY: A NOVEL. London: Ward and Downey, 1893 BMC.

A beautiful artistic girl, raised in the depressing, deadening atmosphere of London suburbs, marries a clerk and is miserably unhappy. When he becomes sick, she supports him and her children by going on the stage. She resists the advances of a noble, but her husband dies from the shock of believing she is unfaithful. She leaves her old life and marries the noble. Twenty years later, a widow and leader of society, she learns her stepson is about to seduce a young woman, warns the woman who consequently kills herself and who is none other than Stella, her own daughter. Sympathetic portrayal thoughout.

GASKELL, CATHERINE HENRIETTA (WALLOP) MILNES.
United Kingdom.

1146   A WOMAN'S SOUL. London: Hurst and Blackett, [1919]
NUC BMC.

Women run military hospital.

GATES, ELEANOR. 1875-1951. United States.

1147   THE BIOGRAPHY OF A PRAIRIE GIRL. New York:
Century, 1902 NUC. London: G. P. Putnam, 1904 BMC.

The life of a young woman in the Northwest who is
physically active (horse riding, cattle stampeding, etc.) and
"consumed with an anomalous craving for a college
education." No love interest.

1148   PHOEBE. New York: G. Sully, [c1919] BMC NUC.

Contemporary problems facing young people. Heroine is
fourteen when she is called from school to travel with her
mother because her parents have separated. Her loneliness,
her view of the adult world, her adjustment to a new
mother after her parents divorce.

1149   THE PLOW-WOMAN. New York: McClure, Phillips,
1906 NUC. London: Methuen, 1907 BMC.

Dallas Lancaster does a man's work at the plow. She is a
farmer in Dakota. Describes the tough rude life of
pioneering, Dallas's fear of losing the land, her love for
her childish sister and care of her tyrannical, bad
tempered crippled father who turned her suitor from the
door.

GAUNT, MARY. See MILLER, MARY ELIZA BAKEWELL
(GAUNT).

GAY, MAUDE (CLARK). 1876-1952. United States.

1150   PATHS CROSSING; A ROMANCE OF THE PLAINS.
Boston: C. M. Clark, 1908 NUC.

Two women teaching in an Indian school.

GEORGE, HELEN.

1151 THE CLAY'S REVENGE. London: Stephen Swift, 1912
BMC.
Bertha marries a man who loves her "with his brain"; after
a time the clay in her asserts itself. She then has a purely
physical relationship with a brute. Author is sympathetic
to her.

GERARD, D. See DE LONGGARDE, DOROTHEA (GERARD),
also DE LASZOWSKA, JANE EMILY (GERARD) AND
DOROTHEA (GERARD) LONGARD DE LONGGARDE.

GERARD, DOROTHEA. See DE LONGGARDE, DOROTHEA
(GERARD) LONGARD.

GERARD, E. See DE LASZOWSKA, JANE EMILY (GERARD)
AND DOROTHEA (GERARD) LONGARD DE
LONGGARDE.

GERARD, LOUISE. B. 1878. United Kingdom.

1152 DAYS OF PROBATION. London: Mills and Boon, 1917
BMC NUC.
Life of a probationer in a hospital—unattractive picture of
inside life of a large hospital, the hard daily routine,
severe discipline, the tyranny of sisters and nurses, and
the bad food. Also a love story.

1153 LIFE'S SHADOW SHOW. London: Mills and Boon, [1916]
BMC NUC.
Lorraine marries, discovers husband is already married.
She runs away but still sees him, has a child. The author
says, "she had done wrongly, and the fruit was joy."
Lorraine goes on to become a writer.

1154 THE SWIMMER. London: Mills and Boon, [1912] BMC
NUC.
The heroine is a genius from the lower class who struggles
in London as a writer.

1155   A TROPICAL TANGLE. London: Mills and Boon, [1911]
       BMC NUC.
       Nurse practices first in London, then in West Africa.

1156   THE WITCH-CHILD: A ROMANCE OF THE SWAMP.
       London: Mills and Boon, [1916] BMC.
       Luliya is stolen as a child by a group of West African
       witches. They send her to England to study medicine. She
       returns to Africa, but when she discovers that Blacks have
       killed her family, she goes back to England and founds a
       medical mission. The author believes that a "regiment of
       women" is the proper order of nature in Europe and
       Africa.

GERRY, MARGARITA (SPALDING). 1870-1939. United
States.

1157   HEART AND CHART. New York and London: Harper,
       1911 BMC NUC.
       Experiences of an American nurse related in first person.
       Somewhat sentimental at times.

1158   THE MASKS OF LOVE; A NOVEL. New York and
       London: Harper, 1914 BMC NUC.
       Marjorie wants the adventure of living life independently,
       and she goes on stage, living on her salary. Her
       relationship with the theater manager reveals to her that
       "there must be something of the primitive brute in the
       manly man, while (he) learns that a woman can be a real
       comrade."

GERSTENBERG, ALICE. B. 1885. United States.

1159   THE CONSCIENCE OF SARAH PLATT. Chicago: A. C.
       McClurg, 1915 NUC.
       "A woman's movement novel dealing with the expression
       of one's own individuality and the human being first and
       woman afterward ideas." Author poses the question "How
       far can a woman be herself untrammeled by the weight of
       her childhood's narrow training?" Sarah is middle-aged,

single, a primary school teacher in New York City, lonely, shy and out of touch. An old flame, now married, comes back into her life, takes her about, opens her mind to modern ideas. First they are "comrades"; then they fall in love and the end is tragic. "The author's purpose is evidently to make a preachment in favor of feminism, of the right of a woman to the expression of her own individuality...."

1160   UNQUENCHED   FIRE;   A   NOVEL.   Boston: Small, Maynard, [c1912] NUC. London: J. Long, 1913 BMC.

Young woman gives up comfortable life and social position for a career on stage. The story describes her struggles and her success. Her marriage is one of comradeship until she becomes a star; then personal problems arise.

GESTEFELD, URSULA NEWELL. 1845-1921. United States.

1161   THE   WOMAN   WHO   DARES.   New   York: Lovell, Gestefeld, [1892] NUC BMC.

The author "holds that women are responsible for their bondage to man, and specially points out to wives the duty of maintaining their individuality and asserting the rights of their womanhood in the marriage relation....Not suitable for the general novel reader."

GHOSAL, MRS. See GHOSAL, SRIMATI SVARNA KUMARI DEVI.

GHOSAL, SRIMATI SVARNA KUMARI DEVI. 1857-1932. India.

1162   THE FATAL GARLAND. BY MRS. GHOSAL (SRIMATI SVARNA KUMARI DEVI). S. K. Lahiri, 18— NUC. Calcutta: Kuntaline Press, [1910] BMC NUC.

The garland means betrothal. Skabti considers herself married when the prince throws the garland around her neck, but he takes the act lightly. He marries another;

unhappy, she sacrifices herself. The author deplores the inequality of men and women, notes reviewer.

1163   AN UNFINISHED SONG. BY MRS. GHOSAL (SRIMATI SVARNA KUMARI DEVI). London: T. W. Laurie, 1913 BMC. New York: Macmillan, [1913] NUC.
Insight into pyschological life of a Hindu girl, whose marriage is arranged by her father. (Mrs. Ghosal was a pioneer in the movement for education and emancipation of Indian women.)

GIBB, ELEANOR HUGHES.

1164   THE SOUL OF A VILLAIN. London: J. Long, 1905 BMC.
Minute study of a certain kind of mother love—an undisciplined affection that leads the mother to strange lengths. The mother—silent, reserved, strong-willed—and her bright irresponsible daughter Sara love each other enormously. For the mother, that love is a master-passion, a jealous protective instinct that makes her commit a sin to save her daughter.

GIBBONS, LOUISE ELISE.

1165   TRUTH: A NOVEL. BY LOUIS DE VILLENEUVE. New York: Published By Author, 1894 NUC.
Truth marries a man, has a son, and divorces. Then she marries her godfather, an aristocratic doctor. He publishes her books, defends her against her critics. But when he abuses his washerwoman, Truth dies in a sensational manner.

GIBBS, EDITH A.

1166   A DAUGHTER IN JUDGEMENT. London: J. Long, 1910 BMC.
Two women wronged by the same man. Their friendship.

GIBERNE, AGNES. 1845-1939. United Kingdom.

1167 MISS DEVEREAU, SPINSTER: A STUDY IN DEVELOPMENT. London: Longmans, 1893 BMC.
Character study of narrow-minded, talkative, confused, authoritarian woman in her late 40's.

1168 THE PRIDE O' THE MORNING. London: S. C. Brown, 1905 BMC.
Phyllys is raised in an atmosphere of repression. She refuses to live out the grey days she sees ahead of her. She leaves home, and a whole new life opens up for her that includes two men who love her.

GIBSON, L. S. See GIBSON, LETTICE SUSAN.

GIBSON, LETTICE SUSAN. B. 1859. United Kingdom.

1169 THE OAKUM PICKERS. BY L. S. GIBSON. London: Methuen, [1912] BMC NUC.
The stories of two women which illustrate the tragic consequences of unsatisfactory divorce laws.

GIFT, THEO. See BOULGER, THEODORA (HAVERS).

GILBERT, LADY. See GILBERT, ROSA (MULHOLLAND).

GILBERT, ROSA (MULHOLLAND). 1841-1921. United Kingdom.

1170 AGATHA'S HARD SAYING. BY ROSA MULHOLLAND (LADY GILBERT). New York: Benziger, 1912 NUC.
A woman whose family died from alcoholism and who fears her children might inherit the need for drink—if she were to have children—decides never to marry. Instead she devotes her life to orphaned children of alcoholics.

1171 NANNO: A DAUGHTER OF THE STATE. BY ROSA MULHOLLAND (LADY GILBERT). London: G. Richards, 1899 BMC NUC.
Nanno, born in a Dublin workhouse, leaves at 16 and

returns at 17 after she was betrayed and deserted. "For the girls to come back burdened as Nanno was burdened is only too common an experience." She leaves her child at the workhouse and full of fierce resolve goes out to win respectability for herself. She falls in love but breaks off the relationship rather than reveal her past. She cheats, forges, deceives and lies, labors on a farm, makes a home for her child, wins the respect of her neighbors and is happy in hard work.

1172   THE TRAGEDY OF CHRIS. London: Sands, 1903 BMC. St. Louis: B. Herder, 1904 PW.

Friendship between two women: Sheila and Chris sell flowers till Chris gets into bad company and disappears. Sheila searches all of London for her.

GILBREATH, OLIVE. United States.

1173   MISS AMERIKANKA; A STORY. New York and London: Harper, [1918] BMC NUC.

Young American woman goes to Russia during first months of the war.

GILKISON, ELIZABETH.

1174   THE STORY OF A STRUGGLE: A ROMANCE OF THE GRAMPIANS. London: A. and C. Black, 1892 BMC NUC.

James is a pragmatic, priggish Scotchman with ambitions for the ministry. Elsie, who has been trained to be self-sacrificing, releases him from their engagement so that he can go to Aberdeen to study for Holy Orders. She dies of a broken heart, and her mother brings up her sisters differently. James marries Mary; she is unhappy and turns to opium and alcohol. James has an epiphany when, in one of her periods of insanity, the expression on Mary's face reveals to him "how frightfully she must have suffered from distress, compression, and intimidation." They are eventually happy.

GILL, MARY (GILL). D. 1937. United States.

1175 A STRANGE RECORD. BY MOUNT HOUMAS. New York: Neale, 1908 NUC.

A woman doctor who attempts to practice in the U.S. has two patients in one year. She disguises herself as a male, changes her name on her diploma, and moves to Barbados and a successful practice.

GILLMORE, INEZ HAYNES. See IRWIN, INEZ (HAYNES).

GILMAN, CHARLOTTE (PERKINS) STETSON. 1860-1935. United States.

1176 MOVING THE MOUNTAIN. New York: Charlton, 1911 NUC.

Utopia created by women who won the vote and men who were converted and helped them.

1177 WHAT DIANTHA DID; A NOVEL. New York: Charlton, 1910 NUC. London: T.F. Unwin, 1912 BMC.

The illustration of Gilman's reform of households and housework in fiction.

1178 THE YELLOW WALL PAPER. BY CHARLOTTE PERKINS STETSON. Boston: Small, Maynard, 1899 NUC.

"...a woman's gradual mental unbalancing; she goes with her husband to a quiet country place for rest and sleeps in a room papered with a hideous yellow paper; her mind dwells upon its ugliness, and she imagines things about it, till she becomes insane."

GILMAN, DOROTHY FOSTER. B. 1891. United States.

1179 THE BLOOM OF YOUTH. Boston: Small, Maynard, [c1916] BMC NUC.

Leslie encounters radical ideas in her education at Radcliffe; reviewers agree she is "none the worse" for it.

GLASGOW, ELLEN ANDERSON GHOLSON. 1874-1945.
United States.

1180 THE BUILDERS. London: J. Murray, 1919 BMC. Garden
City, N.Y.: Doubleday, Page, 1919 NUC.
Conflict between Angelica Blackburn, who poses as a
martyred wife but is in reality a terribly selfish woman,
and Caroline Meade, a wise, courageous trained nurse of
thirty-two who comes to care for Angelica's sick daughter.
For a long time Caroline is fooled by Angelica's pose.
Caroline loves Angelica's husband, but Angelica will not
give her husband his freedom.

1181 THE DELIVERANCE; A ROMANCE OF THE VIRGINIA
TOBACCO FIELDS. New York: Doubleday, Page, 1904
NUC. London: A. Constable, 1904 BMC.
Blind woman deceived by family into believing she is still
wealthy, Confederate States are still a nation, and she still
has 300 slaves. "Caustic comments on marriage and
husbands."

1182 THE DESCENDANT: A NOVEL [ANONYMOUS]. New
York: Harper, 1897 NUC. London and New York:
Osgood, McIlvaine, 1897 BMC.
Contrast between two women through their relations with
Micheal Akershem. Rachel Gavin is an artistic genius, a
Bohemian who meets the radical journalist, Akershem,
loves him and lives with him until he meets a different
woman—"the best domestic type." Instead of realizing that
Rachel sacrificed herself to his anti-marriage ideals, he
turns on her and questions her easy "giving-in."

1183 LIFE AND GABRIELLA; THE STORY OF A WOMAN'S
COURAGE. Garden City, N.Y.: Doubleday, Page, 1916
NUC. London: J. Murray, 1916 BMC.
Described by reviewer Florence Kelly as the second in a
series of family biographies planned by the author, the
first of which was Virginia and portrayed an earlier era in
which the heroine was a victim. Gabriella is not in the
avant-garde of feminism but rather is part of a group
which supports it and enjoys what it has won. She refuses

to be a victim either of her family or a bad marriage and at 38 is a successful, independent business woman. The third biography will describe a more advanced woman.

1184   THE MILLER OF OLD CHURCH. London: J. Murray, 1911 BMC. Garden City, N.Y.: Doubleday, Page, 1911 NUC.

Molly Merryweather is the daughter of a poor woman and an aristocratic father who would not marry her mother but left her a trust fund. Molly is complex—wild, passionate loveable, with a deep longing to be free and to see life. She inherits the money and travels, but returns to her hometown. For a long time she feels only distrust of men and a wish to avenge the wrong done to her mother.

1185   PHASES OF AN INFERIOR PLANET. New York and London: Harper, 1898 NUC. London: W. Heinemann, 1898 BMC.

Mariana comes to New York to train her voice for opera. She marries a scientist; they suffer poverty, their child dies, and she leaves him. She continues her career successfully. The story ends with her death. "In different forms we all know the type—the slight, dazzling, restless woman whose brilliance is the result of her unstable nervous equilibrium."

1186   THE ROMANCE OF A PLAIN MAN. New York: Macmillan, 1909 NUC. London: J. Murray, 1909 BMC NUC.

Describes the empty lonely life of a rich American woman who feels she has no purpose in life. Sally Mickleborough marries Ben Starr. She is close to her husband only when his business is ruined. When he is busy making a fortune, she feels estranged from him and utterly bored. She welcomes the chance to maintain him and her child when his business is ruined.

1187   VIRGINIA. A NOVEL. Garden City, N.Y.: Doubleday, Page, 1913 NUC. London: W. Heinemann, 1913 BMC.

The influence of feminism on Southern women in the

early 1880's. Virginia Pendleton marries when she is very young. She lives the ideals of traditional womanhood, living for her husband and children completely. When her children are grown and distant from her because of their modern ideas and when her husband has mentally outgrown her, her slow growing misery and disillusionment begin. She is at first bewildered by modern ideas concerning women; then her illusions about ideal womanhood are shattered. Being an old fashioned woman, she does not rebel, but wears a mask of outward serenity while she aches inside for her husband's infidelities and her disappointment in her children. "A more powerful argument for justice to women than all the suffrage pleas...."

1188   THE WHEEL OF LIFE. New York: Doubleday, Page, 1906 NUC. London: A. Constable, 1906 BMC NUC.

A "study of temperament" in a "half-dozen mismated men and women." One of the women is from Virginia; she publishes a book of poems.

GLASPELL, SUSAN. See MATSON, SUSAN (GLASPELL) COOK.

GLAZEBROOK, ETHEL.

1189   THE DOWER OF EARTH. London: Percival, 1891 BMC NUC.

Modern story of Stella Graham who marries the wrong man and pays dearly for her mistake. She gives up the man she loves to please her father who, she believes, prefers Mortimer Ashton, a successful politician. She is the patient Griselda for the year or two of married life that prove him a real brute. Then, half bewildered by a violent headache, she poisons herself. "She does not consider the effect on her father of this action of his only child," says one critic.

GLENTWORTH, MARGUERITE LINTON. B. 1881. United States.

1190 THE TENTH COMMANDMENT; A ROMANCE. Boston: Lee and Shepard, 1902 NUC. London: Gay and Bird, 1902 BMC.

An actress whose marriage fails to satisfy her aspirations leaves her husband and four children after nine years of marriage because she no longer likes them. "Question of divorce and remarriage fearlessly handled."

GLOVER, ELIZABETH. See BENNETT, MARY E.

GLYN, ANNA L. United Kingdom.

1191 FIFTY POUNDS FOR A WIFE. Bristol: J. W. Arrowsmith, [1892] BMC. New York: H. Holt, 1892 NUC.

Objective tale of crime focussed on Winifred, who is "an intermittent maniac who has murdered her mother and abducts herself." Gerald rescues her from "inhuman whipping" by buying her from a proprietor of traveling shows.

GLYN, ELINOR (SUTHERLAND). 1864-1943. United Kingdom.

1192 THE CAREER OF KATHERINE BUSH. New York: D. Appleton, 1916 BMC NUC. London: G. Newnes, [1929] BMC.

She is a "shorthand typist" for a London moneylender, daughter of an auctioneer, who sees life as a game in which the strong win and is determined to win. But she is never deceitful or conniving. It is her courage, logical brain, common sense and honesty that bring her success. She moves "up" to a position as secretary to a great lady, meets a duke who dismisses all the mindless aristocratic husband-snatchers once he meets Katherine. When he proposes, she explains that she had an earlier affair. He loves her the more for her honesty.

1193 THE DAMSEL AND THE SAGE; A WOMAN'S WHIMSIES. New York and London: Harper, 1903 NUC. London: Duckworth, 1903 BMC.

A young woman visits a sage with whom she exchanges ideas about men and women. Her great intuition and courageous logic outwit the sage's arguments concerning women's proper place.

1194 FAMILY. New York: D. Appleton, 1919 NUC.

Amaryllis Ardayne marries a wealthy man who fails to "unfreeze her," so she looks elsewhere. And Henrietta Boleski is a "vamp" married twice.

1195 THE REASON WHY. London: Duckworth, [1911] BMC NUC. New York: D. Appleton, 1911 NUC.

Zara's first marriage left her bitter and scornful against all men because her husband treated her as a toy. She makes a second marriage only in order to get help for her crippled brother. She is cold and scornful toward her new husband. Gradually she learns he is a fine man, and they are drawn together.

1196 THE SEQUENCE, 1905—1912. London: Duckworth, 1913 BMC NUC. (Also published as Guinevere's Lover. New York: D. Appleton, 1913 NUC.)

Guinevere Bokun tells her own story. Her parents forced her to marry at 16 a man of 50 whom she feared. At 31 she still fears him and is bullied and dominated by him; at the same time she is very conscious of the problems in her marriage. She falls in love with another man but remains loyal to her husband. She breaks off the relationship with this man when her son discovers the relationship. Two days before her husband dies, the man she loves marries on the rebound, but Guinevere and he are eventually reunited when his wife drowns.

1197 THREE WEEKS. New York: Duffield, 1907 NUC. London: Duckworth, 1907 BMC NUC.

An aristocratic woman married to a brutal husband meets

a man much younger than herself, feels a strong sudden passion for him, and after five days the two live together. She withholds her identity; he is not to interfere in her life in any way; he is to treat the relationship only as an episode; and she is to leave when she wishes. She provides every luxury for their stay together after which she returns home, has a child and is murdered by her husband. The author glorifies and exalts the passion between the lovers.

1198 THE VICISSITUDES OF EVANGELINE; A NOVEL. London: Duckworth, 1905 BMC. New York and London: Harper, 1905 NUC.

Red-haired, exciting, unconventional Evangeline tells her own story in this "outspoken diary of her feelings." Raised in a worldly environment, she's uninhibited, not warped by the conventions she spurns. At 20, she states outright that she will be an adventuress. The story includes "all the audacities of a dozen up-to-date women."

GODFREY, ELIZABETH. See BEDFORD, JESSIE.

GOETCHIUS, MARIE LOUISE. See HALE, MARICE RUTLEDGE (GIBSON).

GOLDIE, HENRIETTA TAUBMAN.

1199 THE VEILED LIFE. London: W. Heinemann, 1914 BMC.

A detailed account of Laura's experiences as a kitchenmaid, an unhappy marriage, an attempted suicide, divorce, remarriage and two confinements, "the long and particular account of which," says one reviewer, is an example of a story "overloaded with small and even petty details."

GOLDWIN, AGNES.

1200 IN DUE SEASON. London: Digby, Long, 1894 BMC.

Alice Evans, past 30, wants to be a hospital nurse. Persevering, she is "constantly driven back by physical unfitness from the tasks to which she would soonest put her hand to than the uncongenial drudgery of the schoolroom." Her love for Dr. Arkwell, a married man, is a further complication.

GOODWIN, MAUD (WILDER). 1856-1935. United States.

1201 WHITE APRONS: A ROMANCE OF BACON'S REBELLION, VIRGINIA, 1676. Boston: Little, Brown, 1896 NUC. London: J. M. Dent, 1896 BMC.

Bacon's Rebellion; Penelope crosses the ocean to intercede with the king to get lover's pardon; succeeds.

GORDON, JULIEN. See CRUGER, JULIE GRINNELL (STORROW).

GORDON, LESLIE HOWARD.*

1202 THE GATES OF TIEN T'ZE. London: Hodder & Stoughton, [1920] BMC.

Spirited young woman develops an amazing capacity as a detective.

GORST, MRS. HAROLD E. See GORST, NINA C. F. (KENNEDY).

GORST, NINA C. F. (KENNEDY). United Kingdom.

1203 AND AFTERWARDS? London: Greening, 1901 BMC.

"A woman's revenge and opinions on life and men and manners." Sexual ethics.

1204 THE LEECH. BY MRS. HAROLD E. GORST. London: Mills and Boon, [1911] BMC NUC.

Tragic picture of hardships of London working women. Charlotte Barnes is deserted by her husband, seeks help from her sister-in-law, Susannah, moves into Susannah's flat and takes over. Susannah is a wretchedly poor widow who dies. Her daughter Elvina is left to the mercy of her cruel aunt and cruel cousin. Elvina first works in a library, then in a draper's showroom. She becomes ill and anemic from exhaustion. She is burned to death.

1205 THE LIGHT. BY MRS. HAROLD E. GORST. London: Cassell, 1906 BMC NUC. New York: B. W. Dodge, 1907 NUC.

A 16 year old unwed mother struggles to keep her self respect and to support her child. This purpose novel depicts a maternity ward for unwed mothers and includes statistics.

1206 POSSESSED OF DEVILS. London: J. Macqueen, 1897 BMC.

Demoniacal heroine. Lady Radclyffe hates her husband. She feels misunderstood; sees visions. She persuades Francis Ingelow to elope with her. "From the cradle, the female infant, child, girl, woman, is not, and never has been, what she appears. She is a creature evolved out of an age of shams and unrealities." (quote from novel)

1207 THE SOUL OF MILLY GREEN. London: Cassell, 1907 BMC.

Dedicated to "the average respectable man." Decline and fall of a poor pretty girl to a ragged, disreputable woman—precipitated by a respectable man.

1208 THE THIEF ON THE CROSS. London: Nash, 1908 BMC.

The story of Eve Ridgefoote, the daughter of a drunken mother of the slums. Eve's courageous but short history includes her life on the street, prison, the care of her children "under circumstances where infanticide would appear almost laudable." Described as "a moving and painful study, uncompromising in its realism."

1209 THIS OUR SISTER. BY MRS. HAROLD E. GORST. London: Digby, Long, 1905 BMC NUC.

Nell's misfortunes are treated with sympathy in this study of her character. After her father murders her mother, Nell is left to care for her infant brother. She "sells herself" to support him, but he dies. She becomes an artist's model, falls in love with the artist who "casts her off in her hour of need," and she kills herself. This realistic study of sordid poverty is never sentimental.

GOULD, ELIZABETH PORTER. 1848-1906. United States.

1210 A PIONEER DOCTOR; A STORY OF THE SEVENTIES. Boston: R. G. Badger, 1904 NUC.

Young woman physician goes to Syria to heal women.

GOWING, EMILIA AYLMER (BLAKE).

1211 MERELY PLAYERS. London: White, 1897 BMC.

At eighteen, Ena appears on the stage as Juliet and as Desdemona. She falls in love with a young actor, and after several misunderstandings and separation, they are reunited. She also writes a play—in blank verse.

1212 A TOUCH OF THE SUN. London: T. Burleigh, 1899 BMC.

English woman marries Indian prince. Much discussion of the differences between European and Oriental ideas of marriage.

GRAEME, VIOLA.

1213 VIVIANNE'S VENTURE. F. Griffiths, 1908 EC.

Young journalist becomes editor of Fashionable Flutterings; her methods of finding copy are not always respectable. She also writes the season's successful novel, "Sin and Cinders," and falls in love.

GRAHAM, EFFIE. See GRAHAM, SARAH EFFIE.

GRAHAM, MRS. HENRY. See ASKWITH, ELLEN GRAHAM.

GRAHAM, SARAH EFFIE.

1214 AUNT LIZA'S "PRAISIN GATE". BY EFFIE GRAHAM. Chicago: A. C. McClurg, 1916 NUC.

An old crippled Negro woman works for suffrage in Kansas, although she can't go beyond her gate.

GRAHAM, WINIFRED. See CORY, MATILDA WINIFRED MURIEL (GRAHAM).

GRAND, SARAH. See MACFALL, FRANCES ELIZABETH (CLARKE).

GRANT, DOUGLAS. See OSTRANDER, ISABEL EGENTON.

GRANT, ETHEL (WATTS) MUMFORD. 1878-1940. United States.

1215 OUT OF THE ASHES. BY ETHEL WATTS MUMFORD. New York: Moffat, Yard, 1913 NUC.

Mrs. Marteen is a modern thoroughly sophisticated widow with a grown daughter and an unconventional way of earning a living. She is a blackmailer by choice, and she knows precisely what she is doing. Her sufferings as a woman and a mother win the reader's sympathy.

GRANT, SADI.

1216 THE SECOND EVIL. London: J. Long, [1906] BMC NUC.

Story of two sisters, their life in a boarding school, their teashop, and their trip to Japan.

GRAVES, CHARLOTTE ELIZABETH. B. 1846. United States.

1217 MAUD HARCOURT; OR HOW SHE BECAME AN ARTIST. Syracuse, N. Y., 1897 NUC.

The career and many adventures of an art student in New York.

GRAVES, CLOTILDE INEZ MARY. 1863-1932. United Kingdom.

1218 THE DOP DOCTOR. BY RICHARD DEHAN. London: W. Heinemann, 1910 NUC BMC. New York: G. H. Doran, [c1910] NUC. (Also published as One Braver Thing. By Richard Dehan. New York: Duffield, 1910 NUC.)

Lynette, a nurse in the Boer War, has a horror of all men

as a result of an unhappy marriage. She finally consents to marry a surgeon in name only. The last part of the book is a study of this marriage and her realization that he loves and needs her.

1219   A FIELD OF TARES: A NOVEL. New York: Harper, 1891 NUC.

Heroine a widow and adventuress. With female partner, robs a man of much money. The two women part. She starts a new life, marries but her past catches up to her. Turns to crime again.

1220   MAIDS IN A MARKET GARDEN. BY RICHARD DEHAN. London: W. H. Allen, 1894 NUC. New York: Wycil, 1912 NUC.

Four young women embark on a business of fruit growing and market gardening under the supervision of middle aged Rosevear Trevelyan. They are to keep the insidious man as well as the destructive wireworm out of this Eden. They have had one previous failure, the United Gentlewomen's Work Emporium—failed from neglect. They all fall in love—tragic consequences to one of them.

1221   A WELL MEANING WOMAN. London: Hutchinson, 1896 BMC.

Humorous treatment of Lady Baintree, matchmaker. Farce.

GRAY, ANNABEL. See COX, ANNE.

GRAY, ANNIE JOSLYN. United States.

1222   FIREWEED. BY JOSLYN GRAY. New York: C. Scribner's Sons, 1920 NUC.

Erica, "spoiled and beautiful," wins a contested divorce from her husband. She is denounced by his lawyer in court, meets the lawyer later when travelling in Europe, and subsequently marries him.

GRAY, JOSLYN. See GRAY, ANNIE JOSLYN.

GRAY, MAXWELL. See TUTTIETT, MARY GLEED.

GRAY, PHOEBE. United States.

1223 THE GOLDEN LAMP. Boston: Small, Maynard, [c1916] NUC. London: Jarrolds, [1917] BMC.

Prohibition novel in which the heroine uplifts the city from drunkenness and vice.

GREEN, ANNA KATHARINE. See ROHLFS, ANNA KATHARINE (GREEN).

GREEN, E. EVERETT. See GREEN, EVELYN EVERETT.

GREEN, EDITH M.

1224 ELIZABETH GREY. Edinburgh and London: W. Blackwood, 1905 BMC.

True picture of a living woman, of her courage and humor. Elizabeth Grey is a writer. At first she has great difficulties publishing her work. Down to her last shilling, she bombards editors with her manuscripts with no success. She retires to a farm but eventually lives by her pen.

GREEN, EVELYN EVERETT. 1856-1932. United Kingdom.

1225 THE HOUSE OF SILENCE. London: Hutchinson, 1910 BMC.

Silence is secretary to a writer to whom she is engaged but who marries an heiress. Silence then inherits a house, lives in it by herself and develops her own writing talents.

1226 THE LADY OF SHALL NOT. London: Hutchinson, 1909 BMC.

Lady Sheila Knott is widowed on her wedding day and tries to run her husband's estate.

1227 MARCUS QUAYLE, M.D. London: Hutchinson, 1913 BMC.

One of the two heroines is a feminist who refuses to marry the doctor of the title because of his old fashioned views. She discusses the women's movement at great length.

1228 MISS LORIMER OF CHARD. London: Melrose, 1907 BMC.

She is a typewriter who works for the poor but loves a man who has no sympathy with such charitable work. End is tragic.

1229 MRS. ROMAINE'S HOUSEHOLD. Edinburgh and London: Oliphant, 1891 BMC. Boston: Bradley and Woodruff, 1891 NUC.

Clare Chesterton becomes a governess in this household after her mother dies. Eventually she becomes the strongest influence on the family. Everyday events, a love story and a tragedy.

1230 THE SIGN OF THE RED CROSS: A TALE OF OLD LONDON. BY E. EVERETT GREEN. London and New York: T. Nelson, 1897 BMC NUC.

Plague in London. Two young women nurse the victims.

1231 URSULA TEMPEST. London: R. T. S., [1910] BMC.

Sympathetic description of the lives of educated working women; author supports suffrage.

GREEN, MARYON URQUHART. United Kingdom.

1232 A TRAGEDY IN COMMONPLACE. BY M. URQUHART. London: Methuen, 1905 BMC.

Sympathetic account of the gradual demoralization of Sophia, mother of six. She bears the full weight of the care of the children; her weak husband is no help. She struggles with poverty and the drudgery of overwork all the while they grow up. One son is crippled; her other sons are ordinary. Her daughter is unattractive but develops into a wild genius of a girl. Sophia loses the love of her children, especially of her daughter, through the years along with her youth, because she's the one who nags, overworks and becomes squalid in their eyes. The children turn more and more to the father. Sophia's long feud with her daughter ends with the daughter's leaving home. Sophia dies unreconciled to any of her children.

GREENE, ALICE CLAYTON.

1233 MIRIAM AND THE PHILISTINES. London: L. Parsons, 1920 BMC.

Miriam's views are at odds with those of conventional society. She is disowned by her father when she becomes a member of a touring company. She lives with another man after her marriage.

GREENE, FRANCES NIMMO. 1850-1921. United States.

1234 THE RIGHT OF THE STRONGEST. New York: Scribner's Sons, 1913 NUC.

Mary Elizabeth returns to the Alabama mountains to teach and help her people after her ten years of studying in the city. Her chance to help comes when she opposes the man she loves in his effort to exploit the area for water power in order to make money.

GREENE, MARY ELLEN (BROWN). B. 1848.

1235 THE DOOR WHERE THE WRONG LAY. Boston: C. M. Clark, 1909 NUC.

Father turns out daughter who marries against his will.

GREENE, SARAH PRATT (MACLEAN). 1856-1935. United States.

1236 STUART AND BAMBOO: A NOVEL. New York and London: Harper, 1897 BMC NUC.

Margaret Stuart, accustomed to luxury, comes to Mrs. O'Ragan Stuart's boarding house in Yarmouth with $1.75. Here she works and dies. "The beauty of human sympathy and universal sisterhood" is the theme.

GREENSLET, ELLA STOOTHOFF (HULST). B. 1873. United States.

1237 THE NIGHTINGALE; A LARK. BY ELLENOR STOOTHOFF. Boston: Houghton Mifflin, 1914 NUC.

Hilda Manely is essentially a woman of strong purpose

who comes to feel useless in her marriage. One day she tells her husband she is going to Europe, and he must ask no questions. She makes him understand her longing to roam the world alone. She has many exciting adventures in her travels in her second-hand car. She sets her time of return at the first sound of the nightingale. Her husband is patient through the several months that represent her break for freedom.

GREGG, HILDA CAROLINE. 1868-1933. United Kingdom.

1238   HIS EXCELLENCY'S ENGLISH GOVERNESS. BY SYDNEY C. GRIER. Edinburgh and London: W. Blackwood, 1896 BMC NUC.

Cecil, who has a B.A., goes to Bagdad as teacher of 10 year old Azim Bey. Her adventures there include political intrigue on an international scale and romance.

1239   LIKE ANOTHER HELEN. BY SYDNEY C. GRIER. Edinburgh and London: W. Blackwood, 1899 BMC NUC. Boston: L. C. Page, 1902 NUC.

In letter form. Bengal in the terrible years 1755—7. Sophie Freyne "like another Helen finds another Troy" and writes about it.

1240   PEACE WITH HONOUR. BY SYDNEY C. GRIER. Edinburgh and London: W. Blackwood, 1897 BMC. Boston: L. C. Page, 1902 NUC.

Georgia Keeling is a doctor on a European mission to the court of Ethiopia. She goes to practice in the sultan's harem. With her is Major Richard North who at first is completely prejudiced against new women like Georgia.

1241   THE REARGUARD. BY SYDNEY C. GRIER. Blackwood: 1915 NUC BMC.

One of three daughters of a tyrannical minister in East Indies, a small shy woman, achieves great fame as a novelist writing under a pseudonym.

GREGORY, SACHA. See STOLZENBERG, BETSEY (RIDDLE) VON HUTTEN ZUM.

GREVILLE, BEATRICE VIOLET (GRAHAM) GREVILLE. 1842-1932.

1242 THE FIGHTERS. A NOVEL. London: Chapman and Hall, 1907 BMC.

Story of the Peninsular war, Heroine is an adventuress who marries a British officer in order to spy on U.S. troops.

1243 THE HOME FOR FAILURES. London: Hutchinson, 1896 BMC NUC.

Oriza, discontented with life, opens her home to lonely failures. She has a friend, Hon. Rachel Cator who has good sense, vitality, and a bike, "which latter is becoming a tiresome intrusion in a class of fiction which aspires above all to be modern." Tragic conclusion.

GREY, EVELYN.

1244 OUTRAGEOUS FORTUNE: BEING THE STORY OF EVELYN GREY, HOSPITAL NURSE. London: Greening, 1900 BMC.

She has misfortunes which involve a seducer but eventual happiness.

GREY, ROWLAND. See BROWN, LILIAN KATE ROWLAND.

GRIER, SYDNEY C. See GREGG, HILDA CAROLINE.

GRIFFIN, E. ACEITUNA. See GRIFFIN, EDITH ACEITUNA.

GRIFFIN, EDITH ACEITUNA. B. 1876. United Kingdom.

1245 LADY SARAH'S DEED OF GIFT. BY E. ACEITUNA GRIFFIN. Edinburgh and London: W. Blackwood, 1906 BMC.

Lady Sarah gives her nephew's wife money to leave her husband during a contest of wills as an experiment in human nature. There is a reconciliation at the end.

1246　MRS. VANNECK. BY E. ACEITUNA GRIFFIN. London: E. Nash, 1907 BMC.

Beautiful, unscrupulous young widow avenges her half sister by scheming with a young peer.

GRIFFITH, CECIL. See BECKETT, CECIL (GRIFFITH).

GRIMSHAW, BEATRICE ETHEL. 1871-1953. Australia.

1247　VAITI OF THE ISLANDS. London: A.P. Watt, [1906] BMC. New York: A. Wessels, 1908 NUC.

Vaiti, daughter of an Englishman and a Maori princess, is captain of her father's ship and has "unique and perilous adventures" which include being marooned on a lepers' island where she searches for prehistoric skulls in caves.

GROVE, JESSICA, jt. au. See RACSTER, OLGA AND JESSICA GROVE.

GRUNDY, MABEL SARAH BARNES. United Kingdom.

1248　HILARY ON HER OWN. London: Hutchinson, 1908 BMC. New York: Baker and Taylor, 1908 NUC.

Hilary, tired of the monotony of domesticity, leaves home and goes to London in search of a position as secretary. Her experiences end in matrimony.

1249　THE THIRD MISS WENDERBY. London: Hutchinson, 1911 BMC. New York: Baker and Taylor, [1911] NUC.

Diana, governess, falls for married man, unhappy for a year, finds real happiness with an old friend.

1250　TWO MEN AND GWENDA. London: [1910] NUC.

Natural and generous young woman marries a man involved in society. She becomes rapidly disillusioned. Triangle ensues. Her letters describe her unhappy marriage.

GYP. See DE JANVILLE, SYBILLE GABRIELLE MARIE ANTOINETTE (DE RIQUETTI DE MIRABEAU) MARTEL.

H., A. K. See HOPKINS, ALICE (KIMBALL). SANDERS, ELLA KATHERINE.

HACK, ELIZABETH JANE (MILLER). 1878-1961. United States.

1251   DAYBREAK; A STORY OF THE AGE OF DISCOVERY. BY ELIZABETH MILLER (MRS. OREN S. HACK). New York: C. Scribner's Sons, 1915 NUC.
Antonia de Aragon is one of four "intrepid knightly damsels" who followed the queen through wars. She is a female spy disguised as a male page; she rescues a Spanish nobleman from a Moorish prison. Historical romance.

HACK, MRS. OREN S. See HACK, ELIZABETH JANE (MILLER).

HADDON, A. L.*

1252   WHAT AILS THE HOUSE? A NOVEL. London: W. H. Allen, 1893 BMC.
Mrs. Perkins is a novelist in need of fresh material. She appeals to her cousin Judith Minchin, a "pious spinster" living in seclusion. From Judith's old love letters, Mrs. Perkins creates a new novel. Satire on the novelist's art.

HAINES, ALICE CALHOUN. United States.

1253   FIRECRACKER JANE; A NOVEL. New York: H. Holt, 1918 NUC. London: Hurst and Blackett, [1919] BMC.
Fiery spirited American young woman, red haired, elopes to Mexico with a cousin partly out of pique because her father remarries. A war breaks out, in which Mexican

"women must win by intrigue the influence and independence that society accords them as their birthright in our northern world." Her adventures include the murder of her husband, her capture and escape from brigands.

HALDANE, WINIFRED AGNES. United States.

1254 A CHORD FROM A VIOLIN. Chicago: Laird and Lee, [c1896] NUC.

Romance, of Hester, a great singer, whose father had owned a rare violin, which she had had to sell when he was dying. Hears it at a concert years later and meets its owner.

HALE, BEATRICE (FORBES-ROBERTSON). B. 1883. United States.

1255 THE NEST-BUILDER. New York: F. A. Stokes, [c1916] NUC.

The study of a marriage. She sees herself as the creator of the race, to which all else in life should be subservient. He cares for life only as it helps him express beauty in art forms.

HALE, LOUISE (CLOSSER). 1872-1933. United States.

1256 THE ACTRESS; A NOVEL. New York and London: Harper, 1909 NUC. London: A. Constable, 1909 BMC.

Realistic intimate account of an actress' way of life, her career, success, work. Rhoda Miller describes her own successful career. At one point she has a chance to marry, but a leading role in London appeals to her more. Eventually she marries Aaron.

1257 HER SOUL AND HER BODY. New York: Moffat, Yard, 1912 NUC. London: G. Routledge, 1913 BMC.

A realistic description of a young woman who goes to Boston to study for the stage. Her struggles and eventual success.

1258   THE MARRIED MISS WORTH; A NOVEL. New York and London: Harper, 1911 BMC NUC.

Marriage and career clash: actress marries leading man; they are happy until she gets a better part and he won't play the lesser role. They separate. One reviewer says she finally resigns to be a full-time wife; another says that the story "may carry a moral unawares, but it is the reader who finds it in the story, not the author who presents it."

HALE, MARICE RUTLEDGE (GIBSON). B. 1884. United States.

1259   ANNE OF TREBOUL. BY MARIE LOUISE GOETCHIUS. New York: Century, 1910 BMC NUC.

Anne is a hunchback with a great longing for love. She refuses to marry the man who is responsible for her pregnancy because she learns he doesn't love her, and she raises her son by herself.

1260   THE BLIND WHO SEE. BY MARIE LOUISE VAN SAANEN. New York: Century, 1911 BMC NUC.

Nona is married to a blind violinst. She craves a fuller sexual life than her genius of a husband gives her. She meets a man and runs off to Paris with him, taking him for her lover and forgetting all about her husband. When she realizes her love affair is simply sexual, she returns to her husband who loves and needs her more than ever.

1261   WILD GRAPES. BY MARIE LOUISE VAN SAANEN. New York: Moffat, Yard, 1913 NUC.

Lucia makes a secret marriage to David Ghent, then leaves immediately for Europe with her mother Emily, while her husband remains at home to make and remake fortunes as fast as she can waste, squander and gamble them away. He's kept so busy making money that she soon takes a lover and the marriage ends in divorce. Indictment against this type of marriage.

HALES, A. M. M. See HALES, ADA MATILDA MARY.

HALES, ADA MATILDA MARY. B. 1878.

1262   THE PURITAN'S PROGRESS. BY A. M. M. HALES. London: A. Melrose, 1920 BMC.

Frances, "originally with the non-moral bias of a free Greek," experiences Christian restraints as a child, goes to Oxford and becomes a Nietzschean. One critic says Frances remains an "eerie shadow," but the book is an interesting experiment.

HALL, ELIZA CALVERT. See OBENCHAIN, ELIZA CAROLINE (CALVERT).

HALL, EVELYN BEATRICE. B. 1868. United Kingdom.

1263   LOVE LAUGHS LAST. BY S. G. TALLENTYRE. Edinburgh and London: W. Blackwood, 1919 NUC BMC. New York: G.H. Doran, [c1919] NUC.

Women characters are independent and self reliant: Camilla King, the hero's mother, left poor when her husband dies; Theodora ambitious blue stocking who declines a proposal of marriage and who holds Bible classes for the servants and reading classes for poor young women. Reconstructs early 19th century village life.

HALL, GERTRUDE. See BROWNELL, ANNA GERTRUDE (HALL).

HALLOWAY, MARY.

1264   CROSS ROADS; OR ISABEL ALISON'S HISTORY. Philadelphia: American Sunday School Pub. Union, [c1891] NUC.

Isabel must leave her comfortable home at an early age to earn her own living. The novel concerns her many problems as a governess and teacher.

HALSTED, LENORA B. United States.

1265 A VICTORIOUS LIFE. New York: Metropolitan Press, 1910 NUC.

Bertha Henley, tricked into a disagreeable marriage, writes verse and achieves fame and money. She divorces her husband finally and marries a Congressman who is killed. A third marriage is satisfactory, and when her husband dies, she becomes a minister.

HAMILTON, ANNIE E. (HOLDSWORTH) LEE. United Kingdom.

1266 THE BOOK OF ANNA. London: Hutchinson, 1913 BMC.

Sensations and thoughts of an introspective and imaginative young woman who wants to write.

1267 THE GODS ARRIVE. BY ANNIE E. HOLDSWORTH. London: W. Heinemann, 1897 BMC. New York: Dodd, Mead, 1897 NUC.

Careful study of a modern woman, Katharine Fleming, successful journalist and leader of a labor movement. Her fellow worker Richard believes she's "outside her proper sphere" even though her abilities are far superior to his. Eventually she's forced back to work the family farm, work she knows is beneath her powers. Two critics suggest the novel argues in favor of love and marriage for women.

1268 THE IRON GATES. London: T.F. Unwin, 1906 BMC.

In this story of the London slums the workers are motivated by the memory of a dead woman, the victim of a selfish husband, who gave her life to a cause. She becomes a cult after her death.

1269 JOANNA TRAILL, SPINSTER. BY ANNIE E. HOLDSWORTH. London: W. Heinemann, 1894 NUC BMC. New York: C. L. Webster, 1894 NUC.

Joanna is over 30 when an inheritance brings to an end

her life of dependency. She wants to be useful in her new life; she meets Mr. Boas, a philanthropist, and becomes interested in his work. She undertakes the rescue of Christine, a young woman who had been greatly wronged. Christine falls in love but is heartlessly rejected by her lover when he learns of her past.

1270 LADY LETTY BRANDON. London: J. Long, 1909 BMC.
Wholly sympathetic heroine married to a passionless judge, yearns for a great passion. Under an assumed name, she travels with a woman friend, falls in love with an artist, and marries him. She then proceeds to live a double life as wife to two men.

1271 THE YEARS THAT THE LOCUST HATH EATEN. BY ANNIE E. HOLDSWORTH. London: W. Heinemann, 1895 BMC. New York and London: Macmillan, 1895 NUC.
Young Priscilla is full of hope when she marries a writer named Momerie—even though her clergyman father disapproves. She and her husband move to a working people's community—the Regent's Building in London. Priscilla is a successful novelist with great literary ability, but her husband, a lazy weak person, considers himself the writing genius though he produces nothing. Worst of all, he ignores Priscilla's talents and makes a drudge of her. The story traces her disenchantment with her husband, the birth and death of their sickly child, her husband's paralysis which enables him to watch his wife work without self reproach, her chance for true love, rejected because by then she is a broken woman, poverty, misery, and her death. Reminds one of Story of an African Farm.

HAMILTON, CATHERINE JANE. United Kingdom.

1272 A FLASH OF YOUTH. London: Sands, 1900 BMC.
Alethea, an amateur curate, becomes a clergyman's assistant. She marries, leaves her husband when she finds him making love to another. She goes into rescue work.

HAMILTON, CICELY MARY. 1875-1952. United Kingdom.

1273 DIANA OF DOBSON'S. New York: Century, 1908 BMC NUC.

Diana, leading the monotonous life of a London shop girl, inherits 300 pounds. Posing as a young widow, she spends it all in one short month on Paris gowns, a trip to Switzerland, and two love affairs. Then she must return to London to look for another position and reassume the daily struggle. Ends in marriage to one of the men she met on her trip.

1274 JUST TO GET MARRIED. London: Chapman and Hall, 1911 BMC NUC.

Georgina Vicary is totally dependent upon relatives; she has no way to earn a living and no future but marriage. An eligible man comes on the scene, and she makes a play for him, feeling bitter and ashamed even as she does so. She tells the man the truth and refuses his proposal. In the end it turns out that they really love each other.

1275 A MATTER OF MONEY. London: Chapman and Hall, 1916 BMC.

Matrimonial unfaithfulness—the wife is the victim.

1276 WILLIAM—AN ENGLISHMAN. London: Skeffington, [1919] BMC. New York: F. A. Stokes, [c1919] NUC.

Griselda is a militant suffragette who marries William in 1914 and goes with him to the Forest of Arden in France for her honeymoon. They know nothing about the outbreak of war, until they learn that everyone has cleared the area and they meet Germans. William is taken captive and his worst fears of what might happen to Griselda become fact. He manages to escape, finds her, but she is knocked down and crushed by a motorcycle, and dies. William gives up his pacifist ideas, joins up and is killed.

HAMILTON, EDITH HENRIETTA (FOWLER). 1865-1963. United Kingdom.

1277   A CORNER OF THE WEST. BY EDITH HENRIETTA
        FOWLER. London: Hutchinson, 1899 BMC. New York:
        Appleton, 1899 NUC.
        Lavinia Garland, 30, gives up the man she has been
        engaged to for nine years to care for her "old tyrant of a
        mother." Lovelife of two other heroines included. One is
        Petronel, a fast, vulgar, slangy cigarette-smoking hoyden.

1278   PATRICIA. BY EDITH HENRIETTA FOWLER (HON.
        MRS. ROBERT HAMILTON). New York: G. P. Putnam's
        Sons, 1915 NUC. London: G. P. Putnam, 1915 BMC.
        At 28, Patricia Vaughan has established a literary career
        when a noted publisher asks her to write her father's
        biography. Being a genius, she writes it well. She marries
        the son of a man whose letters to her father she included
        in the biography. At the end, when she is pregnant, she is
        assured by her husband that the child girl or boy will
        inherit alike.

HAMILTON, HELEN.

1279   THE ICONOCLAST. London: C. W. Daniel, [1917] BMC.
        Maud Larkin a high school teacher reads in the newspaper
        that teaching is "the withered vestalhood" and that women
        have vital human needs. She immediately plans to run off
        with a clerk in order to escape dead and monotonous
        respectability. Both are relieved when their plan fails.
        Kindly satire.

1280   MY HUSBAND STILL; A WORKING WOMAN'S
        STORY. London: G. Bell, 1914 BMC NUC.
        The theme is the necessity of access to divorce for the
        poor as well as the rich.

HAMILTON, HON. MRS. ROBERT. See HAMILTON, EDITH HENRIETTA (FOWLER).

HAMILTON, LILLIAS.

1281 A NURSE'S BEQUEST. BY LILLIAS HAMILTON, M.D.
      London: J. Murray, 1907 BMC.
      Nurse and children in a workhouse infirmary. Theory that
      "pauper" children should be sent to Canada, raised on
      farms, taught trades so that they will be self supporting.

1282 A VIZIER'S DAUGHTER. A TALE OF THE HAZARA
      WAR. BY LILLIAS HAMILTON, M.D. London: J.
      Murray,. 1900 BMC NUC.
      Gul Begum, the daughter of an Afghanistan mountaineer,
      is sold as a slave. She plans and executes the escape of the
      ameer's secretary and herself, dressed in male attire, to
      India, where she is killed. (The author was court physician
      to the ameer of Afghanistan.)

HAMILTON, M. See LUCK, MARY CHURCHILL
(SPOTTISWOODE-ASHE).

HAMILTON, MARY AGNES (ADAMSON). 1884-1966.
      United Kingdom.

1283 DEAD YESTERDAY. London: Duckworth, [1916] BMC
      NUC. New York: G. H. Doran, [c1916] NUC.
      The novel focuses on Nigel, the young editor of a
      prestigious magazine, and his perceptions of persons and
      events before and during World War I. Contrasted with
      Daphne and and her mother, Nigel, although sensitive and
      intelligent, is ultimately seen as superficial and weaker
      than either of the two women, both strong characters. He
      shares with other men a fascination for war games, and it
      is his kind of thinking which appears to be responsible for
      the war. Both mother and daughter are strongly anti- war;
      the mother who devotes full-time to international pacifist
      efforts is the author's mouthpiece.

1284 FULL CIRCLE. London: W. Collins, [c1919] BMC NUC.
      The story of Bridget's development into a successful
      modern woman, including an unsuccessful liaison with a
      socialist poet.

1285   THE LAST FORTNIGHT. London: W. Collins, [1920] BMC.

Young wife lives with selfish husband and mother-in-law. She rescues a lame white kitten which she sees as a symbol of her own misery. When her husband and his mother drown it, she kills herself.

HAMLET, EDITH. See LYTTLETON, EDITH SOPHY (BALFOUR).

HAMMOND, FRANCES. See CROAL, FRANCES A.

HAMMOND, L. H. See HAMMOND, LILY (HARDY).

HAMMOND, LILY (HARDY). 1859-1925. United States.

1286   THE MASTER-WORD; A STORY OF THE SOUTH TODAY. BY L. H. HAMMOND. New York: Macmillan, 1905 NUC.

Woman married for eight years learns her husband fathered a child not hers; she slowly overcomes her hatred of him. But the story really concerns her relation to that child—a girl—and the girl's resentment toward being part black. The author has written with sincerity and high purpose.

HANDASYDE. See BUCHANAN, EMILY HANDASYDE.

HANKS, BEULAH DOWNEY. United States.

1287   FOR THE HONOR OF A CHILD. New York: Continental, 1899 NUC.

Margaret Laurence, poor herself, loves poor Fairfax Marmion. When he goes off without confessing his love, she marries a wealthy Spaniard who subjects her to absolute torture, which she bears for the sake of her child. Ends in tragedy. Serves to warn against marrying for social and economic reasons.

HAPGOOD, NEITH BOYCE. 1872-1951. United States.

1288 THE BOND. BY NEITH BOYCE. New York: Duffield, 1908 NUC. London: Duckworth, 1908 BMC.

Teresa, an artist, marries another artist, keeps her own quarters in case the marriage doesn't work out. The marriage is unhappy, she leaves him, they are eventually reconciled.

1289 THE FORERUNNER. BY NEITH BOYCE. New York: Fox, Duffield, 1903 NUC BMC. London: Hurst & Blackett, 1907 BMC.

The first year of Anna's marriage to Dan goes well; her passion for luxury is satisfied by his for money-making. But she's secretly repelled by his love making, and he is hopelessly blind to her moods because his business comes first. Then his business fails, and they separate while he goes East to start anew. Their reunion brings on a bitter quarrel in which Anna pours forth all her accumulated wrath. They separate never to be reconciled.

1290 A PIONEER OF TO-DAY. London: Hurst and Blackett, 1907 BMC.

Sober realism of an unsuccessful marriage.

HARBAND, BEATRICE M.

1291 JAYA: WHICH MEANS VICTORY. THIS IS THE STORY OF A HINDU GIRL OF HIGH DEGREE, TELLING OF HER LIFE'S STRUGGLES AS A MAIDEN, WIFE, AND WIDOW. London, New York: Marshall, [1914?] BMC NUC.

Women missionaries in India.

HARDEN, ELIZABETH.

1292 THE SPINDLE. London: J. Long, 1912 BMC.

Woman doctor keeps outside petty circles in seaside town

and "relinquishes lover."

HARDING, D. C. F. See HARDING, DOLORES CHARLOTTE FREDERICA.

HARDING, DOLORES CHARLOTTE FREDERICA. B. 1888. United Kingdom.

1293   ORANGES AND LEMONS. BY D. C. F. HARDING. London, New York: Cassell, [1916] NUC BMC.

Delores, impoverished, becomes a wealthy and famous dancer. She develops a weakness for gambling, loses her money, her child, and dies of consumption.

HARDY, A. S. F.*

1294   PRINCESS AND PRIEST (A TALE OF OLD EGYPT) AND MADEMOISELLE ETIENNE. London: Downey, 1895 BMC NUC.

Princess Ita has the wonderful power to heal sick people. She practices her art extensively, but in the end "descends to the ordinary life of wife and mother."

HARGRAVE, KATHARINE EDITH SPICER-JAY. 1896-1915.

1295   HILARY'S CAREER. BY L. PARRY TRUSCOTT. London: T. W. Laurie, [1913] BMC.

The law that gives the father alone the right to decide on careers for the children is attacked. A couple do not agree on their son's future. The father wants him to be a publisher like himself. The mother and son prefer a career in the navy. The battle goes on; neither parent gives way. When the father's first wife shows up and the marriage is proved illegal, the wife has full control and allows her son the career of his choice.

1296   MOTHERHOOD. BY L. PARRY TRUSCOTT. London: T. F. Unwin, 1904 BMC.

The story of an unwed mother whose "instincts of motherhood are stronger than her love for Everhard, stronger even than her fear of social ostracism." She refuses to give up her child.

1297   OBSTACLES: A NOVEL. BY L. PARRY TRUSCOTT.
        London: Chapman and Hall, 1916 BMC.
        Susannah becomes a munitions worker to see what being
        poor is like before she marries a soldier who has no
        money. She meets Gwenny, a fellow worker who has an
        alcoholic mother.

1298   STARS OF DESTINY. BY L. PARRY TRUSCOTT.
        London: T. F. Unwin, [1905] BMC.
        A gifted married woman establishes a new kind of relation
        with a younger male artist, not her husband. Their
        "whole" love is spiritual and intellectual—it transcends sex.
        The novel analyzes a different sort of triangle when a
        younger woman awakens the man's sexual nature.

HARGROVE, ETHEL C.

1299   THE GARDEN OF DESIRE; A STORY OF THE ISLE OF
        WIGHT. London: Grafton, 1916 BMC.
        At 25, Agnes Lister is ready to move out of her small
        village on the Isle of Wight because she is in a rut and is
        determined to change the direction of her life. Just then
        she gets a proposal of marriage, but she knows she wants
        more than marriage. She refuses in order to go to London
        to write. In London she lives in a women's hostel, goes to
        art school, becomes a pavement artist, joins a women's
        club and becomes an author. In the end she meets the
        right man.

HARKER, L. ALLEN. See HARKER, LIZZIE ALLEN (WATSON).

HARKER, LIZZIE ALLEN (WATSON). 1863-1933. United Kingdom.

1300   ALLEGRA. BY L. ALLEN HARKER. London: J. Murray,
        1919 BMC NUC. New York: C. Scribner's Sons, 1920
        NUC.
        Young actress, egotistic but thoroughly likeable, well-
        trained in her five years with Westingley Repertory
        Theatre is completely devoted to her art. She resents the
        intrusion of people in her life except as they lead to the

advancement of her career. She throws over a playwright who dramatized a novel for her. Then she throws over the novelist when she reads the rest of his works. Her dog patiently listens to the endless outpourings of her mind. "The author has had the good sense to avoid the conventional happy ending which in this instance would have led to almost certain misery."

HARLAN, MRS. M. R. B. 1879. United States.

1301   IN THE LAND OF EXTREMES. BY MARIE COTTRELL. New York: Cochrane, 1909 NUC.
Concerns a teacher.

HARRADEN, BEATRICE. 1864-1936. United Kingdom.

1302   THE FOWLER. Edinburgh: W. Blackwood, 1899 BMC. New York: Dodd, Mead, 1899 NUC.
Fine study of two women, one of whom comes under the power of the Fowler. Nora Penhurst is brilliant, splendidly educated, modern to her fingertips and full of the great joy of life. Nevertheless she falls victim to "intellectual seduction" by Theodore Bevan, an evil decadent man who has the power to control women and whose object is to break their individuality. Only when Nora reads the Fowler's diary does she free herself of his domination. The other fine character "has not appeared in fiction before." Nurse Isabel is a woman of keen humor born to be fashionable but forced by circumstances to take up nursing.

1303   THE GUIDING THREAD. New York: F. A. Stokes, [c1916] NUC. London: Methuen, 1916 BMC.
Joan, uneducated but with a good mind, is married to a man who has trained her to be a Renaissance scholar. For seven years they work together, withdrawn from the world. Then one day she sees a parrot and understands that this is all she has been. She burns her notes, telling

her husband that none of it is really hers and leaves him to become her own person. She goes to the United States.

1304   HILDA STRAFFORD AND THE REMITTANCE MAN. TWO CALIFORNIAN STORIES. Edinburgh: W. Blackwood, 1897 BMC. (Also published as Hilda Strafford; a California Story. New York: Dodd, Mead, 1897 NUC.)

Hilda's bitter history: "she is consumed with regret for a life she deems misspent and with longing to be home again." She comes to dusty colorless Southern California to marry her fiance who left England in bad health to settle on a lemon-tree ranch a few years earlier. Hilda, strong and in bounding health, is immediately disheartened with the place and unsuited to the isolated life. Things go badly—the crop fails, her husband's health gets worse. On the night she tells him she does not love him and wants to return to England, he dies. Then she falls in love with her husband's friend, Ben, but they part because he blames her for hurrying Robert's death. Hilda returns to England.

1305   INTERPLAY. London: Methuen, 1908 BMC. New York: F. A. Stokes, [1908] NUC.

The theme is equal morality for men and women; the author insists on the "conception of woman as an independent being." Harriet, a talented woman, leaves her husband for another man. The husband refuses to give her a divorce until the other man is dead.

1306   KATHARINE FRENSHAM; A NOVEL. Edinburgh and London: W. Blackwood, 1903 NUC BMC. New York: Dodd, Mead, 1903 NUC.

Katharine Frensham, happy, young at heart, and unmarried at 40 without a past is distinctly modern—wholly new to fiction. She is the new woman with "the calm independence of a man." She takes over her brother's organ business, and she meets a man she can love. The story gives the "fine psychology of the courtship itself."

1307   OUT OF THE WRECK I RISE. London, New York: T. Nelson, [1912] BMC NUC. New York: F. A. Stokes, [1912] NUC.

Male hero's victimization of two women who become friends. One is Tamar Scott, a shrewd dealer in precious stones and antique jewelry; the other is Nell, head of a large philanthropic office. Together they work to outwit those who would destroy the weaker man.

1308   THE SCHOLAR'S DAUGHTER. New York: Dodd, Mead, 1906 NUC. London: Methuen, 1906 NUC BMC.

Her mother left her father. He has surrounded himself with men, all of them working on a dictionary on which she, too, must work. She rebels, makes friends with a celebrated actress (who is her mother).

1309   SHIPS THAT PASS IN THE NIGHT. London: Lawrence and Bullen, 1893 BMC. Chicago: Donohue, Henneberry, [1893] NUC.

Bernardine Holme, exhausted from teaching, writing and participating in a socialist group and in political discussions, goes to the Alps to a health resort where she meets a man who is her intellectual equal. After she returns to London, she realizes she loves him, as he learns he loves her, but she is killed by an automobile just before they marry.

1310   SPRING SHALL PLANT. London, New York: Hodder and Stoughton, [1920] BMC NUC.

Patuffa, a rebellious and gifted incorrigible expelled from many schools, at last makes good in Dresden, to the advantage of her musical talent.

1311   WHERE YOUR TREASURE IS. London: Hutchinson, 1918 BMC NUC. (Also published as Where Your Heart Is. New York: Dodd, Mead, 1918 NUC.)

T. Scott is a middle-aged dealer in precious stones and antique jewelry. Her interest in her business consumes her entirely. Her friendship with the Thornton family results in her gradually becoming less withdrawn and more outgoing.

HARRINGTON, KATHERINE. See BENNETT, MRS. ROLF.

HARRIOT, CLARA MORRIS. 1848-1925. United States.

1312 THE NEW "EAST LYNNE". BY CLARA MORRIS. New York: C. H. Doscher, [c1908] NUC.
Menage a trois. The former wife, believed dead, returns five years later as governess for her children.

1313 A PASTEBOARD CROWN, A STORY OF THE NEW YORK STAGE. BY CLARA MORRIS. New York: C. Scribner's Sons, 1902 NUC. London: Isbister, 1902 BMC.
An actress becomes the mistress of the stage manager, continues after discovering he is married. She doesn't suffer for it; her life is contrasted with the domestic monotony of her sister's life.

HARRIS, CORRA MAY (WHITE). 1869-1935. United States.

1314 THE CO-CITIZENS. Garden City N.Y.: Doubleday, Page, 1915 NUC. London: Wayfarer, [1919] BMC.
Sara Mosely leaves her money to the cause of gaining the vote for women in a very conservative district: the state has a very low literacy, the public school lasted only five months because the farmers opposed schools and there is only one suffragette in the district. But Susan Walton organizes the Co-Citizens League and gets to work. All the wives who had attended nothing but husbands attend the meetings. How the women won, the methods they used, is the story.

1315 EVE'S SECOND HUSBAND. Philadelphia: Altemus, [c1911] NUC. London: Constable, 1911 BMC.
Eve, a widow, knows men are not to be respected even if one loves them. She cures her second husband of his unfaithfulness by running up bills of such magnitude that he cannot afford to buy things for other women. She comments, "Being a good woman does not pay except in goodness."

1316   IN SEARCH OF A HUSBAND. Garden City, N. Y.: Doubleday, Page, 1913 NUC. London: G. Richards, [1913] BMC.

Opens with the debut of Joy Marr, Southern belle who at an early age is determined to marry rich. She is a "parasite"—wanting comfort, ease, the good things through scheming to marry a wealthy man, in spite of the fact that she loves a poor man. Years go by with no success; her last effort fails; she marries the poor man.

1317   JUSTICE. New York: Hearst's International Library, 1915 NUC BMC.

Shows the prejudice, inequality and "one sexedness" of laws made by men.

1318   MAKING HER HIS WIFE. Garden City, N. Y.: Doubleday, Page, 1918 NUC. London: T. Nelson, [1924] BMC.

John and Olive marry. She is restless; he is determined to reduce her to his ideas of wifely duty. Conflict arises. They separate but eventually reunite, "but the reader remains skeptical as to their future happiness...but does not take sufficient interest in them to care whether they were wretched or not."

HARRIS, CORRA MAY (WHITE) AND FAITH HARRIS LEECH.

1319   FROM SUNUP TO SUNDOWN. Garden City, New York: Doubleday, Page, 1919 NUC.

Letters between a mother "who runs a big farm and knows how and a recently married daughter who is helping her husband run his farm and does not know how."

HARRIS, LINNIE SARAH. B. 1868. United States.

1320   SWEET PEGGY. Boston: Little, Brown, 1904 NUC.

A love story in which the wife becomes a public singer after her marriage.

HARRIS, MARY KERNAHAN.

1321 DR. IVOR'S WIFE. BY MRS. MARY HARRIS. London: G. Allen, 1914 BMC.

Margaret, teacher, marries her favorite pupil's truculent parent. A "delicate situation handled with reticence."

HARRISON, CONSTANCE (CARY). 1843-1920. United States.

1322 SWEET BELLS OUT OF TUNE. BY MRS. BURTON HARRISON. London: T. F. Unwin, 1893 BMC. New York: Century, 1893 NUC.

Unfavorable view of fashionable world of New York's 400—the dog-eat-dog social climbing, the marriage market. Eleanor Halliday of an old Knickerbocker family marries a man who is a social climber—the history of their marriage, the arguments, her disillusionment in finding him selfish and ordinary, his affair with a divorcee Hildegarde de Lancey, a principal character, their estrangement, his penitence and change of character.

1323 THE UNWELCOME MRS. HATCH. A DRAMA OF EVERY DAY. BY MRS. BURTON HARRISON. New York: C.G. Burgoyne, 1901 NUC. New York: D. Appleton, 1903 BMC NUC.

Mrs. Hatch leaves her unfaithful husband, divorces him and twelve years later returns begging to see her daughter. She must disguise herself in order to be at her daughter's wedding. She dies in her daughter's arms.

HARRISON, MARIE.

1324 THE WOMAN ALONE. London: Holden & Hardingham, [1914] BMC.

A woman doctor who is not interested in marriage deliberately has a child as a single parent. Her friends stand by her, and her patients accept the fact of her unorthodox motherhood. The book shows "some of the causes which lie at the roots of feminine unrest today."

HARRISON, MARY SAINT LEGER (KINGSLEY). 1852-1931. United Kingdom.

1325   ADRIAN SAVAGE; A NOVEL. BY LUCAS MALET. New York and London: Harper, 1911 NUC. London: Hutchinson, 1911 BMC.

Two unusual women: Gabrielle St. Leger, whose husband was twice her age and whose marriage was a misery, forty, well-off, devoted to her daughter who is interested in the feminist movement, loved by Adrian Savage, but in no hurry to remarry; Joanna Smirthwaite, plain, gauche, believes Adrian loves her, an illusion that dominates her whole life. She pours all her feelings into her diary. The manner of her coming to know the truth is through a dream.

1326   THE FAR HORIZON. BY LUCAS MALET (MRS. MARY ST. LEGER HARRISON). London: Hutchinson, 1906 BMC NUC. New York: Dodd Mead, 1907 NUC.

Poppy St. John is a study of an audacious, unconventional actress. She is contrasted to Serena Longrove, "faded, elegant, well in her 40's, the typical middle-class English woman—limited, narrow." Serena hopelessly pursues the hero "as a Victorian woman might pursue a man," while Poppy, who is married, offers the hero her frank comradeship.

1327   THE HISTORY OF SIR RICHARD CALMADY. A ROMANCE. BY LUCAS MALET. New York: A.L. Burt, [c1901] NUC. London: Methuen, 1901 BMC NUC.

Sir Calmady, deformed and repellent, is but the prism showing the several colors of woman's sexual nature: Katherine, the mother majestic, calm martyr; Helen, "witch of the sexes," artistic, selfish, taking the most from life; and Honoria, the virgin, "splendid in her freedom" and direct manner. The three women are the novel; they, not Calmady, are treated sympathetically in this psychological study.

1328   THE SCORE. BY LUCAS MALET (MRS. MARY ST. LEGER HARRISON). London: J. Murray, 1909 BMC. New York: E.P. Dutton, 1909 NUC.

Two stories: one concerns a man's futile passion for a woman. He nearly crushes her to death when she rejects him: "love and brutality seem interchangeable." The second concerns Poppy St. John at the zenith of her acting career. She's over 30, loves her work, refuses marriage to an M.P. because she sees it won't work.

1329   THE WRECK OF THE GOLDEN GALLEON. BY LUCAS MALET (MRS. MARY ST. LEGER HARRISON). London: Hodder & Stoughton, 1910 NUC BMC. (Also published as The Golden Galleon. By Lucas Malet (Mrs. Mary St. Leger Harrison). New York: Hodder and Stoughton, [c1910] NUC.)

Miranda Povey, an older woman who keeps a lodging house in London, falls in love. "Her spiritual development after she learns of the unworthiness of the man is vividly and sympathetically drawn." A "sentimental story of old maids" is the reviewers' consensus.

HARRISON, MRS. BURTON. See HARRISON, CONSTANCE (CARY).

HARRISON, MRS. DARENT.

1330   MASTER PASSIONS. London: T. F. Unwin, 1899 BMC.

Madge Wilton's life in the Conservatorium in Germany where she follows a musical career and becomes a fine pianist.

HARROD, FRANCES (FORBES-ROBERTSON). 1866-1956. United Kingdom.

1331   THE HIDDEN MODEL. London: Heinemann, 1901 BMC NUC.

Heroine commits a crime.

1332   THE HORRIBLE MAN. A NOVEL. London: S. Paul, 1913 BMC. (Also published as The White Hound. By Frances Forbes-Robertson. New York: Dodd, Mead, 1913 NUC.)

A fantasy. Heroine is transformed into a milk-white hound to revenge herself against the villain, a land agent and lawyer. As the hound she springs at his throat and kills him. She marries the one witness to her act. Considered an "allegory of the rise of the militant female against horrible men."

HART, MABEL.

1333   FROM HARVEST TO HAY-TIME. London: Hurst and Blackett, 1892 BMC.

Rose Purley runs her widowed mother's farm, gives work to a tramp who is ill with sunstroke.

1334   IN CUPID'S COLLEGE. London: Hurst and Blackett, 1894 BMC.

Ethel is very beautiful, has an income of 8000 pounds a year but has so little mind that she only just escapes idiocy. She bears the penalty of her father's vice. There is a passion of love between Ethel and her mother; her mother is concerned to find someone who will take care of Ethel after her own death. She becomes engaged to a young man who has fallen in love with her beauty, but he breaks the engagement when Ethel, in love with another man, physically attacks that man's fiance. The young man marries someone else, but they are both fond of Ethel and end up sharing their home with her for life.

1335   SACRILEGE FARM. London: W. Heinemann, 1902 BMC. New York: D. Appleton, 1903 NUC.

A young wife is so ill-treated that she revolts. Her husband is found dead, and her family burns the house to cover up "her" crime. Actually, his ex-mistress killed him.

1336   SISTER K. London: Methuen, [1909] BMC NUC.

Hilary Gale is a hospital nurse. Fine detailed decription of nursing profession.

HARTE, EDITH BAGOT.

1337 WRONGLY CONDEMNED: A NOVEL. London: Jarrold, 1896 BMC.

Henry is secretly married to Ruth, and they have a child. In spite of this he engages himself to Rita. When Rita discovers the truth, she kills him. Suspicion falls on Ruth and her brother.

HARWOOD, FRYNIWYD TENNYSON (JESSE). 1889-1958. United Kingdom.

1338 THE MILKY WAY. BY F. TENNYSON JESSE. London: W. Heinemann, 1913 NUC BMC. New York: G. H. Doran, [c1914] NUC.

Picaresque tale full of frank irresponsibility, gaiety, comradeship, adventure. Viv is an artist commissioned to do a book of Provence. She's a strolling player, "an open air model" and a "journalistic detective" as well.

HASANOVITZ, ELIZABETH.

1339 ONE OF THEM; CHAPTERS FROM A PASSIONATE AUTOBIOGRAPHY. Boston: Houghton Mifflin, 1918 NUC.

The pilgrimage of a Russian Jew to the United States. A teacher in Russia, she rebelled against prejudice there and forced her parents to consent to her leaving by a hunger strike. In the United States she learns dressmaking and joins the Garment Workers Union. She describes her experiences with fellow workers, employers, and strikes. She is for unions and against capitalism. She loses her health and her job, is disillusioned in America. Nonfiction?

HASKELL, HELEN EGGLESTON. B. 1871. United States.

1340 O-HEART-SAN: THE STORY OF A JAPANESE GIRL. Boston: L. C. Page, 1908 NUC.

Young Japanese woman saved from suicide becomes a

nurse in a Japanese hospital. She subsequently makes friends with an American woman with whom she exchanges ideas. A "dainty little tale."

HASTINGS, ELIZABETH. See SHERWOOD, MARGARET POLLOCK.

HAULTMONT, MARIE [pseud.].*

1341 THROUGH REFINING FIRES. BY MARIE HAULTMONT. London: Sands, [1914] BMC.

A careful study of the sufferings of two women of the middle class—little lovemaking, not sentimental, sloppy, or sensational.

HAVERFIELD, ELEANOR LUISA. Australia.

1342 A HUMAN CYPHER. London: Hodder & Stoughton, 1909 BMC.

Tragedy of a woman who feels useless and ignored as a wife and the development of her character under the stress of trouble and loneliness. Ursula Bryanston leaves her husband because of their incompatibilty, goes to live alone in London and acquires knowledge of art and sociology. Eventually she and her husband reach an understanding.

HAWEIS, MARY ELIZA (JOY). 1852-1898.

1343 A FLAME OF FIRE: A NOVEL. London: Hurst and Blackett, 1897 BMC.

"I wrote this story to vindicate the helplessness of womankind," says the author in her foreword. "Another addition to the foolish effusions with which women writers attack the eternal marriage question. The usual hysteria over the inequality of the sexes is painfully prominent," says one reviewer. Aglae suffers in her marriage, goes one better than her husband when she falls in love with a soldier—but her relationship with him and other male friends is platonic.

HAWKER, BESSY.

1344 OVERLOOKED; A STORY OF NORTH DEVON.
London: W. Gardner, 1898 BMC.
Rosamond loves an actor whose career is ended by illness.
Together they operate a home for unfortunate actors.

HAWKER, MARY ELIZABETH. SEE HAWKER, MORWENNA PAULINE.

HAWKER, MORWENNA PAULINE. 1848-1908. United Kingdom.

1345 MADEMOISELLE IXE. BY LANOE FALCONER. London:
T. F. Unwin, 1891 BMC. New York: Cassell, [c1891]
NUC.
She is a Russian nihilist who sacrifices her comfortable life
to devote herself to the cause of suffering humanity; she
becomes a member of a secret society that rules a certain
count must die and that she must kill him; she follows the
count to England, becomes a governess at the home he
visits, and finding the right opportunity at the grand ball,
fires at him but misses; "so cool a hand as hers should
have taken more accurate aim." She is then arrested but
makes good her escape. The author's sympathy for her
character is clear in the contrast she makes between "the
narrowness of the English and the large experiences and
still larger sympathies of this woman."

HAWKINS, BATTIE.

1346 NEW WINE: NEW BOTTLES. A NOVEL. London: Digby,
Long, 1898 BMC.
Bride stands "like a white goddess of war on her bed." She
shoots her "would-be ravisher, a Roman Catholic priest."

HAWTREY, EDITH.

1347 MY SILVER SPOONS. London: H.J. Drane, [1901] BMC.
Woman tries to establish a different kind of relation with

a man. She attempts to keep their friendship platonic rather than have it "degenerate into vulgar passion."

HAWTREY, VALENTINA. United Kingdom.

1348   HERITAGE: A NOVEL. New York: Duffield, 1912 NUC. London: Constable, 1912 BMC.

A man who hates women quarrels with his heir, marries. He picks out a wife as he would a horse, judging her points as the mother of his future heir. A study of temperament unsympathetic to men, according to one reviewer.

1349   IN A DESERT LAND. London: Constable, 1915 BMC. New York: Duffield, 1915 NUC.

Restlessness of a married woman shows up in generation after generation of her descendants. Eleanor of the 14th century is a genius, burning with ambition for her son who turns out to be a failure. Her frustration relived in the next generation in a man, in the one after in June who dreamed of being a martyr, almost marries, rejects the man, and kills herself. The restlessness is then inherited by a man and finally by a present-day Eleanor who joins a nunnery and is apparently the first to succeed in her religious aspirations.

1350   IN THE SHADE. London: J. Murray, 1909 BMC.

Henrietta Harris poisons her husband and is acquitted for the murder. Begins with family's reactions—they do not believe she is innocent. She resents them, moves away, assumes another name, meets a man who has been to prison for fraud, and they marry. Both reveal their pasts completely—Henrietta has no pangs of remorse. They settle down happily and have a daughter. The rest of the novel relates the effect of the mother's crime on her daughter.

1351   PERRONELLE. London and New York: J. Lane, 1904 BMC NUC.

Young woman married against her will breaks away for

other man, fights against penance imposed by church, works as servant for four years, finally ends up on church steps with dead child in her arms ready for penance.

1352 RODWELL. London: J. Murray, 1908 BMC NUC.
The Rodwells are charming gentry with a weakness for gambling. Rodwell has spent his first wife's fortune; on her deathbed she attempts to save a young heiress from the same fate by extracting a promise from her son that he will not marry her. But his father marries her instead and dissipates her fortune. The results are tragic.

HAY, MARIE. See VON HINDENBERG, AGNES BLANCHE MARIE (HAY).

HAYCRAFT, MARGARET SCOTT (MACRITCHIE).

1353 GILDAS HAVEN: A STORY. London: Jarrold, 1896 BMC.
Dissenting heroine and high-church hero work out their differences while they work as missionaries in foreign country.

HAYDEN, ELEANOR G. United Kingdom.

1354 LOVE THE HARPER. London: Smith, Elder, 1914 BMC NUC.
Ruth, a secretary in London, loves John, the same man her half-sister loves. Ruth has a child; she had married a man in Australia who told her he was already married. When she goes to Australia at his death, she learns this was untrue. She comes back to London and marries John.

1355 ROSE OF LONE FARM. London: Smith, Elder, 1905 BMC.
Rose is in search of her parentage—in the process sleeps in workhouses, gathers with tramps, etc.

HAYWARD, RACHEL. See CHAMBERS, ROSA.

HEALY, CHRIS.*

1356 MARA: THE STORY OF AN UNCONVENTIONAL WOMAN. London: Chatto & Windus, 1906 BMC.

Mara is left penniless at the death of her father. She struggles to support herself in London. Author's sympathy is with women and against the machinations and injustices of the male. Traditional happy ending.

HEANLEY, CHARLOTTE ELIZABETH.

1357 THE GRANITE HILLS. London: Chapman and Hall, 1920 BMC.

A "psychological study" of Lilla who marries a farmer in Cornwall and then develops a passion for a wandering novelist. "The slow building of a heroine at one with Cornish sea and granite hills."

HEARD, ADRIAN.* United Kingdom.

1358 THE IVORY FAN. London: T. F. Unwin, [c1920] NUC BMC. New York and London: G. P. Putnam's Sons, 1921 NUC.

Catherine Arslea is isolated from books, education, and friends by a possessive and unloving mother. To escape this prison, she leaves with Swaine, a rich and successful actor, and lives with him in Paris, where she develops her talent as a writer. She never feels any dishonor, nor does she allow Swaine to feel he possesses her. She refuses to marry him because of his dishonesty and leaves him to live alone and write. Two men who love her believed from the beginning that her friendship with Swaine would have only positive results: her development and independence.

HEATH, HELENA.

1359 PROPULSION OF DOMENICA. A NOVEL. London: J. Ouseley, 1908 BMC.

Domenica leaves her uncle's farm and goes to London where she opens a lodging house for women factory workers. She eventually marries the curate of the slum district.

HEATHCOTE, MILLICENT.

1360 ENTERTAINING JANE. London: Mills and Boon, [1914] BMC NUC.

Young woman tries to earn her living first as a typist then as an entertainer. When she fails, the handsome hero rescues her in the nick of time.

HECTOR, ANNIE (FRENCH). 1825-1902. United Kingdom.

1361 BARBARA, LADY'S MAID AND PEERESS. BY MRS. ALEXANDER. London: F. V. White, 1897 BMC. Philadelphia: J. B. Lippincott, 1898 NUC.

An inheritance story in which Barbara is first an apprentice to a milliner and dressmaker, then a lady's maid.

1362 BROWN, V.C. BY MRS. ALEXANDER. London: T. F. Unwin, 1899 BMC. New York: R. F. Fenno, 1899 NUC.

He goes in search of his mother who turns out to be his general's wife as well as a famous Hungarian actress.

1363 A CHOICE OF EVILS: A NOVEL. BY MRS. ALEXANDER. London: F. V. White, 1894 BMC NUC. (Also published as Broken Links: A Love Story. By Mrs. Alexander. New York: Cassell, [c1894] NUC.)

The man, unwittingly bigamous, is able to get a divorce from his first wife, when she shows up. The second wife, however, refuses a remarriage. She has found he is not the kind, generous man she thought him to be during courtship, but a selfish prig. She is legally free. "There are readers who will doubt whether she was justified in refusing to return to her bondage when the worthless stone of offense was removed from her path."

1364 THE COST OF HER PRIDE. BY MRS. ALEXANDER. London: F. V. White, 1898 BMC. Philadelphia: J. B. Lippincott, 1899 NUC.

Leslie marries the wrong man out of pride. He is

unfaithful; she divorces him and remarries. He is the "sort of husband who makes the magnanimity of the heroine almost incredible."

1365　THE CRUMPLED LEAF: A VATICAN MYSTERY. BY MRS. ALEXANDER. London: H.J. Drane, [1911] BMC.
Concerns divorce.

1366　FOR HIS SAKE: A NOVEL. BY MRS. ALEXANDER. London: F. V. White, 1892 BMC. Philadelphia: J. B. Lippincott, 1892 NUC.
Sybil's husband, whom she no longer loves, dies conveniently. She marries the man of her choice and becomes a writer of children's books.

1367　FOUND WANTING: A NOVEL. BY MRS. ALEXANDER. London: F. V. White, 1893 BMC. Philadelphia: J. B. Lippincott, 1893 NUC.
May Riddell is left penniless when her father dies. She becomes a companion to a woman in Scotland in order to earn her living. She meets and is loved by Mr. Oglivie who shortly announces his coming marriage to May's best friend but who is anxious to arrange a menage a trois to include May. May refuses; in fact, she is not even tempted. A minor character, Mme. Falk, is a journalist.

1368　THE STEP-MOTHER. BY MRS. ALEXANDER. London: F. V. White, 1899 BMC. Philadelphia: J. B. Lippincott, 1900 NUC.
The usual roles are reversed: the father neglects and dislikes his own son, but the stepmother is genuinely devoted to the boy. Deen is a cultured, broadminded woman whose love for her stepson almost estranges her husband.

1369　THROUGH FIRE TO FORTUNE. BY MRS. ALEXANDER. London: T. F. Unwin, 1900 BMC. (Also published as Thro' Fire to Fortune. By Mrs. Alexander. New York: R. F. Fenno, 1900 NUC.)
Cara, a milliner's apprentice, is believed dead after a fire and takes this opportunity to escape from a drunken

stepmother. She gets a job as a maid. Mrs. Bligh, a retired actress, is her teacher, guide, and friend, and Cara becomes a successful actress. It is also discovered that she is an heiress to a peer.

HEDDLE, ETHEL FORSTER. United Kingdom.

1370 THE PRIDE OF THE FAMILY. London: J. Bowden, 1899 BMC.
Heroine rescues the hero from drowning; becomes "a typewriter" to earn her living.

1371 STRANGERS IN THE LAND. London: Blackie, 1903 BMC NUC.
Two "spinsters" journey to Java accompanied by a girl.

1372 THREE GIRLS IN A FLAT. London: 1896 NUC.
Margaret, teacher, marries her favorite pupil's truculent parent. A "delicate situation handled with reticence."

HEILGERS, LOUISE. United Kingdom.

1373 THE NAKED SOUL, THREE YEARS IN A WOMAN'S LIFE. London: S. Swift, [1912] BMC NUC.
In diary form, described as a "warped and bilious outlook of a selfish and disappointed woman." "Sordid," similar to The Dangerous Age.

1374 THAT RED-HEADED GIRL. London: H. Jenkins, 1917 BMC NUC.
Julia works in a hat shop, and Sheila, referred to in the title, is an artist's model.

HENNIKER, FLORENCE ELLEN HUNGERFORD (MILNES). D. 1923. United Kingdom.

1375 FOILED. London: Hurst and Blackett, 1893 BMC NUC.
Renee Gore, a passionate loving woman married to a man she barely tolerates, takes an unworthy man for her lover and commits forgery for him. Her husband commits suicide when he learns she loves another man.

1376 SECOND FIDDLE. London: E. Nash, 1912 BMC.

Woman whose husband is unfaithful to her comforts and shares the pain of the woman who has striven to take him away from her.

HENRY, MARY H.

1377 THE BENHURST CLUB, OR, THE DOINGS OF SOME GIRLS. BY HOWE BENNING. Boston: Pilgrim Press, 1897 NUC.

The story of a number of young women who establish a "working girls' club" which will give help and companionship to members in various situations.

1378 GOSHEN HILL; OR, A LIFE'S BROKEN PIECES. BY HOWE BENNING. New York: American Tract Society, [c1895] NUC.

Helen Edwards craves more than what farm life at Goshen Hill offers. She gets a teaching post in Illinois. Later when her mother becomes ill, Helen returns home, makes a new plan for life on the homestead and rescues Zoe Moore from the dangers of New York life.

HEPPENSTALL, R. H.*

1379 THE MALICE OF GRACE WENTWORTH. London: J. Long, 1900 BMC.

An heir takes revenge on a man who has scorned her proposals.

HERBERT, ALICE. United Kingdom.

1380 GARDEN OATS. London and New York: J. Lane, 1914 BMC NUC.

A woman's wild oats, sown before and after marriage. Narrated in the first person, the heroine describes her sensations "with gusto." She closes on a note of repentance and a determination to turn over a new leaf, and one reviewer is assured that she is "mildly wild," but another predicts her "wildly controlled character...may lead her yet further astray."

HERBERTSON, AGNES GROZIER.

1381 A BOOK WITHOUT A MAN! London: E. Stock, 1897 BMC.

Four heroines: Rose, Morda, The Limpet and Eena—the emancipated one. Their discussions of men and other subjects. One writes a book without a man but gives it unfinished to the curate she marries.

1382 PATIENCE DEANE, A STUDY IN TEMPERAMENT AND TEMPTATION. London: Methuen, 1904 BMC.

A capable self-reliant teacher plans to marry a man for his money until he insults her. A "tale of thoughtful workmanship."

1383 THE SHIP THAT CAME HOME IN THE DARK. London: Methuen, 1912 BMC.

Marjorie, married to a blind man whom she doesn't love, elopes with another man. Her cousin Margaret agrees to take her place with her husband. When he discovers the truth, he is not appreciative. Marjorie is unreformed, and Margaret is about to marry someone else when book ends.

1384 THE SUMMIT. London: Hutchinson, 1909 BMC.

"A drunken wife, a slatternly home, children that despise their parents," and a pathetic relationship between husband and wife.

HERBERTSON, JESSIE LECKIE. United Kingdom.

1385 BORROWERS OF FORTUNE. London: W. Heinemann, 1912 BMC.

The story of a "cruelly wronged" young woman living in a village with the shadow of her past as governess.

1386 JUNIA. London: Chatto and Windus, 1908 BMC.

The story of two women, egoists and friends. Described by one reviewer as "vulgar, sordid, unpleasant." Another says that the author "sees the world as it is felt by women."

1387　THE STIGMA. A NOVEL. London: W. Heinemann, 1905 BMC.

Susan's chief desire is to be self-sufficient. When her mother dies, she refuses help from her father—she is "illegitimate." Instead she moves in with relatives and takes a job as teacher to mentally retarded children. (She is an artist, but her poor eyesight prevents her career in art.) When she decides to marry a doctor, she fears that marriage amounts to evading her life. Good character analysis.

HERRICK, CHRISTINE (TERHUNE). 1859-1944. United States.

1388　MY BOY AND I. BY HIS MOTHER. Boston: Estes, [c1913] NUC.

Woman is single parent.

HERRINGTON, MRS. M. J.

1389　THE STORY OF A TELEGRAPH OPERATOR. BY M. L. New York: J. S. Ogilvie, 1893 NUC.

Heroine wants a college education, but she must work. First she is employed by Western Union in New York, later in Pennsylvania, still later in Kansas where a disappointing experience concludes the story.

HESTON, WINIFRED ESTELLE THOMAS. United States.

1390　A BLUESTOCKING IN INDIA; HER MEDICAL WARDS AND MESSAGES HOME. BY WINIFRED HESTON, M.D. New York: F. H. Revell, [c1910] NUC. London: A. Melrose, 1910 BMC.

Letters of a woman—a medical missionary in India who is passionate about her work.

HEYWOOD, EVELYN F.*

1391　PASSIONS OF STRAW. London: Methuen, 1913 BMC.

Julia Ponsfort's battles with her husband are described in detail. She leaves him early in the marriage because he is unfaithful and devotes herself to her son. Twenty years later father and son love the same woman, a young actress Peggy Haslam.

HIGGINS, ELIZABETH. See SULLIVAN, ELIZABETH (HIGGINS).

HILDYARD, IDA (LEMON).

1392 A DIVIDED DUTY. BY IDA LEMON. London: Warne, 1891 NUC. Philadelphia: J. B. Lippincott, 1892 NUC.

Young Englishwoman Leslie Mansell living as a governess in Paris and Miss Duckworth, governess who becomes a painter. Reviewers disagree about the meaning of the title, whether it refers to Leslie's divided duty to lover or father or her lover's duty to her or his own brother.

1393 MATTHEW FURTH. BY IDA LEMON. New York: Longmans, Green, 1895 NUC.

Sad story of Selina Pask of London's poor East End. She earns her living by pawning neighbor's treasures, marries a dock worker, recently made stevedore, though she knows he killed a man in a rivalry over another woman. Her marriage is miserable. Her husband deserts her before her child is born. Selina dies.

HILL, CECILIA. United Kingdom.

1394 THE CITADEL. London: Hutchinson, 1917 BMC.

Dinant, Belgium. Catherine Buckland found exquisite relief from the monotony of parents and school in music. She becomes a school teacher, visits successful schools with her sister and together they establish their own school.

1395 STONE WALLS. London: Hutchinson, [1919] BMC NUC.

Struggle of a young girl, Petra Penrose, a repressed musical genius. Her great love of music frightens her mother and sets her father against her. Her life is lonely because she is instinctively an artist and has only one friend. Her later teens are spent in a kind of numb apathy. Her first painful struggle is when her violin and music are taken from her by her father. At the end she is just beginning to overcome some of the problems that separate her from her art.

HILL, ETHEL.

1396   THE UNLOVED. London: Greening, 1909 BMC.

Mary Penrose has much to say to her neighbors on the subject of the position of women. She moves to London, inspired by a social mission and her quest for freedom and love. When she returns to her hometown, she falls madly in love and lives with a man dispensing with the formality of a marriage ceremony. It turns out that he is a married man and a thief who kills himself. We leave Mary with the perfect peace that has come to her soul, and the "true harvest of womanhood"—a child.

HILL, GRACE LIVINGSTON. See LUTZ, GRACE (LIVINGSTON) HILL.

HILL, MARION. 1870-1918. United States.

1397   MCALLISTER'S GROVE. London: J. Long, 1917 BMC. New York: D. Appleton, 1917 NUC.

Annie Laurie McAllister invests all her money in a Florida orange grove. She knows all about oranges. She also knows Sanskrit and is a crack shot with a revolver. She is told to give up the grove when she runs into problems. But she refuses and wins through. She also supports her grandfather and stops his attempts to rule her. There is a slight love story in the background.

1398   SUNRISE VALLEY. Boston: Small, Maynard, [c1914] BMC NUC. London: J. Long, 1914 BMC.

Leaving the luxurious comfort of her aunt's residence in New York, a young woman goes to a small town in Pennsylvania to earn her living as a schoolteacher. She succeeds in teaching, solving a mystery, and falling in love.

1399   THE TOLL OF THE ROAD. New York: D. Appleton, 1918 NUC. London: J. Long, [1918] NUC BMC.

Gertrude Hall, a conventional schoolteacher, joins a travelling theatrical company. The story of how her character develops to a wider view than Puritanism. Finally, she chooses career over wifehood.

HINE, MURIEL. See COXON, MURIEL (HINE).

HINKSON, KATHARINE (TYNAN). 1861-1931. United Kingdom.

1400   A DAUGHTER OF THE FIELDS. BY KATHARINE TYNAN. London: Smith, Elder, 1900 BMC NUC. Chicago: A.C. McClurg, 1901 NUC.

Heroine comes home from a French convent, and she and her mother run a farm.

1401   THE DEAR IRISH GIRL. BY KATHARINE TYNAN. London: Smith, Elder, 1899 NUC BMC. Chicago: A. C. McClurg, 1899 NUC.

Traditional love story except for some fresh touches. Biddy O'Connor, the Dublin girl of the title, has no taste for house cleaning; her house is always untidy. And there is Miss Lucy Holt, the famous Amazon "who had fought the League with a courage and ferocity unequalled by the most militant of landlords." She is described as an "overbearing mannish eccentric elderly spinster," but is sympathetically drawn.

1402   THE HOUSE. BY KATHARINE TYNAN. London: W. Collins, [1920] BMC NUC.

The romance of a medical student disguised as a milkmaid.

1403   THE HOUSE OF THE CRICKETS. London: Smith, Elder, 1908 BMC NUC.

Two daughters escape their father's tyranny to seek fame and fortune; they find men instead.

1404   KITTY AUBREY. London: J. Nisbet, 1909 BMC.

Young woman becomes an M.D. "...if it does not inculcate any heroic ideals of the suffragettes, it depicts a capable young woman who has a soul above clothes and jewels."

1405   MARY GRAY. BY KATHARINE TYNAN. London and New York: Cassell, 1908 BMC 1909 NUC.

Supports self and brothers and sisters. Traditional love story.

1406   PRINCESS KATHARINE. BY KATHARINE TYNAN. New York: Duffield, 1911 NUC. London: Ward, Lock, 1912 BMC.

Young woman, educated beyond what is usual for young people in her Irish neighborhood, returns home to find her mother has taken to drink, and devotes herself to rehabilitating her mother.

HIRSCH, CHARLOTTE (TELLER). B. 1876. United States.

1407   THE CAGE. BY CHARLOTTE TELLER. New York: D. Appleton, 1907 BMC NUC.

The awakening of a young Chicago woman, Frederica Hartwell, to the workers' cause through her love for and marriage to a Hungarian socialist. Concerns the Haymarket riots.

HOBBES, JOHN OLIVER. See CRAIGIE, PEARL MARY TERESA (RICHARDS).

HOBSON, CORALIE (VON WERNER). B. 1891. United Kingdom.

1408   THE REVOLT OF YOUTH. BY MRS. C. HOBSON. London: T.W. Laurie, 1919 BMC NUC.

First-person narrative of Louise Swan, a rebel all her life. Unhappy at home and unable to make friends or find love, she leaves to join an acting company. But she fails as Ophelia, returns home to her relatives, and finally marries. Realistic account of the morals and miseries of a third-rate touring company. Theme: the awakening of womanhood in a young woman with a highly developed sexual instinct. Feminist views reflected throughout.

HOBSON, MRS. C. See HOBSON, CORALIE (VON WERNER).

HOCKING, SALOME. See FIFIELD, SALOME (HOCKING).

HOLDING, ELISABETH (SANXAY). 1889-1955. United States.

1409 INVINCIBLE MINNIE. New York: G. H. Doran, [c1920] NUC. London: Hodder & Stoughton, [1920] BMC.

Frances and Minnie, sisters, are two strong characters, in opposition with each other. When their father dies, Frances is unable to attend medical school as she had planned. She strongly desires a career, something which Minnie is not sympathetic to. Minnie, unlike Frances, is neither bright nor capable; she is, however, clever and determined. She seduces the man Frances is engaged to and marries him; she then marries a second man in order to support the first husband and herself. After bringing much unhappiness to a number of people, she ends up happily, running a boarding house. She is not particularly maternal but remains in possession of her child. Reviewers describe Minnie variously as a "vampire type," a "slow-witted bovine...run amuck—plunging, trampling, in a grotesque nightmarish fashion," and a "monster."

HOLDING, ELIZABETH E. United States.

1410 JOY, THE DEACONESS. New York: Hunt & Eaton, 1893 NUC.

Mehitable Joy Lawrence, trained in hospital work, accepts a position in the Deaconess' Home in a large city. The story traces her career and shows the nature and methods of the Order of American Deaconesses.

HOLDSWORTH, ANNIE E. See HAMILTON, ANNIE E. (HOLDSWORTH) LEE.

HOLDSWORTH, ETHEL CARNIE. United Kingdom.

1411 THE HOUSE THAT JILL BUILT. London: H. Jenkins, 1920 BMC.

Jilted by a man for someone with 500 pounds, when Jill inherits 10,000 pounds, she builds a home in Ireland for tired mothers.

HOLDSWORTH, GLADYS BERTHA (STERN). 1890-1973. United Kingdom.

1412 A MARRYING MAN. BY G. B. STERN. London: Nisbet, [1918] BMC NUC.

Kathleen accidently gets into a compromising situation with Gareth, a weak man. When he proposes, she refuses, but sets up housekeeping with him instead. She is still housekeeping long after she is utterly weary of him. He falls in love with another woman, and they marry, after the two women have talked it over. History repeats itself in this marriage, and on the last page Kathleen comments, "And I stood this sort of thing for sixteen years."

1413 PANTOMIME. A NOVEL. BY G. B. STERN. London: Hutchinson, 1914 BMC [1931] NUC.

Jewish heroine is brought up in well-to-do circumstances. When her family falls into financial misfortune, they must scrimp and save. She yearns for happiness. Wanting a lover, she finds a philanderer. Seeking a career, she joins the Academy of Histrionic Art but is not a success. She falls in love with a fellow student and elopes. Stormbound in Dover, she gets cold feet and slips away to return to London, to discover that he had preceded her.

1414 SEE-SAW. London: Hutchinson, 1914 BMC [1931] NUC.

A study of the effect of marriage on a talented woman with a career. Jaconne is described as "riotously happy, enjoying the freedom of unconventional theatrical life"; she believes this will continue after her marriage. The story ends with "the ultimate victory of the superficial and selfish artist husband."

HOLLEY, MARIETTA. 1844-1926. United States.

1415 AROUND THE WORLD WITH JOSIAH ALLEN'S WIFE. New York: G.W. Dillingham, [1905] NUC. London: T.F. Unwin, 1905 BMC.

1416 JOSIAH ALLEN ON THE WOMAN QUESTION. New York: F. H. Revell, [c1914] BMC NUC.

1417 SAMANTHA AT CONEY ISLAND AND A THOUSAND OTHER ISLANDS. BY JOSIAH ALLEN'S WIFE (MARIETTA HOLLEY). New York: Christian Herald, [c1911] NUC.

1418 SAMANTHA AT THE ST. LOUIS EXPOSITION. BY JOSIAH ALLEN'S WIFE (MARIETTA HOLLEY). New York: G.W. Dillingham, [1904] NUC. London: T.F. Unwin, 1904 BMC.

1419 SAMANTHA AT THE WORLD'S FAIR. BY JOSIAH ALLEN'S WIFE (MARIETTA HOLLEY). New York, London, and Toronto: Funk and Wagnalls, 1893 NUC BMC.

1420 SAMANTHA IN EUROPE. BY JOSIAH ALLEN'S WIFE (MARIETTA HOLLEY). New York, London, and Toronto: Funk and Wagnalls, 1896 NUC BMC.

1421 SAMANTHA ON CHILDREN'S RIGHTS. BY JOSIAH ALLEN'S WIFE (MARIETTA HOLLEY). New York: G. W. Dillingham, [c1909] NUC.

1422 SAMANTHA ON THE RACE PROBLEM. BY JOSIAH ALLEN'S WIFE (MARIETTA HOLLEY). New York: Dodd, Mead, [c1892] NUC. London: B. F. Stevens, [1892] BMC.

1423 SAMANTHA ON THE WOMAN QUESTION. BY MARIETTA HOLLEY "JOSIAH ALLEN'S WIFE". New York: F. H. Revell, [c1913] BMC NUC.

Samantha advocates women's rights as well as temperance.

HOLLIS, MARGERY.

1424 THROUGH THICK AND THIN. London: R. Bentley, 1893 BMC NUC.

Gay Rushton is devoted to her mother. When her wayward father is reported dead, her mother remarries, and when her father turns up alive, Gay keeps the news from her mother. A minor character Miss Fanny Gresham acts at the Bijou Theater.

1425 UP IN ARMS. London: R. Bentley, 1896 BMC NUC.

Noel discovers on her wedding day that her husband is a fortune-hunter who has married her without love. She acts on a "recent legal judgment empowering a wife to live on her own without molestation" and by separation converts him to a loving husband. "A gentler, milder, and more irreproachable story of conjugal revolt has never been penned."

HOLMES, ELEANOR.

1426 LIFE'S FITFUL FEVER. London: Hurst and Blackett, 1898 BMC.

Two sisters on their own. The older one is a singer and a villain; the younger is a journalist. Wholesome, for the younger person.

HOLMES, MARA GORDON.

1427 SILVIA CRAVEN; OR THE SINS OF THE FATHERS. London: E. Stock, [1895] BMC.

She and her brother, orphans, must support themselves. She becomes a governess, "falls a victim to her altruism"—dies of consumption after caring for sick child.

HOLMES, MARGRET. See BATES, MARGRET HOLMES (ERNSPERGER).

HOLNUT, W. S.*

1428   OLYMPIA'S JOURNAL. London: G. Bell, 1895 BMC NUC.

Introspective study of Olympia Colville Daw, a very modern young woman of 25, of cosmopolitan education. More than anything, she wants to be a great author; therefore, she sacrifices herself to her art by marrying a man she cares nothing for in order to study him first hand for her novel. Later she does feel remorse for what she did to George.

HOLT, ADELAIDE.

1429   OUTSIDE THE ARK. New York and London: John Lane, 1913 NUC BMC.

Three people who are different—"outside the ark." Margaret Stair is a great actress and a brilliant woman. She has a lover and a friendship with another man, Hugh, critic and playwright. When an auto accident leaves Margaret a cripple, Hugh writes a very successful play for her, the leading role of which is a crippled woman. He refuses to end his play with suicide. Hugh is married to Iris who hated her Sunday-school life with her minister father. She is immediately and wrongly jealous of his relation to Margaret—as she learns after much spying. Iris sends Hugh away for the duration of her pregnancy and birth of her child, during which time he dies at sea. Iris raises her child by herself and opens a school.

1430   THE VALLEY OF REGRET. New York and London: J. Lane, 1911 BMC NUC.

Betty's husband kills a man who insults her. While he's in prison, she meets and helps a doctor working in the slums. They love each other but Betty returns to husband when he's released.

HOLT, EMILY SARAH. B. 1836. United Kingdom.

1431   ALL'S WELL; OR, ALICE'S VICTORY. Boston: Bradley and Woodruff, [1892] PW. London: Shaw, [1893] BMC.
Alice Benden, the heroine, is one of the Canterbury Martyrs, Protestants persecuted during the reign of Mary, 1556-1558. She was burned at the stake, delivered to justice by her husband.

HOLT, LEE.*

1432   GREEN AND GAY. London and New York: J. Lane, 1918 BMC NUC.
War story, of a hospital directed by Madame la Marquise de Savigny for wounded soldiers.

HOME, FRANCES.

1433   AN AWAKENED MEMORY. London: Ward, Lock, 1909 BMC.
Mrs. Barnes drinks to forget the past. Her medical student husband also drinks. She can not obliterate the memory of her daughter Dorothy.

1434   THE EXPERIENCE OF DOROTHY LEIGH. London: G. Routledge, 1899 BMC.
The life of a hospital nurse—her efforts to reform an alcoholic man and her eventual marriage to the resident surgical officer.

HOOD, AGNES ELIZA (JACOMB). B. 1866. United Kingdom.

1435   ESTHER; A NOVEL. BY AGNES E. JACOMB. New York: H. Ober, 1911 NUC. London: W. Heinemann, 1912 NUC BMC.
A minister sees his love for his wife as a threat to his purity and goes to Africa for the good of his soul. She

"falls" during his absence. He realizes his error when he returns and their marriage is restored.

1436 THE FAITH OF HIS FATHERS: A STORY OF SOME IDEALISTS. BY A. E. JACOMB. London: A. Melrose, 1909 BMC. New York: Dodd, Mead, 1909 NUC.

"A finely wrought study" of a woman married to a Methodist who treats their daughter and son by the book. The woman begins to hate her husband's religion when she sees her son deteriorate because the father forced him to marry a barmaid the son had slept with. And when the father tries to break up the daughter's relation with a man of little religion, the mother rebels. She takes her daughter's part and enables the daughter to marry the man. In the end, she "loses her reason."

1437 JOHNNY LEWISON. A NOVEL. BY AGNES E. JACOMB. London: A. Melrose, 1909 BMC.

Jewish—Christian marriage. Wife revolts against "materialism and luxury with which Johnny's father oppresses her." She turns to Dick Chard, her old friend.

1438 THE LONELY ROAD. BY AGNES E. JACOMB. London: A. Melrose, 1911 BMC.

Full-length presentation of a correct suburban wife in an intolerable position. Helen Andrews goes from the rule of her father to marriage with a man of a lower social status. Her love for him cools when she finds how crude and unrefined he is. The end is tragic.

HOOPER, I.

1439 THE MINISTER'S CONVERSION. London: A. and C. Black, 1898 BMC.

He was called upon in the course of his duty to admonish his wife publicly. The novel "shows how, in the midst of his agony at humiliating the woman he loves, there is the savage joy of denouncing what he considers her guilt. Her lover springs to her side and faces the congregation with her." Reconciliation follows.

1440 NELL GWYN'S DIAMOND. London: A. and C. Black, 1899 BMC NUC.

Historical romance set in 17th century, two thirds of which concern the adventures of Aysgarth trying to find Charles II's stolen diamond. "But the convent scenes are too much for our credulity. A woman is not capable at one moment of cold blooded murder, in whatever cause, and at another of extreme gentleness and gratitude. The Abbess makes a very good villain, but we are outraged by the tale of her sainthood a few pages further on."

HOOVER, BESSIE RAY. B. 1874. United States.

1441 OPAL. New York and London: Harper, 1910 BMC NUC. Romantic story of a teacher.

HOPE, FLORENCE.

1442 THE TWO POWERS. London: J. Long, 1910 BMC. Unhappy marriage.

HOPE, LILITH.

1443 THE ANVIL. London: Chapman & Hall, 1914 BMC.

A "pleasure-loving" young woman who is a governess wants to be a dancer like her sister. She falls into the "white slave peril" but escapes.

1444 BEHOLD AND SEE! London: Hurst & Blackett, 1917 BMC NUC.

Sister Rose is an English nun forced to stay in Belgium when the Germans invade. She is raped by a German soldier, has a child and must then decide between keeping her child and leaving the sisterhood or remaining a nun. She keeps her child and returns to society.

1445   SIMOON. London: S. Swift, [1913] BMC.

First person narrative by Miriam who runs a school. "Study not without poignancy and insight of neurotic femininity with its power to attract man side by side with its lack of balance without his protection."

HOPE, MARGARET.

1446   CHRISTINA HOLBROOK. London: Methuen, 1912 BMC.

Somber, marries a man younger than herself and is so afraid of the marriage turning out badly that she helps it to happen.

1447   MESSENGERS. London: Methuen, 1914 BMC.

Woman is sent to prison for stealing a ring. Unable to conceal her guilt from her daughter, and at the sight of her daughter's misery, she runs away from home in the vain hope that she may retrieve the past. She comes to a miserable end.

HOPKINS, ALICE (KIMBALL). B. 1839. United States.

1448   A DAUGHTER OF THE DRUIDS. BY A. K. H. Boston: [A. K. Mudge], 1892 BMC NUC.

Allice de Kymber has a love of astronomy. Her experiments lead her to be suspected of witchcraft. She must flee England; eventually she meets a scientist, their romance.

HOPKINS, MRS. HERBERT MUELLER. See CAVENDISH, PAULINE BRADFORD (MACKIE) HOPKINS.

HORLICK, JITTIE.*

1449   JEWELS IN BRASS. London: Duckworth, 1913 BMC. New York: Brentano's, 1913 NUC.

Young woman makes a marriage in name only to escape

"dull, grandmotherly influence." The arrangement works well till she really falls in love. The artist-husband dies. Good insights into women's psychology.

HORN, KATE.

1450 THE LOVE-LOCKS OF DIANA. London: S. Paul, [1911] BMC.

Diana Ponsonby does drudge work in boarding house to pay father's debt, later "serves as a decoy" in a beauty shop where she dances.

1451 LOVE'S LAW. London: S. Paul, 1916 BMC.

Author wishes to reinforce belief in universal motherhood.

1452 THE MULBERRIES OF DAPHNE. London: S. Paul, [1910] BMC.

Daphne runs away from family, society, and an arranged marriage to a wealthy man to live in a cottage. She works as a housekeeper.

1453 THE WHITE OWL. London: S. Paul, [1911] BMC.

Demeter is a famous writer who turns her daughter Persephone over to an aunt when her husband dies and devotes herself exclusively to her art.

HORT, DORA.

1454 TIARI; A TAHITIAN ROMANCE. London: T. F. Unwin, 1893 BMC NUC.

Tahiti and the "degradation of the native races at the hands of their conquerors." Tiari, a half-caste, marries the Frenchman Selwin. His "priggish philistinism" and domineering nature cause her death. Another young woman who believed she loved Selwin ends up in sympathy with his wife.

HOSKEN, ALICE CECIL (SEYMOUR). B. 1877. United Kingdom.

1455 THE ADVENTURESS. BY CORALIE STANTON. New York: T. J. McBride, 1907 NUC.
She is a former cafe singer, widow of a wealthy man who killed himself. She is very rich and means to become richer. She loans money, and when the men cannot repay, she makes them work for her.

HOUGHTON, BEATRICE YORK. United States.

1456 THE SHELLEYS OF GEORGIA. Boston: Lothrop, Lee & Shepard, [1917] NUC.
Rose Shelley learns her fiance has seduced a poor young mountain woman named Minnie, tries to educate him to his obligation to Minnie, secretly educates Minnie to make her a more attractive person, and ends up marrying a different man because her fiance marries Minnie.

HOUK, L. C. VIOLETT.* B. 1866.

1457 THE GIRL IN QUESTION; A STORY OF NOT SO LONG AGO. New York: J. Lane, 1908 NUC.
Heroine comes to Washington on a political mission; mystery.

HOUMAS, MOUNT. See GILL, MARY (GILL).

HOUSMAN, CLEMENCE ANNIE. United Kingdom.

1458 THE UNKNOWN SEA. London: Duckworth, 1898 BMC NUC.
Man saves his brother from werewolf woman at the expense of his own life.

HOUSTOUN, MATILDA CHARLOTTE (JESSE) FRASER. 1815?-1892. United Kingdom.

1459 THE WAY SHE WON HIM. A NOVEL. London: F. V. White, 1891 BMC NUC.
Ettie Cranston sings at Coventry Music Hall. Mystery of

her parentage solved; she marries and her marriage is tame.

HOVEY, JEAN EDGERTON.* United States.

1460 JOHN O'PARTLETT'S; A TALE OF STRIFE AND COURAGE. Boston: L. C. Page, 1913 NUC.

A woman befriends a fierce dog (referred to by title) and gives a home to a small black boy. For these acts she is tormented by the villagers who call her Witch Beevish. Things are set right at the end when the dog does the town a service.

HOWARD, BLANCHE WILLIS. See VON TEUFFEL, BLANCHE WILLIS (HOWARD).

HOWARTH, K. A.*

1461 PHILIP HELMORE, PRIEST. London: Downey, 1899 BMC.

After eight years of marriage and children, Mrs. Helmore learns that her minister husband has renewed a relationship with a mistress he had discarded when they married. She leaves him, moves to Belgrave Square, paints, and makes a good living for herself. In the end she and her husband are reconciled, after he confesses, repents and is rehabilitated.

HOWELL, CONSTANCE.

1462 CHESTER CHASE. London: Everett, 1914 BMC.

A man and three women. At the close he has been abandoned by all three; one has become an imprisoned suffragette.

1463 MRS. CHARTERIS. London: J. Ouseley, [1911] BMC.

Injustice and unwisdom of divorce laws. Mrs. Charteris deserted by her husband goes through a form of marriage with another man who, discovering the deception, leaves her.

HOYER, MARIA A.

1464 WHAT HAPPENED AT MORWYN. London: Digby, Long, [1893] BMC.
Heroine pays off her dead father's debts by illustrating botanical works. As a "painter of specimen flowers," she "distances all rivals at her work."

HUARD, FRANCES (WILSON). B. 1885. United States.

1465 LILIES WHITE AND RED. New York: G.H. Doran, [c1919] NUC.
Two stories about life in France. One tells of a French woman who leads a very quiet life until the war and her great act of heroism. In the other a small boy sees the horrors of war.

HUDSPETH, ROSA. United States.

1466 THE JUGGERNAUT OF THE MODERNS: A NOVEL. Boston: Arena, 1896 NUC.
The heroine is a stenographer in a law firm in the rural West; the purpose is a single standard of morals for men and women.

HUESTON, ETHEL (POWELSON). B. 1887. United States.

1467 SUNNY SLOPES. Indianapolis: Bobbs-Merrill, [c1917] NUC BMC. London: Skeffington, [1918] BMC.
Compares two sisters. Carol married to a minister in St. Louis moves with him to New Mexico when he gets TB; Connie is a reporter who struggles to keep from marrying.

HUGHES, M. E.*

1468 MARGOT MUNRO. London: Mills & Boon, 1910 BMC.
Margot makes a foolish marriage but remains with her
husband for ten years for the sake of her blind stepson.
The stepson then persuades her to divorce his father.

HULL, E. M. See HULL, EDITH MAUDE.

HULL, EDITH MAUDE. United Kingdom.

1469 THE SHEIK; A NOVEL. BY E. M. HULL. London: E.
Nash, [1919] BMC NUC. Boston: Small, Maynard, [1921]
BMC NUC.
Diana Mayo—willful, headstrong, raised and dressed as a
boy—meets her match in the sheik who kidnaps her. She
hates the taming process.

HUMPHREY, ZEPHINE. See FAHNESTOCK, HARRIETTE
ZEPHINE (HUMPHREY).

HUMPHREYS, ELIZA MARGARET J. (GOLLAN). D. 1938.
United Kingdom.

1470 BETTY BRENT, TYPIST. BY "RITA". London: T.W.
Laurie, [1908] BMC.
Secretary spends weekend in country house with
fashionable society. Simple minded heroine.

1471 THE COUNTESS PHARAMOND; A SEQUEL TO
"SHEBA." BY RITA. New York: U. S. Book, [c1891]
NUC. London: F. V. White, 1893 BMC.
Sheba is a successful novelist condemned by the "leading
critical journal on the strength of a few botanical errors
that have nothing to do with plot, style, or character."
The novel reveals "the atrocities of Mr. Mixson, the
publisher."

1472 DIANA OF THE EPHESIANS: A NOVEL. BY "RITA".
London: S. Low Marsten, [1919] BMC NUC. New York:
F.A. Stokes, [c1920] NUC.
Diana is the illegitimate daughter of an English professor
and a Greek woman. When her mother dies, she writes to
her father who is then obligated to bring her to England,
though he presents her as his ward, daughter of an old
friend. She is 17, arrogant, self-centered, hated, "ugly in
face and form." She announces that she is writing the
greatest novel. Her struggle for fame and position follows.

1473 THE ENDING OF MY DAY, THE STORY OF A
STORMY LIFE. BY RITA, AUTHOR OF "SHEBA" "THE
COUNTESS PHARAMOND" "MISS KATE" "ASENATH
OF THE FORD". London: F. V. White, 1894 NUC BMC.
Extracts from Belle Ffolliott's journal. Belle, who has a
knowledge of Latin and Greek, comments on society,
folly, immorality. She marries, and "though innocent in
the narrowest sense of the word, is publicly and
disgracefully divorced." She marries the corespondent.

1474 A GENDER IN SATIN. BY "RITA". London: T. F. Unwin,
[1895] BMC. New York: G. P. Putnam's Sons, 1895 NUC.
Paula Drewe marries an artist, Christopher Hope, who
knows she does not love him. Then she falls in love with
his best friend, a wicked ambitious doctor who uses
women to get on with his career. She tells her husband
who patiently waits for her to release herself from
Grantley Daring's power.

1475 THE HOUSE CALLED HURRISH. BY RITA. London:
Hutchinson, 1909 BMC.
Lady Moonrake eventually dies of her morphia habit.
Judith Sarsefield, the heroine, is her companion.

1476 KITTY THE RAG. BY "RITA". London: Hutchinson, 1896
NUC BMC. New York: R. F. Fenno, [c1897] NUC.
Irish waif is raised by a junk collector. She is beautiful

and ambitious, gets an education for herself, becomes an heir and marries happily—though she discovers she is the illegitimate daughter of a woman named Hermia who loved a youth (Kitty's father) but who was forced to marry Lord Ellingsworth.

1477 THE MAN IN POSSESSION. BY "RITA". New York: Hovendon, [1891] NUC. London: F. V. White, 1893 BMC.

Kate O'Brien is a lively young woman, a gifted actress with a beautiful voice. Her romance with a woman-hater is depicted.

1478 PEG, THE RAKE. BY "RITA". London: Hutchinson, 1894 BMC. [New York]: [P. F. Collier], 1895 NUC.

Emilia, clever, lively woman of the world, is 40 years old, and too much for her father and stepmother to handle. She marries to escape their tyranny, but she is miserable. The author sets her free by revealing a secret marriage of twenty years ago that even Emilia didn't know about.

1479 PETTICOAT LOOSE. A NOVEL. BY RITA. London: Hutchinson, 1898 BMC.

Brianna was a "daughter of the people...unspoilt, untampered with, fed on ideals, educated on Shakespeare." She becomes a highly successful actress. An actor "exercised hypnotic influence on her, culminating in downright rape." Men only succeeded in impressing the tedious idiocy of their sex upon the indifference of her own. Three lovers persevered. In the end one is dead, the other is dying, and the third is taking her for a walk.

1480 THE SILENT WOMAN. BY "RITA". London: Hutchinson, 1904 BMC.

Dr. Quarn is sapping the life of his invalid wife with the medicine he prescribes.

1481 THE SINNER. BY "RITA". London: Hutchinson, 1897 BMC. Chicago: [c1897] NUC.

Routine of hospital life of nurses well described. Nellie Nugent's patient Mrs. Langrishe is poisoned by her doctor husband, who has a weakness for women and would be rid of his wife. Nellie Nugent and Deborah Gray, both trained nurses, are the heroines.

1482   VANITY! THE CONFESSIONS OF A COURT MODISTE. BY RITA. London: T. F. Unwin, 1900 BMC NUC. New York: F. M. Buckles, 1900 NUC.

Narration of a court dressmaker.

1483   A WOMAN IN IT. A SKETCH OF FEMININE MISADVENTURE. BY "RITA". London: Hutchinson, 1895 BMC. Philadelphia: J. B. Lippincott, 1895 NUC.

Nina Garbett's diary begins in divorce court where the decision goes against her and she is left without income and reputation. Through the help of a woman, she gets work as a companion to an invalid woman but leaves this work when the woman's husband, mad for Nina, murders his wife. She then becomes a beauty products demonstrator. Her diary records the various business and social ventures of this dare-devil Irish adventuress. It ends with her meeting her good angel—a rich breezy American named Bertha Planefield who tells her "Where our sisters are friendless, desperate, forsaken—there, Nina, lies our country and our work."

1484   A WOMAN OF SAMARIA. BY "RITA". London: Hutchinson, 1900 BMC.

Vicar's daughter betrayed and abandoned, obliged to flee home. Her career in the world, stage life.

HUMPHREYS, ELIZA MARGARET J. (GOLLAN) AND LOUISA ALICE BAKER.

1485   LOOKING-GLASS HOURS. BEING THE TRUE AND FAITHFUL REFLECTIONS OF TWO FEMININE MINDS—WHAT LED THEREUNTO—AND THE RESULT THEREOF. BY "RITA" AND "ALIEN". London: Hutchinson, 1899 NUC BMC.

Letters: gradual estrangement and final reconciliation of a husband and wife.

HUNGERFORD, MARGARET WOLFE (HAMILTON). 1855?-1897. United Kingdom.

1486 THE HOYDEN: A NOVEL. BY THE DUCHESS (MRS. HUNGERFORD). Philadelphia: J. B. Lippincott, 1893 NUC. London: Heinemann, 1894 BMC.

The hoyden is a very wealthy and very young woman, girl bride of an impoverished English lord. When he tells her he married her only to pay his debts, she strikes him on both cheeks and leaves. Her revolt causes him to fall in love with her and beg her pardon.

1487 LADY VERNER'S FLIGHT: A NOVEL. BY THE DUCHESS (MRS. HUNGERFORD). London: Chatto and Windus, 1893 BMC. New York: J. A. Taylor, [1893] NUC.

A patient Griselda finally revolts; Lady Rhoda Verner is married to an impossible and monstrous husband who spends all her fortune, boasts to her of his infidelities, tries to get her seduced so that he can win a divorce, and even beats her. She finally says enough, leaves him, and becomes housekeeper of a handsome squire whom she eventually marries.

HUNGERFORD, MRS. See HUNGERFORD, MARGARET WOLFE (HAMILTON).

HUNT, ISOBEL VIOLET. 1866-1942. United Kingdom.

1488 THE CELEBRITY AT HOME. BY VIOLET HUNT. London: Chapman and Hall, 1904 BMC NUC.

The diary of a "wide-awake and intensely disenchanted" 14 year old "flapper woman" who reveals her father as a famous novelist who poses and lives in the world as a bachelor, neglecting his wife and children.

1489 THE CELEBRITY'S DAUGHTER. BY VIOLET HUNT. London: S. Paul, [1913] BMC NUC. New York: Brentano's, 1914 NUC.

Comic history of the social success of Tempe Taylor, "one

of the most impossible young women who have ever been evolved in fiction." At 18, she declares herself mature, becomes involved with a corespondent in a divorce case, is paid to break off the relationship, but ends up an heir engaged to the prime minister—in spite of her shady past. She is described as a flapper.

1490   THE DOLL; A HAPPY STORY. BY VIOLET HUNT. London: S. Paul, [c1911] BMC NUC.

Minnie Hawtayne is a rebel defying conventions. She's a divorcee whose second marriage is threatened by divorce. Her daughter Isabel, also divorced, makes a visit after a long separation. Disagreeable entanglements involving herself and her daughter and her two men work out in the end.

1491   A HARD WOMAN: A STORY IN SCENES. BY VIOLET HUNT. London: Chapman and Hall, 1895 BMC NUC. New York: D. Appleton, 1895 NUC.

The "gradual moral descent" of Lydia Munday, called vulgar, unfaithful, selfish, shallow and despicable by some reviewers; clever, brilliant, successful, by others. "In the final scene, when she and her husband are left at last alone with the truth—and very little else—one's pity comes very near to liking after all." Dramatic use of male narrator. Interlacing of scenes, some narrative, some formal or informal dialogue appropriate for the individual episodes.

1492   THE HOUSE OF MANY MIRRORS. BY VIOLET HUNT. London: S. Paul, [1915] BMC NUC. New York: Brentano's, 1915 NUC.

The story of a wife's "utterly useless sacrifice" to see that her husband is provided for after her death. She is a strong woman, retired from the stage with money, and married to a man whom she loves but who cannot earn a living. She believes he has been disinherited by his uncle because of her past. Her husband does not impose his values on her, although she lives in many ways that he would believe, if done by him, would sully his good name.

1493 THE HUMAN INTEREST. A STUDY IN INCOMPATIBILITIES. BY VIOLET HUNT. London: Methuen, 1899 BMC.

Phoebe Ellis miserably married has read Ibsen, wants to start a salon, yearns for a grand passion, leaves home disguised as a French general, takes a new name, throws herself at artist, meets Egidea a successful novelist, is divorced and happy at the end. "Satire on the problem novel describing the vague longings of a discontented wife." An "English Emma Bovary."

1494 THE LAST DITCH. BY VIOLET HUNT. London: S. Paul, [1918] BMC NUC.

The story is told in letters exchanged by a set of aristocratic and independent women. They are interested in futuristic art; one becomes engaged to a man on the condition that he promises never to kiss her, one becomes a bus conductor.

1495 THE MAIDEN'S PROGRESS: A NOVEL IN DIALOGUE. BY VIOLET HUNT. London: Osgood, McIlvaine, 1894 BMC.

Moderna remains unmarried for nine years, during which time she sees the world for herself, acquiring her own experience, making her own mistakes. She eventually is bored with this existence and marries her cousin. The novel is almost entirely free of narrative or description, mostly dialogue, in the style of Gyp.

1496 THEIR LIVES. BY VIOLET HUNT. London: S. Paul, [1916] BMC NUC. New York: Brentano's, [1916?] NUC.

The story of two sisters, Christina and Virgilia, the daughters of a pre-Raphaelite artist. Descriptive rather than dramatic style.

1497 UNKIST, UNKIND! A ROMANCE. BY VIOLET HUNT. London: Chapman and Hall, 1897 BMC.

Narrated by Janet Freeman, governess. Concerns the wild heath country of Northumberland and the secluded life of Sibella Drake adept at alchemy, astrology and demonology, completely devoted to her teacher and master. When a woman of fashion threatens to take him, Sibella "wreaks deadly vengeance" on her.

1498 THE WAY OF MARRIAGE. BY VIOLET HUNT. London: Chapman and Hall, 1896 BMC.

Marital histories, "mostly unequal and unhappy," of a group of dinner guests, narrated by Mr. St. Jerome, novelist. "Cynical," "hardness and brilliance in character delineation."

1499 THE WHITE ROSE OF WEARY LEAF. BY VIOLET HUNT. New York: Brentano's, 1908 NUC. London: W. Heinemann, 1908 BMC NUC.

Amy, who has a good figure and bad complexion, has been a dressmaker, a typewriter, an amanuensis in Russia, a nurse in South Africa, an actress, and a lecturer, becomes a house keeper-companion. Although she is "passionless and loathes the attentions of men," she dies bearing her employer's child, and he kills himself. A serious work, in the tradition of Jane Eyre, but there is no salvation for Amy in the men who claim to love her.

1500 THE WIFE OF ALTAMONT. BY VIOLET HUNT. New York: Brentano's, 1910 NUC. London: W. Heinemann, 1910 BMC NUC.

The wife of a murderer provides a home for his mistress and her two children.

1501 THE WORKADAY WOMAN. BY VIOLET HUNT. London: T. W. Laurie, [1906] BMC NUC.

Portrayal of a working woman.

HUNT, MARGARET (RAINE) AND ISOBEL VIOLET HUNT.

1502 THE GOVERNESS. BY MRS. ALFRED HUNT AND VIOLET HUNT. London: Chatto & Windus, 1912 BMC NUC.

HUNT, MRS. ALFRED W. See HUNT, MARGARET (RAINE).

HUNT, VIOLET. See HUNT, ISOBEL VIOLET, also HUNT, MARGARET (RAINE) AND ISOBEL VIOLET HUNT.

HUNTINGTON, GLADYS THEODORA (PARRISH).

1503 CARFRAE'S COMEDY. BY GLADYS PARRISH. London: W. Heinemann, 1915 BMC. New York: G. P. Putnam's Sons, 1916 NUC.

Blanche Benwell is a divorced actress living peacefully in a convent where her friends visit and where her religion is her strength. She is a mystical kind of person—tender, simple and childlike. Eventually she becomes restless and realizes that of the three men who pursue her, she loves Julian, but she gives him up, holding to her determination not to remarry. Carfrae writes a play about her life as told to him by Blanche.

HUNTINGTON, HELEN. See BARKER, HELEN MANCHESTER (GATES) GRANVILLE.

HUNTLY, HOPE. See HUNTLY, KATE HOPE.

HUNTLY, KATE HOPE.

1504 KAMI-NO-MICHI; THE WAY OF THE GODS IN JAPAN. BY HOPE HUNTLY. London: Rebman, 1910 BMC NUC.

A young woman who breaks her engagement in order to become a missionary in Japan makes friends with a young Japanese woman. Together they discuss Shintoism and Christianity. A young woman breaks her engagement and becomes a missionary in Japan. Kami-No-Michi, the Japanese heroine, holds her own in conversations with the Englishwoman on Shintoism.

1505 OUR CODE OF HONOUR: A ROMANCE OF THE FRONTIER WAR. London: S. Low, 1899 BMC.

Anglo-Indian romance—"a loveless marriage and lawless affinities"—that condemns the theory "that every married woman is fair prey if she yield to aught save brute force."

HURD, GRACE MARGUERITE. United States.

1506 THE BENNETT TWINS. New York: MacMillan, 1900 BMC NUC. London: Macmillan, 1900 NUC.

Agnes and Don, orphans, go to New York with $100; she is determined to be a singer, he an artist. Both are students and live at "The Hive" with a group of other students who study hard and work enthusiastically at their chosen art. They show humour in meeting failure; one doesn't doubt their ultimate success. Not sentimental, not a love story.

HUSSEY, EYRE.*

1507 JUST JANNOCK. London: J. Macqueen, 1899 BMC. Philadelphia: J. B. Lippincott, 1900 NUC.

Heroine races horses (against other women), races boats and wins (against men), nurses, boxes, and sings.

HUSTON, ETHELYN LESLIE. B. 1869. Canada.

1508 THE TOWERS OF ILIUM. New York: G. H. Doran, [c1916] NUC.

Somber work depicting the hardships women and their children face without the benefits of financially secure husbands; at the same time the author is outspoken about the immorality of most women's marriages which are for financial security and not a great love. June refuses to marry, supports her invalid father and herself by a succession of jobs: running a nursing home, editing a medical dictionary, and free-lance art work. She is tricked into a marriage but renounces her husband and raises her child without marriage. She has a close friend who is a woman M.D. Ellen Key and George Eliot are frequently quoted. She finally meets a man whom she can love.

HUZARD, ANTOINETTE (DE BERGEVIN). B. 1874.

1509 THE DOCTOR WIFE: A NOVEL. BY COLETTE YVER. London: Hutchinson, 1909 BMC. (Tr. by Anna, Comtesse de Bremont.)

Concerns women doctors and the innumerable difficulties

to be overcome by women taking up the profession of medicine. A study of the conflict between the demands of a woman's professional life and her "duty" as a wife of a doctor.

1510 A KING'S CALLING. BY COLETTE YVER. London: T. Nelson, [1913] NUC BMC. (Tr. by Hugh M. Miller.)
Clara is the science governess in the court of the King of Lithuania.

1511 LOVE VS. LAW. (LES DAMES DU PALAIS). BY COLETTE YVER. New York and London: Putnam, 1911 NUC BMC. (Tr. by Mrs. Bradley Gilman.)
The principal character is a plain woman, a very modern type of French heroine, and she's a lawyer—a better lawyer than her husband. The novel is a serious study of the marriage vs. career problem.

HYLAND, M. E. F.

1512 THE DREAM WOMAN. BY KYTHE WYLWYNNE. London: T. F. Unwin, 1901 BMC.
The heroine is a writer whose husband fabricates an heroic past just so that she will write a book about him.

ILES, SYBIL M.

1513 THE SCHOOL OF LIFE. A STUDY OF THE DISCIPLINE OF CIRCUMSTANCE. London: E. Stock, 1905 BMC.
Woman estranged from her husband goes on the stage.

IMHAUS, ELIZABETH VIGOUREUX. United States.

1514 EXILED BY THE WORLD; A STORY OF THE HEART. New York: Mutual, [1901] NUC. London: Gay & Bird, 1902 BMC.
Concerns an actress.

INCHBOLD, A. CUNNICK. United Kingdom.

1515 LOVE IN A THIRSTY LAND. London: Chatto and Windus, 1914 BMC.

Julie is forced into a convent by her family, is unhappy. She is taken to the Holy Land by the nuns. An American feminist journalist, visiting the Holy Land to inquire into the position of women there, and Julie's lover search for her. The novel "portrays the bitterness and rancour of opposing needs" in the Holy Land.

1516 PRINCESS FEATHER. London: Hutchinson, 1899 BMC.

"Mr. Inchbold's concern is to make us feel what it was to be a peasant's wife in years before the battle of Trafalgar. He succeeds. The picture is sinister, but it convinces." Elizabeth is a refined young woman who marries Michael Tagg, the captain of the sheep shearers, a boor and a brute. Elizabeth's tragedy is that her background insists she submit to her duty as a wife, however disgusting it is to her. Michael is bestial, drunken; he beats her and finally sells her by auction to a soldier. "The horrible auction of wives...is doubtless drawn from credible tradition; the newspapers report such occurrences even today." Set in Sussex.

1517 THE ROAD OF NO RETURN. London: Chatto & Windus, 1909 BMC.

Vounia Petrovna Martinoff becomes a disciple of Tolstoy after her imprisoned husband becomes a monk and thereby annuls their marriage. She becomes part of a revolutionary group and joins a pilgrimage to the Holy Land to hide; she believes she murdered an official who insulted her.

1518 THE SILVER DOVE. London: Hutchinson, 1900 BMC.

Temperance story. Young wife runs away from drunken husband, robs a shop and is condemned to prison. The shock straightens him out.

IOTA. See CAFFYN, KATHLEEN MANNINGTON (HUNT).

IRELAND, MARY ELIZA (HAINES). B. 1834. United States.

1519 WHAT I TOLD DORCAS: A STORY FOR MISSION WORKERS. New York: E. P. Dutton, 1895 NUC BMC.
Mrs. Atheling, active mission worker, tells her experiences. Written to be read at missionary and sewing society meetings.

IRONSIDE, JOHN. See TAIT, EUPHEMIA MARGARET.

IRWIN, FLORENCE. B. 1869. United States.

1520 THE MASK; A NOVEL. Boston: Little, Brown, 1917 NUC.
The slow disillusionment of Allison. She is an intelligent married woman living a shabby life in a New York boarding house with her writer husband. She sees him gamble their money away. She sees her son die in an accident caused by her husband. In her misery, she turns to writing and eventually saves her husband from ruin the source of which is his guilt.

1521 POOR DEAR THEODORA! New York and London: G.P. Putnam's Sons, 1920 BMC NUC.
Theodora endures social snubs and hardships in her job as governess. When war comes she does Red Cross work and finds romance.

IRWIN, GRACE. See IRWIN, MARY GRACE.

IRWIN, GRACE (LUCE). D. 1914. United States.

1522 THE DIARY OF A SHOW GIRL. New York: Moffat, Yard, 1909 NUC.
Woman starving on a salesclerk's salary in New York, gets a job in a chorus line, rises to fame and fortune, keeps her good name, and marries in the end.

IRWIN, INEZ (HAYNES). B. 1873. United States.

1523 ANGEL ISLAND. BY INEZ HAYNES GILLMORE. London: G. Bell, 1914 BMC. New York: H. Holt, 1914 NUC.

"An impressive and rather daring allegory, yet treated in such a view of poetic imagery and shown through such a mist of shimmering light, that one scarcely realizes until sober second thought that it says things in regard to feminism which it would not be easy to say in any less indirect way." The story concerns an island inhabited by a superior race of women and their capture by five men who are shipwrecked.

1524 JUNE JEOPARDY. BY INEZ HAYNES GILLMORE. New York: B. W. Huebsch, 1908 NUC.

Thethry, whose mother died when she was 10 and whose father is a jewel thief, has spent most of her life in a convent. She buys a house on Beacon Street in Boston, invents a past, and brings five young working women into the house to live with her. The book opens with the women talking about men. They are agreed that all men who think that "woman's place is in the home" or that any other activity makes a woman "unfit for the position of wife and mother" are impossible for them as companions or lovers. Thirsting for adventure, Thethry leaves the group for an evening walk. The story relates the night's adventures which involve a diamond necklace, a gang of jewel thieves, and six men who pass the tests the women have devised for them. Romantic comedy.

1525 THE LADY OF THE KINGDOMS. New York: G. H. Doran, [1917] NUC.

Two young women friends rebel against their restrictive Cape Cod homelife and escape to New York. Southward Drake is beautiful; she has lots of suitors, but is indifferent to marriage and dislikes children. She shoots one suitor when she finds him with another woman, but ends up marrying him. Hester Crowell is unattractive with no suitors, but she wants a child and claims the right to be a mother without marriage. She has her child. Both women are happy.

1526 THE OLLIVANT ORPHANS. BY INEZ HAYNES GILLMORE. London: Methuen, 1915 BMC. New York: H. Holt, 1915 NUC.

Two years in the lives of a down and out family of six orphans, three of them young women. Beckie struggles for employment which seems everywhere to be denied to unattractive young women; Ann mixes with Bohemian types; and Lainey revolts.

IRWIN, M. E. F. See MONSELL, MARGARET EMMA FAITH (IRWIN).

IRWIN, MARY GRACE. B. 1891.

1527 BROWN-EYED SUSAN. BY GRACE IRWIN. Arlington, N. J.: Little Book Publisher, 1917 NUC.

"An open-eyed study of the relation between a modern young woman and her mother." They love each other but cannot understand each other's needs and feelings.

IRWIN, VIOLET MARY. B. 1881. United States.

1528 WITS AND THE WOMAN. Boston: Small, Maynard, [c1919] BMC NUC.

Clarissa Kendall is a former department store saleswoman and an expert in slang. She tells her adventures "whose pace and convolutions make a whirlwind seem slow and straight."

JACKSON, IDA.

1529 WHEN HYACINTHS BLOOM. Edinburgh and London: Oliphant, 1898 BMC.

Romance of a governess. Scotland.

JACKSON, MARGARET (DOYLE). B. 1868. United Kingdom.

1530 A DAUGHTER OF THE PIT. Boston: Houghton, Mifflin, 1903 NUC. London: Cassell, 1903 BMC.

A teacher's struggles in a mining town.

JACKSON, MYRTLE BEATRICE STRODE.

1531 KATE MITCHELL. Merry-thought Press, 1914 EC.

The life of Kate Mitchell in the form of a novel. A college and high school teacher, she became famous throughout Europe for the discovery of a new star. "If all Higher Feminists were as attractive and efficient (a rare combination), their various 'causes' soon would be won."

JACOB, MRS. ARTHUR. See JACOB, VIOLET MARY AUGUSTA FREDERICA (KENNEDY-ERSKINE).

JACOB, VIOLET MARY AUGUSTA FREDERICA (KENNEDY-ERSKINE). 1863-1946. United Kingdom.

1532 THE HISTORY OF AYTHAN WARING. BY VIOLET JACOB (MRS. ARTHUR JACOB). New York: Dutton, 1908 NUC. London: W. Heinemann, 1908 BMC.

Character study of Hester Bridge and Aythan Waring who contest an estate; her relentless hatred for him. Her "delineation is a sombre study of the madness which may arise from a woman's jealousy."

1533 IRRESOLUTE CATHERINE. London: J. Murray, 1908 BMC NUC. New York: Doubleday, Page, [1909] PW.

A farm servant and her two suitors.

JACOBS, CAROLINE EMILIA. 1872-1909.

1534 JOAN OF JUNIPER INN. BY EMILIA ELLIOTT. Philadelphia: G. W. Jacobs, [1907] BMC NUC.

Fun loving story of widow and children who run an inn.

JACOBS, ESTHER.

1535 LOVE AND LAW: A STORY OF THE JOY AND WOE IN A SINGER'S LIFE. New York: G.W. Dillingham, 1895 NUC.

Esther Jacobs writes her own life story describing her career as an opera singer and such events as the time she was plaintiff in a breach of promise case against Henry Sire.

JACOMB, A. E. See HOOD, AGNES ELIZA (JACOMB).

JACOMB, AGNES E. See HOOD, AGNES ELIZA (JACOMB).

JAMES, DOROTHY A BECKETT (TERRELL). United Kingdom.

1536 EMANCIPATION; THE STORY OF A GIRL WHO WANTED A CAREER. BY DOROTHY A BECKETT TERRELL. Funk & Wagnalls, 1914 PW. London: Cassell, [1914] BMC.

The experiences of a young woman in search of a career.

JAMES, FLORENCE ALICE (PRICE). 1857-1929. United Kingdom.

1537 THE BARONET'S WIFE. BY FLORENCE WARDEN. London: T. F. Unwin, 1908 BMC.

The Baronet's wife, unknown to her husband, becomes a fence in this story of crime and mystery.

1538 THE BOHEMIAN GIRLS. A NOVEL. BY FLORENCE WARDEN. London: F. V. White, 1899 BMC.

Four young women driven to earn a living in London. Three go on the stage. They smoke, gamble, drink champagne and play billiards, but at the end they marry.

1539 THE DAZZLING MISS DAVISON. BY FLORENCE WARDEN. London: T.F. Unwin, 1908 BMC NUC. New York: H.K. Fly, [1910] NUC.

She has a mysterious income—she appears to be a pickpocket.

1540 THE GREY MOTH. BY FLORENCE WARDEN. London: Ward, Lock, 1920 BMC.

The Grey Moth, also known as The Cobra, is a "masterful and exceptionally although not impossibly wicked old woman" who "baffles investigation."

1541 THE HOUSE BY THE RIVER. BY FLORENCE WARDEN. London: T.F. Unwin, 1905 BMC. New York: J.S. Ogilvie, 1905 NUC.

A typewriter goes to work for invalid in house by river, mysteries abound.

1542 A HOUSE WITH A HISTORY. BY FLORENCE WARDEN. London: F. V. White, 1901 BMC.

Concerns white slavery.

1543 THE INN BY THE SHORE. A NOVEL. BY FLORENCE WARDEN. London: Jarrold, 1897 BMC NUC.

A "quiet little old maid" named Nellie turns out to be a jewel thief.

1544 A LIFE'S ARREARS. BY FLORENCE WARDEN. London: Cassell, 1908 BMC. New York: Cassell, 1909 PW.

Jane, 32, inherits money and goes to Monte Carlo where she encounters adventures and romance.

1545 LITTLE MISS PRIM. A NOVEL. BY FLORENCE WARDEN. London: F. V. White, 1898 BMC NUC.

Governess and lady-help engaged to doubtful family, but she wraps them around her finger and finds a ring for it too.

1546 THE MARRIAGE BROKER. BY FLORENCE WARDEN. London: T.W. Laurie, [1907] BMC NUC.

Exposes marriage as a trade.

1547 MISS FERRIBY'S CLIENTS. BY FLORENCE WARDEN. London: T. W. Laurie, [1910] BMC NUC.

Miss Ferriby is a wealthy philanthropist whose income is augmented by her popularity amongst society as a fortune teller and by her even more clandestine activities as a leader of a gang of criminals. The qualities which contribute to her success on all three fronts are a keen and shrewd intelligence, personal magnetism, and bravery in the face of danger. She is undone by an infatuation for her young male secretary, a passion which is unrequited. She is described as a dwarf possessing much physical strength with a voice which could be either full of feminine charm or masculine authority, and although her face and hands are young and beautiful, her hair is gray.

1548   A PASSAGE THROUGH BOHEMIA. BY FLORENCE WARDEN. London: Ward and Downey, 1893 BMC. New York: Hovendon, [c1893] NUC.

Includes a circus dwarf "Red Jack," a woman disguised as a man. She is also an eloquent speaker whose great speeches stir up revolt of the poor.

1549   SEA MEY ABBEY. BY FLORENCE WARDEN. New York: J. W. Lovell, [c1891] NUC. (Also published as A Wild Wooing. A Novel. By Florence Warden. London: F. V. White, 1893 NUC BMC.)

The heroine Freda Mulgrave is lame; she was raised in a French convent after her mother died. Her vivid adventures and brave actions with her smuggler father after she leaves the convent at age 18.

1550   THOSE WESTERTON GIRLS. BY FLORENCE WARDEN. London: R. Bentley, 1891 NUC BMC. New York: J. W. Lovell, [1891] NUC.

Rector's three daughters run the farm successfully while he wastes money. One marries a man who comes to the farm to be taught farming.

JAMES, GERTIE DE S. WENTWORTH. United Kingdom.

1551   THE CAGE UNBARRED: BEING THE STORY OF A WOMAN WHO WAS DULL. London: Everett, [1913] BMC.

Hypochondriacal suburban wife is so bored with her marriage (the cage) that her husband trumps up a case of infidelity so that she can divorce him. She loses the man she expected to marry and in the end returns to her now successful husband.

1552 THE DEVIL'S PROFESSION. London: Everett, [1914] BMC.

Lionne, a steno-typist who is having difficulty with her eyesight, gets a job as assistant to a doctor in an asylum. She discovers that the patients are made to appear insane by the injection of a drug.

1553 THE ESCORT; A FARCICAL COMEDY. London: Everett, [c1912] BMC NUC.

When the heroine is faced with the choice of becoming a rich man's mistress or a grass widow's escort (dressed in male attire), she chooses the latter.

1554 GOLDEN YOUTH. London: T. W. Laurie, [1916] BMC.

A woman detective plays a prominent part in this drama set in a beauty parlor.

1555 SCARLET KISS; THE STORY OF A DEGENERATE WOMAN WHO DRIFTED. London: T.W. Laurie, [1910] BMC NUC.

A woman of 30, the editor of a low-class paper called Home Comfort, marries, but does not settle down to an uneventful life.

1556 THE SECRET FLAT. London: T.W. Laurie, [1914] BMC.

The "sexual infatuations" of a successful composer of love lyrics. When the war comes, she loses her job, she divorces her husband, her lover leaves for the front, and her relation with a third man is broken. Heroine tells her own "unpleasant" story.

1557 VIOLET VIRTUE. London: T.W. Laurie, [1916] BMC.

Eighteen year old marries rich older man and is unhappy. She leaves, divorces husband, and remarries happily.

1558 WHITE WISDOM. London: Everett, [1913] BMC.

Office of the Flashlight and the young women employed in the folding department—not a "nice" story.

1559 THE WILD WIDOW. London: T. W. Laurie, [1908] BMC. New York: Empire Book, [c1908] NUC.

A successful adventuress, she defrauds her husband's life insurance company, wins at Monte Carlo, speculates and wins on the exchange. She may not be a widow.

JAMES, WINIFRED. See DE JAN, WINIFRED LEWELLIN JAMES.

JAMESON, ANNIE EDITH (FOSTER). 1868-1931. United Kingdom.

1560 THE GOSSIP SHOP. BY J. E. BUCKROSE. London and New York: Hodder & Stoughton, 1917 NUC BMC. New York: G. H. Doran, [c1917] NUC.

Wendlebury is another Cranford. Gossip initiated by heroine in all innocence comes close to ruining a man's life, but the story is serious for only a few pages at a time.

1561 THE ROUND-ABOUT. BY J. E. BUCKROSE. London and New York: Hodder & Stoughton, 1916 NUC BMC.

Lucy in the 19th century married whom she pleased; her daughter learns a trade and goes to war as a nurse.

1562 THE SILENT LEGION. BY J. E. BUCKROSE. London and New York: Hodder & Stoughton, [c1918] NUC BMC.

Barbara returns to her family from work in the hospital during the war to help with the finances—her father has been financially ruined during the war—and to be a companion to her mother who has been devastated by the loss of her son in the war. The title refers to the British middle class and the sacrifices they are called on to make during wartime.

1563 SPRAY ON THE WINDOWS. BY J. E. BUCKROSE. London: Mills & Boon, [1915] BMC NUC. New York: G. H. Doran, [c1915] NUC.

Ann Middleton is a secretary whose marriage is unhappy but ends well.

JAMESON, MARGARET STORM. B. 1897. United Kingdom.

1564 THE POT BOILS; A NOVEL. BY STORM JAMESON. London: Constable, [1919] BMC NUC.

Young woman in a northern university in England, her career there and in London until she marries. Margaret's student days are "erotic, beery, highbrowed." She moves to London where she has a good time writing for suffrage newspapers. She presides over a group of English intellectuals who discuss Bolshevism, Nietzsche, Fabianism and Feminism. All of which, including her erotic dreams, indicates the sanity of the new renaissance.

JAMESON, STORM. See JAMESON, MARGARET STORM.

JANIS, ELSIE. 1890-1956. United States.

1565 LOVE LETTERS OF AN ACTRESS. New York and London: D. Appleton, 1913 NUC BMC.

A popular American actress writes letters to all kinds of men who love her. She marries none of them, holding up to the end the dream of an ideal man. Her career, she says, is her first love.

JAY, EDITH KATHARINE SPICER.

1566 A MASK AND A MARTYR. BY E. LIVINGSTON PRESCOTT. London: E. Arnold, 1896 BMC NUC.

Capt. Harradyne resigned from the army with rumours of war; his brother officers sent him a white feather. He was, although a Sunday school teacher, seen coming out of public houses and was believed to be a drunk and a wife-beater. His wife never went out. He was convicted of stealing a jewel. He was seen frequently with fresh wounds and bruises. What was going on? His wife Violet was a "raving murderess" when drunk, and he was protecting her. She finally dies, and he enlists as a private, dies fighting in Egypt. "Since 'Poor Nellie'—a book of a very different method and manner with a somewhat similar motive—we have seen nothing at all in fiction that seems at all to touch the real aspect of the subject." The author fails to make the husband completely sympathetic—a few jarring notes.

JENKINSON, EMILY J. B. 1879. United Kingdom.

1567 THE SOUL OF UNREST; A NOVEL. London: E. Arnold, 1912 BMC NUC. New York: Duffield, 1913 NUC.

Bride was raised in Inis Gloria, a wild island of the sea,

where she developed a love for all things beautiful. She went to Angel Meadow, a slum in a manufacturing town, to help the poor.

JENNER, KATHERINE LEE (RAWLINGS). B. 1853. United Kingdom.

1568 LOVE OR MONEY: A NOVEL. BY KATHERINE LEE (MRS. HENRY JENNER). London: Bentley, 1891 BMC NUC. New York: D. Appleton, 1892 NUC.

The two oldest of a clergyman's eleven children are two daughters completely different in personality. One is super-angelic; the other, Phil Ferrars, is super-diabolic. She marries a nobleman for his money, but soon runs through his fortune. She is at the point of leaving for the continent with another man, when she finds her husband shot. She is accused of the murder, tried, sentenced to be hanged, and finally exonerated.

JENNER, MRS. HENRY. See JENNER, KATHERINE LEE (RAWLINGS).

JESSE, F. TENNYSON. See HARWOOD, FRYNIWYD TENNYSON (JESSE).

JOHNSON, ANNA. 1860-1943. United States.

1569 AGNES GRANT'S EDUCATION. BY HOPE DARING. Cincinnati: Jennings & Pye, [1902] NUC.
Her efforts to become a teacher.

JOHNSTON, ANNIE (FELLOWS). 1863-1931. United States.

1570 MARY WARE'S PROMISED LAND. Boston: L. C. Page, 1912 NUC BMC.
Mary gives up love for the sake of her work; later she marries when it doesn't interfere with it.

JOHNSTON, GRACE L. KEITH. United Kingdom.

1571 A LOST ILLUSION. BY LESLIE KEITH. London: Methuen, 1891 BMC. New York: United States Book, [1891] NUC.

Loveday Penn, raised by strict Quakers, is a gentle, loyal woman. But when she learns after her marriage that her husband is a brute and has done wrong, she leaves him only to return to comfort his last hour. A worthier man awaits her.

1572 A TROUBLESOME PAIR. BY LESLIE KEITH. London: R. Bentley, 1894 BMC.

Mary married a parson for his sermons, and when she discovered he didn't write them, she wouldn't speak to him for twenty years. She tries to fill her life with pets and flowers. She is described by one reviewer as an "addled Heavenly Twin," and by another as "too strong to attempt any risky experiment in the way of emancipation."

JOHNSTON, MARY. 1870-1936. United States.

1573 CEASE FIRING. London: Constable, 1912 BMC. Boston: Houghton Mifflin, 1912 NUC.

The Civil War, from a Southern woman's point of view. She sees the war as sad and useless; "It wasn't worth it," is the theme that recurs throughout.

1574 HAGAR. Boston: Houghton Mifflin, 1913 NUC. London: Constable, 1913 BMC.

Brilliant argument for feminism. Hagar Ashendyne was raised in Virginia and sent to an old-fashioned girls' finishing school when her mother died. But she breaks with all Southern traditions concerning women and rebels against authority. She moves to New York to start her literary career, and here she awakens to her full responsibility and opportunity as a person. She becomes a successful author, works for the feminist movement and marries late—after her career as a writer is well established. Fine study of the inner growth and convictions of a feminist.

1575 THE WANDERERS. Boston: Houghton Mifflin, [1917] NUC. London: Constable, 1917 BMC.

Nineteen episodes tracing the gradual enslavement and the emancipation of women from primitive times to French Revolution. Shows the changes in the love relationship, the eternal duel of sex, and the position of typical women at various points in history. The early episodes, written in the style of sagas, describe the essential arts of women and show cave women and children living separate and independent lives from men.

1576 THE WITCH. London: Constable, 1914 BMC. Boston: Houghton Mifflin, 1914 NUC.

Joan, a young English woman living alone with a cat, is tried and sentenced to burning for witchcraft. She makes her escape disguised as a man in a ship bound for Virginia. The story is of her subsequent adventures.

JOHNSTONE, EDITH.

1577 A SUNLESS HEART [ANONYMOUS]. London: Ward, Lock and Bowden, 1894 BMC.

Gasparine is left inconsolable after her brother Gaspar's death. Lotus, a college lecturer, becomes her closest friend. Lotus says of her life that "her soul was born old and outraged by man's villainy." Described by reviewers as powerful, painful, repellent, and nauseating, showing a French influence, and like African Farm (although one reviewer feels it lacks the intellectual content), the novel studies first the relationship of Gasparine and her brother and subsequently the friendship between Gasparine and Lotus.

JOLY, MRS. JOHN SWIFT.

1578 THOSE-DASH-AMATEURS. London: J. Long, 1918 NUC BMC.

A satire of titled ladies who act as nurses in wartime. They are contrasted with Janet, a professional nurse who is far-seeing, competent, and firm.

JONES, ALICE ILGENFRITZ. D. 1906. United States.

1579 BEATRICE OF BAYOU TECHE. Chicago: A. C. McClurg, 1895 NUC.

Anti-slavery novel: life of a slave who is white, her life with her grandmother, her ignorance that she is part black, her treatment as part of the plantation master's family to whom she is related. Talented and well educated, Beatrice obtains her freedom, goes through various episodes that test her character, and faces prejudice both in the North and South.

JONES, AMANDA THEODOCIA. 1835-1914. United States.

1580 A PSYCHIC AUTOBIOGRAPHY. New York: Greaves, [1910] BMC NUC. London: W. Rider, [1911] BMC NUC. (BMC: Theodosia.)

A feminist psychic. Describes the destruction of the Women's Company for Working Women by men.

JONES, CONSTANCE EVAN.

1581 THE TEN YEARS' AGREEMENT: AN EXPERIMENT IN MATRIMONY. London: J. Nisbet, 1907 BMC.

A woman with her own ideas concerning marriage insists upon a ten-year contract rather than a life-long one.

1582 WOMAN'S LOOKING GLASS: A SPINSTER'S CHRONICLE. London: J. Nisbet, 1909 BMC.

Margaret Darcy in her thirties lives a dreary isolated life in London with her hyprochondriac aunt upon whom she is dependent and for whom she is a slave. She falls in love with a doctor—the first man she meets outside her aunt's house—but he is indifferent to her. When her aunt dies, Margaret is rich and much sought after but remains alone because she still loves the doctor who is now engaged. Author's view is that men are narrow, selfish, and vain.

JONES, D. EGERTON. See CALLAHAN, DORIS EGERTON (JONES).

JONES, E. B. C. See LUCAS, EMILY BEATRIX COURSOLLES (JONES).

JONES, ENID (BAGNOLD). 1889-1981. United Kingdom.

1583 THE HAPPY FOREIGNER. BY ENID BAGNOLD. London: W. Heinemann, 1920 BMC NUC. New York: Century, 1920 NUC.

Fanny, English, goes to France at the end of the war to drive a car for the French army. She is a new heroine, almost without fear, a pioneer who sees, feels, thinks, hears, yet is full of the sap of life. She remains from first to last an unknown young woman, secret, folded within herself.

JONES, GERTRUDE (WARDEN). United Kingdom.

1584 AN ACTRESS'S HUSBAND. BY GERTRUDE WARDEN. London: C.H. White, 1909 BMC.

Michal Garth poisons her husband, goes on to be a great actress, falls in love, later learns she didn't poison her husband.

1585 THE MILLIONAIRE AND THE LADY. BY GERTRUDE WARDEN. London: J. Long, 1907 BMC.

Young actress who loses heart and money but is rescued by young M.D.

1586 THE SENTIMENTAL SEX. BY GERTRUDE WARDEN. London: J. Lane, [1896] BMC.

Cattle-raiser seeks out his ideal woman, a poet of passion, and marries her. She is very modern; he is old-fashioned and puritanical, won't allow her to look at pictures or statues not fully clothed. "Clever comedy which develops into a tragedy."

JONES, SUSAN CARLETON AND HELEN MILECETE.

1587 THE CAREER OF MRS. OSBORNE. BY CARLETON-MILECETE. New York and London: Smart Set, 1903 NUC.

A bored wife goes off to Europe with her sister, and the

two have a riotous time. She masquerades as the beauty Mrs. Osborne, meets a former lover, dances, flirts and, at the very end, returns to her husband.

JONES, W. BRAUNSTON.*

1588   MITHAZAN: A SECRET OF NATURE. London: T. F. Unwin, 1891 BMC.

Heroine has been bitten by a snake in her youth. She was cured but the poison in her blood transforms her into a "human snake." Even after the death of two husbands she is unaware that her kiss kills the recipient.

JONSON, DOROTHY (FORSYTH).

1589   AS A MAN IS ABLE: A STUDY IN HUMAN RELATIONSHIPS. BY DOROTHY LEIGHTON. London: W. Heinemann, 1893 BMC.

Title alludes to Elizabeth Browning's poem and the idea that women love more passionately and durably than men. Iris Hope and Vere Vandeleur love each other, but his parents send him to India because they oppose the match. Iris goes with him with the plan to marry in Paris. When legal difficulties prevent their marriage, Iris decides "it's ever so much nicer—more ideal—to be bound only by love." They live together in India for three years, after which Vere returning to England to claim an inheritance meets and loves Beatrice but returns to Iris. She in turn discovers his love for Beatrice, gives him up, meets Beatrice, and the two women become great friends. Beatrice learns only on her wedding day that Vere and Iris were lovers; she kills herself. The man is blamed.

1590   DISILLUSION: A STORY WITH A PREFACE. BY DOROTHY LEIGHTON. London: Henry, 1894 BMC.

Linda is a typewriter and a member of the Spade Club, a combination of the Pioneer Club and the Fabian Society. She and Mark are "comrades"; they collaborate on a play. Mark loves his wife Celia, whose remarks are "original, pungent, and entertaining," although she does not feel bound by her marriage vows.

JORDAN, ELIZABETH GARVER. 1867-1947. United States.

1591   MAY IVERSON'S CAREER. New York and London: Harper, 1914 BMC NUC.

Sequel to previous May Iverson books. May goes to New York to become a journalist. The story is of her development, from her convent background to a time when she is more interested in what she sees than in her own attitude towards it. She becomes a successful journalist, novelist, and dramatist. At 25 she leaves it all behind for marriage.

JORDAN, KATE. See VERMILYE, KATE (JORDAN).

JOSIAH ALLEN'S WIFE. See HOLLEY, MARIETTA.

JUDD, A. M.*

1592   THE WHITE VAMPIRE. London: J. Long, 1914 BMC.

The "White Vampire is one of the pseudonyms of a beautiful Russian woman who, in revenge of her own ruin as a girl, takes delight in luring men into her disastrous toils. Sometimes she acts as an agent for the government, and at other times for the nihilists. Most of her victims end in suicide or Siberia."

JUDSON, JEANNE MARGARET ANTONIA. B. 1890. United States.

1593   BECKONING ROADS. New York: Dodd, Mead, 1919 NUC.

The story of a young woman who leaves her husband and goes to New York to live with a friend, a divorced woman. She becomes a cloak model and is involved with a gambler. She eventually returns to her marriage.

1594   THE STARS INCLINE. New York: Dodd, Mead, 1920 NUC.

The story of a young woman artist in New York in a circle of clever Bohemians.

JUDSON, KATHARINE BERRY. United States.

1595 WHEN THE FORESTS ARE ABLAZE. Chicago: A. C. McClurg, 1912 NUC.

A young woman teacher takes up residence in a forest preserve with the intention of acquiring the land in 3 to 5 years under the Homestead Act. She passes through "many terrifying experiences, the climax of which was the great forest fire."

JUTA, RENE. United Kingdom.

1596 "THE TAVERN". London: W. Heinemann, 1920 BMC NUC.

Dr. James Barry, a surgeon-major who was a notable figure in South Africa a century ago, a person with a "quick tongue and a rasping wit," is, in fact, a woman whose son is a leper.

KAUP, ELIZABETH BARTOL (DEWING). B. 1885. United States.

1597 A BIG HORSE TO RIDE. BY E. B. DEWING. New York: Macmillan, 1911 NUC BMC.

The effect of marriage upon a famous dancer whose career is the prime factor in her life. Rose Carson's stormy childhood, the whole technical side of her profession, and her moral development. She marries a man she finds unbearable, breaks off with a lover she finds too self-controlled but who returns after two years changed to her liking. Simulates memoir form.

1598 OTHER PEOPLE'S HOUSES. BY E. B. DEWING. New York: Macmillan, 1909 NUC BMC.

Striking and absorbing study of Emily Stedman, a woman writer who achieves enormous success with her first book.

KEATS, GWENDOLINE. D. 1910. United Kingdom.

1599 THE WHITE COTTAGE. BY ZACK. Westminister: A. Constable, 1901 BMC. New York: Scribner, 1901 NUC.

Significant moments in the lives of four characters, two of them women. Luce marries Ben, a reckless daredevil, and has a child—only to discover that he's already married. When another man offers to marry her and adopt her child, she refuses. Hester is Ben's legal wife, an alcoholic driven to drink by her misery. She exposes her husband's bigamy, and half-mad, steals Luce's child. Later she and the child are found dead. A sensitive tragic study.

KEAYS, H. A. MITCHELL. See KEAYS, HERSILIA A. MITCHELL (COPP).

KEAYS, HERSILIA A. MITCHELL (COPP). 1861-1910?. United States.

1600 THE ROAD TO DAMASCUS; A NOVEL. BY H. A. MITCHELL KEAYS. Boston: Small, Maynard, 1907 NUC BMC. London: G. Richards, 1912 BMC.

Fine psychological study of Richarda Homphrey. Married two years, she is visited by the former mistress of her husband who begs Richarda to adopt her illegitimate child. She does so because she is drawn to the child. She raises the child as her own and keeps the secret of the boy's identity from the boy and from her husband.

1601 THE WORK OF OUR HANDS. BY H. A. MITCHELL KEAYS. London and New York: McClure, Phillips, 1905 BMC NUC.

The ideals of a woman conflict with those of her easygoing, morally-lax husband. He objects to her taking a "woman of ill repute" into their home; her life is devoted to the cause of down-trodden mill workers.

KEDDIE, HENRIETTA. 1827-1914. United Kingdom.

1602 A CRAZY MOMENT. BY SARAH TYTLER. London: Digby, Long, 1899 NUC BMC.

Young childless woman kidnaps a baby who, when she's

grown up, runs off on learning the truth, but returns when she finds she and real mother dislike each other.

1603 FRIENDLY FOES. BY SARAH TYTLER. London: Digby, Long, 1903 BMC.
They are "three old maids." Murder story.

1604 A HONEYMOON'S ECLIPSE. BY SARAH TYTLER. London: Chatto and Windus, 1899 NUC BMC.
Young woman marries a minister in order to wed as young as her sisters had. He is awkward and dull. They part immediately but are reunited in the end.

1605 HONOR ORMTHWAITE; A NOVEL. BY THE AUTHOR OF "LADY JEAN'S VAGARIES" [ANONYMOUS]. New York: Harper, 1896 NUC.
Lady Ormthwaite abandoned her dissipated husband and gave their child to a cousin to care for. She remarries, believing both are dead. The child turns out to be alive; she eventually sends for her, passing her off as a dependent to husband.

1606 IN CLARISSA'S DAY. BY SARAH TYTLER. London: Chatto & Windus, 1903 BMC NUC.
Two women at Oxford—their adventures and loves.

1607 KINCAID'S WIDOW. BY THE AUTHOR OF "CITOYENNE JACQUELINE" [ANONYMOUS]. London: Smith Elder, 1895 BMC NUC.
Based on two historical crimes: one in which a wife kills her husband through the hands of the serving man who is broken on the wheel; the other, a niece who stabs to death her uncle and seducer. Point of view is to demonstrate the domestic cruelty of the Scotch lord. Sympathy is with the women.

1608 LADY JEAN'S VAGARIES: A NOVEL [ANONYMOUS]. London: R. Bentley, 1894 BMC.
A sympathetic study of the sister of a tyrannical duke. She disguises herself as a man and goes to France. She marries secretly outside the church; her brother refuses to acknowledge the legitimacy of her twin sons.

1609 "THE MACDONALD LASS". A STUDY FROM LAST CENTURY. BY SARAH TYTLER. London: Chatto and Windus, 1895 NUC BMC.

Flora Macdonald tells her own story which takes place about 1750 in Long Island and Skye. She saved the life of the young Pretender, Charles Edward, an act that did great harm to the Jacobite cause.

1610 MANY DAUGHTERS. BY SARAH TYTLER. London: Digby, Long, 1900 BMC.

This novel presents a thoughtful woman's idea of the ultimate ideal for the perfect and complete education of her sex. The Woman's Institute of Technical Knowledge and its Productions covers the ground not only of Newnham and Girton but includes domestic science as well. The heroine, Delia, has a Cambridge degree in math, applies it to the science of cooking.

1611 MISS NANSE. BY SARAH TYTLER. London: J. Long, 1899 BMC.

"Homely dignity of provincial gentlewomen" in the tradition of Cranford. Two old Scotch gentlewomen who have lost their fortunes take up high-class dressmaking.

1612 MRS. CARMICHAEL'S GODDESSES. BY SARAH TYTLER. London: Chatto and Windus, 1898 NUC BMC.

Capable, managing widow becomes a cabinetmaker to support her daughters, is very successful. She is equally proud of her family and the honour of her business. She raises her daughters as though she expected them to marry dukes, and when they don't, she is satisfied. "Written in the Scotch language with translations of all the hard words given in brackets."

1613 THE WITCH-WIFE. BY SARAH TYTLER. London: Chatto and Windus, 1897 NUC BMC.

"Sibylla Bethune is a dignified and gracious woman, whose knowledge and spirit are too rare for the atmosphere of dull fanatacism in which she lives and whose end...is alleviated by the skill which provides her with an anaesthetic counterpoise to her sufferings." She is burned as a witch, her only sins being her love of animals, her knowledge of herbs, her self reliance, her discovery of the merciful uses of morphia, chloroform and hypnotism, and her lack of relatives.

KEELING, ELSA D'ESTERRE. 1860-1935. United Kingdom.

1614   APPASSIONATA: A MUSICIAN'S STORY. London: Heinemann, 1893 BMC. New York: R. Bonner, 1893 NUC.

"...story of an artist, a beautiful Finlander, of her love for her art, her infatuation for a sister artist, her very moderate affection for her husband, and the tragedy of her married life, brought about directly by the treachery of the woman she had loved not wisely but too well, and by the stubborn prejudice of her husband....Her after life, bereft of art, and love, and even justice, therefore fills us with indignation....Miss Keeling only tells us of a man knowingly marrying a girl who loved art better than himself, of how he put cramping fetters on her, and...punished her brutally, and with quite special meanness. Things were to improve, it is suggested at the end. We doubt it." The Bookman (London), 5 (1894), 126.

1615   OLD MAIDS AND YOUNG. London and New York: Cassell, 1895 BMC NUC.

A "tangled" tale of diverse women in youth and middle-age: Miss Onora and Miss Mariabella "old maids," a sweet and frivolous bride, Cambridge female students, etc.

1616   ORCHARDSCROFT: THE STORY OF AN ARTIST. London: T. F. Unwin, 1892 BMC. New York: Cassell, [c1892] NUC.

Ally, the wife of an English gardener out of work because he drinks, supports the family by washing.

1617   A RETURN TO NATURE: A KENTISH IDYLL. London: Jarrold, Daffodil, 1896 BMC.

Educated at Cambridge, the heroine becomes a governess in a remote Kentish village.

KEENE, LESLIE.*

1618 THE SUFFRAGE AND LORD LAXTON. London: Digby, Long, 1914 BMC.

Lord Laxton's first wife is a militant suffragette who was killed in an accident at one of their meetings. His second wife belongs to the opposite camp and restores his happiness.

KEITH, ALYN YATES. See MORRIS, EUGENIA LAURA (TUTTLE).

KEITH, KATHERINE. United States.

1619 THE GIRL. New York: H. Holt, 1917 NUC.

A series of impressionistic pictures representing incidents in the life of Marion Crosby that show her vivid imagination, the intense quality of her nature, the shame she learns in the hands of an older woman to feel for nature, and the men she is attracted to. Ends the "darker sides" of her inconclusively.

KEITH, LESLIE. See JOHNSTON, GRACE L. KEITH.

KELLEY, ETHEL MAY. B. 1878. United States.

1620 OUTSIDE INN. Indianapolis: Bobbs-Merrill, [c1920] NUC BMC.

A young woman runs a restaurant not for profit but humanity. The food is so good, however, that she is also financially successful. She adopts a daughter, has an unhappy love affair, marries at the end.

1621 TURN ABOUT ELEANOR. Indianapolis: Bobbs-Merrill, [1917] NUC BMC.

Three young women and three young men are determined not to marry. They adopt a child with the plan that each will care for her two months of the year and that they are collectively responsible for her education. Eleanor, the child, grows up to be such a beautiful person that the three men fall in love with her. She marries one of them.

KELLNER, ELISABETH WILLARD (BROOKS). D. 1916. United States.

1622 AS THE WORLD GOES BY. Boston: Little, Brown, 1905 BMC NUC.

Both mother and daughter are unusual. The mother is an actress who drives at break-neck speeds; the daughter, a college woman who earns a Ph.D. and divorces a husband she considers too conventional. The novel studies the relationship between the two: from their learning fencing together to the mother's jealousy of her daughter's youth and opposition to her relation to an older man.

KELLOGG, MARGARET AUGUSTA. United States.

1623 LEO DAYNE: A NOVEL. Boston: James H. West, 1899 NUC.

Heroine is impulsive and independent. After her father commits suicide, she moves to a manufacturing town with her mother and brother and becomes a forewoman of a tailoring place. She has two suitors; neither is worthy of her. One gives her up when he learns she has taken up new ideas; she gives up the other. Study of the conditions of wage earners and the religious and charitable work done for them. Set in New England.

KELLY, FLORENCE (FINCH). 1858-1939. United States.

1624 THE FATE OF FELIX BRAND. Philadelphia: J. C. Winston, [c1913] NUC BMC.

Henrietta Marne is a young business woman, a secretary, who works hard and is quite successful. She supports her semi-invalid mother and her sister. She rejects Felix Brand, a man with a dual personality, because she senses that he is evil.

1625 RHODA OF THE UNDERGROUND. New York: Sturgis and Walton, 1909 NUC. London: Gay and Hancock, 1910 BMC.

Rhoda devotes herself to abolition. She and her father run an underground railroad during the Civil War. Her principles lead her to help in the escape of the slaves owned by the man who loves her. Rhoda goes to jail for her activities.

KELLY, JOAN COLLINGS. B. 1890. United Kingdom.

1626 BEAUTY FOR ASHES; A NOVEL. BY JOAN SUTHERLAND. London: Hodder & Stoughton, [1920] BMC NUC. New York: G. H. Doran, [c1922] NUC.

Upon obtaining her divorce, Madge discovers that her lover now wishes to marry someone else. She goes to India and dies.

1627 WINGS OF THE MORNING. BY JOAN SUTHERLAND. London: Hodder & Stoughton, 1919 BMC.

Anti-war story: "the fault of the war," says the author, "lay with the politicians who had gambled with public monies, kept their mistresses with public funds, and betrayed the people who elected them."

KELLY, MYRA. 1876-1910. United States.

1628 THE ISLE OF DREAMS. New York: D. Appleton, 1907 NUC BMC.

Young artist successfully sells all her paintings only to learn that the man who loves her bought all of them. Her confidence is restored after further study in Europe and after her fiance successfully sells all the paintings.

KELSEY, JEANNETTE GARR (WASHBURN). B. 1850. United States.

1629 CLOUDED AMBER. BY PATIENCE WARREN. Boston: R.G. Badger, [c1915] NUC.

Young woman's friendship with older actress.

KELSTON, BEATRICE.

1630 BERTHA IN THE BACKGROUND. London: J. Long, 1920 BMC.

Miss Bishop visits her friend Hilary, a novelist. Bertha is

always in the background, communicating words of wisdom by telegram when called upon. Spy mania.

1631 THE BLOWS OF CIRCUMSTANCE. London: J. Long, 1915 BMC.

Amelie Gayne's story, from childhood to her career on stage and marriage made to escape her many suitors. "Ultimately finds herself in the dock."

1632 THE EDGE OF TO-DAY. London: J. Long, 1918 BMC.

Isabel Beamish marries a man she only likes and is very unhappy. She then meets and passionately loves another man with whom she plans to run off. But when she sees her husband kissing her sister's shoulder, she has a change of heart. She runs off by herself instead and pursues a career in dancing.

1633 SEEKERS, EVERY ONE. London: J. Long, 1913 BMC.

Alicia Gunning's acting career with a provincial touring company.

KENDALL, MAY.

1634 WHITE POPPIES: A NOVEL. London: Ward, Lock and Bowden, 1893 BMC.

Story of the criss-crossed loves of three women and of their tragic end. Elsie Everard loves a man she claims she knew in a past life. Vi Romilly loves John who loves Elsie. Vi turns her back on love and joins the Salvation Army. Henrietta Norland, plain, passionate blue stocking, advocates Spencer and attacks religion and politics. In the end, Vi is murdered in a drunken scuffle; Elsie considers suicide but apparently dies of natural causes; Henrietta commits suicide.

KENDELL, JANE ANNE TORREY. B. 1868.

1635 ALICE IN SUNDERLAND. BY JANE ANNE TORREY. New York: Cochrane, 1909 NUC.

Experiences of a country schoolteacher.

KENEALY, ANNESLEY.

1636   THE POODLE-WOMAN. A STORY OF "RESTITUTION OF CONJUGAL RIGHTS". London: S. Paul, 1913 BMC.

"A votes for women novel" concerning the Cockspur's marriage. "Throughout that curiously uninstructed outlook upon practical life that marks some suffragist writers."

1637   THUS SAITH MRS. GRUNDY. London: J. Long, 1911 BMC.

Young woman rebels against Mrs. Grundy and goes off with duke's son and then a sailor; "unwholesome" story.

KENEALY, ARABELLA. 1864-1938. United Kingdom.

1638   DR. JANET OF HARLEY STREET. London: Digby, Long, [1893] BMC NUC. New York: D. Appleton, 1894 NUC.

So revolted is Phyllis Eve of her new husband's kiss that she deserts him one hour after their wedding never to return. She is 17; he is an elderly dissipated French marquis. In London, Phyllis makes friends with Dr. Janet Doyle who helps her become a doctor and tries to teach her the true mission of women—not to be "undeveloped men" but to be womanly "in the highest sense." "A pleading for a recognition of women's equality with men."

1639   THE HONOURABLE MRS. SPOOR: A NOVEL. London: Digby, Long, [1895] BMC NUC.

Woman with disreputable past marries a man of good social position but is so stifled by the respectability of her new life that she escapes to the woods where she sings and "acts up with drunken abandonment." When she meets a young woman she fears knows all about her and will tell, she leaves her husband. Reviewers describe her in turn as evil, coarse, gross, repulsive, pitiable, understandable.

1640   A SEMI-DETACHED MARRIAGE: A NOVEL. London: Hutchinson, 1899 BMC. London: Hutchinson, [1901?] NUC.

Celia Welldron is an heiress who marries Sir Latimer on a part-time basis; that is "to keep up two separate establishments." But the marriage goes bad when she learns he is a bigamist. Then she loses her baby, Sir Latimer dies, and she marries her father's partner.

1641   THE WAY OF A LOVER: A NOVEL. London: Hurst and Blackett, 1914 BMC.

Surgeon gives his bride, a nurse, a scientifically equipped nursing home. His modern views affect their marriage adversely.

1642   WOMAN'S GREAT ADVENTURE: A NOVEL. London: Hurst & Blackett, 1917 BMC.

Story of nurse Stella: author intends her as a selected mother. Because she is richly endowed in mind and body, she will bear a child best fitted to develop the best human characteristics.

KENNARD, MARY E. 1850-1914. United Kingdom.

1643   FOOLED BY A WOMAN: A NOVEL. London: F. V. White, 1895 BMC.

Bianca, bad and beautiful Italian widow, murders her mother-in-law and makes it appear as though George did it. He is condemned but twice the gallows refuse to work to hang him.

1644   THE GOLF LUNATIC AND HIS CYCLING WIFE. BY MRS. EDWARD KENNARD. New York: Brentano's, 1902 NUC. London: Hutchinson, 1902 BMC.

Wife has the temperament of a man; husband should have been born a little girl, comments reviewer.

1645   THE HUNTING GIRL: A NOVEL. BY MRS. EDWARD KENNARD. London: White, 1893 BMC NUC. New York: J. A. Taylor, [c1893] NUC.

Rose Darlington begins her story with the statement: "I am a horrid girl." She is also unscrupulous, vulgar and beautiful, a flirt, and a "come-on" for her cardsharp uncle. But in spite of all her "moral deficiencies," in the end she marries a fine wealthy young man and lives happily.

1646 A RIVERSIDE ROMANCE. London: F. V. White, 1896 BMC. London: F. V. White, 1898 NUC.

"Here Mrs. Kennard's pet hobby, the naughtiness and wickedness of man considered as a husband, displays itself." Mrs. Carson has had an unhappy marital history, is strongly opposed to marriage for her daughter Agatha. While she and her mother are staying in Norway, Agatha falls in love unwittingly with her father's illegitimate son. Mrs. Carson must tell Agatha the truth. Tragedy follows with the death of both.

1647 THE SORROWS OF A GOLFER'S WIFE. BY MRS. EDWARD KENNARD. London: F. V. White, 1896 BMC NUC.

Spirited wife, who has watched her husband's pleasure in golf become a passion, takes to the links herself along with the cook, leaving dinner to look after itself. Humorous.

1648 THAT PRETTY LITTLE HORSE-BREAKER: A NOVEL. BY MRS. EDWARD KENNARD. London: F. 'V. White, 1891 BMC NUC. London: F. V. White, 1892 NUC.

When financial ruin leads her father to kill himself, Katherine Herrick becomes a rider and a horse-breaker in a large horsemarket. She wants to be independent of relatives and friends. She takes a lot of risks in her work, but she knows she understands horses better than most men do. Of her two lovers, one backs out on learning she has no money.

1649 WEDDED TO SPORT: A NOVEL. BY MRS. EDWARD KENNARD. London: F. V. White, 1892 BMC. New York: National Book, [c1892] NUC.

Bligh Burton, a governess, writes two successful novels, "Such Is Man" and "Such Is Woman." She makes an unhappy marriage, leaves her husband and loves another. Said of the author, "She holds a perpetually standing brief for that portion of the feminine world which, if not altogether meriting the contemptuous title of 'the shrieking sisterhood,' is at all events dissatisfied with the conditions under which the Almighty has placed it...."

KENNARD, MRS. ARTHUR. See KENNARD, NINA H.

KENNARD, MRS. EDWARD. See KENNARD, MARY E.

KENNARD, NINA H.

1650   THE SECOND LADY DELCOMBE. BY MRS. ARTHUR KENNARD. London: Hutchinson, 1900 BMC. Philadelphia: J. B. Lippincott, 1900 NUC.
       The Delcombes move in a society where divorce appears to be as common an event as marriage, and both institutions are regarded with a fine impartiality. The second Mrs. Delcombe is friendly and hospitable to her husband's first wife.

KENNY, LOUISE M. STACKPOOLE. United Kingdom.

1651   AT THE COURT OF IL MORO. London: J. Long, 1911 BMC.
       Brilliant court of Beatrice D'Este and her husband in 15th century. Hero is an Englishman who loves Beatrice.

KENT, NORA. B. 1899. United Kingdom.

1652   THE GREATER DAWN. London: L. Parsons, 1920 BMC.
       Lavender writes songs.

KENT, WINNIFRED. United States.

1653   SELL NOT THYSELF: A NOVEL. Chicago: Laird and Lee, [c1894] NUC.
       Stella Dinsmore, a young woman of limited means who has a cherished project, advertises and makes a marriage that is strictly a business arrangement. Concerns other women's issues as well.

KENTON, EDNA. 1876-1954. United States.

1654   CLEM. New York: Century, 1907 BMC NUC.
Clem Merrit was raised in the rough environment of western ranches and mining camps. When she joins the conventional social world of Chicago, she receives a proposal of marriage from a man of exclusive family. But high society sees her as "loud, overbearing, shriekingly insistent" and through its snubs and slights hopes to convince her that she's crude and unworthy of the man. Instead Clem comes to realize her superiority to that petty world and to reject that suitor. Thus she's free to choose the right man. Clem is a highly individualized characterization of an unconventional woman.

1655   WHAT MANNER OF MAN? Indianapolis: Bowen-Merrill, [1903] NUC BMC.
In this psychological study, a woman loves and marries an artist, who married her solely to paint the one portrait that will make him famous. He torments her because he wants to portray pain. When she learns his motive, she leaves him.

KENYON, CAMILLA EUGENIA LIES. B. 1876. United States.

1656   SPANISH DOUBLOONS. Indianapolis: Bobbs-Merrill, [c1919] NUC BMC.
Virginia Harding accompanies her aunt on a treasure. digging expedition, planned and directed by them. Virginia finds the treasure and a husband.

KERNAHAN, MARY JEAN HICKLING (GWYNNE). 1857-1941. United Kingdom. (Identified as Jeannie Gwynne Bettany Kernahan in BMC.)

1657   ASHES OF PASSION. London: J. Long, 1909 BMC.
Marriage intrigue and revenge: Christobel Moore, actress, vain, married to good-natured man who trusts her blindly.

1658   THE CHANCE CHILD. London: Everett, [1914] BMC.

Philista Follingay, beautiful, accomplished and apparently rich actress, is followed by detectives. "All her doings are strange."

1659   THE MYSTERY OF MERE HALL. BY MRS. COULSON KERNAHAN. London: Everett, [1912] BMC NUC.

Two young women, both deceived by the same man. One is a prisoner of her stern grandfather and runs away; the other turns out to be of royal blood.

1660   THE WOMAN WHO UNDERSTOOD. London: Everett, [1916] BMC.

"Foolish babyish woman" runs away from an austere disapproving daughter and her husband with a man with whom she has a platonic relationship. Then the daughter falls in love, leaving the husband to the woman he has loved in silence for twenty years.

KERNAHAN, MRS. COULSON. See KERNAHAN, MARY JEAN HICKLING (GWYNNE).

KERR, SOPHIE. 1880-1965. United States.

1661   THE BLUE ENVELOPE; A NOVEL. Garden City, New York: Doubleday, Page, 1917 NUC. London: J. M Dent, 1919 BMC.

Leslie must learn a profession and earn her own living for two years before she can receive her inheritance.

1662   THE GOLDEN BLOCK. Garden City, New York: Doubleday Page, 1918 NUC. London: J. M. Dent, [1919] BMC.

Margaret Bailey loves the world of business and is exceedingly competent in it. She points out to her admiring male associates that there is "no sex in brains." She saves the Golden Block Co. and becomes a full partner. She is not interested in marriage or love, but there is an inference at the end of the book that she will eventually marry.

1663 LOVE AT LARGE: BEING THE AMUSING CHRONICLES OF JULIETTA CARSON. New York and London: Harper, [1916] BMC NUC.

A comedy wherein a young woman writes stories to get even with people. The novel "pictures suburbia as a community of women where men are in actuality aliens to the life of women."

1664 THE SEE-SAW; A STORY OF TO-DAY. New York: Doubleday-Page, 1919 NUC.

Married life among the prosperous, fast-living younger set of Americans. Marcia divorces her husband who drinks and who chases after women, but in the end she takes him back after his second wife divorces him.

KERRUISH, JESSIE DOUGLAS. United Kingdom.

1665 MISS HAROUN AL-RASCHID. New York: G. H. Doran, [c1917] NUC. London: Hodder & Stoughton, [1917] BMC NUC.

Her adventures in Turkey until she marries include foiling a group of spies and allowing herself to be nailed into a coffin to save a whole community. Background: her work on an archeological expedition.

KEY, HELEN ABERCROMBIE.

1666 A DAUGHTER OF LOVE. BY MRS. K. J. KEY. London: Hutchinson, 1913 BMC. New York: Duffield, 1914 NUC.

A daughter of unmarried parents becomes a peeress. Alone and penniless she starts out as a housemaid, is betrayed, dismissed from her job, but befriended by a French woman. In the end she is reunited to the father of her child who has come to know and love his daughter.

KEY, MRS. K. J. See KEY, HELEN ABERCROMBIE.

KILVERT, MARGARET (CAMERON). 1867-1947. United States.

1667 THE INVOLUNTARY CHAPERON. BY MARGARET CAMERON. New York and London: Harper, 1909 NUC BMC.

Woman past 30 chaperones girl of 17 in South America; in letters.

KING, K. DOUGLAS. See KING, KATHERINE DOUGLAS.

KING, KATHERINE DOUGLAS. D. 1901. United Kingdom.

1668 THE SCRIPTURE READER OF ST. MARK'S. BY K. DOUGLAS KING. London: Hutchinson, [1895] BMC. New York: Merriam, [c1896] NUC.

Alexandra, affectionate and clinging, lives with a man till her husband appears "out of her unknown past."

1669 URSULA. BY K. DOUGLAS KING. London: J. Lane, 1900 BMC NUC.

Ursula is narrator. Her Russian adventures include murder, mystery, lovers. Ends with her marriage.

KING, MADGE.

1670 COUSIN CINDERELLA: A NOVEL. London: R. Bentley, 1892 BMC.

Americans in London. Beulah (Cousin Cinderella) is a Becky Sharp. "She is an extremely clever person, and she does not make the common mistake of exhibiting her cleverness for mere ostentation; she knows that her resources are great, but she uses them with economy and refrains from profligate extravagance of expenditure." She is "admirable," according to one reviewer. Mr. Basset, a rich American, and his cousin Naomi (beautiful but stupid) are in London to introduce Naomi to society. She had her debut in Boston but no success came of it; because of her stupidity, she failed to make an impression.

KING, MAUDE EGERTON (HINE). 1867-1927. United Kingdom.

1671 THE CONVERSION OF MISS CAROLINE EDEN. London: J. M. Dent, 1900 BMC.

An elderly spinster belonging to the Church of England is impressed by a modern Congregational minister.

KING, PAULINE. United States.

1672 ALIDA CRAIG. New York: G. H. Richmond, 1896 NUC. London and New York: E. Mathews, 1896 BMC.

Alida is a successful young painter living in New York. Her love affair.

KING, RACHEL.

1673 THE COMMON PROBLEM. London: Lynwood, 1912 BMC.

Narrated by Lady Ann, an "old maid in old-maidish style," concerns the London art world. Also an account of how Lord Kingsford tries to keep his wife out of the succession.

KINGSBURY, ELIZABETH. United States.

1674 TALE OF AN AMATEUR ADVENTURESS: THE AUTOBIOGRAPHY OF ESTHER GRAY. ABRIDGED AND EDITED BY ELIZABETH KINGSBURY. Cincinnati, Ohio: Editor Pub. Co., 1898 NUC.

Daughter of an Indiana editor "relates her efforts to gain a living as journalist, business woman, book agent, guide at the World's Fair of Chicago, as private secretary, actress, and travelling companion."

KINGSBURY, SARA. 1876-1948. United States.

1675 THE ATONEMENT. Boston: Eastern Pub. Co., [c1905] NUC.

Marion renounces her fiance because he betrayed a young sweatshop worker, and she gives up her life of luxury as a millionaire's niece to work among the poor.

KINGSCOTE, ADELINE GEORGINA ISABELLA (WOLFF).
D. 1908. United Kingdom.

1676 BILLY'S WIFE. BY LUCAS CLEEVE. London: J. Long, 1906 BMC.

Unhappy marriage, spirited wife, concession to sentiment at the end.

1677 BLUE LILIES. BY LUCAS CLEEVE. London: T. F. Unwin, 1902 BMC.

Problem novel. Heroine manages her affairs too successfully to be appealing. Unhappy marriage.

1678 BRUISED LILIES. BY LUCAS CLEEVE. London: F. V. White, 1909 BMC.

Dorothy Trevelyan is married to a man she does not love. She loves another, but social pressures keep her from taking the leap that would bring happiness.

1679 THE CONFESSIONS OF A WIDOW. BY LUCAS CLEEVE. London: F.V. White, 1907 BMC.

Because her first marriage of 10 years to an old man was an unhappy one, the widow has no intention of making a second marriage. She keeps meeting old lovers who propose, but she declines all offers. She lives by herself on a farm and decides to devote her life to the poor.

1680 A DOUBLE MARRIAGE. BY LUCAS CLEEVE. London: T.F. Unwin, 1906 BMC.

Marriage, separation. Then former wife and husband meet again and marry without recognizing each other.

1681 EILEEN. BY LUCAS CLEEVE. London: J. Long, 1903 BMC.

Eileen, married, devours novels on the sex question; morbid story of matrimonial infidelity.

1682 EPICURES. BY LUCAS CLEEVE. London: Downey, 1896 BMC.

Character study of Eileen, an epicure, and of her relations

first with her husband and subsequently with her lover. "Sickly and negative," comments reviewer.

1683   THE FOOL KILLER. BY LUCAS CLEEVE. London: T.F. Unwin, 1904 BMC.

Claire, unfaithful to her first husband, marries a man fifteen years younger than herself. Study of her growing awareness; she is raised to a "thinking, reasoning woman" only to finally kill herself.

1684   THE FOOL'S TAX. BY LUCAS CLEEVE. London: T.F. Unwin, 1907 BMC.

An American woman married to a French count compares French and American attitudes toward divorce and decides the more liberal American attitudes are preferable.

1685   THE INDISCRETIONS OF GLADYS. BY LUCAS CLEEVE. London: J. Long, 1903 NUC BMC.

Contains several sensational episodes. Besides Lady Gladys' indiscretions, there is the quieter story of Phoebe who is first a florist, then a typist, and when she marries, is very unhappy.

1686   THE MAN IN THE STREET. BY LUCAS CLEEVE. London: T.F. Unwin, 1903 BMC NUC.

Actress subject to hypnotic influence. Story of politics, occultism, and a tangle of love.

1687   THE ONE MOMENT. BY LUCAS CLEEVE. London: J. Long, 1909 BMC.

Concerns the affinity theory of marriage (a pair agrees to part when one has an affinity elsewhere). Mr. and Mrs. Carlyon Smith try it and fail. Two other women play with it.

1688   PLATO'S HANDMAIDEN. BY LUCAS CLEEVE. London: J. Long, [1901] BMC.

Heroine starts a hat shop, but her business is unsuccessful.

1689   SELMA. BY LUCAS CLEEVE. London: J. Long, 1907 BMC.

Rival claims of love and money. Selma is a singer the

hero marries for love; Lena a singer he marries for money.

1690 WHAT A WOMAN WILL DO: A SOCIETY DRAMA.
London: F. V. White, 1900 BMC.

Woman lets her husband divorce her so that he can marry
an heiress and supply her with money he does not have
for the children.

1691 WHAT MEN CALL LOVE. A STORY OF SOUTH
AFRICA IN THE DAYS OF CETEWAYO. BY LUCAS
CLEEVE. London: F.V. White, 1901 BMC.

Psychological and moral problems of marriage are
explored. The husband is lazy. He is portrayed in a
negative way. The wife is the hard worker.

1692 WOMAN AND MOSES. BY LUCAS CLEEVE. London:
Hurst and Blackett, 1902 BMC.

Divorce.

1693 THE WOMAN WHO WOULDN'T: A NOVEL. BY
LUCAS CLEEVE. London: Simpkin, 1895 BMC. London:
Simpkin, Marshall, Hamilton, Kent, 1896 NUC.

Opalia wants her marriage to be a platonic relationship,
but her husband can not find satisfaction in such an
arrangement. She finally "sacrifices her noble ideal in the
interest of her husband's morals" when she learns he is
tempted by a "purely animal woman." "Lucas Cleeve is a
type of that mentally diseased class which finds 'Purity' in
the systematic disuse of the sexual aspect of the physical
human being." Opalia is presented as sweet in temper and
superb in health. Reviewers further describe the novel as
"a nympholeptic" story, an offense against propriety, an
essay in "serious pornography."

KINGSLEY, FLORENCE (MORSE). 1859-1937. United States.

1694 THE GLASS HOUSE. New York: Dodd, Mead, 1909
NUC.

Woman takes up writing on a friend's urging. She gives
up her housework and the care of her three children until
one of them gets in trouble.

1695   THE HEART OF PHILURA. New York: Dodd, Mead, 1914 NUC.

Further adventures of "Miss Philura" who solves the village mystery.

1696   HURRYING FATE AND GERALDINE. New York: F. Bigelow Corp., [c1913] BMC NUC.

Amusing story of "a primary teacher" whose family is near ruin, and her disguise as one of the lawyers of the client to whom her family is in debt and with whom she falls in love.

1697   MISS PHILURA'S WEDDING GOWN. New York: Dodd, Mead, 1912 NUC.

Miss Philura is an older woman who lives alone in a small community. She is impoverished. Her romance. Sentimental and very sweet.

1698   NEIGHBORS. New York: Dodd, Mead, 1917 NUC.

More of Philura and her community—a strange assortment of people like the dressmaker. Sentimental.

1699   THE PRINCESS AND THE PLOUGHMAN. New York and London: Harper, 1907 BMC NUC.

"Mary falls romantically in love with a sister-student."

1700   THE SINGULAR MISS SMITH. New York and London: Macmillan, 1904 NUC BMC.

A club woman works as a servant in order to understand conditions better.

1701   THOSE QUEER BROWNS. New York: Dodd, Mead, 1917 NUC.

Annie Smith has altruistic ideals and socialist convictions. She and her professor husband devote their lives to the poor people in New York slums.

1702   TRUTHFUL JANE. New York: D. Appleton, 1907 NUC BMC.

Governess, poor relation to rich family, leaves because of injustices, becomes companion to a woman-smuggler, twice refuses her suitor, searches a long time for employment, takes position as house maid, inherits a fortune and marries.

KINKAID, MARY HOLLAND (MACNEISH). 1861-1948. United States.

1703 THE MAN OF YESTERDAY; A ROMANCE OF A VANISHING RACE. New York: F.A. Stokes, [1908] NUC.

The heroine, daughter of an Indian mother, marries a man from the East. Although he loves her, he cannot face making his marriage known to his mother and friends in the East. He leaves and doesn't return, even when their child is born and she is very ill. The tribe adopts the child, cutting off any claim of the father, and she devotes her life to the education of her people.

1704 WALDA; A NOVEL. New York and London: Harper, 1903 NUC BMC.

Woman is trained by her religious community to reject love and marriage and to become a prophetess. But she awakens to love, forsakes her religion and is excommunicated.

KINKEAD, ELEANOR TALBOT. See SHORT, ELEANOR TALBOT (KINKEAD).

KINTZEL, MRS. A. G. See KINTZEL, MRS. ALBERT GASTON.

KINTZEL, MRS. ALBERT GASTON. B. 1854. United States.

1705 LEAVE ME MY HONOR. BY MRS. A. G. KINTZEL. New York: Broadway, [1904] NUC.

A woman who cannot be confined to a monogamous relationship marries three times; her former husbands understand she is a "constitutional flirt," and she continues to be good friends with them all.

KIRK, ELEANOR. See AMES, ELEANOR MARIA (EASTERBROOK).

KIRK, ELLEN WARNER (OLNEY). 1842-1928. United States.

1706 GOOD-BYE, PROUD WORLD. Boston: Houghton Mifflin, 1903 NUC.

Woman's career in newspaper work from editor of a woman's column, through years of hard work until she's indispensible to the management of the business. She also inherits an estate that she runs successfully.

1707 MARCIA, A NOVEL. Boston: Houghton Mifflin, 1907 NUC.

First person account of a woman who rejects the large estate she inherits because she prefers to support herself. She is a college graduate who works as a secretary and who writes plays. "Loving freedom, Marcia sets aside the judgment alike of old friends and new and follows her own life of purpose...vivid picture of a free woman, mistress of her own destiny."

1708 OUR LADY VANITY. Boston: Houghton Mifflin, 1901 NUC.

Joan lives for adulation—she wants the world at her feet. She carries on an "intrigue" though she is married, neglects her child, does as she pleases until her father puts her "in her place." Joan dies in the end.

1709 THE STORY OF LAWRENCE GARTHE. Boston: Houghton Mifflin, 1894 NUC.

Constance considers the question of whether one should marry a divorced man whose wife is still living and decides in the affirmative.

KIRKE, GENEVIEVE.

1710 AN UNWEDDED WIFE. Chicago: Morrill, Higgins, 1892 NUC.

Jessie a typewriter loves her employer a married man.

Story of her life before and after yielding to temptation.

KIRKLAND, WINIFRED MARGARETTA. 1872-1943. United States.

1711 INTRODUCING CORINNA. New York: F.H. Revell, [c1909] NUC.

Corinna is the head of a boarding school and, at a time of difficulties, saves the school.

KIRSCHNER, LULA. 1854-1934. Russia.

1712 A LEAFLESS SPRING. BY OSSIP SCHUBIN. Philadelphia: J. B. Lippincott, 1893 NUC. (Tr. from the German by Mary J. Safford.)

Italian model, unhappily married and separated from her husband, meets an Englishman studying art in Paris. When he learns she is married, he makes a hurried marriage to an English woman, but he is murdered by the model's husband on his honeymoon. Sensational.

KITCAT, MABEL (HICKSON).

1713 A LATTER-DAY ROMANCE. London: Bliss, Sands and Foster, 1893 BMC.

Heroine neglects, leaves, and forgets her husband for another man. Reviewer calls it "the story of a woman's mistake" and says the author blames the heroine's "agnostic and rationalistic training."

KNAPP, HARRIET LORETTA. United States.

1714 MIRIAM'S TOWER. New York: G. W. Dillingham, 1897 NUC.

Allegory: Miriam lives with Peace. Is tempted by a stranger to explore Elysian Fields. Her lover leaves her. Back to Tower to live with Despair till Hope comes.

KNOCKER, GRATIANA LONGWORTH.

1715 THE WITCH OF WITHYFORD: A STORY OF EXMOOR. BY GRATIANA CHANTER. London: J. M. Dent, 1896 BMC. New York: Macmillan, 1896 NUC.

Real witch, spells, familiars, etc. in connection with murder and child-stealing. Happy ending.

KNOWLES, MABEL WINIFRED. 1875-1949. United Kingdom.

1716 THE DESTINY OF CLAUDE. BY MAY WYNNE. London: S. Paul, [1913] BMC.

Claude is a young and adventurous woman. In this historical romance set in 16th century France, she runs away from home to escape the convent, goes to the court of Henry II, enters Marie Stuart's service, and experiences numerous exciting adventures.

1717 QUEEN JENNIE. BY MAY WYNNE. London: Chapman & Hall, 1918 BMC.

The spirited heroine, a champion of the Stuart cause, becomes the wife of the so-called King Robert Bruce—in name only. In reality she is the queen of his adherents and leads the band of Highland Rovers on midnight forays.

1718 A SPY FOR NAPOLEON: A ROMANCE. BY MAY WYNNE. London: Jarrolds, [1917] BMC.

The spy is a woman who plays the chief part in many intrigues between France and England. She is one of Napoleon's spies at the time of the Cadoudal-Pichegru conspiracy.

KNOWLES, R. B. SHERIDAN.*

1719 GLENCOONOGE: A NOVEL. Edinburgh and London: Blackwood, 1891 BMC.

Love story of Jane Johnson, bookkeeper.

KOVALEVSKY, SOPHIA. See KOVALEVSKYAYA, SOF'YA VASIL'EVNA (KORVIN-KRUKOVSKAIA).

KOVALEVSKYAYA, SOF'YA VASIL'EVNA (KORVIN-KRUKOVSKAIA). 1850-1891. Russia.

1720 VERA BARANTZOVA. FROM THE RUSSIAN OF SOPHIA KOVALEVSKY. London: Ward & Downey, 1895 NUC BMC. (Also published as Vera Vorontzoff. Boston: Lamson and Wolffe, [c1896] NUC BMC.)

Involves the changes in an aristocratic Russian family after the emancipation of the serfs and, more particularly, Vera's love affair with an older teacher, her marriage to a nihilist, her devotion to the revolution and her choice to live in Siberia and work for the exiles.

KRIKORIAN, JESSIE.

1721 A DAUGHTER OF MYSTERY. London: Grifith, Farran, 1892 BMC.

Cleopatra Gunn "believes herself to be a limb of Satan in spite of all her friends' efforts to humanize her." She is in love with the squire who is already married. She mesmerizes his wife and causes her to throw herself in front of an engine. He remains true to dead wife. Filled with remorse and foiled, she chooses the same death. Her grandmother, Granny Gunn, has already been murdered by the villagers for possessing the evil eye.

KROUT, CAROLINE VIRGINIA. 1853-1931. United States.

1722 DIONIS OF THE WHITE VEIL. BY CAROLINE BROWN. Boston: L.C. Page, 1911 NUC.

Young woman forced to be a nun, leaves the convent for love. The novel describes her adventures and struggles as a pioneer woman in Louisiana.

1723 KNIGHTS IN FUSTIAN: A WAR TIME STORY OF INDIANA. BY CAROLINE BROWN. Boston and New York: Houghton, Mifflin, 1900 NUC.

Civil War. The Knights of the Golden Circle, a secret society of the secessionists, conspiracy. No heroes. Author exalts the heroism of the women; they outstrip the men in valor and determination and possibly intelligence.

KYLE, RUBY BERYL. United States.

1724 PAUL ST. PAUL, A SON OF THE PEOPLE: A NOVEL. Buffalo: C. Wells Moulton, 1895 NUC.

Young woman becomes a famous opera star. About to marry a celebrated tenor who has been her guardian, she learns that he is her half-brother.

L., M. See HERRINGTON, MRS. M. J.

LAGEN, M. J. See LAGEN, MARY JULIA AND CALLY THOMAS RYLAND.

LAGEN, MARY JULIA AND CALLY THOMAS RYLAND.

1725 DAPHNE AND HER LAD. BY M. J. LAGEN AND CALLY RYLAND. New York: H. Holt, 1904 NUC.

Two editors of women's pages correspond, at first casually, then passionately; he finally visits her and discovers she has a drunken husband.

LAGERLOF, SELMA OTTILIANA LOUISA. 1858-1940. Sweden.

1726 THE EMPEROR OF PORTUGALLIA. Garden City, N.Y.: Doubleday, Page, 1916 BMC NUC. London: Hodder and Stoughton, [1916] BMC. (Tr. by Velma Swanston Howard.)

Daughter left to earn money to save parents' home. After a few letters containing needed money, nothing more is heard from her. Father refuses to believe ill of her, telling neighbors she is reigning over her empire of Portugallia. When he learns she has gone wrong, he goes mad.

1727   GOSTA BERLING'S SAGA. London: Chapman and Hall, 1898 NUC BMC. (Tr. from the Swedish by Lillie Tudeer. Also published as The Story of Gosta Berling. London: Gay and Bird, 1898 NUC BMC.)

When the story opens, Margarita Samzeiuls, an elderly Amazon, is the Lady of Ekeby. She is the vigorous ruler of the district, she has a passionate love for her people, and in her lavish benevolence keeps twelve ne'er do wells as her pensioners. She is driven out of the position by her husband and these twelve men, the cavaliers. The story is of the year of ruin that followed until rule had been restored to a woman. "The men, strong and wild as Vikings, do not apparently feel safe unless they have placed their rugged natures and impulsive passions under some orderly mother-guidance. Here we seem to return to very primitive instincts; indeed, the original difference between the sexes shines out in this book in a manner very striking to our modern eyes."

LAING, JANET. United Kingdom.

1728   THE BORDERLANDERS. London: J. M. Dent, 1904 BMC.

Inmates of a home for eccentrics, diary of the heroine who works there and has a grand passion for the mistress. Witty, style reminiscent of Rhoda Broughton.

LAMBERT, BRITON.*

1729   LOVE IN A MAZE; THE WAY OF A MODERN GIRL. London: Greening, 1908 BMC.

A 27 year old woman novelist interested in "righting the world and the relations of the sexes" writes letters to a male friend about it.

LA MOTTE, ELLEN NEWBOLD. 1873-1961. United States.

1730 THE BACKWASH OF WAR: THE HUMAN WRECKAGE OF THE BATTLEFIELD AS WITNESSED BY AN AMERICAN HOSPITAL NURSE. New York and London: G.P. Putnam's Sons, 1916 BMC.

Terrible in its realism, dreadful description of gas gangrene. Author's abhorrence of war.

LANE, ELINOR (MACARTNEY). B. about 1864-D. 1909. United States.

1731 KATRINE: A NOVEL. New York and London: Harper, 1909 BMC NUC.

Gifted woman becomes opera star. Her studies, loves.

1732 MILLS OF GOD: A NOVEL. New York: D. Appleton, 1901 BMC NUC.

A wife's extra-marital relation and her illegitimate child. Elinor is married to the wrong man. She takes a lover, and when their child is born, she raises him as though he were her husband's. And she sees her lover marry a younger woman. Elinor is sympathetically drawn—a fine, strong, unconventional woman of great emotion and intellect.

1733 NANCY STAIR; A NOVEL. New York: D. Appleton, 1904 BMC NUC. London: W. Heinemann, 1905 BMC.

Nancy Stair, a genius, is raised by men and given a man's education, in classics, logic and law. She also writes poetry and is a social worker, is in love with three men simultaneously, but in the last few pages renounces (without adequate preparation by the author) all activities outside those of the traditional wife and mother.

LANE, ROSE (WILDER). 1887-1968. United States.

1734 DIVERGING ROADS. New York: Century, 1919 BMC NUC.

Honest portrayal of a woman alone. Helen Davis is engaged to a man too poor to marry. She decides, therefore, to go to work. She learns telegraphy but is bored with it. Then she moves to San Francisco, meets, marries and is separated from a rich man. Story traces her unsophisticated reactions to the big city, her marriage, the years of hard work as a real estate agent in the oil fields, as an advertising writer, and as a newspaper reporter.

LANG, LOUISA LOCKHART (STEUART). United Kingdom.

1735 KNIGHT CHECKS QUEEN. BY MRS. L. LOCKHART LANG. London: A. Rivers, 1911 NUC BMC.

Anne Maitland is impulsive, wayward, bursting with life. She marries a scientist to be free to train her voice and to be free from her tyrannical father. She's about to complete her training when her husband's nervous breakdown forces her to earn money as a gymnast.

LANG, MRS. L. LOCKHART. See LANG, LOUISA LOCKHART (STEUART).

LANG, P. S.*

1736 WHERE THE SOLDANELLA GROWS. London: Heath, Cranton and Ouseley, [1915] BMC.

The snowy Austrian mountain heights represent "the goal of life for Avis Beaumont." She becomes an art student in Frankfurt.

LANGBRIDGE, ROSAMOND. B. 1880. United Kingdom.

1737 THE AMBUSH OF YOUNG DAYS. London: Duckworth, 1906 BMC.

A "character study" of women living in what one reviewer calls a "squalid residential hotel," and another, "a private temperance hotel," managed and owned by a woman.

1738 THE FLAME AND THE FLOOD. London: T.F. Unwin, 1903 BMC.

Heroine must choose between love of an actor and the child of the man who is her husband.

1739 IMPERIAL RICHENDA: A FANTASTIC COMEDY. London: Rivers, 1908 BMC NUC.

Richenda, in order to escape an unwanted marriage,

applies as a housemaid at a hotel and runs it. A comedy set in Ireland.

1740   THE STARS BEYOND. London: E. Nash, 1907 BMC.

Verity leaves and then divorces her husband just before her child is born. For her a husband and children represent fleeting passions.

LANGBRIDGE, V.*

1741   AN ELUSIVE LOVER, A STUDY IN PERVERSITY. London: J. Milne, 1909 BMC.

Nan Golding goes to London alone and works in art and drama. Also a love story.

LANGER, ANGELA. 1886-1916. United Kingdom.

1742   RUE AND ROSES. London: W. Heinemann, 1913 NUC BMC. New York: G.H. Doran, [c1913] NUC.

Anna leaves her very poor German family to become a servant, but while she scrubs floors and minds children, she writes fine poetry. When love comes, it is not the romantic love she dreamed of but the friendship of a man who helps her with her poetry and education and who does not go beyond friendship because he believes she is the kind of woman love kills.

LANGWORTHY, FERRIER.

1743   SLAVES OF CHANCE; A NOVEL. London: L. Smithers, 1899 BMC. Boston: L. C. Page, 1900 NUC.

Poor widow in London desires that her five daughters marry, throws them in the way of many temptations. One runs away and makes her living in an unusual way.

LATHBURY, EVA. United Kingdom.

1744   MR. MEYER'S PUPIL. London: A. Rivers, 1907 BMC.

Lady Violet is married, bored, with much vitality and no way to use it. She is about to run off with a lover when her child's tutor kidnaps the child just so Lady Violet will not elope.

1745 THE PEOPLE DOWNSTAIRS. London: A. Rivers, 1908 BMC.
Described by one reviewer as "unconventional, great psychological drama," in which two "commonplace husbands" listen to what another reviewer describes as the "long and egotistical harangues of their wives."

LATHROP, ANNIE WAKEMAN.

1746 THE AUTOBIOGRAPHY OF A CHARWOMAN AS CHRONICLED BY ANNIE WAKEMAN. London: J. Macqueen, 1900 NUC BMC. (Also published as A Gentlewoman of the Slums; Being the Autobiography of a Charwoman, as Chronicled by Annie Wakeman. Boston: L. C. Page, 1901 NUC.)
A housekeeper at 16, she is betrayed by her employer who repudiates her child. Her first marriage, although bigamous, is to a good man who dies. She then marries a brute who mistreats and deserts her. Her entire life is a hand-to-mouth struggle against poverty. She is not, however, beaten down by her experiences but demonstrates the "cheerful patience of the poor," as one reviewer puts it. Written in Cockney dialect.

LAUDER, MARIA ELISE TURNER. Canada.

1747 AT LAST. Buffalo: C.W. Moulton, 1894 NUC.
Noble and unselfish work of the Women's Christian Temperance Union, set primarily in France and the Riviera.

LAUGHLIN, CLARA ELIZABETH. 1873-1941. United States.

1748 CHILDREN OF TO-MORROW. New York: C. Scribner's Sons, 1911 NUC.
New York working women—actresses and shop-girls, their hardships, problems, and poor pay. A group of young

women and men who live in the East Side slums are interested in art and literature, but more concerned with bettering the social conditions of the poor.

1749 FELICITY, THE MAKING OF A COMEDIENNE. New York: C. Scribner's Sons, 1907 NUC.

Life of a successful actress for whom love is subordinate to fame. Felicity Fergus had a precocious childhood. Though she was repressed on all sides, she escaped through playacting. Her career was well worth the price—the work, sacrifices, demands of acting, the isolation and loneliness that came with success, the slim opportunities for love.

1750 "JUST FOLKS." New York: Macmillan, 1910 BMC NUC.

Betts Tully is a probation officer in the Chicago slums, "realistic."

1751 THE PENNY PHILANTHROPIST; A STORY THAT COULD BE TRUE. New York: F. H. Revell, [c1912] NUC.

Story of Haymarket slums, 18 year old female keeps a "news emporium," sets aside a penny a day for philanthropy.

LAURENCE, FRANCES ELSIE (FRY). B. 1893. Canada.

1752 HALF A GIPSY. BY CHRISTINE FIELD. London: A. Melrose, [1916] BMC NUC.

An English governess in Russia; her love for singer who is half gypsy.

LAW, LEDA.

1753 AND THE WORLD SAITH. London: Digby, Long, 1895 BMC.

Immoral characters. Leading idea is "that the woman who longs to sin and refrains through cowardice and not through virtue is a poorer kind of creature than the woman who bravely sins and takes the consequences." "The day of such books is drawing to an end and a purer taste is reasserting itself."

LAWLESS, EMILY. 1845-1913. United Kingdom.

1754   GRANIA, THE STORY OF AN ISLAND. BY THE HON.
       EMILY LAWLESS. New York & London: Macmillan, 1892
       NUC. London: Smith, Elder, 1892 BMC.

       Grania and her consumptive sister live on the Isle of
       Arran, a desolate, narrow life where "the utmost that a
       woman can hope for is that her 'man' shall not drink, or
       beat her, or neglect to provide for her children." Grania,
       strong and able, was kissed by her lover once—between
       two drags on his pipe—and her passion was awakened;
       she knew what love might be like, while knowing it
       would not be like that with him. She suspects his
       worthlessness but cannot admit it to herself; he is her one
       chance for the future. She dies in a harrowing attempt to
       get help for her sister.

1755   MAELCHO, A SIXTEENTH CENTURY NARRATIVE. BY
       THE HON. EMILY LAWLESS. New York: D. Appleton,
       1894 NUC. London: Smith & Elder, 1894 BMC.

       Essentially the work is a character study of the Saxon and
       Celtic temperament. Unrelieved portrayal of the horrors of
       war. No love story.

LAWRENCE, ALBERT. See LAWRENCE, ALBERTA ELIZA
       INEZ (CHAMBERLAIN).

LAWRENCE, ALBERTA ELIZA INEZ (CHAMBERLAIN). B.
       1875. United States.

1756   THE   TRAVELS   OF   PHOEBE   ANN.   BY   ALBERT
       LAWRENCE. Boston: C. M. Clark, 1908 NUC.

       Older woman.

LAWRENCE, ROSAMOND (NAPIER). B. 1878. United
       Kingdom.

1757   THE FAITHFUL FAILURE. BY ROSAMUND NAPIER.
       New   York: G.   H.   Doran,   [1910?]   NUC.   London:
       Duckworth, 1910 BMC.

       Discovers on honeymoon she doesn't love her husband.

Beautiful picture of sisterly devotion.

LAWSON, M.*

1758   CONEYCREEK. London: Digby and Long, [1895] BMC.
Trials of two blind young women, their torturous ordeals through which they triumph.

LEA, FANNY HEASLIP. 1884-1955. United States.

1759   QUICKSANDS. New York: Sturgis and Walton, 1911 NUC.
Woman out of love with husband of lower social class, in love with male author, must choose between them.

LEAF, A.*

1760   A MAID AT LARGE. London: E. Nash, 1905 BMC.
She says outrageous things, is like Elizabeth. The book takes us into the Country House marriage market. Satire.

LEAN, FLORENCE (MARRYAT) CHURCH. 1837-1899. United Kingdom.

1761   AN ANGEL OF PITY. BY FLORENCE MARRYAT. London: Hutchinson, 1898 BMC.
Rose, a hospital nurse, protests a surgeon's experiments on a pauper patient. The surgeon's interest in her is aroused, and he asks her to marry him. Rose has no interest in marriage but is deeply committed to her profession, and when he offers to establish a nursing home and make her the head of it, she accepts. Once married, she discovers he wants her only as a decorative accessory. She submits, but continues to worry about his experiments. When she discovers his secret laboratory and that he is a vivisectionist, she refuses to live with him as his wife. He retaliates by operating on her pet dog. She breaks in, puts the dog out of pain, throws a knife at her husband,

wounding his hand. He repents, establishes the nursing home, and forswears vivisection.

1762 AT HEART A RAKE. BY FLORENCE MARRYAT. London: H. Cox, 1895 BMC. New York: Cassell, [c1895] NUC.

Author here "takes up her parable versus men," says one reviewer, "especially military men who make the worst husbands." One character, Cissy Barnard, is married to a man who beats her. She leaves him and runs off with a kind man. The main character Lady Phyllis McNaughton is a "lady cyclist" who joins a women's club against her husband's wishes. She leaves him when she learns he runs around with other women. But on page 494, they are reconciled for the sake of their child. Reviewers describe the novel as "nauseous," "unsavory," "unspeakably distasteful," with "too much female smoking, drinking and bad language."

1763 A BANKRUPT HEART. BY FLORENCE MARRYAT. London: F. V. White, 1894 BMC. New York: C. B. Reed, 1894 NUC.

Ruined country maid attempts suicide when her lover marries. She is rescued, has adventures, foils the villain, kills herself with carbolic acid sheepwash.

1764 THE BEAUTIFUL SOUL. BY FLORENCE MARRYAT. London: Digby, Long, 1894 BMC. New York: Cassell, [c1895] NUC.

Felicia Hetherington is 35. She's plain, gets engaged to a young journalist of 24, who proceeds to make love to 19 year old Mab Selwyn. Matters are well-arranged by the end.

1765 THE BLOOD OF THE VAMPIRE. BY FLORENCE MARRYAT. London: Hutchinson, 1897 BMC. Leipzig: B. Tauchnitz, 1897 NUC.

"Vulgar people with loose principles." Heroine is daughter of a quadroon and Jamaican planter whose grandmother has been bitten by a vampire. She has inherited the vampire's power without its inclination.

1766 THE DREAM THAT STAYED. BY FLORENCE MARRYAT. London: Hutchinson, 1896 BMC. Leipzig: B. Tauchnitz, 1897 NUC.

Mrs. Raynam, after leaving her husband many years previously, is now living in Scotland, with an illegitimate daughter May. General Raynam, their legitimate daughter Mary and her fiance, unaware that Mrs. Raynam is living there, visit the area. Sir Guy, the fiance falls in love and engages himself to May. The General feels May has no right to Sir Guy because of her illegitimacy. May suicides; Sir Guy returns to Mary. Mrs. Raynham loses her mind. The indignant reviewer states, "we are expected to sympathise with her. If a woman plays battledore and shuttlecock with the seventh commandment in the irresponsible, motiveless way that she does, she ought to take the consequences."

1767 A FATAL SILENCE. BY FLORENCE MARRYAT. London: Griffith and Farran, [1891] BMC NUC. New York: Street & Smith, [1902] NUC.

Village school teacher marries a wealthy landowner believing her first husband is dead. She changes her name in order to bury the past but is persecuted by the church warden, his colleagues and their wives. Finally she accepts dismissal by the parish committee rather than reveal her history.

1768 IN THE NAME OF LIBERTY. BY FLORENCE MARRYAT. London: Digby, Long, [1897] BMC.

Jane Farrell is a private detective married to a wicked anarchist who plots with his friends to kill the lost heir who returns to claim an inheritance. Jane saves the earl and rehabilitates Maurice, her husband.

1769 IRIS THE AVENGER. BY FLORENCE MARRYAT. London: Hutchinson, 1899 BMC. Leipzig: B. Tauchnitz, 1899 NUC.

Iris Bevan is in turn a governess, actress and typist. She marries an earl "on whom she is resolved to wreak vengeance for the betrayal of her sister." As it turns out the husband's friend, not the husband, is the man she seeks.

1770 THE NOBLER SEX. BY FLORENCE MARRYAT. London: F. V. White, 1892 BMC. New York: U.S. Book, 1892 NUC.

The record of a career "as distasteful as it is objectionable," says one reviewer. Written in the first person, the story is of a woman who is a novelist, an actress, and a public speaker. She "marries a man she cannot love, then loves a man she cannot marry, then lives with a man while her divorce is pending, then marries him and later divorces him."

1771 A RATIONAL MARRIAGE. BY FLORENCE MARRYAT. London: F. V. White, 1899 BMC. New York: F. M. Buckles, 1899 NUC.

Joan Trevor is a strong-minded young woman who is bored with her relatives and insists upon earning her own living. She becomes a secretary and then learns that she will inherit 7000 pounds a year if she remains single. This incentive as well as her own ideas about reformation of marriage lead her to persuade Larry to marry her secretly and to sign a contract that they will not live in the same house. The problems that arise from a secret marriage. One reviewer says Joan realizes she has been all wrong.

1772 THE STRANGE TRANSFIGURATION OF HANNAH STUBBS. BY FLORENCE MARRYAT. London: Hutchinson, 1896 BMC. Leipzig: B. Tauchnitz, 1896 NUC.

Hannah is a domestic servant taken in hand by Signor Ricardo because she has hypnotic powers. The spirit of the she-devil who was his former wife possesses her; much havoc until she again returns to herself and dies.

LEBLANC, GEORGETTE. 1869-1941.

1773 THE CHOICE OF LIFE. New York: Dodd,Mead, 1914 NUC. London: Methuen, 1914 BMC. (Tr. by A. Tiexeira de Mattos.)

An older woman attempts to enlarge the life of a young woman, Roseline. She wants to train her to work for other oppressed women, freeing them from traditional conventions and the "burden of their own apathy." She is defeated, however, because Roseline lacks the capacity for "great feeling." She finds contentment in a village shop caring for the cat, the flowers, and the customers. One reviewer says, "One must be an ardent feminist not to feel, after reading the book through, that there is a little too much scent in the room."

LE BRETON, FARREN. See BLAKE, MABEL P.

LE CLERC, M. E.*

1774 A BOOTLESS BENE. London: Hurst and Blackett, 1895 BMC.

Rachel is an artist of aristocratic birth who chooses rural seclusion and a tradesman for a husband. Reviewers call her arrogant, reckless, independent, insolent, a vulgar prig, birth-proud, impetuous, warm-hearted. Story of the rise of nationalism in Ireland.

LEE, ALICE LOUISE. B. 1868. United States.

1775 A SOPHOMORE CO-ED. Philadelphia: Penn, 1911 NUC.

Coeds write a "girls' edition" for local paper; it wins support for co-education.

LEE, ANNE. B. 1871. United States.

1776 A WOMAN IN REVOLT. New York: D. Fitzgerald, [c1913] NUC.

Heroine is a musical genius who demands all the freedoms rightfully hers. "Expresses the most advanced phase of feminine evolution, having for a background the working of the social evil in which the woman's side of the subject is particularly emphasized."

LEE, AUBREY.*

1777 JOHN DARKER: A NOVEL. London: A. and C. Black, 1894 BMC.

Rosamund tells her story, how she experiences life as a

steerage passenger in a homeward-bound vessel from Australia, as an inmate of a low lodging in Liverpool, as the girl of the house in a small huckster's shop in a country town in Ireland, as a poor pupil in a ladies' school, as hostess in a rich Manchester man's country house, as the wife of a rich man in a first-class villa, as French mistress in a third-class school, and as the wife of a country squire in a comfortable mansion in Devonshire. John Darker murdered her father and was acquitted, when she was seven.

LEE, GEORGINA.

1778 INHALING. London: Chatto & Windus, 1911 BMC.
Biddy Winter loves her husband but he dominates her whole life. Her radical feminist friends convince her she has no independence. The novel ends in a compromise.

LEE, HELENA (CRUMETT). B. 1867. United States.

1779 ACROSS SIBERIA ALONE; AN AMERICAN WOMAN'S ADVENTURES. BY MRS. JOHN CLARENCE LEE. New York and London: J. Lane, 1914 NUC.
An account of the author's journey from Shanghai to Moscow, describing her adventures, the mystery of a letter in Russian, and people she met in Siberia.

LEE, JENNETTE BARBOUR (PERRY). 1860-1951. United States.

1780 THE AIR-MAN AND THE TRAMP. New York: C. Scribner's Sons, 1918 NUC.
Gabriell Eaton, a tired working woman who has spent herself working for her invalid mother and is strangely desolate after her mother's death, inherits a neglected old estate and decides to live on it. Romance follows.

1781 AUNT JANE. New York: C. Scribner's Sons, 1915 NUC. London: Methuen, 1916 BMC.
She is a middle-aged, tactful, efficient, strong-willed woman who is in charge of an endowed hospital in an inland city. Her capabilities and personality and her

delayed love story form the theme.

1782   THE GREEN JACKET. New York: C. Scribner's Sons, 1917 NUC. London: Skeffington, [1918] BMC.

Milly Newberry, head and founder of Millicent Newberry Detective Agency, solves a crime involving missing jewels that baffled other detective agencies for years. And she is a detective with a difference. Those who employ her must agree that she alone will decide what is to be done with the culprit. She is tired of turning criminals over to the police who send too many people to prison.

1783   KATE WETHERILL: AN EARTH COMEDY. New York: Century, 1900 BMC NUC.

A character study of an educated young woman who marries a factory foreman whose pleasures are eating and watching ball games. She has mistaken passion for love; the miseries of her marriage drive her to the verge of suicide.

1784   A PILLAR OF SALT. Boston: Houghton Mifflin, 1901 NUC.

The wife and husband never understand each other; their goals are opposite. She's practical, poverty-threatened; he's a visionary. "The moral is that education and environment of men and women are too one-sided and separate."

1785   THE RAIN-COAT GIRL. New York: C. Scribner's Sons, 1919 NUC. London: Hurst and Blackett, [1921] BMC.

Isabel Merton is a "phenomenal" stenographer, a "master" of merchandising, a community organizer, and an "artist in costume and coiffure, able to visualize a mill girl's transformation, sketch it on paper, and then bring it about." She opens a cooperative laundry in a factory town.

1786   THE WOMAN IN THE ALCOVE. New York: C. Scribner's Sons, 1914 NUC.

In this story of married life the self-centered husband keeps a tight rein on the purse strings while building up a fortune. His wife, forced to scrimp and save, becomes a faded drudge. One day in an expensive restaurant he sees the woman his wife could have been if she had had "all the countless little comforts and luxuries he could so easily have given her."

LEE, KATHERINE. See JENNER, KATHERINE LEE (RAWLINGS).

LEE, MARY CATHERINE (JENKINS). D. 1927. United States.

1787 IN THE CHEERING-UP BUSINESS. Boston and New York: Houghton, Mifflin, 1891 NUC. London: Lily Series, 1891 BMC.

Rebecca Parmelee, orphan thrown out by step-mother, tries to make her own living. Can't get work. Aunt asks her to come live with her and cheer her up. Rebecca starts that business. Goes to Quaker settlement in New Jersey.

1788 A SOULLESS SINGER. Boston and New York: Houghton, Mifflin, 1895 NUC.

A woman's whole existence is centered upon being a great singer. She has a beautiful voice but "sings without soul." A summer in a secluded Quaker settlement and her meeting with a young boy with a fine voice introduce her to feelings that give her voice "soul." She wants to adopt the boy. Ends up loving the boy's father.

LEE, MRS. JOHN CLARENCE. See LEE, HELENA (CRUMETT).

LEE, SUSAN RICHMOND. United Kingdom.

1789 THE GIRL AND THE MAN. BY CURTIS YORKE. London: J. Long, [1904] BMC 1906 NUC.

The heroine, who has learned all about mining from her uncle, promises him on his deathbed to go to Canada and find his lost silver lode. She becomes a co-owner and partner of the mine.

1790   ONLY BETTY. BY CURTIS YORKE. London: J. Long, 1907 BMC. London: J. Long, [1908] NUC.

Well educated young Welsh woman must earn her way, takes charge of young girl for three months.

1791   A RECORD OF DISCORDS. BY CURTIS YORKE. London: Jarrold, 1894 BMC.

Vampire woman, Katrine Delahaye.

1792   THE UNKNOWN ROAD. AN EVERYDAY STORY. BY CURTIS YORKE. London: Hutchinson, [1920] BMC.

The heroine, an orphan, goes to work, becomes the manager of an antique shop, marries.

1793   VALENTINE: A STORY OF IDEALS. BY CURTIS YORKE. London: Jarrold, 1897 BMC.

Follows her life from year to year beginning at age seven. By the time she reaches her teens, all her ideals are destroyed. At the end she has her consolation prize—a husband. The end is "far from the fancies she wove."

1794   THE VISION OF THE YEARS. BY CURTIS YORKE. London: J. Long, 1913 BMC.

Berenice, 27, "not good looking" lives in a Bloomsbury lodging-house, is looking for another job. Traditional end.

1795   WAYWARD ANNE. BY CURTIS YORKE. London: J. Long, 1910 BMC. Boston: D. Estes, [c1910] NUC.

Anne and Brian writers—their romance. Sentimental and silly, according to reviewer.

LE FEUVRE, AMY. D. 1929. United Kingdom.

1796   A DAUGHTER OF THE SEA. New York: T.Y. Crowell, [1902] NUC. London: Hodder & Stoughton, 1902 BMC.

Disguised, an independent young woman makes an occupation of rescuing sailors on stormy nights. She keeps this a secret from her husband; she is discovered but all ends happily.

1797   THE MAKING OF A WOMAN. London: Hodder and Stoughton, 1903 BMC.

The woman is first an artist, then a missionary.

1798   ON THE EDGE OF THE MOOR. BY THE AUTHOR OF
       PROBABLE SONS, THE ODD ONE, DWELL DEEP,
       ETC. ANONYMOUS]. New York: F.H. Revell, [c1897]
       NUC.

       Rhoda Carlton sets up her little establishment on the edge
       of the moor. Earns 140 pounds a year. Sets herself to
       redress wrongs of her tyrannical landlord.

LEFROY, ELLA NAPIER.

1799   JANET DELILLE. BY E. N. LEIGH FRY. London: Hurst
       and Blackett, 1894 BMC.

       Janet is an artist, the widow of a brilliant painter and a
       worthless man. She leads a happy Bohemian existence
       with Katie, a younger woman who has been left in her
       charge. Katie marries the wrong man, is soon bored and
       takes up with an older man, a friend of Janet's. Janet
       loves him, but nothing comes of it.

1800   THE MAN'S CAUSE. BY ELLA NAPIER LEFROY ("E. N.
       LEIGH FRY"). London: J. Lane, 1899 BMC.

       Mrs. Chesney, recently freed from the smothering horror
       of a bad marriage, learns from a young baronet that his
       former fiance is about to marry a man with a past. She
       writes to the young woman, but by chance the letter
       reaches her months after her wedding. The young woman
       drowns herself. "Advocates the cause of women against
       husbands   who   have   sown   wild   oats."   "Tedious
       conversations about women's suffrage."

LEGGE, MARGARET. United Kingdom.

1801   THE PRICE OF STEPHEN BONYNGE. London: A.
       Rivers, 1913 BMC.

       A young woman and man study art at the London Art
       Institute. Their "Bohemian" relationships, the conflict
       between morality and the artistic temperament. Heroine
       dies.

1802   THE REBELLION OF ESTHER. London: A. Rivers, 1914
       BMC NUC.

       Esther, who has "literary abilities," falls in love with a

married man; they live together. Then she is torn by her mother's unhappiness, and, feeling that her mother needs her sympathy and protection from her father, "strong and emancipated" Esther returns home to battle for her "poor crushed" mother.

1803   A SEMI-DETACHED MARRIAGE. London: A. Rivers, 1912 BMC.

Janet, "sensible, strong, and self-reliant," leaves her husband to lead her own life and join the women's movement.

1804   THE WANE OF UXENDEN. A NOVEL. London: E. Arnold, 1917 BMC NUC.

Hermoine Cheadle is a journalist, a fine modern woman of exceptional ability. After a tragedy in her life, she returns to her home town where she finds all has changed but where she nevertheless finds the peace and strength to go on.

LEIGHTON, DOROTHY. See JONSON, DOROTHY (FORSYTH).

LEIGHTON, MARIE FLORA BARBARA (CONNOR). D. 1941. United Kingdom.

1805   THE BRIDE OF DUTTON MARKET. London: Ward, Lock, 1911 BMC.

One of the principal characters is a remarkably successful woman detective.

1806   THE DUCHESS GRACE. London: Ward, Lock, 1918 BMC NUC.

A murder mystery in which the murderer is known in the fifth chapter. The remainder of the book is a grimly realistic portrayal of the wrongfully accused heroine's experiences in a women's prison.

1807   THE HAND OF THE UNSEEN, A ROMANCE OF REAL LIFE. London: Ward, Lock, 1918 BMC.

Murder mystery. Ellaline condemned to penal servitude.

1808 JOAN MAR, DETECTIVE. London: Ward, Lock, 1910 BMC.

1809 LUCILE DARE, DETECTIVE. London: Ward, Lock, 1919 BMC NUC. She uses several disguises to solve crimes, and in solving the murder of her friend's father she faces the difficulty of reconciling her duty to her friend, to her profession, and to love. Vivid adventures.

1810 THE MARKED WOMAN. London: Hodder & Stoughton, 1916 BMC.
Heroine is shot in the side at one point and at another pinked in the arm in a duel with her step-sister. The villain was of such muscular strength that she had grappled with two men more than once in a life-death struggle and come out victorious. Story culminates in a desperate duel between the two women.

1811 THE MYSTERY OF THE THREE FINGERS. London: J. Long, 1916 BMC.
The heroine, a worker in a lace factory, ends as a peeress. A young woman from British Columbia solves a mystery and unmasks the villain.

1812 THE OPAL HEART. London: Ward, Lock, 1920 BMC.
Mystery, the detective is a woman.

1813 RED GOLD. London: Ward, Lock, 1919 BMC.
About a young actress "Angel May" and her kidnapped adopted child. Includes her love story.

1814 THE WAY OF SINNERS. London: Ward, Lock, 1914 BMC.
The story is of a millionaire who wreaked vengeance on those who tried to get rid of her while she was in a home for inebriates.

LEITH, ALICIA AMY.

1815 A PLANT OF LEMON VERBENA: A SOMERSETSHIRE IDYLL. London: Gibbings, 1895 BMC.
Romance of her youth told by an old woman of the

beautiful Briton sailor who came, made promises, and left, and how she followed, found him, and suffered. In dialect. Set in West Somerset.

LEMON, IDA. See HILDYARD, IDA (LEMON).

LEONE, M. L.*

1816 DEAD LEAVES: A SKETCH OF THREE SOULS. London: Digby, Long, [1895] BMC.

Diaries of three people: the Principessa Laura Montecco who had an affair with a wealthy English merchant Clarence Ashton while her husband was alive. When her husband dies, she presents her story to Ashton and a poor admirer Solario. Of the two, she chooses the rich one because she is now poor. She is the subject of the two men's diaries which contain endless discussions of her. Solario met her when she smoked and declared "vulgarity" to be part of her program.

LEROY, AMELIE CLAIRE. B. 1851. United Kingdom.

1817 THE POWER OF THE PAST. A NOVEL. BY ESME STUART. London: R. Bentley, 1894 NUC BMC.

Inez has a youthful affair and shoots her lover when he attempts to blackmail her. Married, she confesses her remorse to her prig of a husband and, in despair over his response, takes an overdose of laudanum. She immediately regrets her act and attempts to walk it off. Conclusion is vague, but "we infer that Inez is successful...and lives happily ever afterwards."

1818 A WOMAN OF FORTY; A MONOGRAPH. BY ESME STUART. London: Methuen, 1893 NUC BMC. New York: Appleton, 1893 NUC.

Magdalen Cuthbert is awakened to a "second summer of love" by a man engaged to Griselda Foy, age 20. Magdalen, the more beautiful and attractive of the two women, is tempted to win him but decides against it. She risks diptheria and scandal to nurse him; both die. A "one character" novel.

LESLIE, HENRIETTA. See SCHUETZE, GLADYS HENRIETTA (RAPHAEL).

LETHBRIDGE, SYBIL CAMPBELL. United Kingdom.

1819   THE JOURNEY HOME. London: Skeffington, [1919] BMC.
Violet is totally indifferent to conventions. She runs off with a man and has a child outside of marriage. When she and her lover die, her sister Mattie adopts the child, and her intense love for the boy conflicts with her love for her husband. Strong psychological study.

1820   MIDDLE LIFE. London: Holden & Hardingham, [1915] BMC.
Anne-Marie Dasant is 42, candid, sensible, intelligent. Her romance is treated without sentimentality.

1821   THE SINS OF THE CHILDREN. London: Holden & Hardingham, [1918] BMC.
Edith, pregnant, asks Adolph to marry her. He refuses, Joe strikes him, and he falls over a cliff. Edith threatens Joe, who doesn't like her, but he marries her. Years later, Adolf shows up.

LETTS, WINIFRED M. B. 1882. United Kingdom.

1822   CHRISTINA'S SON. London: Gardner, [1915] NUC BMC.
Sympathetic study of mother and son. Christina had artistic leanings, but tradition brought her to marry an older man who soon dies, leaving her without means. She has become "a commonplace woman, a unit in that vast army of sober matrons," with all her passion centered on her son. His unhappy marriage becomes her tragedy.

LEVERSON, ADA. 1865-1933. United Kingdom.

1823   LOVE'S SHADOW. London: Richards, 1908 BMC.
Leverson "after her own fashion is a feminist and seldom gives her sex the worst of the situation. Egotisms and fidgetiness in their more masculine mainfestations engage

her and she describes them, if anything, a little too well."
A satire.

1824   TENTERHOOKS. London: G. Richards, [1912] BMC
NUC.
A wife, tied to insufferably fatuous and errant husband
and offered the fullness of life for which she hungers,
rejects it because it would mean his degradation. He is a
"greater ass" than he was in Love's Shadow, notes one
reviewer.

LEWALD, FANNY. See STAHR, FANNY LEWALD.

LEWIS, ELIZABETH PORTIA (GOODSON). United States.

1825   LORENZO OF SARZANA. Boston: R. G. Badger, 1907
NUC.
Mary Mortimer of Boston goes to Italy to study painting.
Includes her love story.

LEWIS, EMILY GWYNNE.

1826   AS ONE FLESH. london: J. Ouseley, 1909 BMC.
A young woman runs off when she suspects her husband
is unfaithful. She earns her living in England and the U.S.
and finally marries her ex-husband's brother.

1827   TEMPORARY INSANITY. London: Murray and Evenden,
[1913] BMC.
Sympathetic study of a woman with a dual personality
who cuts her husband's throat because he tried to kiss her
when he was drunk. She experiences a series of shocks
that make her remember her act, but then it is wiped from
her memory. She remarries, gets a fortune and a title.

LEYLAND, MARIE LOUISE (MACK) CREED. 1874-1935.
Australia.

1828   IN A WHITE PALACE. London: Rivers, 1910 BMC.
A woman falsely charged and sent to prison impersonates
another and gets a job as secretary to the man who

convicted her—he's blind. Eventually they marry and he discovers her innocence and recovers his sight.

1829 THE MUSIC MAKERS; THE LOVE STORY OF A WOMAN COMPOSER. BY LOUISE MACK. London: Mills and Boon, [1914] BMC NUC.

Established and successful woman composer produces a friend's opera. Through a misunderstanding he thinks she has tried to claim it as hers. The misunderstanding is eventually cleared up.

1830 THE WORLD IS ROUND. BY LOUISE MACK. London: T. F. Unwin, 1896 BMC.

Jean, a writer, and her two lovers.

LILJENCRANTZ, OTTILIA ADELINA. 1876-1910. United States.

1831 THE WARD OF KING CANUTE; A ROMANCE OF THE DANISH CONQUEST. Chicago: A. C. McClurg, 1903 NUC. London: Ward, Lock, 1904 BMC NUC.

Young woman disguises herself as a man, becomes Canute's page, goes into battle with him, saves his life, is wounded, sees justice done for her father's murder, and marries.

LILLIE, LUCY CECIL (WHITE). B. 1855. United States.

1832 A FAMILY DILEMMA: A STORY FOR GIRLS. Philadelphia: Porter and Coates, [c1894] NUC.

There is an inheritance problem between two women, both fine characters. The fortune is used by Jean in founding a model academy.

LINCOLN, JEANIE THOMAS (GOULD). 1846-1921. United States.

1833 A JAVELIN OF FATE. Boston: Houghton, Mifflin, 1905 BMC NUC.

Widow wants to revenge herself against man who once deserted her.

LINCOLN, NATALIE SUMNER. 1881-1935. United States.

1834   THE LOST DESPATCH. New York and London: D. Appleton, 1913 BMC NUC.

Nancy Newton is a spy for the Confederate army, knows telegraphy, disguises herself as Union trooper, meets a Union secret agent, knocks him down with butt of her revolver, escapes, is arrested, charged with treason and murder, found guilty, but pardoned by Lincoln. Her love for a Union officer complicates the plot.

1835   THE MOVING FINGER. New York and London: D. Appleton, 1918 BMC NUC.

A sick man, Bruce Brainerd, is murdered. Vera Deane, a trained nurse who is taking care of him, is one of the suspects.

LINDEN, ANNIE.

1836   GOLD: A DUTCH INDIAN STORY FOR ENGLISH PEOPLE. London: J. Lane, 1896 BMC. New York: Century, 1896 NUC.

Concerning the Dutch East Indies and a search for gold which ends in madness or death for all but Jan who is rescued by the heroine, this story also describes the sexual exploitation of native women by Dutch men. It includes an incident in which a Malaysian woman, seeing the European who has deserted her drive by with his new bride, flings her baby against the wall. The child dies, and the mother never recovers her sanity.

1837   A WOMAN OF SENTIMENT. London: Methuen, 1904 BMC.

A disillusioned wife in the fashionably social world of Holland is married to an unfaithful husband. At first she tries to convert him to her way of love; she fails and tries flirtation; falls in love. After much struggle, she remains with her husband.

LINDSAY, CAROLINE BLANCHE ELIZABETH (FITZROY). 1844-1912. United Kingdom.

1838   BERTHA'S EARL: A NOVEL. London: R. Bentley, 1891 NUC BMC.

Bertha Millings supports herself and her sister by painting. She marries an earl—"a dry stick the wrong side of 50." Trouble comes because he is not demonstrative about his love, his sister interferes and an anonymous letter reveals that Bertha has an admirer.

1839   A TANGLED WEB. London: A. and C. Black, 1892 BMC.

Lady Grissel is bored with her castle in Scotland and in revolt against an arranged betrothal to her cousin, so she escapes to London and lives under the name of Marjory Smith, from Australia. Meets cousin, they fall in love.

LINNET, BROWN.*

1840   THE SHARER. J. Murray, 1912.

The story of a woman poacher who is ultimately caught and unmasked.

LIPPMANN, JULIA MATHILDE. 1864-1952. United States.

1841   "BURKESES AMY". New York: H. Holt, 1915 NUC.

Young woman raised in wealthy circumstances decides against travelling in Europe to work with her father in the thick of New York East Side tenement district.

1842   MAKING OVER MARTHA. New York: H. Holt, 1913 NUC.

She's a "big, kindly charwoman" who moves her family to a New England village. Her humorous experiences there.

1843   MARTHA AND CUPID. New York: Holt, 1914 NUC.

Martha, launderer, marries and has children, one of them "wayward."

1844   MARTHA BY-THE-DAY. New York: H. Holt, 1912 NUC. London: G. Richards, 1913 BMC.

Martha is a launderer with a "homely philosophy."

LISLE, DAVID. See WARDELL, MRS. VILLIERS.

LISTER, EDITH.

1845   AMONG THORNS. A NOVEL. BY NOEL AINSLIE.
London: Lawrence and Bullen, 1898 BMC.
Bohemian life in Bloomsbury. Lesbia, a journalist, decides
against love but marries for the comforts marriage offers.
However she finds marriage boring because of the
numerous social obligations. Her friend Peggy, a true
Bohemian, elects for comfort and lovemaking without the
drawbacks of marriage.

1846   AN ERRING PILGRIMAGE. BY NOEL AINSLIE. London:
Lawrence and Bullen, 1896 BMC NUC.
Dolly is a successful music-hall actress and singer who
takes what she wants.

1847   THE SALVATION SEEKERS. BY NOEL AINSLIE.
London: Methuen, 1901 BMC.
Eve and Val represent "new departures for the American
heroine." Eve is a woman of "hysterical self-devotion and
caculating coldness"; Val is undisciplined and
unconventional as well. She's a dancer, who leaves her
husband when he fails her and never returns.

LITCHFIELD, GRACE DENIO. 1849-1944. United States.

1848   THE BURNING QUESTION. New York and London: G.
P. Putnam's Sons, 1913 BMC NUC.
A young woman runs away from her husband and baby
daughter because she wants to be a great violinist. Her
husband pursues her until she has her maid tell him she is
dead. At the end she is brought to life to make a happy
close.

LITTLE, FRANCES. See MACAULAY, FANNIE (CALDWELL).

LITTLE, MAUDE.

1849   A WOMAN ON THE THRESHOLD. London: Chatto & Windus, 1911 BMC.

Theodosia has two selves, one the aspiring imaginative spirit of the rebel, the other timid and conventional. She writes a novel, the heroine of which is herself, rebellious against commonplace domestic surroundings. Theodosia suppresses her writing gift when she marries a conventional school master. Then she has a son who lives the life she portrayed in her novel.

LITVINOVA, IVY (LOW). United States.

1850   GROWING PAINS. A NOVEL. BY IVY LOW. London: W. Heinemann, 1913 BMC NUC. New York: G. H. Doran, 1913 NUC.

Frank and outspoken life study of Gertrude Wilson from childhood to maturity—her questions, doubts, dreams, "the early freakishness of a child's imagination, her later violent adoration of an older girl, and the customary outbreat of unreasoning self-torment." Also vivid picture of London middle-class life.

1851   THE QUESTING BEAST. London: M. Secker, 1914 BMC.

Rachel Cohen is a typist whose landlady gives her free board so she can write novels. She is a "female rake"; the novel describes her "erotic career." She ends up comfortably as a successful novelist at 27.

LLOYD, EDITH M. J.

1852   WAS IT DESTINY? London: R. T. S., 1913 BMC.

Young woman becomes a famous singer. Her love story.

LLOYD, THEODOSIA.

1853   INNOCENCE IN THE WILDERNESS; A ROMANCE. London: Chatto & Windus, 1912 BMC.

The women stand out against a shadowy background of men. One develops character and power in the artistic and journalistic world of London. Another woman becomes an embroiderer.

LOANE, M. E.

1854 THE QUEEN'S POOR: LIFE AS THEY FIND IT IN TOWN AND COUNTRY. New York: Longmans, Green, 1905 PW. London: E. Arnold, 1905 BMC NUC.

Nurse's experience with English poor.

LOCKE, GLADYS EDSON. B. 1887. United States.

1855 THAT AFFAIR AT PORTSTEAD MANOR. Boston: Sherman, French, 1914 NUC.

A woman detective solves the crime; a male guest who is a student of Sherlock Holmes furnishes humor by his attempts.

LOMBARDI, CYNTHIA. See LOMBARDI, GEORGINA MARIE (RICHMOND).

LOMBARDI, GEORGINA MARIE (RICHMOND). D. 1942. United States.

1856 A CRY OF YOUTH. BY CYNTHIA LOMBARDI. New York and London: D. Appleton, 1920 BMC NUC.

A young American woman living in Rome teaching takes a job at the Castle of Belmontes. There is a mystery; she never sees the family.

LONG, GABRIELLE MARGARET VERE (CAMPBELL) COSTANZO. 1888-1952. United Kingdom.

1857 BLACK MAGIC. A TALE OF THE RISE AND FALL OF ANTICHRIST. London: Rivers, 1909 NUC BMC. New York: Hodder & Stoughton, [1913] NUC.

History of a refractory young nun Ursula, an "effeminate and hysterical artist" Dirk, and a diabolic Pope. The heroine robs and bribes the college of cardinals, works to excommunicate the emperor. Story of witches, relics, violence.

1858 THE BURNING GLASS. BY MARJORIE BOWEN. London: W. Collins Sons, [1918] NUC BMC. New York: E. P. Dutton, [1920] NUC.

An historical romance about Julie de Lespinasse, a celebrated French wit and writer.

1859 THE SWORD DECIDES! A CHRONICLE OF A QUEEN IN THE DARK AGES: FOUNDED ON THE STORY OF GIOVANNA OF NAPLES. BY MARJORIE BOWEN. New York: McClure, 1908 NUC. London: A. Rivers, 1908 BMC.

Giovanna "thirsts for powers, and resents the dominion of a husband..(although) the author insists she is charming." She refuses to marry and declares herself queen. Her "ruin"is not "complete enough for poetic justice."

LONGMAN, V. I.*

1860 HARVEST. A NOVEL. London: K. Paul, 1913 BMC.

Hasil Latham is a student at Oxford when she first learns her mother was a high-caste Indian, a fact that causes her fiance to break their engagement. She marries another man but is unhappy—she misses the intellectual life, and, worse, her child dies. Hasil becomes more and more estranged from her husband and removed from reality. Oxford from woman's point of view.

LOOMIS, ANNIE ELISABETH. 1850-1940. United States.

1861 MORRIS JULIAN'S WIFE. A NOVEL. BY ELIZABETH OLMIS. New York: R. Bonner, 1892 NUC. London: Hutchinson, 1893 BMC.

Satia, a schoolgirl, marries a 35 year old man. At first their marriage seems ideal; then because of his oppressive indulgence, she has a revulsion of feeling and leaves him to "cultivate her own individuality." She travels in Europe, leaving her son and husband. After years of pursuit, her remorseful and atoning husband is reunited with her. "A more utterly foolish and conceited little egotist does not exist in fiction."

LOOTA [pseud.].* United States.

1862 MONTRESOR: AN ENGLISH-AMERICAN LOVE STORY, 1854-1894. BY LOOTA. New York: F. T. Neely, 1897 NUC BMC.

A willful young woman nearly wrecks her life by an imprudent marriage. Her mother's diary, which forms the chief part of the novel, has little influence on her.

LORD, M. L. See LORD, MARIA L.

LORD, MARIA L. United Kingdom.

1863 LYDIA. BY SYDNEY CHRISTIAN. London: S. Low, 1893 BMC. Chicago: F. T. Neely, 1895 NUC.

Lydia is a "plain" young woman with a genius for art and a strong personality. For 11 years she works hard to support her destitute family. She meets a young artist she loves but rejects him because he is married. Later she meets his wife, Gertrude, and becomes involved in Gertrude's works of charity. These works are Gertrude's whole life; they are the reason she married for money. At the end Gertrude gets ill and dies wishing her husband and Lydia the joy of love she did not have.

1864 PERSIS YORKE. BY SYDNEY CHRISTIAN. London: Smith, Elder, 1896 BMC. New York: Macmillan, 1896 NUC.

Persis combines two types of heroine: the traditional long-suffering woman and the "later development with modern mind and heaven-questioning spirit." Her struggles include a despotic father, poverty, and an experience which has left her with a horror and distrust of men. The author shows "a marked intention to portray the inner as well as the outer life of a woman as subjectively as it may be possible for a man to do it," comments one reviewer; "his open-mindedness, his generosity, and his delicacy in dealing with difficult subjects are rare," comments another.

1865 TWO MISTAKES. BY SYDNEY CHRISTIAN. London: S. Low, 1895 BMC.

In the first story, "The Wordlings," Bess Appleton is a servant who reads Spencer and Newman. A rake ruins her.

LORIMER, NORMA OCTAVIA. B. 1864. United Kingdom.

1866 CATHERINE STERLING. London: W. Heinemann, 1903 BMC.

Catherine Sterling falls in love with a man whose wife is incurably insane. She and her lover see the foolishness of marriage; they live together bound only by their love. When her lover dies, Catherine falls in love again but won't tell her new lover about her past.

1867 JOSIAH'S WIFE. London: Methuen, 1898 BMC.

Camela, "one of the highly strung complex women of fiction just now". with a "warped nature," is an artist who "confides the workings of her untrammelled, uncomprehended soul to her piano in outbursts of Chopin or wild Hungarian melodies." She wants to live life fully, and she takes a year's vacation from her Baptist husband. She meets her "affinity" in Sicily. Her outraged husband wants a divorce; the "affinity" suggests the husband should first spend a year in Europe on holiday. He does and is so changed by it that he and Camela are reunited. One reviewer warns, "The relations that subsist between the husband and wife are of a kind not easily treated in the English novel."

1868 A MENDER OF IMAGES. A NOVEL. London: Hutchinson, [1920] BMC NUC. New York: Brentano's, [c1921] NUC.

A romance in which the author shows the ill-treatment of women and animals in Sicily.

1869 MIRRY-ANN: A MANX STORY. London: S. Paul, 1900 BMC. New York: D. Appleton, 1900 NUC.

Mirry-Ann is an educated Methodist preacher on the Isle of Man. She is in love with a man who works as a "nursery governess." Another man loses his sight saving her life; she feels she ought to marry him.

1870 ON DESERT ALTARS. London: S. Paul, 1915 NUC BMC. New York: Brentano's, [1915] NUC.

In order to save her sick husband's life—he needs to move to a better climate—Alice Lindsay sells herself to a wealthy Jew and has a child. When her husband learns what she has done, he turns her and the child out. She moves into a "Bohemian" world, living with a former admirer until all is forgiven and she is reconciled with her husband.

1871 THE PAGAN WOMAN. London: Chatto & Windus, 1907 BMC.

Contrast between two women. Martha is a housekeeper who worked for a professor for years. She is exhausted from her years of household drudgery and has no other life. Marian Houston is the pagan, intelligent, has a live-life-to-the-dregs philosophy, is aggressive towards men. She, not Martha, marries the professor.

1872 THE SECOND WOMAN. A NOVEL. London: S. Paul, 1912 BMC.

A woman decides if another woman gains her husband's love, she will give him up. She does so. Many complications.

1873 A SWEET DISORDER. London: A. D. Innes, 1896 BMC.

In the tradition of Mrs. Hungerford. Molly tries earning her living in a variety of ways; as governess (she concludes "Hell must be full of other people's children"), waitress, "skirt-dancer," and novelist. In the end she confesses to Dacre that love is almost as good as independence.

1874 WITH OTHER EYES. London: S. Paul, [1919] BMC NUC. New York: Brentono's, [c1920] NUC.

A love story which gives an answer to the problem of whether women should be stuck with men they no longer want merely because they have been in the war. Alix has left her husband, with whom she had emigrated to Canada and who has squandered their money. She is on her way back to England to open a boarding house when she meets Evangeline; their fortunes are interwoven.

LOTHROP, HARRIET MULFORD (STONE). 1844-1924. United States.

1875 SALLY, MRS. TUBBS. BY MARGARET SIDNEY. Boston: Lothrop, [1903] NUC.

An expert launderer determined to marry by age 50 so she won't be an "old maid" proposes to Mr. Tubbs.

LOUGHEAD, FLORA (HAINES) APPONYI. B. 1855. United States.

1876 THE BLACK CURTAIN. Boston and New York: Houghton, Mifflin, 1898 NUC. London: Duckworth, 1899 BMC.

An artist who is color blind and a singer who has lost her voice take up the same government claim on land in California. They are squatters and argue about their rights. Traditional happy ending.

1877 A CROWN OF THORNS. San Francisco: C.A. Murdock, [c1891] NUC.

Young San Franciscan woman attends a meeting in which the Society for the Prevention of Cruelty to Children is investigating Chinese adoption of babies for immoral purposes. She finds her own child in the act of having her feet crushed, the child she had four years earlier abandoned and whom she now courageously acknowledges to be her own.

LOUIS, A. B.*

1878 MALLERTON. London: Bliss, Sands, 1897 BMC.

Everyday life of everyday people in the town of Mallerton. Judith Estcourt, among them, is an able woman of letters.

LOUTHAN, HATTIE (HORNER). B. 1865. United States.

1879   IN PASSION'S DRAGNET: A NOVEL. Boston: R. G. Badger, 1903 NUC.

Plea for co-education and independence for women in order that women will be less vulnerable.

LOW, IVY. See LITVINOVA, IVY (LOW).

LOWENBERG, BETTIE (LILIENFELD). B. 1845. United States.

1880   THE VOICES. BY MRS. I. LOWENBERG. San Franscisco: H. Wagner, 1920 NUC.

A woman who is born with the word "mission" on her lips listens to voices and becomes a political and industrial leader.

LOWENBERG, MRS. I. See LOWENBERG, BETTIE (LILIENFELD).

LOWNDES, MARIE ADELAIDE (BELLOC). 1868-1947. United Kingdom.

1881   BARBARA REBELL. BY MRS. BELLOC-LOWNDES. London: W. Heinemann, 1905 BMC NUC. New York: B.W. Dodge, 1907 NUC.

Traces Barbara Rebell's life from girlhood to womanhood. As a girl she is well educated in France. As a woman of strong character and temperament, she leaves her scoundrel husband and elopes with her lover.

1882   THE CHINK IN THE ARMOUR. BY MRS. BELLOC LOWNDES. London: Methuen, [1912] BMC NUC. New York: Scribner's, 1912 NUC.

Two women at a gambling casino. One, a confirmed gambler, is murdered. The younger woman risks her life solving the mystery.

1883 THE END OF HER HONEYMOON. BY MRS. BELLOC LOWNDES. New York: C. Scribner's Sons, 1913 NUC. London: Methuen, 1914 BMC NUC.

Spiritualism; a modern young woman with great powers as a medium makes a discovery of murder.

1884 THE HEART OF PENELOPE. London: W. Heinemann, 1904 BMC NUC.

She loves one man, marries another with whom she works in an Eastside settlement till he dies. Then she's attracted to a third man.

1885 LILLA: A PART OF HER LIFE. BY MRS. BELLOC-LOWNDES. London: Hutchinson, 1916 BMC NUC. New York: G.H. Doran, [c1917] NUC.

Marriage for Lilla Singleton meant the stifling of her individuality, but she was strong enough so that nine years of marriage did not ruin her. When her husband is reported killed in action in the war, she meets and marries another man after a short courtship. And when her first husband turns up alive, she solves her problem by taking up relief work in France while the men go their separate ways.

1886 MARY PECHELL. BY MRS. BELLOC LOWNDES. London: Methuen, 1912 BMC NUC. New York: C. Scribner's Sons, 1912 NUC.

Cranford-like in its depiction of the love story of an older woman.

1887 THE RED CROSS BARGE. BY MRS. BELLOC LOWNDES. London: Smith, Elder, 1916 BMC NUC. New York: G.H. Doran, [1918] NUC.

Jeanne, a noble, patriotic heroine, is in charge of the Red Cross Barge; love, war and the Germans.

1888 STUDIES IN WIVES. BY MRS. BELLOC LOWNDES. London: W. Heinemann, 1909 BMC. New York: M. Kennerley, [c1910] NUC.

Six stories dealing with unhappy marriages, one a "tragedy

of a leasehold marriage," which the woman will not consent to renew. A "cool, patient investigation."

1889 THE UTTERMOST FARTHING. BY MRS. BELLOC LOWNDES. London: W. Heinemann, 1908 BMC NUC. New York: M. Kennerley, [c1910] NUC.

Wife goes off with man, dies of heart disease on journey, he arranges to protect her reputation.

LOWNDES, MRS. BELLOC. See LOWNDES, MARIE ADELAIDE (BELLOC).

LOWTH, ALYS.

1890 A DAUGHTER OF THE TRANSVAAL. London: Hutchinson, 1899 BMC NUC.

Strange story of race hatred in a girls' school in Cape Colony. Some of the girls are daughters of Dopper farmers, some of Johannesburg Jews, of French missionaries, and of English officers. The succession of violent encounters—physical as well as verbal—between the English and the Dutch girls, the author siding with the English.

1891 DOREEN COASTING. WITH SOME ACCOUNTS OF THE PLACES SHE SAW AND THE PEOPLE SHE ENCOUNTERED. EDITED BY ALYS LOWTH. London: Longmans, Green, 1912 NUC BMC.

Irish heroine's voyage to East and South Africa, described in a series of letters.

LUCAS, EMILY BEATRIX COURSOLLES (JONES). B. 1893. United Kingdom.

1892 QUIET INTERIOR. BY E. B. C. JONES. London: R. Cobden-Sanderson, [c1920] BMC NUC. New York: Boni & Liveright, [1921] NUC.

Claire Norris is fastidious, emancipated. She and her sister are "tepid" conscientious objectors; they live quietly in their interiors and feel no necessity to do war work. When

Claire gives up the man she loves to her sister, she fully discovers her inner world and is at last in harmony with life.

LUCK, MARY CHURCHILL (SPOTTISWOODE-ASHE). Fl. 1895-1914. United Kingdom.

1893 ACROSS AN ULSTER BOG. BY M. HAMILTON. London: W. Heinemann, 1896 BMC. New York: E. Arnold, 1896 NUC.

Ellen, a young Irish woman, is seduced by a curate and is a mother at 16. Her brothers beat the curate one night until he dies, allowing his body to sink into a bog. "Truly Irish," comments one reviewer; another describes the story as "disgusting, sordid, and repellent."

1894 CUT LAURELS. BY M. HAMILTON. London: W. Heinemann, 1905 BMC NUC.

Katharine, separated from her husband for 18 years, has worked, saved, and with her daughter, established a famous dressmaking business. We follow her mind point by point as she learns of her husband's release from prison in Egypt (where he went to make a fortune), travels there with her daughter, and discovers that he married to save his life and has children. In time this strong woman forgives her weak husband.

1895 THE FIRST CLAIM. BY M. HAMILTON. London: Methuen, 1906 BMC. New York: Doubleday, Page, 1907 NUC.

Married to an old man at 17, the heroine leaves him and her child. Remarried, she is torn between the claims of her new husband and her child, who now has a hateful personality and is disliked by her stepmother. To do anything will bring to life the scandal of her first marriage. She steals the child.

1896 THE LOCUST'S YEARS. BY M. HAMILTON. London: Skeffington, [1919] BMC.

The troubled marriage of Susan, a shy author of 40, to a man 17 years younger than she.

1897   MCLEOD OF THE CAMERONS. BY M. HAMILTON. London: W. Heinemann, 1897 BMC. New York: D. Appleton, 1897 NUC.

Christina is married to a man who is intellectually her inferior. During his three year absence she becomes friends with McLeod, an intellectual who is struggling with insanity. She helps him fight homicidal mania in the face of gossip until his death by suicide. At the same time, although she is completely disillusioned in her husband, she struggles to make the best of her marriage.

1898   MRS. BRETT. BY M. HAMILTON. London: S. Paul, 1913 BMC.

Both mother and daughter take lovers. Mrs. Brett after her long martyrdom with her cruel husband—a kind of penance for an early lapse which separated her from her daughter—loves a much younger man who has been discarded by her daughter. The mother is the more sympathetic character.

1899   THE WOMAN WHO LOOKED BACK. BY M. HAMILTON. London: S. Paul, [1914] BMC NUC.

Sara is married for twelve years when it is discovered that a first wife exists. She looks back at her past and yearns for a former lover, but remains for the sake of her children. The novel has a "sub-acid flavour."

LUDLUM, JEAN KATE. United States.

1900   LIDA CAMPBELL; OR, DRAMA OF A LIFE. A NOVEL. New York: R. Bonner's Sons, 1892 NUC.

"Strangely endowed" woman writes a novel hoping "to ventilate her ill-balanced action and strange theory of being." Sensational incidents involved in her attempts to publish.

LUEHRMANN, ADELE. United States.

1901   THE CURIOUS CASE OF MARIE DUPONT. New York: Century, 1916 BMC NUC.

Marie is a beautiful and clever young woman; people suspect her of being a Parisian dancer who was supposedly murdered. When Gavoch sees her dance, he remembers seeing her in a vile Montmartre cafe—the mistress of a notorious Rumanian prince and a leader of the demi-monde.

LUSK, ALICE FREEMAN.

1902　A WOMAN'S ANSWER TO ROOSEVELT; A STORY ON RACE SUICIDE. Los Angeles, Cal.: Commercial Printing House, 1908 NUC.

Description of the life of a woman with eleven children, her endless labor and early death. Her wealthy husband quickly marries another woman.

LUTTON, ELIZABETH MILLER. United States.

1903　THE CRACKER BOX SCHOOL. Chicago: Reilly & Britton, [c1917] NUC.

Love story of a teacher.

LUTZ, GRACE (LIVINGSTON) HILL. 1865-1947. United States.

1904　"A DAILY RATE". BY GRACE LIVINGSTON HILL. Philadelphia: Union, [c1900] NUC.

Celia, sales woman and boarder at a slovenly house. She inherits a little money and takes charge of house, improving food, manners, morals.

1905　THE ·ENCHANTED BARN. Philadelphia and London: J.B. Lippincott, 1918 BMC NUC.

Heroine, a stenographer, supports her family; they live in a barn. While on a business trip to Washington, she is kidnapped. She meets the owner of the barn; their romance solves all her problems.

1906　THE RED SIGNAL. Philadelphia and London: J.B. Lippincott, 1919 BMC NUC.

Spirited young woman foils a diabolical German plot which threatens the safety of the United States and, with the help of a young engineer, gets secret information she has gathered to Washington.

1907   A VOICE IN THE WILDERNESS: A NOVEL. New York
        and London: Harper, [1916] BMC NUC.

        A young school teacher in Arizona with a mission to
        civilize the wild West has adventures and a "pretty" love
        story.

LYALL, DAVID [pseud.].   (Works under this pseudonym
        are attributed in BMC to Annie S. (Swan) Smith; in
        NUC to Helen Buckingham (Mathers) Reeves.)

1908   THE GRAVEN IMAGE. BY DAVID LYALL. London:
        Hodder and Stoughton, [1919] BMC.

        Selfish bully of a husband. Saintly wife.

1909   THE ONE WHO CAME AFTER; A STUDY OF A
        MODERN WOMAN. BY DAVID LYALL. London:
        Hodder and Stoughton, 1910 BMC.

        Christine runs away from her husband a few weeks after
        marriage because she is bored. Women's rights play a
        minor part. She comes back. Abrupt change from militant
        suffragist to ardent theosophist.

1910   THE SHIPS OF MON DESIR. BY DAVID LYALL.
        London: Hodder and Stoughton, 1910 BMC.

        Mon Desir is a hostel for young English women; their
        stories.

LYALL, EDNA. See BAYLY, ADA ELLEN.

LYNCH, HANNAH. C. 1862-1904. United Kingdom.

1911   AUTOBIOGRAPHY OF A CHILD [ANONYMOUS]. New
        York: Dodd, Mead, 1899 NUC. Edinburgh and London:
        W. Blackwood, 1899 BMC.

        Autobiography of a battered child told by a mature
        woman who can now forgive her mother. The love and
        attention Angela receives from her stepfather the first five
        years of her life enable her to avoid being warped by
        what followed. Angela is beaten mercilessly by her mother
        who hated children. At eight, she moves from her Irish
        mother's home to a convent run by English nuns of Ladies

of Mercy. Here the nuns starve, mistreat, and even torture her. She cries out in anger and resentment against the brutal treatment.

1912 CLARE MONRO: THE STORY OF A MOTHER AND DAUGHTER. London: J. Milne, [1900] BMC.
Mother and daughter, tragic.

1913 DAUGHTERS OF MEN. New York: J. W. Lovell, [c1892] NUC.
Against the background of Athens and the Isle of Terror are drawn the love stories of Photini Natzelhuber, the pupil of Liszt and the rival of Rubenstein, a genius half-mad and wholly kind-hearted, and Inarime, daughter of a Greek scholar, who has been trained intellectually and gymnastically on the most approved classic lines.

1914 DENYS D'AUVRILLAC. A STORY OF FRENCH LIFE. London: J. Macqueen, 1896 BMC.
Troubles and unhappy love of an young English woman studying art in France. Characters are not Bohemians but serious, almost Germanic types.

1915 AN ODD EXPERIMENT. London: Methuen, 1897 BMC.
A middle-aged woman meets young Blanche, her husband's mistress, insists that she come to live with her and her husband, and tries to reclaim her.

1916 THE PRINCE OF THE GLADES. London: Methuen, 1891 BMC.
Story of the revolutionary Irish Fenian movement. Camilla Knoys is a "veritable hero in petticoats." She is completely involved in the movement to the extent of a sixty mile midnight ride. She is beautiful, but chilly—to all but the cause. She does love Godfrey O'Moore, but he goes to prison and then shoots his own brother who is attracted to Camilla.

1917 ROSNI HARVEY: A NOVEL. London: Chapman and Hall, 1892 BMC.
Rosni, a young Irish woman who reads Greek and German philosophers in the original languages, would like

to be a medical student. She goes to Greece with her cousin Annie. "Her one great pleasure lay in her studies. As a girl character, Rosni is a little over-drawn on the intellectual side."

LYNCH, HARRIET LOUISE (HUSTED). 1864-1943. United States.

1918 A LITTLE GAME WITH DESTINY. BY MARIE ST. FELIX. New York: Nocton, 1892 NUC.

Written in diary form by a young woman of sixteen whose rich Boston parents believe is an innocent schoolgirl pursuing her studies. She is in fact living a dual life, is a restless drinker and gambler and the mistress of an elderly married man. "A vivid picture of what is happening about us every week of the year."

1919 TWO BAD BROWN EYES. BY MARIE ST. FELIX. New York: Merriam, [c1894] NUC.

Possessor of eyes in title is a respectable country girl seduced by a clergyman who repents, is filled with horror at her immorality and deserts her. She drifts into a life of sin and Bohemian Paris. Fifteen years later she returns to Chicago during Columbian Fair, meets clergyman's daughter, and takes vengeance in a horribly cruel, wicked way.

LYNCH, LAWRENCE L. See VAN DEVENTER, EMMA MURDOCH.

LYND, SYLVIA (DRYHURST). 1888-1952. United Kingdom.

1920 THE CHORUS: A TALE OF LOVE AND FOLLY. London: Constable, 1915 BMC. New York: E. P. Dutton, [1916] NUC.

Nellie Hayes, 16, falls in love with a 40 year old artist whose wife's friends (the chorus) finally separate the two. He returns to his wife; she's left destitute, "to go to the bad on the streets of London."

LYNN, ETHEL GRACE ALSPICE.

1921　THE ADVENTURES OF A WOMAN HOBO. BY ETHEL LYNN, M.D. New York: G.H. Doran, [c1917] NUC.

Adventures of a couple on a tandem bike: Dr. Ethel Lynn out of work in Chicago in 1908 because of depression and suffering from TB must get to California. With no money available, she and her husband go by bike and on freight cars. Nonfiction?

LYSTER, CORA.

1922　PAUL HEINSIUS: A STUDY FROM LIFE. London: T. Unwin, 1896 BMC.

"The illustration of human frailty as exhibited in the male species." "Breaks fresh ground," "a cold and observant eye carefully noting the squirmings of a few Germanic characters." "One of the ideas of the plot is entirely revolting." Heinsius is a bank cashier who victimizes the women who love him but is finally scorned by them and utterly fooled by a clever woman.

LYTTLETON, EDITH SOPHY (BALFOUR). B. 1865. United Kingdom.

1923　THE TOUCH OF SORROW. BY EDITH HAMLET. London: J. M. Dent, 1896 BMC. New York: H. Holt, 1896 NUC.

The study of the effects of the death of her child on happy, selfish, and thoughtless young woman. One reviewer finds there is too much insight into obstetrics, a subject "best left in the shadow."

M., A. S. See MACNEILL, NEVADA.

MABEL. See PARKS, MABEL E.

MABIE, LOUISE (KENNEDY). D. 1957. United States.

1924 THE LIGHTS ARE BRIGHT. "FOUR BELLS AND THE LIGHTS ARE BRIGHT." (NIGHT CALL OF LOOKOUT ON THE ORE-BOATS OF THE GREAT LAKES.) A NOVEL. New York and London: Harper, 1914 NUC BMC.

Theodora at 18 is owner and operator of immense mines of iron ore and big steel works on Lake Erie. Her father has left her with a sense of responsibility and obligation that the property be administered to serve society in every sense. A rival concern attempts to gain control of the Trevor Works; a suave man has been assigned the task of influencing her to sell. Rivalry in love between him and her forceful manager.

MACALILLY, ALICE.

1925 HILDA LANE'S ADOPTIONS. Cincinnati: Jennings & Graham, [c1905] NUC.

Misunderstanding keeps Hilda from the man she loves for twenty years. She adopts a boy and a black girl and educates them. The girl gives her life to white fever sufferers; the boy discovering upon marriage that he's part black gives his life to uplifting the blacks.

MACAULAY, ALLAN. See STEWART, CHARLOTTE.

MACAULAY, FANNIE (CALDWELL). 1863-1941. United States.

1926 THE HOUSE OF THE MISTY STAR; A ROMANCE OF YOUTH AND HOPE AND LOVE IN OLD JAPAN. BY FRANCES LITTLE (FANNIE CALDWELL MACAULAY). New York: Century, 1915 NUC. London: Hodder & Stoughton, 1915 NUC.

Ursula Jenkins has taught English in Japan for 30 of her 58 years. She opens her home to two women. One is Jane Grey, a missionary; the other a Japanese-American girl. "Pretty."

1927 THE LADY MARRIED. BY THE AUTHOR OF "THE LADY OF THE DECORATION" [ANONYMOUS]. London: Hodder & Stoughton, 1912 BMC.

Sequel to Lady of the Decoration. Descriptions of Japan and revolution in Peking. Sentimental letters.

1928 THE LADY OF THE DECORATION. BY FRANCES LITTLE. New York: Century, 1906 BMC NUC. London: Hodder and Stoughton, 1906 BMC NUC.

Kentucky woman's experiences as kindergarten teacher in a mission school in Japan and later as a nurse in the Russo-Japanese War. Sentimental and romantic.

1929 LITTLE SISTER SNOW. BY FRANCES LITTLE. New York: Century, 1909 NUC. London: Hodder & Stoughton, 1909 NUC BMC.

Study of a young Japanese woman from childhood to betrothal in grave Japanese style to suitor of parents' choice. Her diary, "that naive, pathetic, exquisite confession." The story is "a powerful brief for the emancipation of women of the Orient from the unnatural laws governing marriage."

MACAULAY, R. See MACAULAY, ROSE.

MACAULAY, ROSE. 1881-1958. United Kingdom.

1930 POTTERISM, A TRAGI-FARCICAL TRACT. New York: Boni & Liveright, [c1920] NUC. London: W. Collins, 1920 NUC BMC.

A satire on the commercially successful sale of sentimentality to the public. The Potter family have an "invincibly successful" publishing firm. Mrs. Potter writes sentimental and spiritual novels; her daughter Jane is a journalist. The book is divided into six parts; the first and last are narrated by the author, the other four by different characters. One of the parts is a "burlesque of the Florence Barclay-Ethel Dell-Ruby Ayres school of fiction."

1931 VIEWS AND VAGABONDS. BY R. MACAULAY. New York: H. Holt, 1912 NUC. London: J. Murray, 1912 NUC BMC.

An aristocrat sets himself up as a blacksmith and marries Louie, a mill hand. She is inarticulate, unapproachable, self-sufficient but shut-in. She gets fed up with her husband's pompous friends and family; she tells him off and joins a group of vagabonds. Later on he becomes a human being and they are reunited. "She stands out against a company of shrewd and amiable worldlings, faddists, and social experimentalists."

1932 WHAT NOT: A PROPHETIC COMEDY. London: Constable, 1919 NUC BMC.

A prophecy about Civil Service life in a future when there will be street aeroplanes in London. Kitty Grammond is a thoroughly efficient and independent young business woman who helps run the Ministry of Brains, an organization that registers the people of England by intelligence and that decides who shall marry whom. Kitty's brain is registered at the highest order. Her fiance is a deficient, but she marries him anyway. The marriage works. May be a satire on Big Brother kind of official control.

MACCALL, SIDNEY. See FENOLLOSA, MARY (MACNEIL).

MACCARTER, MARGARET (HILL). 1860-1938. United States.

1933 THE RECLAIMERS. New York & London: Harper, [1918] BMC NUC.

Geraldine, "beautiful and business-like," seeks an independent life on 1200 acres in Kansas. When she learns the land is worthless, she becomes a math teacher, overcomes the prejudices of the town, and succeeds.

MACCHESNEY, DORA GREENWELL. 1871-1912. United States.

1934 BEATRIX INFELIX: A SUMMER TRAGEDY IN ROME. New York and London: J. Lane, 1898 BMC NUC.

Beatrice and Horatia spend the summer in Rome with Beatrice's mother, a novelist. Horatia narrates the story of Beatrice, a restless, unhappy Marie Bashkirtseff type. Beatrice hopes death will bring Nirvana. She has many lovers, can accept none of them. Her mother forces her into a loveless marriage, and she takes an overdose of chloral.

MACCHESNEY, ELIZABETH STUDDIEFORD. 1841-1906. United States.

1935 UNDER THE SHADOW OF THE MISSION: A MEMORY OF SANTA BARBARA. BY L. STUDDIEFORD MCCHESNEY. London: Methuen, 1897 NUC.

Conversations of a chorus of intensely interesting women and two men, all of whom have symbolic names and are invalids in Esperanza Hotel. Ultimata, the speaker, paints her own portrait through her beautiful relation to her daughter, her love of nature, and her part in the discussions on women's place. She says that falling in love with women has been her life-long weakness. Her appreciation of women is intense.

MACCHESNEY, L. STUDDIEFORD. See MACCHESNEY, ELIZABETH STUDDIEFORD.

MACCLELLAN, HARRIET (HARE). United States.

1936 BROKEN CHORDS CROSSED BY THE ECHO OF A FALSE NOTE. BY MRS. GEORGE MCCLELLAN (HARFORD FLEMMING). Philadelphia: J. B. Lippincott, 1893 BMC NUC.

Young woman runs away from home and her clergyman-father. She becomes an actress, is seduced by a man, marries another "to save herself from disgrace," but he dies. When the fiancee of the man who seduced her learns his secret, she refuses to marry him—"sends him to make reparations." He marries the young actress. Unhappiness and complications follow, but all ends well.

MACCLELLAN, MRS. GEORGE. See MACCLELLAN, HARRIET (HARE).

MACCLELLAND, M. G. See MACCLELLAND, MARY GREENWAY.

MACCLELLAND, MARY GREENWAY. 1853-1895. United States.

1937   MAMMY MYSTIC. BY M. G. MCCLELLAND. New York:˙ Merriam, [c1895] NUC.
The mystic is a "quadroon" slave who marries a Scandinavian though the law forbids such marriages. When her child is born, she substitutes her ˙for her mistress' dead child. The child grows up, has a daughter named Eugenia in whose life "the effects of this act are seen and the laws of heredity traced." Set in New Orleans.

MACCONNELL, SARAH WARDER. 1869-1953. United States.

1938   MANY MANSIONS. Boston: Houghton Mifflin, 1918 NUC.
Raised in a gloomy boarding house, the heroine earns her living as an interior decorator. Her love story.

1939   WHY, THEODORA! Boston: Small, Maynard, [1915] BMC NUC.
Intimate study of a young woman who is unconventional—she thinks for herself and makes her own way.

MACCULLOCH, CATHARINE (WAUGH). B. 1862. United States.

1940   MR. LEX; OR, THE LEGAL STATUS OF MOTHER AND CHILD. Chicago and New York: F. H. Revell, 1899 NUC.
Related to the woman question and suffrage.

MACCULLOUGH, MYRTLE (REED). 1874-1911. United States.

1941 LAVENDER AND OLD LACE. BY MYRTLE REED. New York & London: G. P. Putnam's Sons, 1902 BMC NUC.

Described as an American Cranford by one reviewer, and as crude and dreadful by another.

MACDONALD, LUCRETIA S.

1942 CHECKERBERRY. New York: Cochrane, 1908 NUC.

Rachel was kidnapped in her infancy and trained for the circus. A spinster makes a home for her and eleven other young orphaned young girls.

MACDONALD, LUCY MAUD (MONTGOMERY). 1874-1942. Canada.

1943 ANNE OF AVONLEA. BY LUCY MAUD MONTGOMERY. Boston: L.C. Page, 1909 NUC. London: I. Pitman, 1909 BMC.

Teacher marries a man who has all the books she wants and more.

1944 ANNE OF GREEN GABLES. BY LUCY MAUD MONTGOMERY. London: Pitman, 1908 BMC. Boston: L.C. Page, 1908 NUC.

Anne from eleven to seventeen, focus on first two years. She is adopted, educated, becomes a school teacher, supports another woman. Written for adults. Includes a cross, narrow minded spinster.

1945 KILMENY OF THE ORCHARD. BY LUCY MAUD MONTGOMERY. Boston: L. C. Page, 1910 NUC. London: I. Pitman, 1910 BMC.

A young woman who is deaf and mute is a musical genius. She learns to speak. Love story.

MACDONELL, ANNE.

1946　THE STORY OF TERESA. London: Methuen, 1902 BMC NUC.

Epic of a woman's life—a Hardy woman. Teresa is "almost as rare as Hardy's Sue," says another reviewer.

MACDONNELL, MRS. A. J.

1947　DID SHE DO RIGHT? A ROMANCE OF THE 20TH CENTURY. London: S. Paul, 1909 BMC.

Unwitting rivalry of two friends, one 35 and one younger, who both love same man.

MACELROY, LUCY (CLEAVER). 1860-1901. United States.

1948　JULETTY; A STORY OF OLD KENTUCKY. New York: T. Y. Crowell, [c1901] NUC.

Heroine is a moonshiner.

MACFADDEN, G. V. See MACFADDEN, GERTRUDE VIOLET.

MACFADDEN, GERTRUDE VIOLET. United Kingdom.

1949　THE HONEST LAWYER. BY G. V. MCFADDEN. New York and London: J. Lane, 1916 BMC NUC.

A high-spirited woman possessing ancient family privileges asks a lawyer to marry her; he rejects her. She subsequently sends him to the stocks. He commits a technical felony for her sake and is sentenced to deportation for life. She marries him in prison and has him pardoned.

MACFALL, FRANCES ELIZABETH (CLARKE). 1862-1943. United Kingdom.

1950　ADNAM'S ORCHARD: A PROLOGUE. BY SARAH GRAND. London: W. Heinemann, 1912 BMC NUC. New York: D. Appleton, 1913 NUC.

An appeal for the "back to the soil" movement, but

embracing many modern causes, prominent among them, feminism.

1951 THE BETH BOOK. BY SARAH GRAND. New York: D. Appleton, 1897 NUC. London: W. Heinemann, 1898 BMC. (Bookseller subtitle: Being a Study from the Life of Elizabeth Caldwell Maclure, a Woman of Genius.)

Few heroines are so completely described as Beth: 300 pages are given to her childhood, 129 to an intense study of the first eight years of this exceptionally gifted girl. At 16 she marries a detestable brute who spies on her. Claiming that sex with her husband ruins her health, she leaves him and goes to London where she becomes a novelist and joins the sisterhood as a public speaker on women's rights.

1952 A DOMESTIC EXPERIMENT. BY THE AUTHOR OF "IDEALA: A STUDY FROM LIFE" [ANONYMOUS]. Edinburgh and London: Blackwood, 1891 BMC NUC.

Agatha, a clear-sighted, cultured woman, is disgusted with her husband and attracted to Paul Oldham. "She goes a great deal too far with him." "Distasteful." "Vulgar, foolish, impossible."

1953 THE HEAVENLY TWINS. BY MADAME SARAH GRAND. London: W. Heinemann, 1893 BMC. New York: Cassell, [c1893] NUC.

The twins are Diavolo and Angelica, two geniuses for mischief. Their growing up is woven in and out of the more important story of Evadne Colquhoun who refuses to be a wife to her husband when she learns he slept with women in the past. Later she gives in to the pressure of her family and returns to her husband, but he is not to touch her. One of Evadne's friends, married to a dissipated man, has a child that looks like a "speckled toad," and when she learns her husband had children before their marriage, she gets ill from the shock and dies. The author believes girls should have full knowledge of sex, that men no less than women should be virgins when they marry, and that women should refuse to be wives if they learn their husbands had sex before marriage—all in order to remove the double standard by elevating men's morals to those of women.

1954 SINGULARLY DELUDED, A ROMANCE. BY THE AUTHOR OF "IDEALA", ETC. [ANONYMOUS]. Edinburgh: W. Blackwood, 1893 BMC. New York: G. Munroe, [c1895] NUC.

Suspenseful, nightmarish adventures of Gertrude Sommers who plays detective when her husband disappears. She pursues a man from England to France, believing he is her husband gone mad. She proves to be a woman of extraordinary endurance.

1955 THE WINGED VICTORY. BY SARAH GRAND. New York: D. Appleton, 1916 NUC. London: W. Heinemann, [1916] BMC NUC.

Ella, an energetic Englishwoman, is supported by the duke and duchess in a London town house and a place of business where she sells lace. She hopes to reform the lace trade, freeing it from sweating conditions. She sees the duke frequently, and there is talk about her being his mistress. An attack is made on her honor, and she kills the man involved. She marries the duke's son, Lord Melton. When they discover that the duke is Ella's father, Melton kills himself.

MACGEE, AGNES POTTER. United States.

1956 DOROTHY ANGSLEIGH; A STORY OF WAR TIMES. Chicago: W. B. Conkey, 1907 NUC.

Nurse is married to a soldier who deserts her.

MACGILL, MARGARET (GIBBONS). United Kingdom.

1957 THE BARTERED BRIDE. London: H. Jenkins, 1921 [1920] BMC.

Molly runs from brutal stepfather, then from her drunken husband who forced her to marry him. Faithful young miner in background.

MACGLASSON, EVA WILDER. See BRODHEAD, EVA WILDER (MACGLASSON).

MACGOWAN, ALICE. 1858-1947. United States.

1958 THE LAST WORD. Boston: L.C. Page, 1903 NUC. London: Hutchinson, 1903 BMC.

Young lively woman travels on horseback in Texas, goes to New York to be a journalist, writes a successful book and marries the man who illustrated her book, but only after breaking with him because of his views on women and converting him to her views. The agreement includes the proviso that she will keep her career and her individuality instead of making sunshine for his exclusive benefit. A minor character—a woman friend of the heroine—is learned in the classics, in biology and astronomy.

MACGREGOR, A. LYNDSAY. See MACGREGOR, ANNIE LYNDSAY.

MACGREGOR, ANNIE LYNDSAY. United States.

1959 'BOUND, NOT BLESSED'. BY A. LYNDSAY MACGREGOR. New York: G. W. Dillingham, 1892 NUC.

Unhappy marrriage of a good wife and scoundrel husband.

MACGUIRE, C. See MACGUIRE, CATHAL.

MACGUIRE, CATHAL.*

1960 AMABEL: A MILITARY ROMANCE. BY C. MACGUIRE. London: T. F. Unwin, 1893 BMC. Chicago: Rand, McNally, 1893 NUC.

"Well-born" refined young woman marries a coarse army sergeant. They live in a barracks town under social standards very different from what she is used to. Miserably unhappy, she deserts her husband and children, runs off with an officer friend of her husband, and later takes one of her children, a daughter who learns the true identity of her father only at the time of her mother's death.

MACHA, VERA.

1961 ONE OF MANY. London: Digby, Long, 1900 BMC.
Ester Armytage becomes a governess, considers it a calling. Autobiographical form.

MACILWRAITH, JEAN NEWTON. 1859-1938. Canada.

1962 THE MAKING OF MARY. BY JEAN FORSYTH. London: T. F. Unwin, 1895 BMC NUC. New York: Cassell, [c1895] NUC.
Beautiful young woman, selfish, friendless, taken in hand by a woman who can do nothing with her. She becomes a nurse, gets smallpox, loses her beauty. Her fiance leaves her, and she devotes herself to her patients.

MACIVOR, MARY A. United States.

1963 THE UPPER TRAIL. Boston: Roxburgh, [c1912] NUC.
A schoolteacher with strong prejudices from the South in the West.

MACK, LOUISE. See LEYLAND, MARIE LOUISE (MACK) CREED.

MACKAY, HELEN GANSEVOORT (EDWARDS). B. 1876. United States.

1964 HALF LOAVES; A STORY. New York: Duffield, 1911 NUC. London: Chatto & Windus, 1912 BMC.
Florida Marvin wants a great love. She tires of her husband who takes her for granted and who is interested in other women. She leaves this man (capable of only a half-loaf of love), goes to Italy to live by herself. There

she meets and loves a man who gets her involved in working for the poor. At the very end she returns to her husband.

MACKAY, ISABEL ECCLESTONE (MACPHERSON).
1875-1928. Canada.

1965 THE HOUSE OF WINDOWS. London, New York: Cassell, 1912 BMC NUC.

A woman, whose husband and daughter have been ruined by the business methods of a store, kidnaps the owner's daughter. She becomes a shophand in the store.

MACKAY, MARY. 1855-1924. United Kingdom.

1966 INNOCENT, HER FANCY AND HIS FACT; A NOVEL. BY MARIE CORELLI. London and New York: Hodder & Stoughton, 1914 BMC NUC. New York: G. H. Doran, [c1914] NUC.

At 18, Innocent learns she is an orphan with no name or past. She refuses Robin's offer of marriage, because she wants a career. In London, she becomes a successful author and eventually learns about her parents. Love destroys Innocent, as it did her mother. She falls in love with an artist who paints her portrait, saps her of her creativity, destroys her career and leaves her. Innocent dies in the end.

1967 JANE: A SOCIAL INCIDENT. BY MARIE CORELLI. London: Hutchinson, 1897 BMC NUC. Philadelphia: J. B. Lippincott, 1897 NUC.

Jane Belmont inherits a fortune at 57 and "comes out" under the guidance of a social promoter, Mrs. Maddenham. But when she discovers what London society is like, she causes an "incident." She throws out royalty from her home and returns to her house in the country.

1968 THE MURDER OF DELICIA. BY MARIE CORELLI. London: Skeffington, 1896 BMC NUC. Philadelphia: J. B. Lippincott, 1896 NUC.

"The author claims that there are a large proportion of

men who live by their wives' earnings and yet deride women in public and consider them 'unsexed' when their merits are publicly acknowledged." Delicia, a famous and very financially successful novelist (she gets 8,000 pounds advance for a novel), freely placed her income at her husband's disposal, adoring him completely. When she learns of his infidelity with others, the disappointment kills her.

1969   THE SORROWS OF SATAN; OR, THE STRANGE EXPERIENCE OF ONE GEOFFREY TEMPEST, MILLIONAIRE. BY MARIE CORELLI. London: Methuen, 1895 BMC NUC. Philadelphia: J. B. Lippincott, 1896 NUC.

Mavis Clare, the heroine, writes successful books. It is the unsuccessful literary hack who forms a bond like that of Faust's to Prince Lucio Romanas. And Lady Sybil falls under his spell, poisons herself after writing a 75-page farewell, warning others of the devil and decrying contemporary social evils.

1970   THE SOUL OF LILITH. BY MARIE CORELLI. London: R. Bentley, 1892 BMC NUC. New York: J. W. Lovell, [c1892] NUC.

Irene Vassilius was a genius, an author whose books were unfairly reviewed by male critics because she was a woman. "And at last she condescended to marry a very handsome clever good rich man, who understood, and frequently told her, how very much he was her inferior, morally and intellectually. She being a woman of genius and he only a duke."

1971   THE YOUNG DIANA; AN EXPERIMENT OF THE FUTURE. BY MARIE CORELLI. New York: G.H. Doran, [c1918] NUC. London: Hutchinson, 1918 BMC NUC.

Diana May, at 40, unmarried, lives with her parents and takes care of them. Although she is intelligent, generous, a fine musician, they are conscious that all their friends regard her as an "old maid" and they are not grateful for her care. An independent friend urges her to move in with her in London and look for work, which she finally does. Then, through being a subject of an experiment, she becomes endowed with youth, beauty, and an ethereal quality which raises her above such trifles as human vengeance or love. There is a great deal about the despicable qualities of men.

MACKENZIE, HANNAH B.

1972 CROWNED VICTOR: A STORY OF STRIFE. Edinburgh and London: Oliphant and Anderson, 1894 BMC.

Daughter of an English professor is a trained nurse in Edinburgh. Her love story.

MACKENZIE, JEAN KENYON. 1874-1936. United States.

1973 BLACK SHEEP: ADVENTURES IN WEST AFRICA. Boston: Houghton Mifflin, 1916 NUC.

Young missionary in African jungle writes letters to her father in which she describes the people—with full appreciation for personalities.

MACKERLIE, H. G.*

1974 THE RADICAL'S WIFE. London: J. Macqueen, 1896 BMC.

Katherine is a new woman who writes stories, articles, speeches, labors for the poor. She is a politician on whom powerful men depend. But righting the wrongs of women is the most engrossing part of her work. One reviewer says she is "the ideal figure of a woman's dream." Her husband is brutal to her.

MACKIE, PAULINE BRADFORD. See CAVENDISH, PAULINE BRADFORD (MACKIE) HOPKINS.

MACKINNEY, ALICE JEAN CHANDLER (WEBSTER). 1876-1916. United States.

1975 DEAR ENEMY. BY JEAN WEBSTER. New York: Century, 1915 BMC NUC. London: Hodder & Stoughton, [1915] BMC.

Sallie McBride, used to wealth and luxury, takes charge of

an orphanage of 113 orphans. She breaks all the traditional rules about orphanages beginning with treating her charges as individuals. In introducing modern reforms she does 101 radical and astounding things.

MACKIRDY, OLIVE CHRISTIAN (MALVERY). D. 1914.

1976   THE SPECULATOR. London: T. W. Laurie, [1908] BMC. A young wife goes on the stock exchange as Mr. Otto Martini to make money for herself and her children while her husband is in Arabia. Light and amusing.

MACKOWAN, EVAH MAY (CARTWRIGHT). B. 1885. Canada.

1977   JANET OF KOOTENAY; LIFE, LOVE & LAUGHTER IN AN ARCADY OF THE WEST. New York: G. H. Doran, [c1919] NUC. Toronto: McClelland & Stewart, [c1919] NUC.

Janet Kirk is a teacher and reporter, and she runs an 80 acre fruit farm in western United States. There's some gossip about her and the neighbor farmer who helps her out—they marry.

MACLAGAN, BRIDGET. See TURNER, MARY BORDEN.

MACLANE, MARY. 1881-1929. United States.

1978   I, MARY MACLANE; A DIARY OF HUMAN DAYS. New York: F. A. Stokes, [c1917] BMC NUC.

"Morbid, analytical to the swirling point, weird, stubborn, selfish, conceited, what a magnificent Russian revolutionist she might have been!"

1979   MY FRIEND ANNABEL LEE. Chicago: H. S. Stone, 1903 NUC.

Title refers to a statue to whom the author pours out her views on all subjects.

1980   THE STORY OF MARY MACLANE. BY HERSELF. Chicago: H. S. Stone, 1902 BMC NUC. London: G. Richards, 1902 BMC.

A young woman in Butte, Montana, thoroughly bored and unhappy. She is alienated from her family and neighbors, admires Nietzsche, does not believe in God or marriage, has a passion for a woman and the devil. One reviewer says of this book, which all reviewers found repellent, "Heavy responsibility rests on the man who allowed a poor girl to parade a girl's green sickness and shout in the streets the symptoms which should have been whispered in the consulting room." Journal form.

MACLAREN, EMILY.

1981   OUT OF THE DUST OF BATTLE. London: Murray & Evenden, [1920] BMC.

Canadian girl nurses hero at the front. Love is dominant interest.

MACLAURIN, KATE L. United States.

1982   THE LEAST RESISTANCE. New York: G. H. Doran, [c1916] NUC.

Evelyn, married to a drunken actor, leaves him and takes up acting herself. She has no love for it but must support herself. She drifts away, following the line of least resistance, has one success, dies.

MACLAWS, EMILY LAFAYETTE. 1821-1897. United States.

1983   WHEN THE LAND WAS YOUNG. BEING THE TRUE ROMANCE OF MISTRESS ANTOINETTE HUGUENIN AND CAPTAIN JACK MIDDLETON IN THE DAYS OF THE BUCCANEERS. BY LAFAYETTE MCLAWS. London: A. Constable, [1901] BMC. Boston: Lothrop, [c1901] NUC.

Brave, dauntless, incredible Antoinette. She is captured by Spaniards, taken to Florence, dons a man's court suit (awarded for her prowess in fencing), escapes, rules a ship, meets, attacks and disarms a pirate—all the while masquerading as a man.

MACLAWS, LAFAYETTE. See MACLAWS, EMILY LAFAYETTE.

MACLEAN, CLARA VICTORIA (DARGAN). United States.

1984 LIGHT O' LOVE. New York: Worthington, 1891 NUC.
Christine Trescott is rebellious because of several misfortunes. First she becomes a governess with a rich family whose total lack of sympathy for her changes her from a loving to an embittered person. Then she marries a man who is killed on the way home from the wedding after which she virtually becomes a prisoner in his family's house and suffers from the coldness of her sister-in-law, a religious fanatic. Through her physician the light of love finally breaks into her "rebellious soul."

MACLEOD, A. IAN. See RANDALL, MRS. HENRY W.

MACLEOD, CLARA NEVADA. United States.

1985 THEN, AND NOT 'TIL THEN: A NOVEL. New York: Authors' Pub. Association, [c1897] NUC.
"The foundation of a true society will be laid only when the husbands and fathers are as pure as they wish their daughters to be: then and not until then." Sensational.

MACLEOD, IRENE RUTHERFORD. See DE SELINCOURT, IRENE RUTHERFORD (MACLEOD).

MACMAHON, ELLA J. United Kingdom.

1986 THE DIVINE FOLLY. London: Chapman and Hall, 1913 BMC.
Blanche Adeane cannot forgive her erring husband; she has only cold contempt for him. He disregards her

feelings. Things get worse between them when she learns her husband's most recent affection is for her intimate friend Elma Fancourt.

1987 FANCY O'BRIEN. London: Chapman and Hall, 1909 BMC.
Poor Irish woman Bridget wronged by rogue of title, treated despicably. Sympathetic treatment of her.

1988 A MODERN MAN. New York & London: Macmillan, 1895 NUC. London: J. M. Dent, 1895 BMC.
Muriel is loved by a young successful lawyer who has an affair with a young Welsh woman, Miss Sibyl. When the two women discover that Merton Byng is about to give up Muriel to "do the right thing" and marry Miss Sybil, Muriel announces that she knows about the affair and does not fuss about such things "like the women in books nowadays" and Miss Sibyl declines the offer because she is already engaged to someone else.

1989 A NEW NOTE. London: Hutchinson, 1894 BMC. New York: R. F. Fenno, [c1895] NUC. (Published anonymously in England.)
Victoria Leathley is energetic, strong in purpose, is of a wealthy family, but she wants her own career. Her violin recital is not a great success, but she then goes on to write an opera, Sappho, which takes London by storm. Although there are two men in whom she is interested, she is uncommitted at the close of the book.

1990 A PITILESS PASSION. New York and London: Macmillan, 1895 NUC. (Also published as A Pitiful Passion. London: Hutchinson, [1896] BMC.)
Georgie Fitzroy is an alcoholic whose husband becomes interested in another woman. Reviewers are divided in seeing her husband as either "a cad, chiefly concerned with scandal" or as acting "heroically, endeavoring to save his worthless and wretched wife from a fire."

1991 THE TOUCHSTONE OF LIFE. London: Hutchinson, 1897 BMC. New York: F. A. Stokes, [c1897] NUC.
One dark night, Susan Romer rides sixteen miles on her

bicycle to warn her fiance's half brother that there is a conspiracy to kill him. She thereby saves his life. The incident stands out as an "unconscious tribute to the widespread popularity of the wheel." The novel concerns the governor and prime minister of the colony of New Britain, both of whom love Susan.

MACMANUS, CHARLOTTE ELIZABETH. United Kingdom.

1992   THE RED STAR. BY L. MACMANUS. London: T. F. Unwin, 1894 BMC. New York: G. P. Putnam's, 1895 NUC.
Captain Pahlen of the Imperial Russian Guard marries the Polish Countess Halka on the Tsar's orders. He informs her immediately after the ceremony that he has a first wife. She disguises herself as a male, joins the French army, and becomes a lieutenant on the general's staff. Described as the everlasting duel of sex against the grim background of war in all its horror.

MACMANUS, L. See MACMANUS, CHARLOTTE ELIZABETH.

MACNAB, FRANCES. See FRASER, AGNES.

MACNAMARA, RACHEL SWETE. United Kingdom.

1993   DRIFTING WATERS. London: Chapman & Hall, 1915 BMC NUC. New York & London: G.P. Putnam's Sons, 1915 NUC.
Anne Tudor rebels against her mother's tyrannous and demanding love. Her mother now divorced was miserably married to a man who was unfaithful and who abandoned her. As a consequence, she makes such great demands on her daughter that Anne marries secretly, staying with her mother until her mother dies. Her own marriage, meanwhile, suffers but there is reconciliation in the end.

1994   LARK'S GATE; A NOVEL. London: Hurst & Blackett, 1918 BMC.
Rosny experiences passion, separation, motherhood,

loveless marriage, and divorce. At seventeen, romantic, ignorant of life and with little knowledge of parental love, she is sent to a farm. Marriage to the farmer's son is prevented by his father; they are separated, and her mother takes the baby, telling her it is dead.

1995 A MARRIAGE HAS BEEN ARRANGED. London: E. Arnold, 1917 BMC NUC.

Reviewers react to red-haired, golden-eyed, sharp-tongued Toye Tempest with the strongest language. She is a hard, pleasure-loving, selfish, unmaternal wife, moved to passion but to nothing else, she is simply repellent, unrelievedly detestable and odious, a woman of heartless egoism and selfish soullessness. One reviewer claims we are not meant (by the author) to sympathize with the character. Another claims we have no sympathy for her victims and that no man was capable or strong enough to be her equal mate.

1996 THE SIBYL OF VENICE. Edinburgh: W. Blackwood, 1908 BMC.

La Strega, a Venetian wisewoman—her spells and charms.

1997 THE TORCH OF LIFE. New York & London: G.P. Putnam's Sons, 1914 NUC.

Titian Fleury has been the wife of a man hopelessly paralyzed for ten years; he has denied her all contact with others. She "finds a good man's love after a too avid enjoyment of some of the pleasures she has been denied."

MACNAUGHTAN, S. See MACNAUGHTAN, SARAH BROOM.

MACNAUGHTAN, SARAH BROOM. 1864-1916. United Kingdom.

1998 THE EXPENSIVE MISS DU CANE. BY S. MACNAUGHTAN. New York: P.R. Reynolds, 1906 NUC. London: W. Heinemann, 1907 BMC NUC.

Studies several women characters: Florence Ellis, a

husband-hunter; Charlotte Balfour, a self confident, keen, intelligent, energetic and likeable modern woman; and Hetty Du Cane, sweet, reserved. Hetty's fiance gives her up when he learns she is not wealthy. The best women in the novel remain single.

1999   THE GIFT; A NOVEL. BY S. MACNAUGHTAN. London: Hodder & Stoughton, 1904 BMC NUC.

"One of the ever-growing class of women who seem to be avoiding marriage" is an independent social worker. Her love for a celibate clergyman "leads to a painful, humiliating scene and tragedy."

2000   SNOW UPON THE DESERT. BY S. MACNAUGHTAN. London: Hodder and Stoughton, [c1913] BMC NUC.

Focuses upon two women: the financial difficulties of a single woman and the love problems of a married one. Mrs. Antrobus is the most beautiful Englishwoman in India. She is married to a man who does what he likes and is willing that she does the same. She fascinates men, one of whom kills himself. It is through men's eyes that she is portrayed. The other young woman, Hecules, is extremely unconventional. Raised by her father, she has ideals very different from those upheld in the girls' school she attends. Later these ideals are warped by social influences under which she is forced to live.

2001   SOME ELDERLY PEOPLE AND THEIR YOUNG FRIENDS. BY S. MACNAUGHTAN. London: Smith, Elder, 1915 NUC BMC. New York: E.P. Dutton, [19—?] NUC.

Character studies, principally through dialogue, of four older people and three young women. Julia is 40, lives in a comfortable home with servants, gives big dinner parties, drinks. She gives financial assistance to her married sister. Her sister and her friends are older than 40. The young women are Jim and Jack, intelligent and independent journalist and drama critic, and Clemmie who joins the suffragettes.

2002 THREE MISS GRAEMES. BY S. MACNAUGHTAN. London: J. Murray, 1908 BMC NUC. New York: E.P. Dutton, 1908 NUC.

Three sisters, raised on a lonely Scottish island by their father, educated in an unusual way. When he dies, they seek employment in London. Their adventures and love stories.

MACNEILL, NEVADA. United States.

2003 THE RED ROSE OF SAVANNAH: A NOVEL. BY A. S. M. New York: G. W. Dillingham, [c1894] NUC.

Elsie, a 17 year old orphan, finds employment in Washington. Her supervisor marries her in a false ceremony and leaves her. "The way his sins are told makes the book almost unsuitable for circulation."

MACQUOID, KATHARINE SARAH (GADSDEN). 1824-1917. United Kingdom.

2004 THE STORY OF LOIS. London: J. Long, 1898 BMC NUC.

Lois is determined to become an actress and persists despite her father's fears, initial failure, a devastating affair with a scoundrel. Nothing sways her from her commitment to the art she loves beyond all other loves.

MACVANE, EDITH. B. 1880. United States.

2005 TARANTELLA. Boston: Houghton Mifflin, [1911] NUC. London: Hurst & Blackett, 1912 BMC.

Theme: a woman's right to happiness. Cynthia Godfrey is the victim of an unfortunate marriage to a loathsome man. Religion keeps her bound to him. She goes to Rome to seek an annulment. In the end, however, she is free.

MADESANI, GRAZIA COSIMA (DELEDDA). 1871-1936. Italy.

2006 AFTER THE DIVORCE, A ROMANCE. BY GRAZIA DELEDDA. New York: H. Holt, 1905 NUC BMC.

Woman takes a second husband while her first is serving a prison sentence of 27 years. He refuses to divorce her, but cannot prevent the new marriage. The woman soon tires of her new husband, and when he is killed, she returns to her first husband now proven innocent and released. Anti-divorce?

2007 ASHES (CENERE), A SARDINIAN STORY. BY GRAZIA DELEDDA. London and New York: J. Lane, 1908 NUC BMC.

Male hero is the illegitimate son of a young woman who has been betrayed and banished from her father's house. She drifts, finally abandons her child. Her son grows up and marries, hoping she is dead. Then he meets her, provides her with lodging, loses the woman he loves; he then hears his mother is ill, but she has in fact killed herself. He is left with a sense of overwhelming self-reproach.

2008 NOSTALGIA. BY GRAZIA DELEDDA. London: Chapman and Hall, 1905 BMC. (Tr. by Helen Hester Colville.)

Young woman, unhappy living with husband and his family and unhappy still when they move to a small apartment, returns to her family home in the country, prepared to remain until husband can afford better. But she finds she loves him too much, returns to him and his new spacious apartment, has a child and then learns of the sordid arrangement her husband made with a rich woman to obtain the apartment.

MAGEE, VIOLET.

2009 SCHOLAR'S MATE: A STORY. London: Downey, 1895 BMC.

"An Oxford beauty flirts away her time with successive generations of undergraduates until finally at the age of 34 she consents to marry a middle-aged professor." Mollie

Dorothea then rediscovers an old admirer and forms a close relationship but one "devoid of any actual breach of the commandments." Other reviews suggest instead that she commits adultery, that she "displays little restraint in her conduct," and that "with such a husband as she is fortunate enough to get, her treachery is slightly revolting."

MAGOUN, JEANNE BARTHOLOW. B. 1870. United States.

2010 THE LIGHT. New York: M. Kennerley, 1911 NUC.
Letters that trace a woman's conversion to the cause of suffrage and that respond to the anti-suffrage arguments.

2011 THE MISSION OF VICTORIA WILHELMINA. New York: B. W. Huebsch, 1912 BMC NUC. London: G. P. Putnam, 1912 BMC.
Written in diary form by a young woman who trusted a conventional villain and bears an illegitimate child. The child lives only one day, but after her death the mother, a New York working woman with an active spirit and eager mind, is able to face the world bravely and calmly.

MAGRUDER, JULIA. 1854-1907. United States.

2012 DEAD SELVES. Philadelphia: J. B. Lippincott, 1898 W. London: J. Bowden, 1898 BMC.
Opens on Rhoda Gwyn's second marriage. She was married in her youth to a semi-imbecile for his money. She is now a widow and has an imbecile child. Duncan Fraser, a brilliant scientist, has exhausted his fortune on his research, is on the verge of a great discovery. He has nothing but contempt for the widow who has so degraded herself, but he offers marriage as a business transaction; her money for position and protection. She accepts and they marry. Then a few years go by. She begins to take an interest in his work and the world. Reads Eliot. Husband buys her all of Eliot's works; she reads Jane Eyre. Makes friends with a Mrs. Fraser to whom she can really talk. She and husband very gradually overcome

their coldness toward each other. There's a setback when she decides to bring her child to their home. Title refers to past selves of a developing individual.

2013   THE PRINCESS SONIA. New York: Century, 1895 BMC 1896 NUC.

Young American woman studying art in Latin Quarter in Paris meets a Russian princess on whom the story focuses.

2014   A SUNNY SOUTHERNER. Boston: L. C. Page, 1901 NUC.

The young woman "tramps and rides." She considers herself progressive. The man she loves is a student—one of those "dull heroes" that are "best loved by modern women."

MAIRET, MADAME JEANNE. See BIGOT, MARIE (HEALY).

MALET, LUCAS. See HARRISON, MARY SAINT LEGER (KINGSLEY).

MALLET, MAUD. United Kingdom.

2015   THE FLY IN THE BOTTLE. London: Mills & Boon, [1920] BMC [19—] NUC.

Anna is mistress to the owner of petite maison not in a position to marry. She longs to escape. She becomes engaged to young man but doesn't tell him the truth. She is discovered and resigns herself to the bottle.

MANDER, JANE. 1877-1929. New Zealand.

2016   THE STORY OF A NEW ZEALAND RIVER. New York and London: J. Lane, 1920 BMC NUC.

A study of Alice and the conflict of her reserved, ultra-conventional and somewhat puritanical nature with life in an isolated lumber camp in New Zealand from the moment of her arrival until she is "able to look on without any attempt at interference while (her) 18-year old daughter goes to live with a married man."

MANIATES, BELLE KANARIS. D. 1925. United States.

2017 AMARILLY OF CLOTHES-LINE ALLEY. Boston: Little, Brown, 1915 BMC NUC. London: Hodder & Stoughton, 1917 BMC.

Amarilly Jenkins is the mainstay of the Jenkins family—a widow and eight children. She gets help for her family from a young woman doing social work in the slums and help for herself by way of a college education. After college she moves to the city and writes a successful play.

MANN, MARY E. (RACKHAM). 1848-1929. United Kingdom.

2018 ASTRAY IN ARCADY. London: Methuen, [1910] BMC NUC.

A famous author Charlotte Poole lives in an "incredibly dull village" and writes incredibly dull letters in spite of her incredible literary success.

2019 AVENGING CHILDREN. London: Methuen, [1909] BMC NUC.

A patient daughter who finally rebels against a tyrannous father. Grace Blore is dutiful to her father though she has independent views. She accepts her father's choice for her husband, though she loves another man. But faced with the prospect of a marriage with a man she does not love, she persuades the man she does love to run off with her, but they are caught. She is returned to her father, but finally bullied by this patriarch into rebellion.

2020 THE CEDAR STAR. New York: R. F. Fenno, [c1897] NUC. London: Hutchinson, 1898 BMC.

The first half of the novel focuses on Betty, one of four motherless children, growing up in a rectory. She is described as "selfish, passionate, domineering, a prey to sudden gusts of temper and of emotion, but withal generous, brave, and true as steel." In the second half, she is a promising young painter who has fallen in love with her cousin's husband. They are on the point of eloping when the three of them are overturned in a boat. The wife drowns. Betty, shocked, flees. A year later he seeks her out and they marry. On their wedding night, he confesses that he deliberately permitted his wife to drown, striking her off when she rose to the surface. Betty flees again and returns to her work. Eventually she forgives him, but he has died.

2021   THE MATING OF A DOVE. London: T. F. Unwin, 1901 BMC.

About Monica and her unsuccessful marriage to Reverend Bell. She would have given him a dozen times over to have her mother back.

2022   THE MEMORIES OF RONALD LOVE. London: Methuen, 1907 BMC.

An illegitimate child is accepted and loved by Eleanor, the father's wife who has forgiven her husband's relation to Nancy, the child's mother.

2023   MOONLIGHT. London: T. F. Unwin, 1898 BMC.

Heroine, reduced to poverty, works in a grocery and drapery shop, "the humours and squalors of which are described with considerable skill." She marries the wrong man; the ending is tragic. "Seems calculated to please women more than men."

2024   PERDITA: A NOVEL. London: R. Bentley, 1893 BMC.

Perdita Sant's husband disappears on their wedding day, and she has good reason to believe he is dead. To earn her living, she becomes a teacher in a women's school in suburban London where she becomes close friends with the headmistress—Pauline Ashford. When she is about to remarry, her first husband shows up, but she learns he is a bigamist married to Pauline. At the end, he is imprisoned for the murder of Pauline. Story focuses upon the two women and their close relationship.

2025   SUSANNAH. London: Henry, 1895 BMC. New York: Harper, 1896 NUC.

She's a new kind of heroine, shows individuality in speech and manner. She tends her drug ridden brother in the lodging house in Great Kirby Street, works in a variety of positions including maid-of-all-work and is engaged in end.

2026 THERE WAS A WIDOW. London: Methuen, [1911] BMC NUC.

Widowed Julia Delane with three children "too weak to fend for herself." Her difficulties in supporting herself, how a rich cousin tyrannized her, how a gruff doctor won her. Reviewers describe her as a "muddlehead," "stupid and as insensitive as a conscientious cow."One says the author has a "warm regard for her."

2027 THE VICTIM. London: Hodder & Stoughton, 1917 BMC.

Woman deserts her husband for another man. The title refers to the daughter born out of wedlock who is handed over to a foster mother. In her charge she becomes a drudge. The mother deserted in turn is taken back by husband. Years later, when her husband dies, she meets her lover; together they search for their child.

2028 WHEN A MAN MARRIES. New York: Hodder & Stoughton, [1916] BMC NUC.

The story of a man's mistaken marriage told by the woman whom it injures.

MANNING, FRANCES DUNCAN. B. 1877. United States.

2029 ROBERTA OF ROSEBERRY GARDENS. BY FRANCES DUNCAN. Garden City, New York: Doubleday, Page, 1916 NUC BMC. London: Constable, 1916 BMC.

Roberta, the secretary to an owner of a nursery, learns the horticultural trade. Love story as well.

MANTLE, BEATRICE. United States.

2030 GRET: THE STORY OF A PAGAN. New York: Century, 1907 BMC NUC.

Independent young woman who is more successful in business than in love. She knows the lumber business very well and uses her knowledge and practical experience to make a prosperous shingle business. At the same time she rebels against her father's efforts to tame her—and in defiance makes a hurried marriage to prove her independence. When the marriage fails, she simply forgets about the man and marries another man she really loves. End is tragic.

MARCH, ELLA.

2031 MY SUITORS. London: Digby, Long, [1891] BMC.
Romance of a governess who marries a baronet.

MARCHBANK, AGNES.

2032 RUTH FARMER: A STORY. New York: Cassell, [c1896] NUC. London: Jarrold, 1896 BMC.
Totaly misunderstood by her husband, Ruth leaves him and is believed to have drowned. She endures poverty, "strange experiences," and the near loss of her child. On the verge of marrying another woman, he becomes convinced she is still alive. They are eventually reunited.

MARCY, MARY EDNA (TOBIAS). B. 1877. United States.

2033 OUT OF THE DUMP. Chicago: Charles H. Kerr, 1909 NUC.
First person narrative of the hard life in the stockyards region of Chicago. It tells of the death of a father due to a rotten chute and the experience of the family with charities. The author is convinced all this wretchedness is due to capitalism.

MARQUIS, REINA (MELCHER). B. 1881. United States.

2034 THE TORCH BEARER. New York and London: D. Appleton, 1914 NUC.
Sheila, "a girl of rare literary gift and passionate idealism realizes too late that her husband is intellectually her inferior." She is writing secretly against her husband's wishes (he refuses to recognize a woman's right to self-expression) when a nurse takes her son out and he gets a contagious disease. She, feeling guilty, vows never to write again if he lives. Many years later, she and her husband reflect that her talent has not been lost because her son has it; she is a torch-bearer.

MARR, KATE THYSON. D. 1907. United States.

2035 BOUND BY THE LAW. New York: G. W. Dillingham, 1898 NUC.

Portrayal of a marriage in which the wife bears the ill treatment of her husband rather than bring disgrace upon her children with a divorce. But after he has squandered all her money, he proposes a legal separation, and then she is forced to struggle to feed and clothe her children.

2036 CONFESSIONS OF A GRASS WIDOW, A NOVEL. New York and London: F. T. Neely, [c1900] NUC.

Letters describing the adventures of a young divorcee and the unhappy marriage of her friend, a restless and "startlingly audacious young woman."

MARRYAT, FLORENCE. See LEAN, FLORENCE (MARRYAT) CHURCH.

MARSDEW, THALIA.

2037 IDONEA. London: Eden, Remington, 1891 BMC.

Reviewer finds it "incredible" that Idonea, critical of her father's treatment of her mother and his relation with another woman, should live with a married man on weekends. Yet the same reviewer considers the tragic deaths of Idonea and her infant as "quite natural events." Story of Idonea's moral and physical struggles.

MARSH, FRANCES.

2038 THE IRON GAME. A STORY OF THE FRANCO-PRUSSIAN WAR. London: A. C. Fifield, 1909 BMC.

Heroine is a surgical nurse in this anti-war story.

MARSHALL, EMMA (MARTIN). 1830-1899. United Kingdom.

2039 BY THE NORTH SEA; OR, THE PROTECTOR'S GRANDDAUGHTER. London: Jarrold, 1896 BMC. New York: Whittaker, 1896 NUC.

The fictionalized biography of Mrs. Bridget Bendyst, the

granddaughter of Oliver Cromwell, in the form of a diary by Albinia Ellis, one of the household. Mrs. Bendyst "made herself conspicuous by her manual labor."

2040 CASTLE MEADOW; A STORY OF NORWICH A HUNDRED YEARS AGO. London: Seeley, 1897 BMC NUC. New York: Macmillan, 1897 NUC.

Focus of the story is Hyacinth—the 19th century type of woman, "but not a young woman who screamed at the sight of a spider or caterpillar, nor went into hysterics if she thought she did not receive sufficient admiration." Her godmother, "a new woman of most advanced order, single handed chases away four ruffians who have been hired to steal Hyacinth...and frightens (Hyacinth's) imprudently ardent old lover into an attack of paralysis."

2041 AN ESCAPE FROM THE TOWER: A STORY OF THE JACOBITE RISING OF 1715. London: Seeley, 1896 BMC NUC. New York: Macmillan, 1896 NUC.

Lady Nithsdale rescues her husband from the tower. "Stirring heroism"; he by contrast seems "almost weak."

2042 KENSINGTON PALACE IN THE DAYS OF QUEEN MARY II. New York: Macmillan, 1894 NUC. London: Seeley, 1895 BMC NUC.

Character study of Queen Mary the Second.

2043 LADY ROSALIND, OR FAMILY FEUDS. London: J. Nisbet, 1897 BMC.

Proud young English woman learns at her father's death that his money went to blackmail—he had been secretly married—and that her fiance has left her. She is given custody of two children of her father's secret marriage. Though "it was not her destiny to marry, she finds a measure of happiness in dignified spinsterdom."

2044 THE LADY'S MANOR, OR BETWEEN BROOK AND RIVER. A TALE. London: J. Nisbet, 1896 BMC. New York: E. P. Dutton, [n.d.] NUC.

Myrtle Cameron seeks an education superior to that offered to women. She is coached for Oxford by Miss Brown, who prizes womanly graces.

2045 THE TWO HENRIETTAS. London: Partridge, [1896] BMC.

Two young women are contrasted. One goes to London to support herself and her sister by writing. She is successful. The other writes because she is restless and ambitious, publishes a problem novel at her own expense, but doesn't succeed. There are love affairs for both.

MARSHALL, FRANCES (BRIDGES). United Kingdom.

2046 BONNIE MAGGIE LAUDER. BY ALAN ST. AUBYN. London: F. V. White, 1899 BMC.

Mother and daughter love the same man. He marries the daughter. He had been engaged to the mother.

2047 FORTUNE'S GATE. BY ALAN ST. AUBYN. London: Chatto and Windus, 1898 BMC.

College life at Newnham and Cambridge. Phillipa has won two scholarships to Newnham, is a science student. "Picture given of the miserable life of poor women students is ridiculously overdrawn."

2048 THE HARP OF LIFE. BY ALAN ST. AUBYN. London: F. V. White, 1908 BMC.

Cambridge University life—two women students.

2049 THE JUNIOR DEAN: A NOVEL. BY ALAN ST. AUBYN. London: Chatto and Windus, 1891 BMC NUC.

Life at Cambridge. The subject of women's higher education is treated with a judicious lightness of touch and playful irony. Many mixups involving Molly Grey, a student at Newnham, the junior dean she's engaged to, her brother, and Rosey, a "wicked" actress "in a shady house" where gambling takes place.

2050 THE MASTER OF ST. BENEDICT'S. BY ALAN ST. AUBYN. London: Chatto and Windus, 1893 BMC. Chicago and New York: Rand, McNally, 1893 NUC.

Concerns university life at Cambridge—the best parts are the descriptions of women's lives at Newnham. Pamela Gwatkin, Capability Stubbs and Lucy Rae are "Newnham girls," but the focus is on Lucy. She is grandniece of the old master who dies leaving his wife Rachel to make a happy marriage after 40 years of waiting for her true love. Lucy is attracted to the master of the title, Wyatt Edgall, but he commits suicide while suffering the d.t.'s. Lucy is studying to be a teacher, and her ambition is to try for a Tripos. Story traces her life as a university student.

2051 MODEST LITTLE SARA. BY ALAN ST. AUBYN. London: Chatto and Windus, 1892 BMC. Chicago and New York: Rand, McNally, 1892 NUC.

Young woman resident of Cambridge, music teacher, fascinates undergraduates and manages to levy a considerable amount of blackmail from them.

2052 THE OLD MAID'S SWEETHEART: A PROSE IDYL. BY ALAN ST. AUBYN. London: Chatto and Windus, 1892 BMC. London: 1892 NUC. (Also published as For the Old Sake's Sake. By Alan St. Aubyn. Chicago and New York: Rand, McNally, 1891 NUC.)

Letitia, a 50 year old spinster, gives up the man she is to marry because he falls for her young and beautiful sister. One reviewer says the author has made her "thoroughly lovable and sympathetic," has portrayed "the tragedy of her life while allowing her to be in some measure ridiculous."

2053 A PROCTOR'S WOOING. BY ALAN ST. AUBYN. London: F. V. White, 1897 BMC NUC.

Concerns young women at Cambridge—"Newnham girls."

2054 TO HIS OWN MASTER. A NOVEL. BY ALAN ST. AUBYN. London: Chatto and Windus, 1893 BMC NUC. New York: Cleveland, 1893 NUC.

Two interesting women: one is the villain with a "ferocious and sensual nature...whom we are asked to think particularly fascinating." The other is Mary Grove, who has been at Girton and who "gives up a certain first to tend a drunken father and forlorn mother." She beomes a nursery governess. She gives up Stephen Dashwood, the curate in the East End; "she accepts the freedom which he offers...and consoles herself quickly."

MARSHALL, MARGUERITE MOOERS. 1887-1964. United States.

2055 THE DRIFT. New York and London: D. Appleton, 1911 BMC NUC.

Letters of a young writer to a married man she loves. She goes to New York to pursue her writing career expecting that he will obtain a divorce, but he changes his mind when he learns his wife is pregnant. The young writer kills herself.

MARSLAND, CORA. B. 1859. United States.

2056 THE ANGEL OF THE GILA: A TALE OF ARIZONA. Boston: R. G. Badger, [c1911] NUC.

Esther, a teacher in Arizona, converts a mining town to a respectable community.

MARTENS, MARY E.

2057 A DAUGHTER OF SIN. A SIMPLE STORY. London: E. Stock, 1915 BMC.

Dedicated to those women of Nepal "who have suffered under an injust, one-sided and most iniquitous law." "Question of the relation between white women and black men."

2058 A WOMAN OF SMALL ACCOUNT. A SOUTH AFRICAN SOCIAL PICTURE. London: W. Scott, 1911 BMC.

Hester is a powerfully drawn character, a woman of strong enough views on the woman question to break up her home. Her "calm and flawless superiority" is very "fatiguing" to one critic. Hester becomes a famous author. Much discussion of women's rights.

MARTIN, DOROTHY.

2059 FATHER FOX: A STORY OF THE PRESENT DAY. London: E. Stock, 1899 BMC.

He seeks to bring money to Anglican Church by trapping

young women in a nunnery. If they don't bring money, they are not nicely treated. Anti-Romanism.

MARTIN, EMILY.

2060 EVEN MINE OWN FAMILIAR FRIEND. London: S. Low, 1892 BMC.

Una, a young woman of strong-minded determination and character, is misled into marriage to a man she doesn't love. She divorces him and marries another.

MARTIN, GEORGE (MADDEN). 1866-1946. United States.

2061 SELINA: HER HOPEFUL EFFORTS AND HER LIVELIER FAILURES. New York: D. Appleton, 1914 BMC NUC.

Selina, a young woman of the 1880's, is the daughter of a hard-working man who, despite his efforts, is never able to pay all the bills. After graduation she teaches, but her wages do not substantially help. Some of her family see a solution in a marriage to someone with money, but this she refuses to do. She is "not at all aware that she is of those who are blazing the way for a new order of things."

MARTIN, H. R. See MARTIN, HELEN (REIMENSNYDER).

MARTIN, HELEN (REIMENSNYDER). 1868-1939. United States.

2062 BARNABETTA. New York: Century, 1914 BMC NUC.

Barnabetta has been a household drudge for five years for her father and brothers, when her father marries a woman with an income of her own which he expects to take charge of. This woman has very different ideas and carries them out. She relieves Barnabetta of her work and sends her to school and to college. Here begins a new life for Barnabetta.

2063 THE CROSSWAYS. New York: Century, 1910 BMC NUC.

A high-strung cultured woman marries a Pennsylvania

Dutch doctor, knowing only his professional side. She is physically delicate, and in accordance with his male attitude towards marriage (he refuses to pay for women's work), he thinks he is acting for her own good when he heaps all the burdens of housework upon her. In spite of her physical weakness she finally bends him to her will.

2064   THE ELUSIVE HILDEGARDE: A NOVEL. BY H. R. MARTIN. New York: R. F. Fenno, 1900 NUC.

Hildegarde, eccentric and unconventional, attempts to educate herself to teach.

2065   FANATIC OR CHRISTIAN? A STORY OF THE PENNSYLVANIA DUTCH. Garden City, N.Y.: Doubleday, Page, 1918 NUC. Toronto: T. Langton, [1918?] NUC.

Family has amassed fortune through factory. Stella is traditional; Gertie has been to college and wants to apply modern welfare methods to factory.

2066   THE FIGHTING DOCTOR. New York: Century, 1912 BMC NUC.

Heroine is a schoolteacher.

2067   HER HUSBAND'S PURSE. Garden City, N.Y.: Doubleday, Page, 1916 NUC. London: C. Brown, 1916 BMC.

Margaret Berkeley moves from a home in the South to a Pennsylvania Dutch household when she marries. Her husband is a pennypincher who treats her like a breeder, allots her $10 a month, and expects her to account for every penny. His two sisters share his views.

2068   HIS COURTSHIP. New York and London: McClure, Phillips, 1907 NUC BMC.

Eunice has worked as a drudge from the time she was a child, but is discovered to have a very keen mind and to be quite well self-educated. A young college professor visiting her Pennsylvana Dutch community makes the discovery. A further discovery is that she is heir to a fortune.

2069 MAGGIE OF VIRGINSBURG; A STORY OF THE PENNSYLVANIA DUTCH. New York: Century, 1918 BMC NUC.

Maggie and Henry rebel against the sordidness and meanness of their surroundings and leave Virginsburg. She becomes a secretary to a bishop and then a teacher in a church school. Both are radicals, and the story is a criticism of the Christian church.

2070 MARTHA OF THE MENNONITE COUNTRY. Garden City, N.Y.: Doubleday Page, 1915 NUC. London: C. Brown, 1915 BMC.

She does drudge work but, as the famous novelist who visits her community discovers, she is a keen, intelligent young woman. Another woman character, also a newcomer to the community, is an heir who is determined to have a career in teaching. She becomes the assistant principal in the high school.

2071 THE REVOLT OF ANNE ROYLE. New York: Century, 1908 BMC NUC.

Gifted Anne, raised by domineering aunt and father who hates the sight of her, good scholar at college, accepts an unworthy suitor out of sheer loneliness, discovers her true feelings; her revolt follows.

2072 TILLIE A MENNONITE MAID: A STORY OF THE PENNSYLVANIA DUTCH. New York: Century, 1904 NUC. London: Hodder & Stoughton, 1905 BMC.

Tillie is the daughter of an ignorant farmer, whom she defies, and makes a strong, educated woman of herself. She sees that women are treated as beasts of burden, their lives hideously narrow, and she opposes the injustice. "Love for her teacher, Miss Margaret...grew into a passion."

2073 WARREN HYDE. BY THE AUTHOR OF "UNCHAPERONED" [ANONYMOUS]. New York: R. F. Fenno, [c1897] NUC.

He is divorced from a woman he loved and free to marry Nelda Chase, but she is against the marriage because of a "radical flaw in the first contract, the pair being, without knowing it, brother and sister."

MARTIN, MARY EMMA. United Kingdom.

2074 FORTUNE AT THE HELM. London: Hurst and Blackett, 1899 BMC.

Welsh girl driven from home because of her evil drunken father. Gaynor Williams is friendless in London—her struggles, adventures and perils. Meets emancipated young female artist. Wins a gallant lover.

2075 HER DEBUT. BY MRS. HERBERT MARTIN. London: Hurst and Blackett, 1895 BMC NUC.

Ermengarde Laniska is the daughter of a Polish count and countess. Her mother, an adventuress, marries an English landlord, has a child, and then dies of shock when her husband the count turns up. Ermengarde is a beautiful silent young woman, careless of her appearance. Early in life she is resolved to be a great musician, runs away from home and for a time is distracted by love until she learns the man "could never have fulfilled the ideal of her life." She returns to her training and makes her debut. Set in part in a Bloomsbury boarding house.

2076 A LOW-BORN LASS: A NOVEL. London: Hurst and Blackett, 1898 BMC.

The life and character of Sukey, a factory worker.

MARTIN, MRS. HERBERT. See MARTIN, MARY EMMA.

MARX, MAGDELEINE. See PAZ, MAGDELEINE (LEGENDRE).

MASON, CAROLINE (ATWATER). 1853-1939. United States.

2077 A LILY OF FRANCE. Philadelphia: Griffith & Rowland, 1901 NUC.

An historical novel set in Netherlands in late 16th and early 17th centuries in which "the heroine is more emancipated than the newest woman of today."

2078 THE WHITE SHIELD. Philadelphia: Griffith & Rowland Press, 1904 NUC.

A Christian who undergoes suffering and tortures for her

faith, slaps a priest who touches her, is thrown to the tigers, survives.

2079 A WOMAN OF YESTERDAY. New York: Doubleday, Page, 1900 NUC. London: Hodder & Stoughton, 1901 BMC.

Anna Mallison is an "austere, ardent" missionary in a utopian settlement. The story is about a gradual change in her, from a position of strict orthodoxy to an acceptance of her love of literature and art as not sinful.

MASON, EDITH HUNTINGTON. United States.

2080 THE GREAT PLAN. Chicago: A.C. McClurg, 1913 BMC NUC. London: C.F. Cazenove, 1913 BMC.

"An American girl's deeply laid plot for the political enfranchisement of her downtrodden German sisters who have no vote or other women's rights." She makes her headquarters in a castle on the Rhine and works out her plan with another young woman.

MASON, GRACE (SARTWELL). B. 1877. United States.

2081 HIS WIFE'S JOB. New York and London: D. Appleton, [c1919] BMC NUC.

Anne Henderson with her friend Marian Beal opens a shop on Fifth Avenue while her husband is in the service. She had been a traditional feminine type and dependent wife—a bore even to her husband who is very happy with the change he finds in her on his return.

MASSON, ROSALINE ORME. United Kingdom.

2082 LESLIE FARQUHAR. London: J. Murray, 1902 BMC.

Leslie, brought up by her father, is always outdoors, acts like a boy, never thinks of marriage. "One can hardly believe that there is such a thing as a grown-up girl who has never thought of marriage, and if there is such a thing, one cannot believe she would be attractive."

MASTERS, CAROLINE.

2083 THE DUCHESS LASS. London: F. Warne, 1896 BMC NUC.

Frances, penniless after the death of her parents, lives with her father's family, who have always looked down on her mother's family as North Country mill hands. Goaded by their treatment of her, she leaves and becomes a Lancashire weaver, as her mother was before her marriage.

MATHERS, HELEN. See REEVES, HELEN BUCKINGHAM (MATHERS).

MATHESON, C. M. See MATHESON, CHARLOTTE MARY.

MATHESON, CHARLOTTE MARY. B. 1892. United Kingdom.

2084 CHILDREN OF THE DESOLATE. BY C. M. MATHESON. London: T.F. Unwin, 1916 BMC.

Study of a woman artist and her unhappy marriage.

2085 THE GENERATION BETWEEN. BY C. M. MATHESON. London: T. F. Unwin, [1915] NUC BMC. New York: Brentano's, 1915 NUC.

Thomasine Latimer is the personification of all unrest and rebellion of women. She resents giving up her plans just so that her brothers can be educated for careers, decides to make gardening a profession, loves and enjoys freedom, marries in a hurry, and leaves her child and husband for Dyleshort, an all women's community founded by a woman with the purpose of developing a nation within the nation where women with no thought of rivalry with man should fulfill a magnificent ideal, which ideal would in time become the standard of the country. One reviewer says she discovers she's been wrong and returns to her family in the end.

MATHESON, E. REID. See MIDGLEY, MRS. LLEWELLYN.

MATHEWS, FRANCES AYMAR. 1865-1925. United States.

2086   BILLY DUANE; A NOVEL. New York: Dodd, Mead, 1905
       NUC.
       The marital problems of the Duanes begin when the wife
       goes abroad with her sick son where she meets and likes a
       pianist. She returns to find her husband mayor of New
       York City, immersed in politics. Her love for roulette and
       involvement in a gambling scandal are two of the
       problems that keep them apart.

2087   FANNY OF THE FORTY FROCKS. Philadelphia: J. C.
       Winston, [c1913] BMC NUC.
       Fanny leaves her up-state small town to find work in New
       York. She finds herself on board a ship bound for
       England, becomes deeply involved in international
       intrigue, adopts successful disguises, and saves an English
       duke from a French plot.

2088   IF DAVID KNEW; A NOVEL. London: T. F. Unwin, 1910
       BMC. New York: G. W. Dillingham, [c1910] NUC.
       Woman addicted to morphine keeps this a secret from
       husband.

2089   MY LADY PEGGY GOES TO TOWN. London: B. F.
       Stevens & Brown, [1901] BMC. Indianapolis: Bowen-
       Merrill, [c1901] NUC.
       Peggy is an unconventional young woman, "one of our
       problematic women." She masquerades as a man for a
       time. And when a man falls in love with her, she toys
       with him rather than return his love. "If she ends as a
       wife, she's more fortunate than she deserves to be."

2090   MY LADY PEGGY LEAVES TOWN. New York: Moffat,
       Yard, 1913 NUC.
       Successor to "My Lady Peggy Goes to Town." She tires of
       the social life of New York City, moves West for the
       simple life, poses as a widow of former admirer reported
       dead, is claimed and carried off by him when he shows up
       alive hunted as a spy, and helps him escape, taking on the
       disguise of a man. More amazing adventures of this
       modern daring heroine.

2091   PAMELA CONGREVE; A NOVEL. New York: Dodd, Mead, 1904 NUC.

Young woman, half dead, vows vengeance on fiance who allowed her father to hang for his murder. Starts as barmaid, becomes an actress and finally is able to bring him to a tragic death.

MATSON, SUSAN (GLASPELL) COOK. 1882-1948. United States.

2092   FIDELITY; A NOVEL. BY SUSAN GLASPELL. Boston: Small, Maynard, [c1915] BMC NUC.

Ruth Holland, daughter of an important family, falls in love with an older married man while she is still very young. For awhile she leads a double life: with her young friends at parties and with her lover in secret meetings. When she learns that he has bad lungs and must move to Arizona, she goes with him and lives with him for eleven years. Then her father's death brings the two back home where the townspeople are against them. When her lover is divorced, Ruth refuses to marry him because she believes marriage will ruin their relationship.

2093   THE GLORY OF THE CONQUERED; THE STORY OF A GREAT LOVE. BY SUSAN GLASPELL. New York: Stokes, [1909] NUC BMC.

Ernestine Stanley is a successful artist, famous in Paris. She marries a scientist from Chicago, and much pain comes into her life. Her child dies at birth, her husband goes blind, and she must give up her career to train herself to continue his research. She makes great discoveries in the laboratory—without his realization of the work she is doing. Then he dies, and she becomes irreligious and bitter, but the act of painting his portrait, her great and successful painting, helps clear her mind of bitterness.

2094   THE VISIONING; A NOVEL. BY SUSAN GLASPELL. New York: Stokes, [1911] NUC. London: J. Murray, 1912 BMC.

Katy Jones rescues a young woman from suicide and

treats this "fallen" woman like a sister. She gives Annie a home, clothes and money and becomes her friend. Annie eventually marries Katy's brother who breaks with family tradition by marrying someone not of army family. Katy also meets a socialist, a kind of hermit whose ideas affect her strongly. She learns he was once an army prisoner for striking an officer. Eventually Katy's ideas turn against the United States' army, against militarism and war.

MATTHEWS, MARY ANDERSON. United States.

2095 LOVE VS. LAW. New York: Broadway Publishing, [c1905] NUC.

The woman is a lawyer who establishes a successful practice. She pleads the case for equal suffrage before the U.S. Senate and secures a majority vote.

MAUD, CONSTANCE ELIZABETH. United Kingdom.

2096 A DAUGHTER OF FRANCE. London: Methuen, [1908] BMC NUC.

A young French wife with a dominating husband leaves, ultimate reconciliation.

2097 FELICITY IN FRANCE. London: W. Heinemann, 1906 BMC. New York: C. Scribner's Sons, 1906 NUC.

Boyish aunt of 60 travels with niece.

2098 NO SURRENDER. London: Duckworth, 1911 BMC. New York: J. Lane, 1912 NUC.

"Two typical heroines of the suffragette movement—one a mill hand and the other a woman of wealth and rank. The characters are a little too obviously 'made to order' but the story is nevertheless very interesting...." Author says her characters move among events that are historically true and that events touching prison and law court experiences related to women are factual. Relates to suffragist and suffragette movements.

MAUDE, F. W.*

2099   A MERCIFUL DIVORCE: A STORY OF SOCIETY, ITS
       SPORTS, FUNCTIONS AND FAILINGS. London:
       Trischler, 1891 BMC. New York: D. Appleton, 1891
       NUC.
       Society novel. Fanny Banning runs away to Egypt to
       break from her husband who loves another woman. They
       are divorced, and he remarries.

MAURICE, GABRIELLE FITZ.

2100   MRS. FITZ-MAURICE ON LEAVE. London: Greening,
       1908 BMC NUC.
       Wife spends her time in the arms of other men while her
       husband is away and is able to convince him of the justice
       of it.

MAXWELL, BEATRICE ETHEL HERON. D. 1927.

2101   THE ADVENTURES OF A LADY PEARL-BROKER.
       London: New Century Press, 1899 NUC.
       Exciting story of a woman who sells pearls on commission
       and who runs the risk of being robbed of 20,000 pounds
       of jewels at a time. Series of efforts to rob her. No
       character study.

MAXWELL, ELLEN BLACKMAR. See BARKER, ELLEN (BLACKMAR) MAXWELL.

MAXWELL, MARY ELIZABETH (BRADDON). 1837-1915. United Kingdom.

2102   ALL ALONG THE RIVER. BY M. E. BRADDON.
       London: Simpkin, Marshall, Hamilton, Kent, 1893 BMC
       NUC. New York: Cassell, 1893 NUC. (Published
       anonymously in England.)
       Isola Disney, a child-wife, is left alone immediately after
       her marriage to a major who goes to Burma. She meets a
       fascinating rake, goes to his yacht, but whether they sleep
       together or not is left unclear (perhaps, as one reviewer
       says, because the author wants us to like Isola). When her

husband returns, she lies to him. The truth comes out only at her death when her husband forgives her, the author forgives, we're meant to, but at least one reviewer refuses to.

2103   THE INFIDEL; A ROMANCE. BY M. E. BRADDON. New York: Harper, 1900 NUC. London: Simpkin, Marshall, [n.d.] NUC.
Antonia and her father William Thornton, during the reign of George II, pursued the profession of letters. They wrote plays and essays, made translations and furnished smart paragraphs for the society journals. Antonia raised like a boy, an atheist with high ideals. Also her love for a man she refuses to marry because of a former marriage.

2104   A LOST EDEN. London: Hutchinson, 1904 NUC BMC.
In the tradition of Jane Eyre, the heroine is a governess.

2105   MIRANDA. BY M. E. BRADDON. London: Hutchinson, 1913 NUC BMC.
She's up-to-date, well educated and precocious. She reads Newman, Darwin and Spencer. There's a great love and sympathy between her and her mother, who is opposite to the restless, energetic Miranda. Her life is traced from early childhood to a second marriage.

2106   THOU ART THE MAN. BY THE AUTHOR OF "LADY AUDLEY'S SECRET", ETC. [ANONYMOUS]. London: Simpkin and Marshall, [1894] BMC NUC.
Coralie Urquhart, lady's companion, solves mystery wherein epileptic lunatic is accused of murder. Sybil, who loves the suspected man, arranges his escape; she is assisted by the murderer.

MAY, DANAE.

2107   THE INCONSEQUENCES OF SARA. London: A. Treherne, 1902 NUC BMC.
Young woman, clever, undisciplined, reads Aurelius for pleasure, writes persiflage for money.

MAY, GEORGIANA MARION (CRAIK). 1831-1895. United Kingdom.

2108 PATIENCE HOLT. BY GEORGIANA M. CRAIK (MRS. A. W. MAY). London: R. Bentley, 1891 NUC BMC.
She is a lively, restless young woman who is misunderstood at every turn, first by family, particularly her very conservative Quaker father who is shocked by her manners. At school she shocks everyone by bathing near nude in the fountain. And when she marries, she gets little understanding from Ralph, who is shy and timid. Patience's mother preferred that Patience marry a more intelligent man than the dull but kind son of the landlord. One critic found the mother's attitude "unnatural." But Ralph had saved her life, so Patience proposes to him. Once married, she finds him boring and is impatient with his stupidity and incapacity to understand her very different nature.

MAY, MRS. A. W. See MAY, GEORGIANA MARION (CRAIK).

MAYNARD, CORA. United States.

2109 SOME MODERN HERETICS: A NOVEL. Boston: Roberts, 1896 NUC.
Winifred Gray, novelist and dramatist and something of an anarchist meets Vida, daughter of a millionaire.

MAYNARD, LUCY.

2110 THE PHILANTHROPIST. London: Methuen, 1898 BMC.
"The melancholy of the teaching profession lies heavily on this book." The lovers marry and become proprietors of a boys' school on Lake Geneva. The philanthropist appears to be a fake, the discovery of which is part of the plot. Author's purpose is "to show up the hideousness of life in benevolent institutions."

MAYNE, ETHEL COLBURN. 1870-1941. United Kingdom.

2111 THE CLEARER VISION. London: T. F. Unwin, 1898 BMC.
A "powerful" story, showing an "unusual courage of

unreserve" and revealing the point of view that love, wifehood and motherhood are "a poor business for a woman."

2112   THE FOURTH SHIP. London: Chapman & Hall, 1908 BMC.

Allegory. A woman who doesn't marry ends up living with the man she once loved and his wife and children. The final part of the book contrasts mid-Victorian and late Victorian young women.

2113   GOLD LACE, A STUDY OF GIRLHOOD. London: Chapman & Hall, 1913 NUC BMC.

Feelings and relations between young women and servicemen at a naval station and garrison town in Ireland. Rhoda is a feminist. She believes she is superior to the young officers she meets.

2114   JESSIE VANDELEUR. London: Allen, 1902 BMC.

Jessie Vandeleur pursues one quest: that of personal happiness. She steals the plot of her lover's book, destroys his manuscript, and feels no remorse or pity for him at his death. Nor does any of this matter to her second lover when he is told.

2115   ONE OF OUR GRANDMOTHERS. London: Chapman & Hall, 1916 NUC BMC.

She is a piano player, born of a stupid English father and a coarse Irish stepmother. The year is 1860, and she struggles to get out of her commonplace surroundings so she can pursue her music. She yearns for more freedom than 1860 can give her. Psychological study of a woman who can find no escape from the traditional role she has been assigned.

MAYO, ISABELLA (FYVIE). 1834-1914. United Kingdom.

2116   A DAUGHTER OF THE KLEPHTS; OR A GIRL OF MODERN GREECE. London: W.R. Chambers, [1897] BMC.

Patience Hedges, raised in England by woman who left her a fortune, travels to Greece at the time of struggle for independence to be reunited with her parents, finds herself in the thick of the war, devotes her fortune to the cause, and escapes disaster in the disguise of a "pallibar."

MAYOR, F. M. See MAYOR, FLORA MACDONALD.

MAYOR, FLORA MACDONALD. B. 1872. United Kingdom.

2117 THE THIRD MISS SYMONS. BY F. M. MAYOR. London: Sidgwick & Jackson, 1913 NUC BMC.

The depressing life story of Henrietta Symons, well-to-do daughter of a mid-Victorian country solicitor: her sad childhood, her relations to her married sisters, her deterioration, a series of dull periods with no chance for happiness—a plain record of her 63 years.

MEADE, L. T. See SMITH, ELIZABETH THOMASINA (MEADE).

MEADOWS, ALICE MAUD. D. 1913.

2118 I CHARGE YOU BOTH. London: Digby, Long, 1905 BMC.

After her husband is put in an asylum, Lena takes an alias, exploits her beauty, becomes a bigamist and a murderer.

2119 AN INNOCENT SINNER. London: Digby, Long, 1910 BMC.

Young wife in league with a gang of criminals.

2120 THE ROMANCE OF A MADHOUSE. Bristol: J. W. Arrowsmith, [1891] BMC.

Young lawyer meets beautiful young woman unjustly accused of murder and confined to institution on grounds of insanity. Convinced of her innocence, sets out to clear her and succeeds. Wedding.

2121 A TICKET-OF-LEAVE GIRL. London: Digby, Long, 1911 BMC.

Crime story: Brenda wrongly suffers five years of imprisonment.

MEARS, A. GARLAND. See MEARS, AMELIA GARLAND.

MEARS, AMELIA GARLAND.

2122   MERCIA, THE ASTRONOMER ROYAL: A ROMANCE. BY A. GARLAND MEARS. London: Simpkin, Marshall, 1895 NUC BMC.

Mercia becomes Empress of India in this science fiction story of 2002 AD when instead of wars there are tournaments where the opponent is paralyzed in the right arm and not killed.

MEARS, LOUISE.

2123   CONCERNING SOME FOOLS AND THEIR FOLLY. BY NEWTON SANDARS. London: Sands, 1901 BMC.

Two actresses marry clergymen, but refuse to play typical role of clergyman's wife. Neither believes in marriage; one leaves her husband.

MEARS, MADGE.

2124   THE CANDID COURTSHIP. London and New York: J. Lane, 1917 NUC BMC.

"A feminist love story." Joan is a leader in the feminist movement committed to the "ideals of universal sisterhood." She lives in a boarding house in Hygate. She loves a male architect, but when he confesses to having had an affair, she remains true to her ideas of equality and refuses him. In the end circumstances bring about a satisfactory basis of agreement.

2125   THE FLAPPER'S MOTHER. London: J. Lane, 1918 BMC NUC. New York: J. Lane, 1918 BMC NUC.

Concerns unreasonable marriage laws. A woman married to a despicable husband who leaves her without a word falls in love with a worthy man but must wait six years—says the law. Vera, the flapper, falls in love with a married man whose wife is insane. They cannot marry because of the law. Vera lives with the man, but does not find happiness in this unconventional arrangement.

2126 THE JEALOUS GODDESS. London: J. Lane, 1915 NUC BMC. New York: J. Lane, 1915 NUC.

Protests idea of woman's proper place and questions whether women would choose marriage if all things were equal between men and women. Title refers to art or work. A young woman wants to paint; she finds that homelife and then married life hamper her career. When she realizes she is pregnant, she becomes desperately despondent. She is totally estranged from her husband—an artist who is free to devote himself to his work.

2127 THE SHELTERED SEX. London and New York: J. Lane, 1916 NUC BMC.

Ruth goes off with Jolivard to escape the prison of her home. They are comrades travelling together to London to find work. There is a train wreck, he is hospitalized. When he is well, they live together; she works and takes care of him while he is disabled. They are still comrades. Author seems to believe British philistinism is the root of women's enslavement.

MEARS, MARY MARTHA. B. 1876. United States.

2128 THE BIRD IN THE BOX. IKE 2 New York: F. A. Stokes, [1910] NUC.

A young woman goes to New York to work. She has a difficult time and marries a millionaire. She is unhappy and meets again an inventor she had loved earlier. She uses her husband's money to help him with an invention. Disaster follows.

2129 THE BREATH OF THE RUNNERS; A NOVEL. New York: F. A. Stokes, [1906] NUC.

Careers of two young sculptors—Beulah and Enid—from the time they first felt the ambition through the years of toil, discouragement and uncertain progress. Beulah gives up a great chance at success rather than take unfair advantage of Enid, while Enid destroys Beulah's work out of jealousy. Beulah finds contentment in marriage.

2130 EMMA LOU—HER BOOK. New York: H. Holt, 1896 NUC.

Diary of Emma Lou, an 18 year old school teacher who

also helps a minister, occasionally writing his sermons. She has "lofty views."

2131 ROSAMOND THE SECOND, BEING THE TRUE RECORD OF THE UNPARALLELED ROMANCE OF ONE CLAUDIUS FULLER. New York: F. A. Stokes, [1910] NUC.

Fantasy. Claudius, who can't win Rosamond, makes an electric model of her in wax. He has improved on her; she is predictable and loving and doesn't contradict him. But he finds that opposition was dearer than he had imagined.

MELLOR, DORA.

2132 BEAUTY RETIRE; AN HISTORICAL ROMANCE. London: Greening, 1909 BMC NUC.

Time of James II: Hetty, daughter of a country curate, her move to London, love, and her life as a slave in Jamaica.

MENDL, GLADYS. See SCHUETZE, GLADYS HENRIETTA (RAPHAEL).

MEREDITH, ELLIS. See CLEMENT, ELLIS (MEREDITH).

MEREDITH, ISABEL. See AGRESTI, OLIVIA ROSSETTI AND HELENE ROSSETTI ANGELI.

MEREDITH, KATHARINE MARY CHEEVER. United States.

2133 GREEN GATES: AN ANALYSIS OF FOOLISHNESS. New York: D. Appleton, 1896 NUC BMC.

The sad tale of a crippled young woman with a puzzling personality. Reviewers are agreed on the low morals of the characters in this story which takes place in a Long Island country home.

MERREL, CONCORDIA. United Kingdom.

2134 JULIA TAKES HER CHANCE. London: Selwyn & Blount, 1920 BMC. New York: T. Seltzer, 1921 NUC.

Julia, full of rollicking laughter and life, is a great success as an actress. But after a failure she rejects a matrimonial proposal and escapes into the obscurity of a clerical job, eventually marrying her employer.

MERRICK, HOPE (BUTLER-WILKINS). D. 1917. United Kingdom.

2135 MARY-GIRL. A POSTHUMOUS NOVEL. London: W. Collins, Sons, [c1920] BMC NUC.

Ezra and Mary are Quakers and have a great ambition to rebuild the barn used for a meeting house. The manor family needs someone to suckle a new baby, the doctor suggests Mary, Ezra consents, and the building is started with the first paycheck. Agony, shame and trouble follow. There is an episode concerning Mary and Latimer: "Had Mary been younger, one might have thought her lapse with Latimer probable...she had not hated Ezra nor even thought of leaving him."

METHLEY, ALICE A.

2136 LA BELLE DAME. London: J. Long, 1906 BMC.

Heroine steals family jewels, commits murder, drugs niece and tries to force her into marriage and finally poisons herself.

MEYER, ANNIE (NATHAN). 1867-1951. United States.

2137 HELEN BRENT, M.D.: A SOCIAL STUDY [ANONYMOUS]. New York: Cassell, [c1892] NUC. London and New York: Gay and Bird, 1893 BMC.

Helen loves Harold, a lawyer, but he cannot reconcile her public life with his private requirements. She refuses to give up her career for marriage and becomes head of the Hospital and College for Women. Harold marries someone else who eventually leaves him because she is tired of his neglect of her in his involvement in his career. By the end of the story he sees the fallacy of his reasoning.

2138 ROBERT ANNYS: POOR PRIEST. A TALE OF THE GREAT UPRISING. New York and London: Macmillan, 1901 NUC BMC.

Contrast between Mathilda, a woman of affections, and Rose, a woman of passion who loves love and power. Rose is described as "sex incarnate," "vital"; "she thrills responsively to passion whenever she finds it."

MEYER, LUCY JANE (RIDER). 1849-1922. United States.

2139 MARY NORTH. A NOVEL. New York: F. H. Revell, [c1903] NUC BMC.

Romantic young woman deluded into a bogus marriage is soon disillusioned. She leaves husband and moves to Chicago. Includes struggle of earlier lover to find her.

MEYNELL, VIOLA. See DALLYN, VIOLA (MEYNELL).

MEYRICK, DIANA.

2140 PEACE ALLEY. London: Sidgwick and Jackson, 1910 BMC.

Village of "sweet old maids" and their love affairs.

2141 PHYLLIS AND FELICITY. London: Sidgwick and Jackson, 1911 BMC.

Two stepsisters get to know each other after they are grown up and establish a close relationship. Ends with their marriages.

MICHAELIS, KARIN. See STANGELAND, KATHARINA MARIE BECH (BRONDUM) MICHAELIS.

MICHELL, SYBIL C.

2142 INGA OF MORDANGER. London: J. Ouseley, [1910] BMC.

A simple Norwegian young woman comes to England as a companion; she is decoyed into a bad marriage but escapes to Norway and a former lover.

MICHELSON, MIRIAM. 1870-1942. United States.

2143 ANTHONY OVERMAN. London and New York: Doubleday, Page, 1906 BMC NUC.

The heroine is "keen, alert, self-reliant, brilliant, up-to-date," a journalist with a future. She gives it all up to marry the socialist hero.

2144 IN THE BISHOP'S CARRIAGE. Indianapolis: Bobbs-Merrill, [1904] NUC BMC. London: A. Constable, 1904 BMC.

A female "Raffles," a thief and confidence woman who goes almost straight and becomes an actress.

2145 MICHAEL THWAITE'S WIFE. New York: Doubleday, Page, 1909 NUC.

As children, twins Tess and Trix often exchanged names and personalities. Tess was always good, unselfish; Trix, brilliant but vain. In later life, Trix deserts her husband for another man. When she dies, Tess takes her sister's place as wife to the deserted husband to save her sister's good name. She wins happiness in the end.

2146 A YELLOW JOURNALIST. New York: D. Appleton, 1905 NUC BMC.

Rhoda Massey, star reporter for the News, has one ambition; to "score a beat" on rival reporter Ted Thompson. Her job takes her "cross country with a murderer in an open buggy, with a lynching party in full pursuit," involves her in disguises, Senate secrets, dozens of audacious escapades. There is no love story.

MIDGLEY, MRS. LLEWELLYN. United Kingdom.

2147 THE UNCONSCIOUS QUEST. BY E. REID MATHESON. London and Toronto: Sidgwick and Jackson, 1913 NUC BMC.

Dorothea is 40ish, widowed after twenty years of marriage. She travels, falls in love with a man young enough to be her son, but returns home at the end, forgetting him as easily as she had her husband. According to one review, she is a strong woman reasserting her individuality; according to another, a silly old woman.

2148 THE WORLD'S VOICES. BY E. REID MATHESON. London: Sisley, [1908] BMC.
A nun leaves the convent and becomes a nurse.

MIGHELS, ELLA STERLING (CLARK). 1853-1934. United States.

2149 THE FULL GLORY OF DIANTHA. BY MRS. PHILIP VERRILL MIGHELS. Chicago: Forbes, 1909 NUC.
Theme: love does not guarantee compatibility in marriage. Diantha is a strong healthy bookkeeper who rejects several suitors because she wants to marry an innocent "unsullied" man. She travels west to find her man.

MIGHELS, MRS. PHILIP VERRILL. See MIGHELS, ELLA STERLING (CLARK).

MILECETE, HELEN.

2150 A DETACHED PIRATE; THE ROMANCE OF GAY VANDELEUR. London: Greening, 1900 BMC. Boston: Little, Brown, 1903 NUC.
Gay found marriage to Colonel Gore dull and "playing the part of a woman so cumbersome to my development (I am quoting the new woman's jargon now) that I decided to be a man." Her male disguise results in misunderstanding and a divorce which for a time leaves her unencumbered until her identity as a divorcee is known. She travels, flirts, dances, drinks, smokes, makes scathing attacks on her husband and The System. She rides a horse in snow, toboggans, dresses like a man for three months to get around town, and even wears a mustache. She travels until her money is exhausted and then finds work first as a rider in a circus and then as a riding teacher. The book is written in the form of letters to a close female friend who eventually is the agent for a reconciliation with Colonel Gore. She believes the divorce

has saved their marriage from a relationship of indifference.

2151 A GIRL OF THE NORTH; A STORY OF LONDON AND CANADA. London: Greening, 1900 NUC BMC.
Laura Archer, a Canadian, is French, English and Indian. The novel is a protest against the monotony of domestic joys and convention in the relations of men and women.

MILECETE, HELEN, jt. au. See JONES, SUSAN CARLETON AND HELEN MILECETE.

MILLER, ADDIE LETTIE (PECK). B. 1867. United States.

2152 LETTIE; OR THE WHIRLWIND'S CAPER. Naugatuck, Conn.: The Author, 1916 NUC.
Lettie leaves her husband on their wedding day. Story follows her career of independence to their reconciliation.

MILLER, ALICE (DUER). 1874-1942. United States.

2153 THE BLUE ARCH. New York: Scribner's Sons, 1910 NUC.
Nina is an astronomer, who devotes herself to her work against the wishes of her family. She also takes the initiative in her relations with a man.

2154 CALDERON'S PRISONER. New York: C. Scribner's Sons, 1903 NUC.
The first of two modern society novelettes concerns a young, restless woman, who, bored with New York society, travels to South America, becomes involved in a revolution and is taken prisoner. In the second, a wife argues with her husband about how much freedom a man should have, falls out of love with him as a consequence, and leaves him.

2155 THE HAPPIEST TIME OF THEIR LIVES. New York: Century, 1918 BMC NUC. London: Hodder & Stoughton, [1919] BMC.
Satire, contrasting types of women, examination of the

question of women's relationships to men and to society. Records the simultaneous love affairs of three generations to show that real love can occur at any stage of maturity.

2156   THE MODERN OBSTACLE. New York: Scribner's Sons, 1903 NUC. London: G.P. Putnam's Sons, 1904 BMC.

A worldly woman cannot overcome the obstacle that keeps her from the man she loves—money. She must have wealth, yet she despises herself for her crude ambitions. The author uses the woman's predicament to show a form of modern enslavement of woman.

2157   THINGS. New York: C. Scribner's Sons, 1914 NUC.

Mrs. Royce runs her house and household with great efficiency, managing so completely that her family is overwrought. She consults a specialist on the state of her daughter's nerves, and he, after observing the daughter, advises Mrs. Royce to go away for awhile. When she returns she finds her family well and happy to see her. She realizes that things and not ideas have filled her life.

MILLER, ANNIE (JENNESS). B. 1859. United States.

2158   THE PHILOSOPHER OF DRIFTWOOD: A NOVEL. BY MRS. JENNESS MILLER. Washington, D.C.: Jenness Miller Publications, 1897 NUC.

A daughter learns to understand why her mother divorced her father when she herself has to break her engagement to one man because she really loves someone else. The "legal and moral right to divorce for incompatibility is upheld as a duty to both husband and wife, and the children."

MILLER, ELIZABETH. See HACK, ELIZABETH JANE (MILLER).

MILLER, ESTHER. United Kingdom.

2159   WILLOWWOOD. London: Harper, 1899 BMC.

After her husband is disfigured in an explosion, Frances Deltry is so upset that her husband advises her to travel. On her trip, she presents herself as a widow, meets a man she loves, and marries him. When her first husband meets her and husband #2 at a party, he is so despondent that he kills himself. Apparently the only "punishment" Frances receives is that the second husband gives her up.

MILLER, IRENE.

2160 SEKHET. London and New York: J. Lane, 1912 BMC NUC.

Evarne Stornway is raised by her father according to the Greek tradition of physical beauty. She is on her own at 16, is befriended and then cast off by Lord Winborough. She tries to make her way in London in several occupations, but she can't live without love. She becomes engaged to a man who turns out to be the nephew of Lord Winborough, who threatens to reveal her past and prevent her marriage. She attempts to murder him, discovers she has murdered the nephew in error; she loses her mind. She is under the influence of the Egyptian goddess of love and cruelty.

MILLER, MARY ELIZA BAKEWELL (GAUNT). 1872-1942. Australia.

2161 KIRKHAM'S FIND. London: Methuen, 1897 BMC NUC.

Phoebe Marsden is an independent young Australian woman who keeps bees. Includes much of Australian life, the search for gold, the fights with the natives.

2162 THE UNCOUNTED COST. BY MARY GAUNT. New York: E. J. Clode, [1910] NUC. London: T. W. Laurie, 1910 BMC.

Anne is a successful novelist "always yearning for new experiences." She believes in trial marriage; lives with a man for two years, but he doesn't want to continue. She and a group of friends go to Africa, where they have adventures.

2163 A WIND FROM THE WILDERNESS. BY MARY GAUNT. London: T. W. Laurie, [1919] BMC NUC.

Stella Chapman and Rosalie Grahme are doctors in a

missionary compound in Yang Ching, China, in the early days of the war. Rosalie is there not to spread Christianity—she does not profess to be a Christian—but to heal bodies. Descriptions of the poverty and suffering, an uprising, their wanderings in Tibet, their struggles through Arctic wastes, and the tragic end.

MILLER, MINNIE (WILLIS) BAINES. B. 1845. United States.

2164　HIS COUSIN, THE DOCTOR: A STORY. BY MINNIE WILLIS BAINES. Cincinnati: Cranston and Stowe, 1891 NUC.

His cousin is Dr. Sarah Katherine Spencer, a professional of the healing art after the doctrines of Christian Science.

MILLER, MRS. JENNESS. See MILLER, ANNIE (JENNESS).

MILN, LOUISE (JORDAN). 1864-1933. United States.

2165　A WOMAN AND HER TALENT. London: W. Blackwood, 1905 BMC.

At Vassar, Helen astonishes her professors with her genius. They encourage her to pursue her studies, but she marries. All goes well till her husband realizes she's the better writer and she becomes famous. Helen supports the family; he wastes money, wrecks the home and their son. There are painful scenes and ugly arguments in this close study of the "storms and strifes of domesticity."

MILTON, C. R.*

2166　THE EYES OF UNDERSTANDING. London: A. Melrose, 1919 BMC.

Young woman takes post as superintendent of a training school in India and is "face to face with a melange of unrest, attempted revolution and official muddling."

MINNETT, CORA. Australia.

2167 THE DAY AFTER TO-MORROW. London: F. V. White, 1911 BMC.

Utopian novel set in socialist England where all manner of progress has been accomplished, including the full political equality of women. One heroine is Clutha, six feet tall, superior in intellect, a psychic and a music teacher. The other is Emerald Vernay, green eyed, red haired, daring and passionate; she is a great parliamentary leader and orator. Both love Derrick who loves Clutha. On the eve of being appointed governor-general of Australia, Emerald is discovered to have murdered two lawyers who cheated Derrick. She goes off scene exclaiming she would be willing to go to hell if Derrick would love her there.

MIRRLEES, HOPE. United Kingdom.

2168 MADELAINE, ONE OF LOVE'S JANSENISTS. London: W. Collins Sons, 1919 BMC.

Set in mid-17th century France. Young woman, ardent, instinctive, intelligent, is obsessed with the idea of becoming Mlle. de Scudery's intimate friend. "Madelaine apes Mlle. de Scudery with the devoted folly of youth until she is completely divorced from reality." When she finally meets her, she is disillusioned and disappointed.

MITTON, G. E. See SCOTT, GERALDINE EDITH (MITTON).

MIX, JENNIE IRENE. United States.

2169 AT FAME'S GATEWAY; THE ROMANCE OF A PIANISTE. New York: H. Holt, 1920 NUC.

Girl from oil town comes to New York for musical fame. She is a musical prodigy. Usual love interest and traditional ending, but story is more about her music and her teacher, Anton Brandt.

MOBERLY, L. G. See MOBERLY, LUCY GERTRUDE.

MOBERLY, LUCY GERTRUDE. B. 1860.

2170   DAN AND ANOTHER. London: Ward, Lock, 1907 BMC.
        Edith does not know who the father of her child is. When
        she marries, her husband adopts the child.

2171   HEART OF GOLD. BY L. G. MOBERLY. London: Ward,
        Lock, 1911 BMC NUC.
        Nancy Marchmere with voice of gold works in a factory,
        becomes a great opera star.

2172   PHYLLIS. London: Ward, Lock, 1911 BMC.
        Phyllis's mother murdered her (Phyllis's) father and is
        sentenced to 20 years in prison. Phyllis believes her
        mother is innocent but there's the slow realization of her
        mother's guilt.

2173   A WAIF OF DESTINY. London: Ward, Lock, 1910 BMC.
        Sensational exploits. Young woman of extraordinary
        vitality, made to stay a night with an unknown corpse, is
        injured in railroad collision, assumes identity of fellow
        passenger who is killed, escapes a house by climbing down
        a water pipe, is run over while hypnotized, is twice
        hospitalized. She's a spy in the pay of a certain foreign
        power. She possesses hypnotic powers. Everyone resists
        this adventuress but one man.

2174   A WOMAN AGAINST THE WORLD. London: Ward,
        Lock, 1909 BMC.
        Margaret Merivale, a penniless widow, takes a position as
        nurse-companion without revealing that she is suspected of
        murdering her husband ten years earlier. She falls in love
        with her employer whose child is her charge and whose
        wife is in an asylum. Nevertheless the novel ends happily.

MOLE, MARION.*

2175   FOR THE SAKE OF A SLANDERED WOMAN.
        Edinburgh: W. Blackwood, 1895 BMC.
        Widow is ostracized because of accusation that she lives
        off money her husband swindled before he killed himself.
        But she really earns her living as a writer. She must also
        contend with the bitterness of the man she jilted. Set in
        Norway.

MOLESWORTH, MARY LOUISA (STEWART). 1842-1921.
United Kingdom.

2176 THE STORY OF A YEAR. BY MRS. MOLESWORTH.
London: Macmillan, 1910 BMC NUC.
Wife and daughter fend for themselves due to loss of
husband's fortune. Plucky wife embroiders while he is in
West Indies.

MOLESWORTH, MRS. See MOLESWORTH, MARY LOUISA
(STEWART).

MONK, THYMOL.*

2177 AN ALTAR OF EARTH. London: W. Heinemann, 1894
BMC. New York: G. Putnam, 1894 NUC.
Daphne and Theo, socialists, reject men so that they can
work for the good of humanity. One of them is a medical
student. When they learn that Daphne has an incurable
disease and only two years to live; they retire to the
country to make the most of the remaining time. "The
book is the direct outcome of Sarah Grand's
teaching—much of her nonsense being reproduced here."

MONROE, ANNE SHANNON. 1877-1945. United States.

2178 EUGENE NORTON: A TALE OF THE SAGEBRUSH
LAND. Chicago: Rand, McNally, [c1900] NUC. London:
A. E. Hubsch, [1900] BMC.
Young American singer returns home after her first
triumph in Berlin and marries a man connected with
mining interests to please her father.

2179 MAKING A BUSINESS WOMAN. New York: H. Holt,
1912 NUC.
A young woman leaves her country town to escape
boredom and to lead an independent life in Chicago. She
knows and likes the business world, she can type very
well, and she rises to success.

MONROE, HARRIET (EARHART). 1842-1926. United States.

2180 THE HEROINE OF THE MINING CAMP. Philadelphia: Lutheran Soc., [c1894] NUC.

Jennie goes to a mining area in Colorado to teach school. Her romance.

MONSELL, MARGARET EMMA FAITH (IRWIN). 1889-1967. United Kingdom.

2181 OUT OF THE HOUSE. BY M. E. F. IRWIN. London: Constable, 1916 BMC NUC. New York: Doran, [19—?] NUC.

Carolin Pomfret, an orphan, is raised by aunts and cousins—all women. The story begins when she is five and describes the family environment. Their principal interests are whist and rereading family diaries (they are insanely proud of the family). A marriage for Carolin is arranged—a few days before the wedding she walks out of the house to meet someone else.

MONTAGU, LILIAN HELEN. 1874-1963. United Kingdom.

2182 NAOMI'S EXODUS. London: T.F. Unwin, 1901 NUC BMC.

Young woman from the ghetto in West London breaks with all her old ties successfully. Describes the lives of English working class women.

MONTAGUE, MARGARET PRESCOTT. 1878-1955. United States.

2183 LINDA. Boston: Houghton, Mifflin, 1912 NUC. London: Constable, 1913 BMC.

Linda Stillwater is an uneducated mountain girl who marries a middle aged man because he threatens to beat her mother if she does not. When her father learns the man has another wife, he demands Linda's return. Linda wanders off, has her child without scandal, goes to Boston where she is educated by a woman who introduces her to society.

MONTGOMERY, K. L., jt. pseud. of KATHLEEN AND LETITIA MONTGOMERY.

MONTGOMERY, KATHLEEN AND LETITIA MONTGOMERY.

2184 THE CARDINAL'S PAWN: HOW FLORENCE SET, HOW VENICE CHECKED AND HOW THE GAME FELL OUT. BY K. L. MONTGOMERY. London: T.F. Unwin, 1903 BMC. Chicago: A.C. McClurg, 1910 NUC.

"A tale of the Florence and Venice of the Renaissance. The Cardinal's pawn is a girl of wit and daring. In order to save her brother from death at the hands of a faithless wife who wishes to be rid of him so that her social ambitions may be realized, the girl enters the Cardinal's game disguised as the brother she would save."

2185 COLONEL KATE. BY K. L. MONTGOMERY. London: Methuen, [1908] NUC BMC.

During Charles Edward's uprising, a woman of action is taken prisoner, is brutally mistreated by her husband and is involved in daring conspiracies, in return for which she is named "Colonel Kate" by the Chevalier.

2186 THE GATE-OPENERS. BY K. L. MONTGOMERY. London: J. Long, 1912 BMC.

Story of the Welsh toll-gate riots of 1843 and their leader, Rebekah.

2187 MAIDS OF SALEM. BY K. L. MONTGOMERY. London: J. Long, 1915 BMC.

New England witch hunt—the raw vehemence of the time.

MONTGOMERY, LETITIA, jt. au. See MONTGOMERY, KATHLEEN AND LETITIA MONTGOMERY.

MONTGOMERY, LUCY MAUD. See MACDONALD, LUCY MAUD (MONTGOMERY).

MONTRESOR, F. F. See MONTRESOR, FRANCES FREDERICA.

MONTRESOR, FRANCES FREDERICA. D. 1934. United Kingdom.

2188 THE BURNING TORCH. BY F. F. MONTRESOR. London: J. Murray, 1905 BMC. New York: E.P. Dutton, 1907 NUC.

Dolores Ellerson, awkward, timid, eccentric orphan, is a prophetess who has visions and foretells disasters but whom no one believes. Ends with her death.

2189 FALSE COIN OR TRUE? BY F. F. MONTRESOR. London: Hutchinson, 1896 BMC. New York: D. Appleton, 1896 NUC.

Study of Moreze, a French magician, and Linda, a workhouse girl he has rescued from the streets and has trained as a medium. They work together. A young Scotsman, Maclean, falls in love with her; she returns his love, but Moreze doesn't want to lose her. MacLean publicly denounces Moreze for his exploitation of her. She leaves to marry MacLean but returns to Moreze to nurse him when he becomes ill.

2190 A FISH OUT OF WATER. London: J. Murray, 1910 BMC.

A young woman cutting loose from her family.

2191 INTO THE HIGHWAYS AND HEDGES. BY F. F. MONTRESOR. London: Hutchinson, 1895 BMC. New York: D. Appleton, 1895 NUC.

Character studies. Cultured, impressionable, wealthy Margaret Deane, disappointed in love, is caught on the rebound by the religion of a street preacher named Barnabas Thorpe. She gives up her family and luxury to live an ascetic life and travels with him as he preaches his gospel. She is married to him but will not sleep with him. She learns to love him when she sees him ready to sacrifice his life for another.

2192 THE STRICTLY TRAINED MOTHER. BY F. F. MONTRESOR. London: J. Murray, 1913 BMC 1916 NUC.

A woman rebels late in life—when she is a grandmother. Mrs. Betterton spent most of her life under someone's thumb. First her husband tyrannized her; then her daughters did the same—unknowingly, because they have her health in mind above all else. Mrs. Betterton's two daughters have no tact or understanding of their mother—who escapes to her granddaughter (a modern type). Mother and daughters are reconciled at the end.

2193 THROUGH THE CHRYSALIS. BY F. F. MONTRESOR. London: J. Murray, 1910 BMC NUC.

Babette is a Becky Sharp, who doesn't have a downfall; she snatches at luxury but the reader likes her.

MOORE, BERTHA PEARL. 1894-1925. United States.

2194 SARAH AND HER DAUGHTER. BY BERTHA PEARL. New York: T. Seltzer, 1920 NUC. London: L. Pearsons, 1921 BMC.

Sarah, who works by the day when she can, finally takes her husband Elias, who refuses to work on the Jewish Sabbath, to a court dealing with refractory husbands. He is sentenced to ten days, and she is disgraced in the eyes of her neighbors. The family is poverty-stricken, and when Sarah has work, Minnie, her eight year old daughter, must do all the work at home. Sarah has outbursts of temper with Minnie which she later regrets. When Elias dies, Sarah becomes temporarily insane. She becomes a money-mad mistress of a sweatshop in which she exploits her own children. Minnie, sensitive, leaves home at 16, seeking financial independence and struggling against sexual exploitation. Hospitalized, her health ruined, she decides to fling decency aside and becomes a man's mistress. This, too, ends in failure, and she finally marries — a man no better than her father.

MOORE, CAECILIA.

2195 THE SHADOW OF THE DRAGON. London: Chapman and Hall, 1913 BMC.

"A story concerned with the white slave traffic in Shanghai. The horrors detailed are indeed terrible, but there is no reason why, as the author appears to think, readers should become suffragettes." Hespie McLeod on her way to her uncle in Australia is persuaded by a young man to see a bit of life. He sells her to a brothel keeper in Shanghai.

MOORE, E. HAMILTON. United Kingdom.

2196   THE RUT. London: E. Macdonald, 1913 BMC.

Futile, hopeless story of a young woman who drifts into marriage. She doesn't realize that she has never lived, that her life is in a rut, until in middle age she becomes infatuated with a man. He's amused by her passion, her husband is cold and unforgiving and her children curious.

MOORE, EDITH.

2197   A WILFUL WIDOW. London: Constable, 1913 BMC.

Mary Lavender is a widow whose great fortune will be forfeited if she becomes a socialist. She does, and the testator's design is thwarted.

MOORE, EDITH MARY.

2198   THE BLIND MARKSMAN. London: Hodder & Stoughton, [1920] BMC.

A character study of Jane, her lonely childhood, her intense friendship with her uncle, a misogynist, her intellectual energy which can find no outlet in the narrowly confined life in the home of her mother. She marries a weak and dreary husband with a mother who enslaves her.

2199   THE LURE OF EVE. London: Cassell, 1909 BMC NUC. New York: Cassell, 1909 PW.

"Too outspoken for open shelf fiction." Beautiful impassive Annabel Summers marries a writer who hopes to learn the Secret of Woman through her. But she is conventional with no mind and no inspiration to him. Their disillusionment with each other grows. Finally the husband learns the secret through Lora, the "real" woman in the novel. He writes his great novel Woman and Destiny to present his theories of a new world in which women will play the leading part.

2200 THE SPIRIT AND THE LAW. London: Chapman and Hall, 1916 BMC.

The pure minded daughter of a farmer follows her own law with a reflective and silent shoemaker who has a passion for drink and who is unhappily married. Greek drama figures of tragedy.

2201 THE WRONG SIDE OF DESTINY. London: Cassell, 1909 BMC.

Rose Esquilant married a much older man when she was very young. Falls in love with another man but duty to her two sons keeps her in place. When her sons are grown, she accepts the fact that one lives with a woman writer. But when she tells this son about her love, he shoots himself.

MOORE, EVELYN (UNDERHILL). 1875-1941. United Kingdom.

2202 THE COLUMN OF DUST. BY EVELYN UNDERHILL. London: Methuen, [1909] BMC NUC.

"Supernatural realities" in modern London. A spirit takes hold of Constance Tyrrel. It makes her restless, energetic, hungry for adventure. Author supports doctrine that it is ennobling for women to have children outside marriage.

MOORE, JUSTINA.

2203 WITHOUT SIN. A NOVEL. BY MARTIN J. PRITCHARD. London: W. Heinemann, 1896 BMC. Chicago: H. S. Stone, 1896 NUC.

Mary Levinge, the heroine, is an innocent young Jewish woman who believes she is destined to be the mother of the future Messiah. She becomes the victim of "man's depravity." Reviewers describe the story in terms of "contempt for conventionality," "ugly perversity," "nausea." The events of the story are not relatable in the columns of a review.

MOORE, LESLIE. United Kingdom.

2204 AUNT OLIVE IN BOHEMIA; OR, THE INTRUSIONS OF A FAIRY GODMOTHER. New York: Hodder and Stoughton, [c1913] NUC. London: A. Rivers, 1913 BMC NUC.

At 60 inherits a fortune, realizes a life long dream to study art, rents a studio in Chelsea, and plays fairy godmother to the neighbors.

2205 THE GREENWAY. New York: P.J. Kenedy, [1919] NUC. London: Sands, [1920] BMC.

Romance of Elizabeth Dacre, 35, who tells her own story. Poor and untrained at father's death, becomes companion, dislikes the work, trains herself to type, works in an office for two years, and then inherits Greenway.

MOORE, MONICA. See WILSON, MONA.

MOORE, MRS. STUART. See MOORE, EVELYN (UNDERHILL).

MORDAUNT, ELEANOR. See BOWLES, EVELYN MAY (CLOWES) WIEHE.

MORDAUNT, ELENOR. See BOWLES, EVELYN MAY (CLOWES) WIEHE.

MORDAUNT, ELINOR. See BOWLES, EVELYN MAY (CLOWES) WIEHE.

MORGAN, EMILY MALBONE. 1862-1937. United States.

2206 MADONNAS OF THE SMOKE; OR, OUR "MARY'S MEADOW". New York: A. D. F. Randolph, [c1893] NUC.

Group of young working women in a large manufacturing city form a working women's club. One of their projects is to rent a meadow. Story tells what use they put it to. Title refers to the name the group takes after the women see a photo of Raphael's madonna.

2207 A POPPY GARDEN. Hartford: Belknap and Warfield, 1892 NUC.

The love story of an older woman, tender and suggestive, set in New England.

MORRIS, ANNA VAN RENSSELAER. United States.

2208 THE APPLE WOMAN OF THE KLICKITAT. New York: Duffield, 1918 NUC.

Experiences of a woman who develops an orchard in Washington.

MORRIS, CLARA. See HARRIOTT, CLARA MORRIS.

MORRIS, EUGENIA LAURA (TUTTLE). B. 1833. United States.

2209 A HILLTOP SUMMER. BY ALYN YATES KEITH. Boston: Lee and Shepard, [c1894] NUC.

Life of Hilltop people described somewhat in the style of Cranford.

MORROW, HONORE (MACCUE) WILLSIE. 1880?-1940. United States.

2210 LYDIA OF THE PINES. BY HONORE WILLSIE. New York: F. A. Stokes, [c1917] NUC. London: Hodder & Stoughton, [1923] BMC.

About ten years of Lydia's life. She returns to Missouri after college, blazes her own trail of reform to success. She attacks the liquor interests and the treatment of Indians in the nearby reservation. She cleans up the political graft and inspires a Congressional investigation of the way whites took Indian land. She personifies and expresses "the feeling of the feminist toward public affairs: 'I did it because I felt responsible.'"

MORSE, LUCY (GIBBONS). 1839-1936. United States.

2211 RACHEL STANWOOD: A STORY OF THE MIDDLE OF THE NINETEENTH CENTURY. Boston and New York: Houghton, Mifflin, 1893 NUC BMC.

Rachel and her husband are Quakers in New York; the time is 1850-60. Their home is a station of the underground railroad, and their children consider "nigger" a swearword and call their church "The Abolitionist Church." Famous people like Garrison and Mrs. Child figure in the story.

MORTIMER, LESLIE.*

2212 THE MEN WE MARRY. London: J. Long, [1910] BMC NUC.

An indictment of the monstrousness of man. A man marries and deserts three women.

MORTON, L. CURRY.*

2213 THE HERO AND THE MAN. Chicago: A. C. McClurg, 1912 NUC.

Woman journalist and novelist. A man has crossed her path and impressed her so deeply she has made him hero of her novel. Scene is Northwestern town struggling for law and order.

MORTON, VICTORIA. United States.

2214 THE YELLOW TICKET. FROM THE PLAY OF THE SAME NAME BY MICHAEL MORTON. New York: H. K. Fly, [c1914] BMC NUC.

A young Jewish woman must carry a yellow ticket issued to prostitutes though she is not a prostitute.

MOSS, MARY. 1864-1914. United States.

2215 A SEQUENCE IN HEARTS. Philadelphia and London: J. B. Lippincott, 1903 NUC.

Marriage and children change restless Violet into a commonplace woman—an "abominably perfect" young wife and mother—while her women friends, a model and a poster-ad painter, look on and criticize.

MOYER, ALICE CURTICE.

2216   A ROMANCE OF THE ROAD; MAKING LOVE AND A LIVING. Chicago: Laird & Lee, [c1912] NUC.
Story of a widow who travels for a commercial house. Nonfiction?

MUENSTERBERG, MARGARETE ANNA ADELHEID. B. 1889. United States.

2217   ANNA BORDEN'S CAREER. A NOVEL. New York and London: D. Appleton, 1913 BMC NUC.
An active eventful career of a restless woman who thirsts for new experiences. She's a millionaire's daughter who gives up social success in Berlin to become first a hospital nurse, then actress, factory hand, champion of the Toilers Brotherhood, and finally, wife of a strike leader. She samples other activities "even down to the squalid depths."

MUHLBACH, LOUISE. See MUNDT, KLARA (MUELLER).

MUIR, OLIVE BEATRICE. United States.

2218   WITH MALICE TOWARD NONE. Chicago: Rand, McNally, [c1900] NUC.
Lal North, who became an actress after her father's death, marries an actor in her company. Soon after, she learns he is already married. Her ideal in life is honor and she takes action.

MULHOLLAND, ROSA. See GILBERT, ROSA (MULHOLLAND).

MULLINS, ISLA MAY (HAWLEY). 1859-1936. United States.

2219   THE BLOSSOM SHOP: A STORY OF THE SOUTH. Boston: L.C. Page, 1913 NUC.
Mother and blind daughter support selves selling flowers. Sentimental.

MUMFORD, ETHEL WATTS. See GRANT, ETHEL (WATTS) MUMFORD.

MUMMA, ROSA MEYERS. United States.

2220   ANGELA: A SALVATION ARMY LASSIE. New York: Neale, 1907 NUC.

Woman who killed a man hides away in the Salvation Army.

MUNDT, KLARA (MUELLER). 1814-1873. Germany.

2221   A CONSPIRACY OF THE CARBONARI. BY LOUISE MULBACH. New York: F.T. Neely, 1896 NUC. (Tr. by Mary J. Safford.)

A plot of the Carbonari to assassinate Napoleon is foiled by a beautiful woman and her father, spies in Napoleon's service.

MUNGER, DELL H. B. 1862. United States.

2222   THE WIND BEFORE THE DAWN. Garden City, New York: Doubleday, Page, 1912 NUC. London: Hodder & Stoughton, 1912 BMC.

The soul and body-killing grind and monotony of a woman's part in Kansas prairie farm life because husbands "own" their wives and treat them like beasts. Elizabeth Farnshaw is a school teacher who gives up her ambitions to marry a man who turns out to be a selfish tyrant. Elizabeth falls in love with her husband's partner who gives her money so that she can be free, for as the heroine says, "There is no other way...a woman to be free must have money of her own. She must not be supported by a man."

MUNN, MARGARET (CROSBY). United States.

2223   THE PATH OF STARS. New York: Dodd, Mead, 1903 NUC.

Heroine has a voice that thrills Liszt, but ill health spoils her career. Later she conquers her illness and becomes a famous opera singer—her chosen life's work. She has much to say on the subject of her reluctance to become romantically involved with men.

MUNN, MARGUERITE (BRYANT). United Kingdom.

2224 ANNE KEMPBURN: TRUTHSEEKER. BY MARGUERITE BRYANT. New York: Duffield, 1910 NUC. London: W. Heinemann, 1910 BMC.

Anne wants to make a better world. She is interested in economic theory and the regeneration of society. She studies the relationship between capital and labor in order to become the secretary of a labor leader. "Of Anne we remember nothing more weakly feminine than the impassioned handshake with which she and the long suffering Max cement their matrimonial pact."

2225 THE DOMINANT PASSION. BY MARGUERITE BRYANT (MRS. PHILIP MUNN). London: Hutchinson, 1913 NUC BMC. New York: Duffield, 1913 NUC.

Artist believes he needs Honor's inspiration for his work. She is a novelist who averts tragedy only by destroying the manuscript of her book and whose marriage is almost ruined by the artist's selfishness.

2226 FELICITY CROFTON. BY MARGUERITE BRYANT (MRS. PHILIP MUNN). New York: Duffield, 1916 NUC BMC. London: W. Heinemann, 1916 BMC.

Felicity is a 38 year old widow, mother of an 18 year old daughter. Felicity skates, toboggans, dances, has great vitality. She makes a sacrifice to protect a younger woman who is taking drugs. "Love interest" is completely unimportant.

2227 A GREAT RESPONSIBILITY. BY MARGUERITE BRYANT. London: Hurst and Blackett, 1895 NUC BMC.

Cecil Lestrange is the only grandchild of Sir Cecil Lestrange who is bitterly sad that his only son had but one daughter. Sir Cecil sets out to make her "masculine by training." At 16, Cecil gets a tutor instead of a governess, "is much more a boy than a girl, more interested in horses than in gossip," a fine individual. She is trained to be responsible to the family name and estates. "Thanks to her upbringing she remains to the end curiously unconscious of her sex."

2228 THE SHADOW ON THE STONE. BY MARGUERITE BYRANT (MRS. PHILIP MUNN). New York: Duffield, 1917 NUC BMC. London: Methuen, 1918 BMC.

Pauline Paget and two men set out to establish a model republic, and they succeed in spite of their enemy's effort to wreck their scheme.

MUNN, MRS. PHILIP. See MUNN, MARGUERITE (BRYANT).

MUNRO, ALICK.*

2229 A WOMAN OF WILES. London: Ward, Lock, 1902 BMC.

A woman—daring, brilliant, and fascinating—is the head of a gang of adventurers.

MURDOCH, GLADYS H.

2230 MISTRESS CHARITY GODOLPHIN. London: J. Murray, 1914 BMC.

Historical romance, Monmouth, the trial of Alice Lisle, executed by burning.

MURFREE, FANNY NOAILLES DICKINSON. B. 1845. United States.

2231 FELICIA: A NOVEL. Boston: Houghton, Mifflin, 1891 NUC BMC. (Also published as "A Singer's Wife: a Novel". London: Cassell, 1891 BMC.)

A year in the life of a proud young aristocratic woman from a town in western United States who marries an opera singer Hugh Kennell—after considerable hesitation. The trouble between them develops into a crisis. He is so completely devoted to his art that he does not see how miserable she is. She tries to support him but cannot. She is ashamed of his friends, of him in costume, and she hates living in hotels. The crisis comes when her indifference affects his performance and when she becomes aware there is a prima donna interested in him. The novel ends with no resolution, according to one reviewer; with his tragic death, according to another.

MURRAY, EUNICE GUTHRIE. B. 1877.

2232   THE HIDDEN TRAGEDY. London: C. W. Daniel, [1917] BMC.

Young Scottish woman educated at Girton takes up philanthropic work. Story develops into what is really an "out of date" suffrage novel, says one reviewer.

MURRAY, ROSALIND. B. 1890. United Kingdom.

2233   MOONSEED. London: Sidgwick & Jackson, 1911 BMC.

Chloe Warburton secretive, outspoken, jealous and unselfish, "a three-cornered nature." Spends her life in a "dumb resentment against the scheme of things." She loves a young man but repels him so with her rudeness that he turns to another—Augusta "a manly Amazon." Both find him unworthy. Chloe makes a sober marriage with sober middle-aged man, but the freshness of her life is gone, not to be restored.

2234   UNSTABLE WAYS. London & Toronto: Sidgwick & Jackson, 1914 BMC.

Giocosa "is a foreign woman, not belonging to any race or country, not brought up in the security of convention, and lacking the strength needed for a life of freedom....She had not the courage, the passion, and the purpose that they must have who would be a law unto themselves; and she was too restless and individualistic for the sheep folds....She played about with men she could not love; she found nothing real and nothing worth living for; she was, if we may put it bluntly, a very shallow, selfish and silly young person. And therefore, when she comes to grief and is released by death, which she so dreaded, from life, of which she could make nothing, we are left unmoved, either in idea on heart. She is, we feel, not worth our troubling about." Other reviewers see her as an example of the unhappiness caused by the freedom of the modern woman.

MUSGRAVE, H.*

2235 MYOLA. London: Hodder & Stoughton, [1917] BMC.
Saleswoman betrayed, brutally treated by father who murders her child, inherits, travels from New Zealand to England to find her lover, finds him married, returns home, dies.

MUZAKOVA, JOHANA (ROTTOVA). 1830-1899. Czechoslovakia.

2236 MARIA FELICIA ("THE LAST MISTRESS OF HLOHOV") A STORY OF BOHEMIAN LOVE. BY CAROLINE SVETLA. Chicago: A.C. McClurg, 1898 NUC. (Tr. by Antonie Krejsa.)
Bohemia during rule of Joseph II. Maria, daughter of an aristocrat, devotes her life to rights of masses and justice for a persecuted religious society. Love story too.

NALKOWSKA, SOFJA RYGIER. See NALKOWSKA, ZOFIA RYGIER.

NALKOWSKA, ZOFIA RYGIER. 1885-1954. Poland.

2237 KOBIETY-WOMEN. A NOVEL OF POLISH LIFE. BY SOFJA RYGIER-NALKOWSKA. New York and London: G. P. Putnam's Sons, 1920 BMC NUC. (Tr. by Michael Henry Dziewicki.)
The story of three women, in the manner of Bashkirtseff. Analysis of feminine psychology. Women need men's love, but no matter how much supremacy they seem to have, they always lose. But they have honor, a quality men don't share.

NAPIER, EVA MARIA LOUISA (MACDONALD). 1846-1930. United Kingdom.

2238 CAN MAN PUT ASUNDER? BY LADY NAPIER OF MAGDALA. London: J. Murray, 1911 BMC NUC.

Shona Barcaldine doesn't think about marriage, but when several seasons go by and no "husband" comes forth, her parents worry. She's perfectly content to live with her parents. When she learns her parents are anxious, she rushes into a loveless marriage. And there's another woman in her husband's life.

2239 TO THE THIRD AND FOURTH GENERATIONS. London: J. Murray, 1913 BMC.

Hildegard Mauleverer makes a loveless marriage with a marquess and forces her daughter into a loveless marriage with a Russian prince.

NAPIER, ROSAMOND. See LAWRENCE, ROSAMOND (NAPIER).

NAPIER OF MAGDALA, LADY. See NAPIER, EVA MARIA LOUISA (MACDONALD).

NEEDELL, MARY ANNA (LUPTON). B. 1830. United Kingdom.

2240 UNEQUALLY YOKED. BY MRS. J. H. NEEDELL. Edinburgh and London: Oliphant, Anderson, 1891 BMC. Boston: A. I. Bradley, 1898 NUC.

Study of the behavior and character of a woman who marries a man more cultured than herself for security and amusement and who instead finds herself shut away in the country while her husband does his parish work. In addition, the husband is not the demonstrative type. A former lover shows up. One reviewer says the novel warns against marriages of different social classes, but the end is happy.

2241 THE VENGEANCE OF JAMES VANSITTART. BY MRS. J. H. NEEDELL. London: Hutchinson, 1895 BMC. New York: D. Appleton, 1895 NUC.

"The life of a woman with a man whom she has never

loved and cannot respect is described in detail." Diane Charteris marries a hateful man to save her family from ruin, but her husband Maurice is financially dependent on his uncle and disowned by him when he marries Diane. This act is his uncle's planned revenge meant for Maurice's father, but is cast on Maurice because his father died. Fine study of Diane—all her hardhsips.

NEEDELL, MRS. J. H. See NEEDELL, MARY ANNA (LUPTON).

NELSON, KATHLEEN GRAY. United States.

2242 TUEN, SLAVE AND EMPRESS. New York: E.P. Dutton, 1898 NUC. London: Sands, 1899 BMC.
Sold by her father as a slave and then adopted by that family, she is presented to the emperor and marriage follows.

NEMCOVA, BOZENA. See NEMEC, BARBORA (PAMKLOVA).

NEMEC, BARBORA (PANKLOVA). 1820-1862. Czechoslovakia.

2243 THE GRANDMOTHER; A STORY OF COUNTRY LIFE IN BOHEMIA. BY BOZENA NEMCOVA. Chicago: A. C. McClurg, 1891 BMC NUC. (Tr. by Frances Gregor, with a biographical sketch of the author.)
Story of the daily life of an elderly country woman in Bohemia. (Nemcova was active in the 1848 revolution.)

NEPEAN, ELEANOR.

2244 SEA AND SWORD. London: Digby, Long, 1915 BMC.
Young woman disguises herself as the captain of a pirate ship. Time of the Inquisition when English pirates took Spanish nobles prisoners.

NESBIT, E. See BLAND, EDITH (NESBIT).

NETHERSOLE, S. C. See NETHERSOLE, SUSIE COLYER.

NETHERSOLE, SUSIE COLYER. B. 1869. United Kingdom.

2245 MARY UP AT GAFFRIES AND LETITIA HER FRIEND. London: Mills and Boon, 1909 BMC.

Independent and intelligent women of Kent where their labor is valuable. Mary is strong, proud, self-possessed, and capable.

2246 WILSAM. BY S. C. NETHERSOLE. New York: Macmillan, 1913 NUC. London: Mills & Boon, [1913] BMC NUC.

Tragic life of Mercy Pardilow. Her father had wronged her mother's sister before he ran off with Mercy's mother. (It was Hannah Anseed who helped the sister—Milly—through her hard pregnancy.) The infant Mercy survived the ship-wreck that took her mother's life. Story traces Mercy's life—the drudgery, heart-aches, obstacles, bitter trials of her marriage, the death of her child caused by her husband. At the very end, she has a chance for belated happiness.

NEWBERRY, FANNIE ELLSWORTH (STONE). 1848-1942. United States.

2247 THE IMPRESS OF A GENTLEWOMAN. Boston: Bradley and Woodruff, [c1891] NUC. London: Hutchinson, [1894] BMC.

A refined Christian woman Mrs. Raymond goes to a rough western United States town and works wonders in reforming the conditions of Acton—socially, morally, and physically.

2248 JOYCE'S INVESTMENTS. Boston: A. I. Bradley, 1899 NUC.

Joyce inherits a large fortune obtained dishonestly by her father; therefore, she takes her mother's maiden name and proceeds to introduce all types of reforms in the factories she now owns. She builds new homes for the workers and improves their working conditions. She is successful in all these endeavors and marries the man of her choice in the end.

2249 NOT FOR PROFIT. Boston: A.I. Bradley, [c1894] NUC.
New England spinster, Thirza Bascom, inherits money and opens a boarding house in Chicago for the benefit of her guests.

NEWTON, ALMA. United States.

2250 A JEWEL IN THE SAND. New York: Duffield, 1919 NUC.
Realistic story of career of brilliant woman whose talent brings her in touch with people who have no appreciaton of her. Men see in her another Lilith. The story involves her efforts to get away from these "friends." She loses her grip on life. An accident disfigures her face, but her spiritual vision overcomes her circumstances.

2251 MEMORIES. New York: Duffield, 1917 NUC.
Spiritual experience of Zarah Kreeshna who narrates her story. She and her closest woman friend Sarah love the same man. Since the man loves Sarah, Zarah helps bring them together—without bitterness.

NICHOLL, EDITH M. See BOWYER, EDITH M. (NICHOLL).

NICHOLSON, CELIA ANNA. United Kingdom.

2252 MARTIN, SON OF JOHN. London: Sidgwick & Jackson, 1918 BMC.
Wife deserts him; son murders him.

NICHOLSON, VICTORIA MARY SACKVILLE-WEST. 1892-1962. United Kingdom.

2253 HERITAGE. BY V. SACKVILLE-WEST. London: W. Collins Sons, [c1919] BMC NUC. New York: G.H. Doran, [c1919] NUC.
Two sides of Ruth Penniston's nature: the wild passionate side inherited from her grandmother who was a Spanish

dancer and the quiet English side. Her wild nature leads her to marry a cruel man with whom she is so miserable that she shoots (but does not kill) him. There is hope that she may marry a quiet middle-aged Englishman because her frightened husband leaves her. Two male narrators tell different parts of the story.

NICKLIN, CONSTANCE.

2254 THE HOUR AND THE WOMAN. London: Methuen, 1910 BMC.

A plain woman who has set her heart on marriage—any marriage—and is repeatedly disappointed. Her heart overflows with rancor and bitterness. She is in charge of a small girl whom she alternately loves and jealously hates—makes herself indispensable to the child in order to marry the father. "Gloomy."

NIKTO, VERA [pseud.].* United Kingdom.

2255 A MERE WOMAN. BY VERA NIKTO. New York: D. Appleton, 1913 NUC. London: Duckworth, 1913 BMC NUC.

Sonia tells the story of her childhood in Russia, the deadening boredom that led her to marry, the shock and horror of her marriage, her divorce from this man who drinks and in a rage almost kills her, the love of her life which ends brutally, and her marriage to a rich old merchant—because there's nothing else to do. This husband imposes a heartless restriction on her in the end, which is left inconclusive.

NIXSON, EDITH MAY MAYER.

2256 GOLDEN VANITY. BY MAISIE BENNETT. London: Mills & Boon, 1912 BMC.

From orphanage to domestic service to stage, and finally united with a lover.

NOBLE, ANNETTE LUCILE. 1844-1932. United States.

2257   RACHEL'S FARM. New York: American Tract Society, [c1894] NUC.

Rachel, an orphan who worked for her uncle as a typewriter, was constantly made aware of her dependent position. She accepts the offer of an aunt to make her farm her home, learns the daily work of the farm which she puts to use when she eventually inherits it.

NORMAN, MRS. GEORGE. See BLOUNT, MELESINA MARY.

NORRIS, KATHLEEN (THOMPSON). 1880-1966. United States.

2258   HARRIET AND THE PIPES. London: J. Murray, 1920 BMC. Garden City: Doubleday, Page, 1920 NUc.

Harriet, 29, is a governess working for the Carters. They divorce and she marries the husband.

2259   MARTIE, THE UNCONQUERED. Garden City, N. Y.: Doubleday, Page, 1917 NUC. London: J. Murray, 1918 BMC.

Points out the need for educating women for careers. Martie Monroe grows up in the stifling environment of a poor Southern family. She is heartbroken over her first love, makes a hurried marriage, has a child, and is left widowed and penniless in New York. She returns to her hometown where her family, her son, her admirers, and her own longing for self-expression make clashing claims. The last claim proves the strongest. She refuses two offers of marriage, goes to New York to live with her son, works on a newspaper. There is every promise for advancement in her work and happiness.

2260   THE RICH MRS. BURGOYNE. New York: Macmillan, 1912 BMC NUC.

A widow believed to be rich and her children move to a California town filled with women leading aimless lives. To the surprise of all, she becomes a worker and a reformer. Concludes with her marriage to a former sweetheart.

2261 SATURDAY'S CHILD. New York: Macmillan, 1914 NUC. London: Macmillan, 1914 BMC.

Susan works first as a bookkeeper, then as companion, then gets married and is happy doing her housework as wife, having learned that love means service and sacrifice. But before she reaches this view, she nearly elopes with a novelist who wants to divorce his wife for her.

2262 THE TREASURE. New York: Macmillan, 1914 BMC NUC.

The treasure is a servant who is a young woman with a college education in domestic science—the professional approach which Charlotte Perkins Gilman advocates. Although Mrs. Salisbury is forced to acknowledge her ability, she finds it difficult to reconcile her ideas of "mistress" and "help" to this superior young person. Humorous.

NORTH, LEIGH. See PHELPS, ELIZABETH STEWARD.

OAKLEY, HESTER CALDWELL. United States.

2263 AS HAVING NOTHING. New York and London: G. P. Putnam, 1898 NUC BMC.

Elizabeth has studied art in Europe, has a studio in New York and is a very successful book illustrator. She supports her mother. Her love story.

OBENCHAIN, ELIZA CAROLINE (CALVERT). 1856-1930. United States.

2264 AUNT JANE OF KENTUCKY. BY ELIZA CALVERT HALL. Boston: Little, Brown, 1907 NUC. London: Cassell, 1909 BMC.

"The good gospel of women's rights." Recollections of a wise old woman of her youth, her prime and the women she knew: those who bought the church organ though the men in the church opposed the purchase and Millie Amos who refused to sing "Sweet Day of Rest" in church because there is no day of rest for housewives like herself.

O'BRIEN, ALICE.

2265   ANTHONY   BLAKE'S   EXPERIMENT   [ANONYMOUS].
London: R. Bentley, 1896 BMC.

Armande, a French singer, married a novelist who was only interested in her for his writing. While she is in England with him, she discovers the marriage is irregular. She enters a convent for life, never acknowledging herself to her son as his mother.

O'BRIEN, MARY MARVIN (HEATON) VORSE. D. 1955. United States.

2266   AUTOBIOGRAPHY OF AN ELDERLY WOMAN. Boston: Houghton Mifflin, 1911 NUC.

Story of a woman growing old gracefully.

2267   I'VE   COME   TO   STAY: A   LOVE   COMEDY   OF BOHEMIA. New York: Century, 1918 BMC NUC.

Camilla Deerfield is a successful artist living in Greenwich Village. She means to hold off marriage until she has done a lot of living. Eventually she and her neighbor, a male writer, are brought together by a cat. Light and humorous.

OEMLER, MARIE (CONWAY). 1879-1932. United States.

2268   A WOMAN NAMED SMITH. New York: Century, 1919 BMC NUC. London: W. Heinemann, 1920 BMC.

A mystery story. All concerned parties live in Hynd's House run by two "damyankee" business women who take in boarders, manage to win the approval of the community, solve the mystery and find suitable mates. Humorous.

OHL, MAUDE ANNULET (ANDREWS). 1866-1943. United States.

2269   THE WIFE OF NARCISSUS. BY ANNULET ANDREWS. New York: Moffat, Yard, 1908 NUC.

Sophia Van Cort, in the form of a journal, tells of her unhappy marriage to an intensely selfish poet and their Bohemian life in New York.

OLDER, CORA MIRANDA (BAGGERLY). B. 1873. United States.

2270 THE SOCIALIST AND THE PRINCE. BY MRS. FREMONT OLDER. New York and London: Funk & Wagnalls, 1903 NUC BMC.

"Never was vanity so supreme" as in this woman "who drains life of senstion," fears nothing so much as boredom, and daringly reaches out for every new experience. She's ruthless in her disregard for convention, but never punished nor treated unsympathetically by the author.

OLDER, MRS. FREMONT. See OLDER, CORA MIRANDA (BAGGERLY).

OLIPHANT, MARGARET OLIPHANT (WILSON). 1828-1897. United Kingdom.

2271 THE CUCKOO IN THE NEST. BY MRS. OLIPHANT. London: Hutchinson, 1892 BMC NUC. New York: U. S. Book, [c1892] NUC.

Patty, a strong, fiery barmaid, marries Sir Giles' feeble-minded son for his fortune. She is good-natured and loving to her husband who is an alcoholic. After his son's death, Sir Giles makes her his heir. After Sir Giles' death, she routs with spirit those who thought they would benefit financially. But country society is cold to her, and she eventually marries for love, retaining only a part of Sir Giles' fortune.

2272 DIANA TRELAWNY: THE HISTORY OF A GREAT MISTAKE. Edinburgh: W. Blackwood, 1892 BMC NUC. (Also published as Diana; the History Of a Great Mistake. By Mrs. Oliphant. New York: U. S. Book [c1892] NUC.)

Diana, a schoolteacher of 30 unmarried and disinclined to marry inherits a fortune. She is practical and kind to all about her. She sends her aunt and niece to Italy for their health, then follows them. Their adventures.

2273 THE HEIR PRESUMPTIVE AND THE HEIR APPARENT. BY MRS. OLIPHANT. New York: J. W. Lovell, [1891] NUC. London: Macmillan, 1892 BMC.

Searching study of Mrs. Parks whose husband is the heir

presumptive. She attempts to murder a young boy, the heir apparent, to hold on to the fortune.

2274   JANET. London: Hurst and Blackett, 1891 NUC BMC.
Janet Summerhays is vain. Her position as governess soon turns humdrum. She attracts the attention of two men who rival for her affections.

2275   THE MARRIAGE OF ELINOR. BY MRS. OLIPHANT. London and New York: Macmillan, 1892 BMC NUC.
Elinor, a "fin de siecle" heroine, marries too hastily and is miserable. She leaves her husband, raises their son by herself. The husband returns eventually, "to worship at her feet" along with her son and a cousin.

2276   OLD MR. TREDGOLD. A STORY OF TWO SISTERS. BY MRS. M. O. W. OLIPHANT. New York: Longmans, Green, 1895 NUC. London: Longmans, 1896 BMC.
Story of Stella and her sister. Stella is a modern young woman who is a "comrade" to her suitor. One reviewer calls her a spoiled child; another says she "shrieks and fusses too much even for masculine nerves."

2277   THE RAILWAY MAN AND HIS CHILDREN. London: Macmillan, 1891 BMC. New York: Macmillan, 1891 NUC.
Evelyn Ferrance is middle-aged when she makes an "unromantic" marriage to a man with two older children by a first marriage. Interesting details of this domestic problem.

2278   THE SORCERESS: A NOVEL. BY MRS. OLIPHANT. London: F. V. White, 1893 BMC. New York: J. A. Taylor, [1893] NUC.
Laura Lance schemes, takes risks, does anything to get what she wants and succeeds. She marries the wealthy Colonel Kingswood after playing around with his son. "Adventurous as Laura is, Mrs. Oliphant claims our sympathy for her resourcefulness and courage." The men are not to be pitied.

OLIPHANT, MRS. See OLIPHANT, MARGARET OLIPHANT (WILSON).

OLIPHANT, MRS. M. O. W. See OLIPHANT, MARGARET OLIPHANT (WILSON).

OLIVER, AMY ROBERTA (RUCK). B. 1878. United Kingdom.

2279 THE COURTSHIP OF ROSAMUND FAYRE. BY BERTA RUCK. London: Hutchinson, 1915 BMC NUC.
About a club for young women. Rosamund a secretary writes love letters for her employer.

2280 THE DREAM DOMESTICATED. BY BERTA RUCK. New York: Harper's Bazar, 1918 NUC.
"Quiet and thoughtful," the story describes the heroine's education, career as a journalist and her unsuccessful marriage.

2281 THE GIRL WHO PROPOSED! London: Hodder & Stoughton, [1918] BMC.

2282 HIS OFFICIAL FIANCEE. BY BERTA RUCK (MRS. OLIVER ONIONS). New York: Dodd, Mead, 1914 NUC. London: Hutchinson, 1914 BMC. First person narrative of Monica Trout, typewriter, who is paid to pose as her employer's fiance for one year.

2283 IN ANOTHER GIRL'S SHOES. BY BERTA RUCK (MRS. OLIVER ONIONS). New York: Dodd, Mead, 1916 NUC. London: Hodder & Stoughton, [1917] BMC.
A governess and a movie actress exchange places, the former meeting the family of the other's husband as a widowed war-bride. Then he turns up. Comedy.

2284 THE LAD WITH WINGS. BY BERTA RUCK (MRS. OLIVER ONIONS). London: Hutchinson, 1915 BMC NUC. (Also published as The Boy With Wings. By Berta Ruck (Mrs. Onions). New York: Dodd, Mead, 1915 NUC.)
Gwenna Williams comes to London from Wales and moves from her first job as a "typewriter" to a more fascinating one as secretary to the Aeroplane Lady, head of an aircraft factory. She marries a pilot and, when he is

drafted, refuses to leave him. She takes his mechanic's place on the plane. Both are shot down and die.

2285   THE LAND-GIRL'S LOVE STORY. BY BERTA RUCK. London: Hodder & Stoughton, [1919] BMC. New York: Dodd, Mead, 1919 NUC.
Joan and Elizabeth are office workers in London. When Joan loses her job and learns her boyfriend is unfaithful, she and Elizabeth join the women's land army and work on a farm in Wales. In the end both marry. Elizabeth who was a man-hater proposes to the man she marries. Humorous, but the author has great admiration for England's women's land army.

2286   THE YEARS FOR RACHAEL. BY BERTA RUCK. London: Hodder & Stoughton, [1918] BMC. New York: Dodd, Mead, 1918 NUC.
Rachael, after waiting ten years for her fiance, goes to London at the outbreak of war and becomes a successful journalist. He has made a book of his love letters to her. When he finally comes back into her life, she refuses him.

OLMIS, ELISABETH. See LOOMIS, ANNIE ELISABETH.

O'NEILL, ROSE CECIL. B. 1873.

2287   THE LOVES OF EDWY. Boston: Lothrop, 1904 NUC.
Young woman goes on stage, has two suitors.

ONIONS, MRS. OLIVER. See OLIVER, AMY ROBERTA (RUCK).

ORCUTT, HARRIET E. United States.

2288   A MODERN LOVE STORY, WHICH DOES NOT END AT THE ALTAR. Chicago: C. H. Kerr, 1894 NUC BMC.
Not-so-young heroine devoted to art and theosophy and who hates housekeeping refuses to marry minister she loves on grounds of losing her independence. Chapters

record their conversations on the subject, the history of their eventual marriage and its results.

ORCZY, BARONESS EMMUSKA. See BARSTOW, EMMA MAGDALENA ROSALIA MARIA JOSEFA BARBARA ORCZY.

O'REILLY, ELEANOR GRACE.

2289   JOAN AND JERRY. London: W. & R. Chambers, 1891 NUC. New York: T. Whittaker, [1892] PW.
Joan runs a lodging house in London.

ORMEROD, MAUD W. United States.

2290   MADAM PARADOX: A NOVEL. New York: D. Biddle, [c1899] NUC.
Katharine Randolph writes for a magazine under the name of Madame Paradox. Believing her husband is dead, she falls in love with her editor. Her husband returns a physical wreck; Katharine cares for him while the editor waits.

ORPEN, ADELA ELIZABETH RICHARDS. United Kingdom.

2291   PERFECTION CITY. London: Hutchinson, 1897 BMC. New York: D. Appleton, 1897 NUC.
Madam Morozoff-Smith is the founder of a cooperative communist settlement in Kansas, a cause she takes up for the sake of her husband. Problems that arise when Olive joins the community break the settlement apart.

ORSHANSKI, G. (YSTRIDDE) YSTRIDDE.

2292   THREE DUKES. New York and London: G. P. Putnam's Sons, 1904 NUC. London: T. F. Unwin, 1905 BMC.
Three heroines—all governesses in Russia, one to a nobleman and his wife, both of whom are mad. She beats her grown daughter.

OSGOOD, IRENE (DE BELLOT). 1875-1922. United States.

2293 THE SHADOW OF DESIRE. New York: Cleveland, 1893 NUC.

"Unpleasantly suggestive" story of Ruth Parker, widowed at 18 after a year of marriage to a dissolute man twice her age. She makes a second marriage quickly, but "always influenced by her spasmodic and uncontrolled affections," she "gives back kisses hot and fast" to a new love. And when this man kills her second husband in a duel, Ruth rejects him and makes a third marriage to yet another man. "It simply astounds us that any woman could write such a book," says one reviewer.

2294 TO A NUN CONFESS'D. LETTERS FROM YOLANDE TO SISTER MARY. London: Sisley's, 1906 BMC.

Unhappy wife bares soul in letters to her friend who is a nun. Describes her liaison with another man, self-analysis by a victim of hopeless love. "Gushing."

OSMOND, SOPHIE.

2295 AN AUSTRALIAN WOOING. Letchworth: Garden City Press, 1916 BMC.

Australian heroine is killed while fighting Germans with a gyrating hand grenade from an airplane.

OSMUN, LEIGHTON GRAVES.* B. 1880. United States.

2296 THE CLUTCH OF CIRCUMSTANCE. New York: Sully & Kleinteich, 1914 NUC.

Ruth Lawson has been married for only a year when her husband is injured. She is faced with the need to support him and his mother. She goes to New York and becomes a successful actress. He eventually recovers, but believing that she has "fallen," refuses to see her. "When at last they meet, Ruth finds that the man is so changed that he is no longer the man she loved and she has to readjust her life."

OSTRANDER, ISABEL EGENTON. 1883-1924. United States.

2297　THE PRIMAL LAW. New York: M. Kennerly, 1915 BMC NUC.

Mary at 16 has been working in a factory for eight years, but she wants education and a better life. She goes off with a man who promises to hire a teacher for her and to buy her clothes. After that she goes from man to man. Ten years after she left the mill town she returns to use her money to better the conditions of the factory children.

2298　THE SINGLE TRACK. BY DOUGLAS GRANT. New York: W. J. Watt, [c1919] NUC.

Janetta is a rich young woman who undertakes hard work to save the family fortune. She "goes up, into the Klondike, outwits the family enemies, falls in love with the stalwart foreman and, with his able assistance, saves the mine."

2299　SUSPENSE. New York: R.M. McBride, 1918 NUC. London: Skeffington, [1919] BMC.

Betty Shaw—lonely, mysterious young woman with a birth scar on her cheek—risks her life by taking the position of secretary with a woman who heads a gang of crooks and who is blackmailing Betty's father. She has all the courage, tenacity and poise of a professional detective—like the one she ends up marrying.

OVERTON, ELLA EDERSHEIM.

2300　A LADY BORN. New York: E. & J. B. Young, 1893. London: Christian Knowledge Society, [1893] BMC.

Two orphan sisters consider themselves "ladies born." One fails as a governess because she puts on airs. The other succeeds as a house decorator. They eventually learn the truth about their mother's "station" in life.

OVERTON, GWENDOLEN. B. 1876. United States.

2301　ANNE CARMEL. New York and London: Macmillan, 1903 BMC NUC.

Anne Carmel is strong and sexually aggressive. She pursues the man she loves. Since he is in no position to marry, she dispenses with the ceremony. She is thoroughly fearless in face of the community's condemnation. Later when her lover returns married, she promises to go off with him. But she changes her mind either because she wants to save her priest-brother's reputation or because she has lost interest in the man.

2302   THE HERITAGE OF UNREST. New York: Macmillan, 1901 BMC NUC. London: Macmillan, 1901 NUC.
The author unsparingly denounces United States' actions toward Indians in her full character study of Felipa, part Apache. Felipa is a strong, wild, tumultuous woman, restless in spirit, made to adjust to the demands of civilized society. She's never loveable, but completely admirable, educated, intelligent and courageous to her death.

OVINGTON, MARY WHITE. 1865-1951. United States.

2303   THE SHADOW. New York: Harcourt, Brace & Howe, 1920 NUC.
Hertha, the child of an unmarried Southern woman, is raised in a family of Blacks, believing she is one of them. She is employed as a maid when she inherits a small legacy and learns her true parentage. She goes to New York and tries factory work, stenography and typing. She belongs to neither the white or black world and is very lonely. In the face of a lynch mob she affirms her relationship to her black brother.

OWEN, CAROLINE DALE. See SNEDEKER, CAROLINE DALE (PARKE).

OWEN, MARGUERITE (DE GODART) CUNLIFFE. 1859-1927. United Kingdom.

2304   THE CRADLE OF THE ROSE. BY THE AUTHOR OF THE MARTYRDOM OF AN EMPRESS [ANONYMOUS]. London and New York: Harper, 1908 BMC NUC.
Lady Clanvowe, the wife of an English diplomat, returns to her native Brittany when her husband is called to Asia. She studies the conditions of her people and eventually

becomes the instigator of an insurrection in which she loses her life.

2305 THE TRIBULATIONS OF A PRINCESS; WITH PORTS. FROM PHOTOS. BY THE AUTHOR OF THE MARTYRDOM OF AN EMPRESS [ANONYMOUS]. London and New York: Harper, 1901 NUC BMC.

Raised as a boy, contracted to a marriage at 15, this dashing and courageous woman of the world likes to try the most dangerous forms of horseback riding. Her daredevil adventures and the hardships and perils of the life of an army nurse.

P., A. N. T. A. A. N. T. A. P. [pseud.].*

2306 THEORIES. STUDIES FROM A MODERN WOMAN. London: T. F. Unwin, 1894 BMC. (Independent Novel Series.)

Modern young woman filled with enthusiasm for social reform is disillusioned when the training she gives her children miscarries. She is similar to Marcella, says reviewer, only more impulsive with a less disciplined mind. The modern theories (such as socialism) don't work out for her. "Such women as Beatrice do more harm to the good cause they would serve than is wrought by any amount of masculine opacity and opposition."

PAGE, GERTRUDE. See DOBBIN, GERTRUDE (PAGE).

PAGET, MRS. GERALD.

2307 GOING THROUGH THE MILL. London: Brown, Langham, 1908 BMC.

The narrator, an intelligent 40 year old woman, is so stimulated and emancipated by the Great Teacher that she throws off all merely conventional views and champions the claims of women. The Great Teacher is an "Ideal"; her love for humanity cannot be claimed by any one person. She appears to the narrator in her astral body and sends a dream which depicts a young woman sentenced to death by a jury of unrefined men. The dream prophesies the appointment of female judges.

PAHLOW, GERTRUDE CURTIS BROWN. 1881-1937. United States.

2308 THE CROSS OF HEARTS DESIRE. New York: Duffield, 1916 NUC. London: Methuen, 1918 BMC.

Marcia's development from a "beautiful bore" to an alert and interesting person. She had been taught that "woman's beauty is her power," had been raised traditionally. She leaves a comfortable family to work in New York, finds happiness in her work.

2309 THE GILDED CHRYSALIS; A NOVEL. New York: Duffield, 1914 NUC.

The heroine marries a college professor. Their marriage is unhappy, and she leaves him to work on a farm. She "finds herself"; they are eventually reconciled.

2310 THE GLORY OF GOING ON. New York: Duffield, 1919 NUC.

A strong independent young woman's struggle—both as a married and as a single woman. She is determined to be a singer. At first she fails, becomes disillusioned and marries a tyrant of a man who generally makes life miserable for her. She gets a divorce and lives with her two children, meets a man she really loves but who is killed in the war. At the end of the novel, she is again inspired to make a career in music.

PAIN, AMELIA (LEHMANN). D. 1920. United Kingdom.

2311 SAINT EVA. London: Osgood, 1897 BMC. New York: Harper, 1897 NUC.

Painful story of a saintly country girl—Eva Corona. Born in Italy but raised in a primitive English home: her dreary existence there, her love of solitude and appreciation of beauty, her first sexual feelings and love for the "odious"

Clayton Seaford who meant nothing by the kiss she took so seriously, and her death. Her final letter to him "is one of the most pathetic things in this kind of fiction."

PAINTER, LYDIA (HOYT) FARMER. 1842-1903. United States.

2312 AUNT BELINDY'S POINTS OF VIEW, AND A MODERN MRS. MALAPROP: TYPICAL CHARACTER SKETCHES. BY LYDIA HOYT FARMER. New York: Merriam, [c1895] NUC.
Two women discuss women's clubs and women's suffrage. Aunt Belinda and her husband argue the "woman question" from all sides, among other issues of the day.

PAN. See BERESFORD, LESLIE.

PANSY. See ALDEN, ISABELLA (MACDONALD).

PANTON, JANE ELLEN (FRITH). 1848-1923.

2313 THE RIVER OF YEARS. BY THE AUTHOR OF "LEAVES FROM A LIFE" [ANONYMOUS]. London: Heath Cranton, [1916] BMC.
"Quiet and thoughtful," the story describes the heroine's education, career as a journalist, and unsuccessful marriage.

PARKER, AGNES. United States.

2314 THE REAL MADELEINE POLLARD: A DIARY OF TEN WEEKS' ASSOCIATION WITH THE PLAINTIFF IN THE FAMOUS BRECKINRIDGE-POLLARD SUIT. AN INTIMATE STUDY OF CHARACTER. New York: G. W. Dillingham, 1894 NUC.
Purports to have been written by a female detective who gained access to the home in which Miss Pollard resided during the trial, won her affection and confidence, and by a constant scrutiny of her words and actions tried to determine the exact sort of woman she really was.

PARKER, FRANCES. B. 1875. United States.

2315 HOPE HATHAWAY; A STORY OF WESTERN RANCH
LIFE. Boston: C. M. Clark, 1904 NUC.

Hope refuses to marry the man her parents have chosen
for her; she leaves home and becomes a school teacher.

PARKER, MARGARET.

2316 THE DESIRE OF THEIR HEARTS: A NOVEL. London:
Jarrold, 1899 BMC.

Marjorie studies art in Rome after she loses a fortune and,
consequently, a fiance. She considers painting Tennyson's
women as she envisioned them. Suitable for girls.

PARKER, NELLA.

2317 THE MISTAKE OF MONICA. London: G. Routledge,
[1899] BMC.

She's a musician, pushed into marriage to please her aunt.
"After supporting the wrong man in comfort until he
becomes insupportable," she turns her attention to a
former lover and all is made right when her husband
bicycles into a stone wall.

PARKES, ELIZABETH (ROBINS). 1862-1952. United States.

2318 CAMILLA. BY ELIZABETH ROBINS. London: Hodder &
Stoughton, New York: Dodd, Mead, 1918 NUC.

She is 28; travelling alone abroad, she has separated from
and then divorced her husband. She is now engaged to
marry another man, but wants time to think before their
marriage. Though her fiance objects, she returns to the
United States, meets with her ex-husband, and is almost
reconciled to him when he makes the mistake of saying,
"Women as companions are a failure." She marries the
other man.

2319 THE CONVERT. BY ELIZABETH ROBINS. New York:
Macmillan, 1907 NUC. London: Methuen, 1907 BMC
NUC.

Vida Levering leads an aimless existence in the social circle of Parliament and Cabinet figures, where she hears much talk of "sexless suffragettes who spit at police." One day, by accident, she hears a suffragette speak and is amazed at her intelligence. She attends more meetings and is soon converted to an active member of the movement. The novel is a stirring plea for suffrage.

2320   A DARK LANTERN: A STORY WITH A PROLOGUE. BY ELIZABETH ROBINS (C. E. RAIMOND). New York and London: Macmillan, 1905 NUC BMC.

After wasting much of her youth on a fantasy love for a prince, Katharine, a passionate yet firm, steady high-minded woman, refuses his degrading offer of a morganatic marriage (in which a wife has no claim on her husband's wealth); yet later she marries a brute and allows herself to be dominated. The author strips all disguise from the love passion in women in this study of the problem of separate standards of morality for men and women.

2321   THE FLORENTINE FRAME. BY ELIZABETH ROBINS. New York: Moffat, Yard, 1909 NUC. London: J. Murray, 1909 BMC.

Study of a mother and daughter both modern women. Eugenia Rosco knows what she wants and goes after it directly. In her relations with men, she is always the aggressive one. Her mother Isabella is a woman who knows she has had no chance to live. She remained married to a husband she did not love only for her daughter's sake. She has never had a picture of the right man to put in the frame she carries. Mother and daughter become rivals when they fall in love with the same man. Both assume he loves Eugenia whom he marries, but after her mother's death, Eugenia learns that her husband really loved her mother.

2322   GEORGE MANDEVILLE'S HUSBAND. BY C. E. RAIMOND. London: W. Heinemann, 1894 NUC BMC. New York: D. Appleton, 1894 NUC.

Lois Carpenter, after her marriage, adopted the name George Mandeville and determined to be a novelist, with the missions of progress and women's emancipation. She is married to an artist, very weak and somewhat of a maunderer. George is described as "stout, frowsy, slatternly, at rehearsals of her play roaring directions at all." "To sit down daily to the task of being George Eliot, to rise up the average lady novelist to the end, must, even if only dimly perceived, be a soul-tragedy of no mean proportion." The husband suffers much and turns to Rosina, their daughter; "there is much pathos in their furtive conclaves in the box room." Rosina dies; most reviewers blame George. One reviewer contrasts the husband's "scrupulous cleanliness and love of personal seemliness" with George's "unfeminine squalor of person and mind."

2323 THE MESSENGER: A NOVEL. BY ELIZABETH ROBINS. London: Hodder & Stoughton, [1919] BMC. New York: Century, 1919 NUC.
Concerns the war and pacifism. Greta is a German governess, a spy who matches skill and daring with Scotland Yard, a woman of quick wit, power of self command, and lack of scruples.

2324 THE MILLS OF THE GODS. BY ELIZABETH ROBINS. New York: Moffat, Yard, 1908 NUC. London: T. Butterworth, 1920 BMC.
The story of a woman's revenge after 30 years on an Italian nobleman.

2325 MY LITTLE SISTER. BY ELIZABETH ROBINS. New York: Dodd, Mead, 1913 NUC. (Also published as "Where Are You Going To...?" By Elizabeth Robins. London: W. Heinemann, 1913 BMC NUC. Leipzig: B. Tauchnitz, 1913 NUC.)
Bettina's sister narrates the horror story of white slavery. Bettina is an extremely innocent, sheltered unsophisticated young woman when she and her older sister travel to London on their aunt's invitation. But the woman who meets them is not their aunt but a woman who traffics in white slaves. The older sister escapes and tries to rescue Bettina, but Bettina is gone, as though the earth had swallowed her up.

2326 THE OPEN QUESTION: A TALE OF TWO TEMPERAMENTS. BY C. E. RAIMOND. London: W. Heinemann, 1899 NUC BMC. New York and London: Harper, 1899 NUC.

Val brims with life, wants to experience everything, yearns for love and fame. She falls in love with and marries cousin Ethan, a decadent weakling. Because they have both inherited TB, they agree on double suicide if Val gets pregnant. She does. The novel ends as they sail out to sea. Val's mother-in-law is a study of a powerful ruling woman; in dying, she pulls the sheet over her face.

2327 UNDER THE SOUTHERN CROSS. BY ELIZABETH ROBINS. New York: F. A. Stokes, [1907] BMC NUC.

"Ultra-independent" young woman describes her sea and land voyage. She meets an ocean liner man with old-fashioned ideas of women's dependence. "Half-veiled touch of satire."

PARKMAN, SUSAN.

2328 TWO NOBLE WOMEN. New York: American Tract Soc., [c1897] NUC.

Wife of famous judge and wife of humble tinner join forces for social betterment of several of the poor woman's neighbors "who have fallen from grace."

PARKS, MABEL E. B. 1862.

2329 A SOUL'S LOVE LETTER. BY MABEL. Westwood, Mass.: Ariel Press, 1904 NUC.

"Her demands for social justice reveal the reformer."

PARR, OLIVE KATHARINE. 1874-1955. United Kingdom.

2330 A RED-HANDED SAINT. New York: Benziger, 1909 NUC. London: Washbourne, 1909 NUC.

Title refers to a murderer who becomes a prison visitor on her release from jail. Concerns London slums and Roman Catholicism.

PARRISH, GLADYS. See HUNTINGTON, GLADYS THEODORA (PARRISH).

PARRY, D. H.*

2331 FOR GLORY AND RENOWN. London: Cassell, 1895 BMC.

Marion Ascough growing up in French quarter of Montreal has great beauty that brings as much disaster as good fortune. Goes to Boston to make a career in art world. Has difficult time earning a living posing, moves to New York, finally marries an artist.

PARSONS, FLORENCE MARY (WILSON). 1864-1934.

2332 OVER THE EDGE. London: E. Macdonald, 1915 BMC.

Christian Guildersleeve is a study of a mentally disturbed woman. She loves one man, but when she learns he is married, she marries his brother. Then the darkness begins to set in, with her lost hopes and regrets, her envies and suspicions, her fears and hatred. The whole world seems against her.

PARUK, OLGA.

2333 BEWARE OF PURDAH—A STUDY OF MAHOMMEDAN MARRIAGE. London: Simpkin, Marshall, Hamilton, Kent, 1916 NUC BMC.

Describes the suffering the author says she knows from experience to await an Englishwoman entering a Moslem marriage.

PASTON, GEORGE. See SYMONDS, EMILY MORSE.

PATCH, KATE (WHITING). 1870-1909. United States.

2334 BECAUSE YOU ARE YOU. New York: Dodd, Mead, 1913 NUC.

Jane Spindler is a tired school teacher who goes to board with a spinster in order to restore her health.

PATERSON, ISABEL (BOWLER). 1885-1960. Canada.

2335　THE MAGPIE'S NEST. New York: J. Lane, 1917 NUC. London: J. Lane, 1917 BMC NUC.

Independent, fascinating young artist born in the Rockies comes to New York to make her fortune. Hope Fielding is in search of happiness, which like the magpie's nest, is always just out of reach. "It is difficult to fancy any imprudence of which she was not guilty or any accepted code of womanly virtue that she was not willing to throw over the windmills." She shudders at the "essential brutality" of the permanence of marriage. The author approves of Hope completely, but yet bows to convention at the end with a traditional happy ending.

2336　THE SHADOW RIDERS. London: J. Lane, 1916 BMC NUC. New York: J. Lane, 1916 NUC.

Lesley Johns, a journalist "possessing much cultivation and knowledge," is "persecuted by a married man." One reviewer says that the author regards men as a bad lot, and quotes her as saying, "Perhaps it is that secret sense of guilt in common which makes for the solidarity of men as a sex; they are all outlaws together." Another reviewer notes that the characters and situations described "go far toward indicating that the age old ideals of feminine conduct are fast crumbling to dust."

PATON, J. L.*

2337　A HOME IN INVERESK. London: Methuen, 1896 BMC.

Marion, after discussing Carlyle, Spencer, Darwin and Huxley with him, marries Nigel, only to discover he is the father of an illegitimate child. She is so horrified that Nigel flees to America in remorse. Eventually she decides to forgive him and goes to America to find him. Here she encounters new suspicions, but they prove groundless.

PATRICK, DIANA. See WILSON, DESEMEA (NEWMAN).

PATTERSON, MARJORIE. D. 1948. United States.

2338 THE DUST OF THE ROAD. A NOVEL. New York: H. Holt, 1913 NUC. London: Chatto & Windus, 1913 BMC.

Tony, a young American actress goes to England and joins a Shakespearean touring company. She is an unconventional, ambitious woman who loves her work which is the subject of the novel, but she gives it up at the end apparently to marry a sculptor turned actor.

PAULINA ELIZABETH OTTILIA LOUISA, QUEEN CONSORT OF CHARLES I, KING OF RUMANIA. 1843-1916. Rumania.

2339 EDLEEN VAUGHN: OR PATHS OF PERIL. A NOVEL. BY CARMEN SYLVA. New York: Cassell, [c1891] NUC. London: F. V. White, 1892 BMC.

Story of maternal devotion to a worthless son which is so extreme that the mother allows a servant to go to prison, robs her husband, and finally goes to a premature grave. "The fiction of the last quarter of a century has proved that women will rush in where the average man would fear to tread...."

PAYN, E. M.*

2340 HER STEWARDSHIP. London: Digby, Long, 1914 BMC.

The heroine is raised by her grandfather as a boy so that she will inherit the estate. She maintains her disguise for the rest of her life, although there are complications when she falls in love with the rightful heir.

PAZ, MAGDELEINE (LEGENDRE).

2341 WOMAN. BY MAGDELEINE MARX. New York: T. Seltzer, 1920 NUC. London: G. Allen & Unwin, 1921 BMC. (Tr. by A. S. Seltzer.)

In this novel narrated by a nameless heroine, the author defends women's multiple love relationships and financial independence. She cries out against "the fallacy of the maternal instinct." The woman is a factory worker in war-time.

PEARD, FRANCES MARY. 1835-1923. United Kingdom.

2342 THE BARONESS: A DUTCH STORY. London: R. Bentley, 1892 BMC NUC.

Marriage between Dutch baron and French woman has not been happy; she has taken the "advice of a sinister friend" and obtained a separation. Under Dutch law this is possible if the husband has been violent, and after five years the marriage is dissolved by default if the husband and wife do not appear in court. Story opens here. They are finally reunited; Hilvardine Steen remains the baroness' faithful friend throughout her trouble.

2343 THE CAREER OF CLAUDIA. London: R. Bentley, 1897 BMC.

Claudia's onslaught on the old ways, her self-sufficiency and belief in her own powers qualify her as a new woman. She is well educated, competent, and dedicated to devoting herself to a profession. She becomes a landscape gardener, but marries in the end. "We like her much better at her landscape gardening, and so too, we suspect, did the author....The magazine public would never tolerate a girl who succeeded at landscape gardening."

2344 CATHERINE: A NOVEL. New York: Harper, 1893 NUC. London: Innes, 1894 BMC.

Catherine Armstrong gives up a young soldier for a rich man who loves only her pretty face. Then she falls from a horse while hunting, and her face is disfigured for life. Story traces the difficult adjustments she must make. In the end she marries the former admirer who loved her for herself. Set in small English village, early 1800's.

PEARL, BERTHA. See MOORE, BERTHA PEARL.

PEARN, VIOLET A.

2345 SEPARATE STARS. London: J. Murray, 1910 BMC.

Joan, a painter devoted to her art, gives it up to marry a man who plays cricket. When he dies, she has hopes for her son as an artist. When these hopes are shattered, she refuses a second offer of marriage and, now a mature woman, takes up art again.

PEATTIE, ELIA (WILKINSON). 1862-1935. United States.

2346 THE BELEAGUERED FOREST. New York: D. Appleton, 1901 BMC NUC.

Regina, a lonely sensitive artist, keeps a studio and lives a Bohemian life till her small savings run out. She marries a lumberjack she hardly knows because life in a lumber camp with 70 loggers promises excitement. Her brief loveless marriage, her efforts to help her addict husband and his death are the record of her growth and great strength. Her story ends with her lone exit from the forest.

2347 THE PRECIPICE: A NOVEL. Boston: Houghton Mifflin, 1914 NUC.

Kate, in spite of her family's objections, goes to college and develops a career as a social worker. Then she falls in love and faces the inevitable conflict. Both she and the man refuses to give up career for marriage, and they solve the problem by marrying and living in separate cities. A "novel dealing almost wholly with the feminist problems of the day. In its chief character it dramatizes the opposing calls to woman of love and the independent career and attempts to reconcile the two. It pictures other phases of the modern feminine unrest in other characters."

PECHELL, MARY, jt. au. See DICKSON, F. THORALD AND MARY PECHELL.

PECK, THEODORA AGNES. B. 1882. United States.

2348 THE SWORD OF DUNDEE. A TALE OF "BONNIE PRINCE CHARLIE". New York: Duffield, 1908 NUC.

Historical romance in which the "gallant" heroine "convoys" the prince across the sea and "wields the sword with effect."

2349 WHITE DAWN; A LEGEND OF TICONDEROGA. New York: F.H. Revell, [c1914] NUC.

An historical romance of Lake Champlain and the armies of Wolfe and Montcalm, in which the "heroine plays an important part in the war."

PEEL, DOROTHY CONSTANCE (BAYLIFF). United Kingdom.

2350 THE HAT SHOP. BY MRS. C. S. PEEL. London: J. Lane, 1914 BMC NUC. New York: J. Lane, 1914 NUC.

Mrs. Earl, a widow, opens a hat shop in the West End of London. She does so not only because she must support herself but also because it provides her with an interesting occupation. The story describes the internal organization and operation of the shop, the struggles of the employees and the customers from both sides of the counter.

2351 MRS. BARNET-ROBES. BY MRS. C. S. PEEL. London: J. Lane, 1915 BMC NUC. New York: J. Lane, 1915 NUC.

Nellie, a young dressmaker, is seduced, made pregnant, and abandoned, but she is determined that her child not be hurt. She buys a ring, takes the name of Mrs. Barnet and opens a modest dressmaking establishment. The novel concerns her daughter Gladys and Anthea Selincourt, daughter of the man who seduced Nellie. Anthea is a nervous, passionate, neurotic person who kills herself when she fails to win the married man she loves. Gladys is a healthy, normal and prosperous young woman who earns a good income as a fashionplate artist and who marries the man of her choice.

2352 A MRS. JONES. BY MRS. C. S. PEEL. London and New York: J. Lane, 1916 NUC BMC.

Dot is an unhappy, restless wife who leaves her husband and says, "I have taken nothing from my husband that he ever had."

PEEL, MRS. C. S. See PEEL, DOROTHY CONSTANCE (BAYLIFF).

PEILE, PENTLAND.*

2353 THE BLUFFSHIRE COURIER. A WEST HIGHLAND STORY. Edinburgh: W. Blackwood, 1909 BMC.

Miranda Ross owns and runs the provincial newspaper. She becomes radical in her ideas, proclaiming "land for the people" and "abolition of all remaining feudal encumbrances." She marries in the end.

PEMBERTON, JEANNETTE. United States.

2354 BUFFETING. New York: Dodd, Mead, [c1892] NUC.

The financial struggles of a widow and her two daughters after the father's death. They continue to maintain a large house they can't afford to heat and keep the servants because they can't do the work. The story is narrated by one of the daughters who despises their false position. She would like to enter a learned profession but instead must become a governess.

PENDERED, MARY LUCY. 1858-1940. United Kingdom.

2355 DAISY THE MINX. A DIVERSION. London: W.J. Ham-Smith, 1911 BMC.

A music hall artist but the regular fare of love, impersonation, etc.

2356 DUST AND LAURELS. A STUDY IN NINETEENTH CENTURY WOMANHOOD. London: Griffith and Farran, 1893 BMC. New York: D. Appleton, 1894 NUC.

Veronica Grace, middle-aged, single, meets Sylvia Grant at a university extension meeting. The two become good friends and live together. Veronica has many involvements with men because of her "too keen appreciation of masculine charms." In the end she marries a younger man, inferior to herself "in order to escape from a temptation from which her better self revolts." She is a brilliant social success and a famous author, with the world at her feet, and she founds a free college for women.

2357 AN ENGLISHMAN. London: Methuen, 1899 BMC.

Maria chooses to be a governess in order to earn her own living. She is of "aristocratic birth" but chooses to marry a grocer.

2358 MUSK OF ROSES. FROM THE EGO BOOK OF DELIA WYCOMBE. London: Cassell, 1903 BMC.

Retired singer married to gentleman farmer—a philistine who falls asleep during her performance.

2359 A PASTORAL PLAYED OUT. London: W. Heinemann, 1895 BMC. New York: Cassell, [c1895] NUC.

Gylda Mariold, young, inexperienced woman from the country, consents to live with Conway Etheredge when she is 17. Because of debts, he marries a Russian princess. Gylda worried and desperate murders her own child. She starts out alone as a washer-woman but ends as a great actress, a dazzling woman of the world, and is reunited with Conway, when his wife becomes more interested in theosophy than in him and decides Gylda is the better mate for him. Gylda's consciousness of the wrongs done to women develops rapidly. At the end she is on the platform reciting a Ballad of Women, her own composition. Theme: man is the monster and marriage the bugbear.

2360 THE SECRET SYMPATHY. London: Chapman & Hall, 1916 BMC.

A traditional plot with a missing heir, but Katherine, a "chauffeuse," and her sister live together independently.

PENNELL, ELIZABETH (ROBINS). 1855-1936.

2361 THE LOVERS. Philadelphia: J. B. Lippincott, 1917 PW. London: W. Heinemann, 1917 BMC NUC.

Both the heroine and hero are artists.

2362 OUR HOUSE AND THE PEOPLE IN IT. Boston: Houghton Mifflin, 1910 NUC. London: T. F. Unwin, 1910 BMC.

Describes experiences with socialists, suffragettes, domestics, and other help.

PENNINGTON, PATIENCE. See PRINGLE, ELIZABETH WATIES (ALLSTON).

PENNY, F. E. See PENNY, FANNY EMILY (FARR).

PENNY, FANNY EMILY (FARR). D. 1939. United Kingdom.

2363 DESIRE AND DELIGHT. BY F. E. PENNY. London: Chatto & Windus, 1919 BMC NUC.

Rosemary goes to India to marry Maurice Edenhope of the Indian Medical Service. She sees that he is a changed man from the horrors he has seen and therefore suggests the wedding be postponed. But he marries her, then promptly neglects her. Rosemary puts him out of her life. She changes her name, throws off her wedding ring, becomes a V.A.D. nurse, and even pits her art and courage against a harem gang; playing on their superstition, she poses as a white witch and gets the better of them. In the end when her husband is himself again, she rejoins him.

2364 LOVE BY AN INDIAN RIVER. London: Chatto & Windus, 1916 BMC.

India. The main theme is its superstitions. An American woman runs a fruit canning business.

2365 LOVE IN A PALACE. London: Chatto & Windus, 1915 BMC.

Concerns women in India. One woman marries an Indian schooled in England. By custom they have not seen each other before the wedding. She is blind and when her new husband learns of this, he realizes his duty is to love and cherish her more. Other Indian women are depicted in the seclusion of their personal lives, and the inner life of harem women is shown to be influenced by Western traditions.

PENROSE, MARY ELIZABETH (LEWIS). B. 1860. United Kingdom.

2366 AS DUST IN THE BALANCE. BY MRS. H. H. PENROSE. London: A. Rivers, 1905 BMC.

A woman very unhappily married leaves her husband, an

impossibly self-righteous person. Her sister is contemptuous of her action.

2367 DENIS TRENCH. A PLOTLESS HISTORY OF HOW HE FOLLOWED THE GLEAM AND WORKED OUT HIS SALVATION. BY MRS. H. H. PENROSE. London: A. Rivers, 1911 BMC NUC.

Grace Diston is an "insufferably perfect literary woman" who shows up her husband as a "prig"; Stella Trench is an alcoholic who parted from her husband on her wedding day. But focus is on Denis.

2368 THE GREY ABOVE THE GREEN. BY MRS. H. H. PENROSE. London: Hodder & Stoughton, [1908] BMC.

The heroine becomes a successful dramatist and marries happily.

2369 THE HOUSE OF RENNEL. BY MRS. H. H. PENROSE. London: A. Rivers, 1913 NUC BMC.

Single man, a "scamp," gets sister-in-law's maid pregnant. When the maid dies, the sister-in-law raises her child as her own. The problems that arise.

2370 RACHEL THE OUTSIDER. BY MRS. H. H. PENROSE. London: Chapman & Hall, 1906 BMC.

Rachel is an orphan who becomes a successful novelist and marries happily in what one reviewer describes as an "old-fashioned domestic" and another as a "searching novel of character."

2371 THE UNEQUAL YOKE: A STUDY IN TEMPERAMENTS. BY MRS. H. H. PENROSE. London: A. Rivers, 1905 BMC.

Insightful study of the personalities of a woman and her minister husband. She has no sympathy at all for his "cramped theology," and her attitudes shock the parish.

PENROSE, MRS. H. H. See PENROSE, MARY ELIZABETH (LEWIS).

PENROSE, S. E.*

2372 VICTORIA'S VICISSITUDES. London: Simpkin, Marshall, [1912] BMC.

After a period in Germany in the position of governess, Victoria returned to marry the man she had left behind.

PERCIVAL, DOROTHY.

2373 FOOTSTEPS. London: J. Lane, 1918 BMC NUC. New York: J. Lane, 1918 NUC BMC.

Daphne, "has become embittered, degenerated into a sort of feminist and old maid." She goes to the Canary Islands with her father to regain his fortune. Their experience there causes her hatred and distrust of men to grow.

PERKS, LILY.

2374 LIFE'S COUNTERPOINT. London: C. A. Pearson, 1903 BMC.

"Passionate, unstable" woman becomes a great opera singer.

PERRIN, ALICE (ROBINSON). 1867-1934. United Kingdom.

2375 THE HAPPY HUNTING GROUND. London: Methuen, 1914 BMC. Leipzig: B. Tauchnitz, 1914 NUC.

The heroine, after an unhappy love affair, goes to India with the business-like intention of putting herself on the marriage market. But she accepts her lover's proposal almost absent-mindedly, her resolve having failed. An illustration of the dilemma of the moneyless young woman: whether or not to marry.

2376 IDOLATRY. New York: Duffield, 1909 NUC. London: Chatto & Windus, 1909 BMC NUC.

Anne Criviner seeks her mother in missionary work in India. Includes her love story.

2377 INTO TEMPTATION. London: F. V. White, 1894 BMC.

In autobiographical form, story describes the life of a young woman who marries an older man and goes to India with him, in order to get away from an unkind home. He turns out to be foolish and disagreeable; she enters into "pronounced flirtations." He dies; she returns to England and is offered marriage by a man she almost loves. She chooses to live alone in a flat in London.

2378   STAR OF INDIA. London: Cassell, 1919 BMC.

At 17, Stella Carrington is bored almost to despair with her life in a genteel English village. She longs to move to India, for she is part Indian. When she marries an elderly colonel, she moves to India where she is shocked to see women and children massacred. She falls in love with a young writer. The second part of the novel shows her efforts toward political reforms.

2379   THE WOMAN IN THE BAZAAR. London: Cassell, 1914 BMC 1926 NUC.

Innocent, the daughter of a vicar, is married to Captain Coventry, a selfish husband who has divorced his first wife for infidelity. When a roue threatens their happiness, this marriage also would have ended in disaster if he had not been awakened by seeing his abandoned first wife playing the part of a courtesan. "Painful theme—the future of a divorced woman abandoned by her lover."

PETERSON, MARGARET ANN. 1883-1933. United Kingdom.

2380   BLIND EYES. London: A. Melrose, 1914 BMC NUC. Chicago: Browne & Howell, 1914 NUC.

Demonstrates the cruelty of letting young women grow up ignorant of sex. Cynthia Weston at 17 is completely unsophisticated. She knows absolutely nothing about the "facts of life." When she becomes engaged, she has her illusions about life and men ruthlessly shattered by her fiance's sister who learns how naive Cynthia is. She is so shocked that she breaks her engagement, becomes very withdrawn and depressed, and narrowly misses ruining her whole life.

2381   BUTTERFLY WINGS. London: Hurst and Blackett, 1916 BMC.

Stella, an artist, is friends with Billy, who loves Peggy who loves another. When Stella comes to love Billy, she tells him, and they live together, Billy concealing that he still loves Peggy. When Peggy, disillusioned with her first choice, seeks out Billy, a tragedy occurs—but all is straightened out by the war.

2382   LOVE'S BURDEN. London: Hurst & Blackett, 1918 BMC.
Margot, who has always admired and appreciated her self-sacrificing and humble mother, marries unhappily and learns "the un-wisdom of futile self-sacrifice."

2383   THE SWORD-POINTS OF LOVE. London: Hurst & Blackett, [1919] BMC.
The light tone of the opening gives way to tragedy with Mavis' marriage. She is half forced to marry and move to Uganda where her life is full of squalor, cruelty and terror. Shut up in the wilderness, she is forced to watch her husband flog the natives. He is brutal in his treatment of her. She blazes out fiercely against his brutality, but holds back her hatred for the sake of her unborn child. Her husband dies, but there is no conventional happy end.

2384   "TO LOVE". London: Hurst & Blackett, 1915 BMC.
Struggle of an untrained young woman from a village to earn her living and the sordid conditions of such a life. Joan Rutherford is cultured and educated but untrained for work. She gets tired of having nothing to do; she wants the freedom that comes with a good-paying job. She meets a man who betrays her. She then marries a doctor who helps her through her suffering.

PETTER, EVELYN BRANSCOMBE.*

2385   MISS VELANTY'S DISCLOSURE. London: Chapman & Hall, 1916 BMC NUC.
Gretchen is mutinous, independent, aggressive, sensitive, fastidious, and intolerant. She rebels publicly at boarding school, is taken in by an English religious fanatic and his wife, rebels, works for a feminist (as her secretary) and falls for older German man. When her employer resents this, she marries him. Leaves him a few months later when she discovers he has a wife already. Then falls in love with an Englishman but this doesn't work out. Her tragedy is to be a German out of place.

2386 SCOPE. London: Chapman & Hall, 1916 BMC.
Describes scope offered to and accepted by Kate Carruth for wider life than she found in her native country town—"in a strangely concerted marriage which led through tragedy to a subtle development." Sombre, fresh, sincere.

PETTUS, MAIA. 1875-1956. United States.

2387 MEDA'S HERITAGE. New York: Neale, 1906 NUC.
A woman preacher in the South.

PHELPS, ELIZABETH STEWARD. United States.

2388 ARTHUR NORRIS; OR, A MODERN KNIGHT. BY LEIGH NORTH. Milwaukee: Young Churchman, 1915 NUC.
A young woman marries her friend and both become missionaries in China.

PHELPS, ELIZABETH STUART. See WARD, ELIZABETH STUART (PHELPS).

PHILLIMORE, MRS. C. E.

2389 A MILLION FOR A SOUL: A NOVEL OF ANGLO-INDIAN LIFE. London: J. Long, 1915 BMC.
A young woman under stress of work takes to drinking. She marries and is ultimately cured of her drinking habit.

PHILLIPS, F. EMILY.

2390 THE EDUCATION OF ANTONIA. London: Macmillan, 1895 BMC.
"Essentially a woman's book, it is written in the main from the standpoint of impotent sympathy with the sufferings of women who, handicapped by disabilities of sex, have to compete with men in the struggle for life." The tone is "often bitter." "Another omnipresent fault is that inartistic excess of details of minor feminine

experience of which we have complained before." Antonia expresses all the author's ideas.

2391 THE MAN OF THE FAMILY: A STORY OF FORTUNAUS AND THE BARBARIANS. London: Macmillan, 1898 BMC NUC.

Title refers to Barbara, a strong, clever, independent young woman who supports her family by teaching. She is given a two week holiday in Paris for bravery in a fire at school. She meets an artist, Sebastian, and suffers an embittering experience. The novel "has the undercurrent of vehement assertion that women really have a sense of honour and a sense of humour."

PICKERING, PERCIVAL. See STIRLING, ANNA MARIA DIANA WILHELMINA (PICKERING).

PICKERING, SIDNEY.* United Kingdom.

2392 MARGOT. London: Lawrence and Bullen, 1897 BMC. New York and London: G. P. Putnam, 1897 NUC.

Sad story of "illegitimate" Margaret Lee, an art student in Paris, with just a hint of a happy end.

2393 THE ROMANCE OF HIS PICTURE. London: A. Constable, 1895 BMC.

Lesbia poses as artist's model. Romance with artist follows.

2394 VERITY. London: E. Arnold, 1900 BMC.

Three sisters and a clergyman who horsewhips them and keeps them in solitary confinement as discipline. Their love affairs. Final catastrophe in which the father shoots Verity's lover.

PIERCE, LUCIE FRANCE. United States.

2395 THE WHITE DEVIL OF VERDE: A STORY OF THE WEST. New York: G. W. Dillingham, 1898 NUC BMC.

Marcia, a progressive young woman from New York, goes West to recuperate from an illness. She stakes a claim to a lost mine, and her efforts to protect her interests and hold her claim win her the name "The White Devil of Verde."

PIERSON, JANE SUSANNA (ANDERSON). B. 1854. United States.

2396 THE COMING OF THE DAWN. Cincinnati: Standard, [c1917] NUC.

A young Christian woman loves a Russian Jew. Both her parents and his oppose their marriage, and his commitment to Jews in Russia also prevents their marrying. He goes to Russia to fight for his people and dies. She starts a mission in a Jewish ghetto in the United States to help Jews.

PINSENT, ELLEN FRANCES (PARKER). 1866-1949. United Kingdom.

2397 CHILDREN OF THIS WORLD. London: Methuen, 1895 BMC NUC.

Rachel and Janet are "intellectual, upright and thoroughly modern in their outlook." Rachel's "self chosen end is impressive."

2398 JENNY'S CASE. London: S. Sonnenschein, 1892 BMC NUC.

Jenny, a farmer's maid of all work, is seduced by a local policeman on a promise of marriage. She moves to a distant town to have her child and is driven for a time upon the streets for a livelihood. The local poacher who loved her returns from his regiment, kills the policeman but takes to drink and dies himself. Jenny disappears. Realistic account of rural life and suffering. Absence of moralizing.

PIRKIS, CATHARINE LOUISA. United Kingdom.

2399 THE EXPERIENCES OF LOVEDAY BROOKE, LADY DETECTIVE. London: Hutchinson, 1894 BMC.

"A small, keen, not very pretty (we think) not very young (we are sure) lady detective, who is always called in at the last moment in extremely obscure cases which have baffled the best experience and ingenuity of all the professional males of Europe."

2400 A RED SISTER: A STORY OF THREE DAYS AND THREE MONTHS. London: S. Low, 1891 BMC NUC.

Lady Jean Herrick is "an out-and-out bold bad woman." She rejects a poor clergyman to marry a millionaire's heir, thinking the old man will soon die. But he goes on living for 20 years. She sees that her son loves a poor woman and arranges to break up the relationship with the help of the poor clergyman she rejected. Together they have her son's fiancee shut in a convent for Red Sisters, but this young woman is rescued before taking final vows. When her husband gets ill at the same time the old man is dying, she poisons the old man to secure the inheritance for herself. When her son learns about the murder, Lady Jean kills herself.

PLAYNE, CAROLINE ELISABETH.

2401 THE TERROR OF THE MACDURGHOTTS. London: T.F. Unwin, 1907 BMC.

A woman from a fictitious South American republic "where war has been foresworn and the reign of love inaugurated" comes to the northern part of Scotland where feuding has gone on for years. "Expresses an idea that is at once revolutionary and the soundest practical wisdom."

PLEYDELL, KATHLEEN (GROVE) MANSEL.

2402 A VOICE FROM OBLIVION. London: Digby, Long, 1908 BMC.

Hermione, heroine, is nurse and benefactor among the Arabs. Divorces her husband, makes love with another man, "feeble and rather sickly story."

POLLARD, ELIZA FRANCES. United Kingdom.

2403 TRUE UNTO DEATH: A STORY OF RUSSIAN LIFE AND THE CRIMEAN WAR. London: S. W. Partridge, [1894] BMC.

English governess of independent character accepts position with wealthy Russian family. She responds to her student Viera's views on the oppressiveness of the Russian government, and together they develop and promulgate these views. The government retaliates first by banishing Viera from her home, then sending her to Siberia. The governess goes with her and stays with her until her death.

POOL, MARIA LOUISE. 1841-1898. United States.

2404 AGAINST HUMAN NATURE: A NOVEL. New York: Harper, 1895 NUC.

Temple Crawford raised in the wild mountains of North Carolina believes it is madness to marry since she saw her own mother was so miserable. Then she "experiences religion," marries the revivalist preacher, learns to love him, and becomes a revivalist herself—preaching and working among the poor. She is contrasted to Alminy Drowdy, a New England spinster who is conventional where Temple is freer.

2405 IN A DIKE SHANTY. Chicago: Stone and Kimball, 1896 NUC.

Two women on Cape Cod for the summer. Their adventures.

2406 IN THE FIRST PERSON: A NOVEL. New York: Harper, 1896 NUC.

Wilhelmina is 23 and living in New England when her voice is discovered by a great prima donna, Leonora Runciman. She becomes her understudy, but soon Leonora looks on her as a rival and drops her. She refuses to marry the man her drunken father chooses for her, undergoes a secret and unsuccessful marriage to a tenor. When her father dies, she returns home to care for the farm and her mother, who is supportive of her career but has been under her husband's control. Eventually Wilhelmina goes to Europe with her mother to study singing. The story is told by Wilhelmina.

2407 KATHARINE NORTH: A NOVEL. New York: Harper, 1893 NUC.

Katharine is persuaded by her mother to become the

fourth wife of an elderly deacon, but immediately after the marriage ceremony she leaves the new husband she loathes and moves to a summer resort in Massachusetts Bay with another young woman. Here she becomes a waitress and meets her aunt Mrs. Llandaff who is a public speaker on "women's wrongs" and working women. Katharine is strongly influenced by her aunt thereafter. She eventually obtains a divorce from the old deacon.

2408   MRS. GERALD: A NOVEL. New York: Harper, 1896 NUC.

"Another of the author's strong studies of woman's complex nature." Judith, married to a man she doesn't love, and loving another, follows her husband through Africa as he slips into insanity and finally kills himself.

2409   MRS. KEATS BRADFORD: A NOVEL. New York: Harper, 1892 NUC.

Sequel to Roweny in Boston. Roweny separates from her husband for a few years because he is jealous of her art, pursues her career alone in Boston. They are eventually reconciled.

2410   OUT OF STEP: A NOVEL. New York: Harper, 1894 NUC.

A sequel to The Two Salomes, concerns Salome's marriage, which she realizes cannot last because she and her husband don't regard abstract truth in the same way. Although trained as a puritan, Salome doesn't have the puritan code of honor; she has an abnormal conscience. Mrs. Keats Bradford, now a celebrated portrait painter, is her friend.

2411   ROWENY IN BOSTON: A NOVEL. New York: Harper, 1892 BMC NUC.

Roweny goes to Boston to study art. Record of the lives of common workers in the city.

2412   SAND 'N' BUSHES. Chicago: H. S. Stone, 1899 NUC.

Amusing story of Amabel Waldo and her woman friend, both close to thirty, who buy horses at an auction in Boston though they know nothing about horses. Amabel buys a man's saddle and converts her skirt to pants. They ride to uppermost Cape Cod carrying a kitten and put up with much gossip about them.

2413 THE TWO SALOMES: A NOVEL. New York: Harper, 1893 NUC.

Sad, serious and sympathetic study of an "abnormal" young woman. Salome Gerry has no conscience. She forges a check to save her father and confesses to her mother—not because she repents, but because she senses that other people see her act as wrong. Her mother cannot understand her; her doctor orders her to Florida where the sunshine seems to make her better. Her story ends with a question. Another woman character Mrs. Darrah is a novelist.

POOR, AGNES BLAKE. 1842-1922. United States.

2414 BROTHERS AND STRANGERS. Boston: Roberts, 1893 NUC.

Flora Shepherd refuses to marry a man she considers too fickle. He must wait years during which time he becomes more tender and kind before Flora will have him.

2415 UNDER GUIDING STARS; A MASSACHUSETTS STORY OF THE CENTURY END. New York and London: G.P. Putman's Sons, 1905 BMC NUC.

The heroine is a strong-minded salesclerk "born to command."

POPHAM, FLORENCE.

2416 THE HOUSEWIVES OF EDENRISE. New York: Appleton, 1902 NUC. London: W. Heinemann, 1902 BMC.

Portrayal of housewives—"a modern Cranford."

POPP, ADELHEID (DWORAK). 1869-1939.

2417 THE AUTOBIOGRAPHY OF A WORKING WOMAN. London: T.F. Unwin, 1912 BMC NUC. Chicago: F.G. Browne, 1913 NUC. (Tr. by E. C. Harvey.)

Description of women's work in Vienna, narration of a woman's struggle from childhood on.

PORTER, ELEANOR (HODGMAN). 1868-1920. United States.

2418 CROSS CURRENTS: THE STORY OF MARGARET.
Boston: W.A. Wilde, [c1907] NUC. London: G.G. Harrap,
1928 BMC.
"A revealing child-labor document." A lost girl from a
wealthy family is found by a waif from the slums and
grows up among the sordid conditions of sweatshops and
dirty streets.

PORTER, GENE (STRATTON). 1868-1924. United States.

2419 A DAUGHTER OF THE LAND. London: J. Murray, 1918
BMC. Garden City, N.Y.: Doubleday, Page, [c1918] NUC.

Family of sixteen children. The nine sons are at 21 to be
given 202 acres of land, the seven daughters six weeks in
normal school and a bolt of cloth and a dress to be
married in. Kate rebels against this, leaves home for
independence of school teaching, starts a saw mill, finds
happiness in second marriage. Self-confident, not
sentimental. "Every feminist will rejoice in the sudden
emergence of Mrs. Bates, the overworked and repressed
mother of the sixteen."

PORTER, REBECCA NEWMAN. B. 1883. United States.

2420 THE GIRL FROM FOUR CORNERS; A ROMANCE OF
CALIFORNIA TO-DAY. New York: H. Holt, 1920 NUC.
Freda Bayne, brought up in coarse surroundings, makes
her way alone in San Francisco, first as a hairdresser, then
in a bookstore. There is also a romance.

PORTSMOUTH, MARIANNE.

2421 DOCTOR JOHN. London: H. J. Drane, [1903] BMC.
Idle husband lays down all "pretensions to manliness" to
loaf while his wife works.

POST, EMILY (PRICE). 1873-1960. United States.

2422 THE EAGLE'S FEATHER. New York: Dodd, Mead, 1910 NUC.

Vera lives with an artist who is married and cannot get a divorce because he is Catholic. They are happy together until, in order to have the right subject for his poem, he tells her he no longer loves her and uses her pain for his inspiration. By the time he realizes what he has lost, she has left him.

2423 THE TITLE MARKET. New York: Dodd, Mead, 1909 NUC.

The marriage business in the United States and Europe exposed. Nina has an excellent opportunity to discover Italian ideas on the subject of arranging marriages with titled Italian noblemen.

POTTER, FRANCES BOARDMAN (SQUIRE). 1867-1914. United States.

2424 THE BALLINGTONS, A NOVEL. BY FRANCES SQUIRE. Boston: Little, Brown, 1905 NUC.

The Ballingtons are a wealthy middle aged couple in this thorough study of the failure of a marriage in which the husband has all the financial power. Agnes Ballington is forced to deception to help her starving mother. Her struggles and her spiritual awakening concern a wife's right to separate income, separate conscience, and independent action—her struggle for the "rights of the soul."

POTTER, MARGARET HORTON. See BLACK, MARGARET HORTON (POTTER).

POWELL, F. INGLIS.*

2425 THE SNAKE. London, New York: J. Lane, 1912 BMC NUC.

Diary giving the "unsavoury imaginings of a bad woman," a snake woman who is used by the chief priest of a cobra cult. She murders many people including her parents and takes revenge on the man she loves before she is finally killed herself in a tragic ending.

POWELL, FRANCES. See CASE, FRANCES POWELL.

POYNTER, ELEANOR FRANCES. United Kingdom.

2426   AN   EXQUISITE   FOOL   [ANONYMOUS].   London:
Osgood, McIlvaine, 1892 BMC NUC. New York: Harper,
1892 NUC.

"Study of character" of an "unhappy and brilliant" woman,
Helen Bromley, who is "fastidious, elegant, and with fine
perceptions   where   dress,   society   and   literature   are
concerned." The only man she ever loved told her this was
a pretty coating for a vulgar soul. She has a sordid
history. Euphemia, her daughter by her first marriage, is
wholesome, stupid. Fine analysis of character of the
mother and her daughter and the man who hesitates
marrying the daughter. Ends tragically.

PRAED, MRS. CAMPBELL. See PRAED, ROSA CAROLINE
(MURRAY-PRIOR).

PRAED, ROSA CAROLINE (MURRAY-PRIOR). 1851-1935.
Australia.

2427   "AS A WATCH IN THE NIGHT": A DRAMA OF
WAKING AND DREAM IN FIVE ACTS. BY MRS.
CAMPBELL PRAED. London: Chatto and Windus, 1901
BMC NUC.

She has a studio in Chelsea, is the friend of one man, the
mistress of another. She has two historical pasts: a lady of
fashion with an interest in politics and a Roman matron in
the time of Domitian. She has a dual existence.

2428   BY THEIR FRUITS: A NOVEL. BY MRS. CAMPBELL
PRAED. London, Paris, New York, Toronto, Melbourne:
Cassell, 1908 NUC BMC.

Twin sisters, one with a drug habit. She marries; the other
loves and yields to her sister's husband.

2429   CHRISTINA   CHARD.   BY   MRS.   CAMPBELL-PRAED.
New York: D. Appleton, 1893 NUC. London: Chatto and
Windus, 1894 BMC.

Christina, an Australian, comes into a million and is

introduced to London society. She was betrayed at seventeen and has developed an intense hatred for mankind, although she is somewhat softened by the death of her daughter. She meets Lady St. Helier who wants to found a salon, start cooperative nurseries for the poor, and organize guilds for the employment of women. "Christina Chard is represented as being one of those neurotic and abnormal women who are the daughters of much reading of that strange and sickly book, The Heavenly Twins," comments one reviewer.

2430 DECEMBER ROSES. BY MRS. CAMPBELL-PRAED. New York: D. Appleton, 1892 NUC. Bristol: J. W. Arrowsmith, [1893] BMC.

A divorced woman, 32 years old, meets a former lover. Their love for each other is renewed, but he is engaged to someone else. Each of the women struggles with her scruples in finding a resolution.

2431 FUGITIVE ANNE: A ROMANCE OF THE UNEXPLORED BUSH. BY MRS. CAMPBELL PRAED. London: J. Long, [1902] BMC NUC.

Anne, married four months to an odious bully, slips out the window port aboard ship to escape him. She's thought dead; instead, she takes to the bush, her body painted black, meets a Danish explorer and has many unique, chaste but thrilling adventures, including becoming a high priestess. Her husband is done away with at the right moment, and she marries the explorer.

2432 THE GHOST. BY MRS. CAMPBELL PRAED. London: R.A. Everett, 1903 BMC NUC.

The woman in this novel publishes a novel not her own to save her aunt who is an alcoholic. When she becomes a great success, the real author appears. But she's not made to pay for the deception.

2433 THE LUCK OF THE LEURA. BY MRS. CAMPBELL PRAED. London: J. Long, [1907] BMC NUC.

Short stories on the single theme of the terrible side of Australian bush life from a woman's point of view—the strains and demands on women settlers.

2434 MADAME IZAN: A TOURIST STORY. BY MRS.
CAMPBELL-PRAED. London: Chatto and Windus, 1899
NUC. New York: D. Appleton, 1899 NUC.

Heroine is blind till 20, married to a Japanese noble she
has never seen and from whom she was separated
immediately by her family. She travels with Mrs. Bax to
the East not knowing whether she is wife or widow.
Unknown to her, her husband travels with them as a
guide. There is an Australian millionaire who tries to win
her, much travelling around Japan, and a satiric picture of
Theodosia Gotch who tries to save the Geishas.

2435 THE MAID OF THE RIVER. AN AUSTRALIAN GIRL'S
LOVE STORY. BY MRS. CAMPBELL PRAED. London: J.
Long, [1905] BMC NUC.

An innocent young woman rejects a good man for a
scoundrel who betrays her by a mock wedding ceremony.
He's married, and scandal and desertion fall upon Nuni.
But Nuni sues her betrayer for breach of promise when his
wife dies because she wants legitimacy for her child. Her
suit is successful.

2436 MRS. TREGASKISS. A NOVEL OF ANGLO-
AUSTRALIAN LIFE. BY MRS. CAMPBELL-PRAED. New
York: D. Appleton, 1895 NUC. London: Chatto and
Windus, 1896 BMC NUC.

"A type of new woman shrinking from wifehood and
motherhood." When Clare's father loses his fortune and
kills himself, Clare gives up hope of making a brilliant
marriage. She marries a rough Australian rancher who she
soon learns is dull, unfaithful, and an alcoholic. The story
opens when Clare has had several children and can barely
endure her husband. It describes the agony of a sensitive
and cultivated woman forced to live out her life on a
distant station with no social or cultural opportunities.
She almost runs off with another man—only the death of
her child prevents her. Intimate depiction of habits and
daily routine of women's lives in the Australian bush.

2437 THE OTHER MRS. JACOBS; A MATRIMONIAL
COMPLICATION. BY MRS. CAMPBELL PRAED.
London: J. Long, 1903 BMC NUC.

Two women and their relationship as well as marital

difficulties. Susan, an egotistical young woman, is companion to Mrs. Jacobs who writes novels. The setting is Bohemian.

2438 THE ROMANCE OF A CHALET. A STORY. BY MRS. CAMPBELL-PRAED. London: F. V. White, 1892 BMC. Philadelphia: J. B. Lippincott, 1892 NUC.

Constance Van Klaft, rich, travels alone with her St. Bernard. On the verge of marrying Sir Rupert, she discovers her mother was insane and had murdered another woman. She enters a convent.

2439 THE SCOURGE-STICK. BY MRS. CAMPBELL PRAED. London: W. Heinemann, 1898 BMC. New York: J. Chartress, 1898 NUC.

Negatively described by reviewers as morbid, repressed and having a "triune personality," Esther Zamiel relates an unhappy life in which she is first an actress, then an author.

2440 SISTER SORROW: A STORY OF AUSTRALIAN LIFE. London: Hutchinson, 1916 BMC.

Wilkins enslaves his wife Delores because she is a pure psychic. He is satanically evil. Narrated by Agatha, Delores' friend. Delores is a likeable governess.

2441 SOME LOVES AND A LIFE: A STUDY OF A NEUROTIC WOMAN. London: F.V. White, 1904 BMC.

Sympathetic portrayal of a woman who is a morphine addict.

PRAGA, MRS. ALFRED.

2442 LOVE AND 200 POUNDS A YEAR. London: T. W. Laurie, [1913] BMC.

Cynthia Rafferty wishes to prove that marriage on 200 pounds a year can include good meals, a well-kept house, servant, pretty things—the refinements. Science of household management proves a marvel of practical sense.

PRATT, GRACE TYLER. United States.

2443 THE BAINBRIDGE MYSTERY; THE HOUSEKEEPER'S STORY. Boston: Sherman, French, 1911 NUC.
Eliza Carter, middle-aged housekeeper, discovers the murderer of her employer.

PRESCOTT, AUGUSTA.

2444 THE STAIRWAY ON THE WALL. New York: Alice Harriman, 1911 NUC.
Murder mystery. A woman proposes to a man to avoid a detested marriage.

PRESCOTT, E. LIVINGSTON. See JAY, EDITH KATHARINE SPICER.

PRESTON, ANNA. B. 1887. Canada.

2445 THE RECORD OF A SILENT LIFE. New York: B.W. Huebsch, 1912 NUC. London: M. Secker, 1913 BMC.
The story of an intelligent but dumb young woman who, on receiving an inheritance, opens a large house as a haven for children, invalids, old people, but not men between 20 and 70. "It is written with the realism of a diary and the detail of a pathological study, yet the result is cold and detached."

PRICE, A. T. G.*

2446 SIMPLICITY. Chicago: Rand, McNally, [1896] BMC NUC.
The innocent heroine inherits money and goes to live with her impoverished family in a rural district of England. Her experiences with country society lead to her suicide. "The satire is too evident, the position of the author is too palpably biassed. One sees how inimical it is to men, how indeed the simple story is a manifesto against them."

PRICE, ELEANOR CATHERINE. United Kingdom.

2447 THE LITTLE ONE. London: Bentley, 1891 BMC NUC.
Agnes and Nora D'Alby, 17 and over 20, live with their

minister-grandfather. Agnes elopes, learns the man is married and returns home to die. Nora, a novelist of enormously high standards, had in the meantime ignored Agnes for the "violent and enthusiastic" love she felt for Mrs. Murray (Agnes' seducer's mother). Nora full of grief returns after Agnes dies and writes a novel with an elopement very like Agnes'.

2448 OFF THE HIGH ROAD: THE STORY OF A SUMMER. London: Macmillan, 1899 BMC NUC.

Viola Fairfax runs away from guardian to keep from marrying a man chosen by him. She takes a different name, rents a cottage off the high road. Romance follows.

PRICE, ELIZABETH ROBINSON (WALKER). B. 1863. United States.

2449 FREDERICA DENNISON, SPINSTER. Boston: Pilgrim Press, [c1916] NUC.

Diary of a woman who went to Lansing to study music, is a genius at making friends.

PRICE, F. C.*

2450 LORD KENTWELL'S LOVE AFFAIR. London: W. Heinemann, 1909 BMC NUC.

He's a libertine who tries to get Mrs. Gambler, a sweet natured divorcee, to be his mistress. She's disgusted with him.

PRICHARD, KATHARINE SUSANNAH. See THROSSELL, KATHARINE SUSANNAH (PRICHARD).

PRICHARD, SARAH JOHNSON. 1830-1909. United States.

2451 SHAWNIE WADE. Boston: R. G. Badger, 1909 NUC.

A young Southern woman of fiery temper and indomitable spirit comes to a Northern school and changes places with a slave playmate whom she resembles. Afterwards no one believes she is not the slave.

PRIESTLEY, A. E.*

2452 THE MARRIAGE OF NAOMI. London: Digby, Long, 1911 NUC.

Somber story of her unconventional life and her unsatisfactory husband.

PRINCE, HELEN CHOATE (PRATT). B. 1857. United States.

2453 THE STRONGEST MASTER. Boston: Houghton, Mifflin, 1902 NUC.

A young man who has a passion for the reform of marriage lives with a woman who then has a baby. "As far we can understand it, Chris and Clytie are made man and wife in an orthodox manner."

PRINDLE, FRANCES WESTON (CARRUTH). 1867-1934. United States.

2454 THOSE DALE GIRLS. BY FRANCES WESTON CARRUTH. Chicago: A.C. McClurg, 1899 NUC.

When their wealthy father dies, the two sisters must earn their own living. They open a successful baking business. Includes a love story.

2455 THE WAY OF BELINDA. BY FRANCES WESTON CARRUTH. New York: Dodd, Mead, 1901 NUC.

A "slum sister" with the courage of her convictions refuses to marry in her high social class. She marries a reporter.

PRINGLE, ELIZABETH WATIES (ALLSTON). 1845-1921.

2456 A WOMAN RICE PLANTER. BY PATIENCE PENNINGTON. New York: Macmillan, 1913 BMC NUC.

She manages two large plantations with skill, courage and hard work.

PRITCHARD, MARTIN J. See MOORE, JUSTINA.

PROCTOR, GERTRUDE AMELIA. United States.

2457   GLEAMS OF SCARLET; A TALE OF THE CANADIAN ROCKIES. Boston: Sherman, French, 1915 NUC.
Story of a young woman whose brother is tried for a serious crime though he is innocent. She is brought East by a woman physician who helps provide the education and training for her art.

PROUTY, OLIVE (HIGGINS). 1882-1974. United States.

2458   THE FIFTH WHEEL; A NOVEL. New York: F. A. Stokes, [c1916] NUC. London: Cassell, 1918 BMC.
Ruth rejects debutante role, marriage of convenience, goes to little university town and begins to define her own life. Falls in love but does not marry because the man objects to her activism in suffrage. Years later he feels differently and they get back together. Narrated by Ruth and her sister Lucy.

2459   THE STAR IN THE WINDOW; A NOVEL. New York: F. A. Stokes, [c1918] NUC BMC. London: W. Collins, [1920] BMC.
Reba rebels at 25, leaving her New England family for the "Alliance" in Boston.

PROWSE, C. M.*

2460   THE LURE OF ISLAM: A NOVEL. London: S. Low, [1914] BMC. South Africa: [1914?] NUC.
Concerns young white women in Capetown lured into Moslem marriages by the promise of wealth and fear of the powers of black magic. Describes the "true" position of women in Islam: multiple wives, divorce by a statement from the husband, etc.

PRYCE, MYFANWY.*

2461   BLUE MOONS. London: Hodder and Stoughton, 1919 BMC.
Two heroines, one in conflict between love and work—"the girl's realization of the inherent deficiency of the 'devotion to art' ideal."

PUDDICOMBE, ANNE ADALIZA (EVANS). 1836-1908. United Kingdom.

2462 UNDER THE THATCH. BY ALLEN RAINE. London: Hutchinson, 1910 NUC BMC.

Daughter gives mother an overdose when she asks to be relieved of terrible and fatal pain, but it turns out that she really didn't give an overdose as she intended.

2463 A WELSH SINGER: A NOVEL. BY ALLEN RAINE. London: Hutchinson, 1897 BMC. (Also published as Mifanwy (A Welsh Singer). By Allen Raine. New York: D. Appleton, 1897 NUC.)

Mifanwy is a Welsh shepherd who at fifteen can neither read nor write. She leaves her village and joins the circus, but her beautiful voice eventually brings her enormous success as a contralto in London. At this time she is reunited with a young man from her village who is now a famous sculptor. Idyllic.

PUGH, BARBARA TUCKER. United States.

2464 CHRONICLES OF A COUNTRY SCHOOL TEACHER. Baltimore, Md.: Saulsbury, [c1919] NUC.

Concerns Indiana school life.

PUGH, HELEN PROTHERO (LEWIS). United Kingdom.

2465 A LADY OF MY OWN. London: Hurst and Blackett, 1891 BMC.

Woman is married to a brute of a husband. Both she and her daughter Hyacinth are delicate and sensitive women who suffer at his hands. Hyacinth leaves home when her father hits her and returns home to forgive him only after a long time and much wandering.

PUTNAM, NINA (WILCOX). 1888-1962. United States.

2466 ADAM'S GARDEN; A NOVEL. Philadelphia and London: J. B. Lippincott, 1916 BMC NUC.

Adam's garden is a vacant city lot where he raises flowers and cultivates humanity; the heroine is an "aeroplane girl."

2467   IT PAYS TO SMILE. New York: G. H. Doran, [c1920]
NUC.
Freedom Talbot, New England spinster, breaks from the
bonds of tradition in an unconventional way. She is
involved in a mystery on a ranch in the West.

QUINN, E. HARDINGHAM. See SCOTT, PATRICIA ETHEL
(STONEHOUSE).

RACSTER, OLGA AND JESSICA GROVE.

2468   THE PHASES OF FELICITY: A NOVEL OF SOUTH
AFRICA. London: G. Allen & Unwin, 1916 BMC NUC.
Felicity in South Africa first teaching music, then as a
journalist, and her love affair with Bromley.

RADFORD, DOLLIE. B. 1858.

2469   ONE WAY OF LOVE: AN IDYLL. London: T. F. Unwin,
1898 BMC NUC.
Sacha, a lonely young woman, is seduced and abandoned
by a man of the world. She is "left to her lost illusions."

RAE, LUCY M.

2470   THE HEART OF A GREAT MAN. London: F. V. White,
1903 BMC.
Woman is a Russian spy.

RAGSDALE, LULAH. See RAGSDALE, TALLULAH.

RAGSDALE, TALLULAH. B. 1866. United States.

2471   MISS DULCIE FROM DIXIE. BY LULAH RAGSDALE.
New York and London: D. Appleton, 1917 BMC NUC.
She is a gifted dressmaker as well as a great success as an
actress, acclaimed by the critics. Dulcie Culpepper is a
Southern woman who has problems with her Northern
relatives concerning an inheritance.

2472 A SHADOW'S SHADOW. BY LULAH RAGSDALE. Philadelphia: J. B. Lippincott, 1893 NUC.

Heroine goes on stage because her "furious ardor, her nervous force, her eating, burning restlessness found an outlet only in that great source that serves as a safety valve for so many overcharged natures."

RAIMOND, C. E. See PARKES, ELIZABETH (ROBINS).

RAINE, ALLEN. See PUDDICOMBE, ANNE ADALIZA (EVANS).

RAIT, JANET ELDER.

2473 ALISON HOWARD. Westminster: H. Constable, 1903 BMC.

Alison Howard must work two years before she can inherit the fortune left to her. The novel describes the poverty she sees, her work in an employment office and the lives of several poor women. Its purpose is to show how sadly prepared some women are to earn their own living.

RAMSAY, RINA. United Kingdom.

2474 THE STRAW. London: Hutchinson, 1909 BMC. New York: Macmillan, 1909 NUC.

Unhappy marriage. Wife beaten.

2475 THE WAY OF A WOMAN. New York: Dodd, Mead, 1911 NUC.

Love story of an actress.

RAMSDEN, HELEN GUENDOLEN (SEYMOUR). 1846-1910.

2476 SPEEDWELL. BY LADY GUENDOLEN RAMSDEN. London: R. Bentley, 1894 BMC.

Attractive widow doing good works in the London slums thinks herself invulnerable to love until attractive egoless young man comes along. But then he turns to her niece; she has a cruel awakening, but the man gets neither them. In the tradition of Edna Lyall.

RAMSDEN, LADY GUENDOLEN. See RAMSDEN, HELEN GUENDOLEN (SEYMOUR).

RAMSEY, ALICIA (ROYSTON). 1864-1933. United Kingdom.

2477 MISS ELIZABETH GIBBS. London: Mills & Boon, [1915] BMC NUC.

She realizes her fondest dream when she becomes editor of the "Universe," a magazine for "advanced women." Describes her experiences in the main office and her splendid success.

RAMSEY, OLIVIA.

2478 A GIRL OF NO IMPORTANCE. London: J. Long, 1913 BMC.

The second heroine plays the part of a boy; the first is a 16 year old Roman Catholic girl with mystic powers loved by an earl.

RANDALL, MRS. HENRY W.

2479 HACK'S BRAT. BY A. IAN MACLEOD. London: Hodder & Stoughton, 1916 BMC.

He adopts her in an Australian mining camp; he insists on voice training for her. For awhile she breaks away from him but returns to marry him and to a career as a singer.

RANDOLPH, EVELYN SAINT LEGER (SAVILE). United Kingdom.

2480 THE SHAPE OF THE WORLD. BY EVELYN ST. LEGER. New York and London: G. P. Putnam's Sons, 1912 BMC NUC.

The Javelins are a peculiar family in which, generation after generation, the males make their wives miserable and all end in suicide. In the eleventh generation Christopher, who is repeating the pattern, is cured by a brain operation. The author is sympathetic to his wife, who subsequently becomes a successful playwright. "Witty."

RAPHAEL, ALICE PEARL. B. 1887.

2481 THE FULFILLMENT. New York: Sturgis & Walton, 1910 NUC.

The heroine, ardent, brilliant, and high-spirited, finds herself married to a narrow and limited husband. She leaves husband and son to pursue artistic ambitions in Paris. The focus of the book is on her life in Paris; the conclusion finds her "spurned" by her grown up son and husband.

RAWSON, MAUD STEPNEY. United Kingdom.

2482 THE APPRENTICE. London: Hutchinson, 1904 BMC.

The fall of a young woman through passion; she had not the excuse of ignorance and is therefore not a victim, and so leaves the audience irritated and scandalized.

2483 THE ENCHANTED GARDEN. London: Methuen, 1907 BMC.

Sympathetic study of a woman's soul. Joanna Hurst, 35 years old, is unhappily married. To escape her husband's infidelities, she goes to Spain where she falls in love. Her husband shoots the man she loves.

2484 THE LABOURER'S COMEDY. London: A. Constable, 1905 BMC NUC.

Courageous and spirited, Pamela works as a journalist on several women's newspapers and supports her inventor husband. But her strength gives out as does her deep belief in her husband's ultimate success.

2485 A LADY OF THE REGENCY. BY MRS. STEPNEY RAWSON. London: Hutchinson, 1900 BMC. New York: Harper, 1901 NUC.

June Cherier comes from Yorkshire to the court of Queen

Caroline and finds herself surrounded by intrigue. Good character study of the women of the court.

2486   THE MAGIC GATE. London: Hutchinson, 1917 BMC.

Jennet is the energetic and efficient acting manager of an amazing American—Lady Paramount. She comes to a small English community during the war to manage that woman's estate.

2487   THE PRICELESS THING. London: S. Paul, [1914] BMC NUC.

A detective story in which the heroine takes a position as librarian in a country mansion.

2488   SPLENDID ZIPPORAH. London: Methuen, 1911 BMC.

Zipporah Londesbury is six foot two inches tall, she is gawky, she whistles, she sleeps on the floor, and she's an outspoken and ambitious musical genius: "I can play the cello and bass well, the piano a little, the horn tolerably, the clarinet fairly, the viola a bit, the oboe ditto and the drums. I have some acquaintance with the flute; the bassoon I am now studying and I can conduct a band." She teaches music; she tours the world, meets a feminist, and goes up in a suffrage balloon. And she does form and conduct her own orchestra. The whole novel concerns her music career and her "comradeship" with a man. At the end there is some suggestion she will marry—but the man must reach to be equal to her.

2489   THE THREE ANARCHISTS. London: S. Paul, [1912] BMC NUC.

"Psychological study" of a young wife married to a "bleak and sordid" man. Love, birth, and death are the anarchists in their influence on her.

2490   THE WATERED GARDEN. London: S. Paul, [1913] BMC NUC.

Bettina's career from the time she becomes a secretary-gardener to her own inheritance of the house of her employer. The story is just that, an account of her very busy whirlwind of a life.

RAWSON, MRS. STEPNEY. See RAWSON, MAUD STEPNEY.

RAY, ANNA CHAPIN. 1865-1945. United States.

2491 THE BRIDGE BUILDERS. Boston: Little, Brown, 1909 NUC.

Jessica is unconventional, capable, careless of her appearance; risks her life to save a young engineer as an old bridge falls. Also concerns her mother's jealousy of her.

2492 A WOMAN WITH A PURPOSE. Boston: Little, Brown, 1911 NUC. London: S. Paul, [1911] BMC.

Dorcas Sloane, graduate of Smith, refuses to marry until she makes something of herself. She becomes a novelist in New York, tries to support herself by writing, but fails. She marries but is soon estranged from her husband who treats her like a plaything. In the end she is reconciled to her husband and full of high ideals and respect for herself though she failed as a writer.

RAYMOND, EVELYN (HUNT). 1843-1910. United States.

2493 AMONG THE LINDENS. Boston: Little, Brown, 1898 NUC.

Young woman struggles against poverty in New York City flat. Rescue of an old man leads to "ideal existence among the lindens." For girls?

2494 AN HONOR GIRL. Boston: Lee and Shepard, 1904 NUC.

Having won a scholarship to college, she must return home to help family. For girls?

RAYNER, E. See RAYNER, EMMA.

RAYNER, EMMA. D. 1926. United States.

2495 FREE TO SERVE; A TALE OF COLONIAL NEW YORK. BY E. RAYNER. Boston: Copeland and Day, 1897 NUC. London & Boston: G. P. Putnam, 1900 BMC.

Aveline, an 18th century gentlewoman, is brought by circumstances to the position of bond-servant on the plantation of a Dutch patroon in New York.

RE, LUCY. See BARTLETT, LUCY RE.

REA, LORNA. B. 1897. United Kingdom.

2496 SIX MRS. GREENES. New York: Harper, 1919 PW. London: W. Heinemann, 1929 BMC.

They are all wives or widows and members of one family—from old Mrs. Greene, all but bedridden though still active in mind, to the latest married of her grandchildren. "Analysis and contrasts with irony and pleasant humor."

READ, GEORGIA WILLIS. United States.

2497 MEDOC IN THE MOOR. Boston: Sherman, French, 1914 NUC.

Terese is an innkeeper in a Breton village. She is an older woman upon whom all the village depends to straighten out their troubles.

REANEY, ISABEL (EDIS). B. 1847.

2498 A DAUGHTER'S INHERITANCE. London: Heath, Cranton and Ouseley, [1913] BMC.

Efforts of a young woman, who is an alcoholic by heredity and is degraded by the habit, to obtain a living without a character reference and to rehabilitate herself.

2499 DR. GREY'S PATIENT: A NOVEL. London: Bliss, 1893 BMC.

Doctor Grey attends the delivery of a child whose father wants the infant killed. Glory St. Clair is spared, she grows up not knowing her parents, travels about the country alone, becomes a nurse, faces many perils—one from the "libertine propensities of an individual who eventually turns out to be her father." Her mother, she learns, is an alcoholic.

2500 POOR MRS. EGERTON; A STUDY IN ATMOSPHERE. London: Cranton & Ouseley, [1914] BMC.
Life in a small community of widowed women in reduced circumstances.

REBBECK, MRS. ELIZABETH. See REBEK, LILLIE.

REBEK, LILLIE.

2501 THE STRAGGLERS; A TALE OF PRIMAL ASPERITIES. BY MRS. ELIZABETH REBBECK (ANNA CATHARINA). London: F. Griffiths, 1910 BMC NUC.
Study of marriage from a woman's point of view. Mary Faire carries on the battle; Hetty Culver gives in.

REDDEN, HELEN PINKERTON.

2502 M'CLELLAN OF M'CLELLAN. London: Bliss, 1895 BMC.
The fates of a large family of Scottish farmers—the women characters being the most interesting. The young woman becomes a successful painter. Love story included.

REDFIELD, MARTIN. See BROWN, ALICE.

REED, HELEN LEAH. 1860(?)-1926. United States.

2503 MISS THEODORA: A WEST END STORY. Boston: R. G. Badger, 1898 NUC.
The impecunious aunt and nephew of an old Boston family are snubbed by their Brahmin relatives. They live in the West End of Boston. He marries a woman from the West, and all three move to Denver. A still life on the order of Cranford. Quiet, uneventful, realistic environment.

REED, MYRTLE. See MACCULLOUGH, MYRTLE (REED).

REESE, CARA. United States.

2504 "AND SHE GOT ALL THAT!" WOMAN'S SPHERE IN LIFE'S BATTLE. New York: F. H. Revell, 1897 NUC.
Wife of working-man dissatisfied; leaves husband to study nursing. By this she is almost entirely "weaned" from husband and home, goes abroad as nurse companion. Her only child dies; her husband is badly injured in mill accident. She returns home to care for him and reunites in a "chastened life and mended home."

REEVE, KATHARINE ROOSEVELT. United States.

2505 COVERT-SIDE COURTSHIP. Philadelphia: J.B. Lippincott, 1909 NUC.
She races her own horse, has two suitors, one of whom at first thought she was a boy.

REEVES, HELEN BUCKINGHAM (MATHERS). 1853-1920. United Kingdom.

2506 "HONEY". BY HELEN MATHERS. London: Methuen, 1902 BMC NUC.
A "rebel against all that is conventional," the heroine adopts a male disguise.

2507 MY JO, JOHN: A NOVEL. BY HELEN MATHERS. London: F. V. White, 1891 BMC. New York: J. W. Lovell, [1891] NUC.
Colonel and Mrs. John Andrews, married for twenty years, have a serious misunderstanding. They separate, are reunited.

2508 THE SIN OF HAGAR. London: Hutchinson, 1896 BMC NUC.
Hagar, a hypnotic medium, has been "utilized" by her father until she loathes him. After his mysterious murder, she moves into the home of Lord Straubenzee and his impressionable daughter Nadege. Mischief follows; Hagar uses hypnotic power on her. She attempts to gain the love of Will Cassilis, married, through her powers. Finally kills herself. "More sinned against than sinning." Her father had dehumanized her.

2509 A STUDY OF A WOMAN; OR VENUS VICTRIX. A NOVEL. BY HELEN MATHERS. London: F. V. White, 1893 BMC.

Analysis of the character of an introspective person, who, under the tension of keen suffering and suspicion, imagines herself guilty of a crime of which she is innocent.

REEVES, HELEN BUCKINGHAM (MATHERS). See also LYALL, DAVID [pseud.].

REICHARDT, ANNIE.

2510 GIRL-LIFE IN THE HAREM; A TRUE ACCOUNT OF GIRL-LIFE IN ORIENTAL CLIMES. London: J. Ouseley, 1908 BMC NUC.

The author describes her purpose as being "not to tell a sensational tale but to delineate faithfully a Moslem interior and a few months of girl-life in a Damascus harem. As I myself have known it."

REID, CHRISTIAN. See TIERNAN, FRANCES CHRISTINE (FISHER). (FISHER).

REIFSNIDER, ANNA CYRENE (PORTER). 1850-1932. United States.

2511 UNFORGIVEN. St. Louis, Mo.: A. C. Reifsnider Book Co., [c1893] NUC.

Julia Hudson is a very gifted woman. "The author seems to have aimed to prove through her that a woman's greatest happiness is found in congenial work."

REMICK, GRACE MAY. United States.

2512 JANE STUART, COMRADE. Philadelphia: Penn, 1916 NUC.

Story of friendship between women.

RENO, ITTI (KINNEY). B. 1862. United States.

2513   AN EXCEPTIONAL CASE: A NOVEL. Philadelphia: J. B. Lippincott, 1891 NUC.

Young woman rejects a suitor who insults her, even though her father had chosen him as her husband to save the family fortune. Her rejected suitor ruins her father and then shoots himself in her presence so that the world will know what she has done and no man will marry her. His gesture is futile because the heroine wants most of all to paint. She devotes her life to her art.

REYNOLDS, AMY DORA.

2514   THE GIFTED NAME. London: Hodder and Stoughton, [1912] BMC.

Hester, a famous novelist, is "one of the most offensively horsey young women we have ever met in fiction."

2515   THE GREY TERRACE. London: Chapman and Hall, 1912 BMC.

Keith, an M.D., strikes a man who subsequently dies. Jeanne, also an M.D., certifies otherwise. Jeanne is a "particularly interesting study"; Keith's romance is with Maisie.

2516   HAZEL OF HAZELDEAN. London: Hurst and Blackett, 1906 BMC.

Little girl, raised as boy for purposes of inheritance, scoffs at feminine limitations.

2517   THE HOUSE OF REST. London: Hurst and Blackett, 1907 BMC.

After ten years of struggle with poverty in London, Leone Lorraine inherits money. She uses it to establish a home of rest for the poor. When she marries, she and her husband carry on the good work she began.

2518   IN SILENCE. London: Hurst and Blackett, 1906 BMC.

The heroine is a deaf mute who becomes the founder of an institution for the training of children like herself. A study of her character.

2519 IN THE YEARS THAT CAME AFTER. London: Hutchinson, 1899 BMC.

Two sisters contrasted. Irene marries a curate. Greta is a brilliant young woman who writes an anonymous novel. The novel is a success and is so powerful that her liberal father forbids her to read it. Her literary adventures and her romance.

2520 THESE THREE. London: Hodder and Stoughton, 1907 BMC.

Three women, Faith, Hope and Charity, run a farm.

REYNOLDS, ELDRID.* B. 1889.

2521 WHISPERING DUST. London: A. Rivers, 1913 BMC NUC. New York: F. A. Stokes, [1914] NUC.

Woman of 33 feels old, drab, different from other women because her life is dull. She travels to Egypt, writing constantly to "You," a man she creates out of her imagination.

REYNOLDS, GERTRUDE M. (ROBINS). D. 1939. United Kingdom.

2522 ALSO RAN. BY MRS. BAILLIE REYNOLDS. London: Hutchinson, 1920 BS. New York: G. H. Doran, [c1920] NUC.

A mystery story during war time in which the heroine is a war nurse.

2523 A CASTLE TO LET. BY MRS. BAILLIE REYNOLDS. New York: G. H. Doran, [1917] NUC. London: Cassell, 1917 BMC.

Young English woman studies at Oxford and makes friends with a Hungarian woman; the two visit the ancestral home—a castle near a cave said to be haunted by a terrible dragon. She is determined to solve the mystery and does.

2524 THE COST OF A PROMISE; A NOVEL IN THREE PARTS. BY MRS. BAILLIE REYNOLDS. London: Hodder and Stoughton, 1914 BMC. New York: G. H. Doran, [c1914] NUC.

Germaine is a "born suffragette"; she works in an office to support herself and her mother rather than becoming a "down-trodden governess" and is a public speaker for suffrage. Her attempted murder of her cousin as a child causes some minor difficulties later.

2525 A DULL GIRL'S DESTINY. BY MRS. BAILLIE REYNOLDS. New York: Brentano's, 1907 NUC. London: Hutchinson, 1907 BMC.

Avril Eden is anything but dull. She's a brilliant and successful novelist whose works are considered great classics. She writes under the pen name of Jane Smith, and when she marries, she conceals the secret of her authorship from her professor husband.

2526 HER POINT OF VIEW. BY G. M. ROBINS (MRS. BAILLIE REYNOLDS). London: Hurst and Blackett, 1896 NUC BMC.

Stella, a violinist, is loved by two writers, one a distinguished novelist whom she plans to marry. The other, who had formerly rejected her because of her lack of position or money, goes mad with jealousy, lures her to his quarters where "the leering Beardsleyism of the 'Yellow Book' jostled the medievalism of an ivory inlaid bureau," etc. Attempts to force her into a relationship but novelist rescues her. "Overflowing with sentimentality, nice principles."

2527 THE IDES OF MARCH. BY G. M. ROBINS. New York: J. W. Lovell, [1891] NUC. London: Hurst and Blackett, 1892 BMC.

Hope Merion breaks off her engagement when she learns her fiance has treated another woman "dishonorably." Main story involves her relation to a misogynist, young Westmoreland who his father fears will have no heir.

2528   THE LONELY STRONGHOLD. BY MRS. BAILLIE REYNOLDS. London: Cassell, 1918 BMC. New York: G. H. Doran, [c1918] NUC.

In this war-time love story Olwen, who works in a bank, buys a house with her inheritance and turns it into a hospital.

2529   A MAKE-SHIFT MARRIAGE. BY MRS. BAILLIE REYNOLDS. London and New York: Hodder and Stoughton, [c1912] BMC NUC.

Mrs. Brandon is a rare character in fiction—a mother-in-law who helps her daughter-in-law who is unhappily married because her husband married her on the rebound.

2530   THE MAN WHO WON. BY MRS. BAILLIE REYNOLDS (G. M. ROBINS). London: Hutchinson, 1905 BMC NUC. New York: Brentano's, 1907 NUC.

Millie is fully an individual—high spirited and complex. At 16 she shrinks from Bert's passion; years later rebukes him until he disciplines himself to be acceptable to her. Also takes eager delight in her work, studies to be an architect, is self supporting, does marry in the end.

2531   "THALASSA!" BY MRS. BAILLIE REYNOLDS. New York: Brentano, 1906 NUC. London: Hutchinson, 1906 BMC.

Frail but self reliant woman comes to serve as governess for child of an isolated man who has some dark secret in his life. Wins the man but on learning the secret is forced to seek self support where he will not find her; love compels her to return. He is convinced that only a pure man can woo a pure woman. A Jane Eyre kind of story.

REYNOLDS, MINNIE JOSEPHINE. B. 1865.

2532   THE CRAYON CLUE. New York: M. Kennerley, 1915 BMC NUC.

Billy Pen is a school teacher who finds the graft and corruption impossible when teachers are forced to use greasy crayons. She launches a great campaign for honest government. She fights the school board, goes to the state legislature, takes the stump, preaches a great sermon at the Presbyterian Church—in short, demonstrates what a woman can do once she gets going. "The author has been given a lion's share of the credit in getting an ammendment for equal suffrage through the Colorado Senate."

REYNOLDS, MRS. BAILLIE. See REYNOLDS, GERTRUDE M. (ROBINS).

RHOADES, NINA. B. 1863.

2533 RUTH CAMPBELL'S EXPERIMENT: A STORY. Boston: W. A. Wilde, [1904] NUC.

Young woman must support herself.

RHODES, KATHLYN. United Kingdom.

2534 THE MAKING OF A SOUL. London: Hutchinson, 1914 BMC.

Antonia, a typist, is married to a man who does not consider her his intellectual equal. She leaves him; they are ultimately reconciled after his repentance. A "satire on the futility of the intellectual man without perception."

2535 THE STRAIGHT RACE. London: Holden and Hardingham, [1916] BMC.

Dierdre Granville, a young friendless woman must earn her own living. First she works in a shop; then she goes on the stage. The temptations and trials of a chorus girl. Ends happily.

2536 SWEET LIFE. A NOVEL. London: Hutchinson, 1908 BMC 1916 NUC.

A description of the struggle and ultimate failure of an educated young woman to earn her living in London, also her love story.

RHYS, GRACE (LITTLE). 1865-1929. United Kingdom.

2537 MARY DOMINIC. London: J. M. Dent, 1898 BMC. Leipzig: B. Tauchnitz, 1899 NUC.

Mary, a 15 year old in rural Ireland is seduced; she and her child are thrown out of her home to fend for themselves by her father.

RICE, RUTH LITTLE (MASON). 1884-1927. United States.

2538 THE TRAILERS: A NOVEL. New York: F. H. Revell, [c1909] NUC.

Woman works with a religious idealist.

RICHARDS, LAURA ELIZABETH (HOWE). 1850-1943. United States.

2539 A DAUGHTER OF JEHU. New York and London: D. Appleton, 1918 BMC NUC.

Belonging to the "school of Cranford," this novel portrays a young woman who insists on her independence. After working as a cabdriver, she earns her living by running a livery stable.

2540 GEOFFREY STRONG. Boston: D. Estes, [c1901] NUC.

Two "old maids" living contentedly, one sworn to spinsterhood. Sentimental.

2541 LOVE AND ROCKS. Boston: Estes and Lauriat, 1898 NUC.

Romance on New England coast of two students vacationing; he a Harvard student of surgery; she a Smith student trying to decide between literature and medicine as a career.

RICHARDSON, ANNA STEESE (SAUSSER). 1865-1949. United States.

2542 ADVENTURES IN THRIFT. Indianapolis: Bobbs-Merrill, [1916] BMC NUC.

Claire undertakes to run her house for 1/3 less; she tests all the modern methods, marketing, cooperative buying stores, clubs, commercial kitchens. This enables her to marry a man whose income she had formerly thought was impossible to live on.

RICHARDSON, DOROTHY. 1875-1955. United States.

2543 THE LONG DAY. THE STORY OF A NEW YORK WORKING GIRL, AS TOLD BY HERSELF [ANONYMOUS]. New York: Century, 1905 BMC NUC.

A teacher is lured to New York by glamorous ads showing self-supporting women living well. But what she finds is factory work. She describes many kinds of working women, the horrible factory conditions that goad women into prostitution, and her years of struggling her way up to respected business woman.

RICHARDSON, DOROTHY MILLER. 1873-1957. United Kingdom.

2544 BACKWATER. London: Duckworth, [1916] BMC NUC. New York: A.A. Knopf, 1917 NUC.

Miriam's grey life teaching in a London suburban school, her students who hurry toward marriage, the older single sisters that run the school.

2545 HONEYCOMB. London: Duckworth, 1917 BMC NUC. New York: A.A. Knopf, 1919 NUC.

Miriam Henderson's third job—as a governess in the country home of the Corries at Hastings on the Sea: her analysis of marriage through observation of the Corries, the Kronens and her own parents; her analysis of the limits of men's minds through studies of Mr. Corrie, her own father, the men she meets; the tragedy of her mother's suicide.

2546 INTERIM. London: Duckworth, [1919] BMC NUC. New York: A.A. Knopf, 1920 NUC.

Miriam at Mrs. Bailey's boarding house in Bloomsbury, her job with a dentist on Wimpole Street, her solitary life, the people she meets.

2547   POINTED ROOFS. London: Duckworth, 1915 BMC NUC.
New York: A.A. Knopf, 1919 NUC.
Miriam teaches in Hanover for six months—her relations
to her girl students, to Fraulein Pfaff, her school teacher
life.

2548   THE TRAP. London: A.A. Knopf, 1919 NUC. London:
Duckworth, 1925 BMC NUC.
Miriam drifting toward a nervous breakdown, her feelings
of being trapped.

2549   THE TUNNEL. London: Duckworth, 1919 BMC NUC.
New York: A.A. Knopf, 1919 NUC.
All the details of Miriam's work as assistant to three
dentists. No conventional romance.

RICHARDSON, HENRY HANDEL. See ROBERTSON, ETHEL FLORENCE LINDESAY (RICHARDSON).

RICHARDSON, JERUSHA DAVIDSON (HUNTING).

2550   GATES OF BRASS. London: Digby, Long, 1909 BMC.
Concerns a world famous prima donna and her daughter
just out of college.

2551   THEY TWAIN. London: T.F. Unwin, 1904 BMC.
Careful study of a marriage and marital differences,
especially good portrait of the woman. She is hoydenish,
"figures as an exclamation of horror through many pages."

RICHARDSON, MARY RALEIGH.

2552   MATILDA AND MARCUS: A NOVEL. London: Simpkin,
1915 BMC.
Author is venting her enthusiastic feminism. Matilda is an
idealist, married to Marc a poet; she is unhappy, arranges
to marry Sir Henry.

RICKARD, JESSIE LOUISA (MOORE). B. 1879. United Kingdom.

2553   CATHY ROSSITER. BY MRS. VICTOR RICKARD. London and New York: Hodder & Stoughton, [1919] NUC BMC.

Highstrung, unstable and young, Cathy is befriended by Dr. Monica Henstock and then betrayed. The doctor plots with Cathy's husband to have her confined to an insane asylum. Vivid description of her sufferings there. Discussion of women's rights.

2554   THE FIRE OF GREEN BOUGHS. London: Duckworth, 1918 BMC NUC. New York: Dodd, Mead, 1919 NUC.

The title refers to the sacrifice of youth in war, a sacrifice demanded by the older generation of men who are beyond military age. Sylvia is a failure as a war worker; out of a sense of humanity she lies and steals to protect another woman and a dying German soldier. She is denounced as pro-German.

2555   THE FRANTIC BOAST. London: Duckworth, [1917] BMC NUC.

Two wives leave their husbands in Burma and go to London. Lisa Weston is tired of hers; Judith Coleston finds hers intolerable. She is the principal character, in love with a journalist. Author includes her own views on marriage.

2556   A RECKLESS PURITAN. London: Hodder & Stoughton, [1920] BMC. New York: G.H. Doran, [c1921] NUC.

A young Irish woman married to an Englishman leaves her husband when she finds he has brought another woman into the house. The story is about her struggles to support herself. She spends a month in jail for alleged theft.

RICKARD, MRS. VICTOR. See RICKARD, JESSIE LOUISA (MOORE).

RICKERT, EDITH. See RICKERT, MARTHA EDITH.

RICKERT, MARTHA EDITH. 1871-1938. United States.

2557   THE BEGGAR IN THE HEART. BY EDITH RICKERT. New York: Moffat, Yard, 1909 NUC. London: E. Arnold, 1909 BMC.

A female vagabond wanders all over the world when her uncle dies and finally settles in London by the time she is middle-aged. She becomes a potter, lives in a tenement, commands the respect of working people, is extremely outspoken about reforms. This modern older heroine keeps a suitor (a lord) dangling for years before he finally gets a yes from her.

2558   FOLLY. BY EDITH RICKERT. New York: Baker & Taylor, [1906] NUC. London: E. Arnold, 1906 BMC NUC.

Spirited young wife is maddened by husband's virtues. The book opens with his rejoicing that she can regard their first-born without actual detestation. She falls for a poet and leaves her husband in order to nurse the poet when he becomes ill. After the poet's death, her husband gladly accepts her back.

2559   THE REAPER. BY EDITH RICKERT. London: Arnold, 1904 BMC. Boston: Houghton, Mifflin, 1904 NUC.

Character study of strong and weak women in a fishing village. One is an alcoholic; another "defies widowhood."

RIDDELL, CHARLOTTE ELIZA LAWSON (COWAN). 1832-1906. United Kingdom.

2560   THE HEAD OF THE FIRM. BY MRS. J. H. RIDDELL. New York: J. W. Lovell, [c1891] NUC. London: W. Heinemann, 1892 NUC.

Aileen, a vendor of fruits and vegetables, inherits money and hires a governess to educate her for her new position.

2561   A MAD TOUR; OR, A JOURNEY UNDERTAKEN IN AN INSANE MOMENT THROUGH CENTRAL EUROPE ON FOOT. BY MRS. J. H. RIDDELL. London: R. Bentley, 1891 NUC BMC. New York, Chicago: U. S. Book, [c1891] NUC.

Middle-aged woman and young man set out on a walking tour. Though she is the one who has many apprehensions about enduring the trip, she succeeds and ends up nursing the young man. Light and amusing.

RIDDELL, MRS. J. H. See RIDDELL, CHARLOTTE ELIZA LAWSON (COWAN).

RIDLEY, ALICE (DAVENPORT). D. 1945. United Kingdom.

2562 ANNE MAINWARING. London: Longmans, 1901 BMC. New York: Longmans, Green, 1901 NUC.

Anne Mainwaring is a clever, "stormy and strenuous" young woman—a thorn in her mother's side. She feels destined to be a great actress but makes an unsuitable marriage when she's quite young. Her friendship with Lady Katherine.

2563 A DAUGHTER OF JAEL. London: Longmans, Green, 1904 BMC NUC.

A strong young woman justifiably kills her grandfather who is killing her young brother by starvation and beatings. She keeps her secret and bears her guilt alone. Her guilt returns in agonizing proportions later when she is tempted to use the same method when a woman is destroying her marriage.

2564 THE STORY OF ALINE. London: Chapman and Hall, 1896 NUC BMC.

A study of Aline, an intellectual and sensitive woman married to an athletic man with whom she has nothing in common. Her suffering is intensified by her husband's becoming crippled in an accident and the loss of her friend Gerald's companionship when he becomes engaged to her niece. Her yearning for happiness is intensified to a passion. One reviewer calls this a delicate and sensitive work; another describes it as a painful subject handled with commendable restraint.

RIGGS, KATE DOUGLAS (SMITH) WIGGIN. 1856-1923. United States.

2565   A CATHEDRAL COURTSHIP, AND PENELOPE'S ENGLISH EXPERIENCES. BY KATE DOUGLAS WIGGIN. Boston: Houghton Mifflin, 1893 NUC. London: Gay and Bird, 1893 BMC NUC.

Two stories of American women's experiences in England. In the first, Celia Van Tyck and Catherine Schuyler tour the English cathedral towns. In the second, Penelope is an artist. Humorous stories ending in marriages.

2566   MARM LISA. BY KATE DOUGLAS WIGGIN. Boston: Houghton Mifflin, 1896 NUC. London: Gay and Bird, [1896] BMC.

Psychological study of 10 year old girl, called a "half-wit" by one reviewer, a "congenital idiot" by another. She is adopted by a woman who cares for humanity but not for individuals; she doesn't do well. Then she is taken in by a community of women who look after children like her. Study of her mental development under their care.

2567   PENELOPE'S ENGLISH EXPERIENCES. BY KATE DOUGLAS WIGGIN. Boston: Houghton Mifflin, 1900 NUC BMC. London: Gay and Bird, 1901 BMC.

2568   PENELOPE'S EXPERIENCES IN SCOTLAND. BEING EXTRACTS FROM THE COMMONPLACE BOOK OF PENELOPE HAMILTON. BY KATE DOUGLAS WIGGIN. London: Gay and Bird, 1898 BMC. London: Bell, 1898 NUC. Travel-fiction. Penelope and two friends, one a middle aged Bostonian spinster and the other a vivacious New Yorker, in Scotland.

2569   PENELOPE'S IRISH EXPERIENCES. BY KATE DOUGLAS WIGGIN. Boston: Houghton Mifflin, 1901 NUC. London: Gay & Bird, 1901 BMC NUC.

Three women, one married, one engaged and one "to be settled," travel in Ireland, meet a stranded young woman from New England and befriend her.

2570   PENELOPE'S POSTSCRIPTS; SWITZERLAND: VENICE: WALES: DEVON: HOME. BY KATE DOUGLAS WIGGIN. Boston: Houghton Mifflin, 1915 NUC. London: Hodder & Stoughton, 1915 BMC.

2571 PENELOPE'S PROGRESS: BEING SUCH EXTRACTS
      FROM THE COMMONPLACE BOOK OF PENELOPE
      HAMILTON AS RELATED TO HER EXPERIENCES IN
      SCOTLAND. BY KATE DOUGLAS WIGGIN. London:
      A. P. Watt, 1897 BMC. Boston: Houghton Mifflin, 1898
      NUC.

2572 THE STORY OF WAITSTILL BAXTER. BY KATE
      DOUGLAS WIGGIN. Boston: Houghton Mifflin, 1913
      NUC. London: Hodder & Stoughton, [1913] BMC.
      Story of stepsisters and their tyrannical father, a deacon
      whose three wives died mostly to get away from him.
      Waitsell is a drudge to her father. Both she and fiery, red-
      haired Patience are strong young women who refuse to be
      dutiful to their father whose strict morals and narrow
      views are more than the stepsisters can bear. Both revolt,
      refusing to submit to injustice. One does it impulsively;
      the other calmly. Includes their "unconventional love
      affairs" and marriages.

2573 SUSANNA AND SUE. BY KATE DOUGLAS WIGGIN.
      Boston: Houghton-Mifflin, 1909 NUC. London: Hodder &
      Stoughton, 1909 BMC.
      Susanna leaves her husband and son to live in a Shaker
      village with her little daughter Sue. She gets help with her
      marital problems, finds happiness and, in the end, returns
      home.

RINEHART, MARY (ROBERTS). 1876-1958. United States.

2574 THE AMAZING ADVENTURES OF LETITIA
      CARBERRY. Indianapolis: Bobbs-Merrill, [c1911] NUC.
      London: Hodder & Stoughton, [1919] BMC.
      She is a witty, adventurous old woman, unashamed of her
      spinsterhood. She solves a murder mystery. Her two
      friends Lizzie and Aggie are the same age as she and
      single.

2575 THE AMAZING INTERLUDE. London: J. Murray, 1918
      BMC. New York: G. H. Doran, [c1918] NUC.
      When Sara Lee, living in a conventional town, decides she
      wants to be in the front lines, she gets the Ladies' Aid

Society to send her to France to start a soup kitchen. She doesn't ask but tells her fiance she is going. She nurses soldiers and falls in love with a Belgian officer.

2576 A POOR WISE MAN. New York: G. H. Doran, [c1920] NUC. London: Hodder & Stoughton, [1920] BMC.

Lily, after her experiences as a war worker, rebels against her luxurious home and her tyrannical grandfather. She becomes involved in labor problems and is used by an unscrupulous labor leader. Disaster follows.

2577 THE STREET OF SEVEN STARS. Boston: Houghton Mifflin, 1914 NUC. London: Cassell, 1915 BMC.

Harmony Wells studying in Vienna to be a violinist runs out of money. Determined to be a great artist, she refuses to give up her studies and looks for work. She falls in love and shares a home with Peter, Dr. Anna, and a waif named Jimmie. Conflicting claims of love and art.

2578 TISH. Boston: Houghton Mifflin, 1916 BMC NUC. London: Hodder & Stoughton, [1917] BMC.

Stories of three elderly spinsters and their unconventional adventures, which include an auto racing scheme and a woman chauffeur.

2579 WHERE THERE'S A WILL. Indianapolis: Bobbs-Merrill, [c1912] NUC. New York: A. L. Burt, [1914] NUC.

Heroine, a "spring-house girl" in a sanitarium, has strong individuality and pungent humor. The adventure portrayed is the most exciting time of her long and diplomatic career.

RION, HANNA. See VER BECK, HANNA (RION).

RITA. See HUMPHREYS, ELIZA MARGARET J. (GOLLAN). Also HUMPHREYS, ELIZA MARGARET J. (GOLLAN) AND LOUISA ALICE BAKER.

RITCHIE, BARBARA LOGIE.

2580   THE TENANT OF SEA COTTAGE. London: Drane, [1916] BMC.
"Time honored" lady burglar and her accomplice.

RIVERS, RUTH.

2581   SHE WAS A WIDOW. London: J. Long, 1911 BMC.
"She was also a mercenary, deceitful, sensual woman interested above all other things in the effect of her lures upon the sex instinct of the men she met. This story is a nauseous delineation in the first person of a type of character that our plain-speaking forefathers would have summed up in one word."

RIVES, AMELIE. See TROUBETZKOY, AMELIE (RIVES) CHANLER.

RIVES, HALLIE ERMINIE. See WHEELER, HALLIE ERMINIE (RIVES).

ROBBINS, EMMA SHELTON. United States.

2582   OH, YOU ENGLISH! New York: Neale, 1915 NUC.
Amily at her father's death left the Ozarks and went to New York to earn her living. After escaping perils of many kinds, she married Lord Richard and discovered her English relatives.

ROBBINS, MABEL HOTCHKISS. United States.

2583   THE HEART OF A MOTHER-TO-BE. Boston: Pilgrim Press, [c1917] NUC.
Diary telling dreams, hopes and fears preceding motherhood.

ROBERTS, HELEN C.

2584   THE DISCREET ADVENTURE. London: T. F. Unwin, [1917] BMC NUC.
Character study of Alberta Upwey, a woman with a

superior attitude toward "social inferiors," who worships Art. "We are meant to sympathize with her throughout." Story concerns the way she and her two sisters live their lives. Becomes a governess suspected of having designs on her employer's unmarried brother.

2585 SOMETHING NEW. London: Duckworth, 1913 BMC.

Tessa Hastings of high society is engaged, but she tires of the social whirl of teas and dances and yearns for a different kind of life. She gives up her soft life and her fiance for a life with working-class people. Eventually she meets another man.

ROBERTS, MARGARET. 1833-1919. United Kingdom.

2586 NICCOLINA NICCOLINI. BY THE AUTHOR OF "MADEMOISELLE MORI" [ANONYMOUS]. London: Gardiner, Darton, [1897] NUC BMC. (NUC does not indicate anonymous publication.)

Lina is the orphan of an English mother and an Italian painter: her growing up and her love affair. "Love could hardly be altogether absent from any typical study of a woman, but it is of the essence of this conception that love takes a subordinate place, and it is here but slightly touched on." This author's heroines are endowed with talent, the improvement of which is one main object of their lives. "This gives an independence and completeness to a woman's career which it is hard for her to attain in any other way."

2587 A YOUNGER SISTER. BY THE AUTHOR OF "THE ATELIER DU LYS" [ANONYMOUS]. London: Longmans, Green, 1892 BMC NUC.

Guenola, a "fin de siecle young woman," is the daughter of a narrow-minded pedant and egoist. She longs to study Greek and math and to be financially independent. She is considered selfish, but when the older daughter accepts a marriage offer and leaves home, it is Guenola who remains as her father's companion. At last she is free to earn her own living. After experiencing some of the difficulties of working, she is less self-confident and better appreciates home and love. She eventually marries and becomes a manager of her husband's printing shop.

ROBERTSON, ALICE ALBERTHE. B. 1871. United States.

2588   TAMAR CURZE. BY BERTHE ST. LUZ. New York: R. F. Fenno, [c1908] NUC.

Half woman, half tiger, Tamar wins her cousin's love. When he repulses her, the tiger in her kills him.

ROBERTSON, ETHEL FLORENCE LINDESAY (RICHARDSON). 1870-1946. United Kingdom.

2589   THE GETTING OF WISDOM. BY HENRY HANDEL RICHARDSON. London: W. Heinemann, 1910 NUC BMC. New York: Duffield, 1910 NUC.

Laura Rambotham, a young woman in boarding school, dislikes men and is close friends with her room-mate. She determines to become a writer so that, although she is a misfit, she can create her own world in fiction.

ROBIN, E. GALLIENNE.* United Kingdom.

2590   CHRISTINE, A GUERNSEY GIRL. London: Hurst and Blackett, 1912 BMC.

Psychological study of a calculating woman who is a blackmailer and runs an eating house.

ROBINS, ELIZABETH. See PARKES, ELIZABETH (ROBINS).

ROBINS, G. M. See REYNOLDS, GERTRUDE M. (ROBINS).

ROBINSON, SUZANNE (ANTROBUS). United States.

2591   THE KING'S MESSENGER: A NOVEL. BY SUZANNE ANTROBUS. New York and London: Harper, 1901 NUC.

Heroine leaves husband to bear a secret packet to the New France; falls in love with another man. Sentimental.

ROCH, FFLORENS.*

2592   THE CALL OF THE PAST. London: Sands, 1913 BMC.

Humorous account of reorganization of the Welsh Women's Charitable Union. Story concerns Gwenllian and her parents' guidance in her choice of husband.

RODEN, ADA MARIA (JENYNS) JOCELYN. B. 1860.

2593 FOR ONE SEASON ONLY: A SPORTING NOVEL. London: F. V. White, 1893 BMC.

Six foot two, large framed, rough-mannered Georgina Pembrooke is a sportswoman, a paying guest for the horse season at MacFluster Hall where she comes to hunt. She is a direct, capable, self-reliant young woman with large hands, a loud voice, decided opinions, daring manners and mannish ways. "She almost takes one's breath away." She wages a campaign against her host because he neglects his daughter Charlotte. She manages to get Charlotte free from an unsuitable suitor and to arrange a London trip for Charlotte—at the expense of Charlotte's father.

2594 RUN TO GROUND; A SPORTING NOVEL. London: Hutchinson, 1894 BMC.

Lord Goring is accused of cheating at cards; he dies. Princess Dagmar Saravaski, who loved him, comes from Russia to England under an assumed name. Using her mesmeric powers, she brings the guilty person to light and clears Goring's name. Too-perfect Violet and her love affairs are a large part of the story.

RODZIEWICZ, MARYA. See RODZIEWICZOWNA, MARIA.

RODZIEWICZOWNA, MARIA. 1863-1944.

2595 DISTAFF; A NOVEL. BY MARYA RODZIEWICZ. London: Jarrold, 1901 BMC NUC. (Tr. by S. C. de Soissons.)

The woman in this novel is a Russian new woman. At 17, she leaves her home secretly and goes to the university. The story describes several years of her independence, comradeships with men, and her study of medicine.

ROE, V. E. See ROE, VINGIE EVE.

ROE, VINGIE EVE. 1879-1958. United States.

2596   A DIVINE EGOTIST. New York: Dodd, Mead, 1916
NUC.
Velving is a novelist who turns a broken-down farm into
a model settlement and frees her town from corrupt
politicians, one of whom she "thrashes." She rescues a
drunk from the gutter and later marries him. She adopts a
blind baby.

2597   THE HEART OF NIGHT WIND; A STORY OF THE
GREAT NORTH WEST. New York: Dodd, Mead, 1913
NUC. London: Gay & Hancock, [1928] BMC.
Heroine comes under the protection of "a very remarkable
and exceptional old woman who is cook, mother, and
general-in-chief of a certain lumber camp in Oregon."
Includes heroine's love story.

2598   THE MAID OF THE WHISPERING HILLS. New York:
Dodd, Mead, 1912 NUC. London: Gay & Hancock, 1915
BMC.
The story of a young woman who is the leader of a band
of French Canadians in the wilderness, an 18th century
historical romance.

2599   THE PRIMAL LURE: A ROMANCE OF FORT LU
CERNE. BY V. E. ROE. New York: Dodd, Mead, 1914
NUC. London: Gay & Hancock, [c1915] BMC.
Lois Lewayne, described as a superwoman of inexhaustible
energy, has many adventures, beginning with her
imprisonment at a small Hudson Bay Post. Includes an
Indian woman doctor who administers a blood
transfusion.

ROGERS, C. V.*

2600   HER MARRIAGE VOW. London: F. V. White, 1898
BMC.
On discovering that she has been married for her money,
the dowdy-looking heroine leaves her husband before the
birth of her child. A severe illness causes her to lose
weight and transforms her appearance. She then takes on

a new identity, Lady Blanchyre, by assuming the title of a deceased peer. She is successful in society, encountering her husband who falls madly in love with her; she doesn't reveal her identity to him until the end, when she's 60.

ROGERS, MARY HULBERT.

2601 CHILDREN OF THE NIGHT. New York: Duffield, 1911 NUC.

Middle-aged blind woman dictates her life story to her secretary; her digressions and happy reminiscences.

ROHLEDER, GRACE IRENE.

2602 WOMAN ON THE BENCH. Washington, D. C.: 1920 NUC.

(Author is a member of the bar in Washington, D. C.)

ROHLFS, ANNA KATHARINE (GREEN). 1846-1935. United States.

2603 THE GOLDEN SLIPPER, AND OTHER PROBLEMS FOR VIOLET STRANGE. BY ANNA KATHARINE GREEN (MRS. CHARLES ROHLFS). New York: G. P. Putman's Sons, 1915 BMC NUC.

Violet Strange is a successful American detective.

2604 LOST MAN'S LANE: A SECOND EPISODE IN THE LIFE OF AMELIA BUTTERWORTH. BY ANNA KATHARINE GREEN (MRS. CHARLES ROHLFS). New York and London: G. P. Putnam's Sons, 1898 BMC NUC.

Amelia Butterworth, "in some respects an even more original conception than Doyle's Sherlock Holmes" and "much more canny," is assisted by Gryce in detection.

2605 MISS HURD, AN ENIGMA. BY ANNA KATHARINE GREEN (MRS. CHARLES ROHLFS). New York, London: G. P. Putnam's Sons, 1894 BMC NUC.

She makes repeated attempts to run away from her wealthy and devoted husband, each time earning her living by various means. He always brings her back. After a final escape, there is a growing suspicion that he has murdered her.

2606 THAT AFFAIR NEXT DOOR. BY ANNA KATHARINE GREEN (MRS. CHARLES ROHLFS). New York, London: G. P. Putnam's Sons, 1897 BMC NUC.

There is a friendly competition between detective Gryce and the still more astute detective—Miss Butterworth, who unravels the mystery and brings the murderer to justice. She outwits Gryce because he is overconfident.

ROHLFS, MRS. CHARLES. See ROHLFS, ANNA KATHARINE (GREEN).

ROLLINS, CLARA HARRIOT (SHERWOOD). B. 1874. United States.

2607 THREADS OF LIFE. Boston: Lamson, Wolffe, 1897 NUC.

The "heart histories" of Miriam Sard, 27, single; and Mrs. Farnham, 38, a widow and grandmother. The two discuss the nature of men and women, their privileges, rights and duties—in a learned, witty fashion. Scene: a farm near Concord, Mass.

ROOSEVELT, FLORENCE.

2608 THE SIREN'S NET: A NOVEL. TRANSCRIBED FROM LIFE. London: T. F. Unwin, 1905 BMC NUC.

The difficulties and risks a woman faces in a career as opera singer.

ROSMAN, ALICE GRANT. B. 1887. United Kingdom.

2609 MISS BRYDE OF ENGLAND. London: A. Melrose, [1915] BMC.

Helen Bryde and her brother escape the tyranny of their cruel father, move to London, and pursue careers in literature and art.

ROSS, MARTIN. See MARTIN, VIOLET FLORENCE AND EDITH ANNA OENONE SOMERVILLE, also SOMERVILLE, EDITH ANNA AND VIOLET FRANCES MARTIN.

ROSSETTI, CHRISTINA GEORGINA. 1830-1894. United Kingdom.

2610   MAUDE; A STORY FOR GIRLS. London: J. Bowden, 1897 BMC NUC.

The record of a half-hysterical self-occupied young woman who dies early, "somewhat to the relief of the reader," says one reviewer who also describes the story as "fumblings...of a half-learned art and half-developed power."

ROSSI, LOUISE.

2611   AN UNCONVENTIONAL GIRL. London: Lawrence and Bullen, 1896 BMC.

Linda L'Estrange leads a lonely life, reads voluminously as a child, lives alone, smokes, writes, and becomes a famous novelist. Reviewers concur that "nowadays these proceedings are rather conventional than otherwise."

ROUSE, ADELAIDE LOUISE. D. 1912. United States.

2612   THE DEANE GIRLS. A HOME STORY. New York: A. L. Burt, [1895] NUC. London: Hodder and Stoughton, 1895 BMC.

Eight daughters of a poor clergyman help out by teaching, writing for a newspaper, and taking in boarders—until most of them marry.

2613   THE LETTERS OF THEODORA. New York and London: Macmillan, 1905 BMC NUC.

Theodora, a college professor, moves to New York City to write and to avoid John. In the city, she runs into him again, avoids him again, and becomes a lecturer. She almost marries a congressman, but repents and goes abroad, John in pursuit. Independent Theodora does finally marry John but not without enforcing her own ideas of wifehood.

2614 UNDER MY OWN ROOF. New York and London: Funk & Wagnalls, 1902 BMC NUC.
Middle-aged spinster, retired from journalism, builds her own house. She marries the next door neighbor.

ROWLAND, HELEN. 1875-1950. United States.

2615 THE DIGRESSIONS OF POLLY. New York: Baker and Taylor, [1905] NUC.
Polly, a "modern" young woman discusses cigarette smoking, art of proposing, making over of a wife, etc. with her fiance.

ROWLANDS, EFFIE ADELAIDE. See ALBANESI, EFFIE ADELAIDE MARIA.

ROWSELL, MARY CATHERINE. United Kingdom.

2616 PETRONELLA AND MADAME PONOWSKI. London: Skeffington, 1891 BMC. (Two tales.)
Petronella is a Jacobite woman who quarrels with her Hanoverian lover about politics. The two are reunited in middle age. Madame Ponowski is a murderer who collects her victims' heads in a cabinet.

ROY, GORDON. See WALLACE, HELEN.

ROY, JEAN.*

2617 THE FIELDS OF THE FATHERLESS. London: W. Collins, 1917 BMC. New York: G. H. Doran, [c1918] NUC.
Autobiography of a young Scotch-Irish woman living in a poor Scotch village. She leaves home where she is beaten and where her grandmother drinks. Jean Roy was born of unwed parents and thus abused. She earns her own living as a factory worker, a domestic worker, a stewardess on a boat. Her whole sad haunting hopeless hand-to-mouth

existence including severe illness and an operation is depicted. There is no space for love in this life story that is an indictment of the social effects of poverty on parts of Scotland.

ROY, OLIVIA.

2618 THE AWAKENING OF MRS. CARSTAIRS. Edinburgh: G. A. Morton, 1904 BMC.

A diary in which is revealed a lawless, consuming passion. She had "left her home a cold, passionless girl, liking her husband as a friend."

ROZANT, INA.

2619 LIFE'S UNDERSTUDIES: A NOVEL. London: T. S. Clark, [1907] BMC NUC. New York: M. Kennerley, [1915?] NUC.

Actress whose husband becomes insane tells the world and her child that her husband is dead. He goes out of her life when he learns this.

RUCK, BERTA. See OLIVER, AMY ROBERTA (RUCK).

RUDOLF, MRS. E. DE M.

2620 THE BLUE CARNATION. London: Ward Lock, 1916 BMC.

Millicent is a student at a horticultural college.

2621 CURTIS & CO. London: Ward, Lock, 1917 BMC.

Woman married a shopkeeper who is injured in an auto accident. She runs the business so effectively that "Curtis" in the title could refer to her.

RUMSEY, FRANCES. United States.

2622 LEONORA; A NOVEL. New York and London: D. Appleton, 1910 BMC NUC.

Leonora is the child of divorced parents, spends three

months' time with each, and is violently opposed to divorce. She falls in love with a divorced man.

2623 MR. CUSHING AND MLLE. DU CHASTEL. New York and London: J. Lane, 1917 NUC 1918 BMC.

Analysis in Jamesian style of an international marriage. Mlle. Du Chastel married in France, comes to the United States, "forms liaisons," separates and returns to Paris to live in poverty. Ends with her husband proposing they remarry.

RUSSELL, DORA. United Kingdom.

2624 A COUNTRY SWEETHEART. London: Chatto and Windus, 1894 BMC. Chicago: Rand, McNally, [1895] NUC.

Women who propose to men. Vulgar characters elbow out the more refined.

2625 THE DRIFT OF FATE. London: Chatto and Windus, 1895 BMC.

Nell Drummond must marry to save her family's estate. She prepares for her wedding by buying a knife, but instead of killing her husband, she dresses in men's clothing and runs off on her wedding day. She becomes a governess-companion and ends well.

2626 AN EVIL REPUTATION: A NOVEL. London: Griffith, Farran, 1892 BMC.

In a lonely house on the seacoast with an evil reputation for tragedy, a beautiful young married woman is the victim of almost unheard of cruelties. Her husband and his accomplice try to kill her, but she recovers. They subsequently twice abduct her; she survives it all to bring retribution on them. Sensational.

2627 A FATAL PAST: A NOVEL. New York: J. W. Lovell, [1891] NUC. London: Simpkin, Marshall, [1896] BMC.

Lady Ennismore, married, mother of several children, attempts to kill her first husband whom she married at 16 and who reappears after years. Instead she kills the husband she loves. She also dies.

2628   A GREAT TEMPTATION. London: F. V. White, 1894 BMC.

Laura is educated, is writing a novel. She marries a solicitor, tires of him, loves Sir Ralph. She leaves her husband but does not remarry. Her husband identifies a dead woman with a disfigured face as Laura and remarries.

2629   HER PROMISE TRUE. Chicago: Rand, McNally, [c1898] NUC. London: Digby, Long, 1899 BMC.

Belle Wayland is deceived into marrying a man she doesn't love. When she discovers the deception, she runs off with the lover from whom she had been separated. Before they can be married, he dies. She subsequently dies in childbirth.

2630   A HIDDEN CHAIN: A NOVEL. London: Digby, Long, 1894 BMC. Chicago: Rand, McNally, [1896] NUC.

Eva is married to a tyrant clergyman who has been in Africa for so many years she assumes he's dead. He returns the day before her wedding. Clair horsewhips a treacherous banker. (Dora Russell is an heir of M. E. Braddon.)

2631   A TORN-OUT PAGE. Chicago: Rand, McNally, [1897] NUC. London: Digby, Long, 1899 BMC.

Daughter of an English admiral has at 16 a secret and unhappy marriage. She afterwards conceals this "torn-out page" of her life from her father.

RUSSELL, FRANCES E. United States.

2632   A QUAINT SPINSTER. Boston: Roberts, 1895 NUC.

Priscilla Trippings inherits a fortune, "sets up a home for the sisterhood." Together with Misses Lawrence, Pressie, Meekson, and Gildersleeve, she conducts night-classes and cooking schools. Their home becomes a center of great influence.

RUSSELL, LINDSAY PATRICIA. 1870-1949.

2633 EARTHWARE. London: Cassell, 1918 BMC.

The development of a woman through a hard childhood and a hard married life to, for a time, a freer outlook in London.

2634 LAND O' THE DAWNING. London: Cassell, [1917] BMC.

Heroine takes part in Sinn Fein rebellion.

2635 SONS OF ISCARIOT. London: Ward, Lock, 1916 BMC.

Young Australian woman betrayed by priest.

2636 THE YEARS OF FORGETTING. London: Ward & Lock, 1914 BMC.

A young Australian woman is deceived by a priest; she struggles to make a living for herself and her child.

RUSSELL, MARIE.

2637 RUSSIAN REBELS. London: F. Griffiths, 1914 BMC.

Edna is a governess in a Russian family. The story does not end in marriage.

RUSSELL, MARION.

2638 AN EXCELLENT MYSTERY. London: S. Swift, 1912 BMC.

She flees from an uncongenial home and marries a man she doesn't love. He deserts her, she divorces. She is left with the prospect of a happier union.

RUSSELL, MARY ANNETTE (BEAUCHAMP) ARNIM RUSSELL. 1866-1941. United Kingdom.

2639 THE ADVENTURES OF ELIZABETH IN RUGEN. BY THE AUTHOR OF "ELIZABETH AND HER GERMAN GARDEN" [ANONYMOUS]. New York and London: Macmillan, 1904 BMC NUC. Leipzig: B. Tauchnitz, 1906 NUC.

Elizabeth takes a month's vacation from her husband and children each year and travels alone.

2640 THE BENEFACTRESS. BY THE AUTHOR OF "ELIZABETH AND HER GERMAN GARDEN" [ANONYMOUS]. London and New York: Macmillan, 1901 BMC NUC.

Woman comes into money and establishes her estate as a home for unmarried women who are impoverished. Heroine marries; the single women are manipulative.

2641 THE CARAVANERS. BY THE AUTHOR OF "ELIZABETH AND HER GERMAN GARDEN" [ANONYMOUS]. New York: Doubleday, Page, [c1909] NUC. London: Smith, Elder, 1909 BMC 1910 NUC.

Group of German travellers in England, among them a pompous baron oblivious of his faults, Frau Von Eckthum, whom the baron misunderstands to be attracted to him, and an oppressed German wife who gradually revolts.

2642 CHRISTINE. BY ALICE CHOLMONDELEY. New York: Macmillan, 1917 NUC. London: Macmillan, 1917 BMC.

Letters from Christine to her mother from Germany just before and after the outbreak of the war. Her mother sacrificed for Christine's year of violin study in Germany. She is 22 and her music master claims she is a genius. The letters show Christine as a thoughtful and independent young woman. Her early letters are about her art, the people, her love for a German officer. Then she records the state of mind of German citizens, shrewd statements about the Kaiser, the change war brings in the Germans and in her relations to them. In the preface we are told that Christine died of pneumonia in a German hospital and that she was the author's daughter, a statement received with much skepticism by some reviewers.

2643 FRAULEIN SCHMIDT AND MR. ANSTRUTHER; BEING THE LETTERS OF AN INDEPENDENT WOMAN. BY THE AUTHOR OF "ELIZABETH AND HER GERMAN GARDEN" AND "THE PRINCESS PRISCILLA'S FORTNIGHT" [ANONYMOUS]. New York: C. Scribner's Sons, 1907 NUC. London: Macmillan, 1907 NUC.

Rose-Marie Schmidt's letters concerning literary criticism, unconventional ideas, discussions of music, as well as her past experiences written to a man she was secretly engaged to but who jilted her for a rich woman. Her love for him had turned to contempt at that point and she had chosen poverty and independence rather than take him back. She is completed cured of her love for him.

2644   IN THE MOUNTAINS [ANONYMOUS]. Garden City, New York: Doubleday, Page, 1920 NUC. London: Macmillan, 1920 BMC NUC.

A woman who is recovering from losing all she loved in the war goes to a Swiss chalet. By chance she is joined by two widows who become permanent guests. She describes their relations and her recovery from grief in the form of a diary.

2645   THE PASTOR'S WIFE. BY THE AUTHOR OF "ELIZABETH AND HER GERMAN GARDEN" [ANONYMOUS]. London: Smith, Elder, 1914 BMC NUC. Garden City, New York: Doubleday, Page, 1914 NUC.

Ingeborg, the daughter of an English bishop, marries Dremmel, a German minister with an obsessive interest in manure. She has six children in seven years; her health is shattered. On regaining her strength, she refuses to have further sex with her husband. She runs off with an artist, finds him unworthy, and returns filled with remorse to Dremmel. He, however, is so busy with his manure that he barely notes her departure or return.

RUSSELL, MRS. H. E.

2646   JOYCE MARTINDALE. London: Remington, 1894 BMC.

A curate who believes in sexual abstinence is in love with Joyce. Joyce rejects his suit. "Powerful and sometimes trenchant opinions on social subjects." Australia.

RUTHVEN, E. C.*

2647   THE UPHILL ROAD. London: Chapman & Hall, 1906 BMC.

Elaborate analysis of the sensations of an introspective and independent young woman who refuses love "for unconvincing reasons."

RYAN, MARAH ELLIS (MARTIN). 1860(?)-1934. United States.

2648 THE BONDWOMAN. Chicago: Rand, McNally, 1899. London: T. F. Unwin, [1899] BMC.

A French marquise, widow of twenty, idealistic and well educated, buys a southern plantation during the Civil War. She is fiercely resentful for the wrongs of slave women in the United States. She becomes a spy and eventually plots to ruin the man she loved because she believes he owns an octoroon, and in trying to free her fellow-women from the consequences of slavery, she discovers that she herself is an octoroon.

2649 A FLOWER OF FRANCE: A STORY OF OLD LOUISIANA. Chicago: Rand, McNally, 1894 NUC.

Zizi, an African slave, incurs the displeasure of her master and is branded with the fleur-de-lis. The story is of her vengeance and her final act of restitution.

2650 THE WOMAN OF THE TWILIGHT; THE STORY OF A STORY. London: C. F. Cazenove, 1913 BMC. Chicago: A. C. McClurg, 1913 NUC.

Sympathetic portrayal of Monica Wayne married very young to a man who deserted her. She is an artist of genius who later falls in love, but cannot marry this man because of her marriage. The pair "seek happiness outside the law." Includes the heroine's "flaming indignation against certain hideously unjust laws." Takes place first in a Mexican settlement in California, then in New York City.

RYLAND, CALLY THOMAS, jt. au. See LAGEN, MARY JULIA AND CALLY THOMAS RYLAND.

RYLEY, M. BERESFORD.*

2651 "MA'AM". London: Hutchinson, 1917 BMC.

Griselda Cunningham, a suffragette, a near agnostic, and the restless rebellious wife of a narrow pompous husband, is completely out of place as a curate's wife. She leaves him and goes off to Italy, where she falls in love. She is about to live with the man when illness intervenes. At the end her husband comes to his senses, and the man she loved becomes her good friend.

SADLEIR, MARIE M.

2652 SUCH IS THE LAW! A STORY. London: Greening, 1899 BMC.

Condemns the law that gives a man the right to will his property away from his wife and children. The story of Lavender and Sydney Weston.

SADLER, CORA G.

2653 THE PENDULUM: A NOVEL. Boston: Sherman French, 1912 NUC.

Woman loses her mind through husband's blow; avenged by her son.

SAGER, JULIET GILMAN. B. 1873. United States.

2654 ANNE, ACTRESS; THE ROMANCE OF A STAR. New York: F.A. Stokes, [1913] BMC NUC.

Widowed Anne North, leading lady in a stock company in Brooklyn, struggled for years to educate her daughter Elsie. At 18 Elsie joins her mother in theater work just at the point of Anne's great success and happiness in love. Elsie wins her mother's place on stage.

SAGON, AMYOT.*

2655 AN AUSTRALIAN DUCHESS. London: Hurst and Blackett, 1897 BMC.

The young man who jumps from his horse, seizes a whip, lashes a man senseless and dares other men to approach is in reality a young woman in male attire, "one of the most skillful stockriders of the district." Eventually she marries, and we see her in diamonds on Park Lane.

SAINT AUBYN, ALAN. See MARSHALL, FRANCES (BRIDGES).

SAINT FELIX, MARIE. See LYNCH, HARRIET LOUISE (HUSTED).

SAINT LEGER, EVELYN. See RANDOLPH, EVELYN SAINT LEGER (SAVILE).

SAINT LUZ, BERTHE. See ROBERTSON, ALICE ALBERTHE.

SANBORN, KATHERINE ABBOTT. 1839-1917. United States.

2656 ADOPTING AN ABANDONED FARM. New York: D. Appleton, 1891 NUC BMC.
Tired of the city and apartment life, a woman buys a farm for a bargain and runs it successfully. Her various experiences at auctions, buying a horse, raising chickens, etc.

SANBORN, MARY FARLEY (SANBORN). 1853-1941. United States.

2657 PAULA FERRIS. Boston: Lee and Shepard, 1893 NUC.
"...a woman has permitted a man to tell her he loves her and has answered that she loves him," has been "passionately kissed, etc. and returns to loving her husband and to being loved by him without a sign of regret or shadow of remorse." The author believes in women like Paula who can experience outlaw passion and remain pure and good. The reviewer sees her as "hysterical," idle and self indulgent.

SANDARS, NEWTON. See MEARS, LOUISE.

SANDEMAN, MINA.

2658 THE INFATUATION OF AMANDA. London: Digby, Long, [1898] BMC.
Amanda, a plain heroine in love with her husband, discovers he has only a "tepid toleration" of her. He

neglects her and is abusive. She kills him, going mad when she does so.

2659 AN UNCONVENTIONAL MAID. A NOVEL. London: Skeffington, 1904 BMC.

She is plain and piquant, astonishes with the brilliant audacity of her views, marries a famous scientist who is an ardent anti-vivisectionist. In the form of an autobiography, humorous.

2660 WICKED ROSAMOND. London: J. Long, 1899 BMC.

Tries to poison her husband by means of poisoned gloves a music-hall woman gave her. They were made from a recipe of Catherine de Medici. According to one reviewer her fate "provides a salutary moral."

SANDS, BEATRICE. United States.

2661 WEEPERS IN PLAYTIME. New York: J. Lane, 1908 NUC.

A child born of a bigamous marriage is placed in a home. The mother works befriending children in these institutions, at last discovers her child. Institutionalized children are the weepers.

SANDYS, OLIVER. See EVANS, MARGUERITE FLORENCE HELENE (JERVIS).

SANGSTER, MARGARET ELIZABETH (MUNSON). 1838-1912. United States.

2662 ELEANOR LEE: A NOVEL. New York: F.H. Revell, [1903] BMC NUC.

Eleanor Lee works among the poor and rehabilitates her alcoholic husband. The novel covers many subjects pertinent to modern women such as women's clubs.

SATTERLEE, ANNA ELIZA (HICKOX). B. 1851. United States.

2663 THE WONDER GIRL: A TOURIST TALE OF CALIFORNIA. Boston: Sherman, French, 1915 NUC.

She sings, dances, and tours California.

SAUNDERS, MARGARET ELSIE (CROWTHER) BAILLIE.
B. 1873. United Kingdom.

2664 BECKY & CO.: A NOVEL. London: Hutchinson, [1919?]
BMC NUC.
Cultured milliner houses women workers and Franciscan
nuns in her business establishment.

2665 THE BELFRY. London: Hodder & Stoughton, [1914] BMC
NUC.
Wife marries man who is committed to mental asylum,
told his case is hopeless. Finding no pleasure in society,
she is about to join a High Church nunnery when in
Bruges she meets a dramatist whose genius stirs her, and
she becomes selflessly and passionately attached. She
collaborates on a play with him; no credit is given her.
Her huband recovers and to tell him might shatter his
newly gained health. She returns to her husband.

2666 THE BRIDE'S MIRROR. London: Hutchinson, 1910 BMC.
Free love, wife beating, and atheism are the subject
matter.

2667 LADY Q. London: Hutchinson, 1912 BMC.
Heroine is a jailbird and a thief with several aliases. Her
career.

2668 LITANY LANE, A NOVEL. London: Hutchinson, 1909
BMC 1910 NUC.
Woman from the slums separated from husband "triumphs
as artist," becomes the rage as dancer and mimic. Three
men struggle for her, one for her "charms," one for her
soul, and one for her mind.

SAUNDERS, MARGARET MARSHALL. 1861-1947. Canada.

2669 THE GIRL FROM VERMONT. THE STORY OF A
VACATION SCHOOL TEACHER. BY MARSHALL
SAUNDERS. Philadelphia: Griffith and Rowland Press,
1910 NUC.
Heroine is in the "profession of organizing children's
playgrounds and vacation schools"; the theme is anti-child
labor. Includes love story.

SAUNDERS, MARSHALL. See SAUNDERS, MARGARET MARSHALL.

SAVI, E. W. See SAVI, ETHEL WINIFRED (BRYNING).

SAVI, ETHEL WINIFRED (BRYNING). 1865-1954. United Kingdom.

2670 BABA AND THE BLACK SHEEP. London: Hurst & Blackett, 1914 BMC.

Jean lives alone in India, in charge of a plantation. She is respected by the Indians, who look on her as an arbitrator and magistrate. The "black sheep" is a "self-exiled" Englishman; she falls in love with him.

2671 BANKED FIRES. BY E. W. SAVI. New York and London: G.P. Putnam's Sons, 1919 BMC NUC.

Joyce Meredith is 15 years younger than her husband, whose career keeps them in India. Joyce wants desperately to return home to England with her child but her husband refuses to leave. When she is forced to make a decision between her child and her husband, she "puts her child first and her husband nowhere."

2672 MISTRESS OF HERSELF. London: Hurst & Blackett, [1918] BMC.

Two sisters, one is fashionable and artificial. The other, the heroine, has advanced views and is too aggressive, reviewer feels.

2673 WHEN THE BLOOD BURNS. BY E. W. SAVI. New York and London: G.P. Putnam's Sons, 1920 BMC NUC.

Marcelle, a typist, goes to India with David; they live together as a married couple. Their secret is discovered and they meet with disapproval. David's devotion breaks down under the strain and Marcelle leaves him.

SAVILE, HELEN V.

2674 LOVE, THE PLAYER. London: 1899 NUC.

Melodramatic story of an Irish woman who is betrayed and whose rejected lover vows revenge. Her sister Janet Brady adopts the illegitimate child and is severely scorned by society for her action. She is killed accidentally in the revenge attempt.

SAWTELL, ELLA.

2675 THE BREATH OF SCANDAL. London: Greening, 1909 BMC.

Hazel is deserted by her husband who becomes a famous singer. She lives obscurely in London until she too becomes famous—as a violinist. But her career is cut short by her death.

SAWYER, RUTH. 1880-1970. United States.

2676 LEERIE. New York and London: Harper, [c1920] BMC NUC.

Leerie is a nurse who breaks rules when it is in the best interests of her patients. The story is of her job in a sanitarium and then as an army nurse in France. Her love story is incidental.

SAYLOR, EMMA ROSALYN (SUTEMEIER). B. 1863. United States.

2677 THE LAST MILE-STONE. San Francisco: P. Elder, 1917 NUC.

Edith's letters to her friend Jerry concern her sick husband (whose death at the end makes it possible for Edith to marry Jerry), her trip to Honolulu, and the home for the aged she establishes in California.

SCARFOGLIO, MATILDE (SERAO). 1856-1927. Italy.

2678 AFTER THE PARDON. BY MATILDE SERAO. London: E. Nash, 1908 NUC 1909 BMC. New York: Stuyvesant Press, 1909 NUC.

Maria deserts her husband to live with another man and returns home when her passion for her lover burns out. There is no happiness in the reconciliation, although the husband pardons her.

2679 THE BALLET DANCER, AND ON GUARD. BY MATILDE SERAO. New York and London: Harper, 1901 NUC. London: W. Heinemann, 1901 BMC. (Tr. from the Italian.)

Psychological study of a "homely" Italian ballet dancer.

2680 THE DESIRE OF LIFE. BY MATILDE SERAO. London: S. Paul, [1911] BMC NUC. (Tr. from the Italian by William Collinge.)

A young English woman commits suicide as a result of the misery inflicted on her by the man she loved who refused to free himself from another woman.

2681 FAREWELL LOVE! A NOVEL. BY MATILDE SERAO. New York: Minerva Pub. Co., [1892] NUC BMC. (Tr. from the Italian by Mrs. H. Harland.)

Anna Acquaviva, passionate heroine, has much in common with Hedda Gabler, is another "victim of neurotic degeneracy," although Addio Amore, the Italian edition, was published in 1887, before the publication of Hedda Gabler. Anna elopes with a man who delivers her into the hands of her guardian, whom she subsequently marries. She is unhappy, he finds her a bore, she shoots herself.

SCHAEFFER, EVELYN (SCHUYLER).

2682 ISABEL STERLING. New York: Scribner, 1920 NUC. London and New York: E. Nash, [1921] BMC.

Life of Isabel from childhood through college to marriage of young army officer and subsequent life on an army post.

SCHAUFFLER, RACHEL CAPER. B. 1876. United States.

2683 THE GOODLY FELLOWSHIP. New York: Macmillan, 1912 BMC NUC.

The adventures of a young American woman missionary in Persia.

SCHEM, LIDA CLARA. 1875-1923. United States.

2684 THE VOICE OF THE HEART. A ROMANCE. BY MARGARET BLAKE. New York: G.W. Dillingham, [c1913] NUC BMC.

"The biggest thing in sex fiction....A cleverly worded plea for the recognition of passion as a vital necessity in rounding out a perfect marriage." "Romance of a girl who believes marriage is a bond of friendship and comradeship but not of love." Then she is awakened by her lover.

SCHOFIELD, LILY.

2685 CASSANDRA BY MISTAKE. London: Methuen, 1914 BMC.

A psychology professor removes his ward from all social contact in order to prove that her "spirit writing" is indeed derived from no lesser source. She murders a mute attendant defending herself from assault, and the rest of the story is concerned with saving her from the gallows.

SCHOONMAKER, NANCY (MUSSELMAN). 1873-1965. United States.

2686 THE ETERNAL FIRES. New York: Broadway, [c1910] NUC.

A young woman, rebelling against the narrow life of farmers in Kentucky, leaves home, goes to college, and travels. Her experiences in Paris with an artist are disillusioning; she finally marries an American businessman.

SCHREINER, OLIVE EMILIE ALBERTINA (SCHREINER) CRONWRIGHT. 1855-1920. South Africa.

2687 DREAMS. Boston: Roberts, 1891 NUC. London: T. F. Unwin, 1891 NUC BMC.

The subject is women's rights. A woman's eleven dreams are presented in this "classic of feminism."

SCHUBIN, OSSIP. See KIRSCHNER, LULA.

SCHUETZE, GLADYS HENRIETTA (RAPHAEL). B. 1884.
United Kingdom.

2688   A MOUSE WITH WINGS. BY HENRIETTA LESLIE.
London and Glasgow: Collins Clear-Type Press, [1920]
BMC.
Olga, whose marriage is unhappy, raises her son to be
completely unlike his sports-loving "normal" father. Olga
is a Fabian and a pacifist. The son falls in love with
Beryl, a militant suffragist, a "mouse" released under the
"cat and mouse" act. He enlists and is killed in the war.
Although Olga and Beryl are temperamentally
antagonistic, they are united in their hatred of war.

2689   THE ROUNDABOUT. BY GLADYS MENDL. London:
Chapman and Hall, 1911 BMC.
Study of friendship between two women art students and
the unhappy marriage of one of them to a man who
drinks. "Too much rhetoric."

SCHWARTZ, JULIA AUGUSTA. B. 1873. United States.

2690   VASSAR STUDIES. New York and London: G. P.
Putnam's Sons, 1899 NUC BMC.
Twelve studies of twelve types of women students. The
author's purpose is "to embody in literary form for the
alumnae of a particular institution memories and
impressions of their college days." One reviewer's response
is that 300 pages without incident or a single male figure
makes appallingly dull reading.

SCIDMORE, ELIZA RUHAMAH. 1856-1928. United States.

2691   AS THE HAGUE ORDAINS: JOURNAL OF A RUSSIAN
PRISONER'S WIFE IN JAPAN [ANONYMOUS]. New
York: H. Holt, 1907 NUC.
She is a hospital nurse in Japan who reports the war
between Japan and Russia. Her husband is a Russian
prisoner. Nonfiction?

SCOTT, C. A. DAWSON. See SCOTT, CATHARINE AMY
(DAWSON).

SCOTT, CATHARINE AMY (DAWSON). 1863-1934. United Kingdom.

2692 THE AGONY COLUMN. London: Chapman & Hall, 1909 NUC BMC.

Frances Morgan married to middle-aged soldier is bored with common duties of life. She yearns for what she doesn't have, neglects her home, and absorbs herself in a friendship with a young Jew. Her husband refuses to believe he is the father of her second child, but is willing to forgive her. Frances rejects him.

2693 THE BURDEN. BY C. A. DAWSON SCOTT. London: W. Heinemann, 1908 BMC. New York: R. Reynolds, [c1908] NUC.

A character study of a woman married to an elderly scholar. She is unfaithful, but the author condones her action: she "knew that she had ripened into a womanhood more kindly and tolerant than if she had remained the cold and gentle wife of the old scholar."

2694 THE CADDIS-WORM; OR, EPISODES IN THE LIFE OF RICHARD AND CATHERINE BLAKE. London: Hurst & Blackett, 1914 BMC.

Catherine, like the caddis-worm, has created about herself a sheath of all those virtues civilization desires in a woman: meekness, unselfishness, etc. She bears her husband's domination until it is discovered that his first wife was not dead when they married; therefore the children are not legitimate—and therefore her concern, not her husband's. She emerges from her sheath and wins independence for herself and her children.

2695 THE HEADLAND. London: W. Heinemann, 1920 BMC. New York: A. A. Knopf, 1920 NUC.

Roma is a keen-witted denizen of London studios. The novel covers three days seen through her eyes and involves Tavis Hawke, a young farmer, "the natural man calling to the natural woman," and Hendre, a clear-minded, studious man of 40. However, he has a "monstrous passion to which he periodically succumbs." Roma's discovery of his activities leads to an exciting climax in which she narrowly escapes with her life.

2696 MADCAP JANE; OR, YOUTH. London: Chapman and Hall, 1910 BMC.

Bored young wife runs away and works as a servant in her mother-in-law's household. She eventually returns.

2697 MRS. NOAKES. AN ORDINARY WOMAN. London: Chapman & Hall, 1911 BMC NUC.

Middle class woman yearns for the best but has to take second best. Husband ruins the faith she once had in him. Son turns out badly.

2698 THE STORY OF ANNA BEAMES. London: W. Heinemann, 1907 BMC NUC.

At 35 she is seduced by a scoundrel. After a short sordid marriage, he throws her downstairs; she dies giving birth.

2699 WASTRALLS. A NOVEL. BY C. A. DAWSON-SCOTT. London: W. Heinemann, [1918] BMC NUC.

Sabina works her farm Wastralls in rural Cornwall "with the skill of a man," refusing offers of marriage. Eventually she marries a farm hand. When she becomes crippled, she insists on continuing the management of the farm, control of which her husband much desires. A character study.

SCOTT, FLORENCE MARY SEYMOUR.

2700 GWLADYS PEMBERTON. London: Smith, Elder, 1896 BMC.

Gwladys, handsome and clever with original and unconventional ideas, dies nursing in a fever-struck village. There is no love interest.

SCOTT, FRANCINA.

2701 ROMANCE OF A TRAINED NURSE. New York: Cooke and Fry, 1901 NUC.

Studies, graduates, fills several positions.

SCOTT, GERALDINE EDITH (MITTON). D. 1955. United Kingdom.

2702   A BACHELOR GIRL IN LONDON. BY G. E. MITTON. London: A. & C. Black, 1898 NUC BMC.

An "accurate and convincing" portrayal of the world of large numbers of single women working in an effort to live decently, with its "utter loneliness." The heroine goes to London to make her fortune in journalism, stays at a single women's club, gets a job as a typist, endures the drudgery. She eventually makes her fortune through marriage.

2703   THE CELLAR-HOUSE OF PERVYSE: A TALE OF UNCOMMON THINGS FROM THE JOURNALS AND LETTERS OF THE BARONESS T'SERCLAES AND MAIRI CHISHOLM. BY G. E. MITTON. London: A. & C. Black, 1917 BMC NUC.

Journals of two women who were given special permission to go into the firing line to treat the wounded on the site rather than be transported. What was to be a week's experiment was extended for two years. They drove motorcycles, ambulances, cared for injured in the midst of shelling, and lived in a cellar which was bombed three times.

2704   THE GIFTS OF ENEMIES. London: A. & C. Black, 1900 BMC.

Although the first few chapters are devoted to cricket and the focus is on Neil's character, Rosa Wybrow begins the tale by killing a man, and Betty is a modern young woman who revolts against the materialistic atmosphere of her marriage.

SCOTT, PATRICIA ETHEL (STONEHOUSE). 1870-1949. Australia.

2705   THAT WOMAN FROM JAVA. BY E. HARDINGHAM QUINN. London: Hurst and Blackett, 1916 BMC.

Eleanor has been dragged through the divorce court by the treachery of a friend—comes to live in Java. Happy ending with son of Javan friend.

SCOTT, ROSE LAURE (ALLATINI).

2706 DESPISED AND REJECTED. BY R. ALLATINI. London: C. W. Daniel, [1918] NUC.

"Immediately suppressed on publication." A plea for pacifism and for tolerance of those "abnormal in their affections."

2707 HAPPY EVER AFTER. London: Mills and Boon, 1914 BMC.

The emotional history of Olive from childhood. She has literary ambitions but also yearns for a marriage of love but loses the marriage by writing a story containing biographical details.

2708 PAYMENT: A NOVEL. London: A. Melrose, 1915 BMC.

Daughter "doomed to existence with a mother whose chief interest is to kill time."

2709 REQUIEM. London: M. Secker, 1919 BMC.

Cecile is a model, and Olivia a writer. Focuses on young male Bohemian.

SCOTT, WINIFRED MAY.

2710 LOVE AND THE MAN. London: Drane, [1915] BMC.

Woman achieves immense success as an author. Writes of her passion for a married man; "emotion is overdone."

SEAWELL, MOLLY ELLIOT. 1860-1916. United States.

2711 THE DIARY OF A BEAUTY: A STORY. Philadelphia and London: J. B. Lippincott, 1915 BMC NUC.

Beautiful young postmaster inherits a fortune and inspires a playwright to write a play for her as the lead.

2712 FRANCEZKA. Indianapolis, Ind.: Bowen-Merrill, [c1902] NUC. London: B. F. Stevens and Brown, 1902 BMC.

Historical romance about an actress.

2713 THE HISTORY OF THE LADY BETTY STAIR. New York: C. Scribner's Sons, 1897 NUC BMC.

Historical romance set in France 1798. Lady Betty separated from the man she loves, meets him on the battlefield in Algeria where "she fell bleeding from a dozen wounds." She does not die nor marry the hero, but joins a convent.

2714 THE JUGGLERS: A STORY. New York: Macmillan, 1911 BMC NUC.

Historical romance. Includes an opera singer who rescues two men.

2715 THE LOVES OF THE LADY ARABELLA. New York: Macmillan, 1898 BMC NUC.

Lady Arabella, "the human counterpart of a man-slaying tigress, a highly impossible anti-heroine." Most of the story focuses upon a lieutenant in the English navy, swearing, gambling and fighting.

SEDGWICK, ANNE DOUGLAS. See DE SELINCOURT, ANNE DOUGLAS (SEDGWICK).

SEIVER, JULIA A. B. United States.

2716 BIRKWOOD: A NOVEL. Boston: Arena, 1896 NUC.

The purpose of this novel about women's rights in Florida is equality and "the development of the race intellectually, morally, and physically, that future generations may receive their just birthright." Women's rights in Florida.

SELKIRK, EMILY.

2717 THE STIGMA. Boston: G. P. Putnam's Sons, 1906 NUC. London: H. B. Turner, 1906 BMC.

The "stigma" is that of being a mulatto. A young woman school teacher finds it such a curse that she suicides.

SERAO, MATILDE. See SCARFOGLIO, MATILDE (SERAO).

SERGEANT, ADELINE. See SERGEANT, EMILY FRANCES ADELINE.

SERGEANT, EMILY FRANCES ADELINE. 1851-1904. United Kingdom.

2718   THE FAILURE OF SIBYL FLETCHER; A NOVEL. BY
       ADELINE SERGEANT. London: Heinemann, 1896 BMC.
       Philadelphia: J. B. Lippincott, 1896 NUC.
       Sibyl, a successful London painter in water-colors, "fails"
       when her fiance marries another woman. She loses both
       her power to paint and her health. She seeks rest in an
       obscure village, where she meets Michael Drage, an
       uneducated rustic, whom she marries. Reviewers are much
       divided in their opinions of Michael and their marriage.
       Sibyl, however, ultimately regains her "genius."

2719   IN THE WILDERNESS. London: A. Melrose, [1896] BMC.
       Janet, disappointed in her lover, devotes her life to work
       among the poor in the East End of London. Title refers to
       the period of loneliness through which she passes before
       she is strengthened and purified. She is described by one
       reviewer as a mild type of new woman. She eventually
       marries, but at the same time she adopts a child from the
       slums.

2720   IN VALLOMBROSA: A SEQUENCE. London: F. V.
       White, 1897 BMC.
       Cecily Marchmont and her husband are separated by
       mutual consent and with good cause. When he returns to
       Vallombrosa ill and repentent, Cecily admits her love for
       Frank Wycherly. Her dying husband urges her to marry
       Frank and be happy.

2721   THE LADY CHARLOTTE. A NOVEL. BY ADELINE
       SERGEANT. Chicago and New York: Rand, McNally,
       [1897] NUC. London: Hutchinson, 1898 BMC.
       Lady Charlotte Byng, a great traveller and sportswoman
       who rows and is a first-class shot, is an author as well as
       a reader for publishing houses. When her secretary Arthur
       Ellison steals her private family papers and writes a book
       about her, the publishers accidently send her the Ms. for
       review. Her punishment is swift and sure. Armed with a
       revolver, she goes to his rooms and forces him to give up
       the papers and sign a confession. He commits suicide by
       an overdose of chloral. Her husband, her publishers, the
       male world in general are made to tremble at her nod. A

secondary character, Esther Ellison, a college graduate and a new woman, is another fine character study.

2722 MARJORY'S MISTAKE. London: Hurst and Blackett, 1895 BMC.

Marjory Moore's nature is impulsive and reckless, but she is a talented musician. She makes a bad, then a good marriage.

2723 MRS. LYGON'S HUSBAND. London: Methuen, 1905 BMC.

Woman released from mental hospital seeks her husband and daughter. The husband who confined her is an "unmitigated villain."

2724 NO AMBITION. Edinburgh: Oliphant, Anderson and Ferrier, 1895 BMC. Bardley, 1897 NUC.

"Modern girl's world of school and college and professional ambitions." Heroine wins a scholarship at Girton but gives it up without explaining the reason to her family: she believes it will entail financial hardship on them. They then look on her as "spiritless."

2725 OUT OF DUE SEASON: A MEZZOTINT. BY ADELINE SERGEANT. London: Heinemann, 1895 BMC. New York: D. Appleton, 1895 NUC.

Results of a bad marriage. Emmy Blake is unhappy in her marriage to a village working man. She runs off with an officer (who later deserts her) and becomes a prostitute in the Soho slums. Her husband follows her and "rescues her." Their child dies, and the united couple die in a storm.

2726 THE PROGRESS OF RACHEL. London: Methuen, 1904 BMC.

Unattractive wealthy young woman married by man out of pity. A careful and thoughtful study of character.

2727 SIR ANTHONY. London: Hurst and Blackett, 1892 BMC.

When he marries his second wife, he tells her that he has "adopted" the two children in his household. Actually, they are his children by his first marriage, and he intends to "spring" it on his wife that they will disinherit the children by their marriage. Twenty years pass; when she suspects the truth, she poisons him.

2728 THE SIXTH SENSE: A NOVEL. London: Hutchinson, 1905 BMC.

Woman kills her doctor and becomes insane.

2729 THE SURRENDER OF MARGARET BELLARMINE. A FRAGMENT. EDITED BY ADELINE SERGEANT. New York: International News, 1894 NUC. London: International News, 1894 BMC.

Psychological study of a young widow who writes poetry and meditates on religious topics. Her spirit had been crushed by a cold and calculating husband. She awakens after his death, but her lover proves dishonorable. She breaks her engagement, finds peace in religion and renunciation.

2730 SYLVIA'S AMBITION. London: Hodder and Stoughton, 1901 BMC.

Sylvia becomes an actress.

SETON, JULIA. B. 1862. United States.

2731 DESTINY: A NEW-THOUGHT NOVEL. New York: E. J. Clode, [c1917] NUC.

Audrienne Lebaron, dissatisfied with her aimless life, goes to New York to be a writer, but falls in love and, though her husband dies, remains married to his memory. Enters mysticism school and devotes her life to "publicity work in the psychic realm."

SEVERNE, FLORENCE.

2732 IN THE MESHES. London: Osgood, 1894 BMC.

Young woman in London trying to make ends meet in various positions becomes the lover of married doctor and is persuaded to continue the relationship after she learns of his wife, who is dying—then she is suspected of murder.

SEYMER, GERTRUDE CLAY KER.

2733 THE BLACK PATCH. A SPORTING NOVEL. London:
G. Routledge, 1894 BMC.

Clara, who shares her father's love for horses, has
"detective powers equal to any hero of Scotland Yard."
She solves a mystery involving horses and cures her father
of wishing that she had been born a boy.

SEYMOUR, BEATRICE KEAN (STAPLETON). D. 1955.
United Kingdom.

2734 INVISIBLE TIDES. London: Chapman and Hall, 1919
NUC. New York: T. Seltzer, 1921 NUC.

Helena returns to her husband after her lover is killed in
war.

SHAKESPEAR, OLIVIA.

2735 THE FALSE LAUREL. London: Osgood, 1896 BMC.

Daria is a woman for whom the life of the intellect is all-
consuming. She marries without love, destroys her poems
because they are inferior to her husband's. She leaves to
write great plays, wrestles with poverty and insanity, and
finally kills herself.

2736 LOVE ON A MORTAL LEASE. A NOVEL. London:
Osgood & McIlvaine, 1894 BMC.

Rachel insists she is pure even after she has lost her
honour. She is clever; second part of the book is the story
of her marriage. Study of effects of wealth on literary
ambition.

2737 UNCLE HILARY. London: Methuen, [1910] BMC NUC.

Mother and daughter both make several marriages without
formality of divorces. They leave the men and they seem
to choose them.

SHAND, CHRISTINE R.

2738 MISS PILSBURY'S FORTUNE. London: Mills and Boon,
[1909] BMC.

Heroine's wealth leaves her free to marry for love.

SHAPIRO, ANNA RATNER. United States.

2739 THE BIRTH OF UNIVERSAL BROTHERHOOD. Kansas City, Mo.: Burton, [c1916] BMC NUC. (Also published as Red Ruth; The Birth of Universal Brotherhood. Chicago: Arc Pub. Co., 1917 NUC.)

Woman preaches gospel of right living and universal love. Ends with characters' effort to organize world for peace.

SHARBER, KATE (TRIMBLE). B. 1883. United States.

2740 AMAZING GRACE, WHO PROVES THAT VIRTUE HAS ITS SILVER LINING. Indianapolis: Bobbs-Merrill, [c1914] BMC NUC.

Grace is a reporter who burns the love letters of an English woman novelist to her ancestor. Their publication would have made a great difference to her financially, but she refuses to make use of them in this way.

SHARKEY, EMMA AUGUSTA (BROWN). B. 1858. United States.

2741 MAM'SELLE, A MODERN HEATHEN. THE 94TH NOVEL OF THE CELEBRATED SOUTHERN AUTHORESS, E. BURKE COLLINS. Philadelphia: W. J. Benners, 1895 BMC NUC.

A young woman raised in the backwoods of Louisiana is nevertheless a genius as an actress.

SHARP, EVELYN. 1869-1955. United Kingdom.

2742 AT THE RELTON ARMS. London: J. Lane, 1895 BMC. Boston: Roberts, 1895 NUC.

Lady Joan Relton is an "advanced" young woman, a "bachelor," irresponsible, full of daring remarks. She considers and rejects a proposal to run off with her friend's husband; she sees through him in time.

2743 THE MAKING OF A PRIG. New York & London: J. Lane, 1897 BMC NUC.

Katherine Austen is no prig, but a lively, insolent, outspoken, moody, modern young woman who finds living at home dull and goes to London to earn a living where she becomes assistant mistress in a girls' school and lives in a boarding house for professional women, mostly journalists. Her life in London with working women, her aunt who takes an interest in women's rights and her complicated love life make up the story.

2744 NICOLETE: A NOVEL. London: Constable, 1907 BMC. New York: Brentano's, 1908 NUC.

Her story from age six to marriage: her mother's death ends the happy period of her childhood. She then becomes a drudge to her large family and must forsake her interest in drawing. About to marry money for the sake of her family, she is saved by an unexpected legacy. After traveling in Italy for two years, she falls in love and marries. Sympathetic study of the effect of conscience and environment on a girl of artistic genius. Described as "a genius but womanly."

2745 REBEL WOMEN. New York: J. Lane, 1910 NUC. London: A. C. Fifield, 1910 BMC NUC.

Militant English suffragists giving "insight into the soul of the women's movement," "written by an enthusiastic supporter of the cause." Suggests the working people of London strongly supported the suffragists.

2746 THE YOUNGEST GIRL IN THE SCHOOL. New York and London: Macmillan, 1901 NUC BMC.

Twelve year old girl of large family of boys comes into contact with "girl nature" for the first time at school.

SHARP, HILDA MARY. United Kingdom.

2747 A PAWN IN PAWN. London: T. F. Unwin, 1920 BMC NUC. New York and London: G. P. Putnam's Sons, 1920 NUC.

The story of a child of an unwed mother adopted by a poet genius, told by his friend, a journalist. She develops a remarkable gift for poetry. He had adopted her with intent to pass on his inheritance to her, but died without leaving a will. She is faced with a charge of plagiarism.

SHAW, ADELE MARIE AND CARMELITA BECKWITH.

2748 THE LADY OF THE DYNAMOS. New York: H. Holt, 1909 NUC.

The heroine is an extremely intelligent young woman who studies dynamos, is an inventor in Ceylon and a "comrade" to the hero in his work.

SHAW, MRS. DONALD.

2749 SUNSET. London: W. J. Ham-Smith, 1913 BMC NUC.

Set in California. Wife learns of husband's past, refuses to live with him; they separate for five years during which time the husband has amatory experiences with a beautiful Mexican who saves his life.

SHELDON, RUTH LOUISE. 1846-1926. United States.

2750 DOLLY, A DAUGHTER OF NEW ENGLAND. Akron, O.: Saalfield, [c1905] NUC.

Dolly is a lively madcap who is expelled from school and goes abroad. She is unprincipled in her love affairs, makes a bad marriage, and is widowed.

2751 FLEXIBLE MORALS. New York: H. I. Kimball, 1898 NUC.

The young heroine tells her own story of her marriage in which she is first neglected then abandoned by her husband. "A marriage of this kind is given as a just cause for flexible morals on the part of the woman."

SHEPHERD, MARGARET LISLE. B. 1859.

2752 MY LIFE IN THE CONVENT; OR THE MARVELLOUS PERSONAL EXPERIENCES OF MARGARET L. SHEPHERD (SISTER MAGDALENE ADELAIDE). Columbus, O.: [c1893] NUC.

"Real" experiences of a Catholic woman who is betrayed by a priest, enters a convent, leaves, joins the Salvation Army, and becomes a lecturer against Romanism. "The story of convent life is a succession of vulgar, revolting episodes."

SHERWOOD, MARGARET POLLOCK. 1864-1955. United States.

2753 AN EXPERIMENT IN ALTRUISM. BY ELIZABETH HASTINGS. New York and London: Macmillan, 1895 NUC.

Satire on several altruistic types: the anarchist who plays with his children while plotting murders and while his wife does all the work at home; the woman doctor struggling for sanitary reforms; Janet, the doubter who refuses to try to elevate the masses. The effect of these and other types on a woman tailor, the "victim of all this experiment in altruism." Book ends on word of hope—in spite of the satire.

2754 HENRY WORTHINGTON, IDEALIST. New York, London: Macmillan, 1899 BMC NUC.

Annice Gordon shares the social idealism of Henry Worthington, a professor at an American university. She takes a position as saleswoman in her father's department store in order to show it is an oppressive corporation. Henry wants his college to refuse a grant "ground out of the victims of department store methods"—a grant offered by Annice's father. Author implies that "all stores in which women clerks are paid wages on which no woman can decently live and are forced by a system of fines to stand all day despite the seats placed behind their counters, all stores in which goods are bought at starvation prices from sweat-shops should be outlawed."

2755 A PURITAN BOHEMIA. New York and London: Macmillan, 1896 NUC.

The "Puritan Bohemia" is a community of women, living intellectual, artistic, or philanthropic lives in an earnest and austere atmosphere, a place where "man is a memory, a shadow, rarely a reality." Anne, an artist, decides not to marry because marriage has no place in her mission. Boston.

SHEW, ELIZABETH LEILA.

2756 IF MEN WERE WISE. A NOVEL. London: Bentley, 1894 BMC.

Mary Ford, a school teacher whose husband has deserted her, goes to British Columbia, passing as a single woman. She meets Lawrence Wrayburn, a free-thinker from England who has been jilted. Then the husband shows up and brings a tragic termination to the story.

SHIPTON, HELEN.

2757 TWILIGHT. London: A. D. Innes, 1891 BMC.

Louis Lorimer is a weak man who causes much grief, especially to Katherine Lyndhurst: deserts her on eve of wedding day, causing her to live in a kind of twilight world. Story of her awakening from it.

SHOLL, ANNA MACCLURE. United States.

2758 THE GREATER LOVE. New York: Outing, 1908 NUC. London: T. F. Unwin, 1909 BMC.

Eleanor, an artist, returns to a provincial town in the Northeast after a period of study in Paris. She has a daughter; she poses as a widow. The story, "a subject rarely touched upon," is "the passionate love of a woman for her girl-child."

2759 THE LAW OF LIFE. New York: D. Appleton, 1903 NUC. London and New York: W. Heinemann, 1904 BMC.

Barbara Dale, an intellectual young woman married to her guardian, a math professor 25 years older than she, tries to be a wife, but is miserable and restless. All ways seem closed when her baby dies. Then she meets and loves a young professor. But there's no happy end. He's forced to resign; and she pities her husband too much to leave. Barbara is the study of a woman unmarried in spirit. We're left with a feeling of revolt because her story is true to life. Considers the question of separate versus co-ed colleges for women.

2760 THIS WAY OUT. New York: Hearst's International Library, 1915 BMC NUC.

Margaret Carpenter is a detective who solves mysteries and tracks down criminals mainly by virtue of her powers of psychological analysis.

SHORE, FLORENCE TEIGNMOUTH. United Kingdom.

2761 CIRCE'S DAUGHTER. BY PRISCILLA CRAVEN. London: Hurst & Blackett, 1913 BMC NUC. New York: Duffield, 1913 NUC.

Claudia Iverson finds her lawyer husband absorbed in his work and cold toward her. She is attracted to other men who find her attractive. "A fine man helps her, and in the end she finds true happiness." Her youngest daughter Pat is described as "blessedly sexless," able to find life "full of splendid things quite outside of sentiment."

SHORT, ELEANOR TALBOT (KINKEAD). United States.

2762 THE INVISIBLE BOND. BY ELEANOR TALBOT KINKEAD. New York: Moffat, Yard, 1906 NUC.

A powerfully magnetic woman, an adventuress with a "lawless passion," loves and leaves men. The study of a Becky Sharp or a Lily Bart.

SHUEY, LILLIAN (HINMAN). 1853-1921. United States.

2763 DAVID OF JUNIPER GULCH: A STORY OF THE PLACER REGIONS OF CALIFORNIA. Chicago: Laird and Lee, [c1894] W.

Story of Hulda Hardy, her sacrifice for a woman friend, her experiences as a school teacher in California. Happy ending.

SHULER, MARJORIE. United States.

2764 FOR RENT—ONE PEDESTAL. New York: National Woman Suffrage Pub. Co., 1917 NUC.

Young teacher loses her position after making a speech for suffrage. "How she gave her whole time to the cause and made many conversions including that of a certain college professor. Told in the form of letters to an intimate friend."

SHUTE, MRS. A. B. E.

2765   THE CROSS ROADS. London: E. Nash, 1917 BMC.

Heroine is a great success as an actress.

SICKERT, ELLEN MELICENT (COBDEN). 1848-1914.

2766   SYLVIA SAXON. EPISODES IN A LIFE. BY ELLEN MELICENT COBDEN (MILES AMBER). London: T. F. Unwin, [c1914] BMC NUC.

Sylvia, brought up to believe in material rather than spiritual values, searches for meaning in life. Her lover and husband are failures; she finds motherhood a matter of resentment. At the end she is taking "the plunge into the larger world where women consider freedom the ultimate goal." Reviewers dislike her; one calls the novel a "cold and depressing work."

2767   WISTONS: A STORY IN THREE PARTS. BY MILES AMBER. London: T. F. Unwin, 1902 BMC. New York: C. Scribner's Sons, 1902 NUC.

Esther and Rhoda are sisters brought up in the country and given an education by their father. Their mother was a gypsy. Esther marries an egotistical novelist and finally leaves him. Rhoda chooses not to marry but lives with a man, becomes pregnant, and leaves him, claiming the baby as her own. He subsequently tracks her down and kills her.

SIDGWICK, CECILY (ULLMANN). D. 1934. United Kingdom.

2768   ANTHEA'S GUEST. BY MRS. ALFRED SIDGWICK. London: Methuen, [1911] BMC NUC.

Anthea goes to Germany to study music and language, meets Lydia, and brings her back to England with her. Anthea refuses a marriage proposal to be free for several years to help run her uncle's estate. Lydia loses her job as governess, flirts, lies and finally captures the uncle. She's an unscrupulous adventuress, but author makes her "extremely human and interesting."

2769   BELOW STAIRS. BY MRS. ALFRED SIDGWICK. London: Methuen, [1913] BMC NUC.

Priscilla Day: her everyday trials, hardships, and dangers as a modern servant working for several employers. Marries in the end.

2770   THE BERYL STONES. BY MRS. ALFRED SIDGWICK. New York: Longmans, Green, 1903 NUC. London: E. Arnold, 1903 BMC.

Melodrama: Ursula struggles to make a living but must steal jewels in order to eat. The villain who witnessed the theft "schemes to bend her will," but after much action Ursula goes to London and becomes a successful actress.

2771   CYNTHIA'S WAY. BY MRS. ALFRED SIDGWICK. London: E. Arnold, 1901 BMC. New York: Longmans, Green, 1901 NUC.

Heiress, in disguise, takes job as governess, marries.

2772   THE GRASSHOPPERS. BY MRS. ANDREW DEAN (MRS. ALFRED SIDGWICK). New York: F. A. Stokes, [c1895] NUC. (Also published as The Grasshopper. London: A. & C. Black, 1895 BMC.)

Tract on the evils of bringing up women in ignorance of money matters and educating them in utter inability to earn their own living. Mrs. Frere and her daughters Nell and Hilary, accustomed to luxury, are thrown penniless on the world at father's death. Mrs. Frere and Nell have grave difficulties facing poverty. But Hilary is of stronger stuff and very unconventional. She insists upon a college education, for she is inspired by the doctrines of feminism. She alone of the three women has the capacity to take care of herself.

2773   LAMORNA. BY MRS. ALFRED SIDGWICK. London: Methuen, [1912] BMC NUC.

Lamorna is an artist who is raised by an aunt and is being used by her for odd jobs and secretarial work. She gains independence and travels to Italy.

2774 THE LANTERN BEARERS. BY MRS. ALFRED SIDGWICK. London: Methuen, 1910 BMC NUC. Leipzig: B. Tauchnitz, 1911 NUC.

Suburban poverty: middle-aged husband loses job. Men are automatons who sleep, commute, return home angered because they're worked like machines. Women are snobs, complacent. The exception is Mrs. Bryne, strong, lonely, filled with a hopeless courage and practical optimism. She has a motherly sort of love for her weak husband. She doesn't want her daughter Helga to be like other suburban women. A study of their relationships and different outlooks.

2775 THE PURPLE JAR. BY MRS. ALFRED SIDGWICK. London: Hutchinson, [1919] BMC NUC. (Also published as Iron Cousins. By Mrs. Sidgwick. New York: W. J. Watt, [c1919] NUC.)

English governess in German middle-class family before the war.

2776 THE SALT OF THE EARTH. BY MRS. ALFRED SIDGWICK. New York: W.J. Watt, [c1917] NUC.

Brenda Muller is an English woman unhappily married to a German and living in Berlin. She puts up with his bickering about her English manners and the intrusions of her in-laws. But then she learns her domineering husband is unfaithful, and after the loss of her child she leaves him. Story leaves her safe in England, without a husband, facing a happy future.

2777 THE SEVERINS. BY MRS. ALFRED SIDGWICK. London: Methuen, 1909 BMC NUC.

A mother and six grown sons and daughters, one of whom is Selma, a modern rebel studying art in Paris; another is Clotilda, separated from her husband, planning to run off with another man.

2778 A SPLENDID COUSIN. BY MRS. ANDREW DEAN. London: Unwin, 1892 BMC. New York: Cassell, [c1892] NUC.

Theodora is absorbed in her violin, sacrifices mother, cousin, husband to her art. Treats others as though "they were born to serve her interests" but finds she'll never achieve anything with her art for all she sacrificed. She is much admired but does not deserve it. She is run over in a fog.

2779   A WOMAN WITH A FUTURE. BY MRS. ANDREW DEAN (MRS. ALFRED SIDGWICK). New York and London: F. A. Stokes, [c1895] NUC. London: Black, 1896 BMC.

Hesperia is idle, shallow, vulgar, uneducated, false, cold, cowardly, insolent, a charming hedonist—an understandable if not sympathetic woman who leaves her husband and runs off with a millionaire adventurer. "Formerly (fiction) was nearly always about a young woman whose history invariably ended with her marriage....A future still more heartless, hollow and sensual suggests itself as likely to be the consumation of (Hesperia's) career."

SIDGWICK, ETHEL. 1877-1970. United Kingdom.

2780   HERSELF. Boston: Small, Maynard, [c1912] NUC. London: Sidgwick & Jackson, 1912 BMC NUC.

A young woman teaching in a French school is the victim of scandal-making.

2781   JAMESIE. London: Sidgwick & Jackson, 1918 BMC. Boston: Small, Maynard, [c1918] NUC.

The story is told through a collection of letters and brief notes, intimate and informal, between characters. The characters include a range of feminists, from militant suffragist to conservative. Jamesie, an eight year old, dies in the English Channel on a boat that is torpedoed. War—not Germany—is a fiend incarnate. One reviewer comments that Margaret Deland also expressed this way of looking at the war.

2782   A LADY OF LEISURE. London and Toronto: Sidgwick and Jackson, 1914 BMC NUC. Boston: Small, Maynard, [c1914] NUC.

Violet Ashwin, the daughter of a London surgeon, wishes to work and enters a dressmaking establishment. Here she meets Alice, a working-class woman; both are intelligent, and they have a close friendship which endures. Violet's sister Margery is involved with a man in a physically passionate affair which ends in tragedy. "The revelation of woman to woman."

2783 LE GENTLEMAN: AN IDYLL OF THE QUARTER. London: Sidgwick & Jackson, 1911 BMC 1912 NUC. Boston: Small, Maynard, 1912 NUC.

Gilberte is an art student in Paris. She is French, "sane, practical, intelligent." She is contrasted with Meysie, a "silly" young Englishwoman. Their love affairs.

SIDGWICK, MRS. ALFRED. See SIDGWICK, CECILY (ULLMANN).

SIDNEY, MARGARET. See LOTHROP, HARRIET MULFORD (STONE).

SILBERRAD, U. L. See SILBERRAD, UNA LUCY.

SILBERRAD, UNA LUCY. 1872-1955. United Kingdom.

2784 CO-DIRECTORS. London: Hodder & Stoughton, 1915 BMC NUC.

Elizabeth Thain is 35, competent part-owner of a company that puts an invention on the market. She and the inventor share a vast capacity for work and identical moral qualities. Together they fight those who oppose the invention. Criticism of the bitter competitive spirit in business.

2785 DESIRE. BY U. L. SILBERRAD. New York: Doubleday, Page, 1908 NUC. London: A. Constable, 1908 BMC 1909 NUC.

Desire, described as "unconventional," "intelligent," and "a good comrade," finds happiness in business.

2786 THE GOOD COMRADE. New York: Doubleday, Page, 1907 NUC. London: A. Constable, 1907 BMC.

Julia Polkington struggles between honor and the

necessities of her family. First honor keeps her from stealing from a family she serves as a "lady help." But later she steals a formula to pay the family debt. Sympathetic portrayal of Julia. Set in Holland.

2787   THE INHERITANCE. London: Hutchinson, 1916 BMC NUC.

Male legitimate and female illegitimate are joint heirs to property. She is a vagabond, a "coiner," wanted by the law. They eventually marry. 17th century.

2788   KEREN OF LOWBOLE. New York: G.H. Doran, [c1913] NUC. London: Constable, 1913 BMC NUC.

Time of witch hunts in England. Keren is the daughter of a gipsy who escaped fire by suicide. She is raised by her father who teaches her alchemy. Tells of her father's revenge against Dutch enemies and Keren's flight from the witch-hunters of Colchester.

2789   THE LADY OF DREAMS. New York: Doubleday, Page, [1900] BMC NUC.

Agnes' uncle has delerium tremors, more than once attempts murder on his death bed. Succeeds once. Agnes kills him. She marries the hero, a big-hearted doctor who works in the slums. She cannot love him; she has become "strangely elusive and dream-like." She later falls in love with another man. Subsequent tragedy.

2790   ORDINARY PEOPLE. London: Constable, 1909 BMC NUC.

Catherine Santerre separates from her husband because of an argument concerning an affair she had before her marriage. They are reconciled after she dyes her hair and works in his office as a typist unrecognized.

2791   SUCCESS OF MARK WYNGATE. BY U. L. SILBERRAD. New York: Doubleday, Page, 1902 NUC. Westminster: A. Constable, 1902 BMC.

Judith has unusual physical, mental, and emotional strength; she forges iron bars, her recreation is pure mathematics, and she is a scientist. She works with another scientist, a cold man, sacrifices her life for his; success for herself never occurs to her. Tragic ending.

SIME, J. G. See SIME, JESSIE GEORGINA.

SIME, JESSIE GEORGINA. B. 1880. Canada.

2792 SISTER WOMAN. BY J. G. SIME. London: G. Richards, 1919 BMC NUC.

Thirty stories bound together with one theme: women's desire for freedom and self-expression. Most of them concern women working in Canada.

SIMONTON, IDA VERA. 18??-1931. United States.

2793 HELL'S PLAYGROUND. New York: Moffat, Yard, 1912 NUC. London: Gay & Hancock, 1915 BMC.

A critique of colonial rule in West Africa, of the male colonialists' involvement with native women, of their treatment as chattel to be sold or leased by their fathers and husbands. One reviewer notes a "failure in craftsmanship."

SIMPSON, KATHERINE.

2794 THE FUGITIVE YEARS. London: J. Long, 1912 BMC.

Rhoda, in spite of her ideas about free love, refuses to become her cousin's mistress. She has always loved him, but he seeks her out only when he needs her.

SIMPSON, VIOLET A. United Kingdom.

2795 THE BEACON-WATCHERS. London: Chapman and Hall, 1913 BMC NUC.

Development of Sara, her hurried unfortunate marriage. But she wins out in the end.

2796 THE KEYS OF MY HEART. London: Chapman & Hall, 1915 NUC BMC.

Francesca Bellares is an independent young woman who makes a comfortable living by private demonstrations in cookery.

SINCLAIR, B. M. See SINCLAIR, BERTHA (MUZZY).

SINCLAIR, BERTHA (MUZZY). 1874?-1940. United States.

2797 CHIP, OF THE FLYING U. BY B. M. BOWER (B. M. SINCLAIR). New York: G.W. Dillingham, [1906] NUC. London: T. Nelson, [1920] BMC.

A young woman doctor visiting a Western ranch overcomes prejudice of the cowboys with her medical competence. Marries Chip.

2798 THE FLYING U'S LAST STAND. BY B. M. BOWER. Boston: Little, Brown, 1915 BMC NUC.

A determined woman land agent plays a large part in this novel. She convinces a colony of home seekers, made up mostly of women school teachers, to file claims against the land needed by the Flying U Ranch for grazing. In the controversy the Ranch wins out. The "little doctor" in the novel is a young woman.

2799 JEAN OF THE LAZY A. BY B. M. BOWER. Boston: Little, Brown, 1915 NUC BMC. London: Methuen, [1918] BMC.

Jean happens to be doing some fancy horse-riding stunts when a manager of a film company sees her. She joins the company and becomes a movie star featured as Jean of the Lazy A, doing stunts before the camera, risking her life for an ever-increasing salary. With the money she earns, she establishes her father's innocence and gets him out of prison.

2800 LONESOME LAND. BY B. M. BOWER. London: S. Paul, 1912 BMC. Boston: Little, Brown, 1912 NUC.

Valerie is married to a man who drinks; he neglects her and is physically abusive. He is eventually killed by the sheriff. She marries the cowboy who has been her faithful friend throughout her marriage.

2801 THE QUIRT. BY B. M. BOWER. Boston: Little, Brown, 1920 NUC.

Lorraine's parents are divorced; she is a movie actress. She has lived with her mother, but when her mother remarries, Lorraine decides to visit her rancher father. Here she experiences adventures more "chilling" than any she has portrayed on film.

2802 THE RANCH AT THE WOLVERINE. BY B. M. BOWER.
Boston: Little, Brown, 1914 NUC BMC. London: E. Nash,
1916 BMC.
The love story of Billy Louise, who managed a ranch and
"looked out for everyone."

SINCLAIR, MAY. 1870-1946. United Kingdom.

2803 AUDREY CRAVEN. Edinburgh & London: Blackwood,
1897 BMC. New York: H. Holt, 1906 NUC.
Sympathetic portrayal of a vain, callous, "chameleon" type
of woman who cannot help being what she is. She jilts
two men who love her and almost becomes mistress of a
writer who wants to use her only as a model for the
heroine of his new book. Ultimately she marries a
"chinless" country gentleman.

2804 THE COMBINED MAZE. New York and London: Harper,
1913 NUC. London: Hutchinson, 1913 BMC NUC.
Cockney London of underpaid and overworked clerks and
shop-girls whose one respectable meeting place for men
and women was the cooperative clubs—the gymnasium
with its swimming tank and competition between the
sexes. Strong, physically fit Winny Dymond meets Randy
at such a club, but Violet Usher attracts him more. Violet
and Randy marry, but she tires of him immediately. She
neglects her house and children and finally runs off with
another man. Randy realizes then it is Winny he loves,
saves for a divorce but must use the money for his
father's funeral. Violet returns, and Randy takes her back
out of duty. An indictment against English divorce laws.

2805 THE CREATORS; A COMEDY. New York: Century,
1910 NUC. London: Constable, 1910 BMC NUC.
The question explored, "Is it possible for the man or
woman of genius to marry and sacrifice neither family or
success in creative work?"

2806 THE DIVINE FIRE. New York: H. Holt, 1904 NUC.
Westminster: A. Constable, 1904 BMC NUC.
Outspoken about sex, characters do and say shocking
things, women play with fire. Lucia's friendship with Kitty

is strong; Flossie is intelligent, aggressive, independent of men, can view them in a detached way. She supports herself by teaching piano. Proposes to the man in the end. Novel centers on male poet.

2807 THE FLAW IN THE CRYSTAL. New York: E. P. Dutton, [c1912] NUC.

A young woman discovers she has a healing power, the basis of which is her sexual purity. In an attempt to cure a man who is going mad, she realizes the limits of her power and that she must give up on him. She cures a married man who loves her and returns to his wife. She remains alone.

2808 THE HELPMATE. New York: H. Holt, 1907 NUC. London: A. Constable, 1907 BMC NUC.

Ruthless analysis of the conventional good woman—all superficial virtue and hidden faults. Ann Majendie resents the fact that her husband had sexual relations with a woman in the past. Satire.

2809 THE JUDGMENT OF EVE. New York: Ridgway, [c1907] NUC. London and New York: Harper, 1907 BMC 1908 NUC.

Aggie Purcell takes her time choosing between two suitors. Because she's intellectual, she decides in favor of the "struggling London clerk of literary tendencies" and against the sheepherder. The rancher succeeds; the clerk does not. Aggie worn down with maternal cares dies prematurely.

2810 KITTY TAILLEUR. London: A. Constable, 1908 BMC NUC. (Also published as The Immortal Moment: The Story of Kitty Tailleur. New York: Doubleday, Page, 1908 NUC.)

A young woman with a past is rejected by the man she loves when she reveals it to him. She kills herself.

2811 MARY OLIVIER; A LIFE. London and New York: Cassell, [1919] BMC NUC.

She relives all the bitter moments of her life which centers upon her relation to a tyrannical mother. Her earliest recollection is that of being taken from her mother's breast. In girlhood, she broods about babies and how they come to be born. At 14, she still has no idea. As the unmarried daughter, Mary is called upon to sacrifice herself to a mother whom she feels loves her least of the four children. Mary loves and hates her mother, admires her aunt who goes to bed with every man she meets. At 27, Mary is still at her mother's side. Her only escape is her studies and her poetry.

2812   MR. AND MRS. NEVILL TYSON. Edinburgh & London: W. Blackwood, 1898 BMC. (Also published as The Tysons (Mr. and Mrs. Nevill Tyson). New York: B. W. Dodge, 1906 NUC.)

Tyson's love for his wife is in direct proportion to his perception of her physical beauty. When nursing their child seems to affect her looks, he insists on giving the baby to someone else's care, where it dies of neglect. He leaves her then but returns, and she saves his life in a fire which he has started while drunk. Her face is scarred; he is repelled, and leaves permanently.

2813   THE ROMANTIC. New York: Macmillan, 1920 NUC. London: W. Collins, [1920] BMC NUC.

Sharlie and Gwennie, farm workers, travel to the front in Belgium to help in the war, the most romantic thing that has ever happened to them. Here Sharlie becomes involved with two men—both romantic on the surface but basically motivated by a desire for power. One reviewer feels Sharlie is obsessed with her sexual experiences.

2814   THE THREE SISTERS. London: Hutchinson, 1914 BMC NUC. New York: Macmillan, 1914 NUC.

"One realizes...how tragically women are the victims of their very sex" in this "intimate history" of three sisters in a provincial town whose father selfishly wishes to reduce their matrimonial possibilities to a minumum, while their one objective is the snaring of men. In their village there is only one man suitable for them. Their father has been responsible for the death of his first two wives; the third has left him.

2815   THE TREE OF HEAVEN. London and New York: Cassell, [1917] BMC NUC.

The great changes of the years 1910-14 and their effects on Frances Robinson, her daughter Dorothea and her three sons. Political troubles and the war devastate the family. Dorothea is 19, competent, tall, robust; she graduates from college with a degree in economics, takes part in a suffrage raid, is imprisoned in Holloway for three months, joins the Service Corps and has the misfortune of loving an anti-feminist whose opposition to her wish to serve at the front keeps her in London even after he dies in battle. Two of her brothers are also killed in the war.

2816   TWO SIDES OF A QUESTION. New York: Taylor, 1901 NUC. London: A. Constable, 1901 BMC. (Also published as Superseded. New York: H. Holt, 1906 NUC.)

An older woman, a teacher, portrays "the anguish of discovering one has outlived one's usefulness."

SINDICI, MARIA MAGDA STUART.

2817   VIA LUCIS; A NOVEL. BY KASSANDRA VIVARIA. London: W. Heinemann, 1898 BMC. New York: G. H. Richmond, 1898 NUC.

The life history of Arduina, queer, morbid, passionate, sullen, intelligent, visionary and introspective. The daughter of a morose and brutal father, she is placed in a convent school; she spends a year working out the details of a female order of Jesuits, only to discover that she will not be permitted to publish her work. After much conflict between the spiritual and the worldly, she marries a man 17 years older than herself; he soon wearies of her and her love dies. A "minute and exhaustive mental analysis of a progressive human being."

SINGLETON, ESTHER. 1865-1930. United States.

2818   A DAUGHTER OF THE REVOLUTION. New York: Moffat, Yard, 1915 NUC.

Young woman goes to New York to start a career in writing and succeeds. Her first article is published in a newspaper; her first essay, in a magazine. She is more interested in New York social life, the opera, and D.A.R. meetings.

SKELTON, MARGARET. United Kingdom.

2819 THE BOOK OF YOUTH. London: W. Collins, [1920] BMC NUC.

Monica Harthen in London, stirring incidents including some associations with female agitation before the war. Monica marries in closing pages. A character study.

SKINNER, HENRIETTA CHANNING (DANA). 1857-1928. United States.

2820 THEIR CHOICE: A NOVEL. New York: Benziger, 1913 NUC.

Diary of a middle-aged woman who meets a man who falls in love with her.

SKRAM, BERTHA AMALIE (ALVER). 1846-1905. Norway.

2821 PROFESSOR HIERONIMUS. London and New York: J. Lane, 1899 BMC NUC. (Tr. from the Danish by Alice Stronach and G. B. Jacobi.)

A woman comes to the Professor for expert help for her nervousness. He misunderstands her sufferings as a tortured wife and mistakes her rebelliousness for madness. His treatment is to place her in an insane asylum with "lunatics and dangerous maniacs." The Professor is a fanatical tyrant forcing the weak and insane to cringe before his power. "Revolting details of the mental conditions and treatment of lunatics in an asylum."

SKRINE, MARY JESSIE HAMMOND (TOOKE). B. 1856. United Kingdom.

2822 THE HERITAGE OF ELISE. London: E. Arnold, 1917 BMC.

"Takes to the streets" not knowing she's an heir.

SLADE, A. F.*

2823 THE ALTERNATIVE. London: Hutchinson, 1909 BMC.
"Intense meticulous analysis" of a refined woman and her coarse husband. Kate Heriot's unhappy marriage, her false charge against herself of intimacy with old lover made apparently to obtain a divorce. The position of the son between the parents.

2824 A WAYSIDE WEED. London: Hutchinson, 1901 BMC. (Also published as Annie Deane, A Wayside Weed. New York: Brentano's, 1901 NUC.)
A young woman of sixteen, seduced by an artist who never gives her another thought, raises her child by herself and grows into a very forceful woman.

SLOOT, NICOLINA MARIA CHRISTINA. 1853-1927.

2825 THE RESIDENT'S DAUGHTER. BY MELATI VAN JAVA. London: Henry, 1893 BMC. (Tr. by A. Teixeira de Mattos.)
The author is "not afraid to make a half-caste girl the heroine." Concerns colonial life in Java and Batavia and the heroine's marriage of convenience that turns to love.

SMART, MRS IRWIN.

2826 EBB AND FLOW, A NOVEL. London: G. Routledge, 1912 BMC.
Nan married a weak man who, with two whiskeys on an empty stomach, accused her of nagging. She responded by throwing a bread knife at him and leaving. She becomes a literary success; years later when he returns from the Boer War missing a leg, they are reunited.

SMEDLEY, CONSTANCE. See ARMFIELD, ANNE CONSTANCE (SMEDLEY).

SMITH, ANNIE S. (SWAN). 1859-1945. United Kingdom.

2827 ANNE HYDE, TRAVELLING COMPANION. London: Hodder & Stoughton, 1908 BMC.

2828 ELIZABETH GLEN, M.B.: THE EXPERIENCES OF A LADY DOCTOR. London: Hutchinson, 1895 BMC. Dr. Glen makes her practice in Bloomsbury. She is an exceptional doctor with great sympathy for her patients, ministering to minds as well as bodies. She believes men doctors treat the body when the mind is the problem as in Nora Fleming's case. She makes a fortune as a doctor. Finally retires to marry a good man.

2829 A FOOLISH MARRIAGE: AN EDINBURGH STORY OF STUDENT LIFE. BY ANNIE S. SWAN (MRS. BURNETT-SMITH). London: Hutchinson, 1894 BMC. Toronto: W. Briggs, [1894] NUC.
Left penniless she supports herself by helping aunt run a boarding house for medical students; one is the hero.

2830 HESTER LANE. London: Hodder & Stoughton, 1908 BMC.
"Agreeable tale" of how a young woman started an employment agency. She gives it up when she becomes engaged.

2831 MARGARET HOLROYD; OR, THE PIONEERS. London: Hodder & Stoughton, 1910 BMC.
A story of the women's movement: its effect on various lives, those who are awakened by it, those who become weary and drop out.

2832 MEMORIES OF MARGARET GRAINGER, SCHOOLMISTRESS. London: Hutchinson, 1896 BMC. London: Hutchinson, [n.d.] NUC.
In each of the eleven chapters she describes one of her female pupils—all individuals and interesting. Many love stories. Nonfiction?

2833 MRS. KEITH HAMILTON, M.B. MORE EXPERIENCES OF ELIZABETH GLEN. London: Hutchinson, 1897 BMC.
"Experiences of a Lady Doctor" continued. Now she is retired and plans to establish a home for women who work in dressmaking establishments.

2834 A STORMY VOYAGER. London: Hutchinson, [1896] BMC.

Domestic for family reading: although wife runs away from her husband, she comes to see the error of her ways.

2835 WHO SHALL SERVE? A STORY FOR THE TIMES. London: Oliphant, 1891 BMC.

Dorothea Redmond and James Wentworth improve the living conditions of strikers in a shipyard in Malden after the owner's attempts to avoid a strike fail.

SMITH, ANNIE S. (SWAN). See also LYALL, DAVID [pseud.].

SMITH, CONSTANCE ISABELLA STUART. United Kingdom.

2836 THE BACKSLIDER: A STORY OF TODAY. London: Bentley, 1896 BMC.

Reviewer sees this as a "novel of reaction" as opposed to the "novel of revolt." Katherine, a modern young woman, writes and publishes anonymously a "naughty" novel, then marries a serious scholar. A former lover reveals authorship to her husband; estrangement, reconciliation, and forgiveness follow. Reviewer notes that other feminist characters remain unconverted.

2837 PRISONERS OF HOPE. London: A. D. Innes, 1898 BMC.

Linda marries a man dedicated to working in the slums in London's East End. She discovers she can't bear the life in the slums and spends more and more time away from home. He is uncompromising in his expectations; Linda's analysis at the conclusion is that she could not be a different person than she was; his unreal expectations have only made matters worse.

SMITH, ELISE HOWARD. B. 1893. United States.

2838 A KNIGHT OF TODAY. Philadelphia: J. C. Winston, 1919 NUC.

Love story: theme "the danger of a girl's ignorance of vital truths."

SMITH, ELIZABETH THOMASINA (MEADE). 1854-1914. United Kingdom.

2839 ALL SORTS. London: J. Nisbet, 1899 BMC NUC.
Westerna Wickham determines to support herself and her widowed mother when their money is gone. She opens a boarding house in Bloomsbury. Society is outraged by her action; all her friends scorn her, but two. Problems of running the business and the sorts of people that come to the house, suitors among them.

2840 BELINDA TREHERNE. London: J. Long, 1910 BMC.
Young woman answers ad for governess with strong nerves. Ghost story.

2841 BESS OF DELANY'S. London: Digby, Long, 1905 BMC.
Bess does killing factory work. She persuades the man she loves to marry her friend who is too frail for such work. After the marriage, Bess and the man work together to improve the lot of factory workers.

2842 A BRAVE POOR THING. BY L. T. MEADE. London: Isbister, [1899] NUC 1900 BMC.
Story of a "typewriter girl."

2843 THE BURDEN OF HER YOUTH. London: J. Long, 1903 BMC.
Goes to London to make her own way; story closes in marriage.

2844 CATALINA: ART STUDENT. BY L. T. MEADE. London and Edinburgh: W. & R. Chambers, 1896 BMC. Philadelphia: J.B. Lippincott, 1897 NUC.
The story (not a love story) of Catalina's success as an artist.

2845 THE CLEVEREST WOMAN IN ENGLAND. London: J. Nisbet, 1898 BMC. Boston: A. I. Bradley, 1899 NUC.
Dagmar is a brilliant, emancipated woman who devotes all her energies to the cause of her sex, and is the idol of the female multitude. Her husband, a literary prig, holds views diametrically opposed to hers. She dies of smallpox.

2846   ENGAGED TO BE MARRIED. A TALE OF TODAY. London: Griffith, Farran, [1895] BMC.

Three young women in a flat. Helen, practical and absorbed in her work. Dorothea, her sister, an artistic genius. Emany, quiet, engaged to be married with a poor, dependent family at home, is the heroine. "A story we heartily recommend to young ladies of the would-be intellectual and self-sufficing type."

2847   FROM THE HAND OF THE HUNTER. London: J. Long, 1906 BMC.

Mother by a piece of culpable folly has killed her own daughter.

2848   A GIRL IN TEN THOUSAND. BY L. T. MEADE. Edinburgh and London: Oliphant, [1896] BMC. New York: T. Whittaker, 1897 NUC.

Effie wants to be a nurse, but has responsibilities at home (mother is feeble). She goes, but after a time has to give up nursing "to retrieve the family fortunes, ruined by an unconscionable brother." "For girls."

2849   THE GIRLS OF ST. WODE'S. BY L. T. MEADE. London and Edinburgh: W. & R. Chambers, 1898 BMC. New York: Mershon, [1902?] NUC.

St. Wode's is a college for women which prepares them for careers, described by the reviewer as "one aspect of the new order of things."

2850   GOOD LUCK. BY L. T. MEADE. London: J. Nisbet, 1896 BMC. Boston: 1897 NUC.

London East End workers: Grannie Reed earns a scant livelihood by needlework, chiefly by her wonderful feather stitch, a family tradition. Loses use of her arm.

2851   IN AN IRON GRIP; A NOVEL. London: Chatto and Windus, 1894 BMC NUC.

Esther, knowing her uncle has stolen her mother's diamonds, forges his name on a check. He finds her and locks her up. She manages to escape but is sentenced to five years at old Bailey. She comes out none the worse for it but had many adventures in prison.

2852 JILL, A FLOWER GIRL. BY L. T. MEADE. London: Isbister, [1893] BMC. New York: T. Whittaker, 1893 NUC.

Jill Robinson makes a precarious living selling flowers to the rich in the West End. Story tells of her heroic act concerning her alcoholic mother.

2853 THE MAID WITH THE GOGGLES. London: Digby, Long, 1906 BMC.

Private sensational history of female "model" typist in a detective firm.

2854 MARY GIFFORD, M.B. London: Wells Gardner, 1898 BMC.

Mary tells story of her life as a doctor. She is energetic and accomplishes much. One reviewer finds that her "display of expert knowledge somehow detracts from the charm of the story," does not find her "attractive."

2855 THE MEDICINE LADY. BY L. T. MEADE. London: Cassell, 1892 BMC. New York: Cassell, [c1892] NUC.

Cecilia Harvey, a young nurse on probation in a hospital, fails to get a position because she is impulsive and sensitive. She marries a doctor who has been working on a drug called "lymph" as a cure for consumption. When he dies, he tells her to let the drug die with him. When she finds she is a victim of the disease, she tries the drug on herself and is cured. Timidly at first, she begins to dispense it. In the final scene she confesses to a mob in the street that it is imperfect and she has killed her child with it. She is stabbed by a man in the crowd.

2856 MERRY GIRLS OF ENGLAND. BY L. T. MEADE. London: Cassell, 1896 BMC. Boston: A.I. Bradley, [1897] NUC.

Story of three young women running a farm and making it pay.

2857 ON THE BRINK OF A CHASM; A RECORD OF PLOT AND PASSION. BY L. T. MEADE. London: Chatto and Windus, 1898 BMC. New York: F. M. Buckles, 1899 NUC.

A nurse who has studied under a famous Parisian doctor

uses her knowledge of hypnotism to rescue a young boy from the plot of a brain specialist.

2858 OUT OF THE FASHION. BY L. T. MEADE. London: Methuen, 1892 BMC. New York: Cassell, [c1892] NUC.
Three penniless sisters run a boarding house and make it pay.

2859 A PRINCESS OF THE GUTTER. BY L. T. MEADE. London: W. Gardner, 1895 BMC. New York and London: G.P. Putnam's Sons, [c1896] NUC.
Miss Princep, graduate of Girton, works in London's East End for the poor. Because the fortune she inherited was ground out of the poor, she chooses to live in the slums, working to return the money in the form of better homes and living conditions.

2860 THE PURSUIT OF PENELOPE. London: Digby, Long, 1909 BMC.
Penelope is a detective who clears up the terrible secret accusation hanging over Mrs. Forbes' marriage.

2861 ROSEBURY. London: Chatto & Windus, 1903 BMC.
This woman has a passionate "amoral" nature. She commits "two of the worst crimes possible": murder and treachery. Yet she is treated completely sympathetically by her author.

2862 RUFFLES. London: S. Paul, [1911] BMC.
A fifteen-year old precocious young woman plays the part of a female Sherlock Holmes.

2863 A SISTER OF THE RED CROSS. A TALE OF THE SOUTH AFRICAN WAR. BY MRS. L. T. MEADE. London: T. Nelson, 1901 BMC NUC.
Hospital nurse in South Africa.

2864 A SWEET GIRL GRADUATE. BY L. T. MEADE. London: Cassell, 1891 BMC NUC. New York: Burt, [1897] NUC.
Life at Newnham, one of England's most serious and successful colleges for women.

SMITH, ELLEN ADA.

2865 THE BUSYBODY. London: J. Long, 1910 BMC.

Anne Arden, novelist and journalist, retires to a remote village to recover from a disappointment in love. Writes about inhabitants.

2866 THE ONLY PRISON. London: J. Long, 1913 BMC.

One heroine is an art student; the other, a writer whose fiance acts as her secretary and agent.

2867 THE PRICE OF CONQUEST. London: J. Long, 1914 BMC.

A violinist discovers a young woman of talent, gives her music lessons, becomes her guardian and eventually her husband. She becomes famous as a violinist. Subtle analysis of his emotions when he believes that she is surpassing him in skill and personality.

2868 THE UNGOVERNED MOMENT. London: Hutchinson, 1907 BMC.

Betty struggles for employment in London.

SMITH, GERTRUDE. 1860-1917. United States.

2869 DEDORA HEYWOOD. New York: Dodd, Mead, 1896 NUC.

New England village. Dedora and David have been separated for 20 years over religious differences, barely get together again when separated by death.

SMITH, HARRIET (LUMMIS). D. 1947. United States.

2870 OTHER PEOPLE'S BUSINESS: THE ROMANTIC CAREER OF THE PRACTICAL MISS DALE. Indianapolis: Bobbs-Merrill, [c1916] BMC NUC.

Persis is a 36 year old dressmaker who can manage everything.

SMITH, ISABEL. Fl. 1900-1913. United Kingdom.

2871 MATED. London: Digby, Long, 1911 BMC.
Julia, who has had an affair with a chauffeur, must marry within the year to inherit income and property. She succeeds and wins her inheritance.

2872 NEVERTHELESS. London: A. Rivers, 1913 BMC NUC.
Woman torn between conventions and natural inclinations: Sara Gale learns that the man she loves has a wife confined in an asylum. Sara decides to live with the man. After making the decision, she learns the wife has died. One character is a platform champion of women's rights. Thoughtful treatment of subjects like women's suffrage and divorce.

SMITH, MRS. BURNETT. See SMITH, ANNIE S. (SWAN).

SMITH, PHARALL.*

2873 THE WOMAN WITHOUT SIN. A STORY OF PASSION. London: S. Swift, 1911 BMC.
Theme: when love is sincere, it is sinless, and a couple should be free to indulge in it.

SMITH, S. JENNIE. D. 1904.

2874 MADGE, A GIRL IN EARNEST. Boston: Lee & Shepard, 1902 NUC.
Madge rejects the patronage of her aristocratic relatives and supports the family herself.

SMITH, SHEILA KAYE. See FRY, SHEILA KAYE (SMITH).

SMITH, SYBIL CORMACK.

2875 THAT WHICH WAS WRITTEN. London: Methuen, 1913 BMC.
South African farms. Nancy Burke, a nurse, is "really offensive," says one reviewer. Seduced in her youth, she

hides the fact from her fiance, then confesses. Her lover returns but dies and the new pair marry.

2876 THE VELDT WOMAN. London: Murray & Evenden, [1911] BMC.

She is one of many whose lives are blighted by a sordid young man.

SMITHSON, ANNIE MARY PATRICIA. B. 1883. United Kingdom.

2877 BY STRANGE PATHS. London: T. F. Unwin, 1919 BMC. Dublin: Talbot Press, 1919 BMC NUC.

Irish heroine is a nurse, becomes a member of the Gaelic League.

SNEDEKER, CAROLINE DALE (PARKE). 1871-1956. United States.

2878 SETH WAY; A ROMANCE OF THE NEW HARMONY COMMUNITY. BY CAROLINE DALE OWEN (MRS. CHARLES H. SNEDEKER). Boston: Houghton Mifflin, 1917 NUC.

Jessonda Macleod is much in advance of women of her time. At 19, she goes to New Harmony Community to teach music, and Seth is put off by her ideas of independence—for a time.

SNEDEKER, MRS. CHARLES H. See SNEDEKER, CAROLINE DALE (PARKE).

SNEYD, PAMELA.

2879 NEEDS MUST. A NOVEL. London: Osgood, 1894 BMC.

Not a lady in the book—we are allowed to see the foolish side alone of the men. There is a woman who is a revendeuse of clothing, a woman who plays poker and picks up a husband on the Underground Railway.

SNEYD, PAMELA AND BRITIFFE CONSTABLE SKOTTOWE.

2880   AN ISHMAELITE INDEED. London: Hurst & Blackett,
         1893 BMC.
         Beatrix Spenlowe is an intelligent woman who goes to
         England to write, using "family secrets" in order that
         readers will recognize the characters of her novel
         "Joachina." She then tries (and nearly succeeds) in winning
         her friend's fiance.

SNOW, ISABEL. See DI CADHILAC, MARGARET ISABELLA
     (COLLIER) GALLETTI.

SOLOMON, JESSICA.

2881   ISABEL MCDONALD. London: Heath, Cranton and
         Ouseley, [1915] BMC.
         She lives a dull life with her family whose ideas conflict
         with her modern views.

SOMERSET, ISABELLA CAROLINE (SOMERS-COCKS).
     1851-1921. United Kingdom.

2882   SKETCHES IN BLACK AND WHITE. London: T.F.
         Unwin, 1896 BMC.
         Pitiful scenes of lower classes, grim account of woman
         who killed her baby. Story of unfortunate young woman.

SOMERVILLE, E. OE. See MARTIN, VIOLET FLORENCE
     AND EDITH ANNA OENONE SOMERVILLE, also
     SOMERVILLE, EDITH ANNA AND VIOLET FLORENCE
     MARTIN.

SOMERVILLE, EDITH ANNA OENONE AND VIOLET
     FLORENCE MARTIN.

2883   THE REAL CHARLOTTE. BY E. OE. SOMERVILLE AND
         MARTIN ROSS. London: Ward and Downey, 1894 BMC.
         London, New York & Bombay: Longmans, Green, 1901
         NUC.
         Charlotte has no family ties; she remains single. She is a
         landowner and a "man of business." "Given these

conditions in a woman of violent nature, under whose not very admirable social polish lurks a coarse, hungry, self-seeking real ego, and what can the end be but unsatisfactory? Returned love would probably have saved her...it was only when she was undeceived by a cruel disenchantment that her inner nature rose in strength and Charlotte showed herself the selfish and brutal woman she was."

SOUTHWART, ELIZABETH. United Kingdom.

2884 THE STORY OF JENNY; A MILL GIRL'S DIARY. London: Macdonald, 1920 BMC NUC.

The "new realism," a close and intimate record from the Boer War through the Armistice.

SPADONI, ADRIANA. B. 1883. United States.

2885 THE SWING OF THE PENDULUM. New York: Boni & Liveright, [c1919] NUC. London: Hutchinson, [1921] BMC.

Jean, after graduating from the Unviersity of California, becomes first an assistant in a library, then a newspaper reporter, finally a successful social worker in New York where she organizes a national movement for women. She left a man she married and a man she didn't marry; at 39 she makes a happy second marriage which is completely free from romantic love.

SPARHAWK, FRANCES CAMPBELL. B. 1847. United States.

2886 ONOQUA. Boston: Lee and Shepard, 1892 NUC.

Onoqua, an Indian educated in an Eastern school, returns to her tribe hoping to teach what she has learned. She is helped by an Indian of another tribe whom she eventually marries. "Their experiences show that unless work can be provided for the returned students, they must leave the tribe to find it, or fall back into the ways they have tried to outgrow. Enforced idleness robs them of ambition and skill; but no people can learn the arts and industries in a land where neither are."

SPENDER, EMILY. B. 1841. United Kingdom.

2887 THE LAW BREAKERS. BY THE AUTHOR OF A SOLDIER FOR A DAY [ANONYMOUS]. London: F. V. White, 1903 BMC.

The dominant themes are the contrast between women's and men's attitudes toward marriage and the harsh attitude toward single women. Rhoda is 50 and single. She saves her young niece from marrying a man who could never be a real "comrade."

2888 A SOLDIER FOR A DAY. A STORY OF THE ITALIAN WAR OF INDEPENDENCE. London: F. V. White, 1901 BMC.

An Italian girl of the working class disguises herself as a soldier and takes her twin brother's place in the army.

SPENDER, LILIAN (HEADLAND). 1835-1895. United Kingdom.

2889 A STRANGE TEMPTATION. London: Hutchinson, 1893 BMC NUC.

Polly Smith is a dancer whose dying friend Azalea, also a dancer, hears she has inherited a fortune. Azalea dies before she can carry out her wish to make Polly her heir. Polly poses as Azalea (temptation), gets inheritance, and later marries a young squire. Her career as a social beauty, her unmasking by an old admirer, her consequent exile, but a happy end for her.

2890 A WAKING. London: Hutchinson, 1892 BMC NUC. (Also published as Zina's Awaking, a Novel. By Mrs. J. Kent Spender. New York: R. Bonner's Sons, 1892 NUC.)

Zina, a genius who has been trained in all the philosophies, has three awakenings: in her relation to her father, her lover, and her husband, all "fine studies of cold selfishness." Compared to Nora by one reviewer, she revolts after a few months of marriage; she is consoled by Mary Carruthers who supports her own ungrateful and critical husband by what she knows to be third-rate literarary hack work.

SPETTIGUE, H. H.*

2891 THE HERITAGE OF EVE. London: Chatto and Windus, 1898 BMC NUC.

Titania, daughter of a German engineer, moves to Cornwall. She becomes a successful novelist; her career and adventures are "partly recorded by means of her own diary." She is also a philanthropist, marries finally.

SPINNER, ALICE. See FRASER, AUGUSTA ZELIA (WEBB).

SPOFFORD, HARRIET ELIZABETH (PRESCOTT).
1835-1921. United States.

2892 THE MAID HE MARRIED. Chicago: H. S. Stone, 1899 NUC.

Josephine Grey, beautiful, talented school teacher. Her rich aunt and uncle launch her into high society.

2893 PRISCILLA'S LOVE-STORY. Chicago: H. S. Stone, 1898 NUC.

She is a music teacher in a college town, loves a foolish younger man but marries an older and wiser man. Finds happiness in motherhood.

SPOTTISWOODE, SYBIL GWENDOLEN (LAMB). B. 1879. United Kingdom.

2894 HER HUSBAND'S COUNTRY. London: W. Heinemann, 1911 BMC. New York: Duffield, 1911 NUC.

Once Patience Thaile escapes the dull and miserable existence of her English home, she has the time of her life in Germany. She marries a young German despite her family's objections. Then the cultural differences in attitudes towards women becomes apparent to her. She learns her husband is a tyrant, and she learns what is expected of the ideal German hausfrau. Patience is well on the way to revolting against her husband and the marriage, when he dies.

SPRENT, MABEL. Australia.

2895 LOVE'S APPRENTICESHIP. London: Methuen, 1913 BMC.

A young Australian woman named Polly gets right into the whirl of society because she wants love and excitement. But she finds that her own nature conflicts with middle-class conventions. She then moves to Dresden with her brother and a woman friend Sylvia to start an independent life.

SQUIRE, EILEEN HARRIET ANSTRUTHER (WILKINSON). B. 1884.

2896 THE FARM SERVANT. BY E. H. ANSTRUTHER. London: G. Allen & Unwin, [1916] BMC NUC.

Frank leaves and Anna has a baby alone before he returns and they marry. Character study.

2897 THE HUSBAND. BY E. H. ANSTRUTHER. London and New York: J. Lane, 1919 BMC NUC.

Penelope, a very modern young woman befriended by her cousin Margery, goes to London to earn a living. She becomes involved with Margery's husband, and, after Margery's death, is free to marry him. Includes Phoebe, a "blunt tongued suffragette."

SQUIRE, FRANCES. See POTTER, FRANCES BOARDMAN (SQUIRE).

STACEY, MARGARET (WESTRUP). United Kingdom.

2898 TIDE MARKS. BY MARGARET WESTRUP (MRS. W. SYDNEY STACEY). New York: Macmillan, 1913 NUC. London: Methuen, [1913] BMC NUC.

The best scenes are those that describe Phillippa Hamilton's work in a hat shop in London where she finds employment when she is left alone and penniless. She is a bold young woman who holds all the advanced thoughts of the age. She makes an extraordinary marriage with the most casual attitude: marriage in name only on the condition that she will only be housekeeper to the man who loves her. In the end she learns to love him.

STACEY, MRS. W. SYDNEY. See STACEY, MARGARET (WESTRUP).

STACPOOLE, MARGARET (ROBSON) DE VERE. D. 1934. United Kingdom.

2899 THE BATTLE OF FLOWERS. London: Hutchinson, 1916 BMC NUC.

The heroine is a journalist, a secretary, and finally proprietor of the Dial.

2900 MONTE CARLO; A NOVEL. London: Hutchinson, 1913 BMC NUC. New York: Dodd, Mead, 1914 NUC.

Julia Revell rebels against her strict parents. She elopes with an English artist and becomes involved with a group of Bohemians. Though the sort of life she leads soon loses its glamour, the experience serves as material for her first and very successful novel. With the royalties, she takes her husband to Monte Carlo where they are temporarily estranged and where he gambles away much of the money but wins it all back.

STAHR, FANNY LEWALD. 1811-1889. Germany.

2901 THE MASK OF BEAUTY: A NOVEL. BY FANNY LEWALD. New York: R. Bonner's Sons, 1894 NUC. (Tr. by Mary M. Pleasants.)

Extraordinary beauty is the cause of many tragic events in a story of a widow and her daughter who is born after the husband's death.

STANGELAND, KATHARINA MARIE BECH (BRONDUM) MICHAELIS. 1872-1950. Denmark.

2902 THE DANGEROUS AGE: LETTERS AND FRAGMENTS FROM A WOMAN'S DIARY. BY KARIN MICHAELIS. London, New York: J. Lane, 1911 NUC BMC. (Tr. by Marcel Prevost.)

Author presents Elsie Lindtner's case as universal of the dangers of the 40's for women. Elsie married for 22 years for money and security becomes restless and bored, has a strong urge to live alone, gets a divorce and goes to live in solitude on an island from which she writes letters to all her restless married women friends. Her only companion is Jeanne, her servant, who soon becomes her close friend and confidante. She tries to revive a relation with a man who loves her, but he remembers her as a young woman and the change in her gets in the way. She contacts her husband but learns he is about to marry a 19 year old woman. In the end, with confidence and optimism she starts out for a trip around the world with Jeanne.

2903 ELSIE LINDTNER, A SEQUEL TO "THE DANGEROUS AGE". BY KARIN MICHAELIS. New York: J. Lane, 1912 NUC. London: J. Lane, 1912 BMC NUC. (Tr. by Beatrice Marshall.)

Elsie Lindtner keeps young. She gambles in Monte Carlo, travels through Greece with Jeanne, fences in London, rides in New York, and adopts a street orphan to whom she gives all her affection. At the same time she corresponds with her women friends like Lili Rathe, the ideal mother who insists she loves both her husband and her lover, and Magna Willman, who has a child outside of marriage and is proud of her action.

STANLEY, CAROLINE (ABBOT). 1849-1919. United States.

2904 THE KEEPER OF THE VINEYARD, A TALE OF THE OZARKS. New York: F. H. Revell, [c1913] NUC.

Eleanor Dinwoody is a successful Chicago teacher who must support her brother's family of five. This she does as well as improve the school and church. Includes her love story.

2905 A MODERN MADONNA. New York: Century, 1906 BMC NUC.

A story based on the law which permitted a man to will the custody of his child to whomever he chose. The women of Washington help a widowed mother regain custody of her child by getting a law passed making parents equal guardians. "The novel is throughout a plea for equal suffrage."

STANLEY, DOROTHY (TENNANT). United Kingdom.

2906   MISS PIM'S CAMOUFLAGE. BY LADY STANLEY. London: Hutchinson, 1918 BMC. Boston: Houghton Mifflin, 1918 NUC.

Peredita Pim, a spinster of 50, can make herself and anything she touches invisible. When she discovers her gift, she goes to the war office and volunteers her services. She is sent to Germany. Exciting, interesting, not comic. Anti-German point of view.

STANLEY, LADY. See STANLEY, DOROTHY (TENNANT).

STANLEY, MARTHA MELEAN BURGESS. B. 1872. United States.

2907   THE SOULS OF MEN. New York: G. W. Dillingham, [c1913] NUC.

Beth Mannering grows to hate her married life in the wilds of Cuba's unsettled tobacco district. When a wealthy New York club man happens along and promises to help her with a singing career, she goes with him. She becomes a brilliant success. When the man demands his price, Beth almost gives in, but saved by what she believes is a miracle, she returns to her husband.

STANLEY, WINIFRED.

2908   A FLASH OF THE WILL. London: Chatto & Windus, 1904 BMC.

The heroine, a "genius," is unhappily married. One reviewer describes her as a priggish, neurotic 19th century type of heroine.

STANNARD, HENRIETTA ELIZA VAUGHAN (PALMER). 1856-1911. United Kingdom.

2909   A BLAMELESS WOMAN. BY JOHN STRANGE WINTER. London, New York: International News, [c1894] NUC. London: F. V. White, 1895 BMC NUC.

Margaret North secretly elopes with a Russian prince and

lives with him in Berlin for two years, telling her guardian that she is studying German. Then she discovers her husband already has a wife. She returns to England, telling no one of her marriage, eventually marries and has a family. Her secret finally comes out, and her husband divorces her. The author considers her blameless.

2910   GOOD-BYE. A NOVEL. BY JOHN STRANGE WINTER. London: F. V. White, 1891 BMC. New York: United States Book, [c1891] NUC.

Mrs. Adair disappears after her husband divorces her on false evidence. He marries a woman he does not love and who feels only friendship for him. When he learns his first wife was innocent, he goes in search of her, finds her, but she will not return to him. The first wife and the second, old acquaintances, become very good friends, and the husband is left to his own conscience. Only after the second dies, does the first agree to remarry Mr. Adair.

2911   HEART AND SWORD. BY JOHN STRANGE WINTER. London: F. V. White, 1898 BMC. Philadelphia: J. B. Lippincott, 1899 NUC.

Katherine is an ambitious intelligent actress married to a soldier. She is known as the most remarkable actress of the day. Her husband objects to her commitment to her profession. The result is divorce. "An attempt to convince readers that the profession is in every respect superior to society." Katherine becomes the manager of a first-class theater.

2912   I MARRIED A WIFE, A NOVEL. BY JOHN STRANGE WINTER. New York & London: F. A. Stokes, [c1895] NUC BMC. London: F. V. White, 1895 BMC.

Sisters: the younger (the wife of the title), married to an officer, is a philanthropist in the slums who "comes dangerously near to bringing about a mutiny in the regiment by her mistaken philanthropic activity among the wives and children of the soldiers." The older is an advocate of the most advanced women's rights.

2913 THE LITTLE VANITIES OF MRS. WHITTAKER. A NOVEL. BY JOHN STRANGE WINTER. London: F. V. White, 1904 BMC. New York and London: Funk & Wagnalls, 1904 NUC.

The story of a new woman who returns to traditional values, according to one reviewer.

2914 MARTY. A NOVEL. BY JOHN STRANGE WINTER. Philadelphia and London: J. B. Lippincott, 1903 NUC. London: F. V. White, 1903 BMC NUC.

Well educated woman supports family by selling second-hand clothes. She marries "above" her station and is unhappy.

2915 THE MONEY SENSE; A NOVEL. BY JOHN STRANGE WINTER. London: G. Richards, 1900 BMC. New York: G. W. Dillingham, [1900] NUC.

The charming heroine's extravagance, a "vice pushed to the utmost limit," leads to a marriage, a divorce and remarriage, and alcoholism.

2916 A NAME TO CONJURE WITH; A NOVEL. BY JOHN STRANGE WINTER. London: F. V. White, 1899 BMC. Philadelphia: J. B. Lippincott, 1900 NUC.

Mary Lessingham: when her father loses his mind and a fortune, Mary supports the family by writing. She marries a friend who helped her publish, gives up writing for a time, but takes it up again when her husband becomes ill. This time she becomes a famous novelist, her husband serves as her business manager, and the family lives luxuriously. Mary struggles to maintain their way of life and keep up with the pressures of fame, but fears her creative powers are failing. She takes to alcohol as a stimulant and eventually becomes addicted. The novel traces the trials, sorrows, and temptations of this strong woman.

2917 THE OTHER MAN'S WIFE. A NOVEL. BY JOHN STRANGE WINTER. London: F. V. White, 1891 BMC. New York: F. M. Lupton, [n.d.] NUC.

Daughter of Corsican noble is seduced and abandoned by an English army major. Her two sisters organize a vendetta. They follow him all over the world until they trap him in London, and one of the sisters murders him. She is the one who tells the story to a friend of Ethel Mordaunt, who was forced by an ambitious mother to marry that major. This friend had suspected Ethel of murdering the major because he treated her horribly. The widowed Ethel is now free to marry the man she loves.

2918 THE PRICE OF A WIFE. BY JOHN STRANGE WINTER. Philadelphia: J. B. Lippincott, 1901 NUC.

A nurse whose father demands a price for her.

2919 THE SOUL OF THE BISHOP. A NOVEL. BY JOHN STRANGE WINTER. London: F. V. White, 1893 BMC NUC. New York: J. S. Tait, [c1893] NUC.

Cecil Constable postpones her wedding to a loyal broad-church bishop because she protests the church's belief that unbaptized babies don't go to heaven. She also takes exception to some of the 39 Articles. She marries the bishop when he convinces her she is basically a Christian, but breaks up her marriage when she realizes she is agnostic.

2920 THE TRUTH-TELLERS, A NOVEL. BY JOHN STRANGE WINTER. Philadelphia: J B. Lippincott, 1896 NUC. London: F. V. White, 1896 BMC NUC.

A pair of enfants terribles, "even more down on the nail with their searching comments on men and things" than the Heavenly Twins.

STANTON, CORALIE. See HOSKEN, ALICE CECIL (SEYMOUR).

STARK, HARRIET. United States.

2921 THE BACILLUS OF BEAUTY: A ROMANCE OF TO-DAY. New York: F. A. Stokes, [c1900] NUC.

The theme is the turmoil beauty causes. A German professor has discovered how to produce perfect beauty by a bacillus.

Stearns, Amanda (Akin).

2922   THE LADY NURSE OF WARD E. New York: Baker and Taylor, 1909 NUC.

A series of chatty letters from a Civil war nurse.

Steel, Flora Annie (Webster). 1847-1929. United Kingdom.

2923   THE GIFT OF THE GODS. New York: J. Chartres, 1897 NUC. London: W. Heinemann, 1911 BMC NUC.

Margaret is a widow who lives alone on her homestead in Scotland. Her tie to the land represents a fierce love and devotion. Conflict comes when a seaman who has suffered loss of memory comes to her home and then recovers his memory.

2924   MISS STUART'S LEGACY. BY MRS. F. A. STEEL. New York & London: Macmillan, 1893 BMC NUC.

Belle Stuart, educated in England, rejoins her father in India. She is an unconventional young woman—false conventions are often pointed out by the author. Belle loves a "half-caste" who saves his regiment at the cost of his life. She uses her legacy of money to found a home for incurably ill children. Set in the wilds of Afghanistan in the community of Faizapore. Full study of Anglo-Indian society and life.

2925   MISTRESS OF MEN: A NOVEL. London: W. Heinemann, 1917 BMC 1918 NUC. New York: F. A. Stokes, 1917 NUC.

"The long struggle of a beautiful and highly intellectual woman to overcome the artificial disabilities imposed upon her simply and solely because of her sex." Nurjahen was born in a caravan, left to die in the sands, but then rescued. She became a great beauty, desired and then married by the Emperor of India. Mihrunnissa (queen of women) rules in fact, if not in name, as prime minister. She is strong, just and completely capable as the ruler, while her husband is a weak drunkard. She is also a skilled housewife and a great huntress. The time of the story is 17th century.

2926 ON THE FACE OF THE WATERS, A TALE OF THE MUTINY. Rahway, N.J.: Mershon, 1896 NUC. London: W. Heinemann, 1897 BMC.

Fiction based on the Indian Mutiny, historically accurate. Alice Gissing, who one reviewer says "carries the book on her shoulders," takes Major Erlton away from his wife, is pregnant by him. Their relationship is described with "rare and even audacious sympathy." When she dies in an attempt to save a child's life, and Mrs. Erlton helps bury her, "one is made to feel that the injured wife is offering only partial reparation to the person who had deliberately wronged her."

2927 RED ROWANS. BY MRS. F. A. STEEL. New York and London: Macmillan, 1895 BMC NUC.

Set in Scotch highlands: three women all involved with Paul McLeod. Jeanie Duncan is loved and left by him, seeks revenge but dies loving him. Violet is wooed by him because she has money that can rehabilitate his estates. And Marjorie Carmichael, educated as a boy by her scholarly uncle, learned in Greek and Latin, genius in math, studying to enter the university, loves Paul. Tom must console himself with her friendship, which, Marjorie writes, "is bigger than love."

STEEL, MRS. F. A. See STEEL, FLORA ANNIE (WEBSTER).

STEELE, FRANCESCA MARIA. D. 1931. United Kingdom.

2928 LOTTIE'S WOOING. BY DARLEY DALE. London: Hutchinson, 1893 BMC. New York: Cassell, [c1893] NUC.

Charlotte Vaughan is determined to marry her rich landlord because her family is destitute. First she bribes a gypsy to say they are destined to marry; then she manages to put in his hands a letter in which she refuses a proposal; and then she puts an announcement of their wedding in the London Times. She never deceives the man by her tricks, but he turns from the woman he loves to Charlotte, because the more she fails, the better a person she becomes. Light and humorous.

STEFFENS, JOSEPHINE BONTECOU. United States.

2929   LETITIA BERKELEY, A.M.: A NOVEL. New York: F. A. Stokes, [c1899] NUC.

"The erotic in fiction." "An unhealthy story." Letitia is a very intelligent young woman, the daughter of a professor. She is bored with the narrow life in her small New England town, so she leaves to see what the world is like. First she goes to New York, mixes with a fast crowd, and sleeps with Philip Enton though she does not love him. She then goes to Paris to study medicine and meets revolutionary anarchists and theorists of both sexes. Philip tracks her down in Paris to offer to marry her, but she refuses. She now loves a doctor to whom she freely tells all. There is much discussion of sex as sinless—the author's view. The story dwells especially upon the difference of the moral standard held binding upon men and women.

STEPHENS, ETHEL STEFANA. See DROWER, ETHEL STEFANA (STEVENS).

STERN, E. G. See STERN, ELIZABETH GERTRUDE (LEVIN).

STERN, ELIZABETH GERTRUDE (LEVIN). 1890-1954. United States.

2930   MY MOTHER AND I. BY E. G. STERN. New York: Macmillan, 1917 NUC.

A young modern woman grows away from the Polish-Jewish ghetto and her mother's ways. She goes to college, marries—everything contributes to making the gulf between mother and daughter wider as the daughter escapes the drudgery, child-bearing, gossipy sisters of the ghetto.

STERN, G. B. See HOLDSWORTH, GLADYS BERTHA (STERN).

STERNE, STUART. See BLOEDE, GERTRUDE.

STETSON, CHARLOTTE PERKINS. See GILMAN, CHARLOTTE (PERKINS) STETSON.

STETTHEIMER, ETTIE. United States.

2931 PHILOSOPHY: AN AUTOBIOGRAPHICAL FRAGMENT. BY HENRIE WASTE. London: Longmans, 1917 BMC. New York: Longmans, Green, 1917 NUC.

Henrie Waste is a young American woman studying at the University of Freiburg, Germany, for her Ph.D. The degree is to her a mere detail—what matters is the mental quest, for philosophy is to her the science of wonder. When she falls in love, she refuses to interrupt her studies. Her fiance leaves, she finishes her degree. Then she is ready to take up the relationship. Henrie tells her own story.

STEVENS, E. J. C.*

2932 LEENTAS. A TALE OF LOVE AND WAR. London: G. Allen, 1914 BMC.

The heroine, in the Karoo District of South Africa, disguises herself as a British trooper in order to revenge herself on the man who had wronged her sister.

STEVENS, E. S. See DROWER, ETHEL STEFANA (STEVENS).

STEVENSON, G. H.*

2933 THE SILVER SPOON. London: W. Blackwood, 1909 BMC.

Pathetic story of Miriam Westlake's sad marriage to a medical student, his weaknesses, their financial problems, and their deformed child.

STEVENSON, MRS.

2934 A ROMANCE OF A GROUSE MOOR. C. A. Pearson, 1898 EC.

In the style of George Eliot, although reviewer finds it difficult to believe that book was written by a woman.

Includes pen and ink portrait of her in "military dress and tout ensemble."

STEWART, A. L.*

2935   THE MAZE. London: J. Long, 1914 BMC.

The love story of a prima donna and a violinist. She is older than he, is trapped into marriage. He develops love for her; she is passionately devoted to him but absorbs his individuality and stifles his genius.

STEWART, CHARLOTTE. 1863-1918. United Kingdom.

2936   BEGGARS AND SORNERS. BY ALLAN MCAULAY. London and New York: J. Lane, 1912 BMC NUC.

Helen Murray visits Amsterdam after an illness. Her experiences include torture, espionage, and an interview with the Pretender. Not a romance, but intended to show the darker side of political intrigue.

2937   BLACK MARY. BY ALLAN MCAULAY. London: T.F. Unwin, [1901] BMC.

Mary's life of hardship, peril and disappointment nobly borne is pathetic.

STEWART, EDITH ANNE.

2938   LOVE AND THE PEOPLE. London: Lynwood, 1911 BMC.

Novel of social reform, slum settlement life and working-class aspirations. Marjorie Keswick wants more out of life than her working class parents had. She marries an artisan who is killed. Socialism and women's rights are given a large hearing in the novel.

STIRLING, ANNA MARIA DIANA WILHELMINA (PICKERING). 1865-1965. United Kingdom.

2939   A LIFE AWRY. A NOVEL. BY PERCIVAL PICKERING. London: Bliss, Sands and Foster, 1893 BMC NUC.

Focuses completely on Judy whose life began with so much promise: an accident that cripples and deforms her;

her discussions about men and love with Maud who is completely bored with her husband and believes love is a disease; her furious passionate love for her commonplace cousin who is repulsed by her deformity; the strain of her relationship with him and knowledge of his love for another woman; and her suicide.

2940 A PLIABLE MARRIAGE. BY PERCIVAL PICKERING. London: Osgood, 1895 BMC.

"Experiment of a young gentleman and lady who agree to go through the ceremony of marriage as an unavoidable concession to conventionality previous to their becoming business partners for life and her entering upon the duties of confidential housekeeper to look after his establishment and act as hostess to his guests." The woman who makes this platonic marriage is an "advanced" woman who "converses on improper subjects." The man really loves her and tries in a clumsy way to subjugate her. She leaves him, but they are reconciled in the end. Owes much to "New Woman vapours not even yet banished from our literary atmosphere."

2941 THE SPIRIT IS WILLING. BY PERCIVAL PICKERING. London: Bliss, Sands, 1898 BMC.

Heroine is unhappily married to a painter with severe morals. She turns to another man. She gives her husband the following analysis. "I do not know how men are constituted; but for women, love has to be created. Yes, I tell you, planted, tended, compelled into being. You do not know? Oh men like you never know! This love creating is an art, a knack which the worst men possess, a talent which they perfect with care. And so it is they win women's love, while men like you go hungry."

STOCK, GERTRUDE GEORGINA (DOUGLAS). B. 1842.

2942 A WASTED LIFE AND MARR'D. London: Hurst and Blackett, 1892 BMC.

The unhappy life of Maud Deering. Her selfish father passes her off as a foundling when her mother dies. When her husband shoots her dog, she shoots him.

STOCKING, JANE [pseud.].* United States.

2943 VIA P. AND O. New York: Dodd, Mead, 1914 NUC.
Through letters Carola Freiheit relates the problems of her marriage to her sister in England. Five months after her wedding to a German diplomat, she discovers his unfaithfulness. He insists males are naturally polygamous. They live under the same roof but apart, in the foreign quarters of Shanghai. Years pass and she meets a man she loves.

STOCKLEY, CYNTHIA. 1883-1936. United Kingdom.

2944 THE CLAW. London: Hurst and Blackett, 1911 BMC NUC. New York and London: G. P. Putnam's Sons, 1911 NUC.
Heroine is a remarkable woman with a biting wit who tells the story of her life in South Africa where she travelled the veldt alone. Dierdre Saurin used to have an art studio in the Latin Quarter. Then she fell in love with a man, but married another who tricked her into believing her lover was dead. Dierdre is miserable in her marriage, but wins happiness in the end.

2945 THE DREAM SHIP. London: Constable, 1913 BMC NUC. (Also published as Wanderfoot (The Dream Ship). New York and London: G. P. Putnam's Sons, 1913 NUC.)
Brilliant journalist writing under the pseudonym "Wanderfoot" and reporting from all corners of the world marries a doctor after her first husband is reported dead in the Boer War. The doctor expects her to be the housekeeper of his nursing home, but she cannot settle for domestic work. Then her first husband returns, and rather than tell the doctor, she runs off with the children and raises chickens and gardens. She is eventually reunited with the doctor who comes to have a proper sense of her after his initial mistake.

2946 POPPY; THE STORY OF A SOUTH AFRICAN GIRL. London: Hurst and Blackett, [1910?] NUC BMC. New York and London: G. P. Putnam's Sons, 1911 NUC.
History of Poppy from the time she was an overworked orphan to her fame as a writer and novelist. She's a

woman with an artistic temperament whose "fall" the author justifies by Poppy's passionate nature. She is a beautiful woman made attractive to the reader. The story concerns marital complications, divorce and remarriage, single parenthood by a woman who refuses to let the world's scorn crush her.

2947 VIRGINIA OF THE RHODESIANS. London: Hutchinson, 1903 BMC 1910 BMC. Boston: Estes, 1911 NUC.
The narrator's personality connects these South African love stories. She's an unconventional woman with a distaste for chaperones and nonsense of that sort. She invites us to "learn about women" through her.

STOLZENBERG, BETSEY (RIDDLE) VON HUTTEN ZUM. B. 1874. United States.

2948 BEECHY; OR THE LORDSHIP OF LOVE. BY BETTINA VON HUTTEN. New York: F.A. Stokes, [1909] NUC. (Also published as The Lordship of Love; a Novel. By Baroness Von Hutten. London: Hutchinson, 1909 BMC. Toronto: Musson Book, [1909] NUC.)
Career of Beatrice Cavaleone from slums to success as opera star in New York and London. She begins as the cast-off child of a royal Roman house, but she wants a career in opera. She wears male clothes to sing in Carmen, finds them convenient, sells papers dressed in them. In the end she marries.

2949 BIRD'S FOUNTAIN. BY THE BARONESS VON HUTTEN. London: Hutchinson, 1915 BMC NUC. New York: D. Appleton, 1915 NUC.
Amy Dorset at thirty five has been married sixteen years and has never known love. She and her husband who is a dull man much older than she are indifferent to one another. Then Amy falls in love with a rake, and her woman friend saves her from him. Ends in reconciliation of wife and husband.

2950 THE HALO. BY BETTINA VON HUTTEN. New York: Dodd, Mead, 1907 NUC. London: Methuen, 1907 BMC.
Bridgit Mead, sulky, embittered, tired of poverty, sick of her mother's nagging her to marry a wealthy old man,

makes a hasty engagement to Theo, a young rich man who drinks, but soon falls in love with Theo's father, a famous violinist. The father makes her marry Theo when he learns of her engagement, but their passion remains undiminished. Only the death of his wife halts their plans to elope.

2951　HAPPY HOUSE. BY THE BARONESS VON HUTTEN. London: Hutchinson, [1919] NUC BMC. New York: G.H. Doran, [c1920] NUC.

Mrs. Walbridge, past 50, is a writer of popular sentimental romances whose happy endings are no longer in style. She is a "capable, practical woman," whose waning popularity is her "nearest approach to personal tragedy." She writes to support a family of selfish children and an unfaithful husband. Although she is "at times a little exasperating in her meekness, her sentimentality and her continual self-sacrifice," she sees her family for exactly what they are, and she does not divorce her husband because "she regards him as an investment she has paid for in heavy installments until he has acquired the sentimental value of a costly mistake."

2952　MAG PYE. BY BETTINA VON HUTTEN. New York: D. Appleton, 1917 NUC. (Also published as Magpie. London: Hutchinson, 1917 BMC.)

Margaret Pye is a laundry maid who at 16 after proper training becomes a successful painter and supports her ex-artist father now on opium. Falls in love at the end.

2953　MARIA. London: Hutchinson, 1914 BMC NUC. New York: D. Appleton, 1914 NUC.

Maria loves a prince who will not marry her because of the difference in their social status. Her suffering makes her a great rather than good singer.

2954　OUR LADY OF THE BEECHES. BY THE BARONESS VON HUTTEN. Boston: Houghton, Mifflin, 1902 NUC. London: W. Heinemann, 1907 BMC.

A writer whose husband is habitually away hunting big game enters a literary flirtation with a philosopher. She is a 29 year old countess, interested in philosophy, nature, and metaphysics. Their letters are described as "witty, intelligent." They meet by chance, and lady's husband is a good fellow, they presently part, "as they are decent folks, and the never, one hopes, to meet again."

2955   PAM. BY BETTINA VON HUTTEN. London: W. Heinemann, 1904 BMC. New York: Dodd, Mead, 1905 NUC.

This "deliciously unconventional" novel is a searching analysis of the growth and development of Pam. At ten, she's well aware that she's illegitimate and that her mother lives with a married lover in open defiance of convention but is radiantly happy. For a brief (and impatient) period, Pam lives with her conventional grandfather but returns to her mother's irregular life for the next six years. Pam discusses all these matters openly; she developes her own "lawless" creed—she'll take love where she can, but will never marry.

2956   PAM DECIDES; A SEQUEL TO "PAM". BY BETTINA VON HUTTEN. New York: Dodd, Mead, 1906 NUC. (Also published as What Became of Pam. By Baroness Von Hutten. London: W. Heinemann, 1906 NUC BMC.)

Pam is now 27, living alone and writing cheap novels.

2957   YELLOWLEAF. BY SACHA GREGORY. London: W. Heinemann, 1919 NUC BMC. Philadelphia: J.B. Lippincott, 1919 NUC.

Lady Mary Dampiere, an invalid lives in her luxurious home Yellowleaf in London with her daughter-in-law Lila, recently a widow whose new husband is making Lila's life miserable. When Lady Mary dies, we learn that she killed Lila's second husband with her heart medicine.

STONE, JANE. See TRIMBLE, JESSIE.

STOOTHOFF, ELLENOR.   See   GREENSLET, ELLA STOOTHOFF (HULST).

STOTT, BEATRICE.

2958 ROSEMARY AND RUE. London: Sidgwick and Jackson, 1912 BMC.

Rosemary, daughter of Rosemonde of earlier book. Wretched girlhood, falls from virtue, leads double life, marries a man she learns to abhor and enters on a career of misery. She lacks loveable qualities and is as hard as nails. Psychological study.

2959 ROSEMONDE. London: T. F. Unwin, 1903 BMC.

Concentrated psychological study of Rosemonde and her cruel husband. She is tortured mentally and physically by this man to whom she is passionately bound. He's an attractive, charming, Byronic type, selfish and distrustful even after she lets him read the diary she has kept for years. The relationship is one of love and pain.

STRAIN, E. H. See STRAIN, EUPHANS H. (MACNAUGHTON).

STRAIN, EUPHANS H. (MACNAUGHTON). D. 1934. United Kingdom.

2960 A MAN'S FOES. BY E. H. STRAIN. London and New York: Ward, Lock and Bowden, 1895 BMC NUC.

Mrs. Hamilton narrates this true-to-fact story of the hardships of her husband and citizens of Derry during the seige of 1689. Reviewers describe her as a "womanly woman," but she outwits a soldier by wrapping him up, pistols and all, in her mantle until her husband arrives. She saves her husband's life, and when he must escape, she is left alone to defend her children, "when desertion of the cause would save her little ones from starvation." No love story.

STRANNIK, IVAN. See ANICHKOVA, ANNA MITROFANOVNA (AVINOVA).

STREATFEILD, LILIAN CECIL.

2961 EVELYN'S QUEST. BY ELSIE FEILD. London: H. J. Glaisher, 1906 BMC.

Suitable for young readers. A young woman searching for religion, working among the poor.

STREET, LILIAN.

2962 THE LITTLE PLAIN WOMAN AND OTHERS. London: T. F. Unwin, 1895 BMC.

Concerns a literary woman described as young, small, weird, electric: "What a colourless soulless face is mine! I believe I am as sexless as you said!" she exclaims to the man she loves; while to the man who loves her she confides, "I began life in hell, and I haven't admired the road to heaven, so I am sitting on the side to consider the next move." She is uncomfortable in her love affairs, as in all other affairs of her daily life. Everything goes wrong in a dull, vague manner, and the story ends with her as she was at the start. "And Others" are five very short sketches.

2963 THE WORLD AND ONORA. London: Duckworth, 1898 BMC.

Onora is married to a baronet who is cruel to her and kills her baby. She leaves him and falls in love with a music-hall singer, whom she marries when her husband dies.

STRICKLAND, MARGARET.

2964 ELUSIVE PEG: BEING SOME CHAPTERS IN THE LIFE OF PEGGY VERDON, NEE O'HARA. London: Angold's, [1917] BMC.

She is wayward and irresponsible as a child and even as a woman. She uses every devious method she knows to get money. She is a reckless gambler by nature. She marries a responsible type of man, but learns he is not as virtuous as she thought. They have many financial difficulties.

STUART, ELEANOR. See CHILDS, ELEANOR STUART (PATTERSON).

STUART, ESME. See LEROY, AMELIE CLAIRE.

SUKLOVA, MARIYA.

2965 THE LIFE-STORY OF A RUSSIAN EXILE. New York: Century, 1914 BMC NUC. London: W. Heinemann, 1915 BMC. (Tr. by Gregory Yarros.)

Frank revelation of a woman who is a born revolutionary written by an author who was herself exiled to Siberia for her political views.

SULLIVAN, ELIZABETH (HIGGINS). B. 1874. United States.

2966 OUT OF THE WEST, A NOVEL. BY ELIZABETH HIGGINS. New York and London: Harper, 1902 BMC NUC.

The heroine, a stump orator for the Populist Party in Colorado, marries a man and sends him to Congress, where he becomes corrupted.

SULLIVAN, MAY KELLOGG. United States.

2967 A WOMAN WHO WENT TO ALASKA. Boston: J. H. Earle, [c1902] NUC.

A woman who loves to travel goes to the Arctic circle.

SULLIVAN, MRS. A. SHACKELFORD. United States.

2968 A QUESTIONABLE MARRIAGE. Chicago: Rand, McNally, [c1897] NUC.

"Based upon complications incident to the Oklahoma divorce law and the decision of the Supreme Court declaring that law void."

SURBRIDGE, AGNES.

2969 THE CONFESSIONS OF A CLUB WOMAN. New York: Doubleday, Page, 1904 NUC.

The conflict between meetings and domestic duties.

SUTHERLAND, JOAN. See KELLY, JOAN COLLINGS.

SUTHERLAND, MILLICENT FANNY (SAINT CLAIR-ERSKINE) SUTHERLAND-LEVESON-GOWER. B. 1867. United Kingdom.

2970 ONE HOUR AND THE NEXT. London: Methuen, 1899 BMC. New York: 1899 NUC.

Agnes Stanier is an enthusiastic young woman with boundless self confidence who falls in love with a radical agitator named Lester, a married man who neglects his wife. Agnes types for him. Painfully and slowly she comes to realize he regards her only as a tool. The realization makes her cold and hard toward him. The novel ends with her misery.

SUTTON, ELIZABETH M.

2971 CELESTE. New York: G. W. Dillingham, 1895 NUC.

Marie Lascille leaves home with a count who deserts her to marry another woman. Marie then lives a free life in Paris but plots against the count. Eventually she steals his daughter with the intention of raising her to be a prostitute.

SVETLA, CAROLINE. See MUZAKOVA, JOHANA (ROTTOVA).

SWAN, ANNIE S. See SMITH, ANNIE S. (SWAN).

SWAN, ELIZA B. United States.

2972 THE OPAL QUEEN. Cincinnati: Robert Clarke, 1897 NUC.

Purpose is to persuade women to renounce current fashions and wear classic Greek dress.

SWAN, MAGGIE.

2973 LIFE'S BLINDFOLD GAME. Edinburgh: Oliphant, Anderson & Ferrier, 1895 BMC.

Mary Ellsworth mistress of a public school loves David Grey, Presbyterian minister. For a time he is attracted to another woman but comes to realize what a gem Mary is.

2974 A NEGLECTED PRIVILEGE: THE STORY OF A MODERN WOMAN. London: Ward, Lock, 1896 BMC.

Two sisters, very different. Elsie Blair marries without "accepting the responsibility of marriage." She leaves her husband, a doctor, to pursue her own freedom. She is eventually sorry, according to one reviewer.

SWAN, MYRA.

2975 BALLAST: A NOVEL. London: Longmans, 1901 BMC. New York: 1901 NUC.

The story concerns two stepsisters. One is an alcoholic; the other gives up her lover in order to care for her sister.

SWETNAM, FLORA MAY (STAFFORD). B. 1874. United States.

2976 MISS PHENA. New York: American Tract Society, [c1916] NUC.

She is a "quiet but forceful spinster," a leader of movements in her community.

SYLVA, CARMEN. See PAULINA ELIZABETH OTTILIA LOUISA, QUEEN CONSORT OF CHARLES I, KING OF RUMANIA.

SYMONDS, EMILY MORSE. D. 1936. United Kingdom.

2977 THE CAREER OF CANDIDA. BY GEORGE PASTON. London: Chapman and Hall, 1896 BMC NUC. New York: D. Appleton, 1897 NUC.

Candida refused to pray as a child because she got no

response. She is athletic, has boyish tastes, and does not like being told she is pretty. She goes to London and teaches gymnastics until her marriage to a weak, dissipated man. She becomes disillusioned with him and returns to gymnastic instruction, supporting herself and her son. Years later she sees her husband crippled; she takes him home and supports him also, but she isn't happy.

2978   A MODERN AMAZON. A NOVEL. BY GEORGE PASTON. London: Osgood and McIlvaine, 1894 BMC.

Regina, a journalist, at 26 marries a man on the condition that it be a platonic marriage. She has no romantic feeling for him, has never had romantic feelings toward any man. An eminent specialist advises her not to return to her husband unless she can love him as a wife. Actual events are unclear, but one reviewer says she is brought to her senses by a strong dose of suffering and humiliation.

2979   A STUDY IN PREJUDICES. BY GEORGE PASTON. London: Hutchinson, 1895 BMC. New York: D. Appleton, 1895 NUC BMC.

"Satire on the average man who, in his heart, holds the opinion that a woman should be the mere reflex of her husband: that it is a little short of heresy and sacrilege for her to think for herself." Cecily Tregarthen marries such a man thinking marriage offers her an escape from drudgery. She learns that his ideal is a combination of "doll-wife and cow mother." She is deserted by him when he learns she flirted before marriage, but she is gleeful to discover her priggish husband's "irregularities."

2980   A WRITER OF BOOKS. BY GEORGE PASTON. London: Chapman and Hall, 1898 BMC. New York: Appleton, 1899 NUC.

Cosima goes to Bloomsbury to gain experience and to write. She marries, is unhappy, leaves her husband and goes back to writing. She comments in the last chapter, "Love may once have been a woman's whole existence, but that was when a skein of embroidery silk was the only other string to her bow. In the life of the modern woman, blessed with an almost inexhaustible supply of strings, love is no less episodical than in the life of a man." One reviewer notes that the vogue for this kind of novel "has certainly passed."

SYNGE, MRS. HAMILTON.

2981 A SUPREME MOMENT. London: T. F. Unwin, 1905 BMC.

The awakening of a staid, middle-aged woman through a young woman who comes to live with her and her brother, for whom she keeps house.

SYRETT, NETTA. United Kingdom.

2982 ANNE PAGE. London: Chatto & Windus, 1908 BMC NUC. New York: J. Lane, 1909 NUC.

Anne Page, middle-aged, inherits a fortune and goes to Paris. She lives with an artist, offering to stay for as long as their love lasts. She leaves calmly three years later and returns to her English village. The author makes it seem "that the man is lucky who receives such companionship as hers," and even the vicar feels that there is more than one path to heaven.

2983 A CASTLE OF DREAMS. London: Chatto & Windus, 1909 BMC. Chicago: A. C. McClurg, 1909 NUC.

Bridget grows up in a lonely old castle. She refuses to conform to her father's wishes and to his choice of a husband for her. When suitors come to call, she frightens them off by making weird noises and telling wild stories. She eventually chooses her own husband.

2984 THE CHILD OF PROMISE. London: Chapman and Hall, 1907 BMC.

Natasha Heathcote raised in a Tolstoyan colony by parents dedicated to the cause of socialism is "the child of promise." Much of the novel studies her motives and her level of commitment to socialism. She becomes a socialist platform speaker, ignores "the claims of matrimony" with her socialist lover Val, and when he must leave for Vienna, she makes a success of her life through lectures on socialism. One critic determined that the author "considers babies quite incompatible with high intellectual values."

2985   THE DAY'S JOURNEY. London: Chapman & Hall, 1905 BMC. Chicago: A. C. McClurg, 1906 NUC.

Cecily is a brilliant woman who leads a secluded married life. After a few years she learns her literary husband has taken a lover. Her faithful woman friend and an old suitor persuade her to move to London. Here she becomes a writer herself, publishing a book that is more successful than any her husband has written. She eventually takes her husband back when he is penitent, but the new relationship is set up on her own terms.

2986   DRENDER'S DAUGHTER. London: Chatto & Windus, 1911 BMC. New York: J. Lane, 1911 NUC.

The man who tries "wife-culture" is the son of a blue stocking. He trains Nancy Drender to be an ideal wife for his later years. She marries her guardian partly out of gratitude, mostly because wifing is all she can do. But she is a born rebel and very soon refuses to submit to his theories despite her training. She detests him, and the marriage fails. Both eventually find more suitable mates.

2987   THE GOD OF CHANCE. London: Skeffington, [1920] BMC NUC.

Deborah hates the monotony of teaching, has a natural gift for acting. She makes the break from her job too late, but finds happiness in a colony of art lovers.

2988   NOBODY'S FAULT. London: J. Lane, 1896 BMC. Boston: Roberts, 1896 NUC.

Bridget Ruan, an educated young woman in an uneducated family, goes to London and becomes a high school teacher and writes stories. She marries unhappily and leaves her husband. A realistic portrayal of the loneliness and dullness of her life.

2989   OLIVIA L. CAREW. New York: John Lane, 1910 PW. London: Chatto & Windus, 1910 BMC NUC.

A New England teacher with literary ambitions marries, thinking her husband will help her in these ambitions. She is revolted by the realities of marriage and neglects "her duties." There is a novelist whom she meets in Italy who awakens in her a sense of art, life, and beauty. In the unexpected conclusion she finds happiness finally in conventionality.

2990   ROSANNE. London: Hurst & Blackett, 1902 BMC.
        The "neurotic female portrayed with minute care"; "the writer must remember there are men as well as women in the world."

2991   THREE WOMEN. London: Chatto & Windus, 1912 BMC NUC.
        Rosamund, Phillida, and Katherine. Rosamund is "needlessly offensive, a suburban Messalina. Phillida is willing to be a mistress but not a wife. "For this she is very properly punished by discovering that the relationship of marriage is not purely one of sex, but that 'the mutual society, help and comfort that the one sought to have of the other' is unattainable save by a legal tie. It is just as well that women who are, to use the modern phrase, feminists, should have this point brought home to them in fiction, though of course, the novels which preach this moral must necessarily be rather unpleasant reading." Katherine, ultra-modern, "perhaps conveys the most awful warning of all, for she is the brilliant business woman who deliberately stifles all her natural inclinations and refuses to marry lest domestic life should interfere with her business interests."

2992   THE TREE OF LIFE. London & New York: J. Lane, 1897 BMC NUC.
        387 pages of discussion of the sex question: completely sympathetic history of Christine Willowfield. As a child all joy is crushed out of her by her scholar father who believes women have no reasoning powers. As a young woman, Christine goes to college to prepare for teaching. (We are given a "whole gallery" of women being trained to teach school.) As a wife, she revolts against her grey suppressed life, first taking a lover and then leaving her "impossibly heartless" husband.

2993   TROUBLERS OF THE PEACE. London: Chatto & Windus, 1917 BMC.
        Difficulties in the mother-daughter relationship. Isabel Wickham is a successful career woman with little time for

friendship with her daughter Joan. Later when Isabel wants to draw close to Joan, Joan is antagonistic. Joan is a rebel, attracted to every freedom in life—free love, militant suffrage, etc. (Another mother, Margaret Courtney has a full friendship with her daughter Sylvia.) Though Isabel and Joan have a conflict of wills that is not reconciled, the author shows clearly that she favors liberty for young women.

2994 THE VICTORIANS; A NOVEL. London: T. F. Unwin, [1915] BMC NUC. (Also published as Rose Cottingham; A Novel. New York: G. P. Putnam's Sons, 1915 NUC.)

Minute account of Rose Cottingham's life from 9 to 19 which is at the same time a condemnation of the whole system of raising children in mid 19th century. Rose revolts against narrow Victorianism; she is introduced to advanced ideas in London, where she begins her career as a writer.

2995 THE WIFE OF A HERO. London: Skeffington, [1918] BMC NUC.

Ann Templeton, highly educated and well read, spoiled and adored by her aunt, marries a soldier who is beautiful but has no brains. When she hears he has been killed in action, she is secretly relieved. When he returns and his lover learns that Anne does not love her husband, Anne is offered "a rearrangement of partners"—by the other woman.

T., M. I. See TODD, MARY VAN LENNUP (IVES).

TABER, LOUISE EDDY. B. 1890. United States.

2996 THE FLAME. New York: A. Harriman, 1911 NUC.

Gwendolyn Rolfe is saved from a fortune-hunting noble by a music hall singer that the man had seduced in her earlier days.

TADEMA, LAURENCE ALMA. D. 1940. United Kingdom.

2997 THE FATE-SPINNER. London: E. B. Mortlock, 1900 BMC NUC.

"Neurotic" heroine Ginerva, bedridden by the death of her child for five days. Lonely husband begins affair with Althea, the cheerful governess. Ginerva almost elopes with husband's cousin, but at last moment has premonition she won't be happy.

2998 THE WINGS OF ICARUS: BEING THE LIFE OF ONE EMILIA FLETCHER AS REVEALED BY HERSELF IN: I. THIRTY-FIVE LETTERS WRITTEN TO CONSTANCE NORRIS BETWEEN JULY 18TH 188- AND MARCH 26TH OF THE FOLLOWING YEAR II. A FRAGMENTARY JOURNAL III. A POSTSCRIPT. New York and London: W. Heinemann, 1894 BMC NUC.

Emilia is a female prig in her "advancement," her melancholy and her meditations. "An early application of the slipper and an education in sound religion and useful learning would have been the making of her." She has a friend, Constance Norris, who is a maumariee, "a pretty word for an ugly thing of no particular time or language." Emilia has a love who is a poet. She adores Constance and then he does. She sees this, wants to give him up, can't carry it through, marries him, hoping that if they go off everything will work out. At the end of the year she gives up, brings him home with the intention of freeing him to her friend. It is too late; her husband and Constance suicide.

TAINTER, HELEN (DAVIES). United States.

2999 THE REVERIES OF A SPINSTER. BY HELEN DAVIES. New York: F. T. Neely, 1897 NUC.

Marjorie first works hard teaching in New York. Her loneliness leads her to create an imaginary lover she calls Sandalphon. She then becomes an accompanist, and on the occasion that the singer fails to show up, she gets her big chance. She astonishes the audience, finds "her true position, and all the fashionable world of New York wanted to hire her." Even when a real lover comes along, she scorns love for the profession of music.

TAIT, EUPHEMIA MARGARET. United Kingdom.

3000 THE RED SYMBOL. BY JOHN IRONSIDE. Boston: Little, Brown, 1910 NUC. London: E. Nash, 1911 BMC.
Anna Petrovna, Russian nihilist and grand-duchess, is the leading spirit of a league which has as its symbol a five-petaled red geranium.

TALBOT, L. A.*

3001 THE DUKE'S JEST. London and New York: Harper, 1904 BMC.
Adventures, young woman bicycles through strange country, comedy.

TALLENTYRE, S. G. See HALL, EVELYN BEATRICE.

TAMURA, NAOMI.

3002 THE JAPANESE BRIDE. New York: Harper, 1893 BMC NUC.
Frank pictures of Japanese home life. Chapters bear titles like "why Do We Marry?" "Courting" and "The Honeymoon."

TAPNER, ETHEL GRACE.

3003 ONE EVENTFUL SUMMER: A ROMANCE OF NORTH DEVON. London: J. Long, 1907 BMC.
Phyllis tries to support mother by writing poetry.

TASMA. See COUVREUR, JESSIE CATHERINE (HUYBERS).

TAYLOR, H. M.*

3004 "JANE ELLEN" BEING REAL SKETCHES FROM THE LIFE OF A LANCASTER LASS. London: Drane's, [1921] BMC.

Scenes from the life of a cotton weaver, her difficulties at home, her religious experiences, hopes, ideals, loves.

TAYLOR, KATHARINE HAVILAND. 1888-1941. United States.

3005 YELLOW SOAP. Garden City, N.Y.: Doubleday, Page, 1920 NUC.

An unwed launderer and her son, whom she raises to be a "gent" like his father.

TAYLOR, LYDIA JUTSUM.

3006 LAND OF THE SCARLET LEAF. BY MRS. ALFRED EDWARD TAYLOR. London: Hodder & Stoughton, [1915] BMC.

Delia is companion to a wealthy Canadian woman. She very deliberately chooses to marry a wealthy man rather than the man she loves. After her marriage, she becomes very extravagant—she gambles and she forges her husband's signature to a check. The story flouts poetic justice, for the wronged husband dies and Delia is happily reunited with the man she loves.

TAYLOR, M. IMLAY. See TAYLOR, MARY IMLAY.

TAYLOR, MARY IMLAY. 1878-1938. United States.

3007 AN IMPERIAL LOVER. BY M. IMLAY TAYLOR. Chicago: A. C. McClurg, 1897 NUC. London: Gay and Bird, 1899 BMC.

Historical romance of the Russian court of Peter the Great and his romance and marriage to a girl with the "tigress in her nature, passionate, bold, ambitious, a peasant, a slave and Empress of all the Russias," Catherine I.

3008 THE LONG WAY. Boston: Little, Brown, 1913 NUC.
Eva Astry wrongly accuses her sister Rachel of indiscretion with her own lover. Eva's husband insists that the man marry Rachel, and Rachel consents—in order to save her sister's reputation. Slowly Eva realizes her own selfishness and the enormity of her sister's sacrifice.

3009 THE REAPING. Boston: Little, Brown, 1908 NUC. London: Hutchinson, 1909 BMC.
Woman marries for money, divorces; first love is no longer interested.

3010 THE WILD FAWN. New York: Moffat, Yard, 1920 NUC.
A young French woman, a dancer, married to one of the most respected citizens in a Southern town.

TAYLOR, MRS. A. E.

3011 THE PRODIGAL AUNT. London: Digby, Long, 1914.
Diane, a teacher, inherits a 2,000 lb. per year income. She shares this with her niece, a teacher in the same school, enjoying "all the pleasures of freedom, foreign travel, and attractive clothes."

TAYLOR, MRS. ALFRED EDWARD. See TAYLOR, LYDIA JUTSUM.

TEETGEN, A. B. See TEETGEN, ADA B.

TEETGEN, ADA B.

3012 A WHITE PASSION. BY A. B. TEETGEN. London: W. Gardner, [1913] BMC. Toronto: Bell & Cockburn, [1913] NUC.
Alma Norway is a hospital matron in a new prairie hospital founded in Alberta. Shows the trials of wives and mothers miles away from medical care, and the need for central hospitals for the scattered Canadian farming population.

TELLER, CHARLOTTE. See HIRSCH, CHARLOTTE (TELLER).

TEMPLE, LESLIE.*

3013 NOTHING VENTURE. London: Digby, Long, [1917] BMC.
Young woman from rich family works in a factory.

TENNYSON, MARY H. See FOLKARD, MARY H.

TERRELL, DOROTHY A BECKETT. See JAMES, DOROTHY A BECKETT (TERRELL).

TESKEY, ADELINE MARGARET. D. 1924. Canada.

3014 WHERE THE SUGAR MAPLE GROWS: IDYLLS OF A CANADIAN VILLAGE. New York: R. F. Fenno, 1901 NUC. Toronto: Musson Book, [1913] BMC.
A Canadian village not unlike Cranford.

THANET, OCTAVE. See FRENCH, ALICE.

THEOBALD, C. M.*

3015 LENA HALE. London: G. Allen and Unwin, 1915 BMC.
Her life story from infancy to womanhood. Lena Hale makes a poor marriage. When her husband deserts her, she has several affairs and then marries. All her different emotions as she grows up and grows older are given in detail. Her history is "modern in its lack of reticence. The impression left is that the sexes are to be equalized not by restricting the male but by giving equal license to the female."

THOMAS, ANNIE. See CUDLIP, ANNIE HALL (THOMAS).

THOMPSON, LILIAN TURNER. Australia.

3016   BETTY THE SCRIBE. BY LILIAN TURNER. London: Ward, Lock, 1906 BMC. New York: Saafield, [c1907] NUC.

At 16, Betty supports three brothers and a sister. She loves to write. At 21 she sets out to be a writer. "Betty absolutely refuses to be a woman as the story closes."

THOMPSON, MARAVENE (KENNEDY). United States.

3017   THE WOMAN'S LAW. New York: F. A. Stokes, [1914] NUC. London: E. Nash, 1914 BMC.

A woman whose husband has killed a man does all she can to protect her child from dishonor. "Her law—the woman's law—dictates the protection of her child, even though the law of the land be against her." She helps her husband escape and then drives through the streets of New York, picking up and bringing home an amnesia victim who is the double of her husband. She persuades him to impersonate her husband.

THROSSELL, KATHARINE SUSANNAH (PRICHARD). 1884-1969. Australia.

3018   THE PIONEERS. BY KATHARINE SUSANNAH PRICHARD. London and New York: Hodder & Stoughton, [1915] NUC BMC.

Deirdre sells herself to a man to prevent her father, the "schoolmaster," from returning to prison. When she finds she has been cheated and betrayed into becoming this man's wife, she shoots him. She does not suffer for her act, says one reviewer; another says it left a "cloud of pain and horror over all her life."

THRUSTON, LUCY MEACHAM (KIDD). B. 1862. United States.

3019   MISTRESS BRENT: A STORY OF LORD BALTIMORE'S COLONY IN 1638. Boston: Little, Brown, 1901 BMC NUC.

Love plays a small part in Mistress Brent's life.

"Large-brained and strong," she lives her own life; and with courage and enterprise she manages her estates in the new world.

THURSTON, KATHERINE CECIL (MADDEN). 1875-1911. United Kingdom.

3020 THE CIRCLE. New York: Dodd, Mead, 1903 NUC. Edinburgh: W. Blackwood, 1903 BMC.

Young Russian woman in London slums craves action, is bored in her father's curio shop, leaves for adventure, studies for the stage, has a brilliant career, but steps down from topmost height to return to her father.

3021 THE FLY ON THE WHEEL. New York: Dodd, Mead, 1908 NUC. Edinburgh: W. Blackwood, 1908 BMC.

Isabel, a Hedda Gabler type, returns to small Irish village after living in Paris, is unutterably bored with the monotony and narrowness of village life. She and a married man fall in love, but when he loses his nerve and cleaves to his wife, she kills herself with the poison she had briefly intended for him.

3022 THE GAMBLER, A NOVEL. New York and London: Harper, 1905 NUC. Toronto: F. H. Revell, 1905 BMC.

Young widow with an inherited weakness for gambling goes heavily into debt, considers suicide, but with spirit and strength of character resolves her problem.

3023 JOHN CHILCOTE, M.P. Edinburgh and London: W. Blackwood, 1904 BMC 1905 NUC.

John Chilcote arranges for a man who looks just like him to lead his life as a member of parliament so he can pursue his morphia habit. When he dies from an overdose, his impersonator discovers that Chilcote's wife has known his secret. She insists that it is his duty to continue his role as John Chilcote so they can work together politically, and she accepts him as her husband without ceremony.

3024 MAX. A NOVEL. New York: Harper, 1910 NUC. London: Hutchinson, 1910 BMC.

Max, a Russian princess disillusioned in men, comes to

Paris disguised as a man. She is an artist and makes friends with Ned, a fellow artist. As their friendship develops, her male disguise becomes a problem. Eventually, she decides to trust their love and reveal her female identity.

TIERNAN, FRANCES CHRISTINE (FISHER). 1846-1920. United States.

3025 THE CHASE OF AN HEIRESS. BY CHRISTIAN REID. New York & London: G. P. Putnam's Sons, 1898 NUC BMC.

Romance in West Indies. Leslie, the hero, is looking for the heir of Ancram's. She (the heir) has run off with a man to make her lover jealous and has stabbed the man she was travelling with when he tried to kiss her. Katherine, the heroine, is the true detective who tracks her down for Leslie. Everything straightens out and the story ends with two marriages.

3026 THE MAN OF THE FAMILY: A NOVEL. BY CHRISTIAN REID. New York & London: G. P. Putnam's Sons, 1897 NUC.

The man is a young woman who had always supplied the "masculine element" in the family. Yvonne disguises herself as a man and travels by steamer from New York to Haiti to find the ancestral treasure. She meets a man who does not see through the disguise. Together they find the treasure, bring it back to the States, and separate. Much later, Yvonne arranges a way to meet him at a tea party where she will appear as Henri de Marsillac.

3027 WEIGHED IN THE BALANCE. BY CHRISTIAN REID. Boston: Marlier, Callanan, 1900 NUC.

Psychological study of heroine, an idealist who finds the world's motives and standards in direct contradiction to hers. Love, sorrow. Bohemian Paris, American society.

TINAYRE, MARCELLE. See TINAYRE, MARGUERITE SUZANNE MARCELLE (CHASTEAU).

TINAYRE, MARGUERITE SUZANNE MARCELLE (CHASTEAU). 1877-1948. France.

3028 MADELINE AT HER MIRROR; A WOMAN'S DIARY. BY MARCELLE TINAYRE. New York and London: John Lane, 1913 NUC BMC. (Tr. by Winifred Stephens.)

An intelligent wealthy widow of 35, mother of grown son and daughter, gives an account of her life in which "nothing of interest as between one woman and another is omitted." She married when she was very young. She once felt that children fulfilled a woman's life, but finds she wants more.

3029 THE SHADOW OF LOVE. BY MARCELLE TINAYRE. London, New York: J. Lane, 1911 BMC NUC. (Tr. by Alfred Allinson.)

"We search our memories in vain for any fiction matching it in its handling of the physical facts of life....Two girls appear in the story; the one, trained by her father, a physician, to believe firmly in that right, of all others most ignored, the 'right of the child not to be born,' has reached the age of 27 years, a well-poised, calm young woman. How all that her rearing and her own nature have carefully built up within her soul crumbles at the touch of a love far removed from passion, an almost maternal yearning over a dying man, is the dominant theme of the story. The other girl, Fortunade...is of the stuff of which mediaeval saints were made. Her temperament is that of a mystic, her longing is for the cloister." The New York Times Literary Section, 25 June 1911, p.403. "If Mme. Tinayre makes her heroine succumb, in spite of her forceful theories, to so vulgar a sentiment as amorous pity, it is because her theories are too new to have become an integral part of this heroine's being. It is obvious that the author believes that the woman of the future will not be subject to lapses of this nature." The New York Times Literary Section, 4 April 1910, p. 25.

TIPPETT, ISABEL C.

3030   GREEN GIRL. London: J. Long, 1913 BMC.
Young woman resents being tied down by marriage.
Janette Acklebourne studies art in Paris until she marries a
rich man against her better judgment. Once married,
however, she gets restless, leaves her husband, and rejoins
a young man she met and travelled with in France.

TODD, MARGARET GEORGINA. 1859-1918. United
Kingdom.

3031   GROWTH, A NOVEL. BY GRAHAM TRAVERS
(MARGARET TODD, M.D.). London: A. Constable, 1906
BMC. New York: Holt, 1907 NUC.
One of the leading women characters is a successful
actress.

3032   MONA MACLEAN, MEDICAL STUDENT. A NOVEL.
BY GRAHAM TRAVERS. Edinburgh: Blackwood, 1892
BMC. New York: D. Appleton, 1892 NUC.
An "intellectual comedy" of the female medical movement.
Mona's life as a medical student in Scotland. She marries
a physician; they become practitioners together.

3033   WINDYHAUGH. A NOVEL. BY GRAHAM TRAVERS.
London: W. Blackwood, 1898 BMC. New York: D.
Appleton, 1899 NUC.
The mental, spiritual, and physical development of
Wilhelmina. She marries a Cambridge "prig," who, she
discovers, does not feel that she is his intellectual equal.
She leaves him, becomes a governess, studies science,
becomes a successful actress; by end of book she has
brought her husband to his knees. "...a kind of Sartor
Resartus translated into feminine and everyday terms, with
a woman instead of a man as the central character; with
the trials, circumstances and thoughts of the late
nineteenth century given in place of the abstract and
transcendental scenery of Carlyle." The Academy, 55
(1898), 376.

TODD, MARY VAN LENNUP (IVES). B. 1849. United States.

3034 AN AMERICAN ABELARD AND HELOISE; A LOVE STORY. New York: Grafton Press, [1904] NUC.
"Heloise," independent and with her own views on religion, marriage, and women's rights, refuses to marry until she and the clergyman who loves her have, for a period of three years, tested their opinions. One reviewer comments that he is an "involuntary martyr to progressive views of womanly independence, with hope of home and marriage indefinitely postponed.

3035 DEBORAH, THE ADVANCED WOMAN. BY M. I. T. Boston: Arena, 1896 NUC.
"A strong and pathetic story of life among the Mormons...written for the purpose of asserting woman's coequality with man and aiding in her release from that subjection to man's use and passion which has been her lot for years."

3036 THE HETERODOX MARRIAGE OF A NEW WOMAN. New York: R. L. Weed, [c1898] NUC.
An intellectual American woman marries a Russian. She insists on changing the prose in their wedding ceremony from "till death do us part" to "till it shall please God to separate us."

3037 VIOLINA; OR THE PASSING OF THE OLD ADAM AND EVE. A ROMANCE. New York: Broadway, 1904 NUC.
A young woman musician marries a scoundrel, leaves him, and returns to her career.

TOMKINSON, JULIA REDFORD.

3038 DORIS, A MOUNT HOLYOKE GIRL. New York: American Tract Soc., [c1913] NUC.
Her home life on a New England farm, her education at Mt. Holyoke, her life as a teacher and her happy marriage.

TOMPKINS, ELIZABETH KNIGHT. B. 1865. United States.

3039   HER MAJESTY: A ROMANCE OF TO-DAY. New York, London: G. P. Putnam's Sons, 1895 NUC 1896 BMC.

Queen Honoria travels incognito among her people to discover their needs; she meets and loves a duke also travelling incognito. Their relationship is one of comrades. When the revolution comes, she is dethroned, marries the duke. At the end the two are called back to the throne.

3040   THE THINGS THAT COUNT. New York and London: G. P. Putnam's Sons, 1900 NUC BMC.

The heroine, with a small income, survives by visiting wealthy friends. She has expensive tastes, a banjo, and is a little shocking. "The imperfect heroine is one of the most popular arrivals in recent literature."

TOMPKINS, JULIET WILBOR. 1871-1956. United States.

3041   DIANTHA. New York: Century, 1915 BMC NUC.

Diantha and Sylvia are twins, very much alike in childhood. As they grow up, Diantha gains weight and becomes sluggish and lifeless while Sylvia develops beautifully. Men flock around Sylvia while they ignore Diantha, and Sylvia is spoiled enough to attract the one man who comes to like Diantha. Diantha longs to be like her sister; she represses her rebellious feelings. When she becomes ill, it is she who regains her beauty while Sylvia fades. Interesting psychological study of female twins.

3042   DR. ELLEN. New York: Baker & Taylor, [1908] NUC.

Ellen sacrifices her career to take her sick sister to the Sierras. Her patients in the small Western town leave her for a male quack who moves in.

3043   A GIRL NAMED MARY. Indianapolis: Bobbs-Merrill, [c1918] BMC NUC.

The character of a young mother whose child disappeared at two is developed in her search for her daughter. Her long inquiry into the lives and homes of working girls leads to her devoting her time and energy to causes that will benefit children and working women. When she finds her daughter, she discovers she is a stenographer, as proud of her work as another woman might be of her wealth.

3044 JOANNA BUILDS A NEST. Indianapolis: Bobbs-Merrill, [c1920] BMC NUC. London: Page, 1921 BMC.

Joanna arranges her work with a publisher so that she can spend half the week in a small country house she has bought. Humorous account of the delights of remodeling a house and the problems of housekeeping.

3045 OPEN HOUSE. New York: Baker & Taylor, [1909] NUC.

The changes in a woman who must earn her own living after years of luxurious living. She takes a job as a physician's assistant and becomes very capable in her work. Eventually she falls in love with the doctor and he with her.

3046 THE STARLING. Indianapolis: Bobbs-Merrill, [c1919] BMC NUC.

Study of a mother and daughter subjected to the tyranny of a patriarchal father. Sarah Cowthorne and her mother hunger for the companionship of friends, but Professor Cowthorne keeps them shut up and isolated. Sarah is an imaginative person who takes joy in things others take for granted. Her father, a complete rationalist, despises this quality in her. Eventually Sarah has two suitors, about whom her mother says, "It is true my dear, men are not much, but they are all we have in that line." Sarah becomes a novelist.

TOPHAM, ANNE. B. 1874. United Kingdom.

3047 THE BEGINNING AND THE END. London: A. Melrose, 1919 BMC.

Careful study of Anne Arbuthnot—her childhood as an orphan, and her narrow education at a young ladies' seminary, her passionate response to her seducer at 17, and his abandonment of her, her rescue from despair by her old nurse and her happy end. Anne becomes a portrait painter and marries happily; her seducer is left to repent in agonies of remorse.

3048   JULIA AND I IN CANADA. BY THE AUTHOR OF
        "DAPHNE IN THE FATHERLAND" [ANONYMOUS].
        London: A. Melrose, 1913 BMC.
        Julia and Priscilla on a lecture tour in Eastern Canada.
        The problems of women finding living quarters.

TORRANCE, M. E.*

3049   HILDEGARDE'S CAMPAIGN. St. Paul, Minn.: Price-
        McGill, 1892 NUC.
        War, heroine disguised in male attire, sensational.

TORREY, JANE ANNE. See KENDELL, JANE ANNE
        TORREY.

TOTTENHAM, BLANCHE MARY LOFTUS.

3050   A HEART'S REVENGE. London: Hurst and Blackett, 1894
        BMC.
        Miserable tyrant drives son from home, wife to arms of
        lover.

TOWGOOD, EDITH ETHEL. United Kingdom.

3051   THE GOAL OF FORTUNE. London: Sidgwick & Jackson,
        1911 BMC NUC.
        Alison has humor, brains and purpose, but author says it
        was "inevitable that she would fall in love with her first
        serious wooer." Delicate, precise, fidelity to observed life.
        Expresses the woman's view—not based upon male
        models.

TOWNESEND, FRANCES ELIZA (HODGSON) BURNETT.
        1849-1924. United States.

3052 HIS GRACE OF OSMONDE: BEING THE PORTIONS OF THAT NOBLEMAN'S LIFE OMITTED IN THE RELATION OF HIS LADY'S STORY PRESENTED TO THE WORLD OF FASHION UNDER THE TITLE OF A LADY OF QUALITY. BY FRANCES HODGSON BURNETT. New York: C. Scribner's Sons, 1897 NUC. London: F. Warne, 1897 BMC.

The same story and characters of the author's "A Lady of Quality" from the husband's point of view: Clorinda Wildairs through Osmonde's eyes. As a youth he saw her in boy's clothes, heard of her "unrivaled profanity" and fell in love with the swearing beauty but loses her for a time. The notorious Clorinda goes on to crown "the follies of her youth with a capital crime"—murder of a lover. She is in fact "up to her knees in broken commandments," yet the author presents her as a true woman, wife, tender mother and excellent model of England's womanhood. About the murder of her lover—even her husband says he would have done the same. Set in the 18th century.

3053 A LADY OF QUALITY: BEING A MOST CURIOUS HITHERTO UNKNOWN HISTORY, AS RELATED TO MR. ISAAC BICKERSTAFF BUT NOT PRESENTED TO THE WORLD OF FASHION THROUGH THE PAGES OF THE TATLER AND NOW FOR THE FIRST TIME WRITTEN DOWN. BY FRANCES HODGSON BURNETT. New York: C. Scribner's Sons, 1896 NUC. London: F. Warne, 1896 BMC.

Clorinda, whose mother died in childbirth, runs into her father, a drunken bestial baronet, for the first time at age six, during which encounter she curses him and beats him with his own hunting crop. He is quite taken by this and henceforth dresses and treats her as his son. On the occasion of her 16th birthday party, she announces to her father and his drunken companions that she will dress as and be a lady. She quickly becomes the most desired woman in society. On the eve of her wedding to a wealthy duke, one of her father's bestial friends who had seduced her as a child threatens her with disclosure. She invites him to tea to discuss it, reads sermons before he arrives, brains and buries him in the cellar. She then marries, lives a long life happily and is widely respected throughout. "Granting that many a wretched woman has killed her lover, no one of them all has gone on record that by so doing she has blotted out her own shame. The belief that this can be done by the shedding of blood is still a male article of faith...the subsequent argument making the murder committed by this lady of quality 'the accomplishment of love's purification,' and the primary, immediate, and permanent cause of the spiritual transfiguration of the murderess is equally insane and pernicious."

3054   THE ONE I KNEW THE BEST OF ALL: A MEMORY OF THE MIND OF A CHILD. BY FRANCES HODGSON BURNETT. New York: C. Scribner's Sons, 1893 NUC. London: F. Warne, 1893 BMC.

Story of a Manchester girl from the age of three to fifteen—from the time her family moved to the North Carolina mountains so that her brothers might find work to the time when an editor accepted two of her stories for publication. Autobiographical form.

3055   THE SHUTTLE. BY FRANCES HODGSON BURNETT. London: W. Heinemann, 1907 BMC. New York: F. A. Stokes, [1907] NUC.

Bettina is a modern young woman, outspoken, well-educated. She always has the facts at hand. She goes off to England to rescue her sister from her villainous husband Nigel who has cut Anne off from her family and has taken over her income. Bettina saves the estate, takes charge of all repairs, hires and fires workmen. She's a genius at everything and a millionaire. She falls in love with a poor man who nevertheless has inherited an estate. When he lies dying after helping the victims of an epidemic, Bettina calls him back to life. The book has its melodrama—Bettina's battle of wits with Nigel, his attraction for her, his attempt to seduce her. She's rescued by her lover but only after she hides from Nigel, keeps cool and is self-sufficient and quite ready to whip him if he discovers her.

TOYE, NINA. United Kingdom.

3056 THE DEATH RIDER. London and New York: Cassell, [1916] BMC NUC.
Setting is Italy during the time of Pope Julius II. Fiametta is humiliated by a brutal Captain Malviso but designs a gruesome revenge which is his nemesis.

TRAIL, FLORENCE. 1854-1944. United States.

3057 UNDER THE SECOND RENAISSANCE: A NOVEL. Buffalo: C. W. Moulton, 1894 NUC BMC.
Heroine goes on stage in face of family's oppostion. She's a success. Then she falls in love, but leaves the man because of his abhorrence of her career. He follows her, eventually begins to enjoy her triumphs; they marry. A defense of acting as a career for women.

TRAIN, ELIZABETH PHIPPS. B. 1856. United States.

3058 A DESERTER FROM PHILISTIA. London: J. Bowden, 1897 BMC.
Heroine is a rich successful and virtuous dancer. She has educated her daughter in a convent. When Lisa comes out, she condemns her mother for her profession and destroys her mother's plans for marriage to someone she loves because it would involve divorce. She does all this, smugly feeling she has saved her mother's soul.

3059 MADAM OF THE IVIES. Philadelphia & London: J. B. Lippincott, 1898 NUC.
Dorothy, narrator, answers an ad for companion to an elderly woman. There is a mystery in her life. Mad

sensationalism—Jane Eyre plot in modern New York setting.

3060　A QUEEN OF HEARTS. Philadelphia: J. B. Lippincott, 1898 NUC.

Young married woman of vagabond spirit "irks under the humdrum of her life." She leaves her husband and child to become a "danseuse" known as Mlle. Cleo.

TRASK, KATE (NICHOLS). 1853-1922. United States.

3061　FREE NOT BOUND. BY KATRINA TRASK. New York and London: G. P. Putnam's Sons, 1903 BMC NUC.

Historical novel set in Revolutionary times, but good psychological study. A free thinking woman is married to a New England minister of stern religious ideas. She is excommunicated because of her views, but sticks to them. She travels during the war to search for her husband. Finally the two are reconciled with integrity—both learn and bend after a long separation.

TRASK, KATRINA. See TRASK, KATE (NICHOLS).

TRAVERS, GRAHAM. See TODD, MARGARET GEORGINA.

TRAVERS, JOHN. See BELL, EVA MARY (HAMILTON).

TRAVIS, ELMA (ALLEN). 1861-1917. United States.

3062　THE COBBLER. New York: Outing, 1908 NUC.

The secret marriage of the son of a cobbler to a young woman with an interest in "astronomical investigation" which takes her away from home much of the time. He needs companionship and finds it in two very different women. They eventually discover they can be happy together.

3063　THE PANG-YANGER. BY ELMA A. TRAVIS, M.D. New York: McClure, Phillips, 1905 NUC.

Woman deserts both her husband and child for a lover,

and marries him—trusting to her husband's lack of proof of her first marriage.

TREMAYNE, SYDNEY. See COOKSON, SYBIL IRENE ELEANOR (TAYLOR).

TREMLETT, MRS. HORACE. United Kingdom.

3064 EMILY DOES HER BEST. London: J. Lane, 1917 NUC BMC. New York: J. Lane, 1917 NUC BMC.

Light amusing comedy. Emily is 30, single by choice because, she says, she never took to husband hunting. When she learns that her brother is living with Pipsy, she accepts the relationship without hesitation—much to her brother's astonishment. They expected the "spinster" Emily to be shocked. Pipsy returns to Johannesburg as a newly appointed secret service agent. Emily finds romance in the end.

TRIMBLE, JESSIE. B. 1873. United States.

3065 THE NEW MAN. BY JANE STONE. New York: T. Y. Crowell, [1913] NUC.

Subplot concerns white slavery. Frances Stephens, daughter of a Western senator, is kidnapped in Central Park. It affects the main love plot in that Mollie Preston holds some very strong views on the subject of white slavery, and her romance with John Ridgeway is jeopardized because he does not understand her attitude.

TROLLOPE, FRANCES ELEANOR (TERNAN). 1834-1913. United Kingdom.

3066 THAT WILD WHEEL: A NOVEL. London: R. Bentley, 1892 BMC. New York: Harper, 1892 NUC.

In the Hughes family, the women as well as the men are expected to work. One has a position in London, another keeps a boarding school, Barbara begins early in life to earn her living. When all their enterprises fail, they struggle for existence.

TROUBETZKOY, AMELIE (RIVES) CHANLER. 1863-1945.
United States.

3067 BARBARA DERING. A SEQUEL TO "THE QUICK OR THE DEAD?" BY AMELIE RIVES. London: Chatto and Windus, 1892 BMC. Philadelphia: J. B. Lippincott, 1893 NUC.

Barbara is 29, less hoydenish. She marries; she and a friend share the problems of their marriages. Her friend's husband lacks feeling, Barbara's has an excess of feeling. He is physically abusive at times, as is Barbara. "Barbara is a sort of pioneer in an obscure region....Certain scenes and reflections...express what many persons (women, perhaps, particularly) may have felt in a dumb and groping fashion."

3068 THE GOLDEN ROSE: THE ROMANCE OF A STRANGE SOUL. BY AMELIE RIVES (PRINCESS TROUBETZKOY). New York and London: Harper, 1908 BMC NUC.

The mature and sophisticated heroine, who has had one marriage, loves a man and does not want to spoil the relationship by marriage. Their platonic relationship doesn't withstand his absence of a few months.

3069 HIDDEN HOUSE. BY AMELIE RIVES (THE PRINCESS TROUBETZKOY). Philadelphia and London: J. B. Lippincott, 1912 BMC NUC.

A dual personality, Moina and Robina, whose poetry rivals that of Robert Burns.

3070 SHADOWS OF FLAMES; A NOVEL. BY AMELIE RIVES (PRINCESS TROUBETZKOY). London: Hurst & Blackett, 1915 BMC. New York: F. A. Stokes, [1915] NUC.

Sympathetic story of a woman of passionate nature who yearns to be happy. Sophie first marries a morphine addict and then an alcoholic. Through these marriages she suffers miserably. Her second husband is a man younger than herself. When her passion for him burns out, she gets a divorce. At the end she marries an Italian prince who promises to make a good husband.

3071 TANIS, THE SANG-DIGGER. New York: Town Topics, 1893 NUC.

Tanis lives like a savage in the Allegheny mountains where she digs sang—a medicinal root. When she goes to live with a highborn Southern woman, she yearns to be civilized, and to a great extent she succeeds. She knows physical passion, but she now aspires to ideal love. Her efforts to convert her lover in that direction fail. She must renounce the new hopes of the new world. In the end she returns to her primitive life in the mountains. Mostly in dialect.

3072 TRIX AND OVER-THE-MOON. BY AMELIE RIVES (PRINCESS TROUBETZKOY). New York and London: Harper, 1909 BMC NUC.

Woman in Virginia loves horses better than anything else in the world. Trix' favorite stallion is Over-the-Moon. She runs her own farm and breeds horses while her husband writes bad novels.

3073 WORLD'S-END. BY AMELIE RIVES (PRINCESS TROUBETZKOY). London: Hurst & Blackett, 1914 BMC. New York: F. A. Stokes, [1914] NUC.

Phoebe is pregnant by Richard, who deserts her. Then, knowing this, her cousin Owen marries her and makes her happy, hoping that she will eventually trust him enough to confide in him.

TROUBETZKOY, PRINCESS. See TROUBETZKOY, AMELIE (RIVES) CHANLER.

TROUBRIDGE, LADY. See TROUBRIDGE, LAURA (GURNEY).

TROUBRIDGE, LAURA (GURNEY). United Kingdom.

3074 THE EVIL DAY. London: Methuen, 1915 BMC.

Heroine of 40 reaches that day when she feels life is over

and yearns for lost passion. She revolts against her too dull life and too familiar husband and pursues a young man. When she returns home, her husband treats her well.

3075   THE FIRST LAW. London: Mills and Boon, 1909 BMC.
A divorced disreputable wife and her violent death.

3076   O, PERFECT LOVE. London: Methuen, 1920 BMC.
Her husband returns from the war an invalid. She leaves, returns after a year.

3077   THE UNGUARDED HOUR. BY LADY TROUBRIDGE. London: E. Nash, 1913 BMC NUC.
A beautiful young woman of good family "loses her virtue" but still marries happily in the end.

TROUT, GRACE WILBUR. D. 1955. United States.

3078   A MORMON WIFE. Chicago: E. A. Weeks, [1896] NUC.
Set in Utah before polygamy was abandoned: a woman learns that in spite of his promise to her, her husband is about to take a second wife. Ends tragically for the woman and her children.

TRUMBULL, ANNIE ELIOT. 1857-1949. United States.

3079   LIFE'S COMMON WAY. New York: A.S. Barnes, 1903 NUC.
Studies the currents beneath the conventional surfaces of New England life. One woman is unhappily married; another becomes completely indifferent to public opinion because of her marital difficulties; in fact, no marriage is shown to be happy.

TRUSCOTT, L. PARRY. See HARGRAVE, KATHARINE EDITH SPICER-JAY.

TURNBULL, CLARA. United Kingdom.

3080   THE DAMSEL DARK: A FOOL'S ROMANCE. London: Melrose, 1912 BMC.
In this historical romance the heroine raises the fortunes of

her house and strikes terror into evil doers. She unhorses her uncle in a tourney before the king.

TURNBULL, DORA AMY DILLON. 1878-1961. United Kingdom.

3081 A LITTLE MORE THAN KIN. BY PATRICIA WENTWORTH. London: A. Melrose, 1911 BMC NUC. (Also published as More Than Kin. By Patricia Wentworth. London: A. Melrose, [1914] BMC.)

Historical romance of the French Revolution. A woman disguises herself in men's clothes, takes the place of her twin brother, and shows she is very brave.

TURNBULL, MARGARET. D. 1942. United States.

3082 THE CLOSE-UP. New York and London: Harper, [1918] BMC NUC.

Kate goes out West to be a mummer, becomes a movie star. Loves studio life and her career, will probably marry Jeffrey, a secret service agent.

3083 HANDLE WITH CARE; A NOVEL. New York and London: Harper, [1916] BMC NUC.

The assistant in the psychological division of a research laboratory, breaking down from overwork, goes to Covered Bridge to recuperate. Here she meets the subject of the title, a drunken express agent. In the face of the small town's talk, she courageously takes hold of his life.

3084 LOOKING AFTER SANDY; A SIMPLE ROMANCE. New York & London: Harper, 1914 BMC NUC.

Of the "bright domestic type," the story is of Sandy who rises from a shorthand clerk to a successful dramatist.

TURNER, LILIAN. See THOMPSON, LILIAN TURNER.

TURNER, MARY BORDEN. 1886-1968. United Kingdom.

3085 COLLISION. BY BRIDGET MACLAGAN. London: Duckworth, 1913 BMC NUC.

Adventures in India of Maggie, an ultra modern young

woman who is a suffragist leader, and an ex-Labour M.P. in sympathy with her cause.

3086 THE MISTRESS OF KINGDOMS; OR SMOKING FLAX: A NOVEL. BY BRIDGET MACLAGAN. London: Duckworth, 1912 BMC NUC.

The focus is on Barbara's development, beginning with the death of her father during her first year in college. Her first love is for an artist who is married; later she loves and marries a man she meets in India, but she doesn't feel the same passion she had for the artist. She is restless and leaves India for awhile, but she grows to understand her husband and herself more fully. They share the experience of the birth of their child, but they are separated when the child gets sick and Barbara fights a losing battle for its life. A strong counter-theme is the penetrating analysis of Barbara's relationship to her mother.

TUTTIETT, MARY GLEED. 1847-1923. United Kingdom.

3087 IN THE HEART OF THE STORM; A TALE OF MODERN CHIVALRY. BY MAXWELL GRAY. London: K. Paul, 1891 BMC. New York: U. S. Book, [1891] NUC.

Concerns an Indian mutiny, though the author "continually finds the opportunity to talk on women's rights." The exciting adventures of Ada escaping from the Sepoy Rebellion in India and the tragedy of Jessie, an innocent young woman from the village. Shows the harm a man can do an innocent woman that causes gossip about her. Author attacks the double standard.

3088 THE LAST SENTENCE. BY MAXWELL GRAY. London: Heinemann, 1893 BMC. New York: Tait, [c1893] NUC.

Renee is a young woman who marries a man of higher class. He leaves her and her daughter when the marriage proves unhappy, and Renee dies as a consequence. Years later her daughter on trial for murdering her own child faces her father now a judge. He sentences her to death, knowing she is his daughter, collapsing from the ordeal. Ends at the gallows, but her innocence is proven and her life saved.

3089 SWEETHEARTS AND FRIENDS, A NOVEL. BY MAXWELL GRAY. London: Marshall, Russell, 1897 BMC. New York: D. Appleton, 1897 NUC.

Amy Langston becomes a doctor in the 1870's while friends and sweethearts look on with horror. She's an advocate of female suffrage and believes professional women should remain single, theories tested by a young man who believes in the clinging vine type of woman. According to one reviewer, Amy learns that "love and home are best after all."

TWEEDALE, VIOLET (CHAMBERS). 1862?-1936. United Kingdom.

3090 AND THEY TWO. London: G. Redway, 1897 BMC.

"The heroine is of a purity that faints at marriage and kills herself on her wedding day in a fury of spotlessness."

3091 THE BEAUTIFUL MRS. DAVENANT. A NOVEL OF LOVE AND MYSTERY. New York: F.A. Stokes, [c1920] NUC. London: H. Jenkins, 1920 BMC NUC.

Two unattached women living by themselves, a ghost and murder.

3092 THE HEART OF A WOMAN. London: Hurst & Blackett, 1917 BMC.

The customs of certain sections of society. One character is a typist-secretary who has very definite opinions on many subjects and who is a suffragist devoted to the cause.

3093 THE VEILED WOMAN. London: H.Jenkins, 1918 BMC.

The novel centers around feminism and suffrage, topics now "out-of-date."

3094 WINGATE'S WIFE. London: J. Long, 1916 BMC NUC.

Portrays women as victims of tyranny or cajolery of man. Wingate's wife kills her husband when he shows up after twenty years to threaten her present married life; she had deserted him. Gloria Power expresses author's views on feminism.

TWELLS, JULIA HELEN, JR. United States.

3095   A TRIUMPH OF DESTINY. Philadelphia: J. B. Lippincott, 1896 NUC 1897 BMC.,

A study of Helen Wentworth, a "singularly complex character." Both attracted to and repelled by Phenix Loraine, a "school-girl's idol," she marries him and leaves him after one year. After a love affair with a cowboy, she returns to Phenix who has changed and has learned to appreciate her. They agree to live together as brother and sister.

TYBOUT, ELLA MIDDLETON. United States.

3096   THE SMUGGLER. Philadelphia and London: J. B. Lippincott, 1907 NUC.

Three young women vacation in Canada—their adventures do not include love stories.

TYNAN, KATHARINE. See HINKSON, KATHARINE (TYNAN).

TYTLER, SARAH. See KEDDIE, HENRIETTA.

UNDERHILL, EVELYN. See MOORE, EVELYN (UNDERHILL).

UNDERWOOD, EDNA (WORTHLEY). B. 1873. United States.

3097   THE WHIRLWIND. Boston: Small, Maynard, [c1918] NUC BMC. (Also published as The Whirlwind of Passion. London: Hurst & Blackett, [1919] BMC.)

Catharine of Russia is portrayed as all head and no heart, ambitious and able.

UPHAM, ELIZABETH.

3098   SUNSHINE AND COLLEGE GIRLS. New York: Morse, [1901] NUC.

College women about to graduate plan their futures in

terms of careers in writing, in service to the public, and in living for worthy ideals. All but two lose their ambition. The two most idealistic do not marry but devote themselves to working with the poor.

URNER, MABEL HERBERT. 1881-1957. United States.

3099 THE JOURNAL OF A NEGLECTED WIFE. New York: B.W. Dodge, 1909 NUC.

A middle-aged woman gives painful testimony of her feelings of shame and frustrated passion, her pitiful attempts to appear young, the loss of her pride because of her husband's infidelity, and her adjustment to separation.

3100 THE WOMAN ALONE. New York: Hearst's International Library, 1914 BMC NUC.

The heroine loves a married man, a "contemptible hero oscillating between wife and mistress, unable to be faithful to either." The story repeats the truth that the woman pays, and the woman alone.

URQUHART, M. See GREEN, MARYON URQUHART.

V. See FERGUSON, V. MUNRO.

VAILE, CHARLOTTE MARION (WHITE). 1852-1902.

3101 THE M. M. C.: A STORY OF THE GREAT ROCKIES. Boston: W. A. Wilde, [1898] NUC.

New England school teacher trapped in Colorado mining camp by early onset of winter. Her struggle to hold on to a claim for an old friend.

VAIZEY, JESSIE (BELL) MANSERGH. 1857-1917. United Kingdom.

3102 CYNTHIA CHARRINGTON. London: Cassell, 1911 BMC.

She rebels against the restrictions imposed upon her by her family. She falls in love, but the man does not return her love. She goes off to devote herself to settlement work.

3103 THE DAUGHTERS OF A GENIUS. A STORY OF BRAVE ENDEAVORS. London: W. & R. Chambers, 1903 BMC. Philadelphia: Lippincott, 1903 PW.

Father has daughters cultivate their individual talents. They follow his advice.

3104 THE LADY OF THE BASEMENT FLAT. London: Woman's Magazine and Girl's Own Paper, [1917] BMC.

She's a wealthy young woman of 26 who disguises herself as an elderly spinster to do good works for the poor.

3105 A QUESTION OF MARRIAGE. BY MRS. GEORGE DE HORNE VAIZEY. London: Hodder & Stoughton, 1910 BMC. New York and London: G.P. Putnam's Sons, 1911 NUC.

Heroine lives a happy life as a single woman. Vanna Strangeways learns there is hereditary insanity in her family, struggles against herself and the man she loves for strength to give him up, but then finds happiness in visits with her married woman friend, her friendship with the man she gave up, and in good works.

3106 A ROSE-COLOURED THREAD. London: J. Bowden, 1898 BMC.

Janet Graham, a plain governess in Cairo, is wooed and rejected by an English doctor. Her suffering.

3107 SALT OF LIFE. BY MRS. GEORGE DE HORNE VAIZEY. London: Mills & Boon, 1915 BMC NUC.

The heroine wins a prize for her novel. She also wins a husband.

VAIZEY, MRS. GEORGE DE HORNE. See VAIZEY, JESSIE (BELL) MANSERGH.

VAKA, DEMETRA. See BROWN, DEMETRA (VAKA).

VALLINGS, GABRIELLE FRANCESCA LILIAN MAY. B. 1886. United Kingdom.

3108 BINDWEED. London: Hutchinson, 1916 BMC NUC. New York: Dodd, Mead, 1916 PW.

Eugenie Massini is a French convent-bred woman with a wonderful voice; her jealous aunt watches over her, murders a man she thinks is out to get Eugenie. Eugenie then is cared for by Mme. Perintot, a retired opera singer who appreciates Eugenie's talent and devotes herself to training her voice. A tenor interferes with her plans.

VANAMEE, LIDA (OSTROM). United States.

3109 TWO WOMEN; OR, "OVER THE HILLS AND FAR AWAY". New York: Merriam, [c1895] NUC.

"A record of two women's friendship and of their respective love stories." One a widow, the other single, they travel to Europe for self improvement. Reviewer says they are husband-hunting.

VAN BUREN, EVELYN. United States.

3110 PIPPIN. New York: Century, 1913 BMC NUC.

A young actress meets Victoria Alexandra (Pippin) struggling to earn her living and to support her consumptive younger brother. Pippin is a deft, successful, and well trained pickpocket working on London streets.

VAN DEVENTER, E. MURDOCH. See VAN DEVENTER, EMMA MURDOCH.

VAN DEVENTER, EMMA MURDOCH. Fl. 1879-1912. United States.

3111 UNDER FATE'S WHEEL. A STORY OF MYSTERY, LOVE, AND THE BICYCLE, ETC. BY LAWRENCE L. LYNCH (E. MURDOCH VAN DEVENTER). London: Ward, Lock, [1900] BMC. Chicago: Laird and Lee, [c1900] NUC.

Crime, property, love and melodramtic misery. Mad mesmerist, a cyclist, kidnaps child of the Western prairie, encourages her to become a professional cyclist. Everyone cycles, including heroine. On her deathbed Inez explains about her bike ride in male attire, the "air gun with which she did the deed."

VAN DE WATER, VIRGINIA BELLE (TERHUNE). 1865-1945. United States.

3112 THE TWO SISTERS. New York: Hearst's International Library, 1914 BMC NUC.
Julia and Caryl Marvin rebel against their stepmother and come to New York to earn their living. Julia works in a department store, and Caryl takes lessons at a business college and gets a job as a stenographer. She becomes involved with a married man and subsequently dies.

VAN DYKE, CURTIS.* United States.

3113 A DAUGHTER OF THE PROPHETS. New York: Abbey Press, [c1900] NUC. (Also published in London and Montreal.)
A woman lawyer marries a minister.

VANE, DEREK. See BACK, BLANCHE EATON.

VAN JAVA, MELATI. See SLOOT, NICOLINA MARIA CHRISTINA.

VAN SAANEN, MARIE LOUISE. See HALE, MARICE RUTLEDGE (GIBSON).

VAN SLYKE, LUCILLE (BALDWIN). B. 1880. United States.

3114 LITTLE MISS BY-THE-DAY. New York: F. A. Stokes, [c1919] NUC. London: Nisbet, 1920 BMC.
Alone and penniless in Brooklyn, Felicia Day struggles as a seamstress.

VAN VORST, BESSIE (MACGINNIS). 1873-1928. United States.

3115 THE ISSUES OF LIFE. A NOVEL OF THE AMERICAN WOMAN OF TO-DAY. BY MRS. JOHN VAN VORST. London and New York: Doubleday, Page, 1904 BMC NUC.

A novel of the new woman who substitutes clubs and personal freedom for the home.

VAN VORST, BESSIE (MACGINNIS) AND MARIE VAN VORST.

3116 THE WOMAN WHO TOILS. BEING THE EXPERIENCES OF TWO LADIES AS FACTORY GIRLS. BY MRS. JOHN VAN VORST AND MARIE VAN VORST. London: G. Richards, 1903 BMC. New York: Doubleday, Page, 1903 NUC.

VAN VORST, MARIE. 1867-1936. United States.

3117 AMANDA OF THE MILL: A NOVEL. London: W. Heinemann, 1904 BMC. New York: Dodd, Mead, 1905 NUC.

Amanda is almost driven to prostitution by the harsh conditions she endures in a Southern cotton mill. But she rescues an alcoholic man whose mother makes her an heiress. She uses this money to educate herself and her fellow-workers, leading them to better working conditions.

3118 FIRST LOVE. Indianapolis: Bobbs Merrill, [c1910] NUC. London: Mills & Boon, 1910 BMC.

Virginia Bathhurst is loved by a younger man. She is attracted to him but refuses to marry him after her husband's death. She marries an admirer her own age.

3119 THE GIRL FROM HIS TOWN. Indianapolis: Bobbs-Merrill, [c1910] NUC. London: Mills & Boon, 1910 BMC.

Dance hall girl with sordid past marries and lives happily ever after.

3120 MARY MORELAND; A NOVEL. London: Mills & Boon, [1915] BMC. Boston: Little, Brown, 1915 BMC NUC.

She's a secretary to three different employers, one who loves her. She tries to convince him to stay with his wife.

3121 MISS DESMOND; AN IMPRESSION. New York: Macmillan, 1905 NUC. London: W. Heinemann, 1905 BMC.
Love story of a beautiful "spinster" of 30; chaperones niece in Switzerland.

3122 PHILIP LONGSTRETH; A NOVEL. London and New York: Harper, 1902 BMC NUC.
He is torn between Amber Garland, factory forewoman, and a woman of his own class.

3123 THE SIN OF GEORGE WARRENER. New York and London: Macmillan, 1906 NUC. London: W. Heinemann, 1906 BMC.
Mrs. Warrener, bored, unfaithful, and extravagant, drives her husband to theft. The development of·her character from shallow stupidity to triumphant independence.

VAN VORST, MARIE, jt. au. See VAN VORST, BESSIE (MACGINNIS) AND MARIE VAN VORST.

VAN VORST, MRS. JOHN. See VAN VORST, BESSIE (MACGINNIS), also VAN VORST, BESSIE (MACGINNIS) AND MARIE VAN VORST.

VAUGHAN, GERTRUDE ELIZA MARY. United Kingdom.

3124 THE BIRD OF LIFE. London: Chapman & Hall, 1917 NUC BMC.
Rachel Carwardine from childhood to womanhood, through school days, office work and efforts to become a journalist. She's a free-thinker but marries a strict clergyman. After two years of drab marriage, she leaves him without a word, establishes a platonic relation with a doctor, and becomes a famous novelist. War claims both her husband and the doctor, and Rachel is left with her young son.

VEITCH, SOPHIE FRANCES FANE.

3125 MARGARET DRUMMOND, MILLIONAIRE. London: A. & C. Black, 1893 BMC.

She inherits a million and Moyle Island, Scotland, makes her home on the remote island and devotes herself to helping and educating the people. She is self-sufficient and determined to be a model proprietor. "Her powers of mind, her seriousness, her information were altogether abnormal." The whole novel is devoted to her good works, but at the very end she turns over control of the island to her husband.

VENN, MRS. See VENN, SUSANNA CARNEGIE.

VENN, SUSANNA CARNEGIE.

3126 THE HUSBAND OF ONE WIFE. BY MRS. VENN. London: Hurst and Blackett, 1894 BMC NUC.

A psychological study of Victoria Goldenour and "her kaleidescopic moods and contradictions." She is married three times, least happy with Dr. Garfoyle who, filled with protective love, tries to save her from herself.

3127 SOME MARRIED FELLOWS. BY THE AUTHOR OF "THE DAILYS OF SODDEN FEN" [ANONYMOUS]. London: R. Bentley, 1893 BMC.

Through two women characters, two contrasting male types are revealed. Margaret makes us see Chevington Appleton's selflessness. Helen is miserably married to Randal Keltridge, a very self-centered person. At his suggestion, she takes courses at the university and does very well. She is especially interested in philosophy. He leaves her, but when he returns after two years, she will have nothing to do with him. At the very end of the novel, they are reunited at her brother's funeral.

VER BECK, HANNA (RION). 1875-1914. United States.

3128 THE SMILING ROAD. BY HANNA RION. New York: E. J. Clode, [c1910] NUC.

After Libby Trevelyan's husband leaves her, she begins a

new life. She becomes interested in her neighbors' problems, and she makes friends with a man, a friendship that brings her happiness.

VERMILYE, KATE (JORDAN). 1862-1926. United Kingdom.

3129 AGAINST THE WINDS. BY KATE JORDAN. Boston: Little, Brown, 1919 NUC BMC. London: Hutchinson, [1919] BMC.

Naomi Tway is a Southern girl of high ideals. She is a typist in a flour mill, but she hungers for travel and adventure. When she learns that her mother is a prostitute, she runs off to New York. Alone and poor, she drifts into marriage with a traveling salesman who drinks. And though she falls deeply in love with a millionaire, she sacrifices herself to help her husband overcome his problem.

3130 A CIRCLE IN THE SAND. BY KATE JORDAN (MRS. F. M. VERMILYE). Boston and London: Lamson, Wolffe, 1898 NUC.

Anne Garrick, a new woman, is a journalist on a large daily paper. She becomes comrades with the editor; he subsequently marries a more feminine type and the marriage fails. He returns to Anne, but she "refuses to accept the remains."

3131 THE NEXT CORNER. New York: Harper, 1920 PW. Boston: Little, Brown, 1921 NUC.

Unfaithful wife is separated from Spanish lover when the father of a woman he has ruined shoots him. Returns to unknowing husband but lives in fear of discovery.

VERMILYE, MRS. F. M. See VERMILYE, KATE (JORDAN).

VIEBIG, CLARA. See COHN, CLARA (VIEBIG).

VILLARS, MEG. United Kingdom.

3132 BETTY-ALL-ALONE. New York: E.J. Clode, [c1914] NUC. London: G. Richards, 1914 NUC BMC.

She has a bold adventurous spirit and a great sense of humor. Born wealthy, she is left penniless and goes forth in search of the Golden Male, a rich husband. On the way, she works as a companion and is an artist for a newspaper.

3133 THE BROKEN LAUGH. London: G. Richards, 1920 BMC. New York: R.M. McBride, 1920 NUC.

Kissy is the daughter of an unmarried woman whose mother also was unwed. She is seduced while still a child and becomes a servant in a brothel. Then she lives with a man, and they are happy. One reviewer says that the author believes a wife with no legal claim is happier; another says that although Kissy never felt wicked, she never felt worthy of the man. She is killed in an air raid on the eve of her wedding.

VIVARIA, KASSANDRA. See SINDICI, MARIA MAGDA STUART.

VIVIAN, EVELYN CHARLES H.* United Kingdom.

3134 DIVIDED WAYS. London: Holden & Hardingham, 1914 BMC.

Mary North is "strong, maternal, discerning" and represents the big things of life. She seduces Alan Hope, a married man, "in a great pure passion" which had given him "the most wonderful days of (her) life" and leaves him.

VON HEYKING, ELISABETH AUGUSTE LUISE HELENE MELUSINE MAXIMILIANE (VON · FLEMMING). 1861-1925.

3135 THE LETTERS WHICH NEVER REACHED HIM [ANONYMOUS]. London: E. Nash, 1904 BMC. New York: E. P. Dutton, 1904 NUC.

A series of letters to a man in military service from a woman whose husband is insane—"a revelation of unhappiness and anxiety bordering on the morbid." Both men die.

3136 LOVERS IN EXILE. BY THE AUTHOR OF "THE LETTERS WHICH NEVER REACHED HIM" [ANONYMOUS]. London: E. Nash, 1914 BMC NUC. New York: Dutton, 1915 NUC.

Ilse marries a "primitive, old-fashioned" German, cannot keep her individuality and is unhappy. She gets a divorce and marries another, but her first husband persecutes them, ruining her husband's career. In spite of this she is happy.

VON HINDENBERG, AGNES BLANCHE MARIE (HAY). 1873-1938. Europe.

3137 A GERMAN POMPADOUR: BEING THE EXTRAORDINARY HISTORY OF WILHELMINE VON GRAVENITZ, LANDHOFMEISTERIN OF WIRTEMBERG, A NARRATIVE OF THE EIGHTEENTH CENTURY. BY MARIE HAY. London: A. Constable, 1906 NUC BMC.

Wilhelmine, the wife of a duke, takes the reins of power into her own hands—her court taking over vast properties. Then the duke casts her off, and she is subsequently tried for treason, witchcraft, bigamy, grasping land, and attempted murder. But she is eventually pardoned and retires to her Swiss castle.

VON HUTTEN, BARONESS. See STOLZENBERG, BETSEY (RIDDLE) VON HUTTEN ZUM.

VON HUTTEN, BETTINA. See STOLZENBERG, BETSEY (RIDDLE) VON HUTTEN ZUM.

VON SUTTNER, BERTHA FELICIE SOPHIE (KINSKY). 1843-1914. Germany.

3138 "GROUND ARMS!" THE STORY OF A LIFE, A ROMANCE OF EUROPEAN WAR. Chicago: A. C. McClurg, 1892 NUC. (Tr. from the German by Alice Asbury Abbott. Also published as Lay Down Your Arms; The Autobiography of Martha Von Tilling. London: Longman's, 1892 BMC. New York: Longmans, 1894 NUC. Tr. by T. Holmes.)

Written in journal form. Daughter of a general is educated to war and is frustrated that the "laurels of the battleground" are denied to her sex. She marries a soldier who is killed in battle. Out of her personal suffering she questions the justification of any war. Her second husband is falsely accused and shot as a spy. She spends the remainder of her life working for international arbitration. The author emphasizes the need for the education of women, "if the highest degree of civilization is to be obtained."

3139 WHEN THOUGHTS WILL SOAR; A ROMANCE OF THE IMMEDIATE FUTURE. BY BARONESS BERTHA VON SUTTNER. London: Constable, 1914 BMC. Boston: Houghton Mifflin, 1914 NUC. (Tr. by Nathan Haskell Dole.)

Franka devotes herself to the uplift of woman and refuses a prince for the lover who shares her ideals.

VON TEUFFEL, BLANCHE WILLIS (HOWARD). 1847-1898. United States.

3140 DIONYSIUS THE WEAVER'S HEART'S DEAREST. BY BLANCHE WILLIS HOWARD. New York: C. Scribner's Sons, 1899 NUC. (Also published as Vroni, the Weaver's Heart's Dearest. By Blanche Willis Howard. London: F. Warne, 1899 BMC.)

Study of a wild, bright country girl from childhood: Vroni starts out to earn her own living, enters the service of Countess von Vallade where she becomes apprentice to a French chef. Already a heaven-born cook, Vroni becomes a professional cook. She is contrasted to Nelka, the Countess' daughter. Nelka marries a man she does not love and is unhappy. Of her predicament, she says, "I cannot dig, to beg I am ashamed. I have not learned to work...I am too cowardly to die...it is a monstrous thing that girls are left so blind." Vroni was betrayed by a valet, but refuses to marry this man when he offers her marriage—in spite of the fact that he is the father of her two children. She faces the world bravely and supports her children herself.

3141 THE GARDEN OF EDEN. BY BLANCHE WILLIS HOWARD. New York: C. Scribner's Sons, 1900 BMC NUC. Toronto: C. Clarke, 1900 BMC.

Monica, a new woman, loves a married man. Her mother, anti-divorce, persuades her to leave the country. She later falls for another married man who brings her added sorrow. Divorce question.

VOYNICH, E. L. See VOYNICH, ETHEL LILLIAN (BOOLE).

VOYNICH, ETHEL LILLIAN (BOOLE). 1864-1960. United Kingdom.

3142 THE GADFLY. BY E. L. VOYNICH. London: W. Heinemann, 1897 BMC. New York: H. Holt, 1897 NUC.

Gemma, a "masculine" character, is active in the liberal party struggling against the powers of the church in Italy. She gives up Gadfly, a political writer, when she believes he's a traitor to their cause. Novel focuses on Gadfly and his conflict with the Cardinal, his father.

3143 OLIVE LATHAM. BY E. L. VOYNICH. Philadelphia: J.B. Lippincott, 1904 NUC. London: W. Heinemann, 1904 BMC.

Psychological study of a nurse who follows her consumptive lover to Russia to care for him; she is dragged through months of mental agony by his arrest and subsequent death in prison. Final part of book focuses on her after she has returned to England where she hovers on the borderline of insanity.

VYNNE, NORA. D. 1914. United Kingdom.

3144   A MAN AND HIS WOMANKIND. London: Hutchinson, 1895 BMC NUC.

The Cedicssons—the first few months of their marriage. She is older than he and for years has earned her living writing "analytic" novels. She has no taste for housework—leaves all that to her mother-in-law and sister-in-law. All of them spoil the young husband.

3145   THE PIECES OF SILVER. London: Melrose, 1911 BMC.

Beatrice Stallingway is a hard working journalist and politician, a women's rights person. She and a male friend set out to reform the world. A "clever and sanely conceived feminist novel."

3146   THE PRIEST'S MARRIAGE. London: T. Burleigh, 1899 BMC. New York and London: Putnam, 1900 NUC.

Annie Fulton retains our sympathy and interest to the last. She marries a renegade priest from the Roman Catholic Church who has become a Protestant layman. At first the two are content. Then he is in turn affectionate toward her and repelled by her because he believes love is fleshy, base. Annie is disturbed by his attitude, and when he returns to the monastery and refuses her letters, she takes steps for a legal separation. He makes a last minute attempt at reconciliation, but she refuses him, though she has a child.

3147   SO IT IS WITH THE DAMSEL. London: S. Paul, 1913 BMC.

Depicts the evils of white slave traffic, the horrors of this secret trade in South America. A young middle-class woman from London is the victim who manages to escape her bondage and meets the two people responsible.

3148   THE STORY OF A FOOL AND HIS FOLLY. London: Hutchinson, [1896] BMC.

Mrs. Craigh has an invalid husband and a lover who is a clerk. She arranges to compromise herself in order to get a divorce, but her husband dies. She is described by reviewers as monstrous and base. "Although the book is a failure, Nora Vynne shows every sign of becoming the best woman writer since the too brief career of Emily Bronte."

WADSLEY, OLIVE. D. 1859. United Kingdom.

3149   BELONGING. A NOVEL. London and New York: Cassell, [1920] NUC.

Sara Desanges, a widow, has two lovers. One of them is killed; she is wrongly accused and imprisoned. She describes her experiences in prison and in solitary confinement.

3150   THE FLAME. London and New York: Cassell, 1914 BMC NUC.

Toni Saumarez is the child of aristocratic and drunken parents. She moves from the slums of London to Paris schools and on to Italy. At 18 she is the mistress of a 40 year old man whose wife is mad. Later she is an assistant in a Paris shop, then a famous Parisian caricaturist. After a brief passionate episode with an Oxford youth, Toni marries.

3151   FRAILTY: A NOVEL. London and New York: Cassell, [1917] BMC NUC.

A young wife is an alcoholic whose husband makes the discovery after their first few months of happy married life. Her problem is worsened by his disgust. Eventually they make a joint effort to overcome their failings; the husband is himself a reformed drug addict.

3152   INSTEAD. London: Cassell, 1919 BMC NUC.

Annuziata becomes a waitress in Brazil, but the novel seems to focus on her loves and friendships in London and Europe.

3153   NEVERTHELESS. London: Cassell, 1918 BMC.

Viola is loved by a man 12 years younger than she. He wants to marry her; she asks that they dispense with marriage. Believing she has a husband, he agrees. Later he discovers that her husband is dead. He is selfish, unworthy of her.

WAKEMAN, ANNIE. See LATHROP, ANNIE WAKEMAN.

WALCH, CAROLINE C.

3154 DOCTOR SPHINX: A NOVEL. New York: F. T. Neely, [c1898] NUC.

"Impressions and experience of young woman who is making her way in the world without influential friends and under the dual disability of lack of training and an unusual amount of morbid conscientiousness."

WALFORD, L. B. See WALFORD, LUCY BETHIA (COLQUHOUN).

WALFORD, LUCY BETHIA (COLQUHOUN). 1845-1915. United Kingdom.

3155 THE BLACK FAMILIARS. BY L. B. WALFORD. London: J. Clarke, 1903 BMC NUC. New York: Longmans, Green, 1903 PW.

Mother's ambitions for her husband make him turn to their daughter for comradeship. She hates her daughter, tries to marry her off, even starts a rumor that her daughter is guilty of heresy. (The time is the Reformation.) When her plot is discovered, she kills herself.

3156 IVA KILDARE: A MATRIMONIAL PROBLEM. London and New York: Longmans, 1897 BMC NUC.

The Irish widow Lady Tilbury proposes marriage to Mr. Druitt, disappointed suitor of her daughter, and Druitt becomes her third husband.

3157 LEDDY MARGET. BY L. B. WALFORD. London, New York: Longmans, 1898 BMC NUC.

Past 80, physically perfect, has a heart of gold, and lives

to shower benefits on others. Dies and rises to heaven as a saint.

3158   LEONORE STUBBS. BY L. B. WALFORD. London and New York: Longmans, Green, 1908 BMC NUC.

Lenore, a widow at 21 and penniless, returns home to two younger sisters and a father who assumes her life is over. She resents his attitude, marries a rich man he had chosen for one of her sisters. Her "moves are diagonal, not straightforward."

3159   THE MATCHMAKER, A NOVEL. BY L. B. WALFORD. London, New York: Longmans, Green, 1894 NUC BMC.

"Though Mrs. Walford is probably the last person in the world who would consciously harbour such an aim, her description of the Carnoustie household is calculated to place a premium on filial revolt as compared with submission." Three daughters, the lives of two are ruined, the third is accidentally shot. The mother goes mad.

3160   THE MISCHIEF OF MONICA. BY L. B. WALFORD. New York: J. W. Lovell, [1891] NUC. London: Longmans, 1891 BMC.

Shows the effect of training on a young woman. Monica Lavenham is raised in the social world of balls and marriage making and efforts to climb the social ladder. She is beautiful, witty and sometimes rebellious. Her training warps her enough that she sets out to rob Daisy of her lover. But in time she sees what she has done, and her whole character is changed.

3161   STAY-AT-HOMES. BY L. B. WALFORD. London: Longmans, 1903 BMC.

Study of the influence of environment on the characters of three women, daughters of an upper-class family who live a very secluded life. One daughter of 27 is sent to her room for allowing a young man to join her in a walk.

WALFORD, S. E.*

3162 UNTIL THE DAWN. London: Chapman and Hall, 1899
BMC.
Sympathetic portrayal of Judith Marsh who murders the
woman who is blackmailing her husband.

WALL, MARY.

3163 BACK TO THE WORLD. London: Chapman & Hall,
1916 BMC.
Story of a 49 year old woman from the time she is
released from a lunatic asylum until her death.
Autobiographic form. Period is autumn, 1914.

WALLACE, EDNA KINGSLEY. United States.

3164 THE QUEST OF THE DREAM. New York and London:
G. P. Putnam's Sons, 1913 NUC BMC.
Doria French's letters to several people including her friend
Barbara and her imaginary dream man reveal her complex
mind, her modern ideas, and her independent spirit. She's
a composer; in the end, marries an artist.

WALLACE, HELEN.

3165 HIS COUSIN ADAIR. BY GORDON ROY. Edinburgh:
W. Blackwood, 1891 BMC NUC.
A family made up entirely of poor female relatives is
tolerated and patronized by their neighbors and cousins.
Good character studies of cousin Isabel and actress Cicely
Charleris who uses a strong narcotic. Focus on the two
sisters: Adair is conventional, self sacrificing, a contrast to
cousin Isabel and sister Agnes. Agnes is worldly. She
marries an elderly manufacturer for his money. Part of the
arrangement is "that he shall likewise marry her family
and especially her mother into the bargain."

3166 LOTUS OR LAUREL? London: E. Arnold, 1900 BMC.
Karola's mother, a great violinist, cannot bear her

daughter's surpassing her in her art. She asks Karola to postpone her career so as to leave her undisputed first place in the few years left to her. Karola refuses. Then Karola falls in love. Whether she will marry (the lotus) or continue with her career (the laurel) is unresolved at book's close.

WALLER, M. E. See WALLER, MARY ELLA.

WALLER, MARY ELLA. 1855-1938. United States.

3167 A CRY IN THE WILDERNESS. Boston: Little, Brown, 1912 NUC. London: A. Melrose, 1912 BMC.
A 26 year old woman goes to Canada, takes a position of librarian on an estate. She is of illegitimate birth, is "wooed by her mother's husband."

3168 SANNA; A NOVEL. BY M. E. WALLER. New York and London: Harper, 1905 NUC.
A wild fearless young woman who races her own skiff.

3169 A YEAR OUT OF LIFE. New York: D. Appleton, 1909 BMC NUC. London: A. Melrose, 1909 BMC.
Nathalie translates the works of a German author with whom she begins a correspondence. In time he proposes, but when they meet, Nathalie realizes it is the letter writer, not the man, she loves. She rejects him. Later the situation is reversed. In the end nothing comes of the relation. One reviewer describes Nathalie as "a sexless and well informed young person who is by no means scarce in our time and country (and who) goes on her emasculated way...certain to evolve into a perfect specimen of old maid."

WALLING, ANNA STRUNSKY. 1879-1964. United States.

3170 VIOLETTE OF PERE LACHAISE. New York: F. A. Stokes, [1915] NUC.
The record of development of a gifted young woman who becomes an actress and who devotes herself to the social revolution.

WALTHER, ANNA HILDA LOUISE. B. 1878.

3171 A PILGRIMAGE WITH A MILLINER'S NEEDLE. New York: F. A. Stokes, [c1912] NUC.

How she worked her way through France, Germany, Russia and South Africa. Includes her love story.

WALTON, ELEANOR GOING. United States.

3172 SHE WHO WILL NOT WHEN SHE MAY. Philadelphia: H. Altemus, 1898 NUC.

Series of letters and telegrams exchanged by a woman artist and a man. She rejects his suit because of her art and a preference for a platonic relationship. She changes her mind, but just as she does so, a letter arrives announcing his betrothal to someone else.

WALTZ, ELIZABETH (CHERRY). 1866-1903. United States.

3173 THE ANCIENT LANDMARK; A KENTUCKY ROMANCE. New York: McClure, Phillips, 1905 NUC BMC.

The "ancient landmark" refers to matrimonial legislation in Kentucky which permits the husband to brutally maltreat his wife. The story is of the gradual revolt of the wife and the galvanization of the community into taking action against the husband.

WALWORTH, JEANNETTE RITCHIE (HADERMANN). 1837-1918. United States.

3174 FORTUNE'S TANGLED SKEIN; A NOVEL. New York: Baker & Taylor, [1898] NUC. London: F. Warne, 1899 BMC.

A mysterious death and suspicion of murder in rural Mississippi. The case is solved by a Bohemian young woman detective.

WARD, DORA. B. 1878. United States.

3175 THE MARRIAGE OF CLARYS. Letchworth: Garden City Press, 1917 BMC.

Clarys Bailey is a nurse. Her marriage ends in the middle of the novel when she is widowed.

WARD, ELIZABETH STUART (PHELPS). 1844-1911. United States.

3176 AVERY. BY ELIZABETH STUART PHELPS. Boston: Houghton Mifflin, 1902 NUC. London: G. Richards, 1903 BMC.

Unhappy marriage of an egoist to a self-effacing wife. His lack of affection at first makes her sick and almost kills her, except for the intervention of her physician.

3177 CONFESSIONS OF A WIFE. BY MARY ADAMS. New York: Century, 1902 NUC.

Marna reveals herself as the utmost in wifeliness—her husband is her entire world, and they are both miserable. Most reviewers despised this woman who wrote notes to her absent husband every few hours, kissed his socks instead of darning them, and cried a lot; a few saw in this exaggerated portrayal the basic condition of wifehood. Charlotte Perkins Gilman describes the novel as "a vivid expression of what it is like to be a highly—concentrated, double-distilled wife—and nothing else."

3178 THE SUCCESSORS OF MARY THE FIRST. BY ELIZABETH STUART PHELPS. Boston: Houghton Mifflin, 1901 NUC.

The author shows the folly of women's frivolous education when it doesn't prepare them to keep house. The servant problem and the relation of mistress to servant, subjects important to the women's clubs, are seriously debated.

3179 THOUGH LIFE US DO PART. BY ELIZABETH STUART PHELPS. Boston: Houghton Mifflin, 1908 BMC NUC.

Carolyn Sterling is married to a doctor. She is self-sacrificing; he drinks heavily and is interested in another woman. They are unhappy.

WARD, JOSEPHINE MARY (HOPE-SCOTT). 1864-1932. United Kingdom.

3180   GREAT POSSESSIONS. BY MRS. WILFRID WARD. London: Longmans, 1909 BMC. New York and London: G. P. Putnam's Sons, 1909 NUC.

Molly Dexter is described as "a type of adventuress rare in fiction," a "Becky Sharp type," "a natural pagan," "a woman of ruthless egoism" who inherits money and holds on to her wealth passionately. One reviewer says she is penitent in the end.

3181   THE LIGHT BEHIND. BY MRS. WILFRID WARD. London and New York: J. Lane, 1903 BMC NUC.

A "mental history of a splendid, much suffering woman." The novel asks the question "shall a wife give a husband freedom which they both desire, he for the worst, she for the best motives?" Lady Cheriton does get a separation. She has been deeply wronged and "has the courage of her own common sense to face the scandalmongers in her town bravely." The novel carries her history to her death.

WARD, MARY AUGUSTA (ARNOLD). 1851-1920. United Kingdom.

3182   THE CORYSTON FAMILY; A NOVEL. BY MRS. HUMPHRY WARD. New York and London: Harper, 1913 BMC NUC.

Strong Lady Coryston tries to shackle her sons. They turn on her for devoting herself to politics rather than "the place for which (her) better, softer qualities fit her." According to one reviewer, the novel proves "the futility of women in politics."

3183   COUSIN PHILIP. BY MRS. HUMPHRY WARD. London: W. Collins Sons, [1919] BMC NUC. (Also published as Helena. By Mrs. Humphry Ward. New York: Dodd, Mead, 1919 NUC.)

Portrayal of a modern young woman who does canteen work and drives during the war. One reviewer says that Mrs. Ward has no sympathy for this kind of woman and does not understand her; another says that the novel portrays the world young women are faced with in war when all the young men are gone.

3184 DAPHNE; OR, "MARRIAGE A 'LA MODE". London and New York: Cassell, 1909 BMC NUC. (Also published as Marriage a la Mode. By Mrs. Humphry Ward. New York: Doubleday, Page, 1909 NUC.)

Daphne Floyd makes an unfortunate marriage with a foolish and timid Englishman who is more interested in her money than in her. She is independent, up-to-date, an exciting passionate person very different from Roger. She soon tires of him, and the marriage becomes uglier and uglier until Daphne leaves, firmly believing in women's freedom. Then their child dies, the husband dies of TB after turning to drink. One reviewer considers the novel an expose of the dangers of feminism; another, an indictment of American divorce laws; and a third, a criticism of the economic conditions governing marriage.

3185 DELIA BLANCHFLOWER. BY MRS. HUMPHRY WARD. New York: Hearst's International Library, 1914 NUC. London: Ward, Lock, 1915 BMC.

The young heroine becomes fascinated with Gertrude Marvell, militant leader of the suffrage movement in England, and consequently joins the movement. The author gives vivid accounts of the raid on the House of Parliament and the mob's attack on the suffragettes. Gertrude Marvell is presented as an admirable woman. The aims of the movement are supported, but militant means of gaining those aims and focus on the vote as the answer to the woman question are criticized by the author. Delia slowly gives up her belief in militant feminism. Gertrude dies in a fire she set as part of the militant suffrage action.

3186 ELEANOR; A NOVEL. BY MRS. HUMPHRY WARD. London: Smith, Elder, 1900 BMC. London & New York: Harper, 1900 NUC BMC.

Eleanor, an educated and intelligent woman, has ruined her health by overworking for eight years in an attempt to forget the death of her husband and child. She goes to Rome to recuperate, meets Edward, her cousin, a self-centered, arrogant man, and, drawing on her little remaining strength, throws herself into helping him write his book. Then a friend of Edward's criticizes the book, and Edward decides he no longer wants her help. At the same time he falls in love with Lucy, a friend of Eleanor's, and marries her. Eleanor suffers much and dies.

3187 ELTHAM HOUSE. BY MRS. HUMPHRY WARD. London: Cassell, 1915 BMC. New York: Hearst's International Library, 1915 NUC.

Caroline Marsworth runs away from her marriage with Alec Wing, deserting her two children. The younger one dies, people mistakenly think, because of her running off. Husband divorces her. She marries Alec. Theme: How will society receive them?

3188 HARVEST. BY MRS. HUMPHRY WARD. London: W. Collins Sons, [1920] BMC. New York: Dodd, Mead, 1920 NUC.

Rachel Henderson, graduate of an agricultural college, and Janet Leighton, a classmate, rent a farm and run it together successfully. Disclosure of Rachel's past, which she believed dead, results in tragedy for her.

3189 HELBECK OF BANNISDALE. BY MRS. HUMPHRY WARD. London and New York: Macmillan, 1898 NUC. London: Smith, Elder, 1898 BMC.

Agnostic heroine and Roman Catholic hero love each other but cannot reconcile their differences. She tries to accept faith, and when she cannot, suicides. "Freedom is her being," and life with him would not be possible.

3190 THE HISTORY OF DAVID GRIEVE. BY MRS. HUMPHRY WARD. New York and London: Macmillan, 1892 NUC. London: Smith, Elder, 1892 BMC.

David is brilliant, has advanced political and social ideas, and is very generous and sacrificing to women in his life, especially his sister Louie. David lives with Eliee, a sculptor. Louie is seduced by a sculptor; David arranges her marriage, but she is so unhappy she suicides. "Monochrome pessimism."

3191 LADY ROSE'S DAUGHTER; A NOVEL. BY MRS. HUMPHRY WARD. London: Smith, Elder, 1903 BMC. New York and London: Harper, 1903 NUC.

What women want is the theme. Lady Rose leaves her indifferent husband to run off with another man. Her illegitimate daughter Julie has a brilliant education and is highly ambitious. When her mother dies she's left penniless, becomes a companion and slowly wins for herself a center place in high society. She is determined to run off with her cousin's fiance whom she loves, but reluctantly and without love marries a duke, and there begins a long and fierce conflict. Though Lady Rose chose exile with a lover to respectable marriage with a husband she disliked, she still can work only through men, says Elizabeth Forbes Robertson Hale. "Lady Rose is the apotheosis of the parasite class. With all her charms and ability she remains the product of a slave status, the typical expression of a passing order."

3192 MARCELLA. BY MRS. HUMPHRY WARD. New York and London: Macmillan, 1894 NUC. London: Smith, Elder, 1894 BMC.

Marcella, a hospital nurse and an extremely complex character is an ardent socialist. Her involvement in politics and her relation to two men. A gentle introduction to socialism.

3193 THE MARRIAGE OF WILLIAM ASHE; A NOVEL. BY MRS. HUMPHRY WARD. New York and London: Harper, 1905 NUC. London: Smith, Elder, 1905 BMC.

Kitty Ashe is beautiful, reckless, destructive. She flirts, moves with a fast crowd, smokes, and writes a novel exposing husband's political secret. At this point he leaves; she takes a lover who mistreats her, and she dies painfully and penitently. One critic blames the all-too-busy husband's neglect of Kitty; another blames him for being too weak. Author treats her sympathetically.

3194 THE MATING OF LYDIA. BY MRS. HUMPHRY WARD. Garden City, New York: Doubleday, Page, 1913 NUC. London: Smith, Elder, 1913 BMC NUC.

Intelligent, strong minded Lydia Penfold makes several attempts to be independent and live up to her theory that men and women can be "comrades." She supports herself as an artist in the Lake country. She refuses to marry the very wealthy but tyrannical Edmund Melrose though she is tempted, and she tries consistently to maintain relations of comradeship between herself and Melrose and another suitor Faversham. Lydia marries Faversham in the end though she had held that marriage is not necessary; however, she does not give up her art work.

3195 'MISSING'. BY MRS. HUMPHRY WARD. New York: Dodd, Mead, 1917 NUC. London: W. Collins, Sons, [1917] BMC.

Nellie Sarratt, married three weeks, learns first that her husband is missing in action and then that he is dead. She becomes a nurse, self-reliant and independent. Whether she marries or not, she will never be "a plaything or a parasite."

3196 THE STORY OF BESSIE COSTRELL. BY MRS. HUMPHRY WARD. New York and London: Macmillan, 1895 NUC. London: Smith, Elder, 1895 BMC.

Background of misery of poor English village life. Bessie's only feeling toward her stern laborer of a husband is awe. Toward her children she holds only a "feeble" love. She is given an old man's life's savings of 70 pounds to guard, steals it coin by coin, treats the neighbors, and when it is all spent and she must face her husband and the accusers, she kills herself. Grim somber story told with full sympathy for Bessie.

3197 THE WAR AND ELIZABETH. BY MRS HUMPHRY WARD. London: W. Collins Sons, [c1918] BMC NUC.

Elizabeth is a Greek scholar, a trained accountant, knowledgeable in the details of farming, gardening, and estate agency. She is also a good wife and mother, and very patriotic. When the war comes, she persuades her employer to be as patriotic as she is herself.

WARD, MRS. HUMPHRY. See WARD, MARY AUGUSTA (ARNOLD).

WARD, MRS. WILFRID. See WARD, JOSEPHINE MARY (HOPE-SCOTT).

WARDELL, MRS. VILLIERS. United Kingdom.

3198   THE IMPOSSIBLE MRS. BELLEW. BY DAVID LISLE. New York: F. A. Stokes, [c1916] NUC. London: E. Nash, 1916 NUC BMC.
Betty Bellew is impossible because she has a past and is therefore a social outcast. In spite of this, the story ends in her marriage to a man who accepts the scandals in her history and the social ban she is under. "The author's theory is apparently that expressed by the American Senator Willard: 'It might be better to realize that nature is very much the same in both sexes, and to give women full credit for temptations resisted....I find it very easy to overlook a slip, even several slips, in a 'mere woman.'"

3199   WHAT IS LOVE? BY DAVID LISLE. London: Methuen, [1913] BMC NUC.
Isola Dering actress in Paris, marries in the end.

WARDEN, FLORENCE. See JAMES, FLORENCE ALICE (PRICE).

WARDEN, GERTRUDE. See JONES, GERTRUDE (WARDEN).

WARING, ELEANOR HOWARD.

3200   THE WHITE PATH; A NOVEL. New York: Neale, 1907 NUC.
A talented writer defies convention and lives with the man she loves when he is unable to get a divorce.

WARNER, ANNA BARTLETT. 1827-1915. United States.

3201 PATIENCE. Philadelphia: J. B. Lippincott, 1891 NUC.
One year in the life of Patience Hathaway who drowns herself because she longed for a wider life and greater love than life in a small New England town offered her.

WARNER, ANNE. See FRENCH, ANNE RICHMOND (WARNER).

WARREN, CONSTANCE MARTHA (WILLIAMS). B. 1877. United States.

3202 THE PHOENIX. Boston: Houghton Mifflin, 1917 NUC.
Janet makes a bad marriage and almost succumbs to a "great temptation." Her solution to her problems is to become a nurse in a French hospital.

WARREN, MAUDE LAVINIA (RADFORD). 1875-1934. United States.

3203 BARBARA'S MARRIAGES; A NOVEL. New York and London: Harper, 1915 BMC NUC.
Sympathetic heroine: development from a bewildered girl to a strong self-reliant woman. Barbara Langsworthy is extremely unhappy living with her brother and his wife. Because she has no training by which to earn her living, she believes marriage is her only way out. But her first husband dies on the wedding trip, and her second makes a slave of her for six long years until their divorce. A third man she loves brings her much misery, so she gets rid of him. In the end, she finally makes a good marriage.

3204 THE MAIN ROAD; A NOVEL. New York and London: Harper, 1913 BMC NUC.
Janet Bellamy's life from sentimental girlhood to mature womanhood: raised on a Wisconsin farm, she is sheltered from life by her father and gets all her ideas from romantic novels. Story traces her love life, her four years at the University of .Chicago, her involvement in the suffrage movement, her work in a social settlement, her

part in the garment strike, and at the end her marriage.

3205 PETER-PETER, A ROMANCE OUT OF TOWN. New York and London: Harper, 1909 BMC NUC.
Humorous "nursery idyll." A couple used to luxury struggle with poverty. He does all the housekeeping—cooking and washing dishes—while she teaches French and music. Then twins arrive.

WARREN, PATIENCE. See KELSEY, JEANNETTE GARR (WASHBURN).

WARWICK, ANNE. See CRANSTON, RUTH.

WASSERMANN, LILLIAS.*

3206 THE DAFFODILS. London: Chatto and Windus, 1891 BMC.
Two artists, cousins, love the same man. They make a pact that the first of them to succeed as an artist will suppress her love for the man.

WASTE, HENRIE. See STETTHEIMER, ETTIE.

WATANNA, ONOTO. See BABCOCK, WINNIFRED (EATON).

WATSON, AUGUSTA (CAMPBELL). 1862-1936. United States.

3207 DOROTHY THE PURITAN: THE STORY OF A STRANGE DELUSION. New York: E. P. Dutton, 1893 NUC BMC.
Old Salem days of rigid Puritanism. Dorothy is no Puritan in spirit—she is out of place in Salem. She likes to dance, is vain, much tempted, and has pluck. Vivid and accurate description of the witchcraft delusion.

WATSON, ELIZABETH SOPHIA (FLETCHER). D. 1918.

3208 A HIGH LITTLE WORLD AND WHAT HAPPENED THERE. London: R. Bentley, 1892 BMC NUC.

Resemblances to Wuthering Heights. Hard stoical people; Lady Hartley, the heroine in a certain sense, has a brute of a son and a daughter who burdens her with grandchildren. Laura Garnett is a deaf and dumb heiress and one of the central characters.

WATSON, HELEN H.

3209 THE CAPTAIN'S DAUGHTER. London: Mills and Boon, 1909 BMC.

Constance Roper is a strong, high-spirited young woman who is up to any occasion. She can sail a boat, but her aspirations are literary. She becomes a journalist, then "finds herself" married to a schoolmaster. She also finds her marriage does not go well.

3210 WHEN THE KING CAME SOUTH. London: Religious Tract Society, 1912 BMC NUC.

Described as a "story for girls," the novel tells of Molly's adventures in the Cromwellian period. She adopts a male disguise to deliver messages, is captured and becomes a prisoner of war.

WATSON, R. D.*

3211 THE DREAM GIRL. London: Heath, Cranton, [1919] BMC.

Heroine impersonates her brother and manages a farm that her brother inherited.

WATTS, MARY (STANBERY). 1868-1958. United States.

3212 THE BOARDMAN FAMILY. New York: Macmillan, 1918 BMC NUC.

Sandra becomes a professional dancer to support her family; she is successful. She is on board the Lusitania when it goes down and is saved, but her feet are damaged. The story describes her "development and emancipation from the traditions of her family."

3213 FROM FATHER TO SON. New York: Macmillan, 1919 NUC.

Effect of the war on a family. Also a contrast between Hester, charming and spoiled, and Edith, a born executive, cool, capable. She breaks with her German husband after dealing capably with his bullying.

3214 THE LEGACY; A STORY OF A WOMAN. London: Macmillan, 1911 BMC. New York: Macmillan, 1911 NUC.

Fine sympathetic biography. Letty Breen, friendless and poor, marries a clerk who is left weak-minded after an accident and who dies after three years. Letty then marries a man for money rather than love, but this marriage doesn't work out either. Development of her character, her geneology of four generations and the clashing strains of her heredity.

3215 THE NOON-MARK. New York: Macmillan, 1920 NUC.

Mid western city. Nettie is "easily recognized type of American business woman, capable, hard-working, intelligent, and dependable." Her cousin, a contrast to her, feminine, ends up as a leader in the "Altruistic Brotherhood."

3216 THE RISE OF JENNIE CUSHING. New York: Macmillan, 1914 BMC NUC.

Jennie spends her life from 12 to 18 in a Midwest state reform school for assaulting a boy larger than herself to protect a cat. She then has a succession of jobs as a farm worker, a manicurist, an artist's model, and a secretary to a feminist. She lives for a few years with an artist whom she refuses to marry. She finds ultimate content in organizing a model home for young girls.

3217 THE RUDDER; A NOVEL WITH SEVERAL HEROES. New York and London: Macmillan, 1916 NUC BMC.

Eleanor, both charming and intelligent, marries a rich man's son who, lacking other talents, devotes himself to baseball. The marriage ends in divorce, she makes a life for herself and the ending is not unhappy.

WEAVER, ANNE. United Kingdom.

3218 THE CORMORANT. London: A. Melrose, 1919 BMC.

Cynara loses her job as private secretary because she admits stealing pearls. Her further adventures include war work, the establishment of her innocence, and her love story.

WEAVER, BAILLE GERTRUDE RENTON (COLMORE). United Kingdom.

3219 THE ANGEL AND THE OUTCAST. BY G. COLMORE. London: Hutchinson, 1907 BMC.

Lillian and Yan are daughters of a brutalized father and a battered, hopeless mother. Lillian is adopted, raised, and loved by a rich woman, marries a baronet, and ends happily. Yan has a passionate, jealous love for the sister taken from her. She becomes fierce and uncouth in her work in the slaughterhouse, finds escape from her problems in gin, goes to prison, is the outcast. The two sisters meet, and each, on separate occasions, helps save the other.

3220 THE CRIMSON GATE. BY G. COLMORE. London: S. Paul, [1910] BMC.

The "high-spirited" heroine is pro-suffrage and anti-vivisection. She is a hospital nurse who marries her cousin and later discovers that he has murdered her grandfather.

3221 A DAUGHTER OF MUSIC. BY G. COLMORE. London: Heinemann, 1894 BMC. New York: D. Appleton, 1894 NUC.

Rhoda has a miserly grandfather, a farmer who denied Rhoda's mother the drugs, food, etc. she needed to stay alive. Her husband, Paul Garnet, is a savage orphan, with strange cruel patience. Anthony Dexter, a musician who recognizes Rhoda's musical ability, controls her with the power of his music. She goes to Italy with Anthony as his paramour, eventually becomes depressed with this position and goes to London, living in poverty and degradation.

Paul finds her, brings her home where he simultaneously punishes and protects her, where they can go on side by side, together, yet forever apart. Much earlier he had told her it was her potential wickedness that fed his love. One reviewer suggests she has a dual personality, another that the novel is in the tradition of Wuthering Heights.

3222 THE GUEST. BY G. COLMORE. London: E. Arnold, 1917 BMC.

Friendship between two women and their conflicting ideals of love and force. Harriet Marchant meets Pauline Caillaux, and together they travel across the dunes of Belgium to England at the outbreak of the war. Pauline is a German spy masquerading as a French woman. She believes in force; Harriet is a Christian idealist.

3223 A LADDER OF TEARS; A NOVEL. BY G. COLMORE. Westminster: A. Constable, 1904 BMC.

The narrative of a woman married to an old man with two half-witted sons. The "patient and intimate unfolding of her mental and emotional history."

3224 SUFFRAGETTE SALLY. BY G. COLMORE. London: S. Paul, [1911] BMC.

A suffrage novel. Sally, a servant, goes to hear a feminist speak, and a new life opens out before her. An inspiring story giving a detailed and clear outline of the militant women's movement.

3225 THE THUNDERBOLT. BY G. COLMORE. London: T. F. Unwin, [1919] BMC NUC. New York: T. Seltzer, 1920 NUC.

Dorrie, brought up in a "sheltered way," is left defenseless against a doctor's "unscrupulous experimentation." She is innoculated; sores appear first on her arm, then on her lip. Her fiance breaks the engagement. She mustn't be told what is wrong. "Grim" tragedy.

3226 A VALLEY OF SHADOWS. BY G. COLMORE. London: Chatto & Windus, 1892 BMC.

Lucy Saryll "after 10 years of peaceful existence" confessed that she had really murdered her husband. "Gloomy," "oppressively somber."

WEBB, GLADYS MARY. See WEBB, MARY GLADYS (MEREDITH).

WEBB, MARY GLADYS (MEREDITH). 1883-1927. United Kingdom.

3227   GONE TO EARTH. BY GLADYS MARY WEBB. New York: E. P. Dutton, [c1917] NUC. London: Constable, 1917 BMC.

Hazel Woodus loves nature and the woods and has an enormous pity for all suffering things. At each step in her life she becomes aware of more and more cruelty around her. She rebels against her cruel father by marrying the first man who proposes, but the marriage is disastrous. Love comes into her life just before she meets a horrible death trying to save her tame fox from hunting hounds.

WEBLING, PEGGY. United Kingdom.

3228   THE PEARL STRINGER. London: Methuen, 1913 BMC NUC.

Virtue goes unrewarded. Careers of Nannie Mordaunt, quietly virtuous, and Rose Leonard, passionate and unprincipled. Rose has a passionate love affair but finds happiness with her dentist husband while Nannie is left a pearl stringer after the elderly man she befriended dies. Focus on the two women; male characters are of minor importance.

3229   THE STORY OF VIRGINIA PERFECT. London: Methuen, 1909 BMC NUC.

Uncongenial marriage, treachery of husband, "a dangerous theme treated with fact."

WEBSTER, JEAN. See MACKINNEY, ALICE JEAN CHANDLER (WEBSTER).

WEBSTER, NESTA HELEN.

3230 THE SHEEP TRACK, AN ASPECT OF LONDON SOCIETY. New York: E. P. Dutton, 1914 NUC. London: J. Murray, 1914 BMC NUC.
Marcia, living with three aunts in London, revolts against the smug conventions of society and joins a group of friends in Bohemia. She becomes disillusioned with some of her friends and also loses the opportunity of making a socially advantageous marriage. The novel shows the improved working conditions for middle class women which have taken place in the last decade, but for upper class women whose goal is marriage "the emancipation of modern women counts for little or nothing." A satire.

WEED, MARIA.

3231 A VOICE IN THE WILDERNESS. Chicago: Laird and Lee, [c1895] NUC.
"Warning against indiscriminate use of morphine to make a patient's suffering endurable." A woman musical artist becomes addicted but is cured by a doctor whose wife had died of the habit.

WELLS, FLORENCE. United States.

3232 TAMA; THE DIARY OF A JAPANESE SCHOOL GIRL. New York: Woman's Press, 1919 NUC.

WENTWORTH, PATRICIA. See TURNBULL, DORA AMY DILLON.

WEST, V. SACKVILLE. See NICHOLSON, VICTORIA MARY SACKVILLE-WEST.

WESTON, E. MARGARET.

3233 PAMELA'S CHOICE. London: Isbister, [1904] BMC.
A middle-aged woman has pledged her fortune to women

who are willing to ignore the existence of men. When she runs out of money, she gets a job working for a young man who has adopted the disguise of an old woman so that he can be near a young woman the heroine has been helping.

WESTON, KATE HELEN. Australia.

3234 THE PRELUDE. London: Holden & Hardingham, [1914] BMC.
Heroine leaves her husband and child. She buys a newspaper and in it promotes her socialist lover. After the death of her husband, she reclaims her child, but doesn't give up her work.

WESTOVER, CYNTHIA M. See ALDEN, CYNTHIA MAY (WESTOVER).

WESTRUP, MARGARET. See STACEY, MARGARET (WESTRUP).

WETMORE, ELIZABETH (BISLAND). 1861-1929. United States.

3235 A FLYING TRIP AROUND THE WORLD. New York: Harper, 1891 NUC. London: Osgood and McIlvaine, 1891 BMC.
Miss Bisland is sent by a prominent magazine to make a tour around the world in order to better Nelly Bly's famous record for such a tour.

WHARTON, EDITH NEWBOLD (JONES). 1862-1937. United States.

3236 THE CUSTOM OF THE COUNTRY. New York: C. Scribner's Sons, 1913 NUC. London: Macmillan, 1913 BMC.
Reviews differ about the heroine, the custom and the theme: Undine Spragg is "a repellent monster of vulgarity,"

she is full of "inner misery." The custom is rapid mating; it is that business men give more attention to their work than their wives. The novel attacks American divorce laws; it denounces the marriage market; it has no moral—Undine gets precisely what she wants.

3237 THE FRUIT OF THE TREE. New York: C. Scribner's Sons, 1907 BMC NUC. London: Macmillan, 1907 BMC NUC.

Nurse Justine Brent loses her job when she and foreman John Amherst refuse to hush up the matter of the mill hand who lost an arm. Justine and John want factory reforms. He marries the millowner Bessie Westmore, but the fact that she's more interested in clothes than reforms estranges them. When Bessie falls from a horse and is dying in excruciating pain, Justine, her friend, kills her out of mercy. Justine is confident that she did the right thing until years later when she marries John and he learns of the mercy killing.

3238 THE HOUSE OF MIRTH. New York: C. Scribner's Sons, 1905 NUC. London: Macmillan, 1905 BMC NUC.

The downfall of Lily Bart. One part of her yearns for Seldon's love; the other for marriage and wealth. She plays the marriage game (which pits woman against woman) more and more desperately. At 29, she's repelled by Rosendale's offer; at 30, she proposes to him. In those years, her beauty fades; she moves from social secretary to hat shop worker and from the fanciest mansions to the dingy room in which she dies.

3239 MADAME DE TREYMES. New York: Scribner's Sons, 1907 NUC. London: Macmillan, 1907 BMC.

Contrast of French and American attitudes toward divorce. Madame de Treymes, dominated by her French husband's family and miserable in her marriage, wants to return to the U. S. but must remain in France to keep her son, even though the couple have separated. And if she divorces her husband, she must remain unmarried to keep her son. She refuses divorce.

3240   SANCTUARY. New York: C. Scribner's Sons, 1903 BMC
       NUC. London: Macmillan, 1903 BMC.
       A superbly strong woman marries a man she knows is
       morally weak because she loves him and feels "a
       responsibility to the unborn." Her married life is tragic,
       but, forewarned, she devotes her life to saving her son
       who inherited his father's weakness. Thus she saves him
       from the hereditary moral taint.

3241   SUMMER: A NOVEL. New York: D. Appleton, 1917
       BMC NUC. London: Macmillan, 1917 BMC.
       Charity Royall's "fall" is not allowed to ruin her life. She
       is the daughter of a convict father and a "dissolute"
       mother. Raised in a small New England town, she
       becomes mistress to a New York City man who dazzles
       her and who leaves her pregnant. A kind lawyer marries
       her.

WHARTON, SYDNEY.*

3242   THE WIFE DECIDES: A NOVEL. New York: G.W.
       Dillingham, [c1911] NUC.
       She marries to gain freedom, gets divorced to gain
       freedom, and marries a second time disastrously.

WHEAT, LU. United States.

3243   AH MOY, THE STORY OF A CHINESE GIRL. New
       York: Grafton Press, [c1908] NUC.
       Ah Moy, a young Chinese woman, is sold by her father,
       when he falls on hard times, to a slave dealer. Her new
       owner brings her to San Francisco where missionaries try
       to free her in court, but they lose the case. She finally
       uses the knife her father had given her to save herself.

3244   HELEN; A STORY OF THINGS TO BE. New York:
       Grafton Press, [c1908] NUC.
       Helen, the daughter of a rancher, rents the ranch after his
       death and goes to the city to study art.

WHEELER, HALLIE ERMINIE (RIVES). 1876-1956. United States.

3245 AS THE HART PANTETH. BY HALLIE ERMINIE RIVES. New York: G. W. Dillingham, 1898 NUC.

A young woman who is a famous violinist has been close friends with a poet for years. He loves her but believes marriage and home cares should not stand in the way of her art, and so he offers her platonic friendship. She loves him and wants a closer relationship but is too proud to tell him.

3246 A FURNACE OF EARTH. BY HALLIE ERMINIE RIVES. London: G. Richards, 1900 BMC. New York: Camelot, 1900 NUC.

Margaret has been taught to despise her physical responses, and she yearns for spiritual development. "Moods sometimes struck through her like the smell of earth to a wild thing of the jungle." A hospital nurse, she is persuaded her love is not too earthy for marriage only when she sees her lover injured and crippled.

3247 SMOKING FLAX. BY HALLIE ERMINIE RIVES. London, New York: F. T. Neely, [c1897] BMC NUC.

Elliott Harding is a Northerner who is against lynching but comes to understand the Southern point of view when his betrothed is raped and murdered.

WHEELER, HELEN MAUDE.

3248 AN UP-TO-DATE PAUPER. Boston: C.M. Clark, 1907 NUC.

Out of poverty and struggle to a career as a singer.

WHEELWRIGHT, EDITH GRAY.

3249 ANTHONY GRAEME. London: R. Bentley, 1895 BMC NUC.

A marriage fails because the husband, a professor, is completely occupied with his studies. The wife tries to get interested in philosophy, but he remains distant. After she leaves, he realizes his great loss, goes after her, but it is too late: she dies rescuing a child; he dies of a broken heart.

WHISPER, A.*

3250 BLACK MARK. Edinburgh & London: Blackwood, 1909 BMC.

Historical romance of Letty Beander. She dresses in black satin breeches, fences with her brother, has daring, dazzling adventures. At 17, she hears of the Black Mark and promises to fight him. She dresses as a man to seek him out. When her coach is held up, she steps out, draws her sword and challenges the Black Mark. She ends up as his partner in marriage and in his rides as a highwayman.

3251 FFYNON THE SUN-EATER. London: Holden & Hardingham, [1914] BMC.

Wife without a wedding ring is loved by a man who marries her and then learns his antecedents. Tragedy results. Ffynon Morgan is the daughter of a religious maniac, has all the superstition and emotionalism of the Celt, a passionate love for her dying child. Written to show that invariably the woman pays for the sins of others and the man goes free.

3252 KING AND CAPTIVE. Edinburgh & London: W. Blackwood, 1910 BMC NUC.

Nefert, an Egyptian dancer, moves from the position of washing the pharaoh's feet to becoming his mistress. She refuses to share his throne or to accept his offers of jewels and riches, but asks for and gets a house of her own where she can read and write.

WHITBY, BEATRICE. D. 1931. United Kingdom.

3253 IN THE SUNTIME OF HER YOUTH. London: Hurst and Blackett, 1893 BMC NUC. New York: D. Appleton, 1893 NUC.

Cheerless story of the three Trevor sisters—none of whom

have "suntime." Agnes and Elspeth grow up as tomboys. Agnes marries a wealthy man for the family's sake and when he dies, she marries a former admirer. Elspeth is responsible for the family when the father dies and the mother is worn out. She eventually marries a bookworm type. Celia dies in a boat accident caused by Agnes.

3254 MARY FENWICK'S DAUGHTER, A NOVEL. London: Hurst and Blackett, 1894 BMC NUC. New York: D. Appleton, 1894 NUC.

Romance, two suitors. Bab Fenwick had friendly feelings for both, desired neither as a lover, yet accepted both. "Absolutely incapable of any emotion warmer than genial camaraderie." Bab is not a new woman, "which follows from the fact that she is a lady; but she is hoidenal, first, in being very athletic, and, secondly, in not ostensibly feeling the necessity of anything more than comradeship with the opposite sex." She has an accident with a runaway horse and chooses one of the suitors.

3255 ROSAMUND. London: Methuen, [1911] BMC NUC.

Depressing story of Rosamund who went off to India as a young beautiful bride and returns as a widow with twins—a broken, hopeless woman.

3256 THE WHIRLIGIG OF TIME. London: Hurst & Blackett, 1906 BMC NUC.

Feminist spinster marries selfish man with children.

WHITCOMB, JESSIE (WRIGHT). B. 1864. United States.

3257 AS QUEER AS SHE COULD BE. BY JESSIE E. WRIGHT. Philadelphia: Presbyterian Board Of Publication and Sabbath-School Work, 1895 NUC.

When Hilary loses her job on the newspaper in Boston, she opens a house on Cape Cod for "five Boston street Arabs."

WHITE, AMBER (REEVES) BLANCO. B. 1887. New Zealand.

3258   HELEN IN LOVE. London: Hurst & Blackett, 1916 BMC. Title applies to love of herself and her fancies, although she is also interested in a young man whom she invites to kiss her. She rides a motor bike.

3259   A LADY AND HER HUSBAND. London: W. Heinemann, [1914] BMC.
Satire. Mrs. Heyham, at a loss for something to do when her daughters leave home, visits her husband's restaurants. In observing conditions there, she applies the same principles on which she has been nurtured and on which she has brought up her daughters, and she finds much to criticize in his treatment of employees, etc. This brings her into a head-on conflict with her husband, who has two standards, one for his business and one for his family.

3260   THE REWARD OF VIRTUE. London: W. Heinemann, 1911 BMC.
A study of the relationship between mother and daughter. Evelyn's mother is her greatest friend, but this worked out "unfortunately." Evelyn repeats her mother's mistakes with her daughter. Intimate story from childhood to marriage of a heroine who is out for emotion—interested in her own sensations.

WHITE, ELIZA ORNE. 1836-1947. United States.

3261   THE COMING OF THEODORA. Boston: Houghton Mifflin, 1895 NUC. London: Smith, Elder, 1895 BMC.
Theodora teaches political economy and history at a Western college; she has made a name and position for herself in the world. For fourteen months she visits with her brother and his wife, both artists. There is much friction because the couple are slipshod housekeepers and Theodora is a genius for managing. The couple attempt to get her married to be rid of her.

3262   JOHN FORSYTH'S AUNTS. New York and London: McClure, Phillips, 1901 BMC NUC.
Three older women, sisters, live happily together. One

enjoys independence in her work in the greenhouse; another decides to become a nurse. The story is alive to women's right to follow their own bent; its moral, it's women's prerogative to refuse to marry.

3263 LESLEY CHILTON. Boston: Houghton, Mifflin, 1903 NUC.

Opens with a discussion of the woman question. Lesley Chilton is a feminist who has published her advanced views on higher education for women. She uses her arguments to keep at bay an anti-suffrage male. Though she marries him in the end, she remains her own person and continues her active work in the women's suffrage club.

3264 A LOVER OF TRUTH. Boston: Houghton Mifflin, 1898 NUC. London: Smith, Elder, 1898 BMC.

Jean Rycroft, an artist, is neither conventional nor abnormal. Her history, from childhood in New England atmosphere of seriousness and restraint to womanhood where she discovers her love for Alan a delusion. "An intelligent being whose actions and affections are deliberate and conscious," "an acute and sympathetic study of the growth and expansion of a reserved. sensitive and high-minded nature."

3265 WINTERBOROUGH. Boston: Houghton Mifflin, 1892 NUC.

The story of Persis in a New England town, her literary aspirations and disappointments, her initial defiance of her teacher and subsequent engagement to him.

WHITE, GRACE (MILLER). D. 1965. United States.

3266 ROSE O' PARADISE. New York: H. K. Fly, [1915] NUC. London: Mills & Boon, 1918 BMC.

Jimmie is a fiddler and composer. For girls.

3267 THE SECRET OF THE STORM COUNTRY. New York: H.K. Fly, [c1917] NUC. London: Hodder & Stoughton, [1924] BMC.

Continues story of Tess of the Storm Country made

famous by Mary Pickford's movie. Again concerns squatters on Lake Cayuga. Tess works hard at music and studies. Makes a secret marriage with Cornell student.

3268 WHEN TRAGEDY GRINS. New York: W.J. Watt, [c1912] NUC. London: C. Palmer & Hayward, 1916 BMC.
An American girl in Paris without money becomes a night beggar.

WHITING, MARY BRADFORD. United Kingdom.

3269 DENIS O'NEIL. London: R. Bentley, 1892 BMC NUC.
A doctor is deported to Australia for a crime a secret society has forced on him. A nurse follows him; they work together in Australia until she is killed by diphtheria and he is killed by one of the secret society.

3270 MERIEL'S CAREER. A TALE OF LITERARY LIFE IN LONDON. London: Blackie, 1914 BMC.
Meriel comes to London for a literary life: she is a prig. Finances force her to work as editor of "The New Girl," a "startling" American publication. Her employer has hired her solely so that she could be advertised as the "youngest editress." Learns that "love does count and that she is not a great literary genius." "Should appeal to the 'young person.'" "Author makes her succumb at the end, in the proper feminine way, to love."

WHITNEY, ADELINE DUTTON (TRAIN). 1824-1906. United States.

3271 SQUARE PEGS. BY MRS. A. D. T. WHITNEY. London: A. P. Watt, [1899] BMC. Boston: Houghton, Mifflin, 1899 NUC.
Estabel Charlock, wild, unbound by convention from girlhood to womanhood: she begins as a country girl who goes to a private school in Boston and meets her ambitious aunt and snobbish schoolmates. She grows into a strong solid woman and meets a man to match her. The book leaves the two pledged to themselves and to one another to try "to right some of the wrong relations of

men," particularly profitable building speculations which make capitalists rich.

WHITNEY, GERTRUDE CAPEN. 1861-1941. United States.

3272   I CHOOSE. Boston: Sherman, French, 1910 NUC.
She chooses to remain in prison and help her companions, although she had been wrongly accused of a crime.

WHITNEY, MRS. A. D. T. See WHITNEY, ADELINE DUTTON (TRAIN).

WHYTE, CHRISTINA GOWANS.

3273   NINA'S CAREER. New York: Macmillan, 1907 NUC. London: H. Frowde, 1908 BMC.
An art student in London and Paris.

WICKHAM, A. E.*

3274   FORTUNE'S FINGERS. London: Hutchinson, 1896 BMC.
Part One: Friendless young woman among strangers. She lives in a huge house with a Rochester-like master, but worse. He knocks her down. She is subject to terrifying nights; there's a mystery about the master's wife who has been tortured into imbecility. Part Two: The tyrant found shot. Heroine suspected; she denies nothing; is tried, sentenced to death, reprieved. Then we learn it was the mad wife who did it.

WIDDEMER, MARGARET. B. 1880. United States.

3275   THE ROSE-GARDEN HUSBAND. Philadelphia: J. B. Lippincott Co., 1915 NUC. London: Hodder & Stoughton, 1915 BMC.
Phyllis Narcissa is a library teacher who dreams of and gets a rose-garden husband. "Drenched in sugar."

WIGGIN, KATE DOUGLAS. See RIGGS, KATE DOUGLAS (SMITH) WIGGIN.

WIGRAM, EIRENE. United Kingdom.

3276 THE AFFAIR OF THE ENVELOPE. London: Methuen, 1910 BMC.

In this story of international intrigue, Madam Kampine is a nurse and a very financially successful spy.

WILCOX, ELLA (WHEELER). 1850-1919. United States.

3277 SWEET DANGER. Chicago: M. A. Donohue, [c1902] NUC.

Dolores and Helena are school friends. Dolores, loving a man, lives with him but refuses to marry because of her mother's unhappy marriage. Helena finds home and happiness.

WILD, IDA.

3278 HOUSE-ROOM. New York and London: J. Lane, 1916 BMC NUC.

Virginia's husband is in an asylum. She makes a life for herself, teaching cooking and being friends with Dr. Clewes. Everyone advises them they are justified in anything they do. She resists, afraid to ruin Clewes' career.

3279 ZOE, THE DANCER. London and New York: J. Lane, 1911 BMC NUC.

After 14 years in a convent, Zoe goes out on her own. She rejects an offer of marriage, preferring to make her own way. She becomes a famous dancer, marries, but leaves her worthless husband to return to the stage. The novel closes on the question of whether she should return to her husband or break with him for good.

WILKINS, MARY E. See FREEMAN, MARY ELEANOR (WILKINS).

WILLARD, CAROLINE MACCOY (WHITE). United States.

3280 KIN-DA-SHON'S WIFE: AN ALASKAN STORY. BY MRS. EUGENE S. WILLARD. New York: F. H. Revell, [c1892] NUC BMC. London: R.T.S., [1893] BMC.

Based on facts the author presented in an earlier work of non-fiction, this is a story of love and suffering depicting the torture and brutality endured by Eskimos in Alaska where "women are as yet little better than animals." It describes the customs of imprisonment of young girls in caves for months to make them more marriageable, girls of twelve wed to their grandfathers, boys to their grandmothers.

WILLARD, MRS. EUGENE S. See WILLARD, CAROLINE MACCOY (WHITE).

WILLCOCKS, M. P. See WILLCOCKS, MARY PATRICIA.

WILLCOCKS, MARY PATRICIA. B. 1869. United Kingdom.

3281 CHANGE. BY M. P. WILLCOCKS. London: Hutchinson, 1915 BMC NUC.

Intimate and sympathetic study of the various stages of a young woman's adolescence with its restless dissatisfaction and its feelings of self-sufficiency and with the coming of love and disillusionment. Includes a sympathetic portrayal of a type—"the managing woman" who manages and spoils men.

3282 THE EYES OF THE BLIND; A NOVEL. BY M. P. WILLCOCKS. London: Hutchinson, 1917 BMC NUC.

The stories of many different characters blended into one tale. One character is a strong steady young woman who picks out the man she wants, has a child when she wants and wastes no time regretting that she is not married.

3283   THE POWER BEHIND. BY M. P. WILLCOCKS. London: Hutchinson, 1913 NUC BMC.

History of Sophie Revel a woman of strong individuality from her birth to the birth of her second child. It is a history crowded with revolts. Born of French parents, Sophie is adopted by an English country doctor from whom she gets many of her liberal ideas. She learns only after his suicide that she is not his daughter. When she finds it impossible to live with her adopted mother, she leaves to make her own way. She works on a farm ruled by a patriarch, makes a secret marriage with a son of the patriarch, has a son, is widowed, and is forced to give up her son to her husband's family. Her second marriage is to an elderly doctor. Lack of love plot and emphasis on "affairs of the mind."

3284   THE SLEEPING PARTNER. BY M. P. WILLCOCKS. London: Hutchinson, 1919 BMC NUC.

About the publishing world. Silas Brutton is a publisher who suffers from a morbid horror of sex because his father took him to a prison to see a child molester. He comes to a healthier view of sex through Nan Carey, whose passion is biology. The son of a publisher's reader carefully analyzes the women novelists of the time because it is they who make sales if not reputations. Then Mrs. Colquhoun, the novelist, comes on the scene. Her subject she says is man and woman—not sex. She claims to write for well-to-do suburban women, her clients. "What they crave is love stories with the woman at the center, the motive power, with enough spice about the atmosphere to suit married women and enough worship to suggest a lover who was quite unlike the gentleman who supplied fur coats. Advance on the edge of things, combined with a long drawn-out agony for the man." That is Mrs. Colquhoun's recipe.

3285   THE WAY UP. BY M. P. WILLCOCKS. London and New York: J. Lane, 1910 BMC NUC.

Elise, pleasure-loving, is neglected by her husband, who is

absorbed in creating a model factory he has acquired with her money. Long held in check by her affection for him, she eventually leaves, leads a "careless life," and, unable to find the love in others she had been denied in her husband, she finally suicides. Michael's secretary is portrayed as being doubly outside of women's world, having neither love nor opportunity.

3286 THE WINGLESS VICTORY. BY M. P. WILLCOCKS. New York and London: J. Lane, 1907 NUC BMC.

Psychological study of a few years in a woman's life. Wilmot Borlace marries only when she tires of the single life. She is a modern woman who is restless and who craves power. Her marriage is miserable, partly because her husband is wrapped up in his work. Her wild nature leads her to serious flirtations with other men. She leaves her husband, with whom she is eventually reunited; the "other" woman, Johanna, visits Wilmot and helps bring about the reunion of husband and wife. Sympathetic view of the heroine's disregard for convention and working out of her own salvation.

3287 WINGS OF DESIRE. BY M. P. WILLCOCKS. London and New York: J. Lane, 1912 BMC NUC.

Sara Bellen has no children and is indifferent to her unfaithful husband. She is bitterly resentful of her martyrdom to the service of sex; she had wanted a musical career. "Sets forth the new independence of women; all the women in it are moved to do something by themselves with their lives and not be mere appendages to men."

WILLIAMS, ELLEN.

3288 ANNA MARSDEN'S EXPERIMENT. London: Greening, 1899 BMC.

Anna Marsden is "an ugly journalist who thought that life would look more lively through masculine eyes. Her travestissement is so successful that no one recognizes her." She shares the lodgings of the man she loves who loves another woman, gets a job on a newspaper, and discovers that in her writing "a manly mode of expression comes much more easily to her than a feminine style." When the man she loves dies, she runs into misfortunes, and eventually resumes her dress as a woman.

WILLIAMS, FRANCES FENWICK. Canada.

3289   A SOUL ON FIRE. New York and London: J. Lane, 1915 NUC. (Also published as Theodora; A Soul on Fire. London and New York: J. Lane, 1915 BMC.)
Several deaths were traced to this dark, mysterious woman who is the reincarnation of the Witch of Carne. She herself admitted to nine murders. She is cured in the end. The novel brings in the women's suffrage question, which has, says one reviewer, "nothing to do with the reincarnation of medieval witches."

WILLIAMS, MARGERY. See BIANCO, MARGERY (WILLIAMS).

WILLIAMS, NELLA.

3290   MY SISTER TAKES A REST CURE. London: Jarrolds, [1919] BMC.
Letters and diary of life in a French sanitorium written by a young woman who has had a nervous breakdown. A slight love story included.

WILLIAMSON, ALICE MURIEL (LIVINGSTON). 1869-1933. United Kingdom.

3291   THE BARN STORMERS: BEING THE TRAGICAL SIDE OF A COMEDY. BY MRS. HARCOURT WILLIAMSON. London: Hutchinson, 1897 BMC. New York: F. A. Stokes, [c1897] NUC.
Monica is a young convent-bred English woman who joins the Scott Ambler Comedy Company and with the group sails to New York. Describes the squalid actualities of everyday life of a touring company in the states and Monica's deep friendship with Della Thomas, the

Cinderella of the Company. Monica ends up marrying an American millionaire.

3292 THE GIRL WHO HAD NOTHING. London: Ward, Lock, 1905 BMC.

Joan has nothing when she's turned out of her servant position. But she makes her way into fashionable society, and "flashes with brilliant audacity" through the world of high finance and international politics.

3293 HE WHO PASSED. TO M. L. G. [ANONYMOUS]. London: W. Heinemann, 1912 BMC. (Also published as To M. L. G., Or, He Who Passed [Anonymous]. New York: F. A. Stokes, [1912] NUC.)

The autobiography of an actress who comes to realize that all her life she has used men or they have used her. M.L.G., who has come into her life and passed out of it, was an exception; she is writing the book in the hope that he will read it and return to her.

3294 THE HOUSE OF THE LAST COURT. BY DONA TERESA DE SAVALLO, MARQUESA D'ALPENS. New York: McClure, 1908 NUC. London: Hodder & Stoughton, 1908 BMC. (NUC: Marchioness D'Alpens.)

A widow and her daughter rent a house; their neighbors avoid them and they discover there is a mystery about the house which the daughter solves. The court conceals a man who has been convicted of a crime. She clears all that up and they marry.

3295 THE LIFE MASK; A NOVEL. BY THE AUTHOR OF "TO M. L. G." [ANONYMOUS]. New York: F.A. Stokes, [1913] NUC.

First-person narrative of Anita Durrand sentenced to life imprisonment for the murder of her husband—a middle-aged Englishman she married when very young. After 10 years in prison, she is set free because she is very ill, sets up a secret life in Grenada, regains her health, falls in love but refuses to tell the man her secret. She is about to kill herself when she learns she is innocent of the murder.

3296 THE NEWSPAPER GIRL. London: C. A. Pearson, 1899 BMC.

Lucille Chandler, an American heiress, swaps identities with an old school chum she meets in Europe and goes to London to work as a journalist. She gets completely involved in her work by disguising herself in different ways to get the news. When she hears of a newspaper for sale, she buys it and makes her lover the editor. "Pictures of the inner workings of those journals which cater to feminine readers being as entertaining as they are unedifying."

3297 A WOMAN IN GREY. BY MRS. C. N. WILLIAMSON. London: G. Routledge, 1898 BMC NUC. New York: A. L. Burt, [n.d.] NUC.

Reviewers seem to agree that this is the most extravagantly sensational novel that they have ever encountered, with no relief in the breathless and kaleidescopic procession of horror, sensation, and crime. Floria Amory leads an exciting life; one of her aliases is Consuelo Hope; she is also a brilliant novelist.

WILLIAMSON, MRS. C. N. See WILLIAMSON, ALICE MURIEL (LIVINGSTON).

WILLIAMSON, MRS. HARCOURT. See WILLIAMSON, ALICE MURIEL (LIVINGSTON).

WILLSIE, HONORE. See MORROW, HONORE (MACCUE) WILLSIE.

WILLY, COLETTE. See DE JOUVENAL, SIDONIE GABRIELLE (COLETTE) GAUTHER-VILLARS.

WILSON, ANNIE. New Zealand.

3298 ALICE LAUDER: A SKETCH. London: Osgood, McIlvaine, 1893 BMC.

Alice Lauder sings in concert. Early plot hangs on hero's error on hearing she is engaged to a professor—meaning engaged to sing at a concert in Birmingham. Chiefly concerns the love versus work dilemma. Also Lizzie Austin—exuberant in spirit, outrageous in her use of slang—discovers the man she loves is not serious about her.

WILSON, DESEMEA (NEWMAN). United Kingdom.

3299 THE ISLANDS OF DESIRE. A NOVEL. BY DIANA PATRICK. London: Hutchinson, [1920] BMC. New York: E.P. Dutton, [1921] NUC.

Rose has an unhappy marriage; her two daughters both become actresses.

3300 THE WIDER WAY: A NOVEL. BY DIANA PATRICK. London: Hutchinson, 1920 BMC. New York: E.P. Dutton, [1920] NUC.

Veronica, a school teacher, escapes a bounder to marry a German. He dies shortly after the war begins.

WILSON, MONA.

3301 THE STORY OF ROSALIND RETOLD FROM HER DIARY. BY MONICA MOORE. London: Sidgwick and Jackson, 1910 BMC.

An unhappy marriage.

WILSON, MRS. LESTER S. United States.

3302 MRS. SINCLAIR'S EXPERIMENTS. Kansas City, Mo.: H. T. Wright, 1900 NUC.

Mrs. Sinclair, a widow, has little belief in men's honor. In a series of letters she describes experiments she has made on single and married admirers which confirm this view.

WILSON, THEODORA WILSON. D. 1941. United Kingdom.

3303 A MODERN AHAB. London: S. Paul, [1912] BMC.
Sentimental. Baronet is opposed by a woman artist in his appropriation of land for a deer run.

3304 MOLL O' THE TOLL-BAR. London: Hutchinson, 1911 BMC.
Historical romance of the late 17th and early 18th centuries. Moll is a brave, magnetic young woman who holds a strange power over the peasants of Ullerdale, some of whom fear her while others call her a witch. She is a bewitching beauty, strongly independent with deep feelings of both love and hate. She is described as a female Quixote righting wrongs in a world of social misery and oppression.

3305 T'BACCA QUEEN: A NOVEL. London: E. Arnold, 1901 BMC. New York: D. Appleton, 1902 NUC.
The story of a young woman in Carolina, a factory worker.

3306 URSULA RAVEN. London and New York: Harper, 1905 BMC.
Becomes a school teacher when father loses his wealth.

WINN, MARY POLK AND MARGARET HANNIS.

3307 THE LAW AND THE LETTER; A STORY OF THE PROVINCE OF LOUISIANA. Washington: Neale, 1907 NUC.
The practice of sending cargoes of maidens to be married by nuns to soldiers of French army. Story of such a marriage.

WINSLOW, HELEN MARIA. 1851-1938. United States.

3308 THE PLEASURING OF SUSAN SMITH. Boston: L.C. Page, 1912 NUC. London: I. Pitman, 1912 BMC.
A 40 year old woman inherits money and goes to town.

3309 THE PRESIDENT OF QUEX. A WOMAN'S CLUB STORY. Boston: Lothrop, Lee and Shepard, [1906] NUC.
A defense of involvement in women's club activities rather

than domestic duties. Anne North is a leading lady in a stock company in Brooklyn. Left a widow with a child while she was very young, she placed her daughter with a relative in order to follow her career. The daughter, now 18, comes back into her life, just at the point when Anne is successful and in love. Her daughter, also an actress, uses her mother's influence and wins both the man and her mother's place in the stock company. (Conflicting review says Anne finds happiness.)

3310 SALOME SHEPARD, REFORMER. Boston: Arena, 1893 NUC.

Heroine returns from her studies, travels in Europe and is expected to be an "ornament." But when she inherits a big factory and the workers strike, she is awakened to human rights. She introduces model housing, builds a school and library for the workers and establishes a system of profit sharing. Love interest concerns the man who becomes her agent.

3311 A WOMAN FOR MAYOR; A NOVEL OF TODAY. Chicago: Reilly and Britton, 1909 NUC.

"Based on the present-day suffrage question. Her theme is that where women are given the right to vote women will be elected to high office." In the city of Roma where women vote, a woman is elected as reform mayor. She takes office and immediately cleans up the corrupt town, is kidnapped by a gang, escapes, drives the gang out of town, marries her opponent, and is asked to run for a second term.

WINSLOW, ROSE GUGGENHEIM. United States.

3312 THE GLORIOUS HOPE; A NOVEL. BY JANE BURR. Croton-on-Hudson, N.Y.: James Burr, 1918 NUC. London: Duckworth, 1921 BMC.

Young woman seeks artistic career in New York. She marries a socialist artist who never works, leaves him for a job as a typist at $8.00 a week.

3313 LETTERS OF A DAKOTA DIVORCEE. BY JANE BURR. Boston: Roxburgh, [c1909] NUC.

3314 THE PASSIONATE SPECTATOR. BY JANE BURR. London: Duckworth, 1920 BMC. New York: T. Seltzer, 1921 NUC. "An argument for physical love, freely indulged."

WINSTON, N. B. See WINSTON, NANNIE B.

WINSTON, NANNIE B. United States.

3315 THE GRACE OF ORDERS. BY N. B. WINSTON. New York: Abbey Press, [1901] NUC.
The maiden aunt, Miss Rachel, is "one of the racy and charming old maids who are beginning to venture into the realms of fiction."

WINTER, JOHN STRANGE. See STANNARD, HENRIETTA ELIZA VAUGHAN (PALMER).

WINTER, LOUISE. United States.

3316 HEARTS AFLAME. New York and London: Smart Set, 1903 NUC.
A divorced woman struggles to get back into society.

WITHERSPOON, ISABELLA M. United States.

3317 THE TRAGEDY OF AGES. New York: F.T. Neely, 1897 NUC. London: F. T. Neely, 1897 BMC.
Concerns "causes which lead women to shrink from the duties and cares of maternity."

WITTIGSCHLAGER, WILHELMINA. United States.

3318 MINNA, WIFE OF THE YOUNG RABBI, A NOVEL. New York: Consolidated Retail Booksellers, 1905 NUC BMC. London: Gay & Bird, 1906 BS.
Twelve year old Minna runs away soon after her forced marriage to a man she has never met, and her "tendencies toward nihilism cause her to be banished to Siberia and result in the death of the Czar, whose daughter she proves to be."

WOLF, ALICE S. United States.

3319 A HOUSE OF CARDS. Chicago: Stone and Kimball, 1896 NUC.

Loys, a schoolteacher with literary aspirations, develops a problem with her eyes from overwork. She marries an old friend, thinking that she will eventually comes to love him. Their marriage is unhappy; he is selfish and unsympathetic with her literary ambitions.

WOLF, EMMA. 1865-1932. United States.

3320 FULFILLMENT; A CALIFORNIA NOVEL. New York: H. Holt, 1916 NUC.

Two sisters live in a cottage in San Francisco. Gwen Heath, impetuous, slips into a love affair and marriage, a situation that offers nothing but unhappiness and divorce. At 24 she marries to avoid poverty, tolerates then hates husband, is estranged, has a child.

WOOD, A. E.*

3321 THE KING. London: A. Melrose, [1911] BMC.

In this 18th century romance, the center of interest is Julie, a courtesan and a spy. She is contrasted to Queen Sophia with her "wooden and doll-like virtues."

WOOD, ANNIE MARY.

3322 SEAS BETWEEN; OR, CALLED TO THE EAST AND CLAIMED BY THE WEST. London: E. Stock, 1908 BMC.

Missionary life in China. Good portrayal of feminine characters, women genuinely absorbed in religion. Reviewer believes this requires far greater courage than writing a conventionally "daring" study of illicit passions.

WOOD, FANNY MORRIS. United Kingdom.

3323 FIVE YEARS AND A MONTH. [London]: Duckworth, 1913 BMC NUC.

Unhappy marriage, callous husband, separation, flirtations. Wife dies on the last page.

WOOD, H. F. See WOOD, H. FREEMAN WIBER.

WOOD, H. FREEMAN WIBER.* United Kingdom.

3324 AVENGED ON SOCIETY. A NOVEL. BY H. F. WOOD.
New York: J. W. Lovell, [c1892] NUC. London: W.
Heinemann, 1893 BMC.

A convict is liberated, she stumps the country, starts a
newspaper and marries a duke. She's the only child of an
ex-convict and a duchess. Includes a woman who studies
gynecology and "writes letters to the medical press on our
Public Women from the Point of View of Etiology."
Another who talks about "Dephlogisticated Air." Diary
form.

WOOD, JOANNA E. D. 1919. Canada.

3325 A DAUGHTER OF WITCHES. A ROMANCE. London:
Hurst and Blackett, 1900 BMC. Toronto: W.J. Gage,
[1900] NUC.

Beautiful woman marries New England minister, tempts
him, leads him, ruining him before his congregation. She
suffers in the end.

3326 FARDEN HA'. London: Hurst & Blackett, 1902 BMC.

Author feels a man's attitude toward his wife and friend
who have had a child should be to suffer silently and go
on as if nothing had happened.

3327 THE UNTEMPERED WIND. New York: J. S. Tait, [1894]
NUC.

Myron, betrayed by a medical student, attempts to earn a
living for her little boy. Her efforts are blocked by the
hypocritical women of the town who include her own
grandmother. Tragedy results.

WOODINGTON, F. THICKNESSE.*

3328 STRAWS UPON THE WATER. London: G. Allen &
Unwin, 1916 BMC.

Heroine is "betrayed and abandoned." She struggles first as
a shop girl and then in a factory. After many years of

work as a dock laborer, the man wins her forgiveness.

3329   SWAYNEFORD. London: G. Allen & Unwin, [1918] BMC.

Ena Cardonnel is an English spy before the war. She discovers so much she is kidnapped and taken to Germany. She has many exciting adventures during the war. One reviewer says she ruins her past cleverness by getting sentimental and going to pieces.

WOODROFFE, DANIEL. See WOODS, MRS. JAMES CHAPMAN.

WOODROW, MRS. WILSON. See WOODROW, NANCY MANN (WADDEL).

WOODROW, NANCY MANN (WADDEL). 1870-1935. United States.

3330   THE BEAUTY. BY MRS. WILSON WOODROW. Indianapolis: Bobbs Merrill, [c1910] NUC.

In this story of an unhappy marriage, the wife has too much strength of character to be relegated to the role of pretty plaything. She and her husband are separated for awhile, during which time she operates a business establishment, teaching women how to dress.

3331   THE BLACK PEARL. BY MRS. WILSON WOODROW. New York and London: D. Appleton, 1912 BMC NUC.

Love story of a dancer in a mountain mining camp.

3332   THE NEW MISSIONER. BY MRS. WILSON WOODROW. New York: McClure, 1907 NUC.

Frances Benton rejects love for her career as a minister. She moves to the small mining town of Zenith in the Rockies where she is unwelcomed at first. But she wins the full support of the community — including the Ladies Aid Society that appoints her their leader—through her devotion to good works.

3333 SALLY SALT. BY MRS. WILSON WOODROW. Indianapolis: Bobbs-Merrill, [c1912] NUC.
Two widows managing a farm; their love stories.

WOODRUFF, HELEN (SMITH). 1888-1924. United States.

3334 THE LADY OF THE LIGHTHOUSE. New York: G. H. Doran, [c1913] NUC.
Heroine works for the Lighthouse—an institution for the blind.

WOODS, ALICE. B. 1871. United States.

3335 EDGES. Indianapolis: Bowen-Merrill, [1902] NUC. London: B. F. Stevens & Brown, [1902] BMC.
A young woman artist "gifted with rare intelligence which understands and delights in Walt Whitman and Schopenhauer," goes to Paris, is followed by male artist friend.

3336 FAME-SEEKERS. New York: G. H. Doran, [c1912] NUC.
Bohemian student life in Paris. A novel with the purpose of warning women against seeking fame and professional life, according to one reviewer.

WOODS, KATHARINE PEARSON. 1853-1923. United States.

3337 THE CROWNING OF CANDACE. New York: Dodd, Mead, 1896 NUC. London: B. F. Stevens, 1896 BMC.
Candace's first book is a huge success, second one a failure. She learns who are her real friends and discovers that her devotion to her art has really been selfishness. This awakening to love and duty is the real crowning of Candace, according to one reviewer.

WOODS, MARGARET LOUISA (BRADLEY). 1856-1945. United Kingdom.

3338　THE INVADER; A NOVEL. New York: Harper, 1907 NUC. London: W. Heinemann, 1907 BMC.

Study of a woman with a dual personality. She is well-educated, strong in character when she marries an Oxford man. Milly is a conscientious wife and homemaker who sometimes becomes Mildred—unscrupulous, loose-living, fun-loving flirt. The husband comes to love not Milly he married, but the worldlier Mildred, while Mildred wearies of her scholarly husband and runs off with another man. At the end, Milly kills herself. Background: much about women at Oxford, "amazons and bluestockings," hockey-players and women in science.

WOODS, MRS. JAMES CHAPMAN. United Kingdom.

3339　THE BEAUTY SHOP. BY DANIEL WOODROFFE. London: T. Laurie, [1905] NUC BMC.

Satirical view of the social world which supports the shop wherein "physical beauty is sought when time or nature has proved unkind."

WOOLF, ADELINE VIRGINIA (STEPHEN). 1882-1941. United Kingdom.

3340　NIGHT AND DAY. BY VIRGINIA WOOLF. London: Duckworth, [1919] BMC NUC. New York: G. H. Doran, [c1920] NUC.

The love affairs of five people who with no refuge of inherited standards and acceptances to run to, must try everything for themselves and will take nothing for granted." Katharine Hilbery's unconscious protest against family tradition and her realization that falling in love is a betrayal of her dream. Mary Dachet the resolute working woman. Sallie Seal the suffragist.

3341　THE VOYAGE OUT. BY VIRGINIA WOOLF. London: Duckworth, 1915 BMC NUC.

"Late development of sheltered young woman. Rachel Vinrace has only her music...goes on a voyage to South America...spends a few months in a little port." She dies young. "The illogic of her death leaves one desolated by a sense of the futility of life."

WOOLF, VIRGINIA. See WOOLF, ADELINE VIRGINIA (STEPHEN).

WOOLSON, CONSTANCE FENIMORE. 1840-1894. United States.

3342 HORACE CHASE: A NOVEL. New York: Harper, 1894 NUC. London: Osgood, 1894 BMC.
Studies of various women, including a sculptor who smokes. Ruth falls in love with a business acquaintance of her husband. She goes to him only to discover he loves another. Concludes with Ruth "comfortably penitent" in her husband's arms, according to one reviewer.

WORKMAN, MARY CHRISTIANA (SHEEDY). 1859-1926. United States.

3343 AN AMERICAN SINGER IN PARIS; A NOVEL. BY MRS. HANSON WORKMAN. Cincinnati: Tribune Printing, 1908 NUC BMC.

WORKMAN, MRS. HANSON. See WORKMAN, MARY CHRISTIANA (SHEEDY).

WORTHINGTON, VICTORIA. United States.

3344 RANK VS. MERIT. New York: Home Book, [1893] NUC.
Love story. Son of lord marries gardener's daughter. Marriage is annulled by family. She becomes actress and singer. Final reconciliation.

WOTTON, MABEL E. United Kingdom.

3345 A GIRL DIPLOMATIST. London: Chapman and Hall, 1892 BMC.
Barbara believes women should have a wider sphere of

action. She wants to be a diplomat. The hero is a jealous prig. Reviewer says author unintentionally demonstrates "diplomacy is not for women."

WRAY, ANGELINA W. United States.

3346 BETTY TUCKER'S AMBITION. Boston: Lothrop, [1913] NUC.

She is a writer who gets a job as reporter for the local newspaper.

WRENCH, MOLLIE LOUISE (GIBBS) STANLEY. United Kingdom.

3347 BEAT: A MODERN LOVE STORY. London: Duckworth, 1917 BMC.

Story of Beat's unfulfilled hopes. From childhood her great aim is college because she has an insatiable thirst for knowledge. Just as she gets there, her aunt dies, and she must care for her two sisters. She gives up her studies and becomes a Council school teacher in London. The novel describes her struggles to make a home and train her two sisters. With the oldest, she fails, because of this sister's love of luxury. With the youngest, she succeeds.

3348 THE COURT OF THE GENTILES. London: Mills & Boon, 1913 BMC.

The principal character is a brilliant novelist, a woman who marries a wealthy cripple. The story describes their adventures on a North African desert. In the third part of the novel we meet a second heroine who is another novelist more brilliant than the first.

3349 THE DEVIL'S STAIRS. London: Duckworth, 1918 BMC.

Barbara, the daughter of a liaison of her mother and neighbor, claims the right to choose a father for her child. Her lover is killed in war. She marries a lawyer; the child born is not his. A serious theme treated in a serious fashion.

3350   LILY LOUISA. London: Methuen, 1915 BMC.
A young woman becomes an artist.

3351   A PRIESTESS OF HUMANITY. London: J. Long, [1913] BMC.
Margot "is rescued from the streets." She becomes the housekeeper of Clive, a writer, later marries him, and becomes a novelist herself.

3352   RUTH OF THE ROWLDRICH. London: Mills & Boon, 1912 BMC.
Ruth, in this "intimate analysis of conflicting elements," goes to London to become a journalist, knowing that "her faculties will never have a chance to blossom if she settles down to being a wife." Her first book is a success, the second a failure, and she returns home to her "old love."

WRIGHT, JESSIE E. See WHITCOMB, JESSIE (WRIGHT).

WRIGHT, JULIA (MACNAIR). 1840-1903. United States.

3353   ADAM'S DAUGHTERS. New York: American Tract Society, [c1892] NUC.
The purpose of the novel is to help working women and to deter them from leaving rural areas in hope of better prospects in the cities. The story describes the efforts of a mother and three daughters who struggle and finally succeed in earning a living.

3354   MR. GROSVENOR'S DAUGHTER. New York: American Tract Soc., [1893] NUC.
Because of financial reverses in her family, Deborah becomes a working woman in a large city. The way she adapts to the change is the theme.

3355   A NEW SAMARITAN. New York: American Tract Soc., [1895] NUC.
Persis Thrale plans to use her wealth to help the poor in a large city.

WRIGHT, MABEL (OSGOOD). 1859-1939. United States.

3356 AT THE SIGN OF THE FOX; A ROMANCE. BY BARBARA, AUTHOR OF "THE GARDEN OF A COMMUNTER'S WIFE" ETC. New York: Macmillan, 1905 BMC. London: Macmillan, 1905 NUC.

Brooke is strong, resourceful, self-reliant. Father "falls into evil ways"; Brooke supports the family with her tea garden in Boston. Includes a love story.

3357 AUNT JIMMY'S WILL. New York and London: Macmillan, 1903 NUC.

A young woman becomes an artist.

WRIGHT, MARGARET.

3358 THE OTHER SELF; A STUDY IN THE SENSITIVE. London: Murray and Evenden, [1920] BMC.

Young woman chafing for freedom is crippled. Introspection follows. Her "other self" rejects love of a masterful man. Author sees in her creation "a parched, unhealthy state of mind, intensive and narrow in outlook," and one which the heroisms of the war have made a "curio" of the past.

WRIGHT, MARY (TAPPAN). 1851-1917. United States.

3359 ALIENS. New York: C. Scribner's Sons, 1902 NUC.

The daughter of a scholar who has treated her as an intellectual person marries a man in the South with a "Germanic" idea of marriage. The story of their marriage.

3360 THE CHARIOTEERS. New York and London: D. Appleton, 1912 BMC NUC.

Octavia attempts "to steer the chariot of her life with a high hand" in this character study with a college town setting. She loves a married man.

3361 THE TEST. New York: C. Scribner's Sons, 1904 NUC.

A "refined and cultured" young woman becomes pregnant; on her wedding day she discovers the man has become drunk and married another. She raises the child by herself.

3362 THE TOWER; A NOVEL. New York: C. Scribner's Sons, 1906 NUC.

Unmarried 38 year old woman in academic setting meets an old male friend for the first time in twenty years.

WRIOTHESLEY, WILLIAM [pseud.].* United Kingdom.

3363 THE AMBASSADRESS. BY WILLIAM WRIOTHESLEY. London: W. Heinemann, 1913 BMC NUC. New York: G. H. Doran, [c1913] NUC.

Woman smokes, has a weak heart, and goes about with her admirer, her "tame cat" who believes that all women should have a profession—the theme of the novel. She is the "The Ambassadress," and her daughter longs for a profession, then becomes a wife and mother considering this life her chosen profession, then decides marriage should not be considered a profession for a woman any more than it is for a man.

WYE, INA.

3364 MISS WENDER. London: Digby, Long, 1910 BMC.

Eva stands by her mother who is divorced and an alcoholic. She seems to be avoiding marriage. She holds on to discarded lovers, lives in a cottage belonging to one lover while she keeps her eye on another. She is loved by one at the end, engaged to another, but loves a third. Novel ends with no idea whether she marries.

WYLIE, I. A. R. See WYLIE, IDA ALEXA ROSS.

WYLIE, IDA ALEXA ROSS. 1885-1959. United Kingdom.

3365 DIVIDING WATERS. BY I. A. R. WYLIE. London: Mills & Boon, [1911] NUC BMC. Indianapolis: Bobbs-Merrill, [c1911] NUC.

Nora Ingestre, an Englishwoman, escapes the boredom of

her home by taking a position as companion to an invalid girl. She marries the girl's brother, a German, but soon finds him incompatible. She revolts against him and leaves. Only at his death does she return to be reconciled.

3366 THE HERMIT DOCTOR OF GAYA; A LOVE STORY OF MODERN INDIA. BY I. A. R. WYLIE. New York and London: G. P. Putnam's Sons, 1916 NUC. ,

The focus is on the doctor, but the heroine, a dancer, is "splended, courageous, and human." She marries without love, as does everyone else in the story.

3367 THE TEMPLE OF DAWN. BY I. A. R. WYLIE. London: Mills & Boon, [1915] BMC NUC. New York: Doran, [1915] NUC.

Woman murderer.

3368 TOWARDS MORNING. BY I. A. R. WYLIE. London: Cassell, 1918 BMC. New York: J. Lane, 1918 NUC.

"A study of the making of a German soldier." Helmut, taken from his mother and his toys, is turned into a brutalized soldier. But when he is ordered into a hut to "debase" a young woman inside, he rebels. She is a former playmate whom he loved. He is shot for his disobedience.

WYLLARDE, DOLF. D. 1950. United Kingdom.

3369 CAPTAIN AMYAS, BEING THE CAREER OF D'ARCY AMYAS, R.N.R., LATE MASTER OF THE R.M.S. PRINCESS. New York: J. Lane, 1904 NUC. London: W. Heinemann, 1904 BMC.

The captain, returning from a voyage to find the young woman he loves pregnant by another, "henceforth abuses sexually all females."

3370 THE CAREER OF BEAUTY DARLING. London: S. Paul, 1912 BMC. New York: J. Lane, 1912 NUC.

Beauty, a penniless foundling, is "victimized" by a man at 14. She runs away to go on stage, becomes a successful actress, and "drifts from one man to another without thought of passion." She has a dread of motherhood, and when she becomes pregnant, she kills herself.

3371 THE HOLIDAY HUSBAND. London: Hurst & Blackett, [1919] BMC NUC. New York: J. Lane, 1919 NUC.

Vervain Chalmont lives alone and supports herself. She is an underpaid and overworked executive secretary of the Colonial Women's League, a semi-charitable organization. And she is a suffragette. She goes on a holiday for two weeks with a lover, not fully realizing that even women who are single are not free to do so. The affair gets in the way of her making a more permanent relationship with another man. She is an attractive character who holds our sympathy throughout. Theme: the double standard of sexual morality.

3372 MAFOOTA; A ROMANCE OF JAMAICA. London: Hurst & Blackett, 1907 BMC. New York: J. Lane, 1907 NUC.

Described as a "sex problem novel," the story portrays Elise Nillier who has not been educated in a way to prepare her for marriage. She marries, she and her husband go to the West Indies, and several months later she discovers he is unfaithful. She leaves him, assumes another identity, and spends the next three years living with the natives of Mafoota. Here begins her education for life. Three years later she meets her husband again, and they are reconciled.

3373 THE PATHWAY OF THE PIONEER (NOUS OUTRES). London: Methuen, 1906 BMC. New York: J. Lane, 1909 NUC.

A story of seven working women who have banded together for "mutual help and cheer" under the name "Nous Autres." The emphasis is more on their struggles and disappointments than their successes. They represent collectively the professions open to women of no deliberate training, though well educated. They are introduced to the reader at one of their weekly gatherings, and the author depicts the home and business life of each one individually.

3374   TEMPERAMENT. A ROMANCE OF HERO-WORSHIP. London: S. Paul, [1920] BMC NUC. New York: J. Lane, 1920 PW.

Sexual and artistic history of Jean Delamore, musical composer and genius. She dies giving birth to illegitimate child.

3375   THE UNOFFICIAL HONEYMOON. London: Methuen, [1911] BMC NUC. New York: J. Lane, 1911 NUC.

Leslie, a missionary, is cast on a lonely island with an English army officer for six months. First they become "comrades"; then love comes slowly.

3376   URIAH THE HITTITE. London: W. Heinemann, 1904 BMC. (Also published as The Rat-trap. New York and London: J. Lane, 1904 NUC.)

A vital and unconventional woman married to a drunk falls in love with his commanding officer who sends the husband to the front lines, knowing he will be killed. They marry, live together without remorse. "A frank and subtle analysis of a woman's thoughts."

3377   YOUTH WILL BE SERVED. London: S. Paul, 1913 BMC. New York: J. Lane, 1913 NUC.

Gillian Kirby is thwarted in her hopes for a musical career when she marries an army man much older than herself and becomes a mother at 18. She begins to see that any restlessness will reflect on her son and that her role in life is to become more and more passive, sacrificing her own interests in order to serve him. Her problem is where does her chief duty lie: with her son, her husband, or with the other man who has come into her life.

WYLWYNNE, KYTHE. See HYLAND, M. E. F.

WYNMAN, MARGARET. See DIXON, ELLA HEPWORTH.

WYNNE, CONSTANCE.

3378 THE WOMEN OF CEDAR GROVE. London: C.W. Daniel, 1920 BMC NUC.

A portrayal of life in a residential street in a manufacturing district and the problems and comradeship of its working women.

WYNNE, MAY. See KNOWLES, MABEL WINIFRED.

X, LADY.

3379 THE DIARY OF MY HONEYMOON. New York: Macaulay, 1910 NYT. London and New York: J. Long, 1910 BMC.

A degrading marriage, the sale of an earl's daughter to a "rich money lender," her suffering and eventual freedom. In three months she is changed from a childish girl to a self-reliant woman.

YANG PING YU.*

3380 THE LOVE STORY OF A MAIDEN OF CATHAY; TOLD IN LETTERS FROM YANG PING YU. New York: Revell, [1911] BMC.

Letters full of worldly wisdom from a Chinese woman to her female cousin—a medical student in Scotland, violating all the Chinese ideals of womanhood.

YARDLEY, MAUD H.

3381 NOR ALL YOUR TEARS. New York: R.F. Fenno, [c1908] NUC. London: Sisley's, [1908] BMC.

Penniless orphan whose wrongs drive her to murder. Melodrama.

3382 SOULMATES. London: Greening, [1917] BMC.

Kay has a love affair with a man whose wife is in an asylum. When he dies and she learns she is pregnant, she marries another man. When he disappears on their wedding day, Kay is suspected of murder. The novel ends tragically with Kay's death in childbirth.

YONGE, CHARLOTTE MARY. 1823-1901. United Kingdom.

3383 GRISLY GRISELL; OR THE LAIDLY LADY OF WHITBURN; A TALE OF THE WARS OF THE ROSES. London & New York: Macmillan, 1893 BMC NUC.

Grisell Dacre is the daughter of a Scotch lord. An explosion of gunpowder disfigures her when she is 10. The boy contracted to marry her is responsible. But the contract is cancelled because the families are on opposite sides in the War of the Roses. First everyone despises her. Then when her sweet nature wins their love, she is considered a witch. She gives her energies to learning about herbs and potions, escapes to a foreign land, returns years later, weds, is loved and accepted.

YORKE, CURTIS. See LEE, SUSAN RICHMOND, also LEE, SUSAN RICHMOND AND MRS. E. M. DAVY.

YOUNG, AMELIA S. C.

3384 POINT BLANK.

Mother and two daughters beg for invitations to officers' messes, for the unconsumed food left on the table. They also ask women friends for their cast-off clothes.

YOUNG, E. H. See YOUNG, EMILY HILDA.

YOUNG, EMILY HILDA. 1880-1949. United Kingdom.

3385 A CORN OF WHEAT. London: W. Heinemann, 1910 BMC.

Judith is about to have a child and no longer loves the father. She marries someone else impulsively, can't tolerate the marriage, leaves. When her child dies at birth, she wakes to the "cruelty of civilization," has thoughts of killing herself.

3386 MOOR FIRES. BY E. H. YOUNG. London: J. Murray, 1916 BMC. New York: Harcourt, Brace, [1927] NUC.

Miriam and Helen Canipers live a secluded life on the moor with their stepmother. The moor has a mysterious influence on the sensitive nature of these twins. They develop in extreme ways, complements of each other. Miriam grasped at life while Helen gave of herself; when Miriam's life is in danger, Helen sacrifices herself and her lover. A minute study of the twin sisters and a delicate psychological study of Helen's married life in the closing chapters.

3387 YONDER. London: W. Heinemann, 1912 BMC. New York: G. H. Doran, 1913 NUC.

Serious, good work. Two families: Edward and his daughter Theresa, and Clara caring for her weak and drunken husband and strong willed sons. One of the fathers kills the other. Theresa learns to let her imagination serve rather than rule her. "The strong-natured girl is a decisive figure with her all too modern contempt of convention and her longing for all the sensations that life can bring."

YOUNG, ETHEL WINIFRID.

3388 A WITCH OF THE WEST: A NOVEL. London: Sisley's, [1908] BMC.

Neighbors believe Nora is a witch.

YOUNG, F. E. MILLS. See YOUNG, FLORENCE ETHEL MILLS.

YOUNG, FLORENCE ETHEL MILLS. 1875-1954. United Kingdom.

3389 ATONEMENT. BY F. E. MILLS YOUNG. London and New York: J. Lane, 1910 BMC NUC.

A young woman engaged to one man "deliberately ensnares" another. Her terror of exposure leads to suicide.

3390   BEATRICE ASHLEIGH. BY F. E. MILLS YOUNG.
       London: Hodder and Stoughton, [1918] BMC. New York:
       G.H. Doran, [c1918] NUC.
       War brings purpose to her life, and she becomes a nurse.
       She marries a man crippled in the war.

3391   THE BIGAMIST. BY F. E. MILLS YOUNG. London and
       New York: J. Lane, 1916 BMC NUC.
       Pamela Arnott has been married for five years and has a
       daughter of four when she receives a letter from her
       husband's real wife. The novel studies the effects this news
       has upon her. First she can't give him up, but realizes he
       begins to respect her less for staying. Then she decides to
       conceal the truth from friends, but things go badly for the
       couple, especially when the husband becomes interested in
       yet another woman. The real wife dies, Pamela's old love
       shows up, and finally after a good deal of humiliation and
       suffering, Pamela, though completely disillusioned, marries
       the man for the sake of her child. The setting is South
       Africa.

3392   THE BYWONNER. BY F. E. MILLS YOUNG. London and
       New York: J. Lane, 1916 BMC NUC.
       The story of an English farmer in South Africa. Ransom
       and his son Tom and daughter Adela lead a grim
       existence, frequently dependent on others' charity.
       (Ransom is educated but alcoholic.) Adela becomes the
       mistress of an adventurer and escapes disgrace by
       drowning. "The most interesting thing in the book is the
       picture it gives of the monotonous, hard-working lives of
       the women whose lot is cast on the lonely farms of the
       veldt."

3393   CHIP. BY F. E. MILLS YOUNG. London and New York:
       J. Lane, 1909 BMC NUC.
       Chip is a young woman who disguises herself as a man
       and takes a position as overseer of an estate in South
       Africa. The owner of the estate is a misogynist.

3394 COELEBS: THE LOVE STORY OF A BACHELOR. BY F.
E. MILLS YOUNG. London and New York: J. Lane, 1917
BMC NUC.
Peggy is one of three sisters raised by an aunt to be
"capable young persons, able to make their own way in
cheerful independence." They take up gardening,
architecture, and medicine rather than live on their uncle's
money. Peggy's overalls and occupation do not make her
less attractive to Coelebs.

3395 THE LAWS OF CHANCE. BY F. E. MILLS YOUNG.
London and New York: J. Lane, 1918 BMC NUC.
Character study of women in South Africa. Hero is "a
little ridiculous and never unmanaged by one of them."

3396 A MISTAKEN MARRIAGE. BY F. E. MILLS YOUNG.
London and New York: J. Lane, 1908 BMC NUC.
Sara waits for five years for man she loves who is in
South Africa. Then she comes to Africa, and he is too
cowardly to tell her he has been living with another
woman and has a child. Instead he marries her. Later she
discovers the truth and divorces him, eventually marrying
another.

3397 THE PURPLE MISTS. BY F. E. MILLS YOUNG. New
York: J. Lane, 1914 NUC. London: J. Lane, 1914 BMC.
The story of an unhappy marriage in South Africa. The
wife finally leaves.

3398 THE SHADOW OF THE PAST. BY F. E. MILLS
YOUNG. New York: G.H. Doran, [c1919] NUC. London:
Hodder and Stoughton, 1919 BMC.
Honor Kringe, daughter of a Boer family is an earnest
rebel. She hates England (though she's part English) for
robbing her of her father and brother. She believes South
Africa will revolt against England, and her love for a man
loyal to England cannot shake her faith in the cause. She
refuses to marry him until he gives up his English
nationality.

3399   THE TRIUMPH OF JILL. BY F. E. MILLS YOUNG. London: J. Long, 1903 BMC NUC.

A young woman struggles to support herself by teaching.

3400   THE WAR OF THE SEXES. London: J. Long, 1905 BMC.

An early example of feminist science fiction. The time is the end of the 20th century. Only one man has survived the war of the sexes. He's a woman hater, and the novel has much to do with his relations to Bertranda, a man hater. England is populated entirely by women through parthenogenesis.

YOUNG, MIRIAM.

3401   THE GIRL MUSICIAN. London: Digby, Long, [1893] BMC.

Queenie—"destined to do wonders as a musician." Author's "simple, old-fashioned views."

YOUNG, VIRGINIA (DURANT). United States.

3402   A TOWER IN THE DESERT. Boston: Arena, 1896 NUC BMC.

Women in the South—the "rapid broadening" of their ideals and the work of the Woman's Christian Temperance Union.

YVER, COLETTE. See HUZARD, ANTOINETTE (DE BERGEVIN).

ZACK. See KEATS, GWENDOLINE.

ZANGWILL, EDITH (AYRTON). D. 1945. United Kingdom.

3403   THE FIRST MRS. MOLLIVAR. London: Smith, Elder, 1905 BMC.

Middle aged woman marries former lover whose first wife has died. Story of her revolt against the restraint of her new position, the outrages on her taste and health.

3404   THE RISE OF A STAR. London: J. Murray, 1918 BMC.
New York: Macmillan, 1918 NUC.
Study of character. Millionaire Vandeleur, his wife
Imogen, the unmaternal mother of little star Joan.
Imogen's grandmother is an actress and mothers Joan.

3405   TERESA. London: Smith, Elder, 1909 BMC.
Teresa is devoted to her mother, a woman of mid-
Victorian ideas. She is pure and completely ignorant about
sex. Just out of school, she is proposed to by an older
experienced man who is attracted to her purity and
freshness. She marries, but is very quickly disillusioned.
When she revolts against her married state, her husband
turns to other women. In the end, however, the two get
back together and their child is born. Besides Teresa, there
is Clare, an actress. The author gives us some of the
emancipated modern types of women.

ZOLLINGER, GULIELMA. 1856-1917. United States.

3406   MAGGIE MCLANEHAN. Chicago: A. C. McClurg, 1901
NUC.
A strong young Irish woman of great courage and good judgment is forced to support herself and her cousin and does so
successfully.

TITLE INDEX

THE INVADER; A NOVEL, 3338
INVINCIBLE MINNIE, 1409
THE INVISIBLE BOND. BY ELEANOR TALBOT KINKEAD, 2762
INVISIBLE TIDES, 2734
THE INVOLUNTARY CHAPERON. BY MARGARET CAMERON, 1667
IONE: A SEQUEL TO "VASHTI", 673
IRIS THE AVENGER. BY FLORENCE MARRYAT, 1769
IRON COUSINS. BY MRS. SIDGWICK, 2775
THE IRON GAME. A STORY OF THE FRANCO-PRUSSIAN WAR, 2038
THE IRON GATES, 1268
THE IRON WOMAN, 818
IRRESOLUTE CATHERINE, 1533
IS IT ENOUGH? A ROMANCE OF MUSICAL LIFE, 491
ISABEL MCDONALD, 2881
ISABEL STERLING, 2682
AN ISHMAELITE INDEED, 2880
THE ISLANDS OF DESIRE. A NOVEL. BY DIANA PATRICK, 3299
THE ISLE OF DREAMS, 1628
ISLE OF THORNS. BY SHEILA KAYE SMITH, 1123
THE ISSUES OF LIFE. A NOVEL OF THE AMERICAN WOMAN OF TO-
DAY. BY MRS. JOHN VAN VORST, 3115
ISTER OF BABYLON, A PHANTASY. BY MARGARET HORTON
POTTER, 282
IT HAPPENED IN JAPAN, 762
IT PAYS TO SMILE, 2467
IVA KILDARE: A MATRIMONIAL PROBLEM, 3156
I'VE COME TO STAY: A LOVE COMEDY OF BOHEMIA, 2267
THE IVORY FAN, 1358
IZRA; A CHILD OF SOLITUDE, 887

JAMESIE, 2781
THE JAMESONS. BY MARY E. WILKINS, 1110
JANE, 535
JANE: A SOCIAL INCIDENT. BY MARIE CORELLI, 1967
"JANE ELLEN" BEING REAL SKETCHES FROM THE LIFE OF A
LANCASTER LASS, 3004
JANE FIELD: A NOVEL. BY MARY E. WILKINS, 1111
JANE STUART, COMRADE, 2512
JANET, 2274
JANET DELILLE. BY E. N. LEIGH FRY, 1799
JANET OF KOOTENAY; LIFE, LOVE & LAUGHTER IN AN ARCADY
OF THE WEST, 1977
THE JAPANESE BRIDE, 3002
A JAVELIN OF FATE, 1833

ME: A BOOK OF REMEMBRANCE [ANONYMOUS], 147
MEDA'S HERITAGE, 2387
THE MEDICINE LADY. BY L. T. MEADE, 2855
MEDOC IN THE MOOR, 2497
THE MEMOIRS OF MIMOSA. BY HERSELF. EDITED BY ANNE ELLIOT, 969
MEMORIES, 2251
MEMORIES OF MARGARET GRAINGER, SCHOOLMISTRESS, 2832
THE MEMORIES OF RONALD LOVE, 2022
THE MEN WE MARRY, 2212
A MENDER OF IMAGES. A NOVEL, 1868
MERCIA, THE ASTRONOMER ROYAL: A ROMANCE. BY A. GARLAND MEARS, 2122
A MERCIFUL DIVORCE: A STORY OF SOCIETY, ITS SPORTS, FUNCTIONS AND FAILINGS, 2099
MERCILESS LOVE. BY THE AUTHOR OF "FOR A GOD DISHONOURED", 80
A MERE CYPHER: A NOVEL, 862
A MERE WOMAN. BY VERA NIKTO, 2255
MERELY PLAYERS, 1211
MERELY PLAYERS. BY LUCY DALE AND G. M. FAULDING, 757
MERESIA, 643
MERIEL'S CAREER. A TALE OF LITERARY LIFE IN LONDON, 3270
THE MERMAID OF INISH-UIG, 964
MERRY GIRLS OF ENGLAND. BY L. T. MEADE, 2856
THE MERRY HEART. BY HELEN RAYMOND ABBOTT, 231
THE MESSENGER: A NOVEL. BY ELIZABETH ROBINS, 2323
MESSENGERS, 1447
A MEXICAN RANCH: OR BEAUTY FOR ASHES: A PRIZE STORY, 946
MICHAEL LAMONT, SCHOOLMASTER, 1045
MICHAEL THWAITE'S WIFE, 2145
MICHAIL; OR, THE HEART OF A RUSSIAN. A NOVEL IN FOUR PARTS. BY A RUSSIAN LADY [ANONYMOUS], 764
'MID GREEN PASTURES. BY E. RENTOUL ESLER, 992
THE MIDDLE COURSE. BY MRS. POULTNEY BIGELOW, 268
MIDDLE LIFE, 1820
MIDSUMMER MADNESS, 226
MIFANWY (A WELSH SINGER). BY ALLEN RAINE, 2463
MILDRED CARVER, U.S.A, 433
THE MILKY WAY. BY F. TENNYSON JESSE, 1338
THE MILLER OF OLD CHURCH, 1184
A MILLION FOR A SOUL: A NOVEL OF ANGLO-INDIAN LIFE, 2389
THE MILLIONAIRE AND THE LADY. BY GERTRUDE WARDEN, 1585
MILLS OF GOD: A NOVEL, 1732

MY CHINESE DAYS, 32
MY FLIRTATIONS. BY MARGARET WYNMAN, 888
MY FRIEND ANNABEL LEE, 1979
MY HUSBAND STILL; A WORKING WOMAN'S STORY, 1280
MY JO, JOHN: A NOVEL. BY HELEN MATHERS, 2507
MY LADY OF THE CHINESE COURTYARD, 631
MY LADY PEGGY GOES TO TOWN, 2089
MY LADY PEGGY LEAVES TOWN, 2090
MY LIFE IN THE CONVENT; OR THE MARVELLOUS PERSONAL
     EXPERIENCES OF MARGARET L. SHEPHERD (SISTER
     MAGDALENE ADELAIDE), 2752
MY LITTLE LADY ANNE. BY MRS. EGERTON CASTLE, 513
MY LITTLE SISTER. BY ELIZABETH ROBINS, 2325
MY LOVE AND I. BY MARTIN REDFIELD, 416
MY MOTHER AND I. BY E. G. STERN, 2930
MY SILVER SPOONS, 1347
MY SISTER TAKES A REST CURE, 3290
MY SUITORS, 2031
MY WIFE'S HIDDEN LIFE, 83
MYOLA, 2235
THE MYSTERY OF A CORNISH MOOR. BY A NEW AUTHOR, 84
THE MYSTERY OF FRANCES FARRINGTON, 175
THE MYSTERY OF MERE HALL. BY MRS. COULSON KERNAHAN,
     1659
THE MYSTERY OF THE THREE FINGERS, 1811
THE MYSTIC NUMBER SEVEN. BY ANNABEL GRAY, 672

NADINE NARSKA, 843
THE NAKED SOUL, THREE YEARS IN A WOMAN'S LIFE, 1373
A NAME TO CONJURE WITH; A NOVEL. BY JOHN STRANGE
     WINTER, 2916
NAMELESS; A NOVEL, 1076
NANCY STAIR; A NOVEL, 1733
NANNO: A DAUGHTER OF THE STATE. BY ROSA MULHOLLAND
     (LADY GILBERT), 1171
NAOMI OF THE ISLAND, 2
NAOMI'S EXODUS, 2182
A NARROW WAY, 1041
NEEDS MUST. A NOVEL, 2879
A NEGLECTED PRIVILEGE: THE STORY OF A MODERN WOMAN,
     2974
NEIGHBORHOOD STORIES, 1139
NEIGHBORS, 1698
NEIGHBORS IN BARTON SQUARE, 754
NELL GWYN'S DIAMOND, 1440
THE NEST-BUILDER, 1255